# Mother's Heart, Father's Mind

The Sexual Revolution of a Young Man

1955–1985

This is the definitive study of the heterosexual man.
A dissection of man's ego with a male knife.

Written by
John Bassett McCleary

Edited by
Joan Jeffers McCleary

*Mother's Heart, Father's Mind:*
John Bassett McCleary
Slow Limbo Productions, August 2021
First Edition, ISBN: 0-9668687-4-6
*Mother's Heart, Father's Mind* is the third book in the Hippie Trilogy.

Other books by John Bassett McCleary:

*The People's Book*
Library of Congress # 72-82869
Celestial Arts, 1972

*Monterey Peninsula People*
ISBN 0-9668687-0-6
Slow Limbo Productions, 1998

*The Hippie Dictionary: A Cultural Encyclopedia of the 1960s and 1970s*
ISBN 1-58008-355-2
Ten Speed Press/ Crown Press/ Random House, 2002, revised and expanded 2004

*Common Sense And Reason Again*
ISBN 0-9668687-3-9
Slow Limbo Productions, 2020

For more information about this book or John McCleary's other works, please see: hippietrilogy.com, hippiedictionary.com, commonsenseandreasonagain.com, mothersheartfathersmind.com.

SLOW LIMBO
PUBLISHING

# Dedication

This is a love poem to my wife,
Joan
As a woman, she may not fully understand it all,
but I hope she knows that the last woman a man wants to be with
is the one he really loves!

With Appreciation
I have a large group of people who have constantly fed me
theories, ideas, new words and concepts. They didn't always know
that they were doing this, but I hear all and write it down and type it
into rows of words, and use it as my own!

In Alphabetical order thank you
Boo, Jonas Candler, Jim Casteel, Bob Davis, Dotty Davis, Dorothy
Edner, Steve Forker, David Glover, David Grubbs, Ian Heuston,
Nick Lefevre, Joe Lubow, Joan Jeffers McCleary, Kathleen Mc-
Cleary, Pauline McCleary, Siobhan McCleary, Randy McKendry,
John Miller, Richard Miller, Ray Parsons, Kerry Sissem, Candice
Tahara, Gordon Terry, Zoe the cat, and Koie the poodle.

For their professional help in production of this book,
I would like to thank Karl Pfeiffer, my computer techie,
and Patricia Hamilton of Park Place Publications,
who helped with the typeset and design mechanics.
Cover background photo by David Glover.

Most of the photographs and art pieces in this book were created or
directed by the author, unless otherwise noted. For the art or photos
that are uncredited, I thank the creators, and hope the artists will
understand the importance of the story they help portray.

# Contents

**Dedication**    iii

**Introduction**    1

CHAPTER 1    **Blame It All On Your Parents**    6

CHAPTER 2    **Dixie Peach**    19

CHAPTER 3    **Sparky**    60

CHAPTER 4    **Sexual Timelines of Life**    67

CHAPTER 5    **Sex, Society, Religion and Politics**    75

CHAPTER 6    **Tammy**    77

CHAPTER 7    **Sex Is As Easy As Driving A Car, And We All Know How Many People Suck At That!**    78

CHAPTER 8    **Sexy Stories**    82

CHAPTER 9    **Taking Your Sex Life Into Your Own Hands; The Masturbation Chapter**    88

CHAPTER 10    **The Kiss**    95

CHAPTER 11    **Introduction By The Typist**    98

CHAPTER 12    **Psycho Killer**    101

CHAPTER 13    **Coming of Age In The 1950s**    103

CHAPTER 14    **Timing Is Everything!**    113

CHAPTER 15    **When Does a Sex Life Begin?**    118

CHAPTER 16    **I Wasn't Raised On Rock & Roll; Rock & Roll Was Raised On Me**    123

CHAPTER 17    **Jerk or Lover?**    129

CHAPTER 18    **Oh, Oh, Oh, Desiree**    134

CHAPTER 19    **Girls Don't Really Like To Be Tickled!**    135

CHAPTER 20    **I Ain't Handsome, But I Ain't Shy**    139

CHAPTER 21    **To Fathom The Soul of Woman, and Other Parts of Her**    144

CHAPTER 22    **It's All In Your Mind …You Know!**    147

CHAPTER 23    **White Bucks, Flat Tops and Pomade**    148

John Bassett McCleary

CHAPTER 24  **Chicks, Cars and Testosterone--You Know, More Guy Talk**  149

CHAPTER 25  **Influences, Heroes And Role Models**  154

CHAPTER 26  **Becoming a Man**  156

CHAPTER 27  **Cats And Dogs And Girls**  157

CHAPTER 28  **It's Now Or Never Turning Point: Guts**  159

CHAPTER 29  **Back Seat Battlegrounds**  168

CHAPTER 30  **The High School Bubble**  175

CHAPTER 31  **MG TF**  186

CHAPTER 32  **The High School Bubble Bursts Turning Point: Reality**  187

CHAPTER 33  **Hearts and Flowers**  192

CHAPTER 34  **Facial Hair: The Mistaken Identity**  196

CHAPTER 35  **HAIR, Infidelity And Hypocrisy**  196

CHAPTER 36  **My First Time**  199

CHAPTER 37  **Don't Worry, Baby; Volleyball, Beach Boys and California Coolers**  200

CHAPTER 38  **Power And Wisdom**  208

CHAPTER 39  **The Perfect Night: Sex, Drugs And Rock & Roll**  213

CHAPTER 40  **Sex: God Giveth And Society Taketh Away**  215

CHAPTER 41  **Monterey Pop Festival, June 17, 1967**  218

CHAPTER 42  **Sex, Business and Religion**  222

CHAPTER 43  **A Miracle Of Medical Science: Giving God A Helping Hand**  227

CHAPTER 44  **The Longest Chapter In The History of Writing**  235

CHAPTER 45  **Dance As If No One Is Watching**  236

CHAPTER 46  **Cool**  236

CHAPTER 47  **It's Not Quite Love, But It Feels Good Anyway**  237

CHAPTER 48  **Sex And Capitalism**  249

CHAPTER 49  **The Closing**  254

CHAPTER 50 **Childhood Crises, Adolescent Crises, Seven-Year Itch Crises, Midlife Crises, And Old Age Crises** 256

CHAPTER 51 **Alcohol As A Tool, Not A Crutch, Drugs As A Solution, Not As An Escape!** 257

CHAPTER 52 **Sex Will Not Be Denied** 258

CHAPTER 53 **Attitude** 260

CHAPTER 54 **Fuck And Bowl** 261

CHAPTER 55 **Tillie Gort's Coffee House: The Center of the Unknown Universe** 263

CHAPTER 56 **Remember Their Birthdays** 272

CHAPTER 57 **Art Or Sex** 274

CHAPTER 58 **Sex And Nudity** 276

CHAPTER 59 **Cunnilingus Among Us** 283

CHAPTER 60 **A Strict Vagetarian** 288

CHAPTER 61 **Children Do Not Receive Wisdom Through Their Mother's Milk** 291

CHAPTER 62 **Jim And I And Jan** 297

CHAPTER 63 **Jim And I Again** 302

CHAPTER 64 **Mom and Dad** 303

CHAPTER 65 **Sex And Ego** 303

CHAPTER 66 **Sex, Business And Religion** 306

CHAPTER 67 **Hippie Chick Between Love And Inescapable Reality** 309

CHAPTER 68 **Me Tarzan, You Jane** 317

CHAPTER 69 **The Rapist!** 323

CHAPTER 70 **Barbarians Have All The Fun** 324

CHAPTER 71 **Sperm, The River of Life** 328

CHAPTER 72 **I Was Enlightened By Rock & Roll; It Was Enlightened By Me** 333

CHAPTER 73 **Am I A Real Man If ... ?** 335

CHAPTER 74 **Break-up Sex** 344

CHAPTER 75 **A Snap Of The Fingers** 345

CHAPTER 76    **Male Mythology And Anti-Mythology**    346

CHAPTER 77    **The Rejection**    347

CHAPTER 78    **Fear And Hate!**    350

CHAPTER 79    **Young Stuff**    352

CHAPTER 80    **Words Of Love...Words Of Sex**    353

CHAPTER 81    **TV LOVE**    356

CHAPTER 82    **Sex And Guns**    361

CHAPTER 83    **Sexual Revolution As A Hippie Movement**    363

CHAPTER 84    **Boy Scouts And Hippies**    365

CHAPTER 85    **"This Is Where I Want To Be For
The Rest Of My Life."**    370

CHAPTER 86    **The Myth Of One-Night Stands**    370

CHAPTER 87    **Male Silly Day**    375

CHAPTER 88    **OXOXOX X X I Love You Mom And Dad**    377

CHAPTER 89    **Are Sex And Love Related?**    378

CHAPTER 90    **To Each His Own Fetish**    382

CHAPTER 91    **The Erogenous Sneeze**    384

CHAPTER 92    **Signs Of The Times**    384

CHAPTER 93    **Losing A Virginity**    386

CHAPTER 94    **A New York Love Story**    395

CHAPTER 95    **What Is Truth?**    398

CHAPTER 96    **Use Your Drugs; Don't Let Them Use You**    402

CHAPTER 97    **Un-Guilty Pleasures**    405

CHAPTER 98    **Three Degrees Of Sexual Separation**    407

CHAPTER 99    **Is Sex A Growth Industry?**    412

CHAPTER 100    **Homophobia Is For Pussies**    414

CHAPTER 101    **Loss Of Innocence**    418

CHAPTER 102    **What Is Indecent?**    422

CHAPTER 103    **Make Love, Not War**    423

CHAPTER 104    **The ESP Of Sex**    426

CHAPTER 105    **The Macho Thing**    428

CHAPTER 106    **Sex In A Hot Tub**    432

CHAPTER 107    **Busted For Sex**    434

CHAPTER 108 **Hair And Clothes:** *"Dahling, you look mahvelous!"*   441

CHAPTER 109 **Sexual Tension**   450

CHAPTER 110 **Venereal Disease Dance Tonight!**   452

CHAPTER 111 **Lovers Don't Come With Resumes**   453

CHAPTER 112 **Cycles Of Sex**   456

CHAPTER 113 **The Confessional**   458

CHAPTER 114 **Sex, Drugs And Rock & Roll Society**   462

CHAPTER 115 **All The Wrong Things**   464

CHAPTER 116 **Don't Tie An Anchor Around Your Social  Life**   466

CHAPTER 117 **I Yam Who I Yam, I Yam What I Yam**   467

CHAPTER 118 **Competition**   471

CHAPTER 119 **To Do Or Not To Do**   472

CHAPTER 120 **Red-Haired Frustration Power Politics In Bed (1980s)**   473

CHAPTER 121 **Love Without Jealousy**   480

CHAPTER 122 **A Train Full Of Amazons**   481

CHAPTER 122 **The Insanity Of Alone**   483

CHAPTER 124 **The Toilet Seat Chapter**   483

CHAPTER 125 **OJ Could Have Been A Hero**   487

CHAPTER 126 **A Slave To Endorphins**   488

CHAPTER 127 **Do The Right Thing**   489

CHAPTER 128 **Back Tats And Tramp Stamps**   489

CHAPTER 129 **To "Ms." Wright And All Other Conservative Feminists, JBMc, 8.12.06**   490

CHAPTER 130 **Sun's Gossamer Gift**   493

CHAPTER 131 **Satire And Shame**   494

CHAPTER 132 **How To Give Up On A Relationship, How To End A Relationship**   497

CHAPTER 133 **Male, Female, Drugs, Seduction**   499

CHAPTER 134 **Love Is Love, Sex Is Sex**   499

CHAPTER 135 **Coitus Non-Performus**   503

CHAPTER 136   **Less Than A Rock Star Or A Sports Hero!**   504

CHAPTER 137   **Facial Hair, The Mistaken Identity**   505

CHAPTER 138   **Is This A Fantasy Or Am I Remembering?**   506

CHAPTER 139   **The Hitchhiking Chronicles**   517

CHAPTER 140   **My Body**   518

CHAPTER 141   **Computer Sex And Other Deviations**   522

CHAPTER 142   **Profanity Is For Pussies**   525

CHAPTER 143   **Stalking And Sexual Harassment**   526

CHAPTER 144   **Sexual Etiquette**   527

CHAPTER 145   **Fantasies And Fantasy**   529

CHAPTER 146   **Men Behaving Badly**   545

CHAPTER 147   **Interviewing For A Wife**   550

CHAPTER 148   **Marriage And Bitching, And Wishing And Hoping … Also "The Mothering Syndrome And Henpecking"**   558

CHAPTER 149   **My Last Affairs**   568

CHAPTER 150   **What's It All About, Dudley?**   575

CHAPTER 151   **The Theory Of Human Relativity, Life, Sex And Baseball**   583

CHAPTER 152   **Sex and Religion, Sex and Dominance, Sex With Morality**   587

CHAPTER 153   **The Secret To Finding True Love Is...**   600

CHAPTER 154   **Joan's Chapter**   607

CHAPTER 155   **The Snoring Chapter**   619

CHAPTER 156   **Media's Contribution Toward Bad Sex, Sex Crimes, And Immorality**   621

CHAPTER 157   **Researching Sex, A Dangerous Misadventure**   623

**About the Author**   636

*"I know that good sex is not the most important thing in life,*
*yet it rates among the first five, maybe first four, or possibly three or*
*two. But, the first breath you take is the most important thing in life!"*
*The Worm In The Paper*

*"Beware the belle of the ball and the stud in the room."*
*Mr. California, 6.29.21*
*"Or, look for them, if you have the guts.*
*You'll see them, they are easy to spot."*
*Mr. California, 6.30.21*

# Introduction

John McCleary 6.8.2014 to 6.27.2021

I have been writing parts of the chapters, stories and prose in this book for over thirty years. It's a good thing I started back then, because I would not be able to remember them now with the clarity and facts that are written here. The insights and opinions I have about human sexuality have been developing from the moment I first recognized that girls weren't here just to be teased.

And then around 1967 I realized that our culture, religion and politics were all cooperating to marginalize the value of women, demonize sex for profit, and bolster the male ego. So I started researching and writing about this disaster.

Life is difficult enough without creating more problems by making sex, drugs and rock & roll into sins! Killing, stealing, bigotry, greed and corporate crimes are real sins and are immoral. Sex, drugs and rock & roll are the things we do to make life enjoyable by helping us forget the real sins of our society.

You might call this a sexual memoir, but its real purpose has been to figure out, and record for myself and anybody who will listen, the mechanics and emotions of the human desire to live and procreate. In this book I will explain the sexual revolution, and its importance, to those who missed it. I will also try to define good taste, bad taste, morality and immorality. Good luck with that, John!

I lived as a sexually active adult before, during, and after the sexual revolution. Sex itself is really very simple, that is the animal part, but the human part is complex. It is the relationships that create the problems.

Being completely in love with a woman leaves many men feeling vulnerable. But some of us know that true love is worth the effort. Giving your heart to someone is not a weakness, but a strength.

The consequences of our "giving in" are worth the companionship we can share with this mysterious creature, whom we are totally intrigued, enamored, amused and confounded by all at the same time. Women keep us guys alive.

I would hope that women who have been given the unreserved heart of a man, will accept it with reverence, for it is not easy for most men to give up their ego.

*"You don't have to be suave or sophisticated to get laid. Awkward and obnoxious guys succeed all the time. But if you want to have a real "relationship" with a partner, one worthy of a scene from a Bogart and Bacall movie, you better brush up on your tact and sincerity. Jive talk and dishonesty have been known to work on some girls, but your rate of success and the impression you leave behind are going to be embarrassing."* Mr. California

Some men have actually learned to recognize and accept the primal drive of women as right and good. That is why we are somewhat more successful with them. If you don't understand the differences between men and women, you will forever be unsuccessful with this opposite sex. These statements can also be true from women to men!

Humans are the most social of all creatures, and sex is the most complex of all social activities. There are many influences on our lives such as, families, places and economics, but arguably sex is the one that has the most emotional affect on us all and always. If our love life or partnership is good, the rest of the problems can be dealt with or in some cases overlooked.

I am, in this book, humbly trying to help you find happiness in love, sex, fantasy sex, or God forbid, no companionship, love, or sex. The best way to find companionship, love or sex is to be worthy of these glorious things! You are to blame for loneliness, because there are a lot of people, just like you, who want someone who is worthy of their affections. I have written this book for every hopeful young man.

In these pages I have several friends and alter egos whom I quote from time to time; they are Dudley Griffin, Mr. California, JOB a family member, and a 500,000-year-old named Ug.

In this book only the names have been changed to protect the guilty. All the real participants did what we did gladly, within the hippie purity of that time.

If you recognize yourself in any of these stories and want to say 'hi' or give me a piece of your mind, just e-mail me at jcmccleary@

comcast.net. I am happily married and don't want to reconnect, but I would be interested in knowing what you have done with your life. If I have pissed you off at any time, you may mention that too. And also, if you want, I would like to thank you for the part you have played in my life.

As the author of an autobiography about sexuality, coming of age, and romance, I have to use myself as the subject or else I would just be guessing. I am telling this story truthfully so that it can be socially informative.

This book is about love, sex and family, yet I have brought politics, economics and religion into it because these last three are continually fucking up the most important and best part of our lives... love, affection and family.

In order for our society to survive, the capitalists and the consumers have to start cooperating and come together for the good of all. Capitalists actually need the consumers more than the consumers need them. The consumers used to make all of what they needed, and that worked out fine, and yet the capitalists can't exist without people to buy their products.

Many folks are listening to exactly the wrong people. If you respect others only for their aggressive dominance, but not for their cultural intelligence, you will most often end up being lied to and stolen from by those self-important leaders.

A large part of bigotry in America comes from white men concerned that black men might steal or coerce white women into sex, creating more blacks. Strange, but that is what the black men saw during slavery--the white man stealing and raping their women. White men should be ashamed. When a race of men listens to religious doctrine or Wall Street propaganda, they begin to believe everything they do is forgivable, because they feel they are superior. But all too often through their actions, fanatics exhibit the fact that they are not any better than any other race or religion.

The male ego and its accompanying desire for power and its resulting greed is the biggest problem mankind has. If you live with those afflictions, then you are the source of every problem in society. There are going to be greedy and bigoted people, and we will have to control them with logic or social, legal force, if need be, because a rational society must have speed limits on people's actions just as we have speed limits on the highway. If we don't have common sense laws, we will not be able to maintain peace and prosperity for all.

For thousands of years mankind didn't even know that sex produced children. And for thousands of years after that, humans could not seem to control their horny desires enough to keep sex from being more trouble than it was worth. Finally in the last few thousand years, but mostly only in Asia, did people started to control their urges for the sake of common sense. Then in the 1960s and 70s after the invention of easy and trustworthy forms of birth control, a culture arose that started taking sex seriously as positive activity and a pastime that could be controlled to bring about only good results. So now we can celebrate sex as being a possible success story for the human race.

Men, today, are being criticized, rightfully, for being men. I said, rightfully, because man is the perpetrator of most of the bad things that happen on this earth. I am like a parent who wants my family to be happy and live a good life, so I must suggest, cajole, discipline and criticize my fellow sex to get their sack of shit together!

Some of you may consider this book to be too raw, explicit and perhaps profane. You may also think I am too personally involved in the story to be trusted to tell the truth, but I am telling the true story. I had to experience sex in order to know it thoroughly enough to be able to write about it. And people had to believe I knew what I was writing about to be able to listen with conviction. You shouldn't buy a knife from someone who hasn't made a knife.

My father selling the competition's newspaper, Carmel,
California, 1926.

*"We each find our own pleasure and our own pain!"*
JOB

*I have made love with hundreds of women, chicks, and girls,
and all of them were beautiful, regardless of their appearances.
Making love is a sacrament to me, and I think any man who treats a
partner as only a sex object, is an asshole who is missing out.*
Mr. California

*"Man is the only insecure animal!"*
Ug, 498,000 BC

*"The male ego is the single most dangerous weapon on the
face of the earth"*
Dudley Griffin, 9.11.01

*"Much of who you are is not your fault or of your making,
but you better accept responsibility for what your mind and body
does, or you won't ever be able to fit into a square, or a round hole!"*
Dudley Griffin, 4.1.20

*"With the state of the media these days, no one knows what is real. This book is real!"*
JBMc, 6.2.1999

## CHAPTER 1

# Blame It All On Your Parents

*Little Johnny jumped into the world on March 5, 1943, at 6:45 pm West Coast Time. By 7 pm, he was searching for his next adventure. Shortly thereafter, big people in white coats, with sharp, shiny instruments were already snipping away at his manhood.*

My name is John Bassett McCleary, and I spent 7½ months in the womb, and that was more than enough for me, thank you. Since then, it has been my routine; I don't overstay my welcome, and I never sit still for boredom. I don't want to outlive my welcome or my usefulness!

My mother and father knew each other before I was born. On the surface, that sounds obvious, but what I'm saying is that they actually got to know each other before my conception and birth. That, in itself, is quite unique.

It is amazing how many couples conceive a child at their very first meeting, and many lovers copulate before they actually become at all acquainted.

The truth is that the majority of our relationships take place by accident, rather than planning, and it is interesting how many of these accidents and consequences are preordained by our biology, culture and economics.

Even though my mother and father had a number of years to work on their relationship, they still didn't <u>quite</u> work it out.

*Unknown to the rest of the world, they came together. They met by chance, these two animals, surrounded by trees within a grass-carpeted clearing.*

*The shock of seeing each other was replaced by curiosity at how similar, yet different, they were. They knew they were neither food nor predator, so they came closer to inspect.*

*They began by touching the parts of each other that were unique.*

*Soon they were fondling; shortly, they were rubbing their bodies together as feelings grew.*

*Stretched out on the bed of grass, they found and touched all their curves and openings. Eventually, their groins were drawn together by nature, and without their own will or choice, he entered her and they were joined.*

*The feeling was irresistible. They threw themselves together. Man's first passion was consummated! Woman's nurturing began.*

*Their indulgence was so complete that they barely heard the screaming saber-toothed tiger as he pounced. The three creatures fought a battle to life and to death.*

"Will You Still Love Me Tomorrow?" the Shirelles, 1961, Monterey Union High School, Carolyn Martin

Often, after some kind of epiphany, spirits or stimulant, I become convinced that I know everything there is to know about sex and life! Of course, I sometimes have to moderate my opinions, and I will be doing so throughout this narrative. Yet, I must say that, with my life's experiences, I have a fairly accurate understanding of the glue that holds human society together. Water, food, sex, politics, drugs, religion, money, and rock & roll.... Is that right; isn't that the whole thing?

When I say I know a lot about sex and things, this is not a pronouncement of arrogance; it is a realization based on the time of history I have lived and the circumstances of my life. I have lived and observed sex, religion, drugs, politics, rock & roll, advertising and commerce for the past 65 years through, arguably, one of the most vividly provocative, expressive and self-aware times of mankind.

From what I'm saying, you may get the impression that I think sex, drugs and R & R are the foundations of human society.... not exactly, yet I do know that these urges are very prevalent activities because they are very enjoyable activities, yet, at the same time, they are some of the most distracting and destructive of our experiences.

Money, religion, sex and politics, I consider the first, second, third and fourth worst elements of our society. Yet I also know that they are necessary and also unavoidable.

I am trying to make sense of our needs and urges and how they can co-exist with other peoples' needs and urges. I am so concerned about our sexual confusions that I am willing to stick my neck out and try to change the course of romance by offering some solutions to the craziness of sex.

You will notice, lest I appear arrogant, I will never boast about sexual prowess; now that would be arrogant! I'm just telling you what I have personally experienced and observed.

Sexual skill is subjective. Just as with food, everyone has their own method of cooking.

Sex is a matter of taste. Just as with wine and cheese, everyone has their favorite flavor.

Although I am not going to make a pronouncement of my own skills, I will say that I have always been very enthusiastic, experimental and grateful.

1957 to 1985, as a young man I wanted to make love with most every "available" woman I ever met. Most boys do.

To me, "available" has always meant "appropriate," and that is the key. Age, other attachments and desirability are always factors, even with an uncontrolled libido. Of course, most young men have uncontrolled libidos, and don't ever forget it. But it is the deviant libido of which society must be leery.

> *"'Boys will be boys' is a fact, a prediction and a warning."*
> Dudley Griffin, 12/27/13

Girls, please remember this! Most men, as adolescents or young adults, want to screw most women, at any place, and any time; it's hard-wired into our genes. It is how men treat women and/or respect women that separates the creepy predator from the lover.

By my observations, I see that a large percentage of men are incapable of being romantic. They use embarrassing humor or obnoxious aggression as their come-on.

Yet some of us men are actually able to employ common sense and discretion in our sex lives. These men have learned that, to get the true value and feeling of romance, it must be a balance of desire and respect. Why would you want to "make love" with someone you do not respect? At that point it is just like any of the other necessary or distasteful body functions. Masturbation would be just as good, and so I propose that you insensitive lovers just use that form of sex and leave all the sweet and beautiful ladies to those of us who care.

Wanting women is natural; how and why you want them is the sticky subject. Insecurity and competition are not good emotions in a love affair nor good reasons for sex.

I am a man who wanted women. I didn't want them because I thought they would make me look good, or because they would make me a man. I am a man who loves women. I do not lust after them, fear them, or compete with them; I love them.

And that is mostly because of my mother.

Because I loved and respected my mother, I have a high opinion of women in general. Many women have told me that they will not make a commitment to a man unless they know that his relationship with his mother was and is a good one.

*"History that is written by a participant, stories taken from one's own life, observations from the inside are so much more true!"*
DG

I am the love child of the Oklahoma dust bowl working class and the New England intellectual elite. The backgrounds of my parents were as different as wood and stone; her lineage might have come from the Apostle Paul, and my father's, from Marquis de Sade.

*"The word 'Mother' .... What does that mean to you? Is it a good emotion? Is it a good feeling, a bad feeling, or a blur?"*
*"The word 'Father' .... What does that mean to you? Is it a good emotion? Is it a good feeling, a bad feeling, or a blur?"*
DG

Although my mother said I was born prematurely, I know better. I just wanted to get on with it. Being a curious and restless sort, I would not be denied a moment of life; yet I had no idea what I was getting myself into.

I was born before Happy Meals, personal computers and cell phones. I grew up in the 1950s, 60s, 70s, and although most younger people today might think of that as the Dark Ages, that period of time, the 1960s and 1970s, was the renaissance of past glories and the beginning of a newer, brighter future for humankind if we could keep it going. We allowed you to be who you are today by breaking down emotional and social barriers.

The 1950s, 60s and 70s are, to this point, the most important years in the history of humankind. They ushered in the computer age, but they also awakened the emotions and intellect that could save us from the computer age. Man's new technology and ideas are usually double-edged swords. We can use them wisely, or they can begin our destruction as a society.

An old Chinese saying reads, "History is a mirror!" Studying our history shows us who we are, and if we ignore what we read, or do not understand it, we will have to start all over learning old lessons. This is why we have books and teachers, to give us a head start on our education, without having to relive, rethink and relearn all the past.

*"Societies and governments need someone to carry the clipboard. We need a collection of experienced, high-IQ intellectuals to tell as when we are being stupid!"*
DG

During the last hundred years, many social and economic ideas have come and gone. What is important to this world right now is to revisit some older ideas and ideals that have come back to our attention, and to reconsider and reuse them to make our future easier and more democratic for all people.

My mother was always in awe of the concept of the "Renaissance man." The Microsoft Encarta Dictionary, 2001, defines him as "a man who has a wide range of accomplishments and intellectual interests." Webster's 1987 edition defines him as "a man of wide knowledge in many fields."

Because of my mother's influence I have always aimed toward the ideal of the whole man, and the world has nudged me in that direction. My time, my place and circumstance of birth have forced me to become a Renaissance man. In essence, I have had to renew myself, every morning, every day when I awake.

If you are born into privilege, you may never have to be creative to succeed or survive. I am not saying that you will be a dull person or a rich failure, but you may never experience the joys of experimentation, challenge and personal success against great odds.

My parents met in the late 1920s, 14 years before I was born. She was a high school student in Monterey, California, working on the school newspaper. He was a newspaper publisher and journalist who printed her school paper on the presses of his small newspaper, just over the hill in Carmel. My father was 20 years older than my mother, and he was also married to someone else.

In 1929, after graduating from high school, my mother went to work for my future father at his newspaper. Their working relationship eventually, somehow, at some time, became a sexual relationship.

During the 1920s through the 1950s, Carmel was an art colony and the home of many Bohemian writers and personalities. John Steinbeck, Edward Weston, Robinson Jeffers, George Sterling, Man Ray, Gertrude Stein, Salvador Dali and numerous others lived and played in the permissive, liberal atmosphere of Carmel during this time. They drank cheap red wine, made love, ate abalone, and then wrote poems, sonnets and songs about the tasty little mollusk and their other indulgences.

Carmel has now lost most of its Bohemian attitude and quaint appeal since being discovered as a weekend tourist destination and a zip code for the rich to boast about. Postcards and T-shirts for some people, overpriced art, trophy homes, and decorative food for the palate of others.

When my mother and father lived there, Carmel had no industry except art and literature, the activities of geniuses and fools. Then, as now, you could buy a painting for less than the price of the frame to wrap around it. Then, as today, most writers spent more money on paper to write on than they would ever be paid back for the words they wrote on it.

Artists, it seemed, traveled to Carmel to absorb its natural beauty and translate it into their work. Or perhaps it was the other way around.

Which came first, artistic beauty or natural beauty? We can look at art in the context of the tree that fell in the forest. If there were no artists to inform us that what we see is beautiful, would we realize that there was such a thing as beauty?

The love of beauty is what sets humankind apart from all other creatures. After self-preservation is accomplished, the human mind turns to wander over the mysteries and creations of Mother Nature. Natural beauty, the song of a bird and the pastiche of a sunset are suggestions for man's fertile mind.

Art, music, literature and natural beauty transcend all the negative activities of mankind. They put the humanity into humans and place us closer to nature.

Since the fourteenth or fifteenth century, artists have been marginalized and even demonized by dominant business and military cultures throughout the world. Artists are seldom belligerent or violent except within their art and literature. They are often drawn to natural beauty and fight in their own way to preserve it. This is what they have tried to do along the coast of California and other places of beauty. Without artists, we would have to live in colorless cities and ravaged landscapes.

Where you are born and to whom you are born influences what you think of beauty! If your life is a struggle in a tragic and unlovely place, your appreciation of beauty, and therefore your intellectual development, will suffer. My place of birth and my parents' genes were my first, and at times, have been my only, advantage.

I was born with a wooden spoon in my mouth, and most of my spoons have been plastic, tin or pot metal ever since, with only a few silver ones from time to time.

The coast of California seems to overpower any attempts to transform it into man-made entertainment. The rocks, trees and ocean cannot be "packaged," no matter how hard the Chambers of Commerce try.

The soul and beauty of the coast of California create epic stories out of normal lives.

My parents were never a couple in the eyes of the governing bodies of the State of California, but they lived and worked closely together in a very small town for over ten years. I have photographs of them sunbathing on a California beach.

It must have been a little vacation on which they stole away. The photos show each of them separately with a dog I recognize from other photographs. They were alone, with no one else to take the shots, so they appear separately in the photos. Yet, they were actually together with the dog, the sand, the blanket and picnic lunch.

There was deniability; the photos did not show them together. I have only one photograph of my mother and father together. I am sure they were forced into discretion due to their age difference and the fact that he was married. Even so, theirs must have been an idyllic life and a romantic existence, living in one of the most beautiful places in the world, and loving each other as they did. My mother always said my father was the love of her life.

Even the surreptitious aspects of their love affair and the fantasies they lived must have been exciting. But, too often, forbidden fruit is forbidden for a reason, and fantasies that come true soon turn into harsh realities.

The bright sun reflects off white quartz sand. Flakes of crushed abalone mother of pearl shimmer in the tide pools. Intricate filigree cypress trees are outlined by the sun as it smooches down into the Western sea. But, on the coast, as with love, the glorious, crystal clear days must in time give way to the gray, emotive, paisley patterns of damp fog. Those who love, as those who live on the water's edge, must learn to appreciate the melancholy overcast along with the sparkles of bright, prismatic light.

In 1941, my mother, despairing of ever being accepted as his wife, moved to the San Francisco Bay area, away from my father-to-be. He had already divorced one wife and married another during their relationship, and my mother saw this as a bad sign.

Shortly after she left town, he sold his newspaper and moved to Hawaii for a job. They met one last time in the summer of '42. It was the end of their 13-year relationship. One last goodbye in the Hotel Californian in San Francisco, and I was the offspring.

My father later offered to marry my mother, but she declined. She had to remind him that he was already married to someone else.

As I said, my parents got to know each other before I was born and she knew he was unreliable as a father and husband. He was too unpredictable in his affections. She had already seen him divorce and marry someone else. And my father knew that my mother would not put up with his bullshit, so they didn't live happily ever after.

W. K., my father, went off to work as a journalist in Hawaii and advisor to the Mayor of Honolulu. My parents' romance had geographical and social difficulties.

Time and Place; they play more in our lives than we know. It served to establish my place of birth on the liberal shores of California, and that contributed to my intellectual development and attitude toward sex, politics, religion and saving the whales.

Great love affairs are usually defined by their tragic qualities. To be notable, it seems a romance must be fated. Fictional love stories often end with, "And they lived happily ever after." Real ones are a little less cut-and-dried.

My parents' relationship does not rank among the epic romances of our times. They were just "little" people living "small" lives, as so many others. But their coupling and my birth were the height of scandal and tragedy in our family and its little part of the world.

During the 1940s, many women were alone and pregnant; the War had their men. My father was also across the sea, but he was not fighting for his country, he was fighting for its people. W. K. was too old for military service, yet he was also "missing in action."

My father could not actually be called a Renaissance man. From what I know of him, he had few physical abilities other than thinking, writing, typing and printing skills. My mother told me that he learned a new word every day, the definition, how to spell it and how to use it. I know rationally that he did not do this all his life and literally every day, for that would be humanly impossible. He was a "muckraker." He wrote the truth and tried to keep politicians, businessmen and religious leaders strait by exposing their hypocrisy and crimes.

My father wrote many of his newspaper columns and articles on the Linotype machine. That was a real skill. That machine was hot, smelly and loud, and it had a different keyboard than a typewriter. Also, if you made a mistake, you had to reach in and pull out letters with your hand, and then once it was set in lead, you would have to replace a whole column line with a newly typed replacement.

My understanding is that one must be an intellectual/lumberjack, or poet/farmer or some such to be a true Renaissance man, but from reading my father's writing, I know he was a Renaissance thinker.

Birthmarks are not only to be found on the outside of our bodies. The mind is the closet for most family skeletons. What we learn from a loving parent, teacher or friend will stay with us to our deathbed, just as bad habits, a rotten personality or sick mind can be passed on to us.

It is possible to be blessed and cursed by the same incident in your life. I was affected both positively and negatively by my circumstances of birth.

I was fortunate in the geography of my birth and for the parents that I had, but that was about the extent of my advantages! There was no family wealth! But, my mother made up for that by giving me wealth beyond money. Pauline, my mother, read and talked to me as a young child. My brain was exercised; I was given curiosity; I was given a head start.

Educated and engaging parents, and an open, non-bigoted society will give you a good springboard for life. At least you will be more curious and open to new things because change is constant in life, and people who fight it are stagnant. I was fortunate that I had a fertile field of information and experimentation in California.

And parents, if you over-parent your children with the excuse that you are protecting them, you are really holding them back, whether it be from your ego, fear or jealousy. Protect them from the real dangers, not from ones you create in your head. Remember what it was like for you as a child; don't do to your children what you hated your parents for doing to you!

My mother said I got my intelligence and creativity from my father; yet I also inherited his grand ideals, which have made it impossible for me to be comfortable with mankind's bad behavior. I do not breathe easily in the world of greed, corruption and shenanigans, nor do I function well in a capitalist, deadly competitive economy.

People seem to fall into three basic categories, capitalistic personality, religious personality, or moralistic personality. I was not born or raised to be capitalistic or religious; my upbringing was moralistic. I try to do the right thing to help everybody live free and profitable. That was my mother and father's legacy to me.

The truth is, most people don't want a competitive world. It is a small percentage of insane assholes that do! Excuse my profanity, but I do not ask you to excuse my socio-economic political commentary. I am sure that if the people on this planet truly understood capitalism, they would label it a destructive economy and ban its practice.

As I have said, I never lived with my natural father or with a stepfather for long enough to count. Many psychologists will say that a fatherless upbringing is a potential problem for proper personality development in a young man. I call that hogwash.

My mother was all the parent I needed, and, from what I have seen in many families that had both parents, a child's development was often obstructed and perverted by the male influence.

I am not against male influence, as long as it is at least constructive, if not positive. But in my experience, it is all too often judgmental and macho-based, two things that are guaranteed to destroy rather than construct.

My mother had four brothers, one who died young and one who was a nice guy. The other two were macho characters. My mother's two sisters married cowboys the first time around. Both of their husbands were also macho. Real men by society's standards then, but in retrospect and by the awareness of today, they were lacking in human compassion

My most valuable asset from birth was my mother. Pauline was an intelligent and loving mother, yet she failed to teach me the selfishness necessary to excel in this era's economic jungle. She had to raise me on her own, but because of her strength and independence, we survived, and at least I was not cursed by the hypocrisies and conventions of the "Greatest Generation."

I was raised a poor white child, but I didn't know I was poor, nor was I taught that my whiteness was a superior state of being. My mother was a realistic person and a very fair one.

Life, like the heartbeat on a hospital monitor, is a series of ups and downs. Although one might hope for the good life, in reality, perfection soon becomes boring or formless, without contrast by which to gauge it. Boredom is the mother of frivolous choice and foolish invention. It takes pain as well as pleasure to sculpt a truly fruitful life!

I was conceived in the midst of the great Second World War. By that fateful wiggle of a sperm, I was destined to live during the 30 most radical years of moral and social change mankind had experienced in all of its previous time.

Unbeknownst to me, I was born to be a hippie! Out of the hatred and fire of war and death, out of the suppression of universal and sexual desires, sprang a whole generation of shiny-faced little kids, anxious to turn against their parents with peace signs and contraceptives.

By a vortex of chance, people born in The United States and much of Europe within a small window of time from 1941 to 1947 would reach adolescence in the uptight, yet impossibly romantic, 1950s. Then they would be sexually reeducated during the alarmingly real and psychedelically erotic counterculture of the 1960s and '70s.

Because of the date and place of my birth, I lived the best of all worlds, socially and sexually. Along with the other boomers, I was exposed to new and imaginative cultural ideals and physical freedoms.

I experienced both idealistic love and realistic love. I saw the hypocrisy of romance in the 1950s and then the raw bones of spiritual lust in the 1960s.

I have tasted all the flavors, sampled all the aromas and seen all the dimensions of sex and of life, the good and bad, the uptight and the out of sight. I know most all the psychological and physical sexual positions because I have experienced them.

I know the perversions of men and how they got them! There may be some chemical imbalances in some men, but, for the most part, most sins are taught to you by your family. I know how men become liars, cheats, bigots, greedy, sexual predators, wife beaters and rapists!

Every good thing and every bad thing that a person does in their life is ultimately created by the first six or eight years of their life. That is the time when you are most affected by your surroundings, and that means the presence or absence of your family and their influences, good and bad, upon you.

*"I know how all you parents can avoid failing as parents!*
*Teach your children how to read and write;*
*read to them, write down their stories;*
*then you won't have to support them for the rest of your lives.*
*Respect them, and teach them respect for others and their property;*
*then you won't have to bail them out of jail*
*or watch them being executed by the state.*
*Don't force your own values, faults and insecurities on your children,*
*and they won't kill you in your bed."*
*Dudley Griffin, 12-12-2020*

*Don't create arrogant children. Even if you were taught to be arro-*
*gant, break the downward spiral. You don't want your children to*
*hate you, do you? Arrogance breeds contempt.*
*Do you hate your parents? Break the downward corruption of the*
*family. Teach your children respect for themselves, for others and*
*thereby for you"*
*Mr. California*

CHAPTER 2

## Dixie Peach

Between 1955 and 1985, I lived every scenario of teenage childhood, adolescent and young adult activity that you have ever seen in any TV and movie script, even up to this date!

I don't have to write one word of fiction to make my memoir interesting. It has always just happened that way.

I have had the same jar of Dixie Peach "concentrated conditioner & hair dress" for over 45 years. Eat your heart out, Madonna and John Travolta.

This historic jar of "pomade" is a good example of the indestructibility of petroleum products and of my nostalgic nature. I have kept this same container of goop through several fashion rebirths of the duck's ass and "greaser" hairstyle, and long after I ceased to have enough hair on top to construct a flat top. The label reads:
Enriched with lanolin

DIXIE PEACH
POMADE
concentrated
conditioner & hair dress

INGREDIENTS: PETROLATUM, FRAGRANCE,
LANOLIN OIL.
Extra rich to keep hair smooth, silky, fragrant.
For best results apply just a "touch" to scalp and hair with fingertips.
DIXIE PEACH, FORT LEE, N.J. 07024, DIST.
Ingredients and instructions are also written in Spanish.

Nostalgia is what caused me to drag that jar around from pad to pad, through numerous houses and relationships. Unbeknownst to her, my mother also stored this container for long periods of time. Whenever I packed up from some temporary home to go traveling around the world, I would leave boxes of my accumulated essential stuff under my family home. Somehow, that jar of Dixie Peach ended up in this collection of boxes, and sometimes it would show up when I moved some of those boxes back into a new living situation.

My mother didn't know what memories she held, and I didn't know how important those memories were. I was often surprised to find that Dixie Peach still among my possessions, yet I always suppressed the urge to throw it away. That jar has always reminded me of my many adolescent struggles for sexual equilibrium and social identity during the 1950s.

And why should this be of any interest to you? Does it affect you personally? Are you worried about someone? Are you worried about yourself?

Sex is the beginning of life, as well as a highlight of life, yet it is a stumbling block to many people.

Aside from the natural attraction that the word "sex" creates and beyond any prurient interest you might have, there are lessons to be learned from the strange rituals and deep insights of the "Hippie Era." I am a hippie, I am curious, I am concerned for the future of human life, and I am a guinea pig for the effects of sex, drugs and rock & roll!

But don't be concerned that I might demystify sex and thereby spoil it for you. I want to explain sex to the degree that people will stop being hypocritical about their feelings. Come on, let's all stop lying about our emotions! Get a grip on your sexuality, or else it will continue to haunt you, and you will never get any real enjoyment out of it!

I'm not going to tell you anything that will make sex predictable or cause you to become jaded toward it. I won't ruin sex by putting it in a scientific specimen bottle!

I am also not proselytizing for any particular kind of sex life. It is a fact of life, and we must know what we are dealing with.

Likewise, I am not going to try to titillate you or make you horny! I would like to help you experience sex, not as sexy nor illicit, but as normal! I want to help normalize sex, thus putting it in the proper perspective for rational human beings, to help us all see and experience sex as a part of life, not as a problem of life.

If anything, I intend to help you to experience every ounce

of thrill from sex by helping you to understand why you have these physical urges. It is surprising how many people don't know why they like sex or what makes them "feel the urge."

*"We are all sexual.... This is what art and creativity comes from!"*
*Marilyn Monroe, 1962*

Knowing my mother, when she learned that she was pregnant, there was never any question whether she would have this child. It had nothing to do with religion; it had everything to do with love and her primal urge to nurture.

Recently, I have begun wondering if Pauline planned her pregnancy. I know that she was intelligent and introspective enough to have done so, and I know why she would have. She knew that a marriage to my father would probably not have worked. She also knew that she wanted something of him to remember him by. This is the real love in their love story.

I don't know the economics of childbirth in the 1940s, but whatever the expense, it would have been a big obstacle for a single woman with no support from her family. Fortunately, my mother knew one of the last real doctors to walk on the planet.

Dr. Rukke personified the Hippocratic oath. A family friend, the good doctor arranged for my birth, without charge, at the University of California Medical Center in San Francisco.

The actual subject of this book is not the young man in this story. The subject is sex. Sex, which is the most complex aspect of human life and the most prevalent of our emotions.

Sex is complex for humans because it is not only a physical necessity, but also an emotional necessity.

The person in this book, John, is just a normal human being. Because he is normal, he is very much like the fly, the deer, the shark, or the lizard. He responds primarily to the stimuli of life.

Sexual desire is the most powerful stimulus in nature after thirst and hunger. If we try to deny it or rebel against it, it will destroy us. Sexual suppression creates hypocrisies, deviations and unhealthy fixations.

I believe that mankind is the most confused and destrutive animal on earth, and this can be proven by many examples. This destructive nature is due to the fact that humankind has not figured out how to accept and properly respond to the ins and outs of sexual desire. In this respect, the "lesser animals" have a better handle on life than we do. This is why a date with a beagle hound is usually less stressful than one with another human being.

Every fuck has a story. It can be fast food or a love affair. It can be a one-nighter or an opulent feast. As with food, there are many restaurants and many flavors.

But sex has more than just four stars by which to rate it, and, unlike food, each experience has a story worth telling. "The first time," or the last effort of an old couple before they are separated by death; every intercourse has a tale to tell.

*"Moonlight and love songs, never out of date. Hearts filled with passion, jealousy and hate. Woman needs man, and man must have his mate, that no one can deny.    It's still the same old story. A fight for love and glory. A case of do or die. The World will always welcome lovers as time goes by."*

"As Time Goes By" 1931
Words and music by Herman Hupfeld
Suggested by Dudley Griffin

In appearance, I guess I would be right between my father and mother. He had that gaunt, intense, questioning look; she was soft and beautiful with an irony that haunted everyone. Their eyes were intense; hers were beautiful.

Turning points in life are not just opportunities; they can be pitfalls as well. You make what you can of them, according to your abilities, timing and circumstances.

Are you who you are in this life because of what you have been given or because of what you have done yourself? Are you a winner because of what your family gave you in terms of genes, money or environment? Are you a winner because of what you have carved out for yourself? Or are you a winner because of good fortune?

Are you a loser because of what fate has dealt you, or are you a loser because of what you have done with your own life?

What we are given, we can multiply or squander. Over fate, we have no control.

I was born in California, not Texas. It was a close call; the bridge over the Rio Grande was washed out!

Life is like a crap game. Everything we do, from crossing the road to being born is a risk. The fact that any man even exists is a toss of the dice. We throw the dice, and they tell us whether we win or lose, go this way or that. Sure, we have some say in the situation. We can sometimes choose when and where to throw the dice. We can try to rig the dice. But the ultimate control we have over our lives is how we deal with the decision of the dice. And we can also decide how to react to the outcome! We can have rotten grapes, or we can have wine! It's all in our minds, you know!

It's called attitude, positive or negative. Lemons or lemonade. Glass half-full or half-empty....You know!

A full glass is really no better than a half-full one 'cause all you drink at a time is one gulp. I'm the kind of guy who is just grateful to have a glass.

Yet some people need a way to judge how well they're doing in order to establish an attitude, positive or negative. As long as you don't get stuck in a downward spiral, sometimes the negative attitude gives you a jumpstart to get the damn glass filled up again.

Attitude aside, there are things in our lives over which we have no control. Circumstances and choices are made for us, such as who our father is or where we are born.

Sometimes, other people or circumstances throw the dice for us. As with everyone, there were turning points in my life over which I had no choice because they happened before I came of age. The circumstance of my birth was one of these. As everyone else, I woke up one day and was informed that these were my parents, and this was where I lived.

My first inadvertent turning point, which I believe went in my favor, concerns a bridge that washed out. On numerous occasions, my mother said to me, "Thank God, when my family tried to go back to Texas, the bridge over the Rio Grand River was swept away by the rain!"

My mother was born in the Panhandle of Texas, somewhere between Lubbock and Amarillo. That's like the Australian outback or Gobi Desert of America. Normally, this is where a writer is expected to conjure up visual images of the landscape in flowery prose for the reader, but all I can think of to describe this place where my mother was born is to say that nearby is a town spelled "Levelland" which should be pronounced "level land," yet called "Loveland" by the locals using some form of Texas rationality.

At this point in America's subjugation of America, around 1906, when my mother was born, most of the once proud Native Americans were relegated to dusty reservations and obligated to reenact snake dances and weave rugs to earn their keep. Those who would behave themselves and were not killed off were sometimes allowed to contribute to the gene pool of the new American society. My maternal grandfather and mother were both part Native American.

My mother's mother and father moved to Texas from the State of Oklahoma, which was previously named Indian Territory, until the pioneers decided to steal even that sorry-assed piece of land away from the "Indians!" Coming from Oklahoma, my maternal grandmother was part Cherokee or Arapaho; I'm not sure which. Family members also say my mother's father had Native American blood.

I have always been enthralled by the Norman Rockwell magazine cover depicting the family tree of an angelic looking little boy, showing his ancestors as puritans, pirates, dance hall girls, cowboys and Indians. I am all of that.

Sometime in the 1920s, my mother's family went to California from Texas to work in the cotton fields, and, when trying to return to Texas, they were stopped by the flooded Rio Grand River. I am well aware that, if the bridge had been there, my mother could likely have married an alfalfa farmer, and my name would be Clint or Buck.

If that bridge had been passable, my mother would never have met my father, I would have different genes, and I might be named after Daniel Boone rather than John Steinbeck and W. K. Bassett--another roll of the dice over which I had no choice. So I was born in San Francisco, not Lubbock or Dallas. More will be said later about this good fortune.

Everyone has turning points; some turns work for them, some

against. Often, we don't know at the time whether it is a good or bad turn. Many times, the left fork in the road is no better than the right fork, just different.

Each pathway exposes us to alternative political, intellectual, and spiritual sensibilities. These experiences mold our social, economic and sexual personalities.

As you will discover of me, I believe in education, both book learning and life learning. Stay in one town for your whole life, and you posses only the attitude of the rest of those in your town. Go out into the world, and you might find that you are wrong, or even find that you are right, and whatever the truth is, it will strengthen you and make you a better person.

I believe that a person's attitude toward sex has a major effect upon who they really are. Good or evil, happy or sad, greedy or generous.

So, on March 5, 1943, I was born looking for excitement. My next adventure came when the doctors used me as a guinea pig by performing an experimental circumcision. That was the first indication that little Dudley's life was not going to be your run-of-the-mill experience.

"Miss or ah... Mam, we are a teaching and research hospital. We would like to perform an experimental circumcision on your son." I can't imagine what my mother felt when they told her that!

What the young medical students did might be considered invasive, a gamble, and definitely a scary prospect. Yet, I am convinced that the circumcision they performed on me was a good gamble, I believe that it served to create a more physically sensitive feeling for me while making love and, therefore, a more fulfilling sex life for both my partner and for me.

I am sure that, once the public and medical profession realize the attributes of this simple alteration, it will create a gold mine of new business. And I want to make sure it's named after me. Not because I invented it, but because I have the guts to admit it and the perspective to see its value.

We will call it "The Bassett Cut." And later I will describe the actual medical procedure and explain the physical, emotional and social aspects of this simple miracle that could, in the long run, benefit both sexes mutually. It may even create nirvana for mankind!

I know, I just lost some people! I broke the barrier into the "ick factor" or "nasty bits," as the British call them.

I am aware that, whenever someone writes about sexual anatomy, many people automatically place it in a category of salacious, perverted material. But there is another category! It is education. This book is a combination of both.

I probably couldn't get your attention if this were only a textbook, and I wouldn't want your attention if you thought I was only trying to titillate you for my own twisted ego. This book is written to appeal to your curiosity, desire for information, social advancement and, perhaps, sexual fulfillment. I hope you have the fortitude and the intellect to follow it through to the end because it will change your life or make you question what you now believe and feel.

Nothing new is ever created from passively following the rules and instructions. To create something new, you have to break some old rules. Knowing me, you would know that this has been my life's mantra. This philosophy has also been largely forced upon me by my circumstances. If you're not on the guest list, and you want to get in, it's easier, and often necessary, to enter through the back door.

My mother had a saying about me as a child. "Go find Johnny. Find out what he's doing, and tell him to stop." It was her little joke, of course. I was always adventurous, but usually not dangerous.

I have never been in jail for more than a few hours, in total, in my entire life. And that was a gross miscarriage of justice, of course. I was hitchhiking in a foreign State of the Union called Tennessee.

I have never maimed, defamed or killed anyone, yet I have

tempted the laws of nature many times, and broken moral "rules" on a regular basis. Usually, I fracture only rules I consider to be ridiculous anyway.

My transgressions have never been monumental or life-threatening. They just have a tendency to annoy some people, primarily conservative-type folks. But, after all, they annoy the hell out of me too!

I was raised by a single mother, but I never missed having a father. My mother, Pauline, had all the love and wisdom of two people.

The circumstances of my birth may be considered a disadvantage by many. I was born illegitimate to a woman of very little means, yet most of my disadvantages ended there. Pauline raised me to enjoy my life and to ignore all obstacles to a happy, productive existence.

*"If I am ever in dire danger and my salvation requires that I must 'think a happy thought' and thus survive; all I need to do is think of my mother." JBMc*

In observing the lives of some of my friends who were raised with the involvement of fathers, I actually think I may have been fortunate not to have had one. And, as far as being poor as a child, I feel that, if it is handled properly by the parents, a child need never suffer from humble beginnings.

First off, Pauline never laid a heavy trip me about being poor. The money we had, though sparse, was always portioned out to cover reasonable necessities with a little left over for fun and entertainment. My mother never voiced any complaints about what we didn't have or jealousy about what others had. If I told her that Billy had a bright new bicycle, Pauline would always say something like, "How nice for him," and then she would buy me a newly repainted, used bike.

My only memory of feeling deprived was associated with that bicycle. Because we lived on the hills of San Francisco during my first years, I didn't get a bicycle until I was seven or eight years old when we moved to the Central Valley. A child on a bicycle in the windy and hilly City by the Golden Gate could easily, by accident, embark on a journey that would leave him lost and alone, miles from home.

After moving to Chico, a flat town in North Central California, I was finally allowed wheels. My first bike was small, with hard rubber tires and no gears. I had to pedal almost as fast as the wheels of the bicycle were turning just to stay within sight of my friends on their shiny new bikes. I could have just as easily gone as far and as fast on foot as I could on that bicycle.

No, I never got the newest or most expensive. And I never got a lot of toys or clothes at all, but what I did get, I appreciated and treated with great care.

The legacy is that, today, as an adult, I don't suffer from the American mental illness of always wanting everything new and shiny.

I don't feel the need to spend money on all the newest gadgets or the most extravagant adult toys. I also don't worry about money, or the lack of it, as many people do. I am always able to supply the necessities of life and enough frivolous entertainment as well.

Although my mother suffered greatly through the Dust Bowl era and the Depression, she never overreacted as many did. My mother and her family were Dust Bowl immigrants and migrant workers, but I did not suffer from the ego-driven expectations that many children did who had insecure and frustrated fathers.

My maternal grandfather was a carpenter who bought property, built houses, sold them to feed his family, and migrate on. My mother once said that, if all the houses her father built had red roofs, a pilot in a small plane could navigate from Oklahoma through Texas, New Mexico and on up to the Central Coast of California by following his bright red dots on the landscape.

I have a receipt book in James Littleton Meeks' handwriting with notations of money received for the construction of a Piggly Wiggly market in Hot Springs, New Mexico. My maternal grandmother is buried in a cemetery in that town, which is now called Truth Or Consequences.

The story of why that city changed its name is amusing and somewhat relevant to a major theme of this book, which is greed and insecurity. Between 1950 and 1974, there was a radio and TV game show program called "Truth Or Consequences." The promoters of the show thought that they could produce some good publicity by asking a city in America to change its name to the name of their show.

Hot Springs, New Mexico, took the challenge, became Truth Or Consequences, and gained a little fame and a lot of ridicule. The sad point about this was that the town had originally been named for the hot springs that provided comfort for Native Americans of the region for thousands of years.

Up a canyon several miles from town are natural fortifications where Geronimo and his Apache warriors held off the entire U.S. Army for years. The canyons were easily defended by a few braves, and the hot springs helped the tribe to endure the cold winters. Geronimo might have been amused, appalled, and/or philosophical about the new name on the signpost outside of town. *Truth Or Consequences, the new name of the town, had its ironic twist.*

*"The enemy of truth is lies, the consequence of lies is to be forever wrong."* Reportedly said by one of Geronimo's most trusted scouts, just after he lied saying he didn't see the U.S. Army over the next hill. He was paid with a pint of bad whiskey to say the lie.

*"Lies bring consequences, either from the Gods, or from man. Lies are the army of the ego, and sexual status is the domain of the ego."*
These are the words of Geronimo channeled through Dudley Griffin!

The word ego, itself, is often used as a definition of insecurity. From what I know about Native American cultures, sexual hypocrisy was not part of their lives. It took Christianity and alcohol to concoct that brew.

My mother's lessons gave me the eyes to see how destructive arrogance and selfishness are. Her upbringing crafted a realistic ego and a less competitive nature in me. This is where fathers often muck-up a family and destroy their children.

Discipline that bludgeons children, and expectations that are too lofty and not based on love, can damage the psyche of a young person. Fathers sometimes look at children as representatives of their own egos. They often place requirements on children to fulfill their own needs, not the needs of the child.

Don't give your child a challenge you know they can't possibly accomplish. Don't set your child up to fail! Congratulate them on each thing that they do learn. Remember, no one, even you, is ever born with knowledge!

Unreasonable expectations, or even expectations that are reasonable, yet do not take into consideration the desires or aptitudes of the child, can force that child into failure, which in turn damages self-confidence. Degrading, ridiculing or embarrassing a child for not reaching expectations will cripple their self-esteem.

Not having had a father's presence and also not having had a father's displeasure puts me in a unique, objective position to judge the power and influence of fathers. I am not emotionally prejudiced by a bad, nor a good relationship with a father. I am speaking only as an observer, and that, I think, is a more realistic viewpoint to dissect paternal authority, and its effects. I have known far too many men who were destroyed or damaged by an asshole father.

*"It is my pleasure that my children are free, happy, and unrestrained by parental tyranny. Love is the chain whereby to bind a child to its parents!"*
Abraham Lincoln

Many fathers think ridicule makes a child strong, but what it really does is create a thin facade of artificial strength and arrogance that actually hides their insecurity. Tough "love" on a child who does not have the capacity to know more than a soft touch or a painful slap is bad parenting. And you will pay for it, believe me! You will be cursed by your child or blessed by your child; that is your choice.

*"The young man struggled through his school career. It wasn't the academics, social life or sports that caused him grief. Good-looking, intelligent and physically fit, he had only one problem as a child- -his own father.*

*The boy got nearly straight A's, contributed to record-breaking team sports, and was a tall and handsome lad. Yet, his one disadvantage was an insecure parent.*

*His father had been physically and emotionally abused by his own father, for the sake of appearances, for the sake of winning and achieving more than he had. The sins of the father visited upon the child.*

*The sins spoken of here are the ones inflicted upon the child by the father.*

*No just God would blame a child for his father's sins. But fathers often pass their own flaws on to their own children.*

*Insecurity is manifested in masculine posturing. The young man's father "needed" him to excel in sports. Insecurity is also expressed in the false hope that education will make you a more important person. The young man's father drove him to unnecessary academic goals.*

*His father never asked him what he wanted. His father always wanted for his son what he needed for himself.*

*The young man's father had no friends, because he was unlikable, so he bound his children to him with fear and guilt, so he would have someone to salve his own insecurity. What the father created was empty, meaningless devotion. What he left behind were children who could not stand emotionally on their own." Dudley Griffin 12.12.6*

My father did not do this to me! And I don't think he would have done so even if he had lived with us and had the chance to. From what I have read of his writing, I think he had more common sense than that.

But many fathers do demean their children, and they especially do it to their boys. My mother always encouraged, never pushed. She showed interest and appreciation in what I wanted to do, no matter what it was, as long as it gave me pleasure, as long as it made me happy. This gave me self-confidence. If women were the primary disciplinarians in the house, we would create better adults.

The hippie culture tried and is still trying today to ease the macho pressures on children. *Teach Your Children (Well)*, CSN&Y, 1970, was one of many songs of the times that asked parents to guide rather than force their children, and to expand rather than pollute young minds.

In the debate about which is more important to a child's development, blood or environment, I have to say I think it all depends on which is the most dominant. Also, you must realize that the family influence is actually environmental and may have nothing to do with bloodlines. You can come from aristocracy, yet beat your wife and enslave millions of people, or you can be whelped from the Panhandle of Texas and become a deeply loved matriarch of a large, poor family. An aristocratic nature is not based on money or power; it is based on self-confidence and a benevolent nature.

My mother by Sonya Noskowiak

## Love Light

Above all, my mother was respectful and rational to everyone and about everything.

Thanks to my mother, I am a self-confident sort. Even saying that is a breach of self-confidence. To boast is insecurity, but since I am writing about these things, I must use examples. Since I know myself better than I do any other person, I use myself as the blueprint.

Because of my mother and the way I was raised, I don't need to enhance my image with arrogance or new and extravagant commodities. To paraphrase Freud, a real man does not have need of things to make himself a man. These expensive toys are only sexual sublimation, and they indicate insecurity.

Pauline knew that the key to a good life started with a good relationship with yourself. She must have known that happiness required self-confidence and self-respect. Self-confidence and a smile were her solutions to all the disadvantages of life.

My mother taught me self-respect and confidence, primarily by respecting me. She knew that people needed a mirror to see themselves, to see if they were OK. And if parents, whom we trust because they gave us life, reflect love and respect back to us, then we will feel good about ourselves.

But if a person's own family, the first people they know in this life, does not have faith in them, then it is impossible for a child to feel confident and secure. Many families kill their children's spirit before the children have a chance to live.

Pauline knew that, to live a good life, a person also had to have the love and respect of other people. Society is harsh on those who are selfish. The business world may be kind to those who are greedy, but the world of real people is not.

My first lessons in life were about mutual cooperation--sociability, if you will. Pauline taught me respect for other people and their property. She taught me by example. She taught me respect for others by respecting them herself.

She also taught me respect for myself by respecting me. It was all part of helping me to fit into society. You cannot expect to be embraced by other people if you cannot embrace yourself.

Along the same lines, you cannot expect children to obey you if you don't respect them. Children, like animals, still possess the sixth sense, before language and lies become their (our) form of communication, and they know sincerity and insincerity! If you teach children because you love them, they will follow. If you teach them just so they won't embarrass you, they will see your hypocrisy.

Children will not follow your rules if they don't make any sense. Human children are smarter than that. And they are smarter at a much younger age than most parents realize.

We can't expect our children to obey us if we are just on our own power trip! We can't push children around for our own gratification. Well, maybe we can, but in many cases we are then creating a monster.

Discipline is destructive if it is only punishment. Discipline is effective only if it is constructive. Discipline is also only followed, if it makes sense; children are more aware than you think, and if you give them a load of crap, one day they will throw it right back in your face. It must be administered to protect children, give them good habits, and then it will help them cope in the world.

If you discipline without a reason, if you rule with only an iron hand, and without love, you can create a monster--a monster you will have to live with and suffer from for the rest of your life!

*Little Johnny said "No!"*

*It wasn't just that he said it, but it was the defiance that sparked*

35

*from his voice. Recently, he had been trying out that word "No" and negative tone to see how far it would take him. As all children of his age, he was testing his environment to see its limits.*

*As all newborn creatures, he came to life wanting everything. After all, selfishness has its roots in self-preservation. Society would need to mold his desires into perspective with the needs and wants of all the others around him, or else he would become an outcast or psychopath.*

*Johnny didn't want to go home. He wanted to play with the older children on the street. Each afternoon, the neighborhood kids would gather to play kick the can or tag in the little pockets of sun that still remained.*

*As the late afternoon shadows and evening fog crept up the hill from the canyons of the City, the children would scurry before them like sandpipers from the waves. The demarcation of the sun moved up the street toward Coit Tower. Patterns of bright warmth and cold shadow were stenciled on the pavement by the shapes of buildings.*

*Slowly, the small tribe of children moved up the hill, chasing the sun. The morphing mass of giggles and screams changed and evolved as new arrivals joined and others went home to hot meals.*

*The band of comrades slowly shrunk as it ascended the four-block hill toward the park at the top. Only the older boys or those with no parental supervision outlasted the sun and then stumbled back home just before it became too dark to see their footfalls on the steep, treacherous street.*

*Johnny wanted to stay outside with the other children. His mother reached for his hand, and he turned and ran.*

*The child's avenue of escape was downhill, as the easiest path to freedom. Down the steep, slippery sidewalk he ran.*

*Pauline hesitated for only a heartbeat before chasing after her son. In high heels and nylons, her pursuit would be dangerous, but the consequences of not chasing him could be tragic.*

*Headlong, following momentum, Johnny's little feet tried to keep up with the rest of his body. His mother knew that at any moment, gravity could tip her son off balance, and he would fall, bouncing and scraping on the unforgiving concrete. Or worse, he could make it to the next intersection and be struck by a passing car. But Pauline also instinctively knew the deeper consequences of allowing Johnny to succeed with this first dangerous rebellion.*

*His mother knew that little Johnny was measuring his world. Could he get away with ignoring his mother's insistent voice? Pauline knew that if she did not catch him this first time, she might never be able to stop him with her voice again, and soon he would outrun her.*

*With determination and risk, Johnny's mother caught him just at the curb of the intersection. Her first reflex was to slap him, once, hard on the exposed calf of the leg, just below his short pants. Her next response was to gather him into her arms and tell him how much she loved him and how frightened she had been for his safety.*

*Johnny must have cried and clung to his mother. He was saved, and he knew he was wanted, and he would listen to his mother's voice from then on because there was a consequence, but mostly because there was someone who cared about him.*

*Pauline's high heels would never be the same, and the runs in her stockings meant she would have to save up again for the expensive postwar fashion. But she had passed a test that would affect her relationship with her son for the rest of their lives. Johnny knew his mother cared about him, not just because she demanded his discipline, but because the discipline had a reason. She loved him.*

God's greatist gift, a baby's breath upon my face.

My mother never spanked me or yelled at me for her own gratification. She disciplined me only when it was for my own good. She knew that respectable behavior toward others, herself included, was necessary for my acceptance and happiness in the society in which I was to live. Little Johnny would listen to his mother and obey, not because it hurt when I didn't, but because it felt good when I did.

My professional baseball career never had a chance. For the first seven years of my life, I didn't even know what a ball was. Where I lived in San Francisco, any round object that hit the ground ended up either on Market Street nine blocks down that way or six blocks in another direction, floating in the bay.

But I did know the inside of a library. I heard great music in great buildings and saw magnificent art. My mother read to me, and she also wrote down the stories I created.

Because my mother was a single parent, she had to work to feed, clothe and house us. I was, by necessity, in preschool and daycare while my mother worked in the shipyards supporting us and the war effort.

I still have Pauline's shipyard toolbox and some of her tools. One of those is a pair of channel-lock pliers. I carry them in my truck. I use them all the time.

Old tools and old memories are built better than today's tools or today's "experiences." If an experience is hardy enough to stay with you for a few years, it powers up and becomes part of who you are.

Old tools, like memorabilia, are visual and tactile reminders of well-spent time and work, and their value, just like their power, grows with each year. My mother's tools are useful pieces of metal, but they are also even more powerful objects of good "juju."

A preschool education was another positive influence on my life for negotiating the many turns of the world to come. The Phoebe Hearst Preschool Day Care Centers in San Francisco were some of the first childcare facilities in this country, and attending them gave me a head start in many directions.

During the first five years of my education, I was always a minority. A white Anglo-Saxon boy who didn't know I was different or that "they" were different. A liberal ethnic education may seem strange to some people, but please tell me how it can possibly be bad!

I have always been able to speak in numerous English accents or feign different Asian and European languages. As a matter of fact, I spoke with a British accent when I first began to talk

John at the Phoebe Hearst School, 1945.

The reason for this is that, at 18 months of age I was the smallest of the children in my preschool. Because of this, the young English woman who watched over us at daycare would carry me on her hip as she made her rounds. When I first began to speak, I adopted what I heard most, her British voice.

This was cute and all that, but my mother realized that her job was keeping her away from me most of my waking hours. She arose early and returned home late in order to commute to and from the Oakland shipyards. For this reason, my mother looked for another occupation.

Mother eventually found an office job in the financial district just down the hill from our home. Then she could walk to and from work, to the daycare center in North Beach, and up the hill to our cold water flat. She had more time with me.

For those who don't understand "cold water flat," it was an apartment in a building that did not have hot running water. Many of these buildings originally didn't even have cold running water. In the 1940s, these flats were usually being plumbed little by little. Later, in the 1950s, hot water heaters were installed.

Our apartment consisted of a bedroom and living room, a kitchen and an enclosed back porch, used as a laundry room. No dining room, family room, library, study or bathroom. We had a "water closet," a closet that, at some point in the golden dawn of indoor plumbing, had been outfitted with a toilet. You know, one of those quaint contraptions with the box of water up above and a pull chain to release it.

The sucking rush of water down that pipe was so demonstrably loud that everyone on the block knew when we used the toilet. I suspect that may be one of the reasons I don't flush every time even today, and not just to conserve water.

For most of the five or six years we lived in that apartment, we didn't have a hot water heater, bathtub or shower. All water was heated on the gas kitchen stove for cleaning dishes, clothes and bodies.

For bathing, I had a square cement laundry sink in the back porch. I got a few inches of tepid water in the bottom to luxuriate in. My mother took sponge baths standing up in a four-foot-diameter galvanized tub.

We were on the top floor of a three-flat, three-story building. In those days the top floor apartment was the cheapest, because you had to walk up the stairs. No one cared much about the penthouse views at that time. But I can remember fondly the glorious view of San Francisco Bay, the Bay Bridge and the Oakland hills beyond from my cement bathtub.

My mother stood in the galvanized tub and washed herself in the chilly atmosphere of Northern California. One day, after years of these baths, my mother was having a medical checkup when the doctor discovered a dark, diamond-shaped patch in the middle of her back. For all those years my mother was unable to reach that spot with her washcloth.

Just before we moved from that apartment, the owner finally installed a water heater and an aluminum shower stall in the corner of the kitchen. Although I can't precisely remember the experience, I can imagine that my first hot shower must have been a life-altering experience. Hot water has been a sensual indulgence for me ever since.

*"Food, sex and money, in that order, are what make the world go round. Air, water, food and sex are the physical necessities. Beauty in art and nature, drugs and rock & roll are emotional necessities. Power and money (or money and power) are ego-driven necessities."*
Geronimo through Dudley Griffin

Richard was my first masculine influence. My mother met him in San Francisco during the Second World War. He was a soldier passing through, to and from the conflict. He eventually became a highly decorated veteran.

Richard was a medic in the European theater and risked his life crawling out under fire to rescue a number of wounded men. For this, he received the Silver Star for heroism, second only to the Medal of Honor.

My mother was already pregnant when they met, but they spent a lot of time together. He offered to marry her, because to be a woman unmarried and pregnant in the mid-1940s was considered an embarrassment.

My mother declined his offer of marriage. She didn't love him in that way, and if you knew my mother, you would know that she was not embarrassed by her condition. A love child was nothing for her to be ashamed of. She had loved my father deeply, and I was his representative within her.

Richard was an artist. I have illustrated letters written to my mother from him while he was serving in Europe. I have pictures of battlefields, in Bausch-like starkness and pain, and also cartoons of the silly formalities of the military.

After the war, Richard returned to San Francisco, and he and my mother continued their relationship. Richard was the first man to give me a bright red truck. It was a chalk drawing he did of a Reno, Nevada fire engine that hung over my bed for most of my childhood. It hangs in my office today.

The first time I got drunk was with Richard and Pauline. I was three or four years old. We were out for dinner, and I kept secretly stealing sips of wine from their glasses.

As my mother told me years later, they didn't discover my larceny until we began walking up the hill from the North Beach restaurant. I wobbled even more than my three-year-old legs would have normally. I can remember them holding my hands and supporting me between them as we walked home. They swung me up and over each curb, and we laughed a lot.

And here is the twist. Richard was a "flaming" homosexual. An unashamed "queer." I have a photograph of him in his military uniform, as gay as "gay" can be. (photo) And from this man I got my first, and possibly most important, lessons of what it should be like to be a "real man." These were sensitivity, loyalty and self-confidence.

Richard was by far more supportive of my mother's illegitimate pregnancy than her own brothers were. Richard was a gentleman. Richard was a war hero. Richard was a friend. Richard was a lover without asking for benefits.

Don't ask, don't tell...? Hell, ask and tell and live with it! Use a person's strengths; don't prey on what you think of as his weaknesses. If I had to fight a war, I would rather fight next to a homosexual or a woman, than a macho, self-absorbed egotist any time.

Lest you get the impression that this book is about homosexual love, I confess it is about <u>love</u>, all kinds of love. But, I must tell you here and now that I am a straight man, hopelessly, unshakable a serial heterosexual, and yet this book is no more about hetero-sex than it is about homo-sex. This book is also applicable to any of the many sexes. All the basics are the same. This book is about love, with enough sex stirred in to make it a realistic representation of true human life.

Writers, critics or censors who try to separate humans from their sexual activity might just as well try to create a mankind without faces or thoughts. Our sexuality is one of the most interesting things about us. Sex is what motivates over 50% of what we do. Take away our sex, and we are all just dull bags of warm water. Give us sex, that "will to live," that desire to touch someone else, love and eventually, if we wish to procreate, and we become alive.

*"Here it comes, here it comes, here it comes--my sex, like water down a well-worn riverbed. It flows, surging, swirling, powerful, free, unchecked and natural. But then the prohibitions of my society, like a landslide of rocks across the river gorge, block Nature's flow. And then what does my urge do when confronted by boulders of religion? It backs up, it grows stronger by weight of inhibitions building like the volume of water behind a dam. It backs up a powerful body of frustration searching for a release. And when it does release, as it will, it is a power less anticipated, less understood, that breaks the dam. Or, even worse, it deviates around the obstruction and flows into areas of dark obsession upon the object of my sex, my sex, my sex,"*
Dudley Griffin, 12.7.98

Abstinence creates deviations. Anyone who doesn't know this has not been paying attention. Priests deviate, preachers do it, preacher's kids do it, frustrated salesmen do it, and uptight CEOs too.

Sex is like a river. If you build a dam prohibiting its flow, you will create deviations. You don't stop sex, just as you don't stop water with a dam--you just divert it toward something that is unnatural. Good sex, and lots of it, is good for people.

Most people take sex too seriously. Sure, there is a serious side, but if you think about it, that is the dark side, the part that shouldn't even enter into sex.

Sex is one of the most spiritual activities in a person's life. The potential of creating life...the closeness to another creature and the celebration of life.

Sex is the most beautiful and potentially rewarding part of our lives. But, because of what our society has done to it, sex is always going to be nasty to some people and an addiction to others. This is a shame because it should be appreciated for its simple pleasures.

Religious disclaimer: Many people say that they think religious devotion is our most rewarding thing in life. That is fine. They can think that way if they wish; I will not stop them! Yet to be fair, they must also not get in my way when I choose not to believe as they do! Only "God" will judge me if God wants to.

Because of my mother's marital status and the Second World War, I was an early preschool participant. Daycare is often a necessity in the world without extended families, and when mothers have to work outside the home. The social and economic changes caused by the industrial revolution, and now the commercial electronic evolution, have isolated families from familial support systems.

But I feel that preschool and daycare are valuable educational and socializing experiences in a small child's life. It is good to get out into the world early and learn the laws of democracy to prepare for the niceties of diplomacy needed to succeed in today's ever-growing, and ever-diverse population.

In photographs of me in my early school classrooms, I was often the only white face. (Another school photo) North Beach, San Francisco, is a melting pot of cultures. Southern European, Asian, African, South American and all the mixes were already there even as early as the 1940s. It was a valuable education in world cooperation.

Evolution is a primary occupation of every creature. To adapt to the changes of the world around you is important for personal survival as well as survival of your species. Evolving is definitely the most important job of a human being, especially now.

Evolution for man, in particular, is not merely with his body, but with his mind. In prehistory we were prey to many other creatures. We had to out think them. We did, and we survived.

Humans are now the top predator. We have only other human beings to fear at this time in history.

Today, many people still act as if they are prey and act out against the world and other people with mistrust and aggression. But, if we do not evolve in our thinking and embrace cooperation and society, the world will dissolve back into the anarchy and chaos of prehistoric self-preservation.

When I was born, America was at war, and a wartime economy prevailed. Food rationing was a reality. This was before vitamin supplements, but also the beginning of food processed without nutritional value. During the war, eggs were invisible, butter was white, and milk was powdered. I contracted rickets, a calcium deficiency, the least of my disadvantages.

I was basically a skinny kid with bowlegs, no father, bank account or central heating. I had to cope, just like many of the other kids who were born during the Second World War.

But because of my birthplace, my early education was eclectic and international. It was bright with possibilities because it was culturally diverse. Yet my mother knew that a family history and familial culture were also needed for stability.

Mother and I spent a lot of time together. We went out to dinner once a week, we took round trips on the ferry to Oakland, and went to museums. We had little or no money, but we did it all on the cheap.

Even a good family life without a window to the outside to see what the world has to offer can leave a person ignorant of the bear traps of life. Being pushed out on the streets at an early age to fend for oneself can be educational, but it gives you no sense of family stability. Both are necessary for a balanced and acceptable social future.

We must be able to live inside and outside of the cave to survive in a dangerous world. We must know how to negotiate for food outside and to create love inside. Sustenance for the body and love and sex for creating the future generations are both self-preservation.

One of the unexpected advantages of living on the top floor of our building was easy access to the roof that had a small wooden platform deck and picket fence around it. My first of two picket fences. I have photographs of me as an infant with my mother on that roof in the sun.

The sun is my joy, and the sky speaks freedom to me. I used to fly kites from the top of Telegraph Hill, and often set them free to float over the city into the sea.

My first childhood friend was Guido Costello. I imagine that our Italian/Anglo-Saxon friendship was confounding to his parents, because as late as the 1950s, most ethnic cultures in America still lived and played within their own community of countrymen.

My first girlfriend? I remember--her name was Sarah! I have photos of us in Washington Square Park, North Beach, San Francisco. We were about five or six years old. We were picking tiny daisies from the grass.

Our faces were bright and full of love. Yes, love! It is the only way to describe that look on someone's face. No matter how young or old, whether the affection is toward another person or toward the day, love has one recognizable expression! That twinkle!

The familial love of a grandchild, the love of sun on your face, or the sensual memory of lovemaking--all give that glow. The warm feeling of love is universal!

"In this book, sex will only be fun!"

*The Author, 11.22.06*

The 20 years from 1959 through 1979 hold more mysteries, epiphanies, triumphs and tragedies than any other 20-year period in the history of man. There are things I know by living as I did, when I did, that you may not know due to the time and place of your birth.

I am not saying that what I know is my knowledge alone. I am not inferring that this information is sacred or even essential to your life. You <u>can</u> exist without it. But I hope you won't live a frustrated and unfulfilled life, or bitch at me about it, or cut me off in traffic.

We are all basically the same at birth. We are all naive. We are all vulnerable and scared.

Life experiences make us different people. Our experiences make us wise or foolish. They give us confidence or fear, and the world turns on these issues. An ignorant person diminishes this world. A frightened person is often in conflict with many of the other people around him.

Insecurity and sexual frustration are responsible for most of the problems of this world. Half a million little Freuds can't all be wrong!

Although this is written from the perspective of a man, I tried, profoundly, to write for women as well as men. Whether women read it or not, if I speak the truth that touches men, this book will positively affect women as well. If women do read it, that will accelerate understanding between men and women and help the healing process between us.

When I say healing process regarding man/woman relationships, I really do mean healing, because, contrary to what most people fantasize, man/woman relationships are constantly on a life-support system.

Late 1960s, Manhattan Beach, California, waves, volleyball and girls in bikinis. It was part fantasy and all true. One of The Beach Boys lived in my uncle's apartment house! Their music, The Beatles, Judy Collins, Jethro Tull, The Doors, Carole King, Steppenwolf and The Stones were the soundtrack of our indulgences.

For about three or four years I lived one-and-a-half blocks from the LA beach. Much of that time I wore nothing but a pair of surfing "baggies," I surfed and body surfed, played volleyball and peddled my ass up and down the "strand" on my bicycle looking for girls.

Back in the 1980s or 90s, I never watched Baywatch. To me it was the old emotions, the past stumbling mistakes of our culture's attempts to find love. Strangely enough, today sometimes while flipping through channels I run into an episode of "The Watch," and stay for a few frames. I still can't stick with it though, but it is amazing the mysterious appeal the female body holds for a man, even one who has no desire to stray.

I also never read Playboy Magazine, unless it was for the music articles. I did go to the Hollywood Playboy Club a few times for some Advertising Club events, but the environment was almost nauseating to me. From the advertising agency on Sunset Boulevard, we sometimes went to a restaurant for lunch that had telephones on each table so you could get a call or make a call to someone at another table who interested you. That was just humorous to me, and a bit extravagant.

We met, made love, parted and never saw each other again. That was the scenario on the beach.

The young girl facing the sea was swaying back and forth to her own music. Her mid-length blonde, almost white, hair moved poetically with the gestures of her head.

A long, Victorian neck tapered down to meet appealing, rounded shoulders with shiny points of light reflecting from their soft surface. Her lightly tanned back was well-formed with underlying muscles, yet feminine softness. The smooth cascade of her back was interrupted only by a thin scarf tied around and over her breasts, I presumed. The small of her back fell to a slim waist that looked as if my two hands could easily circumnavigate. Her well-proportioned and nicely protruding buns moved independently of each other as she swayed. These two distinctly separate globes were beautifully and individually defined by her gauze skirt as it clung to her.

Her skirt flowed into S-shaped waves as she danced, transferring her movements down its length to a hem just above soft, rounded calves, lightly covered in sun-brightened blond hair. The calves of a woman's legs have always been most appealing to me, and the element that excites my attention most are proportion and vitality.

Nicely formed calves give life to the imagination of what lies beyond. Hers tapered down from a gentle knee to meet the petite, yet strong, ankle and Achilles tendon tight with anticipation of adventures to come.

Below those perfectly shaped legs were the obligatory feet, but with all that had gone before them, I knew that these also would be extraordinary. Her feet were covered lightly in dust and naked in their hippie adolescence. I wanted to be that dust.

The mid-length hair told me one thing. She was young and probably just now testing her independence from parental supervision. The answer to this Sherlockian observation was that the predominant hairstyle of the time was long, flowing locks, and that is what would be worn by any young woman, unless her parents had been recently making her decisions.

A salt pillar in my tracks, I stood a dozen or so feet behind the girl and listened to her singing, "This is the dawning of the age of Aquarius, age of Aquarius, A-quar-i-us, A-quar-i-us. Sympathy and understanding... da da da da, oh, darn!" She said, stomping a foot and turning toward me in wrinkled-nose disgust.

She wasn't frightened by my unexpected presence, or annoyed, or embarrassed. She just smiled and said, "Hi."

I smiled back and then said without hesitation. "Please, come with me. I have something I want to show you."

The moment I saw her face, I knew I could not find anyone fresher and more beautiful by searching a hundred miles of beach, or twenty organic juice bars.

She hesitated for only a moment before smiling and nodding her agreement to go with me. We walked together across the slowly cooling sand and climbed the concrete steps to the promenade along and above the beach. Right, then left, up the hill toward my house we walked.

Side by side, but not too close. Several times the backs of our hands brushed together. I didn't reach out to hold her hand because that would have been too possessive. It would have been taking too much for granted and may have frightened her off. We weren't young lovers yet, we were only considering it.

At one point a car turned the corner, and I reached out for her hand to pull her off the street. At this stage of the relationship, I didn't grab her hand; I gave it to her and let her hold it if she wanted. She held my hand firmly for an extended moment or two and then slowly released it after the car passed. This was all the answer I needed. Leading up to almost every "first time," there is a point at which you know that it will happen.

A warm recognition and an acceptance of the inevitable seems to wash over you. From that point on, you both know it's going to happen, and you would both swim up Niagara Falls to make it happen.

By the time we reached my house, we had names exchanged and our basic personalities developed. Her name was Sandra. We commented on how much easier it was to walk backwards up a hill. We laughed at a seagull in a trashcan.

On entering my house, I walked to a bookshelf and retrieved a booklet from the play *Hair*, that had the words of the song Aquarius which she had been trying to sing on the beach. We looked up the song and sang it a few times.

Sandra then took a walk around the living room, commented on my art collection, picked up a tambourine, shook it once or twice, looked in the kitchen and turned to me.

We both took one step forward and were in each other's arms immediately. The kiss and embrace is always one last test of what is to come. Often, by this point no one really cares if that first encounter rings bells or not, because you are already almost certain to make love, no matter what. But sometimes that first embrace is so electric that you both let out a mutual sigh of appreciation. That is what happened this time.

I remember occasions when a casual hug of someone new turned out to be that special kind of embrace. Sometimes it was embarrassing because you were with someone else at the time and could not hide it, or do anything about it; other times it led to unplanned lovemaking.

If you are open to chemistry, it is unbelievable. It is, at times, unavoidable. Married people can often get into trouble if they haven't shut off their receptors and find themselves in an unexpected sensual embrace with a person who isn't their spouse.

Sandra and I ran our hands over each other. She was firm and round and beautiful. We were only a few steps from the couch.

Normally, I would not make love on a couch if a bed were available. I would, though, actually make love anywhere, and have, when necessity was the father of last resorts. But I prefer the comfort and finality of a bed. A man who knows women knows instinctively whether he can chance the move to a bed. If he makes that move too soon it can break the spell.

Some women cannot be seduced on a bed. It is too frightening to them; it is too final. They probably feel that, once on a bed, they can't turn back. The first time with a new lover, I believe that most women are still in the decision-making process right up to the moment of entry.

I also believe that some women, and men for that matter, don't count some forms of "screwing" as really lovemaking. It gives them some deniability.

Up against the wall is just a fling. It can't be taken seriously. It is not really fornication or infidelity. Or at least some people think not.

Hypocrisy is one of the most damaging of all our sex crimes. "We didn't really do it; we didn't have all our clothes off." "I was drunk." "She was a slut."

The thing about the free-love generation is that we tried not to be hypocritical. We preferred to get naked on the most comfortable surface available and roll around on each other in a ritual of freedom and spirituality.

But Sandra was young and inexperienced. I knew she wanted to make love, but might be frightened by a move to the bed just then. At this point there was no question that we both wanted to make love. The spell could be broken only by an awkward interruption.

I picked Sandra up and lay her on the couch, while our lips were still congealed. Kneeling on the floor, I bent over her beautiful form, spread across the brocade fabric. She lay there, eyes closed, body draped, anxious. One leg cocked up, dusty feet askew on the polyester couch.

Our kisses grew in intensity. Our hands roamed. My T-shirt hit the floor.

When my hand touched her knee, her legs opened like a flower or the side doors of a 1967 Volkswagen van. Slipping down the immaculately smooth skin of the inside of her leg, my hand soon discovered that, as was the habit of most free-spirited young woman of the times, Sandra wore no underwear beneath.

My shorts hit the floor, and my erection was deep inside her before we could both take another breath. The abruptness of this move was against all rules of foreplay and very much contrary to the way that I usually liked to make love. But I really wanted to seal the deal with this girl. I didn't want her to change her mind.

I burrowed deep inside her and shivered once with the knowledge of what was to come. We squirmed to find positions most rewarding for our endeavor. It was not tentative. She was almost new to the experience, but willing.

*"Everyone sins, and those who don't, lie about it!" Dudley Griffin*
*1.3.07*

California is unique in the demographics of mankind because of six historic migrations. The first migration was that of East Asians in search of food. The Spanish came looking for plunder. The third migration was the Gold Rush of 1849. Then, the there was the arrival of dustbowl refugees in the late 1920s and 30s. The next was the migration of soldiers and factory workers from the rest of the United States during the Second World War. Following that was the escape to adventure on the Coast by young hippie wannabes in the late 1960s.

The Gold Rush, the Second World War and the hippie movement were the three most decisive migrations.

To begin with, in 1848, California was at the end of the known civilized world. Spanish Conquerors, a few other immigrants and Native Americans were the only population. And then, in the early 1850s, the Gold Rush brought people from every state in the Union and almost every country of the world.

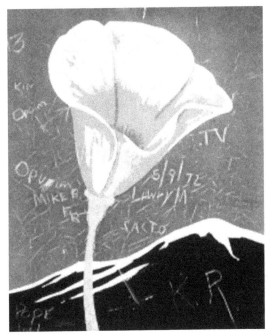

California State Poppy Highway Sign From 1970s

There was no prior historic event in our world that brought as many diverse ethnic populations together as did the California Gold Rush.

And then, WWII drew even more ethnic and racial cultures to California from all of the rest of the United States. Scandinavians from the Midwest, Irish from the East Coast, Blacks from the South and many more came to the West Coast to work in the shipyards and airplane factories. And soldiers from all over the continent passed through California. Many of them stayed, and many came back from the war to live here.

The 1950s were the real "coming out" of ethnic closets. The War had broken up insulated communities and encroached upon isolated pockets of culture and morality throughout America.

The melting pot of moralities and family values was all at once an exciting copulation and, at the same time, a confusion of taboos. It is no wonder that California became, for the next five decades, the Sodom and Gomorrah and the Garden of Eden of America. This cultural and sexual brew soon spread through the media and advertising into the rest of the country and, eventually, the world.

California is the melting pot of the melting pot of the world. America is the cultural soup of the world. California is a golden, some might say pewter, spoonful of the mix.

One of the reasons that the United States has the most confused and perverse sexual identity is because of this conflagration of different religious and ethnic moralities. We suffer from knowing too much and yet not trusting our basic instincts. We fight our natural desires and call them banal and reptilian.

Born as I was into the epicenter of this cultural quake, I made my way at great peril, but learned from my escapades and misadventures. The world knocks off some of our rough edges, while, at the same time, it builds up calluses on some of our other exposed surfaces. It is sometimes a mystery how and why some experiences are lessons learned and others are mistakes.

There are many kinds of sex: First-time sex, forbidden sex, uncontrollable sex, friend sex, I-hate-you sex and break-up sex, to name a few!

This discourse is about "I-hate-you sex." This is not literally a dislike of sex per se, which most men don't, but can be about having sex with someone you personally dislike, which does happen, or if you hate women in general, which is more prevalent than people want to believe. But most often, the kind of sex I am talking about is from a deep-seeded psychological shame or fear of going to hell.

If you have lived a passive, "normal" life, you may not be familiar with "I-hate-you sex." It is often violent, and, in my observations and experience, sex that is violent is most often associated with and perpetrated by a person who is not comfortable with their sexuality or is uncomfortable or unfamiliar with the opposite sex.

Bondage and slapping are exceptions. They are often just a game that people want to try. But real violent sex can be dangerous and even lethal; mostly, I observe it coming from men. Asphyxiation during sex, either self-inflicted or assisted, is something in which no person in their right mind should indulge, unless they have suicidal wishes.

From the homosexual, homophobic world, Jeffrey Dahmer was the poster boy. He was unhappy with his desires to make love with men, so he blamed them and killed them.

On the heterosexual side are men who have been rejected by women or men who were damaged by the Christian attitude toward sex, and have fallen for the Garden of Eden scenario, where a woman is blamed for "our downfall." These men may strike out violently.

I wish I could give you a heads-up about how to recognize a dangerous lover, but that is an instinct you have to acquire. A few clues are a man who won't look you in the eyes, or stares too intently into your eyes. A man who doesn't want to know your name, or is too intrigued by your name. Well, you get the picture!

I would say, ask a guy about his relationship with his mother. That will give you an outline of what he thinks about women. But then keep your senses sharp! At the first indication of violence, prepare for the future possibility of termination. Once a lover displays a propensity for violence, it usually escalates. Get out quickly!

Sparky

## CHAPTER 3

# **Sparky**

I earned the nickname "Sparky" when I was a young actor at a local live theater in my hometown. I was eleven or twelve years old, and a friend of my mother's introduced me to acting and singing. I starred in *Jack And The Beanstalk* and *Six Who Pass While The Lentils Boiled*. As with many of the things I have done in my life, it was all because I was curious. I don't know if I was any good, but I do know I became a good singer.

I played in a few adult productions as well as the children's theater plays. The one I remember best was *Finian's Rainbow*. It was a lively Broadway musical, with several good songs that became popular hits on radio and TV. *How Are Things In Glocca Morra* is one example. It was the mid-1950s, and the music would be considered quaint and mushy by today's standards. I learned all the lead star lines and all the words to all the songs.

60

I was in the crowd scenes and played and sang in a few of the ensemble songs. The cast had a good number of teenage girls and young women. They were apparently attracted by my demeanor, so they began to flirt with me, partly I think because I was less threatening than the older horny young men in the cast.

The girls started kissing me, and I guess they discovered I possessed an aptitude toward oral stimulation. It became quite a regular procedure to kiss me before going on stage.

Of course, this was the most wonderful education I could have received as a pre-pubescent boy. They started calling me Sparky, and I was very appreciative and forthcoming. I believe all young men should have such a pleasant education, and I matriculated gladly and easily into all forms of male/female contact.

After the WWll and the beginning of the Cold War, my mother was worried about the "Red Threat" and "The Bomb." She wanted to move away from "The City," which she knew would be a target in an atomic bomb attack.

Around 1950, we moved to Chico in Northern California, where my mother took a job as office manager of a national insurance company.

As I recall, it was a two-person office, the salesman and my mother. He was gone selling policies most of the time, and she was in charge of everything else. She was a very efficient and self-reliant person. No one who ever met my mother felt sorry for her as a single parent, nor did they feel sorry for me.

My mother was sparing with her discipline. She did not sweat the small stuff. She disciplined me when my actions endangered myself or others or if I showed disrespect for others or their property. Pauline prepared me to live with other people. I was a fortunate child.

Many parents, especially those who don't have self-respect or confidence in themselves, treat their children as scapegoats for their own frustrations. These people feel like victims in this world. They feel like the bottom man on the totem pole, and, since it's not easy for humans to admit such insecurity or to change their emotions, they lash out instead. They try to find someone to look down on, someone else to be the last man on the pole. That's where minorities, homosexuals, people of different religions, or even their own children, come in handy. Yes, even their own children become the victims of insecure people.

Only weak people beat their children. Only parents without confidence in themselves will force their children to do something without a reason. "Don't stick your finger in the fire because I say so," should really be, "Don't stick your finger in the fire because it will burn you, and I love you and don't want you to suffer pain!"

A small child spills milk and gets smacked. God, how stupid a parent is who does that! What lesson does that teach? Children are going to spill; their lack of physical coordination dictates that. The same parent who beats a child for spilling is often the same kind of parent who will ignore a child's cries or questions. Soon, that child will spill a glass of milk just to get some reaction from the parent. Someday that child will vandalize a school or steal a car just to get some reaction from society.

Parents who bully their children do so because their children are the only people in the world over whom they feel they have any power. Because of their own insecurity, they need someone to push around. It makes them feel as if they have some control, as if they have power.

This wouldn't be such a big deal except that most of the problems of our world start with the beating, mistreating or ignoring of just one child.

My mother never forced me to say "no" to something to which she, herself, said "yes." She never told me to "do as she said, not as she did."

Pauline never lied to me unless it was to give me comfort or confidence, and then, of course, it wasn't a lie, but encouragement. "Dudley, we don't have a big house like they do, because we don't need such a big house." "What a beautiful picture that is, my son."

Pauline explained her discipline to me. "Sweetheart, don't go into the street; you might get hit by a car." Not "God dammit, stay out of the fucking street because I say so and I'm the boss!"

The treatment children receive from their parents often translates into how successful or unsuccessful they are with the opposite sex later in life. A child deprived of self-esteem will be insecure, and because of that, he or she will feel threatened by the opposite sex.

Because of that, he or she will be unable to attract a mate readily, and, therefore, will become bitter and resentful, often mistreating a partner when they do find one.

People who beat their children are also often the same people who will beat a spouse. Children in an abusive household will often carry it on into their own adult life and relationships. We have to stop this vicious circle of violence and insecurity or else human society will not survive it.

Wake up, wife beaters and child abusers! You are not just acting out your own frustrations, but you are infecting the world with your poison!

*"What is it with some men and their violence against women? Are these men so insecure that they don't believe their sexual ability is enough to keep a woman's interest, and that they have to dominate, violate and even kill to keep a lover? This is all so childish, immature and self-delusional.*

*If you have ever beaten a woman, or even thought about it, I suggest that you look at yourself in the mirror and repeat after me, 'I am scum, I am not really a man, I am a sniveling pile of insecure crap!' When you realize that and then believe it, then you will be saved from your own stupidity, and then you will become a real man!"*

*Dudley Griffin*


Comfortable relationships and sexual success give us confidence in all social situations, which eventually translates into successful lives. The attitude one has toward the opposite sex is much more important to sexual success than good looks or money. Straight teeth, perfect hair and nice clothes might get you a first look, but if you can't deliver sincerity and affection, then you will forever have bad relationships, if you have relationships at all.

Another childhood trauma that I didn't have to endure was favoritism. As an only child, and also because I had only my mother's love and not a father's expectations, I didn't have to compete for attention with other siblings.

Favoritism, or loving one child more than another, is one of the worst travesties a family can inflict. Relegating one of your children to second place creates a wound from which they may never recover. When they do this, parents often create a monster, one who will probably come back to haunt them, or worse.

My first brush with sexuality took place in Chico, California. I was seven or eight years old. Her name was Darla, as I recall, and she was 11 or 12 years old. We used to walk home together.

My mother had to work her 9 to 5, and I was an early latchkey kid. Then it was just "independent by necessity." Darla came into my empty house with me. We kissed and maybe fondled. It was my first hint of sex. I have very fond memories of Darla.

These moments of early memory are never a concrete step-by-step chronology of visual movements and audible words. They are only snippets of feelings, shadows of movement.

What I see are feelings, what I feel are emotions. Warmth, sincerity and togetherness tied in a bow of the multi-colored ribbon of life.

Later in my adolescence, I would grapple with sexual rules and battle the ambiguities that my society placed on sensual emotions. But, for that brief moment in my life, sex was as pure as a playground swing or childhood laughter.

All of my early life was warmth and togetherness; only a very few times of conflict seem to have left distinct memories. One of my only disturbing pre-adolescent memories of relationship love was when I was going to a primary school, first or second grade, down the coast from San Francisco in Montara.

Some of my mother's closest friends lived in Moss Beach, and I attended a few semesters of school while staying with them. I met a girl by the name of Marsha, and we, in childhood innocence, held hands, and people laughed at us and sang the currently popular "song" by Stan Freberg entitled "John and Marsha."

That was my first experience with the cruelty possible by unthinking people, and the hypocrisy concerning love, sex and human relationships.

*"You cannot understand the pressures on the next generations, just as your parents did not understand your struggles, and the next generation will not understand its children's pathways either.*

*Do we force the status quo on our children? My choice is to make it as easy as I can for my child to make her own way. Change is necessary for the evolution of mankind, but is all change progress? I suggest that it is better for the young to choose their own futures, with a little guidance and warning from the past!" Dudley Griffin*

*I have been bad in my time, but I have never been immoral, never, never.*
*D.G.*

## The Anti-Parent Hormone

Why are we surprised when teenagers rebel against parental prohibitions? It's the hormones, stupid! Mother Nature planned it that way. When children reach adolescence, hormones are created in their bodies that make them want to go out into the world and live their own lives.

The actual mechanism, as shocking as it might seem, causes some children to do exactly the opposite of what parents want them to do. It's the hormones, and that's why people use "Child Psychology" on children to get them to do what they want them to do. "Don't brush your teeth, they will look too bright and shiny and scare people!"

All creatures large and small are "forced" by nature to leave their parents and go out to procreate and rejuvenate their species. "God" makes them reject their parents.

Once you understand this, if you are a rational person, you will realize that it is counterproductive to try to force your teenagers to follow your rules. They will find some way to break your rules. You must lead by suggestion and example, and if you are a bad example of what is good yourself, then you will lead them astray. Their prison time could be your fault; their four divorces, your responsibility!?

After a certain age, your words will not be heard anymore. So if you haven't prepared for that day by teaching them common sense, your children might not have any foundation upon which to deal with the pressures of sex, drugs, rock & roll, greed and selfishness.

When your children are young and looking up to you, you should teach by positive example. Give them reasons, not just rules.

You should socialize them so that they will not become square pegs in a round world that is harsh on them.

If you have taught your children only with an iron hand, but without love and respect, then all those things you have said while they grew up will mean nothing to them. You will have failed as a parent.

At the point of adolescence, it is too late to start guiding children. If they haven't already been prepared with good information, understanding and love, then they just might destroy their own lives through excesses in a natural rebellion against you.

Adolescence is the time when parents should protect children from themselves. The best way to do this is to understand the pressures and pain that growth hormones are inflicting on them. Try to remember your own teenage years.

The less parents say and do to children during adolescence, the better. Parents should have said all the things earlier, when their children could still hear them. Before adolescence is when parents should tell children that they are there for them and that they love them.

One of the extreme consequences of your lack of understanding and overzealous discipline at this point is that you could destroy your relationship with your child forever. Many families are estranged for years or forever because of this.

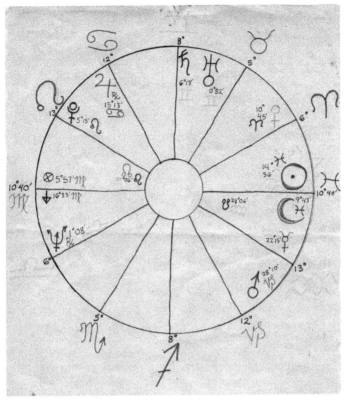

John's star chart

# CHAPTER 4

## Sexual Timelines of Life

At one time in my life, just like every other young man, every girl and woman was my type!

*"At one time when I was very, very young, I thought I knew where I was going. Then one day I realized every step I took put me into new territory, thereby changing where I was headed. Now, I wait until tomorrow to know where I'm going."*
*Dudley Griffin 4.3.11*

This book is an "almost completely accurate" account of my sexual life. Most of my experiences have been dramatic enough that no embellishment is necessary to tell the stories.

For the most part, what is written here is what I can remember. Yet, like most people, I may be susceptible to memory lapses and occasional subliminal delusions of grandeur, so there may be some mistakes or exaggerations regarding size, intensity or duration of the experiences. Remember, objects in this mirror may appear larger than they really are.

Our memories often have a tendency to expand our accomplishments. I, on the other hand, always try to downplay what I remember.

If asked why this book was written, my answer would be, "Sex education!" The next question, obviously, would concern credentials to teach such a complex subject.

No, the writer of this book has no degrees in anatomy, psychology or sociology. I am teaching by example. I am teaching by my failures and successes, by my good fortune, and my bad.

In sex education or the teaching of female/male relations, objectivity has no credibility. If you haven't lived it, you don't know anything about it! The dynamics of sexual relationships and partner politics are so individually strange and sporadically volatile, that anyone who has not been, or is not presently, a player will most likely say something that will make it worse. You already know this if you are at all insightful, and have watched any chick flicks or most sitcoms. "90210," "Friends" and "Two and A Half Men" are good examples of advice gone wrong, over and over and over again. Even if you are experienced, you can only hope that what you say makes people think rationally, and does not cause them to inflict bloodshed irrationally.

I know a gentleman does not brag about his conquests; yet, the day of the gentlemen seems to be long gone. But I don't consider lovemaking a conquest, and I assure you that I am not telling tales for vain reasons. Between 1967 and 1985 I had sex with over 350 girls and women!

If you think for one moment that I am telling you these things for ego gratification, I must confess that I will be getting more grief than satisfaction from these disclosures. I am revealing these things only so that you will know that I am experienced enough to be an authority. This is my university degree, my PhD.

I want you to know you can trust my judgment about male/female sexual relationships. You don't get tips for fixing your car from someone who has limited experience with automobiles, or have a tooth pulled by someone who has never done it before.

This is all for the sake of academics, but it still could be considered juicy by normal, red-blooded boys and girls. Just keep in mind that enlightenment is my intent.

In my life I have had my own fantasies, just like everyone else, and I sometimes have employed them. I masturbated my way through middle school and high school just like all the boys of that time. But then at one point I started to make those fantasies real, and for a number of years I did my best at it.

I finally settled down, yet I still have fantasies, and I still employ them from time to time. But I keep them as fantasies; I have no desire to make them reality anymore.

Within a period of 18 years, I had affairs with an average of one new sexual partner every 18 3/4 days.

That is far below the consumption of rock stars and sports heroes, yet it was good for an average hippie in California. I never paid for sex, I never forced myself on a lover, and I never did it as an obligation of my status.

You should also know that I never counted during those years. It was never a challenge or a contest, and I didn't sit down, remember and count them up until much later and only for this book and this paragraph. I have no gun or lingam statue with 350 notches. Counting is one of the sleaziest things men do.

And I am not by any means advocating quantity. Each person has their own set of sexual necessities, and as long as they are not vicious or dangerous, all is fine. Some libidos are less demanding than mine was, and some, more so.

Sex can be every bit as addictive as alcohol, food or money. Sometime in the late 1990s it was acknowledged that sex could be a problem drug, and some people needed therapy for sex addiction. It now has its own twelve-step program.

The big problem, as with alcohol, is that sex can take up time that could be better used for conducting a productive life. It destroys families, diverts you from pursuing a meaningful occupation, and it can kill you by various means, STDs and the guns of jealous husbands. "Yeah, all that, but sex is the best diversion humans have!"

At one time in my life, sex broke up my family and kept me from my occupation. I almost completely stopped writing and taking photographs, the work that I was always most suited for. It could be considered a character flaw that most men have given in to the drugs that cloak the symptoms rather than finding a cure for the problem. And I'm not trying to justify our male flaws with that statement.

And yet, I will say that the world would be a hipper, happier, and more congenial place to live if everyone did follow the Love.

It is quality, not quantity, that matters. And that is what I am pretentious enough to try to help you with. I know that quantity is not an education; quality and diversity are the teacher. Speaking of diversity, I must restate that I am a serial heterosexual.

I have had my share of offers and propositions from gay friends that I love and respect, but it is just not my thing! I can say with a politically correct straight face that some of my best friends have been homosexuals.

I am not revolted by the gay life. Some of the things I have done with women would be considered every bit as odd as homo sex. I just have always loved girls.

I figure I must have had over two hundred one-night-stands, a dozen one-minute-stand-ups and my share of back seat affairs. I made love with two Jewish girls together in a Catholic Church confessional and with other girls on Greyhound buses, in boats, hot tubs, showers and VW vans, of course. No, I am not a member of the mile-high or one-fathom-deep clubs.

Yet there were dry times along with the wet ones. There were some sparse months and at least one monogamous year.

Often, during that era, sex took the place of a handshake. And names were not exchanged.

Ortho Novum birth control pills

I am not ashamed of any of it. No money ever changed hands, and no force was ever exerted, except maybe to open her bedroom window. I was a slut, but I own it.

During that time I had two, more or less, monogamous relationships off and on for three years. I was in dozens of one-week or one-month relationships and at least two affairs that lasted on and off for over ten years.

I had sex with women that I didn't like in normal social contact, sex with women I wouldn't want to be seen with in public, and with women who wouldn't want to be seen with me in public.

To my knowledge I have only one child; my daughter, Siobhan, who is the warmth of my heart.

I am, I believe, responsible for only two abortions. Both of them were in the same twelve months. My sperm count must have spiked that year.

During the 1960s, 70s, and 80s, most girls had the pill, IUD or a diaphragm. On the few occasions when none of these were present I found other ways to make love. I almost never used a condom. I didn't like them; they are disruptive, anti-intimate and don't always work anyway. I advocate others using them in non-exclusive relationships, of course. I stopped being promiscuous myself, just by circumstance in

1985; right around the time AIDS became a problem for heterosexuals.

I am very familiar with the rhythm method, and quite adept at talking girls out of it, for I was a very persistent sexual partner. When I was with a new lover, I usually wanted to make love four or five times a day for extended durations. I know of only two abortions on my account and one child who is my wonderful daughter.

If you read this without an understanding of that time and place in history, you cannot rationally make a valid judgment of what we were doing. I live today and see things now everyday that are so much more perverted than what we did then, and I know the history of Rome and know we were pure compared to them as well.

I am telling you all of this only so that you will pay attention when I say something about men and women, sex and love. This is not my ego speaking; it is my soul. A man with a big ego would never have been able to have as many pure, emotionally satisfying sexual relationships as I have had.

I am revealing my soul and holding my reputation up for debate, only for your sake, education and future. I want to see mankind survive as an appropriately low impact member of creation.

And when I talk of sex, I speak of the good kind, the kind that has love as its basis. There are those who think that casual sex never carries love, yet they are mistaken. To a man who cherishes women, and respects them for what they offer him, sex is "God-given love." I have never once paid for sex, and maybe that is excessively purist, but there is an extreme difference between sex lovingly given rather than sex paid for or stolen.

I think it is very important to know yourself and not to lie to yourself about your sexuality. It is my theory that there is a proper place for sex for each person and a comfortable amount of sex for each of us to be satisfied, un-frustrated. The second part of this theory is that all of us are different in our needs, of frequency required and type and intensity of sex. I believe that there are as many sexes as there are people.

*"Find yourself and then you can find other people. Until you know where you are, you will not have a platform upon which to observe correctly, learn and then be able to connect properly with other people. Then you will find happiness." DG*

I have said many times that you can have sex without love and love without sex, but sex with a proper amount of love is preferable.

I feel that a person without enough good physical sex will become a deviant. And likewise a person without heartfelt sex will become callous and unable to experience real love.

*"I don't know if it is possible to turn a sex offender into a lover, but I would try!"*
*Dudley Griffin*

## The Sexual Timeline of My Life

**Summer of 1942,** My mother and father made love and I was conceived.

**March 5, 1943,** I was born a male child.

**March 6th or 7th, 1943,** My penis was attacked by doctors, but that was a good thing!

**1943-1955,** I was more interested in food than sex.

**1955,** I began to realize that there was a difference between boys and girls.

**1956,** I didn't know what that difference was.

**1957-1961,** I thought I knew the difference between boys and girls.

**1961,** I was more interested in sex than food.

**1964,** Kathleen and I were married.

**1962-1967,** I began to realize I was wrong about the difference between the sexes.

**1967,** Janis Joplin gave me a glimpse of the differences and similarities of the sexes.

**1967-1972,** I wasn't sure I could handle what I was learning about men and women.

**1972,** Kathleen and I separated.

**1972,** I gave in to the conundrum and began trying to seduce every girl, woman and lady I came in contact with.

**1973-1983,** I learned that the differences between men and women were complicated, but O.K.

**1983,** I became more selective in who I tried to seduce.

**1983-1985,** I started turning down opportunities for sex.

**1985- present,** I married Joan and slowly became comfortable with the differences and similarities of men and women.

**September 18, 1985** I learned that I had no need to make love with every woman. I can love many, but Joan is my mate.

**April 10, 2020** I love the allure of sex, and I am still quite capable of performing the act, with vigor and stamina. But now I have more control over urges, and its called wisdom through experience, a form of sexual pragmatism!

*"It's been said by me and many others many times that each of us will find our own pain and our own pleasure."*
Dudley Griffin, 3.17.15

CHAPTER 5

# Sex, Society, Religion and Politics

What are these doing in the same chapter?

From 1955 to 1985 were the best 30 years for man's efforts at redemption!

But by 1985 Ronald Reagan and his crew of criminals had commandeered the morality of our Ship of State, changing it to read, *"Do to others before they even think of trying to do it to you!"*

From 1980 through today we have been experiencing the de-evolution of humankind. The high point in mankind's awareness during the 1970s was an effort to normalize the human personality. It was a time where we put aside hypocrisy, deception and lies. Many of us wanted to stop lying to ourselves about man's screwed up attitude toward sex, drugs and rock & roll! We were trying to get over and past ignorance, bigotry and religious snobbery.

Our morality during the hippie era was misunderstood by straight society because it was new to the mainstream. It was proactively positive, not reactively negative!

Then came the proactively negative morality of the Neo-Conservatives. These people were trying to find something wrong with everyone who was not like them, and they were trying to validate their own hypocrisy! They lied to their god, they lied to themselves, and they lied to us.

Peace, love and sex, which are not immoral in any other species, have become the primary sins in American society today because it suits the Military-Industrial Complex. Lying, cheating and stealing have been relegated to minor immoralities if you are rich and powerful, and they can be erased from your record if you know the right people and know how to manipulate the media!

In the Bible, Christ never got vocal about people and their sexual actions, but he saved his only recorded criticism for the bankers in the temple.

## But Sex Has Its Pitfalls

*"Most people love sex or are at least, intrigued by it! The real problem is that most people are ignorant of the consequences of sex--pregnancy, STDs, marriage, divorce, abandonment, being demonized or shot for having sex with the wrong person, etc., etc."*
*DG, shortly after his divorce.*

We rarely worry about the pitfalls of sex and are often unconcerned about what will happen tomorrow morning because the urge is so strong that it short circuits our brain. But one thing we agree on is wanting to improve our sex and/or our love life.

Well, to do so we should start with our social skills. How people perceive you is what makes them come to you or run from you. Are you warm and fuzzy or cold and prickly?

### The Perfection Chart

Learn to like people
Learn a good work ethic
Learn to be tolerant of all others
Achieve a reasonable economic stability
Maintain sexual control
Find some sort of spirituality
Achieve a giving spirit
Achieve a volunteering attitude

Politics and our sex life do overlap. Anarchy, poverty and many human conflicts    have an effect on our social life and sexual stability.

Capitalism, religion and bigotry, the three worst sins of mankind, conflict with efforts for a peaceful, successful life on earth and in the home. Overly selfish economics, overly zealous morality and blind national pride separate the large brotherhood of humanity into small competing, conflicting and warring groups of people. Democracy was created and adopted by advanced societies in order to quell these divisions and thus help to save the people of the world from self-destruction and from wasting the resources of the earth for future generations.

Democracy requires one important agreement, and that is everybody is equal and treated equally.

Without democracy you have anarchy, which is painful for everybody except the 1%. The sad thing is that 30% of people think, erroneously, they can do better without democracy, but they are not smart enough to succeed in a rebellious society. They are following their inflated egos and think they can ignore or insulate themselves from negativity on the streets, at the workplace and in the bedroom.

# CHAPTER 6

# **Tammy**

I wish we could go back to the way we thought love was in the 1950s. I wish we could make everybody feel happy ever after, even if it were not true. I wish life were a bowl of cherries instead of prunes. But wishes will only disillusion us when we discover that reality is not actually as bad as we think it is.

*"Love is still as mysterious as it ever was. All these new complications, sexting, and friends with privileges are no different from the confusions with love that we faced sixty years ago."*
*Dudley Griffin, 4.5.16*

What I remember most about the 1950s is the music. The music was pure in its innocence. "It" didn't know that it was an exaggeration. "It" didn't realize that it was a fantasy. Music then was a joyous celebration of its own ignorance.

It wasn't hard to believe in the purity of romance in the songs of the 1950s. Love was the strongest foundation upon which to build one's new life after the horrors of the Second World War.

All the men returning from other countries and continents had memories of different realities to wash away. Love was the only soap.

Me and Violet

My future wife Joan, doing someone's makeup.

Songs of the 50s painted over the blemishes of people in love. The movies performed plastic surgery on sagging fantasies.

When Debbie Reynolds fell in love with Leslie Nielsen in the 1957 film *Tammy and the Bachelor*, it all seemed so simple. Two attractive people met and fell in love against all cultural, economic, and political odds, as well as good taste.

It was no wonder that I had a hard time justifying this outcome with the story line of my own first few romances. It is a good thing I had a strong sense of self-preservation.

In the 1950s and early 60s, girls tasted like powder and grease when you kissed their necks. And they often had rubber padding on their breasts.

But then, for a time during the 1960s and 70s, when you sought love, you got what you saw in a woman. We experienced real love of the spirit of man and womankind. Love had no lies!

And then in the 2000s, women began enhancing their breasts again, and young men began sleeping in beds littered with tiny sparkles of makeup. It is a wonder to me that love can survive with these deceptions.


CHAPTER 7

# Sex Is As Easy As Driving A Car, And We All Know How Many People Suck At That!

*"I don't want to rule the world, I just want to help others learn how to rule their own world. Maybe then they will stop being ₋ such shitheads, so I can relax and enjoy my world." Dudley Griffin 12.8.13*

As the first of many comparisons in this book drawn between sex and driving an automobile, I will refer now to the different methods public schools use to teach drivers' education and sex education. In schools, they teach us how to use a car for fun and profit, yet they don't instruct us in the use of sex for those purposes.

Sex education, as taught in schools or by one's parents, is usually a warning of the dangers of sex and how to avoid them by avoiding sex itself. Drivers' training doesn't mention avoiding driving, and the dangers are usually ignored in favor of teaching driving technique. Sex education in school does not discuss technique, it usually teaches abstinence! And we should all know how self-imposed abstinence works…not. Birth control today, as I see it, is not taught as much as sold, and that is on TV by pharmaceutical companies.

During my sophomore year of high school, a science teacher, who conducted the one and only sex education class I was ever offered, told us boys, "The first thing you need to know about sex is, K Y P I Y P!" And then after some speculation on what that meant he finally told us it stood for "Keep Your Prick In Your Pants!"

Believe me, I will not warn you about sex. If anything, I advocate more of it for a happy, well-adjusted life! And, as far as technique, though secondary to the emotional aspects, I would tell you that good sexual technique is definitely better for everyone involved than being a disassociated amateur.

Demonizing sex is the first mistake our society makes in raising its children. Make kids ashamed of the origin of their birth, mix in hypocrisy by saying that we shouldn't live with sex, yet the fact is, that we can't live without it. And then we send our kids off to try to live happy, well-adjusted lives. Sure, that makes a lot of sense!

Don't get me wrong. There are many dangers surrounding the misuse of sex, but the most prevalent and insidious are not unwanted pregnancy or disease! The psychological perversion of sexual energy by religious, government leaders, and corporate CEOs is by far more destructive to our society than two teenagers fucking in the back seat of a car.

Dreamer that I am, what I would like people to understand is that sex is good for them, unless they suppress it or demonize it. Then and only then, sex becomes a problem.

This is not primarily an instructional manual, though "sexual acts are sometimes explained in vivid detail" in this book. (That quote is supplied for use by the media to help market this product.) No one here is attempting to teach the physical skills of satisfactory sexual copulation solely for the sake of sexual pleasure.

I am not attempting to teach the physical skills of sex, but I am trying to teach the attitude of a good sex partner, for that is what makes good sex or terrific sex! To improve a sex life is an emotional fix. A person has to have the right idea of what the correct relationship between the sexes should be.

Having sex should not be a competition or an effort to harm or humiliate a partner. That is jail sex! Rapists and masochists are screwed up people!

No one who does not care about their partner is going to be a good lover.

My effort is to help mankind be more satisfied, contented with themselves and thus less likely to be assholes and screw up my life. It is a crusade to change the negative perception of the sexual act, and therefore, reverse the damage done by those who demonize it.

This book is an effort to teach the human intercourse part of sex, the communication part of sex. And why would someone ever attempt such a monumentally impossible task? The only answer is some sort of "save-the-world" complex. The "Love Generation" really is a generation of people who believe that the power of love can save the world.

Some of us are basically pissed off by all the stupid things people do because of sex and their misunderstanding of it. We are upset by how frustration and insecurity manifest themselves in the population, and ultimately affect everyone else in the world.

Violence against women, rape, and murder of family members are primary consequences of our screwed-up Christian attitude about sex. Just look at the facts and criminal histories.

Those of us who possess "liberal indignation" think that if we, as a species, learn to communicate better in our sexual relationships, then all the problems of sexual fear, insecurity and frustration will fade away. We liberals think we should treat sex as a fact of life, like walking or breathing. We left-leaners think we should be happy that we can do it, rather than worrying about whether it is right or wrong, good or bad. And we also think this will make us all better citizens of the world.

Why does the "conservative fringe" think sex education is immoral and subversive? Because they are afraid such knowledge will interrupt their little ignorant bubble, and make them have to think. Or perhaps they think sex education may prove that they are the ones who are immoral and socially subversive.

Why does the "liberal fringe" think sex education of this kind is necessary? Because we are "almost positive" most of the problems in this world are caused by sexual frustrations. To simplify, we believe all religious fanaticism, corporate materialism, and wars are caused, on some level, by someone's sexual insecurity.

God nuts, gun nuts, sports nuts, car nuts, porn nuts, buried treasure nuts, ghost nuts and alien nuts all fall into the same category, watch out for these men!

It is O.K. to be interested, or even passionate, about something, but becoming irrationally committed to anything is a dangerous human fault!

Many people like the exhilaration of speed, but competition with other amateurs on the highway is a stupid human act. I have seen a number of winners, dead on the road! More friends and family members have been killed by a man's gun collection, than all the thieves who have been stopped during their crimes! More money and time has been wasted on fanatic searches for aliens, ghosts, buried treasure, God or the perfectly shaped women!

## CHAPTER 8

# Sexy Stories

Sex offers as good an opportunity for storytelling and literature as do a deadly storm, a train wreck, murder and robbery. They are all human interest maybe, yet there is a hell of a lot more sex going on in our lives than there are train wrecks and murders. What's wrong with writing about sex?

Ignorant fundamentalists and conservative family values people think that, if we ignore it, kids will stop screwing. They think that the media's depictions of sex give kids ideas. Sorry, folks, God gave kids those ideas about sex.

Writing about sex is taboo because it might promote sex. But writing about murder is OK. What's up?

We know that seeing or hearing about sex just might give people some ideas, but what is really wrong with sex anyway? What is wrong about sex is violence, rape and pedophilia. I promise not to write about any of those abhorrent sexual deviations in this book, except to condemn them.

How you write about sex, determines whether your words lead toward good, pure, real sex or in the direction of perversions caused by prohibition, insecurity and frustration. Writing about murders and robbery is more destructive to our society. No one has a natural drive to steal or kill. That has to be taught. But sex, on the other hand, is as natural to humans as the next breath we take.

Books and movies about sex don't entice people to go out and have sex. We already want to do that. But a good description of the act of making love just might teach us to be better lovers, and therefore, less frustrated in our lives.

A story exploiting death and violence raises subjects that are not natural, everyday occurrences to any of us. Violent media really gives people ideas. "X" ratings on movies should be for the number of people killed, "X–36", 36 people "Xed" out. Romance should have a love rating, L–3, meaning three love scenes in a movie.

To be very conservative, I will say that at least 25% of our lives has to do with sex. At some times in our lives, it involves as much as 75% or more of our mind or time.

But violence, actual violence committed to or by the normal person, can be nonexistent in a whole lifetime, and for the entire population in our society, it would be hard to prove that it was higher than 1 or 2% of our lives. So why are we glorifying violence? Why are we making it a normal part of our entertainment when it isn't a normal part of our lives?

Why is half of our media pumping out violent stories? I'd rather see more sex, wouldn't you? And a better attitude about how it fits into our lives. A better depiction of pure, emotional sex and a more positive attitude about it would reduce sexual violence, perversion and unwanted pregnancies. But religious fundamentalists would rather have violence than sex in the media. Do you wonder why they dislike sex more than violence?

Books and movies about violence, cop shows, murder mysteries and such are entertaining, but they do not help us with our real lives. Most of us will never experience this sort of drama in our lives, thank goodness!

Even history books and movies about war are only entertainment to most of us, because we will never have anything to do with fighting a war, and this kind of media will never tell us how to live our day-to-day lives. But books and movies about sex and personal relationships can help our lives. A list of such movies might start with: *Bob and Carol, Ted and Alice; Everything You Always Wanted To Know About Sex, But Were Afraid To Ask;* or *When Harry Met Sally.* These are not just chick flicks. Guys can learn more about being a good "provider" through these kinds of movies rather than from *Scar Face, The Godfather,* or *Star Wars.*

And what about those coitus interruptus stories? How insulting to read a love story in a book or see a movie with a couple, kissing passionately, and then, in the next page or scene, you see to them smoking cigarettes. What? Are we ashamed of the act of making love, or are we promoting cigarettes? The media is not ashamed to show someone's guts being blown out by a shotgun blast, yet they are ashamed to show someone making passionate love.

Many books, and movies have been written about how "bad people" are created. Very little media is devoted to how "good people" are created.

It is obvious to those of us with any social awareness that most bad people are created by influences during childhood from family or society. Ignoring possible chemical imbalances, there is usually an environmental reason for bad behavior, which cannot be adjusted by medication.

Many studies have been made about how good people can be made into bad people. *In Cold Blood*, by Truman Capote, is a good example. My book is a study of how people, the raw clay, can be helped and allowed to become good people.

I believe that good is the nature of mankind. And I believe that our sexual desire does not even register in the top one hundred of our sins.

You know that the wildfire, which is desire, cannot be stopped. You must go with it, or it will roll over you and consume your body and soul.

> *"In the 1970s I couldn't let a woman lie beside me for very long before I wanted to make love with her. I was tender and sensitive, yet I was insistent. I would ask if they were sore or too tired... often they lied and said no... I sometimes had to control myself and let us both sleep. In the morning I woke them with my desire."*
>
> *Dudley Griffin 7/30/13*

If you are reading this book to find graphically depicted, provocative stories of sex, you may find what you are looking for, but you will also encounter spiritually motivated sermonettes on love. I have agreed to relate my experiences of sexual encounter, seduction and copulation, but only within the context of their spiritual and educational value. If given the opportunity, I have a tendency to preach with expletives.

First, I consider myself a moral man, but I could never be called a sexual prude. I believe that sex can and should be enjoyed as recreation, and that stories about sex can also be literature.

But I also feel that, if written accounts of sex are explicitly created to titillate, to exist only to supply fantasy for masturbation, then they are worthless ink spots. Yet, if they are love stories of sex that give the heart and head wings to fly, then they are literature.

By nature, the written word is unlike the "acted-out" story. Writing is meant to create visions in a person's mind and, in doing so, to expand the possibilities of that mind. A demonstration can teach, but a written description will implant the elements of knowledge for people to teach themselves.

I feel that stories exploiting the humorous, satirical or erotic aspects of sex can be literature. But they can just as well be meaningless trash if the intent is not thought-provoking. I just happen to prefer the erotic intellectual aspects of sex.

*The Decameron* is a book written in Italy in the 14th century that explores most of the fantasy and farce of human sexuality. "Decameron" in Greek means ten days, which is the period of time that ten young men and women were in quarantine in a villa hiding from the Black Death plague that was raging around them outside the walls. They each took turns telling the most interesting, erotic or tragic stories they knew about sex. It amounted to 100 stories and is both great literature and also an outline for almost every joke you have ever heard about sex.

These tales served to take their minds off the tragedy and death going on outside their protective walls. Stories about the farcical and humorous nature of sex are many, and they are important in order to lighten our spirits.

Such laughter about sex also serves to give us something other than merely depravity or disapproval in our conversation concerning this subject of most importance in our lives. Several TV sitcoms, *Friends, Two And A Half Men* and *Two Broke Girls*, are wonderful examples of how sexual humor can make your life more enjoyable, while being stupid and sleazy.

My intent with this book is to humanize sex as opposed to demonizing or making fun of it. I hope to emancipate the sexual soul of the human animal. And in order to do so, some "'splaining" is necessary, and to do that I must use the correct words. I must use the explicit terms. (The publisher and its multinational corporations are not responsible for the truth or profanity in this book.)

As a writer, I, of course, want to sell books so that people will read these words and receive this information. But, when writing about sex, dilemmas are created. If I were a botanist, no one would be offended by my use of the words "damp leaf" or "pink flower". But, as a writer about sex, I will offend some people by using the words "damp cunt" or "pink clitoris." Did that offend any of you?

As a writer, I know the words well. Shit, Piss, Fuck, Cunt, Cocksucker, Motherfucker, and Tits are the comedian George Carlin's official "7 Dirty Words." Several of those seven I, myself, don't use very often, but I can't imagine writing a proper love scene without using such words as vagina, erection, clitoris, fellatio or cunnilingus. Now that didn't hurt too badly, did it? Why should we be taught to think that sex is nasty, when no other living creature has that same hang-up?

Words, words, we have to use these words! Some people are disturbed by sexual words, but writers need words to create images in readers' minds because those images tell the story.

If we were to try to describe a tree and not be allowed to use the word leaf, the description would suffer. If we cannot use the word vagina, we cannot truly describe a woman, nor without the word penis, a man. A green leaf indicates the time of year; a damp vagina indicates desire.

So, if we are teaching sex, we must use the "improper" words to teach it properly. We have to use these anatomical or sexually explicit words if we are to express what we have to say realistically and in a way everyone will understand.

As messengers, writers choose words for their meaning and the effects they have on people's imaginations. Our own opinion of the word itself has no bearing. If we must use a certain word, it is immaterial whether or not we like the word ourselves.

I have never been a particularly profane person. Sure, I say the "fuck" word in traffic, as most people do, and cuss at my tools from time to time, but I have never been the kind of person who tries to impress others with "bad" language. Yet I am neither afraid of these words nor embarrassed by them.

As a writer, my personal interpretation of words does not matter. It is the reader's "nasty" mind or analytic brain that I am working with.

Fear or hatred of a word only creates a fear or hatred of the activity itself. Yet often the activity is much less objectionable than the word. Dislike or embarrassment toward a word gives it control over our emotions.

Sex is both an emotion and a natural body function. As such, it is more than a clinical term; it is also a poem.

Yes, words evoke feelings of excitement. The word "jugs" creates fond memories of adolescent lust. The term "pussy" is, to me, the kinkiest name for a woman's vagina. The sound alone, coming from my lips, creates nasty, affectionate, forbidden, and appealing emotions within me.

Sex can be a word game or a competitive sport, but it is mostly a spiritual involvement. Without the "sex" in sex it would not be as appealing. The nasty bits are what make us want to do it. But the spirituality of sex is what makes it forever memorable, what makes it Love.

I personally want lovemaking to be a mutual experience. Lovers achieve greater erogenous excitement and a more intense orgasm if their partners are also making the journey. Perfect sex is a cooperative effort, achieved only if there is consideration for each other.

Some men want to dominate, force, and hurt their partners. That may be real primal and animalistic, but isn't very good lovemaking among human beings in the 21st century. If guys with selfish, macho techniques had discovered what they were missing and how little they satisfied their women, I would have lost a lot of lovers over the years.

Somehow, I learned early the technique of romance. It's like seducing a flower, being a Hollywood leading man in the 1940s or selling women's shoes.

Imagine two salesmen in a store selling shoes to women. One of the men is in it only for the money. He just wants to get her in a pair of shoes, any shoes, get her money and move her on. Get it on, get the cream and get her out.

The other guy is interested in the payoff too, but he is also concerned with finding shoes that fit the woman's taste as well as her size. Get her what she likes, get what you like and leave her smiling.

With the first guy, the woman has regrets. She gets home and is unhappy with the results of the shopping trip.

The other salesmen's client is experiencing the afterglow of her acquisition. She is in love with her new shoes.

And so what happens the next time these two women crave another relationship with a shoe salesman? The first woman will go to another store. The second woman will go back, looking for the same salesman in his shining armor.

"Teenage boys' obsession; most of us when we turned twelve started beating our heads against our obsession... sex. It reminds me of the first time I saw a bird pecking at a mirror image of its own reflection on a window, thinking it was a mate, or perhaps a competitor.

The first stages are mired in ignorant obsession. There is something about the form of another person, and then we begin getting as close as we can to their image and heat.

The next step is the deal breaker. Can you overcome utter paralytic fear and step up to your future awakening? And finally we can get up the courage to talk her. And then, taking our lead from the movie we just saw, we ask her out, etc. etc.!

# CHAPTER 9

# Taking Your Sex Life Into Your Own Hands

## The Masturbation Chapter

It eventually happens to all of us. At some point in our lives, we learn how to touch ourselves.

Often, an infant boy finds his penis just by accident, because it's right there, handy. In fact, it is the handiest thing to hold on to, and so, to the discomfort of many parents, small boys constantly touch themselves.

I don't know what kind of pleasure little guys get from this contact, but it sure is a fixation for many of us. Most likely, it's just comforting, just like thumb-sucking. At what point this inadvertent touching turns to masturbation would depend on the child, I assume.

As far as the experiences of little girls, I haven't done the proper research to speak on it. So I'll keep my mouth shut.

To be fair, I guess the only experience I really know of is my own. I can't remember my early feelings about my penis, but I do recall how and when I learned to masturbate.

I had a masturbation mentor. His name was Richard. Another Richard in my young life. He used verbal instructions only, you will be happy to know.

It was at a sleep-over at my house with several other boys, sometime in the sixth or seventh grade, as I recall. I remember that we all lay there in the dark in our prospective beds or sleeping bags, and Richard told us how to do it.

I don't remember the outcome of that first foray into self-gratification, but I do know that it was the start of a full and rewarding life of masturbation. It has not grown hair on the palm of my hand, caused blindness, impotency or insanity!

I am slowly loosing my sight, as do we all. I'm not as interested in sex as I used to be, and some might think I suffer from mental deterioration, but none of this is due to that under-cover lesson I learned from Richard.

When I think of it, I guess the most interesting aspect of the whole experience is Richard himself. Given the gravity of the subject, the person who introduces one to it is even more important than the time or the place.

Richard was a scrappy, little guy. In fact we called him "Little Richard." He looked a lot like Mickey Rooney, without the jovial facade. Of all my friends at the time, Richard was the most derelict, the most unruly and the most likely to know how to masturbate. And yet, there was a sweetness about him that contradicted his outward attitude.

You had to know him well to see his good side, but it was there. As with most competing males, they only let their guard down, only show their real side to you if you are a true friend. A blood brother, maybe a fellow masturbator.

Richard was a great dancer, and he, three other friends and I dominated the dance floor at the Youth Center for three or four years. We won all the contests. I was taught how to dance by a wop, an African-American, a homosexual, a Mexican and an Okie or two.

Richard was a scary competitor, in sports and in social life. All the girls thought he was cute, and all the guys who didn't know him were very scared of him.

Richard probably had a bad home life. His family was one of the few I didn't know about. I believe he kept us away because it was embarrassing for him.

We were quite tight during junior high, but as he grew older, his attitude became more antisocial. During high school we drifted apart. He was short for his age and had a chip on his shoulder. I think he was held back a year, and then he disappeared. Richard is no where to be found in my senior yearbook.

Scrappy little Richard is one of those people I wonder about, and yet I am afraid to find out what has become of him.

If the eyes are the window to the soul, the hands are the window to the sexuality.

The bop, the "dirty bop," the most raw, the most aggressive and sexual of all dances to drive the teenage libido, was perfected, by us, in the 1950s. This was one of the most up-tight periods of mankind otherwise, and yet we learned how to conquer, seduce and dominate the opposite sex on the dance floor without copulation involved.

The picture on the next page, from the 1958 yearbook of Walter Colton Junior High, Monterey, California. The girl with the "me" printed on her images is my now wife, Joan. I didn't make it onto this page, but some of my best buddies are here, including the four dudes in the middle left of this page. It's a wonder that I have been able to skip prison with all my adventures! Joan and I first met in elementary school and went through school together until we graduated from high school in 1962. We re-met in 1985, and were married three months later.

In the 1950s, very few teenagers were getting any sex. But the music, that music, was an extremely compelling aphrodisiac to

90

those who had only one handy release. It was the age of fantasy. We played out our romance on the dance floor and then went home to fantasize what might have been.

8TH GRADE GRADUATES

*"The dance is the stairway to emotions; the kiss,*
*the door to the heart.*
*Eyes are the window to the soul, and hands are the*
*distance to sexuality."*
Dudley Griffin, 1962

Masturbation is one of the most taboo of all taboos, for some unknown reason! U.S. Surgeon General Joycelyn Elders was forced to resign for suggesting it as a reasonable option to intercourse and therefore a deterrent to sexually transmitted diseases (STDs) and unwanted pregnancy.

That would seem reasonable, if not fully sustainable. Which is worse, making your own decision, touching yourself for gratification, or having indiscriminant sex and possibly getting sick or having an unwanted pregnancy?

The same rules apply with all forms of sex, fantasy, self-gratification, or intercourse. If you do any of them without knowing what you are getting yourself into or for the wrong reasons, you may possibly screw the whole thing up. But then, since we can't completely banish all sexual activity from our lives, we must be rational. Ha ha! No one has ever seriously equated sexual activity with rationality!

My only suggestion is that you treat sexual fantasy, self-gratification, or intercourse at least as rationally as you choose a pair of shoes or a tie.

Everybody does it. I don't mean picking your nose and chewing it! Masturbation! Please, if you have never masturbated in some way or other, write me an email and document it. I would like to put it in my next book!

Self-gratification is somehow considered a sin...an abomination even, by some, but who, I ask, is really harmed by it? The first people who are bothered by it are those people who are always worried about what you are doing in your own bedroom, the "fundamentalists!" They should be called the no-fun damentalists!

The second person that can be harmed by masturbating is one who doesn't know how to do it properly!

First and most important, you must do it with a clear conscience. Only recrimination and regrets can spoil good self-gratification. If you make love, in your mind, to your babysitter and your sister together in front of the television, just feel good about it. If she's under age, remember, she is just a figment of your overzealous imagination.

Masturbation is mostly about fantasy, and fantasy is much safer than the reality that might happen were you to do some of the things you fantasize. Besides you can make love to Angelina Jolie when she was 15 years old without time traveling or going to jail.

Most fantasies should be kept as fantasies. They should never make it into reality. In many cases the reality of a fantasy is destructive, the actual acts are immoral, sometimes deadly, and they can ruin your life and the lives of others. Stick with sex that is not perverse. But never ignore or deny the love that you desire!

Desire and fantasy are two different things. Desire is something that is realistically and safely achievable. Fantasy is usually unrealistic and often too dangerous to become reality.

Yet fantasy, kept as fantasy, is a harmless and almost necessary part of our lives. We cannot stop our minds from thinking these things, and we would be hypocritical if we said we didn't think them. We needn't be ashamed of these thoughts because most people have them, but they are only "what if," and they should stay there in our minds.

The Wet Kiss by JBMc

CHAPTER 10

# The Kiss

The kiss is of most importance. The kiss is the first indication of whether the two of you, or the three of you, are going to fit!

The nose, watch the nose…that awkward bumping of the nose thing… that is important to avoid if you are trying to portray experience. The mouth, its softness, yet desire, shows the appreciation of your heart. The uncontrollable, audible breath that escapes you with the kiss is prelude music of lovemaking.

This is from the perspective of a man, yet most of this is unisex. It is international and timeless!

Emotions... reading and feeling emotions, are what the kiss is all about. One of the early 1960s songs, *"It's In His Kiss"* said it.

In the movie *Pretty Woman*, the working girls did not kiss their tricks. The kiss is real intimacy.

It all starts with a kiss or ends with the attempt. The first moment of truth is being truthful about your chances.

A kiss or a touch should be a question: "Do you like me, do you like the way I kiss and touch you?" And, as you continue, each move is an affirmation or a rejection.

I suppose we have all experienced the overly aggressive, and the opposite, a passive kisser, in our lives.

The kiss is the only romantic activity that can truly be equal for both of us. A kiss is the same thing to both lovers. Our body parts are exactly the same doing and experiencing the same thing with each other. We are not doing something to each other, but with each other.

I am convinced that you can never lie with a kiss.

When attempting a first kiss with someone you are not sure about, lean into her, and see if she leans toward you. If she leans in or her eyes beckon, then kiss her. If she starts but then hesitates, take her elbow or shoulder, pull her in slowly, and kiss her. Don't be too aggressive on the first attempt. Draw her in with expectations.

It is a good idea to lean, and not lunge. Reach about an inch from her lips, and if she does not retreat or move away, then you go that inch. Soft, be soft; the first touch, the fervor will come. It is not an attack! It is a search for affection or love, the world's most wonderful pleasure!

Don't start with the tongue, ease into that, my boy! Lick her lips a little, see how that plays. If you can't see it in her eyes or feel it in movements, give it a pass.

Two things you don't do. Never beg! To beg is not a solid place to stand. Never be too aggressive, you appear selfish, not a good start to any relationship. Aggression is also a sign of lack of confidence.

But all of this is immaterial if you do not mean what you say. A kiss is first and foremost an offer of affection. It needs to be sincere or it becomes a slap in her face.

You know that image from movies and media, particularly

when World War II ended, where a couple kisses and the man bends in and the woman bends back, until her spine almost breaks? Well, that is definitely a test of his balance and strength, and her confidence, but it is not comfortable or romantic, it is painful and domineering. In the jungle, women needed us to be strong and dominant, but in society today we men should lose our macho aggression.

Then and only then will the sexes live in harmony together. A good couple is one in which each person does what they are best at for the function and harmony of the relationship. This could be called the Pioneer Family.

I have never understood rape! I cannot understand how a man could go so low as to forsake mutual affection in exchange for a power play! How does a man become a non-emotional animal? How does a man reject the purity and soul-lifting experience of a trusting kiss and a consensual sexual experience? It comes down to a man who is insecure, a wimp, a scared creature, not trusting his own value, and so he must force himself on to a woman who is unable to defend herself.

> *"The difference between man and woman is not to be explained or debated. When a man and a woman come together, it will be heaven and it will be hell! What is most interesting is that the time between heaven and hell is what really excites you, enlivens you and drives you crazy."*
> Dudley Griffin 9.10.04

CHAPTER 11

# Introduction By The Typist

*"I don't have a plan, I have a direction; peace, love, food and drink."*
Dudley Griffin 2-4-2021

All truly good writers expose themselves. In order to fathom the emotions necessary to communicate deeply to readers, an author must strip away his own self-defenses, his own ego. We are always, actually, writing about ourselves, using our own nervous systems to define the feelings.

This book is not literally an autobiography; it is a universal story about growing up as a young man in America during a pivotal period of time for human relations. It is a dramatization of the hopes, dreams, pitfalls, and triumphs of all young men. It also happens to be a true story.

Everything written here is true, except for a few fantasies, which are related as fantasy. After all, a lot of our sex life is fantasy. And fantasy is OK, and it is good to talk about it or write about it because we have much to learn about ourselves from our fantasies.

Nobody could really have lived a life like this, but someone actually did, and so that makes this an historical nonfiction. It is a truly historical novel, but it's just about people, not about wars and nations, nor of politicians and industrial greed, but just about people and their most human of all activities…sex!

As a writer, I appreciate the appeal of sex. "It" is the most provocative subject a writer can employ. But I do not get turned on writing about it, nor am I a voyeur. I do not find titillation in memories or voyeurism.

I am writing this because I have a story to tell, a very important story. And I think it is a crucial enough issue to dispense with my own privacy and my credibility, if need be, in order to get the message across.

I believe most deviations, perversions and sex crimes are committed because people don't know what good sex is. They were never given the chance to experience it, because they were taught to be ashamed of it, or they were too insecure to find a mate or too inexperienced to know what to do when they found a lover.

Some religious folks will condemn this book as justifying and promoting sex for pleasure. But I am just trying to make sense out of a natural body function, given, if you will, to us by God. It is here to stay, and we must put it in its right perspective, or it will eat us up inside. And you know, if God is truly righteous, he or she will not want that to happen.

Everything written here actually, really happened to one person.

I presume, suppose and believe that any person who dissects and studies their own life, as I did for this book, will dredge up a good number of iconic, magic and amazing things that they have seen or done (but forgotten). Yes, this book is based solely on my life, and, as I repeat, everything is true, except for a few fantasies that are labeled as such.

As I have stated earlier in this book: "For the most part, what is written here is what I can remember. Yet, like most people, I may be susceptible to memory lapses and occasional subliminal illusions of grandeur, so there may be some mistakes or exaggerations regarding size, intensity or duration of the experiences. Remember, objects in this mirror may appear larger than they really are."

I slipped this introduction in here because I wasn't sure you would read it up front otherwise. I seldom read introductions myself!

Book introductions often divert my mind from the story or tell me more than I want to know right off the bat. I usually like to set-up mental pictures of my own about the characters and places. The author should be able to explain all that within the tale without digressing right at the beginning of a story.

But, as writers, we often want to emphasize some things outside the context of literature, sort of like historical notes. We often think that a few awkward or orphan facts should be explained. Well, these are mine, and I will use this introduction to express them.

In the final editing of this manuscript, I found the hardest part was placing the different subjects in an order. What order was my dilemma. What's first, what's in the middle and what's at the end? I wanted to tell people about birth control early, so some poor sod might possibly put on a condom and change his life and that of his lover's into one of rational choice, not random mistakes.

I wanted to get readers early, with the news that self-confidence is not arrogance and that confidence will usually find you a lover. I wanted to tell people that macho was insecurity before one more stupid child turned 16 in jail.

I want to explain and emphasize to men how a mature, loving wife is more valuable than a young skirt. Don't give up a whole lifetime of happiness for a few minutes of sexual selfishness.

I want to help people realize that insecurity, impotence and loneliness are self-taught and self-perpetuated. Happiness and love are all in your mind, you know!

There may be people who read this book, and others who don't even read it, who will ridicule me for some of the things I say within. I may likely be shunned or laughed at for my personal admissions and politically incorrect revelations.

Some may accuse me of self-indulgence, others, with self-detachment. Some will pronounce me simple-minded with my self-deprecation, others, self-serving with my self-deprecation.

I already see some discomfort in my wife over the book's content. Yet I cannot find any other way to tell this story or express what I know than by being embarrassingly truthful.

In this book I tell about a lot of kisses, and they are all true. I am not doing this for my own image. I am doing it for the well-being of sex, and therefore the well-being of all our lives and all our egos.

I am not doing this for exposure. I am basically a very quiet person who just feels it is his duty to speak out. My real friends will question this, yet they know the truth.

In this book most of the names and places have been changed to protect the guilty and the innocent. Several of the stories in this book have been "written" more than just recounted.

Inadvertently some of these stories might be compilations of several true episodes in my life. I think I did this only to create a story to which people can relate.

It Is Not All Just One Big Pastoral, Bucolic, Bed Of Whipped Cream! Not everything I have to say about love is positive. Not everything I have done is framed in roses. This is <u>real life,</u> after all!

There are also some fantasies in this book. They are my fantasies, a boy's fantasies, and they will be noted as fantasies.

As usual, this introduction has been primarily a disclaimer. I hope it hasn't damaged your enjoyment of the story. Each generation must be re-educated, it seems. I look at this book as a pop-quiz for the 21st century. In most of this book, I will be using He and She, Women and Men, but many of these scenarios are "almost" as applicable to LBGTQ, relationships.

For those of you who don't know what the acronym LGBTQ means, it stands for: Lesbian, Gay, Bisexual, Transgender and Queer. Now, as of 1/20/20, there is also I for Intersex and A for Ally.


CHAPTER 12

# Psycho Killer

As have most children, I had a few early "sexual" encounters with other children. These were not really sexual as much as they were curiosity.

When I was 7 or 8 years old, a girl in my neighborhood would show you hers, if you showed her yours. It was said that she was a little slow-witted, but that may have been just kids talk. I am not positive whether I exchanged exploration with her, but there is something in my memory about her. That is one thing about early history and memories--they are always sketchy, and often just hearsay.

Later, when I was 10 or 12, I lived, off and on, with a relative who had a daughter who was five or six years younger than I was. Several times while she was asleep, I slipped my hand into her pajamas and touched her between the legs.

I have no justification other than my youthful curiosity.

And then one evening when I was "baby-sitting" this girl, I had thoughts about "exploring" her again, but I didn't. That night, when her parents came home "early," I heard them in her bedroom and I am sure that they inspected their daughter's private parts with a flashlight.

I knew at that moment that I had just dodged a bullet. I never again considered touching her, nor did I ever again indulge in any sneaky sexual exploration of any kind with anyone, woman, man nor beast.

That close call cured me. I was so frightened of her father and what he might have done, that those activities became an instant taboo.

The whole episode could have been completely different. It could have changed my sexual life in a number of different directions.

All children are offered numerous avenues of sexual exploration during their development, some good and some bad. It is never a child's fault that they follow the curiosity of youth. All young creatures test their surroundings to find out what the parameters of life are. It is how their actions are met and dealt with by their society that determines what children will do in their sexual adulthood.

It is often just blind circumstances that veer a young person in one direction or another. There, but for the grace of God, go you! Whether you become a sexual pervert, and thereby a social pariah often depends on a chance, immature decision, and the unplanned reaction it receives from your family or environment.

I could have been caught by the family that night and received such a castigation that my sexual psyche would have been wrapped in an iron grip of guilt that could have crippled my ability to ever successfully join in sex and love with someone. Or I could have continued my midnight explorations until the episodes escalated into rape.

And there is a whole array of perversions and diversions a young man can morph into where sex is concerned. But most often it is how society reacts to your childish or adolescent sexual explorations that produces the pervert or, on the other hand, releases the lover in a person.

That girl's father was an outspoken fundamentalist Christian, and I am sure that he would not have been very philosophical or forgiving about that particular situation. If he had found me "molesting" his daughter, the repercussions would have been devastating and life-altering. I would have been made to feel shame and guilt beyond what any human should endure. And it would have been created by my ignorance, not my diabolical badness. It would be another example of not being educated because of society's embarrassment and the stigmatizing of the subject.

That man, my uncle, had come to Christianity in mid-life after sowing his own wild sperm in younger days, and to me he seemed bound and determined to make everybody else in the world feel ashamed of their lives as a way to cover his own shame. It is within the realm of possibilities that I just barely escaped becoming a sexually frustrated, sexually guilty psycho killer.

People who have been taught to associate sex with guilt will never really enjoy sex, and it will also damage any feelings of love toward their sexual partner. Whether they know it or not, many people in our society don't really experience and express true love in their relationships because, deep inside, they feel that their sexual desire for another person is somehow wrong.

It is natural to be curious about sex, and to be curious about the opposite sex. It is healthy, and it is important to a pure, happy life to learn everything one can about sex.

To be suppressed in one's sexual curiosity can retard one's sexual fulfillment. To be demonized for one's sexual desires can make a psycho killer of a young child.

> "It's not easy being this compassionate and
> introspective."
> Dudley Griffin, 1.11.07

## CHAPTER 13

# Coming of Age In The 1950s

The 1950s were an important period in my sexual development, even though I didn't experience any actual sex during that decade. I did come of age, I did learn to lust, I did learn to kiss, and I first felt the curious emotion evoked by the roundness and firmness of a woman's breast.

Fortunately, I lived to experience the sexually satisfying 1960s and not just the sexual frustration of the 1950s. This time was a stimulating awakening of the libido, and it gave me a perspective on love and sex that very few people during any other age of mankind have had.

Because of my good fortune of birth and sexual enlightenment, I feel it is an obligation to try to enlighten those others who missed the sexual revolution. It is not just a religious crusade; it has selfish overtones. I think the world would be a better place for all to live if there weren't so many damn sexually frustrated people around us. It is my moral crusade to help others understand their sexuality in order to help create a better adjusted world in which to live. I'm a dreamer! And I know all the trite phrases!

In 1955, I turned 12, and my hormones kicked in. Elvis was "The King," and all of us boys wanted to be a king in the eyes of the girls.

We knew there was something called sex, but at 12 years of age in the '50s, we really didn't have a clue about its potential influence. *National Geographic* was our first sex manual; bare, Black breasts were our first titillation.

I remember very little of my sixth grade year, but I remember vividly the summer that followed. In 1956, the 7th and 8th grades were called junior high school. I believe the name was finally changed to "middle school" to soften the embarrassment of kids who would eventually have to sneak into high school with that stigma of "junior high school."

The summer between elementary school and junior high school was the "coming out" party for young people at that time. You have to remember that "coming out" then did not mean what it does today. It didn't mean declaring homosexuality. It meant more-or-less becoming an adult.

Back then, when you came of age, it didn't mean losing your virginity or sticking a needle into your arm. You kissed someone on the lips for the first time, and you smoked tobacco and coughed and tried again for the first time. I will tell you that kissing was a hell of a lot easier to learn than smoking, since it was a much more natural activity.

Aside from a few earlier vague recollections of life, the summer of my 13th year produced many of my first real memories. These memories are of the unique adolescent social dramas.

The teen age is our first awakening of real feelings. The beginning of adolescence is fraught with extreme emotions percolating through us as our adult hormones kick in.

My first memories of that time are all of a sensual nature. They were the parties with girls and stacks of 45 records during the summer of my thirteenth year.

There was an innocence and a naiveté in 1956 that allowed parents to turn 12-and 13-year-olds loose alone in a darkened living room or garage with rock and roll music. We would dance the bop to "Hound Dog" and slow and close to "Moonglow" or "Sincerely." We drank Cokes, ate potato chips and made out indiscriminately in the corner.

At this point, going steady and "petting" hadn't been discovered yet. At the beginning of the summer of '56, we would ask a girl to dance, kiss a little and then get a 7-Up, ask someone else to dance, kiss a little and go get some M&MS, and start all over again with someone else. By the end of the summer, some preferences had developed. Some kids were going steady, some were dancing only with certain people, kissing only certain people, and eating only yellow M&MS because they didn't stain your hands and lips.

Have you ever heard of spin the bottle? Spin the bottle was an acceptable excuse for doing something considered taboo, by giving it the legitimacy of a game. For those of you who don't know how it's played, hold onto your bubble gum.

The participants in a game of spin the bottle (fearful, yet anticipatory) would sit in a circle on the floor arranged boy-girl-boy-girl. In the center of the circle, an empty Dr. Pepper or Mug Root Beer bottle was placed on its side. Starting with the most anxious person, the participants would spin the bottle around on its center axis, and when it stopped and pointed at someone (of the opposite sex, of course), a request would be made of that person.

Now here is where facets of the human social game came into play. First, some basic rules had already been delineated. If it were a new group, it might be simple, such as, if the bottle pointed at someone of the opposite sex; you were required (or as it may be,) allowed to indulge in a short kiss on the lips.

The tastes of each player in the contest came into play, determining the reluctance or desire to kiss a chosen person. The length of the kiss was arbitrarily determined by the mutual or individual attraction of the two people.

More complex spin the bottle games, determined by the experience of the participants, allowed for different kinds of kisses, i.e., French kissing, and the length of the kiss. One memory I have is of a kiss called "one minute of heaven," or two, or three, or however many minutes to which the group had advanced. Sometimes, in more experienced groups, and, of course, considering the tastes of the two participants, the couple could go into a more or less private corner and make out alone for a predetermined period. Often, they would have to endure the jeering and comments of the other players as they did this.

As you can imagine, all kinds of social habits and sexual games developed during these activities. Most importantly, these times provided the first glimmer of sexuality and the beginning of cultural development for these young lives.

Behavioral tastes, visual preferences and social likes and dislikes were learned. I can remember people's reactions when the bottle stopped, and was pointing at the girl with the buck teeth or the boy with freckles and the cowlick. This was before social groups started forming and parties were arranged by cliques.

In elementary school, the guest lists were usually determined by parental alliances, and no one felt discriminated against because of their physical characteristics or social abnormalities. Later, in junior high school, it was all about who you knew, what you looked like, or how much you could spend on clothes that mattered in the embryonic society that would become high school life and, soon enough, our real lives.

During the 1950s, attitudes about others in regard to their appearance and social position first developed during the transitional period between pre-teen and teenage. Now they develop much earlier, what with all the media blitz of sex and social strata. The "Mickey Mouse Club" has been replaced by MTV. National Geographic has been replaced by slick fashion magazines.

To say that the 1950s were a simpler time would be a misrepresentation of the concept of simple. The problems of human intercommunication were no less difficult then than now. We just knew less about the problems.

To say that today is worse than yesterday because we now know too much is a misconception of the function of knowledge. Ignorance may be called bliss by those who don't understand the peace and joy that enlightenment can bring, but ignorance is still the absence of a solution.

Today, though our society may seem jaded, at least we now have the solutions written down on paper someplace and in many places. Recognizing that there is a problem and having the answers available to us is a good start, but now we must apply the solutions. Knowing there is a problem is only the beginning of the solution; as of 2013, we have not even begun to solve the interpersonal dilemmas, which we now know exist.

"Sexually naive" is probably the correct term to describe the world before the sexual revolution happened in the enlightened 1960s. Denial is another good term that describes the '50s sexuality.

What is most interesting about my life is that I have lived from the naive 1950s, through the emancipated 1960s and '70s, and then observed the reactionary retreat back into the dark ages of sex during the 1980s and '90s.

In the 1950s, we lived under the illusion that our politically incorrect activities were, in actuality, correct because they had been going on for so long that no one knew any differently, and no one felt strongly enough to question them or change them. It took the irreverent beatniks, available birth control and the drug enlightenment of the hippie era to expose the hypocrisy of our sexuality.

I have graphic memories of my own social errors and embarrassments during 1950s. I am a human, and I will learn from my mistakes. One of my low points occurred at a dance party at someone's house during that pivotal summer of 1956, between my 6th and 7th grade school years.

After each dance, partygoers would usually break and take a swig of soft drink or eat some potato chips and wait for the next 45 rpm record to drop down and play. We hadn't yet started to pair up on a regular basis; going steady was a development discovered in junior high school.

When the next song started, we would ask one of the girls to dance. Usually, the choice of dance partner was based on the kind of music played, some previous arrangement or whoever was close at hand. On this occasion the other guys were quicker to choose, and I found myself left with "the short, plump girl."

I must have heard it on TV, one of those variety shows like "Red Skelton" or "The Honeymooners," but this joke popped into my head. I know it was meant only to be funny, as were all such jokes that ridiculed someone in the 1950s, and I meant it only in jest, not considering the effect it might have on the person at whom it was directed.

I said loudly enough for all to hear, "You guys emptied the barrel and left me with the barrel." We danced, that plump girl and I, and I don't know for sure what she felt about my comment, but she must not have been happy.

I knew it was wrong the moment I said it. Possibly, her reaction clued me in; possibly, my own moral instincts, likely the influence of my mother. But I do know that I never, ever again made a comment such as that about another person to their face or behind their back, for that matter.

It is hard to remember the exact sequence of events from so long ago. I was affected by that episode, and didn't repeat it again, but what was so much more poignant to the circumstance was what transpired between then and high school.

Within the next few years that girl lost her baby fat, gained sufficient height and became a truly attractive young woman. She dated one of the most popular guys in school and eventually married him to live happily ever after, for all I know. I was truly moved by that episode, and it has guided my treatment of other people, particularly women, ever since.

What is intriguing is the possibility that my comment about her at that time may also have had an effect on her, and may have prompted her to take some interest in her appearance and some action to improve it.

How often do adverse situations in our lives cause positive changes in our direction? This realization doesn't make me want to start calling people fat, just on the off chance it might get them to lose weight, but it does offer a perspective on human nature, my own and others.

A negative education can be every bit as important as positive reinforcement. Finding out what you don't want to do with your life can be as beneficial as learning new possibilities to life.

When others are the messengers of possible change, it can be cruelty or it can be "tough love." Tough love is that new term for the process of making none-too-subtle suggestions to help someone with problems they just can't overcome themselves because of human weakness. It is a good thing when it works, but a tricky job to administer properly.

My next big lesson in humility and social discourse occurred when I was a 7th grader. In junior high school, we started to experiment with both romantic commitment and detachment. It was the age of going steady, of rings on a chain worn around girls' necks, of slow dancing, close, real close, of necking, and of breaking up without a word.

This is how it went; On Friday night, kids would go to a house party or a dance at the Youth Center. They would dance and neck and ask a girl to go steady.

For the next week at school, the girl would wear the boy's ring on a chain around her neck. They would walk around the halls hand-in-hand, sit together at lunch and kiss whenever they could get away with it. Sometimes, a girlfriend would wear the boy's jacket or sweater as well. In junior high, we didn't really have lettermen's jackets, but the girls sometimes wore our coats that were patterned after the high school athletes' jackets.

This "going steady" usually lasted the duration of one week, oftentimes longer or shorter. But often by Friday afternoon, the ring had been returned. This gave everyone the opportunity to "discover" someone new the next weekend and start a new week-long relationship.

Well, very early in my initiation into this process of going steady, I had my eye on this one girl, and decided to make a foray into the world of boy-girl relations. My first mistake was probably timing, as with so many of the errors of social discourse.

I overlooked the advantage of a dark dance floor with seductive music and preliminary kisses, deciding instead to ask this girl to go steady in the noisy, smelly bus park in front of school. I was also most surely too tentative, and possibly a bit vague about what I intended.

I walked up to this girl, cold, and asked her, "Do you want to go steady?" Her answer was, "Who with?" as she looked around for the boy she thought I must be representing.

This embarrassing episode taught me a number of lessons, though they didn't all sink in for a few more years or so. 1. Mood, 2. Timing, 3. Assertiveness, and 4. You have to be your own man, with your own personality, identity and yes, even eccentricities! You must stand out in some way.

As I said, it took me a few years to incorporate these lessons into my social life. For a good part of my early adolescence, I hung out with older, wiser, and, often times, more babe-attractive guys than I. One of the reasons I hung with them was that they were where the girls were. It was good education, but after a while I realized that I was hidden or overshadowed by the popular guy I was with. Sure, sometimes I got their cast-offs or the ones they ignored, but I wanted to come out of the shadows, so to speak, and I eventually did.

Driving back from the college football game, the math teacher and his four, tired, 8th grade students traveled through the night. The trip was their reward for winning math competitions in class.

Two of the boys fell asleep, leaving one boy and one girl to wonder. They began to wonder about each other.

The teacher, though distracted by driving, could still see their heads and faces in the rearview mirror if he wished. As the driver stared straight ahead down the long tunnel of light guiding the car home, the two children began touching each other.

They could not kiss or they would be discovered, so they explored other sensual expressions. He started with her breasts, but this was difficult and tiring for his arm, so his hand slowly fell into her lap. Her hand followed to his lap.

He first pushed his hand and her dress down between her legs. There was nothing much to feel, though it was oddly comforting. She was having more luck in his lap. Her rubbing was creating the desired bulge in his pants.

The boy began to walk the dress up her leg with his fingers. Slowly, it bunched up around her waist until his anxious hand touched the soft flesh of her inner thigh. At that, they both let out a sigh.

Their movement was noted by the driver, but the girl rubbed her unused hand across her face feigning sleepiness. The driver went back to his concentration on the road.

And the boy started concentrating on the thin nylon cloth between the girl's legs. It felt like nothing he had experienced before. Smooth, yet textured and padded by her soft, young pubic hair. Was it the sense of touch or the sense of curiosity?

He began to rub his middle finger up and down, soon finding the crease in her body. As he started warming the spot, she began fumbling with his buttons.

His finger followed the crease down all the way into her crotch and then up to where it stopped and then down again as he began getting the feel of her body. She was unable to get his top button off and so with his free hand he undid it for her. She then rushed to the next button and was able to accomplish its unfastening.

As he rubbed up and down, she spread her legs slightly wider, and a damp sensation reached his finger. This gave them both another ripple of excitement.

She finished undoing the top three buttons and began caressing the front of his cotton jockey shorts. They both became energized with the closeness of sex. They empathized with each other's feelings. The rhythm of their hands synchronized.

Their heads began to roll limply; their eyelids drooped. For all practical purposes, from the rear view mirror they looked as if they were falling asleep, but their hearts pumped, and their minds raced on to eventualities.

He and his friends bragged about scenarios like this, but he had never done this before. He didn't think his friends had either. A strange thought crossed his mind. They wouldn't believe him now even if he told them.

Her girlfriends talked about just such experiences, or at least the eventuality of such things. But to her knowledge none of them had touched it before. Now she was going to. Would she tell them? Could she tell them?

This was fun! No, there was some other emotion involved than just fun! This was more than exciting. This was forbidden! This was forbidden, yet it was destiny. This was a forbidden destiny that was achievable. It was not like wealth or wisdom, which might elude you. It was attainable, and yet it was one of the most sought-after destinations. Sex!

The boy liked this, but it was not enough. He wanted to feel her soft flesh, her juices, her warm insides. Stinky finger! He had heard about it.

The girl liked this, but it was not enough. He was harder now, but it was still frustrating. Feeling the cloth and piping on the front fly of his shorts, she could not really tell what his penis felt like.

The girl wanted to hold it. He wanted to stick his finger inside her. Deep urges and curiosity drove them.

Almost simultaneously, they reached up to the waistband of the others' underwear. They slipped their fingers under the elastic and began to move down into the tangled pubic hairs. It was the most amazing sensation, completely unlike anything they had felt before. It was almost alarming, how exciting it was. They were feeling with their hands and their pounding hearts. Nothing would ever be the same! There was no going back.

Her hand reached his erect penis. His fingers slipped between the damp lips of her vagina. Her fingers wrapped around his body; his finger slipped into hers.

Suddenly, another hand fell upon the girl's hand inside the boy's underwear. They both stifled a scream. The sleeping boy next to the girl had shifted in his seat, and his arm had fallen into their laps.

With several swift moves, the couple's clothing was brushed back into appropriate modest fashion. They both pretended as though they had been startled out of sleep.

The driver looked in the rearview mirror, smiled and said, "Is everyone behaving themselves back there? We'll be home soon, and you can sleep soundly in your own beds, without disturbance."

Two of the passengers were indeed disturbed. She would have to straighten out her undies later, and he would have to button his fly before he could leave the car.

They each carried the scent of the other on their hands. They fell asleep that night smelling each other.

That was the way it was to be an adolescent in the 1950s. You got what little sex you could, when you could. The story was always evolving; it was always going somewhere.

I have lived every scenario of a young man's sex life--sexual contact with a much older girl, puppy love for a teacher, rejection by the most popular girl in school, blowing my first chance at sex, having the best lesson in romance the least likely long haired scruffy K9! I have also been fortunate enough to be able to touch many people intimately and see their needs, hopes and desires, the same as mine.

*"I have been bad in my time, but I have never been Immoral, never, never!"*
Dudley Griffin

## CHAPTER 14

# Timing Is Everything!

*"Knowing when to do, and when not to do something, is the key to a good and happy life."*
Dudley Griffin

Timing phase 1, The logistics…when the objective is to meet someone new. It is universally agreed by social intellectuals that "Timing Is Everything." Songs have been written about it, and people study and strive to improve their social timing. Some people believe in arriving "fashionably late" to a gathering and making a big entrance. Some come at the end to harvest the lost and lonely who are left behind.

I always believed in going to a party early, mostly because the hors d'ouvres were still fresh and the good beer had not yet been decimated, but I also felt it was an advantage to get a jump on the competition.

I was a cerebral seducer, not a physical one. I wanted to talk to a woman and get to know her, and attract her through personality, humor and intelligence. I never considered relying on my "beauty." I have never been considered beautiful, and the intellectual part is also a bit of a stretch, but personality has its value.

Pajama party Pacific Grove, California

Some guys seem think they can arrive at any time, look around the room, see what they want, and conquer. That is usually a fantasy.

<u>When</u> you arrive is never a guarantee you will score. How you arrive has some value; but what you do after you arrive is the answer.

Making a big entrance is good or bad, depending on the type of party, who is attending, and what your intentions are. Read the room! Don't be arrogant at someone else's birthday party. Dress appropriately, unless it is an art opening, and be respectful of the other egos in the room, unless it is a tailgater or sports TV bash.

Know what kind of costume party you are going to. Being available is always the first criteria for having a shot at love, so make yourself available.

Timing phase 2, The logistics…when getting laid is the objective. By timing, I am speaking here of clock timing and a good awareness of the mood. Knowing when to ask a person to go out for coffee or when to put your hand on their knee is an important element of courtship.

114

This kind of social timing is the most complex and also the only one where we have any control. Logistically, we never know whether the right girl, or any acceptable girl, for that matter, will appear, but after she does we have to employ timing to ensure that the scenario will progress toward a satisfactory consummation.

And just because you have gained some control over the situation, it doesn't mean success. If you don't possess the common sense and self-confidence to capitalize on it, you will fail, as most men do, most of the time.

Insecurity is the killer in seduction. You must be confident! But overconfidence is arrogance, and that turns off the sensitive girls. If you want a "bimbo," the "Attila the Hun" approach works, but if you're looking for a "meaningful relationship," an attentive, more romantic repartee is called for.

"What's your sign?" or "What's a beautiful girl like you doing in a joint like this?" are laughable introductory comments, but it is surprising how many men use such ploys. Having a set routine or script to follow is OK as long as it is unique to you, but it's better if the conversation fits the situation.

Everyone knows that the game is on at a bar or party, but a little subtlety is still expected. We have not reverted back to clubbing and dragging women back to our caves by their hair.

What most men don't realize is that the odds of finding a mate are better at the grocery store than at a nightclub. I suggest that you develop your vegetable vocabulary and learn to push a cart without aggression.

Insecurity breeds jealousy, breeds arrogance, breeds selfishness, and these are the worst sins of good timing, and of finding "Someone."

If you don't know what you're doing, turn and walk away. Ego, pride, or insecurity are the most damaging flaws to any relationship. Don't make yourself a laughing stock by being stupid! Haven't you ever watched, *Seinfeld*, *Friends* or *Two And A Half Men*? Although they are among the most sophomoric TV shows ever produced, they do give a rational man a good glimpse of how not to act in a romantic situation.

Timing phase 3, The Cosmic logistics...when finding true love is the objective. And here I am talking about "Cosmic Timing." After all, we are all looking for that perfect person, that soul mate, so to speak.

Here, I am not just speaking about the luck of "hooking up" or finding a bed partner, though that is often cosmic timing, too. I am discussing the profound scenario of finding "true love."

A small birthday party, 1970s, Pacific Grove, California

This chapter is about romantic happenstance...the timing of meeting or not meeting your soul mate. This discourse is about cosmic romantic luck!

And, of course, romantic luck is one of those things over which we have absolutely no control. We can try being at the right place at the right time, but it is capricious; we can turn this corner while our potential life's partner is turning another corner in some other part of the city. Yet we still try to beat the odds by going to every party or trying to figure out when to go to the party, late or early or in between.

For many years, I went everywhere and did everything with the underlining expectation that I was doing my best to "find" my real lover.

But it took me years to realize that it was not just the aspect of being at a place at a time, but there was the element of being at the "right place" at the "right time." And I had no control over the "rightness."

If all you want is to get laid, then all you need is money and a cat house, but, think about it, if you are looking for a lifelong companion who shares your values, hopes and dreams, you might actually have to put some more emotion into it.

It's not going to be easy. You may have to spend more time and money in less exciting environments, like bookstores, pet shops and organic markets, but the odds are better there.

P.S. On-line dating will most likely bring you only fantasy and frustrations.

Timing between couples can change. Romantic timing can go from good to bad within months, years or decades and then back again. I have seen it in my own life.

It must be understood that timing, like good luck, will favor those who are prepared or open to such positive events. Both timing and good luck have cycles. Those of us who play poker are aware of this, and we use it to our advantage.

CHAPTER 15

# When Does a Sex Life Begin?

I don't know what a perfect adolescence is, but mine was as good as anyone could expect. The town where I was raised was ethnically diverse and culturally exciting. My friends were from a dozen different cultures. For many of them, English was not the language spoken at home. There were several military installations in the area, and it was a tourist destination as well. We were not cut off from the world of diverse sexual mores.

I cannot understand why some people and cultures don't want to live in an ethnic mix. Being with people of different religions, languages and colors is the most educational and exciting life, and even so, does not mean that you will or are forsaking your own family and history. I think it comes down to the ego of the father figure. Men should look at history and realize that you can't kill every other culture to save your bloodline. It never has worked, and it never will.

In the early 1950s or 60s, it was impossible to get any kind of sex education from the media. TV and movies were trying to show us what "normal" family values were supposed to be, even though there has never really been a "normal family" then or now, as far as I can tell.

MTV did not exist back then, and the soap operas were tame by today's standards. Yet, even still, sex as it is taught by the media is fraught with deviations and obstructions. I am glad when they don't even try.

I grew up in a small city on the California coast, a good place to be in order to get a perspective on how abnormal life could be. And, because of that, the diversity and all, it was a good place to live in order to make up your own mind about what "normal" would be for you.

When I was in junior high school, all the kids went to the Youth Center on Friday nights. It was the focus of our week. We would go to the Center and dance, drink soft drinks, dance, play pool, dance and dance. Dancing was our life.

Five of my best friends and I won every dance contest, every weekend, for over four years. We competed with one another and took turns in the spotlight every night. Slow dance and bop, we won them all.

I had an exciting group of friends, and I thank each of them for what they gave to me. But not all of us fared well in life.

Putting them into perspective as to their future places in society, they could be described at random as: a hippie, a Viet Nam War vet, a lawyer, a homeless person, a drug lord, a rebellious African-American, a real estate tycoon, a homosexual, and a drug casualty. Yet even if they had all been my same ethnicity, color and religion, the same consequences could have easily befallen them. I have seen that to be true.

One of these guys was the first person I ever knew to have a silver crown front tooth primarily as a fashion statement. Possibly to your surprise, it was not the black guy, by the way.

One friend was gay, though I didn't know it at the time. This guy was not afraid to wear pink sweaters even before there was any "odd" connotation to that color on a man. A lot of us were wearing "gay" colors then. This gay friend taught me how to dance to rock & roll and turned me on to black and soul music, though he was white himself.

Another of this group was the kind of guy who would piss in the punch at a girl's birthday party. Sometimes he would tell you he did; sometimes he wouldn't.

One of my friends taught me how to masturbate (only by example), and he later fought in Viet Nam, but was dishonorably discharged for striking an officer who wanted him to kill civilians. This Viet Nam hero died homeless on the streets.

My Black friend was not the drug lord, homeless, or the drug casualty. He became an artist.

None of these young men came from horrible family circumstances. Some of them were privileged, and most were well-educated and supported by their families. There is no such thing as normal. There are no guarantees, and I was fortunate to learn that early in my life.

A father's sperm determines our sex. He shoots male and female sperm in equal amounts. Male sperm is more vigorous, but female sperm lives longer. The woman's egg awaiting the sperm is without a gender--has no sex. If a male sperm gets there first, the baby is male; if a female sperm gets there after all of the male sperm have died from exhaustion, then the baby will be female. What does that tell you about women and men?

One's real sex life begins the first time you dance to a slow song like "Could This Be Magic?" by the Dubs, Tab Hunter's "Young Love," or Elvis singing "Love Me Tender" from a 45 record turning round and round in a darkened garage with 20 of your classmates, and you just can't resist sticking a tongue in her ear, because that is the only thing you know for sure is really sexy.

During my 6th grade year I went to see the movie, "Blackboard Jungle," and my life was changed. I don't know if I had ever danced before in my life. Sure, a few spins with my mother, some pretend ballet or cotillion, but never real dancing. When the theme music of the movie came on, my friends and I got up and "danced."

From that moment we knew what we wanted to do with the rest of our lives, and that was anything that would give us that same feeling in our groins. Life's desires have expanded somewhat since then, but I defy anyone to deny that their first primary realization of the meaning to life was felt with that initial tickle, that primal, sexual feeling experienced during their first real dance with someone of the opposite sex. The song, "Rock Around The Clock," was for many of my generation the opening lines of the opera of the rest of our lives.

My sex life began in 1956 when my circle of friends became old enough to start going to dance parties and sock hops at the Youth Center. At first, all we wanted to do was dance the bop, but soon we discovered something that gave us even more tickle in the groin. Slow dancing! Then, the next step in the "fall from Eden" the kiss!

I think if a person were allowed to choose a time in history to come of age, to become a romantic and a sexual being both at once, the mid-1950's in America would be that time and place. There was no better music before or since to awaken the love and lust of mankind than at that time.

With artists like Elvis Presley, The Platters, Sam Cooke, The Everly Brothers, The Crickets, The Fleetwoods, Ricky Nelson, Paul

Anka, and, yes, even Pat Boone, how could we ignore our sexuality? With songs like "I Want You, I Need You, I Love You," "April Love," "Don't," "Twilight Time," "Little Star," "It's Only Make Believe," "Mr. Blue," and "To Know Him Is To Love Him," how could one survive without romance?

A sex life can be depraved, distorted and diverted if it is not nurtured by healthy and proper romance. Sexual desire can become sordid and ugly without the possibility and eventuality of emotional love. If people deny or fear their sex drives, they become hypocritical about their needs.

Sexuality is something many people put into a box and hide and say they don't have it. Yet they secretly use it when it suits them, and that makes them ashamed and, therefore, perverted to the world. By ignoring our sexual desire and denying its necessity and importance in our life, we take something that is beautiful and create a monster out of it.

Many "religious" people scorn sex because it makes them feel too much like the other animals to which they prefer being superior. My feeling is that most organized religion is just a way to help insecure people feel superior to something and, therefore, secure.

I suggest a new religion, a religion based on good, clean, consensual sex. Such a religion would never exalt superiority or create conflict. It would celebrate tolerance of life. Our worship would be a slow, fluid, symbiotic dance to a 1950's love song.

The concept of original sin is a ruse that the tyrants of religion, government and industry use to divert our attention away from their hands in our pockets. The conservative and fundamentalist media has us so worried about who, when or why we are screwing that most of us can't see that they are busy screwing us.

Childhood and adolescence are so confusing to most children, yet if you get it right the rest of your life can be a breeze. Who your parents are and how they treat you, and who your friends are and what you learn from them are the biggest asset or the worst detriment to a happy life. I was fortunate in both family and friends, yet with both influences I did not get your normal, boring, follow the leader education.

I have already said much about my mother and father who

were obviously progressive in their thinking. My outside education, in the public world, was even more diverse and radical.

My acquaintances in middle school and high school were very ethnically and economically diverse and also most often sacrilegious, anti-establishment and confrontational. They didn't indulge in hypocrisy or phony painted-on personalities. They seemed to be dedicated rejects, contrary to conformity and committed to the joys of life. Each of my friends, though different in many ways, were individuals of purpose, even though the purpose was to enjoy life, and screw the rules that they did not agree with. In their own way they were juvenile delinquents, yet they were also true to reasonable codes of decency and morality. We were crazy, but not stupid. When we tagged the school, I told them that we could get away with it without consequences if we did not tell anybody we were the perpetrators. I told them we couldn't tell even our guy friends or girl friends or families. They held that code, and to this day our names have never been in the papers for that episode. We were not looking for notoriety, we did it for fun. Anonymously making a point, a silent statement was more profound, more true to the rebellion that we represented on our high school campus!

My potentially marginal friends

At the time I knew I was hanging with potentially marginal

people, and yet I was drawn to them. It could have had disastrous consequences, yet, except for a few anti-social activities, we were lucky and intelligent enough to avoid capital crimes. Some of us moved on up or down, dictated by the reality of life and times. But my education with them was a positive one, and my personality was cemented by knowing those guys and girls.

Over the years I have grown to love those rebels, or at least the memories of who they were and what they did for me.

Trudy Aagren, Michele Arndt, Vicki Breton, Richard Graham, Charley Harraway, Mary Ann Hawkins, Gary Hover, Joan Jeffers, Carolyn Martin, Larry Oda, Bob Palma, Rosolino Prestigiacomo, Shirley Reed, Johnnie Ross, Jesse Rubio, Sandy Scardina, Sue Segali, Tom Verga, Alex Walters and James Wolfenden, I thank you.

CHAPTER 16

# I Wasn't Raised On Rock & Roll; Rock & Roll Was Raised On Me

When we are children and teenagers, we have many different influences--our family, teachers, friends, movies, music and even that "crazy" guy at the pool hall, or the mall girl, or that video arcade champion who trounced us. But we are also an influence on other people, and potentially a good or bad contributor to all the events that are happening around us.

We are all part of everyone else's lives as they are part of ours. You influenced people and things in your own way, and I have influenced lives and events in my way as well.

One of my most notable contributions was to rock & roll. I bought the records, I danced to them, I listened to the radio and bought what they sold, and watched the movies. I supported the music, and therefore more people wrote it, played it, sang it and recorded it.

People like me and many others of my generation built our own musical culture by supporting the music that we loved. We are just as responsible for the music as the music is responsible for us.

I was fortunate to be passing through my adolescence when rock & roll music went through its adolescence. My friends and I empowered the music, and it empowered us! We showed them what we wanted, and they created it. And therefore, music was fortunate to have our sensibilities.

My first orgasm was music.

I didn't even know what my feet were really good for until I heard that song "Tutti Frutti" come out of that little box with the dial on the front. The round, black vinyl sphere spun and changed my life.

And then, when Little Richard choked out the name "Jenny, Jenny," I finally had a notion of what my body was for, "spinning, spinning, spinning, spinning like a spinning top!"

"Havin' me some fun tonight," the lyrics of my life for the next 30 years.

Little Richard was the most effective messenger between Black and white music lovers in America. You know how sometimes the messenger gets crucified? Well, he was too wonderful to crucify by anybody except the religious right.

Hearing Little Richard was one of the first times many white folk ever thought, "well maybe 'they' have a place in our society!" "I will let them sing and play sports, but they can't move into my neighborhood!"

The first thing you had to get over was Penniman's androgynous nature. The fact that he was Black didn't matter after that. Your Uncle George was every bit as sexually conflicted, and George couldn't sing or play piano. Little Richard seduced everyone who has ever heard his voice. But there is no shame in such love. "Miss Ann" was an embodiment of all man's fears and frustrated ego. "Slippin' and a-slidin'" was one of the motivations of my life!

Have you ever heard any other singer, sing so fast and hard that he stumbled over the toes of the next word and reached out fighting for a breath to scream the next lyric? "Jenny, Jenny, ooh Jenny, Jenny...."

What about Chuck Berry? He certainly shared our teenage angst and knew our hearts and the heat within our groins. "Sweet Little Sixteen"... need I say more? Can't keep my mouth shut about Chuck! "School Days." He nailed it!

There are few guitarists more motivating than Chuck Berry and his licks. No one else has been covered by more musicians than CB--by The Beatles, Buddy Holly, The Stones and many, many more. Is "Maybellene" the best automobile song ever written? "That highway sound..," Nadine--we have all known her if we have lived at all. "Seems like every time I see you darlin', you got something else to do!"

Chuck had some of the most moving rhythms in his songs, "Nadine, honey is that you? *boomdadadodo boomdadadodo!*"

Chuck said, "It's gotta be rock and roll music. It's got a back beat, you can't lose it!" Back beat became a sound that we sought out and moved to.

"Johnny B Goode!" That song has always been my theme song.

"Promised Land," "And that hound broke down...in downtown Birmingham." Check out that song! Part of my wanderlust came from that song.

I have no defense against the euphoria where music takes me, and I admit and embrace the sexuality that it produces.

"Blackboard Jungle" at the State Theater, 1955. We all jumped to our feet to dance in adolescent joy and fearful anticipation. Some of us, if the moment worked out, found joy. Some of us, when it didn't, found fear. Even then, the importance of acceptance and peer pressure was high. We all fought the battle to survive.

In everybody's life a song or piece of music was a turning point for them. I have several: "Rock Around the Clock," "Ball and Chain," and "Light My Fire."

Having lived through the 50s into the 80s, I have many musical moments--my mother's Victrola with Caruso's voice coming from it, winding up and then down. I learned tempo from that. Janis stomping her feet, Jimi beating his guitar painlessly into submission of sweet cords and then burning it.

My mother was not a person who loved music for music's sake, but she loved several songs because of what they meant in her life! She loved "I'll Be Seeing You" sung by Frank Sinatra, Cole Porter's "So in Love," and "All In The Game" sung by Dinah Shore, 1951.

The Shirelles "Will You Love Me Tomorrow," 1960, was one of the first rock & roll psychotherapy songs. This beautiful woman asking you to be faithful, yet you both knew the outcome. By the Skyliners "Since I Don't Have You", 1959. The ultimate of loss and loneliness, the words of this song would bring even a Republican to tears. "This Is Dedicated To The One I Love" by The Shirelles, 1961. This song has much to think about.

Sex is not something to be rushed into, yet it, above all, is an emotional, even primal, necessity. In an organized, ordered human society, it should be controlled by some common sense. But since our society has chosen not to properly educate its children about sex, we blunder on through our sex life. We also treat other important human dilemmas such as bigotry, religion and national chauvinism in the same way, and therefore, our existence is always in turmoil.

If Christian fundamentalists were to look deeply into their religious fervor, they would see that their emotions are not always rational, scientific or even moral. Please remember the Golden Rule, folks!

We are a special creature on this earth. We are not better than any other animal or plant in the world. We are important because we are the only occupants of the world that can actually destroy this world.

Everybody has seen the cult of guns or the cults of cars. They are always too extreme and come with dictatorial requirements. You must be self-indulgent and not care about reality. If you have lots of money, you can ignore the realities of most real people. But guns and cars kill more people than most of man's other indulgences, and they also cost more money.

During the 1960s and 70s, many people called hippies cult members. Yes, we had cults, mostly cults of rationality, life, peace and freedom. These were not dictatorial; they were diplomatic, because we realized that democracy promotes peaceful harmony without racial, national or religious bigotry.

And what does all this have to do with a satisfactory sex life? Hang in there, and you'll see that frustrations of any kind, be they conflicts about religion, race, gender, or patriotism, all affect our emotions, and that disturbs love and sex.

I had the melodious good fortune to work for a time in the 1960s and 1970s as a rock and roll photographer. It was the most stimulating part of my lifetime and the least stressful time in my life. I am partially deaf in my left ear from standing up against the stacks of speakers photographing bands. I liked to photograph from the left side view of the stage because I could catch the whole guitar and player. Jimi Hendrix was a lefty and so he was better shot from the front or right side view of the stage.

For a time in late 1969, I was Ike and Tina Turner's photographer. I followed them to some of their gigs in L.A. for Blue Thumb Records. One of their bookings was the L.A. Forum on November 8, 1969, opening for The Rolling Stones.

I introduced Mick to Tina. I don't remember how it came about. I was moving between the dressing rooms connected by a bathroom. Mick, Keith and I smoked in a stall. I went and got Tina and Ike and the Ikettes from the other room, I introduced them, I took some pictures, we danced and sang.

Can we quantify the beat of the drums in our groin? How many lovers met on the dance floor, or dusty tribal square? How many songs have won your heart?

Keith Richards, Ike Turner and Mick

Working with a record label I could not keep most of the good negatives' these are culls, but they show what good fun we were having.

Tina, Mick

CHAPTER 17

# Jerk or Lover?

*"When I Look In Your Eyes, Is It You Baby, or Just The Reflection of My Own Desire?" Dudley Griffin 12.29.07*

During my freshman year of high school, I had a run-in with the law. Normally, I chose crazy, but not stupid friends to run with, but this one night I made a mistake in judgment and went out with some stupid and crazy guys. Bad mix, wild and dumb. From early in life I have been drawn to fun and people who liked to have fun, but not at the expense of others, and definitely not to their own detriment.

Do you understand the appeal of Russian roulette? If so, please don't call me. I'll call you if things get really boring. Take a deadly weapon with six chambers, put in five bullets, spin the chamber, place it to your head and pull the trigger. Gee, are we having fun yet?

Take a syringe with a substance in it that everybody says will kill you eventually, and stick it in your vein. Yippee!

Drink a stupid-making amount of vodka, and drive your car 95 miles per hour. Do you get the picture?

In my high school freshman year, I went out one night with some new "friends." They drove to the valley, drinking beer and throwing water balloons at mailboxes. Then "they" decided to throw some at a passing car.

Our car was going 50 miles an hour, and the other car was traveling at 50. Do you know what a 100-mile-an-hour water balloon will do to the hood of a car? I saw the damage later.

My new "friends" chose me as the patsy. I had to pay the damages. In my recollection, it was about $150. In those days, that was a lot of money. But that was cheap, compared to what could have been paid. That incident could have ruined my life and ended the lives of others.

The woman in the other car was pregnant. The balloons missed the windshield. We were all lucky. I have never again, when I had the choice, put myself in the hands of luck. I figure I have used up most of my share of the stuff.

Because of that incident, my mother felt I needed some masculine discipline, so I was shipped off to spend my sophomore high school year, 1959-60, with my uncle near Los Angeles, California. That year and the next, my junior year, were crucial in the development of my attitude toward women.

During my sophomore year I got my driver's license and began using one of my uncle's pickup trucks. It was a 1956 Ford, and arguably one of the most beautiful pickup trucks ever built. That model is still sought after today as the most popular classic custom truck.

In that year, I started customizing that pickup, and that summer I stayed and worked with my uncle in his masonry contracting business. After doing a lot of bodywork on the truck, I had it painted Thunderbird red. I had parts of the engine chromed, and I painted the undercarriage white. I had big, slick tires on the back, chrome drop pipes, and a black Naugahyde tarp over the bed.

Red Truck, Inglewood, California, 1960

I loved that truck. I cleaned and polished it incessantly. I was furious whenever I had to use it for work.

In Southern California, one of the popular getaways was Big Bear Lake in the mountains. Summer or winter, high school kids by the thousands would ascend upon the mountains to party.

Shortly after I had the truck painted, I drove it up to the mountains with a few friends for some adolescent activity. One of my first important lessons about women was learned on that trip.

The guy friends I traveled with were from either school or church. I can't remember which. But I do know that my activities that weekend were strictly against the rules of my uncle's church, the church I was "forced" to attend when living with him. I expected to drink some beer and neck with some "non-Christian" girls that weekend.

My friends and I were staying at one of their family's cabins and soon hooked up with a party. We drank some beer, danced with the girls, and I ended up making out with one particularly cute young woman. As all this developed, I realized that this girl was some sort of a celebrity, and at one point in the evening a song came on the record player, and it was my "girlfriend" singing it. I am not sure who it was, but my impression was that it was either Shelley Fabares or Shelby Flint, both of whom were singing and recording around that time. But I was possibly misled.

I have always been noted as a good kisser. How I learned, or what I did right, is a mystery to me. I think it may have something to do with sincerity, and a lack of inhibitions. Somehow, it has always been, that if I could kiss a girl, all other opportunities became available to me.

As the evening progressed, I got the impression that this girl was interested in going off someplace with me to get more intimate. It was, of course, my hope that we could go back to my bed at the cabin.

I had, in my wallet, my trusty Trojan rubber. No self-respecting teenage boy of that era was ever without a prophylactic. It was a very important item that we all carried, but which very few of us ever got to use in that frigid time in the history of teenage sex. I thought this might be the time, the first time, the opportunity to use that well-worn, yet never employed, prophylactic, which I had stored with anticipation next to my driver's license.

In an effort to impress the girl further and hasten our departure for what I hoped would be a sinful night of fornication, I invited her and her friends out to see my beautiful, bright red pickup truck. They were all very impressed and wanted to get in the back and take a ride. But to do so, they would have to climb over the fenders. Well, I, of course, went into a fit of indignation about my paint job.

To make a short, and sad story long on heartbreak, the girl, "my girl," my first potential copulation, saw me as a stupid jerk and told me so. How important was an "ol' paint job" anyway? After telling me off, she retreated back into the party, and I went home alone, dragging my ego behind me.

Believe me, I relived that episode many times over the next few months, and, even today, I get a flush of embarrassment from its memory. But it taught me a big lesson.

That night, I learned not to rely on my possessions to supply me with the affections of women. Down deep inside, most women don't give a damn what your car is like. That piece of metal that you have so much of your ego wrapped up in, or those clothes or house really have no effect on the outcome of a relationship. They may, and I say <u>may</u>, get you a look, but if you don't know when to forget them and move on to a more attentive attitude toward the woman of your affections, she will go elsewhere.

You May Have A Shot! She gives every man the impression he could get lucky! Her personality is comfortable so you feel as if you have known her for eternity...as if you were already her lover.

There are girls--women--who are so appealing, outgoing and seemingly obliging that they make every man and boy think he has a shot. But be realistic. Her defenses could be immature. Her outlook may be naive.

These girls are tricky because it often is not as easy as it seems to get next to them. They aren't necessarily manipulative, but their basic attractiveness and outward sincerity may sometimes hide a manipulative history. They have found out, even during their young lives, that they can get what they want by seeming gullible.

If you say the right thing, make the right moves, you may find the golden door. But be careful; the rejection may be more than you can handle. Knowing if you have a chance with a woman is your responsibility. If you misread her kindness, friendship or youth, it is not her fault.

If you are rejected, it is not the girl's fault...it is your mistake. You have not read the signs. You have been too arrogant or too timid, or your timing has been wrong. Don't blame yourself or her. Learn from it and move on. Maybe someday you will have another shot, and you will be worthy.

You must always be certain that you are talking to the person to whom you think you are speaking. If you misjudge the "worldliness" of a girl, you quite likely will say the wrong things, be too forward, and embarrass yourself and her as well, and I might add, you will lose the girl.

Also, if you reach into another economic or educational culture for romance, you must be prepared to raise your I.Q. or prepare to be embarrassed! If you can't communicate in multiple worlds or multiple syllables, just keep you mouth shut. Stand back, see if you are out of your depth, turn and walk away, or maybe try to rise to the level of those around you.

Slumming is done by both sexes, and then there are the gold diggers and the snob's snobbery. 2018, and now we have the web fishers who have no self-respect or respect for anyone else's emotions.

Guys who are in certain guy groups will denigrate one another in humor without any misunderstanding or repercussions. A man must choose carefully the words and subject when speaking with a woman. Forget it with cross-gender-satire. What you think is humor could be considered harassment by many women.

CHAPTER 18

# Oh, Oh, Oh, Desiree

Our life, like a highway, is a path to all possible things. We must each learn what we desire or need to fulfill our idea of a successful life. As an adolescent, I did not know the difference between desire and need. They are both the same to a horny teenage boy. The truth is that they are as different as a scar and a sliver. Desire is a scar, a hard-earned and valuable reminder, whereas need is the sliver, which is an annoying irritation.

To desire is the recognition of emotional feelings. Need is the physical feelings. Desire is the following of your soul, whereas need is the necessities of the body.

So you're cruising down Alvarado Street with a quart of warm beer between your legs, looking for some activity or someone upon whom to express your personality. One problem is that the beer is not a quart anymore, but a splash or two of backwash, and you haven't found a party yet or a girl to confront. The night is close to that point where soon only the losers will be out on the streets.

One of your buddies in the back seat is almost asleep. The guy riding shotgun can't stop talking about the girl he almost met last weekend, and your other rider is becoming more and more maudlin and combative. Soon, the night will no longer be hopeful; it will become impatient.

When our sex life becomes anxious, we loose the spark of life that can attract another person's love. And then we are in a downward spiral that makes us more un-loveable. We overeat or drink too much, we talk too loudly and push too hard.

I experienced this, myself, several times in my life. Fortunately, they were fleeting moments. Thankfully, I was able to pull myself together and out of them. And the experiences were enough to show me that sexual or romantic anxiety, self-pity and insecurity are man's most personally damaging, and our most dangerous, states of mind.


# CHAPTER 19

# Girls Don't Really Like To Be Tickled!

When we were kids together, it was the only way we could show affection. A boy could tickle a girl or squirt her with a water pistol without being teased by his guy friends. It was a none-too-subtle way to show that you were attracted to her, yet it had the deniability factor.

(1950s) At 11 or 12 years of age, boys still suspected that girls had cooties, yet there was a glimmer of attraction surfacing. We wanted to touch them and have some sort of interaction, but we needed an excuse that would be plausible to our buddies. So we teased the girls. We played physical tricks on them. It was part affection and part ridicule.

If we did it right, of if we did it to the right girl, she responded with the proper deniable reaction for a girl. Giggles and screams of delight/terror!

But girls don't really like nasty sounds blown on their bellies! Girls are different from guys. They like only certain guys to squirt them or tickle them.

If she already liked you before you knuckled her head, she would smile and giggle. Yes, but not because she liked what you were doing to her, but because she liked you and having your attention.

But, know the pitfalls! Antics, such as tying pigtails together, are a good way to get noticed, but not to create a romance. Annoying someone is a backward form of communication.

Have you ever heard these words uttered from the lips of a girl? "Get away from me, you creep!" If so, that was your clue that she didn't like you, and you had better devise a more subtle way to break the ice. Yes, ice! That's another one. Ice down the blouse. It didn't work then to get a girlfriend, and it still doesn't work today.

These sorts of tricks, to get attention, are still practiced today by some grown men! It is still the deniability game. "Well, in case she rejects me, I will have given her a good reason to do so. Therefore, my ego will be safe!" Good thinking!

Never, never give a girl a reason to reject you. Believe me, they can find a reason on their own.

Being obnoxious is not a very good way to start a relationship, or to keep one, for that matter. Many guys still haven't learned that.

Girls really do like receiving flowers, having you put your coat over a mud puddle, and candlelight, don't forget candlelight! They don't like wedgies or rubber snakes in their lunch bags.

> *"I was never any good at flirting. Flirting is like stepping into a fast, beautiful car, starting it up, revving the engine a few times, and then turning it off.*
> *I like to drive; I don't like to flirt."*
> *Dudley Griffin, 1.13.7*

Of course, some people believe that flirting is a fun little game and an essential element to courting. It can help you gauge another person's interest in you. It can allow both parties to show their level of intellect or humor. It also, often spoils the moment and turns a potential love affair into a sitcom.

Don't toy with her affections! If you are attracted to her, let her know your intentions, sensitively, of course. Commit to a position.

If she is not interested in you, your best defense is always having mounted a "good" and respectful offense. If you are rejected, your respectable reaction should then be something like, "Oh, OK, I understand. I'll see you later!" You should never say, "You're missing out" or "You'll come around" or even "Maybe next time!"

The downside of any commitment is that you may look stupid when you wimp out. But worse yet is that, if you don't respect a woman's decision, you become a creepy stalker, and then you will never have another chance with her or any of her friends. You might as well move to another town.

Everyone you meet will have a different opinion of you; most probably they will be wrong. You will never, ever talk someone into loving you, but you can easily talk someone out of loving you!

One of the worst mistakes a man can make in this society is to believe that, just because he is a man, he is entitled to control any woman he so wishes, meaning that they must listen to him and do as he says. And, of course, since that is not going to happen, he is going to get indignant, abusive and maybe also violent. Well, there you go! That is a man who will have a lot of lonely nights, unless, of course, he ends up in jail with a cellmate.

*"And so you go out to buy some love, and you find the only thing that will buy love is love itself, and you find that there are no deals made. The rate of exchange is set. So you find out what love is, and you find that it is tolerance, and tolerance is finding a common ground on which to communicate, and to listen, and to hear what someone else is saying and listen long enough to forget what you are thinking and to think about what they are saying." Dudley Griffin, 1971*

Looking back with introspection, I realize I've always had a quirky sense of rebellion. I didn't want to be pigeonholed. And the reason, I believe, was that I had already seen too many cookie-cutter people, and I didn't think that they had the answers or even knew the questions.

By accident, my rebellion just so happened to be what mainly brought me to the attention of the opposite sex. In my last two years f high school, I did a lot of things that just seemed fun to me, I was not inhibited by conventions of the time or any time. The snowball fight in the school hallway after a rare snowfall and the hopscotch game on the senior quad are examples.

The movie *Rebel Without A Cause* came out in 1955. I was 12 years old, and it had an effect on me, just as it did on many young men of that time. I won't say that I acted out any of my rebellion consciously just to emulate James Dean. I can't remember my exact thoughts at the time, but many of the juveniles of that era had these thoughts, and the screenwriters of that movie knew it.

In 1961 and 1962 I was rebelling against what I could see as moldy thinking and backward mentality. I acted out in ironic rebellion and in parody and humorous ways, not in dangerous ways. That was my mother's influence, to have respect for yourself and those around you.

1962, the year I graduated from high school, was the beginning of the end of human hypocrisy. I know it might take another century before the final death of mankind's lying to itself, when we truly become righteous, but we started the process in the early 1960s.

That era was when we started losing our unquestioning loyalty of authorities in religion and politics. We began looking for the truth, in our own souls and in our own mind.

## CHAPTER 20

# I Ain't Handsome, But I Ain't Shy

*"Sometimes we rewrite our past, often we improve it. Sometimes we depreciate it, but most often we get its importance wrong!" DG*

My persona in high school? I guess I could say I demanded respect, but I also gave it back in kind!

By 1959, my sophomore year of high school, I had accumulated what I thought to be a good deal of experience with girls. I had danced with many and kissed them too, but I hadn't yet achieved real equilibrium in communicating with women.

As all adolescent boys, I was still deathly afraid of rejection and therefore reluctant to expose my ego to pain by showing too much interest in girls. The difficult catch-22 of love and relationships is that, in order to get the girl, you have to make some kind of sincere move. You have to commit, and in doing so, you are making yourself vulnerable to the possibility, no, the probability, of rejection. The truth of the matter is that no guy, however attractive or smooth, gets every girl he tries for. It ain't personal! Oftentimes, it is just timing or chemistry.

During my sophomore year, I lived with an uncle in Southern California and attended Inglewood High School.

That year at the school there was one girl who stood out larger than life to me, and to many of the other boys. She was an upperclassman, a junior or senior. She was, if I remember correctly, a cheerleader, and without a doubt, the most popular girl in the whole world, my world at least. She was gorgeous!

She had bouncy, curly, shoulder-length, blonde hair. She made those soft, pink sweaters of hers look like the rolling hills of a cotton candy fantasy land. Her straight, tight, (but not trashy tight), tweed skirts ended just below dimpled knees.

I got to see her knees only once or twice that year and only during lunchtime as she sat at an old green, initial-carved picnic table with her friends. The immaculately shaved and shiny calves of those legs ended too soon for me as they disappeared up into the dark crevasse of her skirt and down into her bobby socks and loafers.

One day, as I sat eating lunch from my brown paper bag, waiting for her to come out and sit at the upper-class picnic table and hopefully show another glimpse of dimpled knees, she appeared and began walking toward me. She was looking in my direction as she floated across the basketball courts where we all gathered each sunny noon to eat, gossip and fight.

I expected her to veer off to her own table or to walk up to one of the other kids between us, but she kept coming toward me. She passed her domain and her lofty friends at their table and kept on coming. I even looked over my shoulder, to see who she was heading for, but, no, she was looking right at me and coming right toward me!

She stopped not two feet away and looked down at me on my bench. Smiling, she said "Hi." Her greeting flowed down over me like water on a dying plant. "I hear you have a yearbook that you want to sell." She said.

I may have stuttered; I know I was staring at the front of her sweater. It must have taken me some time to get into my stride.

It was true. I was at that school for only the one year. I didn't have many friends at school, and I really didn't need the yearbook. I had just bought it out of habit. I must have let it be known to someone she knew that I was willing to sell the book.

For some reason, she forgot to buy a yearbook at the appointed time and now, I was "her savior." We conducted the transaction. It was the most exciting business deal I had made up to that point in my life. It ranks along with the purchase of my first car.

During the proceedings, I was at a loss for words and probably made a fool of myself, but I got to talk to her, and I had my one glorious opportunity to observe, up close, the breathing movements beneath her pink angora sweater.

I don't know for sure, but I must have lived those moments over again many times for the next few months. If I know adolescent boys' habits at the time, I probably masturbated to the memory of that meeting a "time or two." As a matter of fact, I believe, that was the occasion when my amorous activity and the heat of the water and steam cracked the shower stall glass in my apartment.

It was only a few short weeks later that I learned a major lesson in my social life from another encounter with that same girl. I was leaving school for the day and saw her walking off campus in front of me. From my perspective, 15 feet behind, following down that long, concrete corridor, it was the most beautiful walk I had ever seen. When she reached the street a boy was waiting for her.

She walked up to him, and they embraced and kissed. She stood on tiptoes and her leg bent up in back at the knee, just as in all movie images of such kisses. They headed off in the same direction I was going, and I followed as they flirted and walked. I could not hear exactly what they said, but the boy's voice was confident. He was assertive, he teased her, and she laughed a lot. She followed every word he said closely as she clung to his arm.

He was the coolest, most virile, charismatic boy I had ever seen. He had her wrapped around his finger; he was the biggest man on campus, and he was also short, skinny and ugly. Ugly, yes quite ugly, and this most beautiful of all girls was his, and his, as you could easily see, for anything and for as long a duration as he wished.

Why? Self–confidence! He had it!

Bad Boy is a name often given to guys who are really just confident. Self-confidence is sometimes considered arrogance and vice versa. The bad boy persona is often about rebellion. Even if the rebellion is warranted and pure, the straight society brands it unpatriotic, hedonistic or arrogant even though it could really just be confidence.

I watched that boy around campus for the rest of that year. I had the same PE period as he did, and I studied him. He was a surfer and a skateboarder. He carried a skateboard everywhere he went. He wasn't an athlete in any school sport. He wasn't particularly good looking, bright or charming. But he had confidence.

I studied him, but I didn't emulate or copy him. I got into his confidence. I begin to realize that that confidence could never be learned, and it certainly could not be faked. And I also began to realize that I, myself, had that same kind of confidence down inside of me. The only difference between us was that I wasn't using it to my advantage. I began to understand that the key was in knowing how to use confidence, and the way to use it was to accept it, even forget about it, to take it for granted.

You can't ever think, "OK, I am going to become confident now; I am going to be strong now." To have confidence, you must really, honestly, have no fear, and then you will be confident. Having no fear is not as easy as slapping a decal on the back of your car saying that you have "no fear." Many people who rely on decals think that stupid macho actions and a belligerent personality indicate confidence.

Charisma can be created, but it must come from your real image and self-confidence. Some elements of "image" can be purchased at a store. Clothes, a haircut, or a suntan can be acquired, but self-confidence cannot be bought at any price. And wisdom of how to use confidence properly requires years of experience.

After that experience with that beautiful girl and her ugly boyfriend, relationships with girls became easier for me. Why? Because I began to exude self–confidence.

Self–confidence is the most difficult human attribute of all to acquire. As a matter of fact, it may be impossible for some people to ever get there. The reason is that self-confidence is usually either nurtured or destroyed in childhood. Parents and/or circumstances often combine either to make or break the character of a person at an early age.

After negative influences in childhood, the only way to regain confidence is to reverse much of what has been taught. This usually can't even be acquired through conventional means of psychotherapy or self-help seminars. It requires the loss of ego, and killing your ego is a difficult accomplishment. It usually takes a near-death experience or a psychedelic enlightenment to achieve. More about that later.

In my youth I was fortunate to have a nurturing and supportive mother who gave me a good platform upon which to build healthy self–esteem. A few positive circumstances and some early confidence-building episodes also helped out along the way. But confidence can also be a double-edged sword. It is a tool that can become a weapon. In some people, confidence becomes arrogance.

By watching that boy in high school with the dream girl on his arm, and by comparing him to a few other role models and quite a few rejects, I learned to distinguish the difference between being arrogant and being self–confident. There is a fine line between the two. An arrogant person feels that he is the most important person in the world. A self-confident person knows that he is an important person among many other important people.

A truly self-confident person understands limitations. He believes that he is the best person he can be, is happy with his own efforts, and yet realizes that others can and do have their own prominence as well.

An arrogant, self–centered person knocks others over with his or her confidence. Arrogance pushes people away; self–confidence attracts people. There is sometimes a confusion in values because many people have a tendency to be attracted to the noise that an arrogant person makes. This attention from others fertilizes the arrogance of a self-important individual. But soon, the sheer selfishness of an arrogant person will drive other people away, whereas a self–confident person, even an understated one, will attract people.

All this self–righteous verbiage aside, one thing I have learned over time, and definitely the hard way, is that no one can be confident and sincere all the time. There are some people who will never be confident, and some who can never be sincere. There are those who are usually confident, and those who are mostly sincere, but no one is always sincere and always confident.

There are levels and degrees of self-confidence, just as there are levels and degrees of insecurity. But the psychological nature of the mind is that, if you are on one side or the other, either confident or insecure, you will only become more so as time goes on. The weight of insecurity will continue to drag you down, and the lightness of confidence will lift you up.

Once you have been imprinted by your family or childhood experiences, you will, most likely, continue to go in that direction. Positive experiences can lighten insecurity somewhat, just as bad experiences can damage confidence. But very much like physical traits, such as body shape and height, without a drastic reversal of circumstances, you will have your basic personality for your whole life. PTSD is one element that can change a person's soul! Traumatic war experiences or life tragedy may make someone a different person.

Girls, yes, girls, I am now speaking to you!

After all that I have been saying to the boys about how important self-confidence is to them in a relationship and how damaging arrogance is, I must now speak to you ladies. You must learn to recognize the two entirely different emotions of self-confidence and arrogance in men, and this is for your own happiness and well-being.

It is not easy to recognize male sincerity! (And it is different than female sincerity.) Some say it is in their eyes, some say the kiss, and those may be true, but I will tell you several places that men's pronouncement of sincere love will not be found.

A man's sincerity is not found in the money and gifts he gives you, nor in his apologies. After your man has had to apologize to you for being unfaithful more than twice, then it is not love he has for you, it is disdain.

If a man finds reasons to be with you other than just for sex, he might be a keeper! If he finds reasons to be apart from you between sex, and it is not for work, then he should be thrown back into the river of testosterone!

*"Being humble is not just a character trait, it is a means to communicate friendship!*
*Ego is always the unfriendly force!"*
DG

CHAPTER 21

# To Fathom The Soul Of Woman, And Other Parts Of Her

*"Sometimes I think that all my chasing of women was just a biological need. Other times I'm convinced I was actually trying to find out what made them tick!"*
Dudley Griffin 11.6.06

I think it is simplistic to relegate all sex, love and male/female relationships to the place of physical and social necessities. To call sex an urge or a business arrangement is not giving basic human curiosity its due credit.

144

When men and women bump into each other out in the world, it is obvious that the sex drive is present for the man, and the family urge is prevalent in woman. Some people will dust off their hands and call that the whole ball game. But what about the intangible, indescribable, unexplainable fact that men and women sometimes just like to hang out together?

Guys hanging with guys is understandable. We have things in common. Girls hanging with girls is rational because they have similar interests. But, if you strip the sexual part and the child-raising part from the man/woman relationship, what else do we have to discuss?

You may think I'm being flippant in a cavalier, shortsighted, sexist sort of way. I may sound two-dimensional with a four-dimensional subject, but I am truly serious. I am introspective and damn curious about what it is that makes men and women even talk to one another outside of sex and money.

Work with me here. Unless I ask these questions, they are not going to be considered in this book, because I am the author. So I may ask a question or two which I already think I know or raise a subject that I don't even care about. Not that I don't care why women and men socialize, but that I find I think more deeply as I write. By asking a question that is strange or inexplicable, I gain food for thought. What is the true link between man and woman?

What is the true link, if any, outside of procreation, between man and woman? Can we make it stronger, and will it do us any good to become better buddies? As you can tell, this is a subject fraught with confused logic, and it is also mankind, me, crying out!

I'm curious about women, I'm curious about our relationship, and I'm curious to know whether my curiosity is of any value. What will I learn when I finally understand women, and will it do us any good?

Here is an example. Why do women make beds? I can go into the reasons why most men don't make beds, but I can't for the life of me explain why women do. I have heard the words, "It feels good to get into a made bed." "It's neater!" (Neat, now that's a word I want explained to me!) "It seems cleaner!" (Seems cleaner? It's not cleaner, but it seems so. I want that one explained, too.)

For most men, in the time/effort/cleanliness continuum, making a bed makes no sense in the cleanliness, time and effort department. Making a bed falls into a category of the most wasteful uses of time, because soon you will just get back into it again.

Here's another one. Why do women take soup out of a can and heat it up? There are a lot of foods we eat cold. Why heat soup? In the dirty dishes/time/effort continuum, it makes no sense. It also wastes fossil fuels, creating a big ugly carbon footprint on our world's natural resources! Yet, on the other hand, a 380-horsepower motor wrapped up in a pearl essence paint job makes a lot of sense to the male ego.

I'm really serious here. What is it that makes us members of the same species, and should I be concerned about that?

I used to think that making a girl squeal and moan was the highest level of male/female relations. As I matured, I moved on to include watching the sunset together. Balancing the same checkbook was added later in life, and agreeing on bed sheets came along sometime in the last decade.

What I am now trying to rectify is all those other intangible emotions, values and needs. Will we ever mesh, and does it matter?

At this point in time, in my 78th year, I have come to the conclusion and resignation that we probably will never be able to speak the same language regarding some emotions, values and needs. But I am still curious. I am still curious about the deeper parts of woman. And although I may never be able to fathom her, maybe that is what intrigues me most and keeps me coming back for more consternation.

*"If you find your intellectual mate and physical mate in one person, you are blessed. But the chances are slim. Just don't keep looking your whole life, leaving a string of broken relationships behind you."*
*Dudley Griffin, 11.10.06*

If you look at my history, you will see that I have been quite successful with relationships, in their number and duration, quality and quantity, if you will. The ones that were supposed to be long, were long. The ones that were supposed to be fast and furious lived up to that, too.

Only two marriages. The first lasted seven years and the second one is now over 30 years and still evolving. But I have also had a lot of other successful short relationships. Three years, two years, etc.

What makes me a good partner escapes me. I have never been very subservient. I can't stand insanity. I don't make a lot of money.

It might be that I like to see women smile.

As an example of how different men and women are, I bring up vacuuming. If your man vacuums his house or flat before you visit, he is just trying to get laid. If your husband vacuums your mutual home after your affections are a foregone conclusion, then he really loves you.

A husband who vacuums, washes dishes or makes the bed is doing it because he appreciates you and your coupling. Place your own value system on that, but if you think he's a keeper, cut him some slack on a few other things because he may really love you!

CHAPTER 22

# It's All In Your Mind...You Know!

You are now a quarter of the way through this book,... and I know that if I still have your attention at this point in the book, I could start writing about the social life of slugs or the sexual perversion of nematodes, but believe me there is still some good shit ahead in here!

CHAPTER 23

# White Bucks, Flat Tops and Pomade

Looking back on it all now, I'm convinced that I was one of the originators of cool! And until someone proves otherwise, that's my story, and I'm sticking with it. White guy cool at least! Carl Perkins, Elvis, Buddy Holly, Johnny Cash and The Killer showed us it could be done.

I actually owned a pair of white buck shoes, I wore chartreuse pants and used Dixie Peach pomade when few other white guys would touch it.

I was among the first dudes to pull my jeans down to my butt crack on purpose. It was a workingman's style, the sloppy guy in dungarees that slipped down. We adopted it.

Cool, as we know it, often seems to emanate from the Black culture. But it's not exclusively a Black thing. It's rebellion, it's finding something that is exclusively yours until everyone else "discovers" it, and then you and your little gang have to move on.

Adopting ethnic styles or outrageous fashions seems to be what most kids do to be unique. Part of the reason is because it's abhorrent to our elders, and teenagers, it seems, will do anything to piss off their parents and adult society.

Some of you might not think that chartreuse pants, white bucks and greased flattops are cool, and, in retrospect, they may not look like it today, but at that time they were the core of cool. Cool was, and is, that attitude that whatever you are wearing or doing is cool. Cool is not caring, really not caring what anyone else thinks about your style. Cool is confidence! You can tell by the way a man stands, holds his hands or looks you in the eyes. Again, it cannot be faked, and it is not something that a cool person even thinks about.

I am actually blowing my cool by discussing this, by saying I was cool. But, at this point in my life, I have no need for cool anymore, anyway. So I'm talking about it. Hopefully, wisdom will serve me well instead.

I don't even know why I'm trying to explain cool! No one is actually going to learn how to be cool from a definition of cool. You either are or you aren't. In your youth, your cool genes are either crushed or nurtured, and it's all or nothing. But it pays to know cool when you see it. Those are the people you should be following. Those are the people you need to listen to. Who knows? You may become cool by proxy.

After saying all this, I must admit that being cool is not always the magic pill for a successful life. You can be a looser and be cool. You can even be an asshole and be cool. I've seen both, and I've been both, but what I have never seen is a person who says he is cool and really is.

Well, I guess I have just officially blown my cool!

CHAPTER 24

## Chicks, Cars and Testosterone--You Know, More Guy Talk

In high school I liked hoodies. This was the1960s, so remember that kids in the 1990s and 2000s didn't discover them, they rediscovered them. I liked hoodies, but I didn't like the hood, so I learned to sew. I cut off the hoods and rolled them over and sewed them up. I liked to put my hands into the pouch pocket in front but I didn't want to hide inside a hood.

Girls can skip this chapter if they wish, unless they want to grok the male ego better. (Look up grok in The Hippie Dictionary.)

*Mr. Blue* by the Fleetwoods is playing on the radio. It is 1960, I am sitting in my Thunderbird red, 1956 Ford pickup in the front line of cars at the Wich Stand drive-in restaurant with my girl by my side. I am in teenage heaven.

I put all my extra cash into that truck. What money didn't go for hamburgers, cherry Cokes and gas went into bodywork, a paint job, chrome pipes and more chrome, chrome, chrome. It was the coolest looking truck in L.A., or so I thought. And it was fast off the line.

That sucker had the biggest V-8 motor Ford made at the time. It had 10-inch slicks and a crafty driver behind the wheel. But what most of my competition didn't know, was that my truck was mostly smoke and mirrors. It had only a stock carburetor and an automatic transmission.

The truck actually belonged to my uncle, and he wouldn't let me mess with anything under the hood. I couldn't make any mechanical alterations or additions that would increase its speed or change the fuel consumption.

My truck was a paper tiger in a quarter-mile race. I tried racing it once at Lion's Drag Strip in Long Beach. The top speed was good, but elapsed time was disappointing, so I devised a plan of action.

Out on the street, looks were cool, but speed was king. And more than just speed, it was quickness. The real rush was leaving someone behind at the stop sign.

There were some streets where cars could race for the full official quarter mile, but mostly it was just city blocks. Cars couldn't get completely wound up because they had to slow down or stop at the next corner. It was either that or gamble on getting a ticket or smashing into the Cleaver family station wagon.

I wanted a reputation for both speed and looks. My truck had the looks; it just couldn't beat most street racers in a quarter mile.

Every Friday night, the guys in their cars would cruise The City, and I mean the whole city. It was possible to rack up 100 or 175 miles in a night with time out for Cokes and burgers.

Sometimes you went with a girl, sometimes with a buddy or two, sometimes in a group of cars to cruise the drive-in restaurants and racing streets. Sometimes north into Santa Monica, Hollywood and Pasadena, sometimes south to Long Beach or as far as Newport Beach and Balboa Island.

La Brea Avenue, La Cienega, Sunset Boulevard, Santa Monica Boulevard, Los Feliz, Colorado Boulevard, Hawthorne, Pacific Coast Highway and Newport Beach Boulevard, looking for a race, looking for a car to humiliate.

I looked good and fast in my truck, and everyone wanted to try me out, but I had a big handicap. Most of the other street racers were altered and could beat the mud flaps off me in half a city block. But I had tricks up my sleeve.

First, I made a few minor alterations; I removed some restrictions in the transmission shifter on the steering column. On a back street in an industrial area not far from my house in Inglewood, I practiced and experimented with weight in the back of the truck.

Before going out on the weekend cruise, I would load 10 concrete building blocks into the truck bed and take the paper filter out of the big, round air cleaner on top of the carburetor. I always had to do this without the knowledge of my uncle.

Out on the street some 'Vette, GTO or Plymouth Fury would

pull up beside me, and the driver would look over with a curious, but confident, sneer. He would rev his engine and make it known that a race was imminent. With the filter out of the big can on top of the truck's carburetor, my engine sucked in a hurricane of air, which whistled through the metal air cleaner, sounding like a sophisticated fuel-injection system.

Watching the reflection of the yellow light and timing the change from red to green I would floor the accelerator pedal one millisecond before the light and then jam the automatic transmission shifter from neutral all the way down into low gear. The Fordamatic would instantaneously engage the gears, drive shaft, and wheels, and with the precise balance of weight and friction I had calculated, my truck would jump like a frightened bullfrog across the intersection and be six car lengths ahead before that other poor sod stopped burning rubber. I would watch the rearview mirror for the first signs that the other car was gaining on me, and then I would shut it down, coasting on my way. I had won my race, and I would turn and look smugly as my victim, red-faced and crazy, screamed by me at 75 miles an hour.

So humiliated was the poor bastard, that he would be going 90 miles an hour by the next signal. Several times I passed one of these fools moments later as he was getting a speeding ticket. The girl I was with always looked at me with admiration, and, better yet, the other driver's girl was questioning the gladiator she had chosen. I was a teenage God in my chariot of fire. And yet, when I think back now, I realize that I was only a deity to myself. I was an asshole to all those I conquered.

I, myself, would never idolize someone who beat me. Why should I? I would never look at some other guy with a beautiful car or cute girl and say "I want to be just like him." I would always think that guy was a jerk. But if I had that car and that girl, I would be cool. Yet that guy, no matter what, was an asshole in my eyes.

So what value is that car and girl? Your competitors think you're a jerk in spite of what you have, and in spite of your beating them. It's only self-image. So what does one get from all that image? For awhile, it gives a warm feeling in the gut, but how do you stack up to scrutiny when you get out of that car? How do you measure up when you have to say something meaningful to that girl?

That red truck was just a way to get noticed. What I did after that was the important part. Our clothes and cars are just a means to the real end...relationships...with other people, with girls, with the world.

The true irony of the whole situation is that I was not really the macho conquistador I appeared to be. I was not actually the stronger of the two. I was just the <u>smarter</u>. I beat them, not by muscles, but by brains. Strangely, in the youth culture of the 1950s and 60s, that was against the rules. No, it wasn't even <u>in</u> the rules. No one even considered the existence of brains in the game.

The conquest of girls, of races, and of reputations was supposed to be based on appearance and strength alone. That was the culture of the '50s--power and image, the lessons of a war just fought and won.

The value of intelligence was not yet a major issue in the macho endeavors of mating and winning. The importance of education and brainpower was only beginning to be realized among the middle class. Mankind was just then perched on the brink of the intellectual renaissance of the 20th Century.

Times have changed since 1960, yet in some areas of life, things have not changed at all. Image is still as important as always in the minds of immature and insecure people.

I'm not knocking it. Nothing was sweeter than the days when a nice paint job on your car or a sharp pair of shoes was all it took to be happy. The only problem is that life goes on, and the sooner you move on, the better it is for your successful future in the real world.

The sooner you realize that your idea of yourself is not shared by everyone else, the better you will adjust to reality. The more you work on your image, the more it looks like weakness to others. Get over the disillusionment of being who you are, and be the best of who you are. Think about it! What do you feel about other people who try to be what they are not?

Small man, big truck syndrome: The Western World of capitalism offers a perfect solution to the insecure, envious, competitive and greedy personality. All the toys of success and all the cover-ups for deficiencies are available. A car can't make a man, but it can create aspirations. Having "the car of your dreams" has a tendency to kill the incentive for some guys. They stop being idealistic.

And this was the hope of most adolescent boys of the 1960s, that a car could make a woman receptive or excitable!

Fast cars and guns are the toys of insecure men. I'm sorry to tell you this about yourself. Sometimes I realize that I may be telling people things they don't want to hear. Bliss is one of the rewards of ignorance, and often that bliss is easier for our ego than having to admit that we are ignorant.

It would be better if we could do everything right without glorifying our actions. If we could do everything right without thinking it is right or wrong, if there were no question of what right was, we would always do the right thing.

Being right is often more difficult than being wrong. Ignorance makes it easy to lie. Sometimes you have to think to be right. And being right and not admitting it is sometimes the correct move!

As for the subject of male competition, I have been in a number of situations where other men have been jealous of me because of the woman I was with. At times they tried to compete with me for the affections of my date or lover or wife. My reaction has always been ignorance. I was not ignorant of their actions, but I ignored them. If a woman wants to be with someone else, I don't want to be with them! If it comes to a choice, I will always acquiesce. Only twice have I had to initiate this response, and both times it worked out better for me. Once, because she chose me in the end, and the other time I was better off because she was not right for me.

## CHAPTER 25

# Influences, Heroes and Role Models

A young man's influences, heroes and role models can come from any direction. They can be the ones that are expected, or they can be surprises.

My greatest positive influences were my mother and father. One was first-hand, and one, a second-hand influence. I was fortunate that my parents were my most positive influences because they were the most pervasive presence in my young life. Sadly, many children's most dominant influences, their parents, are among the worst influences in their lives.

My first male hero was a gay man who won medals for bravery in the Second World War. My first masculine role model was my uncle, the cowboy. He was the quintessential cowboy. He could have starred in any cowboy movie you have ever seen. Only the strongest horses bucked him off, he once spent 24 hours trapped under a Jeep in a mountain canyon, and he drank Jim Beam. I've seen him punch a horse and knock it down after it kicked him.

In one week I saw Ed Smith put a gutshot deer out of its misery, kill a rattlesnake, cut off the balls of a calf and eat his steak with the same pocket knife. He was a man's man, and everybody knew it.

My first bad role model was one of my other uncles. He would never eat a steak without sending it back at least once, and he turned his back on his first child.

My spiritual role model was Jonas. With Jonas, I made the maiden voyage of my mind.

A role model is just an example of the possibilities of human behavior open to you. The term "role model" could be defined as someone whose actions and personality you <u>might</u> want to emulate--or maybe not. Until you start acting like that role model, you are not really a model of their role! They may just be an influence.

Role models are not always your choice. Most role models are pushed onto you or they may be the only example of human behavior available to you.

A role model is not essential to creating a good personality. Often, they misdirect, sometimes they obstruct, and always, their path is not your path.

A role model is not a necessity, but it is nice when an example of life's possibilities comes along, and even better when it is the example of a good way to live!

CHAPTER 26

# Becoming a Man

### Turning Point: A Mind Of My Own

My sophomore year in high school led to a summer in Southern California, and then I stayed on to start my junior year.

At the beginning of that school year, my self–confidence must have been up a notch or two where women were concerned. Within the first week, I had a beautiful girlfriend on campus who was outside my group of church friends.

My uncle and his family were Pentecostal Christians, and during my visits with him, I had to adhere strictly to my uncle's dictates and the rules of that church. No movies, dances, alcohol, mixed fun, and definitely no dating "outside girls."

Back home, living with my mother, I had no such restrictions. I loved to dance, drink beer and make out with as many different girls as I could get my lips on.

My Inglewood High School girlfriend was in the Drama Club, and we used to go to the theater and make out backstage between the curtains. We were very passionate and would have been having sex very soon if we had been given the chance.

During the second week of school, this girl asked me to take her to the Youth Center for a dance. That was definitely sinful behavior, taboo, outside the realm of the Christian life my uncle planned for me. I couldn't wait to take her!

My customized red pickup stood out like a hickey on a nun. My uncle knew all the police in the city, and one of them saw the truck in front of the Youth Center and called him. Half an hour after my date and I started dancing, in walked my uncle.

You can imagine the embarrassment of this scenario! My very stern and imposing family member walked up to my girlfriend and me on the dance floor and told me to take the girl home "now," then come home and bring him the keys to the truck. The next morning, I bought a bus ticket back to Monterey. I left my uncle, the truck and the girl.

That action was the most confidence-building move I had made up to that time in my life. One very positive move, for I was rebelling against an overbearing parental figure, and one regrettable, yet educational move--I left behind a girlfriend without worrying about whether there would be another girl in my future.

Detachment in relationships is an important lesson to learn, yet it can also be a destructive force. One must know the proper balance. To be forever detached in relationships is never to commit your complete affections, and therefore never to find true love. No one will give you all of themselves unless you will do the same for them.

That exercise in detachment was appropriate to the situation, and it was also empowering for me. But such freedom of feelings can become selfishness and insensitivity if not employed with great care.

My one regret--I have always wondered what that girl thought about my leaving and if it was at all damaging to her self-esteem. I hope not, because I sometimes think about her kisses. They were my first forbidden fruit.

CHAPTER 27

# Cats And Dogs And Girls

I have always been able to "turn on" cats and dogs and girls. I am not boasting; I am just stating a fact. The fact that I can turn them on is not a personal accomplishment; it is actually a personal surrender. The ability to excite someone else is not a jealous act; it is submission and therefore, not done for recognition or self-satisfaction. To get inside someone else's desires, you must lose your own desires and concentrate on theirs.

*"Girls, three things when choosing a man or mate--Do they have a good relationship with their mother, and do they like animals? But mostly, do the animals like them, not just obey them!?*
*Dudley Griffin, 5.11.94*

I sauntered into Sambo's pancake and coffeehouse. Politically incorrect in name, but in 1962 it was the cool place for us high school kids to meet and have coffee on a Friday night.

She sat, bored and trapped in a booth with her parents--the tourist girl. We exchanged glances. I watched her excuse herself to go to the bathroom. In the hallway, we made out. I treated her like an equal, I wasn't a bully like the boys back home.

She needed a friend. Out to my car and around the block to a dark street for half an hour of heavy petting. I understood her; I didn't treat her as her parents and her little brother did.

When we returned to the coffeehouse, her parents were on the verge of calling the police. The young girl smiled at me as her family ranted. She smiled for the first time on their road trip across the entire United States.


In order to satisfy someone else, you almost always have to give up some of your own agenda. You must be willing to do that in return for love. Yet many people are not willing to let their guard down for love. Selfish, arrogant and insecure people have a hard time finding love because selfishness, arrogance and insecurity leave no place for submission to the pleasures of others.

To make a cat purr you must be able to get out of yourself and into what they desire. You have to be strong enough to endure foolishness in the pursuit of that cat's pleasure.

To make a woman purr you must give in to her needs. You must follow her lead. Listen to the small sounds of pleasure her throat makes as you touch her. Forget your own needs for awhile, and you will receive far more in return than your selfishness is expecting.

Men, lose your own needs if you want someone else to need you. No one will trust you if they think you are primarily concerned with your own life and not at all with theirs.

Women, learn this for yourselves and your pleasure. Guide your lover, yet never take advantage by "toying" with a man. Remember, girls, you also get back only what you give into a romance. What's good for the goose is not always good for the gander.

*"There are sensitive people, aggressive, and violent people, with all the steps in between! If you can be sensitive at the right time and aggressive at the right time, you win! But you must rely on timing, and get it right, or else you are 'a stalker' or 'the whimpering reject'!" Dudley Griffin 5.11.94*

*"What is bad manners for the gander is bad manners for the goose!" Dudley Griffin, 11.13.06*

## CHAPTER 28

# It's Now Or Never
# Turning Point: Guts

*"She was the perfect high school dream come true. In her puffy white dress, beautiful round breasts, no eyes could pass her by. She took as much as she gave, and that was more the beauty of it and the education." Dudley Griffin*

Shortly after leaving Southern California, my uncle's oppression, and one very nice kisser, I got right back into the social life at Monterey Union High School. It was 1960-1961. "Theme from A Summer Place," "Teen Angel," "The Twist," "Stuck on You," and "Stay" were the memorable songs on the radio and stacked on the 45-rpm record player.

One night in my junior year, drunk and disorderly at El Patio Drive-In Restaurant, I encountered a couple of girls sitting in their car. One was an old junior high school girl/friend, and the other was a new girl in town. We will call this new girl Carol Morris, She was a senior. She was beautiful and a hell of a lot more sophisticated than most of the other girls I had groped with up till then.

I was hot for her. I gave her all the moves I had. There is a lot to be said for beer courage. I asked her to take a drive with me in my car, which, of course, meant some heavy petting. She said "No." She had to meet someone later that night. I said to her, and I quote, "It's now or never." This, of course, was not very original, since it was the title of a song by Elvis Presley that was being played a lot on the radio at that time. But it was the sentiment that must have gotten through. Carol said she was sorry, she really couldn't come with me that night, but she would be willing to go out with me some other time if I called her. She gave me her number.

I saw her from a distance a few times at school that next week and then I called her.

I could have wimped out; I could have realized she was above my league when I came down from the beer high. I could have told myself it was just her way of brushing me off, but I didn't. I called her, and that confidence was powerful. I called her, and we made a date to go out.

I also asked around and found out a few things about Carol. She was a transfer student; her father was in the Army out at Fort Ord. She was a senior, an upper-class girl. She was also dating a graduate from last year who was going to the local junior college. I felt out of my class, but she still gave me encouragement whenever we met at school.

Our date was set for a Friday night. I can't remember which car I had at the time, but it was either my mom's 1950's model DeSoto or my own 1950's model Chevrolet, which I bought sometime around that period. Neither one of these cars would have been considered a plus to my sex appeal, but at least I was mobile.

The night arrived, and I headed off with great expectations. You would have to be familiar with military family housing to appreciate my difficulty, but I got lost and couldn't find her house. I was devastated, and actually thought that she had led me astray, giving me bad directions because she didn't really want to go out with me.

I drove all the way back home with thoughts of crawling into bed for the next school year. I got home, parked on the street and sat there. I started thinking about that beautiful girl and got a hard–on, so I masturbated.

I sat there for a little while longer, and since I had relieved my frustrations, I began to think more clearly. I wasn't going to let her or this situation beat me. I wanted to take her out. I badly wanted to take her out. So I got mad. I got mad, but I didn't get stupid.

I went into the house and called her number. I figured that if she misguided me on purpose, she wouldn't expect me to call her. I would be too embarrassed to call, and she would be through with me. But I decided that I wasn't going to let it be that easy for her. I was going to be the maker of my own destiny.

I called her. She was wondering why I was so late. I told her, and she gave me better directions. I went back out to the military rabbit warren and picked her up, and we had a great time together that night.

Fate could have dealt my ego a blow that I might not have survived. I very nearly didn't call her; I very nearly convicted her of deceiving me, which would have meant that I would not have been able to talk to her the next Monday at school. I would have blown our potential relationship, and it probably would have distorted future relations with women for me.

On that night I banished all thoughts of feeling sorry for myself forever. I had not given in to groveling.

I was lucky. I made the right decision. I turned against the tide that was pushing me where I didn't want to go. It is all in your mind, and if your endeavor is righteous, you will find a way! It was a turning point in my life with women.

John & Carol

Carol and I dated steadily for maybe six months. We went to a Winter Ball together. I had a carte blanche to all the best parties, and I introduced her to the multi-culture of the Monterey Peninsula.

She was a gorgeous girl, the image of lust all teenage boys strive for. But she was also a bright girl, an interesting girl, someone I could talk to.

Travels with her military family had made her a more worldly person, a more mature mind and a more sensual playmate. Carol was out of my league when I first met her, but I was in her league and climbing fast by the time we ended.

She was my first hand job, and I had all the above-the-waist petting I could ever handle. Today it's called "With Benefits."

We never went "All The Way," but I think I remember a little stinky finger exploration. It was good for my ego and my education. Of all my early experiences, it was most crucial to my future love life.

I learned another important lesson through Carol that year, and it was at the expense of her ex-boyfriend. She had broken up with him when she and I started dating. One night when we were at a party, her ex arrived out in front and started shouting her name, calling to her to come out of the house and talk with him. I wanted to go out myself and tell the guy to leave her alone, even though I knew it probably would mean a fight that I would lose. The ex was a big guy, a football player.

Carol wouldn't let me go alone, or even go outside with her, though I wanted to give the appearance of protection. She went to talk to the guy alone. I watched from the doorway, somewhat ashamed of myself, but ready to rush out and help her if her ex became violent. Instead, when she told him that she was staying with me, the boy leapt up on the hood of his sports car and jumped up and down like a spoiled little kid. In his childish jealousy the young man ruined his reputation for all who saw it or heard about it. And, curse him, he damaged his valuable little sports car!

That image has stayed with me ever since. That night, I promised myself I would never react so foolishly in blind jealousy. It was not that I didn't care; it was because I wasn't willing to end a love affair with a foolish melodrama.

I would practice detachment. If a woman didn't want to be with me, I didn't want to be with her. Somehow, I realized that self-respect was more important to me than a doomed relationship. You can't force someone to love you!

I would do what I could to keep a lover I wanted, but I would never destroy my own personality to do so. I knew that, if I had respect for myself, women would respect me and most likely respond with love. Since then, I have always respected the wishes of women I loved, even if their wish was that I be gone.

I would tell them that when they were through with their fling, they could come looking for me, and I might be available and might consider starting over. "Might." A big might, because I am a man who was never meant to sit at home alone.

Detachment like that is actually healthy, because it is exactly the opposite of jealousy. Jealousy is a horrible affliction. A person who is jealous by nature can never fully appreciate what they have. They will always be thinking that someone else has it better than they do. They will never love well and deeply. Their relationships will always be shallow and often short, if they have relationships at all.

Jealousy is a product of being insecure, and it is a shame and a pox on the possessor and all those around them.

After awhile Carol wanted to move on. After all, it was her senior year, and I was a junior. I let her go. She moved on to one of the basketball stars, and strangely, it didn't hurt my ego at all. In fact, if anything it gave me more status. That year, I dated several seniors, and I learned from each affair.

I use the term affair, but you realize this was 1961. No one in high school had the pill. Sex for us was kissing and feeling.

The next year when I was a senior, I went to several of the local junior college football games and found that four of the five cheerleaders were my ex-girlfriends. Carol was one of them.

**Two Different Kinds of Jealousy—
Love/Jealousy & Envy/Jealousy**

Many stories, books, TV and movies scripts have been written about jealousy, its ups and downs, its good or bad, its truths and lies. Jealousy is like an electro-cardiogram of human behavior.

Love/jealousy (jealousy for somebody) is when you hate

someone for looking at your lover. The extreme solution to that is to not have an attractive mate. "Never make a pretty woman your wife," words from a 1963 song, *If You Want To Be Happy*, by Jimmy Soul.

Envy/jealousy (jealousy against somebody) is when you hate someone for having the lover you want to have. Or having the life you want, the car you want, the hair….

With love/jealousy, a little jealousy is a sign of devotion. You care about someone enough to want them to want you. But too much jealousy makes you a suspicious pain in the ass.

With envy/jealousy, a little should give you some incentive to improve yourself so you deserve having what you want or being like who you are jealous of. But too much misdirected envy/jealousy makes one bitter, vindictive, or even violently abusive.

Herein lies the really stupid thing about vindictive jealousy of somebody. If you like what someone else has, you should be trying to become just like them, and not trying to bring them down. That just draws others' attention to the fact you are not as good as your competition.

There is an envy/love/jealousy that deals only with wanting a particular mate or kind of mate that someone else has. That one is real sticky.

The first reality check about envy/love/jealousy is that you actually must have a chance with the love of your dreams, or else it becomes stalking.

As most human emotional entanglements, jealousy goes both ways. If someone loves you and you don't love them, think about what they must be going through. If you love someone and they don't love you, think about how your actions must seem to them.

Jealousy is one of the windows into how stupid, self-centered and insecure we humans can be. Always try to understand how others might feel.

## I Was A "High Cool" Senior!

In my senior year of high school, I dated numerous girls in the search of that elusive commodity all 1950's era teenage boys sought: a beautiful girl with the reputation of a good girl, but with the instincts of a slut. Guys didn't want to be thought of as someone who dated sluts, but they didn't mind if she was a slut by the time they broke up with her. I didn't quite have this same philosophy, and I think that was my mother's influence. I also don't normally use or approve of the word slut, and apply it only in the context of that time and our, then, adolescent mentality.

You must understand that at this time I was still a virgin. In that era of the 1950s, a 17-, 18- or even a 20-year-old virgin was not an oddity. I was just trying to get on with it, like most guys. I wanted to date girls, touch them, and get my juices flowing.

New girls on campus were a good place to start. They had no reputation at all as yet, and, if you were fast, you could be the first to ask them out. They would always accept because they were new and lonely, and they were likely to be very grateful to you for rescuing them from high school oblivion. At least that was my subplot, theory and formula for getting laid, and I employed it often.

The truth of the matter though, was that very few girls, either new or well-known, were really sluts. It was us guys who were the sluts. But we were the ones who determined reputations. We made sluts at will, through actions or innuendo.

Around this time, I met and started dating a new girl. She was a junior and a transfer from some other town far enough away to have left her reputation behind. We did good "make out." She liked to play on the edge and was fun to party with. But, alas, I was still technically a virgin even after dating her a couple of weeks.

My new girlfriend lived with her single mother in a small apartment, and one night I went to pick her up. As I arrived, her mother was leaving for her own night on the town. The girl was not dressed for our date, and she told me she had to take a shower before we left. That should have been the giveaway to me. But, remember, I was still new at this game.

That very day I had just purchased a cool, full-length raincoat, and I was anxious to get out in public and parade my beautiful coat and beautiful girlfriend around town. When the girl came out of the shower in her robe, she wanted to make out on the couch, but I was distracted. I wanted to go out and posture in public. Another missed message!

She persisted against my protests, and so we necked for a while. I remember her robe falling open several times, and it was obvious that she had nothing on beneath. But I had only my own image in mind. I wanted to be seen in town in my new coat, with my beautiful girlfriend.

I can't quite remember what was going through my mind. I think I couldn't believe she was offering herself to me in that manner. I must have just tried to ignore all the hints, or maybe I was just too stupid or inexperienced to read her. In that day and age, we wanted girls to be sluts, but they were not supposed to be that aggressive. They were supposed to put up a fight and then give in to our manly onslaught with a mixture of feminine frailty and gratitude.

The girl tried for a little while longer to engage my libido, but I wanted to go out on the town and said so, and she said she didn't want to leave the house. She probably asked me to stay with her for a "quiet night," but, I said no and went out on my own to show off my coat. That is the last time that I failed to read a sexual message, though there are times since then when I have chosen not to respond.

That next week at school the girl avoided me. I tried to speak to her, and when I called her on the phone, she was abrupt and non-committal. The next weekend I drove by her house, and saw a familiar car parked in front of her place. I drove by several times, and it was there 'til quite late that night.

Then it hit me! I had blown my first real sexual opportunity! I had gotten sexual sublimation mixed up with real sex. My cool coat was supposed to make me look virile and feel like a real man, and what it had done was lose my opportunity to prove my virility and to perform like a real man. It was practically the same lesson as the paint job on my pickup truck. For the second time I had let possessions get in the way of my love life.

It was the classic example of "The One That Got Away." I had been too inexperienced to see that she was offering herself to me. Since that episode I have watched several scenes in movies illustrating the same scenario. The most memorable was in "Fast Times at Ridgemont High." Every time I see a movie scene like that, I cringe with embarrassment.

My wanting to be cool had gotten in the way of being cool.

That experience and the time I lost the potential girlfriend over the paint job on my truck are the two most embarrassing moments in my sexual education.

We see men making these same mistakes today in adult life. It's also a major theme on TV and in movies, so it's still something men do regularly. And some guys never learn to read women. Even in this day of supposedly relaxed morals and more open communications, men still get it mixed up all the time.

Most men don't know when she is saying yes or no. It gets men in trouble both ways. You can miss out on enjoyment, or you can destroy a friendship and court ego damage if you don't read the signals correctly.

This masculine miscalculation is based either on insecurities or unreasonable expectations. Some men misread invitations for sex because they are insecure; other men misread cordial female friendship as an invitation because they have unreasonable expectations.

The episode of the coat was 1961-62, and, at that point in human sexuality in America, women were not supposed to be obvious with their sexual desires. I was not used to it, but I never made that mistake again, well almost never.

The problem in the '50s and early '60s was that guys had preconceived ideas of what the kind of girl who "put out" was supposed to look and act like. We wanted to be with a "slut," but we didn't want to be seen with a "slut."

You know that old Groucho Marx line, "I don't want to belong to any club that will accept me as a member." Our subconscious was telling us, "I wouldn't fuck a girl who would fuck a guy like me," and "I wouldn't be seen with a girl who would do what I want her to do with me."

We wanted to be able to have sex with a girl without anyone knowing we would be with the kind of girl who would give sex, and yet we wanted everyone know that we were the kind of guy who was getting sex. Now you get the picture of how confused our sexual emotions were in the 1950s and early '60s!

CHAPTER 29

# Back Seat Battlegrounds

*"wild grasses trampled*
*and leaving the impression*
*lovers have been here"*
Dudley Griffin, 1.23.73
Rose Lodge, Oregon

*"damp naugahyde*
*still holding the impression*
*lovers have been here"*
John, 6.26.11

Sex in high school in the 1950s and early 60s was mostly back seat battles. Guys fighting to get her clothes off, and girls battling to keep them on.

It was an interesting scam. It must have been transparent, but we always thought we were being so subtle. "Hey, let's get in the back seat; it's more comfortable. We can stretch out and watch the movie in comfort." Yeah, sure!

Most girls wouldn't get back there with you. But if they did, it was almost as if they had given you the green light, and the battle would begin.

It was possible to neck, pet heavily and even make love in the front seat of most cars of those days, but the back seat was almost like the guarantee that she was willing, or at least open to the possibility.

During the 1950s and early '60s, more cherries were popped in the back seats of cars than anywhere else. Tree houses and back yard forts were a close second. My first experiences were a bit of a combination of the two.

This brings up the term "cherry," one of the most used and misused sexual terms of the '50s era. Virgin girls, of course, were supposed to have a cherry, which was "popped" by their first sexual intercourse.

The actual physical cherry was, in truth, the hymen, a membrane of skin inside the vaginal canal that was torn by the erect penis upon entry. It was not like a curtain that blocked the entry completely, but more like a fleshy ring around the back of the vagina that was stretched until it tore. Sometimes it bled, and that was offered as proof that the woman had lost her virginity. This was not always so, since hymens are often torn through other activities or sometimes not torn during intercourse.

Boys also had cherries, at least in the 1950s vocabulary they did! The term cherry has come to mean inexperienced or unused. During adolescence our erections were definitely used on a regular basis, but it took most of us years before they first saw the inside of a woman.

The author in Jr. high school

1957: We wore our Levi's down at our butt crack. We folded and creased the pant leg bottoms up inside. We wore plain, wide belts with big, heavy buckles. The belt and buckle were to be used as a weapon when you got into a "rumble." For most of us, it was just for looks.

Fortunately, I never got the 'opportunity' to use my weapon.

Although I did lose a tooth in a high school fight, it was fist-to-fist. We were boys proving our manhood. We would never think of shooting an unarmed person. That is the coward's way! That is how you loose your manhood. It does not prove your strength; it proves your weakness!

My first sexual "intercourse" was performed at the expense of two separate girls during my junior year in high school. I lump them both together because neither one of them was satisfactory enough to qualify as a real sexual intercourse.

The first of these experiences was with a girl who was considered by many to be a major school tramp. It was 1960 or '61. You must remember, and any girl who wore tight sweaters or extra-short skirts was thought to be a slut.

The reason I was with this particular girl on that particular night was precisely because of her reputation. I thought that this was going to be my easy chance to score, and yet her reluctance and obvious lack of familiarity with what we were doing belied her promiscuous reputation.

I, of course, had no personal experience myself, so the whole thing was rather awkward. I knew where it was and that I was supposed to insert myself into it in some manner, but that was all I knew.

This girl's defense of her body, though passive, and her obvious discomfort with the procedure once we finally got to it, proved that she was not as much of a tramp as the advertising promised. She "put out" only after a protracted struggle. She did comply and it was not a forced entry. Her reluctance was from fear of the unknown.

The deed was done in very short order on a day bed in the cottage behind my house where my buddies and I had our drinking parties. There were other couples in the room and my "date" and I had to do it on the sly, so we took off, pulled up or pulled down only the minimum clothing necessary.

The actual act was accomplished and ended quickly, because we both were unfamiliar with the process and both apparently embarrassed by what we were doing. It was so unfulfilling that I usually lump it together with the second attempt and call "them" my first sexual intercourse, even though both together would not constitute a decent fuck by any standards.

My first two attempts at sexual intercourse were both only partial penetrations, and so fleeting that they supplied almost no real emotions on which to hang a memory. The social circumstances surrounding these two relationships were actually much more exciting and educational than the actual sexual contact they provided. For example, the fact that this girl had such a bad reputation made it impossible for me to brag about the encounter. Even though I, for one, knew that her reputation was unfounded, I was caught between a social rock and moral hard place.

On the one hand, I could not attest to her being a slut, because that would implicate me as a guy who would be with a slut. On the other hand, I had to go along with the perpetuation of her reputation as a slut. That experience soured me on all gossip and rumors, which was a good thing in the long run.

My second experience with intercourse also had more than its share of humor and pathos. She was a girl I had been dating for awhile. She was a senior, I, a junior. As a junior, I dated mostly seniors for some reason…possibly for the reputation it gave me and also for the experience I expected to get.

Tammy, we will call her, was an Army brat and new at my school that year. She seemed exotic to me because she was part French and spoke with a cute French-like accent. In fact, she looked and acted a lot like the French actress, Brigitte Bardot. All of my friends thought she was weird--cute, but weird. I thought she was the sexiest thing I had laid my hands on.

She bleached her hair and sometimes colored it pink. Ahead of her time! She told me she once had a poodle that she had bleached and colored to match her own hairdo. She had one of the cutest little bodies and wore the shortest skirts and tight pink, nose tickling Angora sweaters over her pointy little breasts.

For several months I tried my damnedest to get into her little cotton panties. I would get her bra off and feel her up. I got my finger into her once or twice, and she would jack me off--you know all the normal, early 1960s vintage high school stuff-- but it was a battle. She was saving it for nuptials.

Then, one night, we were parked on the golf course at Fort Ord Army base. Her father was a sergeant in the army. The course looked out over Monterey Bay at the lights of Monterey and Pacific Grove and was a favorite necking place for high school kids.

I had undone her bra and was fondling her firm little breasts. She was slowly, reluctantly manipulating my erection, and with the other hand trying to keep her panties on.

That night I finally got her underwear completely off and rolled over on top of her. We were in my mother's early 1950s DeSoto, on a front seat so massive it would accommodate the copulation of two grown grizzly bears. I remember her whimpering, and I remember the reluctance of her leg muscles to let me in between them. I found the spot and fingered her a while, and then guided my hard-on toward the "golden doors of ecstasy," so to speak.

Well, the doors had been virtually unused prior to my entry. My visit was fleeting, and I barely made it past the cloakroom. I was trying hard to be a good guest, but Tammy and her anatomy were trying harder to turn me away. I remember penetration of only a few inches of my penis before the red lights began blinking through the back window of my car.

We were rousted by two Military Policemen, who were only slightly older than we were. These two child soldiers were almost as embarrassed as Tammy and I were, but they managed to ask enough questions to determine that she was a military dependent.

They took her in the Jeep, and I was ordered to follow in my car down to the MP station. At the station I was handed over a sergeant who felt none of the embarrassment of his younger colleagues.

He asked me to empty out my pockets, and when one of them issued up Tammy's underpants, his comment was, "Well, I guess we know what you've been doing."

"Excuse me, trying to do it, God dammit!"

Tammy's father was called in, lots of words were spoken, and I was eventually released later that night, fortunately without being beaten to a pulp with a billy club. But it was our last date. Her father would see no more of me.

Several days later I was driving my aunt somewhere in the old DeSoto, and, as she was getting out of the car, she discovered about a dozen long blonde hairs tangled around the inside door handle. As she departed, she gave me that all knowing, disapproving, I-know-what-you've-been-doing look. Excuse me, I gave it the old high school try, God dammit!

Is this my life, or am I watching a situation soap opera comedy? Until I began to go back and dredge up the stories of my past to record for this memoir, I had no idea how ironic, unique and sometimes bizarre my life had been. It is almost as if I knew someday I would need these episodes to illustrate the psychodrama of life! It is almost as if I premeditated myself into situations in order to create scenarios and misadventures for the sake of a book deal in my later life.

The story of interruptus and underwear doesn't just end there. Over 20 years later when I was living the hippie life back on the Monterey Peninsula, I got a call from Tammy. She was visiting her mother from her home in another state, and she asked if I would meet her for lunch someplace?

We met at my favorite coffee house and restaurant. We talked about old times, discreetly avoiding the issue of our struggles and the police encounter. We talked about our present lives. She was "happily" married, had several children, and her husband was back home. She had taken this trip without him.

I could see it coming. Our conversation floated around and toyed with intimacy. Sexual frustration was in her voice. Sensual regrets were in her words. She eventually built up the courage to insinuate that she and I could meet intimately later in the week if I wanted to.

She was still attractive. She hadn't lost her appealing shape. I was tempted. I said "yes," and we made a date for her to come to my house in the afternoon several days later.

In the interim I began thinking about having sex with her after all those years. This was going to be her one fling, her only deviation from her marriage. It wasn't quite right. In recent years I had been slowly acquiring a conscience. I was through with seducing other men's women. Several years earlier, I would have jumped at the chance.

On the day of our date, I stayed away from my house. For all I know she didn't show up either, but I think she did. No one else was home, and no one saw her come or go.

Over the years since then, I have thought about that episode. I have run the gamut of emotions about that affair, not just my rejection of her, but my pursuit of her originally.

Tammy was a very sensitive, almost fragile, personality. I had been hard on her in high school. She had wanted acceptance in a new school. I had shown interest, but the wrong kind of interest. I know that now and I also know, now, that, if I had been a little less demanding, she would have eventually given herself to me willingly, if not without strings attached, expecting forever, for that was the era of forever in relationships.

I have, now, had even more thoughts and revelations about our second meeting 20 years later. In the late 1970s, early 80s I was in my evolution toward becoming a good man. I was almost there. I knew it was not proper for me to have an affair with that man's wife. Yet, I was not thinking straight about her feelings or needs at the time.

Tammy had thought long and hard about her choice. It may have been based on deep-seated needs that were not necessarily good for her marriage, but they were emotions that she needed to explore. She probably felt that her life was missing something. She wanted to explore illicit romance. She wanted to add a new facet to her life.

It was cruel of me not to show up for her coming-out party. I should have at least talked to her or written her a letter. I feel very ashamed looking back now. I hope it didn't cause too much pain or feelings of rejection.

There have been times when I have looked back on that day that didn't happen and wished I had met her in my bed. I have had moments of excitement thinking about making love for hours with this woman that I lusted after so deeply in my adolescent selfishness. It would have been a good closure for our struggles. I might have been able to give her all the adulation and love I was unable to give her as a high school boy. It may have completed her life. It may also have ruined her marriage. For that possibility, I am ambiguous. I would not want to be a part of that, yet I understand the twists of each life and what fate may bring us.

Tammy, and you know who you are, though I have changed your name and place, if you read this, I hope you will know that I do love you very much in the way old lovers do, in the way old friends remember.

What it comes down to is this: men and women need one another. If guys would come on with a little less aggression and girls would display a little less reluctance, things might work out better. "No," would still mean "no," and "maybe" would mean, "If you aren't a complete asshole, maybe we can be lovers."

Guys can learn to be more sensitive to women's needs. It's just a shame that we have to hurt so many girls on our way to learning these things.

*"Love is not a game, but we often play it anyway."*
Dudley Griffin, 5.8.12

CHAPTER 30

# The High School Bubble

High school is like one of those blow-up "bounce houses" filled with ping pong balls at birthday parties and store grand openings. It's not real life. It's more like isolation from real life, but if you learn the right skills in high school, it can help you figure out real life when you finally get off the trampoline!

Vicki and John

Popularity and social status, not algebra, are the true challenges of high school life. Some might think this is reducing adolescence to the most mundane levels of human nature, but because peer pressure is the basis of our self-awareness, it has a big influence on our formative years and therefore on who we will become as an adult.

You have to know yourself in order to really know others; you have to love yourself in order to really love others. What is your basis for love?

*"You have to be able to walk in order to walk with others; you have to be able to talk in order to talk with others. What is your basis for love if you have never loved?*
*You are the first person you ever met. If you don't love yourself, you cannot love another because you don't know the feeling."*
D.G

Reading, writing and arithmetic affect our intellectual and economic lives, but our sex appeal and social skills control what we do with our money and minds. A good life is a good balance of social and functional skills.

What you look like and how you think guide you into different peer groups, and the group you belong to will determine what kind of life you will choose on the outside.

Having already stated that I think self-confidence is the most important contributor to a successful social life, I now wish to add the element of image.

Self-confidence is your own view of yourself; image is the opinion others have of you. They can be independent of each other, but they definitely contribute to one another.

For the most part, during adolescence, popularity is a direct result of image. How people see you affects how they respond to you. Like or dislike, love or hate.

Beauty or appearance contributes greatly to popularity. But some peer groups, like the "goths" or "hippies," try to change the standard of beauty or compensate for physical features they might have that are not considered beautiful by majority standards.

176

Some peer groups are created to give "outcasts" a social life. Some peer groups are formed to justify behavior.

Beauty has a commercial standard. The standard for adolescent beauty comes from teen magazines, Hollywood movies and TV. But real beauty is in the eye of the "holder." Your beauty is in your own eyes. You can be as beautiful as you think you are.

I have known people who were visually perfect, yet they had a lousy self-image, and, therefore, they had rotten social lives. I have met others who were ugly in the eyes of society, yet their healthy self-image gave them wonderful sex and social lives.

The senior quad, a cement patio and a few benches between two buildings, held a solemn place in the minds of a select few who considered it their domain. Though a senior, I was not one who held it as sacred ground. The jocks in their lettermen's jackets looked on with curious disdain as I drew chalk lines on the cement. A series of boxes that looked oddly familiar. Complete, I took a set of keys out of a pocket and tossed them into one of the boxes. I began hopping on one foot in the squares until I reached my keys and picked them up.

Soon several of my cool friends had joined me for a game of hopscotch. The jocks looked on in broiling disbelief. (The word jock means someone who regularly wears a jockstrap.)

I was a member of the Irish mafia, although my core friends were also Black, Asian, Sicilian and Hispanic. We might be called the "rockers" today. We were there, and we held our court as well, yet we didn't take ourselves too seriously. We did not own them, and they did not own us, and that was just fine with us. We lived together within a guarded harmony.

Popularity is a factor of peer acceptance. Peer acceptance is due to: self-confidence, social awareness, style and appearance, somewhat in that order of importance. These basic things create a good image and therefore a successful social life.

Productivity, benevolence, intelligence and moral standing are the true measure of human value, but during adolescent years they are not judged as being that important.

Beauty and popularity are the elements that most affect adolescent development. Sex appeal and social skills are the basic foundations for success in social life. High school is where the defining elements come together for most people, to make them who they are for the rest of their lives.

Style is important in adolescent pop culture. Style does not mean fashion. Style means how you wear something more than what you wear.

Social awareness is the hidden, underappreciated element of a good life. Knowing how to work the social scene is the single most important element of popularity.

Being able to fit in is necessary human behavior. Standing out is important for peer recognition and individual self-confidence. In my observations the truly popular people are those who both fit in and stand out.

Sex and social activity are essential for a good self-image. I am not saying sex and social activity are the only elements of a rewarding existence, but with the pressures of popularity during adolescence, they are necessary to support a healthy ego.

By your senior year of high school, you are usually programmed to be either a social animal or a worker bee. I will, of course, garner ridicule for generalizing this, but the majority of examples will prove me right.

High school is a petri dish creating the real world, and yet it is also a bubble protecting you from the real world. Some people are on the inside, and some are on the outside in high school. Some on the inside never want to leave. Some on the inside want to get out into the world. Some are on the outside want to get in.

Today as then, the high school peer groups come down to three main pigeonholes; "sosh," "greasers & druggies" and "nerds." During the 1950s and early 60s before the introduction of illegal or street drugs into high school life, druggies were called "greasers" or "rejects."

Back then, soshs were the conservative jocks and cheerleaders. They did the "right" things and wore the "right" clothes. Greasers didn't do the right things or wear the right clothes, but we were the innovators.

The term "druggie," even today, is a misnomer like many generalizations. Druggies or greasers are often just outsiders, artists, politically radical, or intellectuals, who are tagged drug-crazed hippies or teenagers.

Nerds are the "students." They are not necessarily intellectual; they complete the assignments.

In the 1960s my generalization would have been that the "soshs" never wanted to leave the bubble. The "druggies" were having fun inside it, but were looking forward to getting out. And the "nerds" did not know whether they wanted to be in the bubble or if they would be better off in the real world.

Today in 2020, these words have slightly different definitions. In my understanding, today a sosh is the same as before, druggies are hopelessly hooked on some form of drugs, greasers are car or motorcycle gear heads, and hippies are intellectuals and computer nerds who also do drugs for mental health and social activities.

In the 1950s, 60s, and 70s, high school, for those of us on the "inside" of a good peer group, was a comfortable place to be. The popular, social and outgoing kids loved high school. To the unpopular students, it was a social purgatory.

Milling about, aglow with the excitement of graduation day, we all looked alike in our caps and gowns. For many, for the first time in their whole high school careers, they felt equal in some way. All colors, shapes and sizes, draped in the same cloth of accomplishment and anticipation.

I strode through the crowed kissing all the girls again for the last time, and a few I had always wanted to kiss. As I tapped her on the shoulder, the beautiful, dark, Asian face turned, recognition became a blank stare and then shock as I stepped into her space and kissed her deep and full upon the lips. Turning away toward the next conquest, I had no idea what I had done. She stood there exploring her feelings, touching her lips, savoring it--her first kiss!

I personally didn't like the schooling part of school; I got my education through social interaction. For what I have done with my life, that was the right education. But my choices in high school also dictated my direction in life.

I didn't know I was going to be a writer at that time. If I had known, I might have concentrated on English and Journalism. But that would have been a mistake. A writer writes about life, not about parts of speech. An exceptional writer might need to know how previous masters worked their craft, but then in the loneliness of his own writing time, he has to exploit his own experiences.

I don't think I read a book during my whole junior high and high school career. I usually stuffed the books into my locker on the first day of class and then turned them in on the last day. They never went home with me. I did very few homework assignments, only the ones essential to passing the class. I participated actively in class, and tested well enough to get by. I graduated, and that is all that mattered to me.

I'm not necessarily proud of my rebellious scholastic record, but it worked for me. The one year I concentrated on schoolwork, my sophomore year in Southern California, I got almost straight A's.

The important thing to note about my particular high school career was that it was conducted during the first few years of the 1960s. Sex was at a minimum, and drugs were nonexistent except for nicotine and alcohol.

Contradictory emotions and opinions arise in me whenever the subject of sex and drugs in high school comes up. On the one hand, I feel that my high school experience was idyllic, simple and uncluttered by some of the pressures of sex and the drugs that appeared only four years after my graduation. On the other hand, I wish the girls had put out a little more when I was 16 and 17.

I regret the turmoil young people must suffer today in these culturally accelerated times. I think they are too young to have to deal with some of the pressures and issues forced upon them by our media. Today sex and recreational drugs are advertised without warning labels and demonized without listing their social, psychological and nutritional values.

Yet, at the same time, I feel that the 1950s and early 60s were too naive. I think that ignorance, hypocrisy and denial concerning sex and drugs were the wrong ways to deal with such important aspects of life. But I also think that, as with so many of our discoveries, we human beings have gone too far the other way by commercializing, sensationalizing and packaging sex. Sex is life itself; it should not be treated with any more fanfare than we do a breath of air!

The "sexual revolution" was a valuable step forward in human relationships at its beginning, but money, greed and religious scrutiny soured it. Since Paul's writings in the Bible, the Christian Church has always served to demonize sex. But the sexual revolution brought the subject out in the open and allowed religious fanatics to further polarize public sentiment.

The way the Christian mentality deals with sex has a tendency to make sex even more desirable. By making it a sin, by "cheapening" it, the church is advertising the rebellious aspects of sex. By making it a counterculture activity, they make it even more attractive to the rebellious nature in young people.

The reverse child psychology of prohibiting sex to hormone-infused teenagers creates a volatile cocktail of rebellion. Mother nature injects hormones into adolescents to make them want to leave the nest, to reject the lifestyle of their parents, and then the parents tell them that sex is a sin and prohibit it. Naturally, what does the child do then? Seek out that which is contrary to their parents, of course!

The teenage years for my peers and me were a bit simpler than today. Our clothing styles were meant to attract attention, not to start bodily fluids flowing. For the girls, the pressure to give out sex was not as institutionalized then. Movies, MTV and advertising campaigns weren't pushing it constantly.

As a teenage boy in the 1950s, sex was always the underlying goal. But most of the time we didn't really know what it was or how to achieve it. And the girls, for the most part, were naive enough to think that the boys were really just attracted to them by their diligently sprayed and teased big hair.

Image was everything when I was in high school. It definitely overshadowed content.

Without sex and drugs as the major focus of our lives, looking good and hanging out was a primary activity. Posturing was our art form.

Image and social status were everything. If you made a mistake, it could ruin your life, or so we thought. And because we thought it, sometimes it did have an effect on the outcome of our lives.

The first three years of high school were just stepping-stones to the pinnacle of our life, reaching the status of "senior." The freshman year was a search for your "look," the time to find your peer group and adapt to their style and habits. The next two years were the process of honing your image, jockeying for status among your peers and the school population as a whole.

A description of my high school career will reveal that I wasn't particularly interested in reading, writing and arithmetic. I definitely did not let academics get in the way of my social life.

I don't think I was shallow, though I may have appeared to be! I was having fun, becoming social, and expressing my creativity.

Social creativity is the ability to deviate from the norm; to take what has been done before, and add to it to make it individually yours. The wild flat tops, white bucks and pegged pants were efforts at social expression. These forms of rebellion were not unlike the in-your-face attitude of the hippie counterculture ten years later.

In the 1950s, status, created by image, was everything! But, of course, status is relative. It is relevant only to those you are trying to impress.

At my high school there were: the science club clique (nerds), the jock and cheerleader clique, greaser clique, the tough black chick clique, the tough black dude clique, the slightly effeminate clique and the "I'm-in-no-clique" clique.

I belonged to the "I'm-in-no-clique" clique, the "so in, we were out" group or what would be called the "druggies" a few years later. A party clique, yet we would have rebelled against the term "clique."

A clique was an "exclusive" group of students drawn together by standards of dress, activity and values. My "group" had no standards, and we weren't very exclusive. If you wanted to drink or dance with us, you were one of the gang for the night or as long as you could handle it. Gang was a better description for us.

My friends and I took the All-American fullback out on his first night on the town and placed him gently on his parent's lawn when he passed out. I got several cheerleaders drunk and taught them the art of French kissing. I didn't care who partied with me as long as they had something to offer to the mix, and as long as their "uncool" didn't rub off on me.

I went to a Key Club meeting on a lark. Everyone there felt I was out of place, including me. I just liked to watch them squirm.

It would be fun to join, just to bug them. But after finding out what the requirements were, it didn't sound like so much fun. That would have put quite a dent in my social life. Besides, I would have to hang out with those guys, and that would have been more difficult than pulling up my grades.

Strangely enough, I most likely could have gotten into the Key Club, on legacy preference. My uncle, Frankie Meeks, had been captain of the football team, and senior class president, thirty-three years earlier. But in my traditional disdain for the good-ol'-boys club mentality, I went back to my own brand of social life. I like to earn what I get on my own efforts.

If I were to assess my status at school during senior year, I would have to say that I was among the top ten most popular boys, the top most misread, envied and most questioned. You notice I didn't use the words "most liked". Popularity has little to do with affections. It often has to do with jealousy.

My school graduated about 420 seniors that year, so there were between 1600 and 1700 students in total. I was at the top of the recognition heap. And do you want to know why? Because I didn't really care about such things as recognition.

I was having fun, letting it "all hang out". I was making friends and rejecting others. Therefore, I had cross hairs on my back.

The most popular boys were the few standout sports jocks and class political representatives. There were about six or seven of them. They were envied by some, looked up to by others and scoffed at by the rest, but popular by virtue of the number of people who thought about them, good or bad.

My main value was that I amused people. I instigated the snowball fight in the hallway on the one and only day of snow in our whole high school career. I organized the hopscotch competition in the senior square. I had the vodka infused oranges at the senior picnic.

I once heard a girl say, "No, I didn't invite John to my party. He knows about it; he'll be there." I grabbed and kissed a Filipino girl on graduation day. Thirty years later, at a reunion, she introduced me to her husband as the first boy to kiss her.

What does all this mean? Do I care? No! I didn't care then; I don't care now.

What it means is that there was an element to my life that transcended image and ego. Ego is one of the strangest drives in our lives. It is important to maintain our lives; it is that which stimulates us to create and produce. Yet, it is also the force in our lives that, when overused, makes us look and act like fools.

In the senior high school yearbook next to my photograph, my name appears, and nothing else. No sports credentials, clubs, or class political achievements. I did some of these things, yet when asked to recount them for the yearbook, I declined. I don't know why. Yet, I remember distinctly doing this as a statement of some kind.

Was that statement a product of my ego? Did it make me look like a fool, or was it an indication of my strength?

*"In high school, the pursuit of sex became my sport of choice!"*

DG

I am considered cute. Or at least I was when my age allowed that term to be used. I have never been though of as handsome.

I was considered smart. I have never been thought of as brilliant. Being average takes some of the pressures off of a person, but it also allows you to surprise the hell out of those who might be your detractors.

The slick magazine photo of Frank Sinatra in Bermuda shorts caught my eye. When could I use this information? The winter ball was two weeks away, I would make some black Bermuda shorts and wear them with my tuxedo to the dance.

I sewed them myself. My date was amused. She has some photos in her high school memorabilia, but I don't know where she is at this point in time.

I didn't make it past Gertrude Rendtorff, the Dean of Girls, at the door. But I had prepared for that probability. I changed into my long pants stashed in the car.

I was popular in high school because I wasn't trying to impress anyone, except for a few girls now and then. I knew my limitations and stuck with them. The only times I ever failed was when I overestimated my abilities. One must at times challenge oneself, but if you don't have wings, don't try jumping off tall buildings.

I was not popular because I made touchdowns or was politically correct, but because I did what other people wanted to do, yet were afraid to try. Not difficult things, achievable things, like dating the sexiest girls, or going to the dance in Bermuda shorts or drinking salty dogs through a rubber hose hidden under my gown at graduation.

I was popular because I didn't know or care what popularity was supposed to be. It was all experience to me.

The need to write this chapter is the first time I have ever thought back about these things. This is the first time I ever tried to assess myself, to assign myself any level of high school strata. It is not easy to do so. It is not comfortable to dissect what you think of yourself, and it is almost impossible to determine what others think of you. I suppose I could be all wrong about my popularity. I don't really know whether anyone was moved by my presence, and I'm not sure I care now or cared then.

But the one thing I did care about was that I didn't want to be completely overlooked. I'm sure I wasn't invisible in school. That was the actor in me, the social animal in me. I like people, and I want to socialize and get to know them.

I don't literally remember most of the people in my high school of 1600 students. The few that I do want to remember fall into four categories. Close male friends, close female friends, and then a few other notables that I wanted to be like, and then some that I didn't want to be like.

The real social value of high school is meeting and watching personalities and choosing what to adopt from them for your own personality. Socialization, learning limitations and available territories... preparing for the outside world.

That is, I believe, why I pushed the envelope. My mother gave me no limitations, except the requirement that I respect other people. I had to find what my boundaries were.

When I broke the bubble of high school, I stepped into a much larger bubble of the real world. There were many more choices, but still there was and always will be the limitations of socially accepted behavior.

## CHAPTER 31

# MG TF

The only photograph, I have of myself and this car.

That was the car I had for most of my senior year of high school and for about three years afterwards! It was what they now call a chick magnet. But once you got her into the car it showed its disadvantages! It was very confined quarters and may have been a contributing factor to why I stayed a virgin as long as I did. I learned to talk and reason in that car. I believe it is part of what molded my personality and made me an aesthetic, a lover of all beauty. End of chapter.

CHAPTER 32

# The High School Bubble Bursts
# Turning Point: Reality

When I finished high school in 1962, I graduated into the kind of limbo that can get a person into real trouble. Not knowing what I wanted to do with my life, I began expressing myself in ways that would eventually have delivered me into systems and institutions that would have made all my choices for me: the penal system, military or unwanted pregnancy scenarios.

I signed my name on a form that was passed around in high school civics class during the last weeks of school, and I was magically enrolled in the local junior college. After a summer of drinking beer and trying to get laid, I matriculated into the Student Union at Monterey Peninsula College.

I say the Student Union because I saw a lot more of the inside of that building than I ever did of my required classrooms. I say required, because when I took the tests, I was automatically commandeered into all the bonehead classes.

I never tested well in school where writing or mathematics were required. I am apparently dyslexic. The wonder of it all is that I have since passed numerous "adult life" tests, including both real estate and building contractor's state license exams. I also have been successful in acquiring a social security card, driver's licenses, two marriage licenses, library cards, and numerous credit cards.

Also, the U.S. military once deemed me sufficiently intelligent to serve my country. I disrespectfully declined their offer, and that's another story.

Long-story-short, at 19 years old, I was not much of a student. I didn't have the aptitude or desire to go to a college or university to improve my intellect or job skills for occupation. I also lacked the finances for advanced schooling or sports skills and grades to receive a scholarship.

At any rate, I was sick and tired of school at 19 and wasn't inclined at the time to embark on anything that wasn't fun for me. So I played whist in the Student Union, and every other waking moment I drank beer and hustled girls.

Needless to say, I wasn't going anywhere very fast. The locations of several of my classes were changed during the semester, and I didn't bother to find out the new room numbers. The high point, which I didn't even appreciate until much later, was the day that Margaret Mead came and spoke in my Marriage and Family class.

It was a 12 X 12 room, and Ms. Mead didn't have a podium or a respectable chair, for that matter, so she sat on the instructor's desk, swinging her legs as she told the class that their concept of love and sex was all screwed up. I read some of her books later, and I agree with her. This book is in some way a result of that experience.

That Marriage and Family class was an effort to keep horny boys and girls from making any rash moves, like getting pregnant or marrying someone for some trumped-up reason like loneliness or rebellion. I am not positive, but I think that the instructor, a pale and self-conscious woman in her 40s, had never been married or even had a meaningful romantic relationship in her life.

One other memory I have of that class is the marriageability test that we were all obligated to take. In my state of mind at the time, I thought that, under the circumstances, I got the highest score. I went off the chart in the category of "least likely to succeed as a husband and father."

Meanwhile, I was still trying to get "totally" laid. I dated a succession of new girls I met in the Student Union. Some of them would kiss me and some would allow me a feel or give me a hand job, but I was still longing to lie down naked in a soft bed with a woman, and touch her and really feel her body.

It was a dangerous point in my life. Staying in one's hometown after high school can lead to self-destructive boredom. It's often a letdown after all the buildup toward the big graduation day and matriculation into adulthood.

And then one day you find that things haven't miraculously changed after high school. If you are not going into college or if you don't have a cushy job waiting for you, the disappointment of unrealized expectations can cause depression. I could have easily become a drunk and/or dope addict and found myself in jail or in an unwanted marriage. I later learned that many of my high school buddies had gone those routes.

At the end of the first semester, the president of Monterey Peninsula College sent me a personal letter suggesting that I should reconsider my efforts at higher education. I agreed with him and dropped out of school.

I was so frustrated and selfish at that point in my life that on one date I kicked the girl out of my car, down at the beach, miles from her home, because she wouldn't let me do what I wanted to do to her.

The next morning, coming out of my alcohol haze, I realized what I had done. My mother had not raised me to treat women that way. I was at a low point in my life, and I didn't want to go any lower.

Always, when thinking about that time in my life, I feel embarrassment. Normally, I am never embarrassed about anything I do. I don't like the feeling, so I just don't do potentially embarrassing things. That was what I learned during those days. I learned to keep my "karma" clean.

At this point you might ask what my definition of embarrassment is! Some guys think that wearing mismatched socks, or a pink belt, or orange sneakers is embarrassing. No, that is ether a fashion statement or a fashion mistake, it is not going to ruin your life. Looking silly, whether you plan it or not, is not embarrassing; being an asshole to someone else is embarrassing.

This was about the time that my inner-self realized I needed a change of venue and direction. I didn't have the padded room of high school anymore. The world was going to eat me up if I didn't challenge it.

I started dating a girl again that I had known in Southern California. We had met in church. What an ominous statement that is when I think about it today.

I spent many summers living with my uncle and attending the Pentecostal Church. I have read the New Testament Bible cover to cover several times and much of the Old Testament. I also have some background with the Apocrypha and Roman history of the early Christian times.

Religion is one of those areas where a little knowledge is a dangerous thing. Most Christians know only a few verses of the Bible, taken out of context, and on these they base their spiritual life.

I was born an agnostic, and becoming biblically literate didn't change that. I acted out the good, clean, church-going young man when I had to, but it was only experience and education for me.

The Old and New Testament are interesting literature, and there are some moral lessons to be learned, but if you were to follow them all literally, you could really get yourself screwed up! A person would actually achieve a much better spiritual path if they were to follow religiously the writings of the beat generation. Ginsberg, Burroughs, Kerouac, Snyder, and Bukowski have a lot to say about morality. They also have the advantage of a couple thousand more years of human history to draw from.

I wanted to get out of Monterey, and I knew and liked the girl in Southern California. So I started looking to Los Angeles as my escape from the hometown quicksand.

I will tell any young person who listens, "When you are young, you should move to a big city. Experience that life. Learn from it. Find out what you do or don't want to do with your life. Stay if it suits you. Don't wake up one morning an old person who's never been anywhere and wish you had."

I drove from Monterey to Los Angeles and back on the weekends for several months. I wanted to see if things would fall into place.

I worked in a restaurant in Carmel on weeknights and on Friday around midnight after closing the kitchen, I would drive my 1956 MG TF down to LA and spend Saturday and Sunday with my long-distance girlfriend. The Big Sur coast is alive in moods and magic, and driving those sweeping turns and tight grooves on an empty road in a dark night with a car that cooperates was ecstasy to the soul of a footloose boy.

To make a very long story, very short, I married that girl and finally got to sleep naked beside a woman. That was not the whole story, of course, and I didn't marry her just to sleep with her.

My life with my first wife was, for all practical purposes, perfect. We looked good. We stimulated each other intellectually. We liked the same stuff.

190

She is a good example of the type of long-term mate that I have always been drawn to; independent, intelligent, opinionated, outspoken and rational. Quite a bit like my mother, and like my mother, they knew what I was doing and though they didn't always approve, they <u>allowed</u> me to do it.

For the first five or six years, it was a steady climb up in economic, professional and social stature. She graduated from UCLA with a degree in education and started teaching. I started in real estate and moved on to employee motivation and then advertising.

During this period of time the world was changing. In 1965, 66, 67, Pandora's box was opened. I was reading things, seeing things and listening to the music.

My creative juices flowed, and I eventually found myself as a copywriter, art director and account executive in several top ten advertising agencies. As I was hired in each successive agency, I was the new resident genius until someone else newer came along. I was living the "Mad Men" TV series script.

How functionally genius can you be at 23? I was creative, but having words in your mind are different than picking up a pen and writing them down. It takes time to apply genius. The corporations take advantage of the things you do create, but if you don't continue to produce or can't handle the corporate world, you are left behind. Moving up in companies and in pay, I reached the point of decision. At a private lunch with the president of the large agency I worked for, the man told me that if I changed my granny glasses to something more conservative, knuckled down and got more competitive, I could be the president of that company one day.

I looked across the table at the arrogant, fat and stressed out executive and asked myself, "Do you want to be just like him in ten or fifteen years?" My answer to myself was, "No!"

I started secretly taking the boss's beautiful secretary out to lunch. I started speaking my "real" mind at meetings. I started being less attentive while partnering in bridge games with my copy chief, Joe Vodnick.

I refused to let them kick another copywriter out of his big office, so I could be the assistant copy chief with a window on Wilshire Boulevard. I started getting too creative! I was writing the type of advertising campaigns that wouldn't be accepted until several years later. I wasn't playing the game by the rules of "The Greatest Generation."

Within several months, I was fired. Months later, I found out that the president had divorced his wife and married that beautiful secretary.

Deep inside I had other plans for my life. I don't know what made me rebel! I don't know what made me buy those granny glasses! I don't know why I started propositioning and seducing other women. Perhaps it was the atmosphere of the times. The year was 1968.

Soon after that, I started smoking dope. My wife and I left the church. I became a rock concert photographer. I started having affairs with other women.

In 1968, wives did not ask you where you were going at 7 pm and why you came home at 3:15 a.m.!


CHAPTER 33

# Hearts and Flowers

When my first wife and I were married, it was a different world from the one we have today. That can be said, to some degree, of any 40 years of recent history. But no other time before or since has been more pivotal, dramatic or revolutionary than the 1960s.

In 1964 when we were married, no one could predict what the next five years would bring. No one could predict it because no five years previously had held so many social changes.

I don't know that if we had met and married in another era, we would have prevailed for a lifetime. Our marriage was like all other hopeful couplings. We entered into it as though it were forever. But we had no clue as to what the culture of our time had in store for us.

Our courtship was similar to that of many couples of that time, the early 1960s, and it hadn't changed much from the previous hundred years. We met as teenagers; we flirted and dated under the restraints of the sexual innocence of the times, and then married out of frustration and social obligation.

Outside of cultures in which marriages are arranged, people on their own venture out searching for affection, needs and love, and find what is closest to their own ideals. If you are emotionally immature, you can sometimes misinterpret affection for love, when it is really only need--both ways, yours and theirs.

We snuck away to make-out. It was Southern California, and we were both mobile with cars and other freedoms. Birth control was not yet widely available and definitely not for the unwed. After I proposed, I became more sexually aggressive and was appropriately chastised by her. We agreed to "wait."

In a way we were "high school sweethearts." We dated when we were both in high school, though we went to separate schools. Our common meeting ground was the church we both attended.

She was a rebel because she, as an adolescent, had chosen that church herself. Her parents did not go to church.

I was a rebel because I was forced to go to that church. Living with my uncle, it was required of me. This was a match made on earth with all of its attending conflicts.

This is not to say that we were not well-matched. We were both rebels in our own way, and, because of this, we were the most obvious two individuals at that place and time. So we got married.

When we married we were both virgins, for the most part. I had only had two or three near copulations. She, from all that I have heard, was a true virgin.

We married in the Pentecostal Church where we had met. That night we drove up the coast to Santa Barbara to spend our first night together at the Miramar Hotel.

How memories manifest themselves. What you remember. What you forget. These are all mysteries. Fifty years is such a long time.

I remember the new pajamas that I never wore again after that night. I remember shaking with anticipation as she prepared herself in the bathroom.

Before that night she had "touched" me a few times. I had "touched" her a few times. Early in our engagement we had talked and agreed to "wait".

Our engagement period of celibacy was still difficult. I was anxious. She accused me several times of being over-sexed. I cannot disagree with that.

That night at the Miramar, I waited under the sheets in my crisp, new pajamas. When she came out of the bathroom in her pure white nightgown and slipped under the covers, we were at an intersection of many roads.

I am almost certain we prayed. I don't know what we said, or who said it, but at that time in our lives, we would have asked God for his help and guidance. We needed it, and, as it turned out, he gave it to us graciously for the next five or six years.

We must have held hands under the covers as we prayed. We probably breathed deeply and fearfully for a short while. I then kissed her and got down to it.

I don't mean to be irreverent. The problem is that the experience was so ecstatic and traumatic for me that I can't remember much of it. I have only emotions of that night.

If I had had more of a concept of what sex was, I might have been able to remember it. You know how they say the first time you get stoned you don't feel it, or don't know you are. The first time Native Americans saw a European ship, they ignored it because it didn't register as reality to them. That is how my first experience with real sex was.

The other thing about sex, at that time and place, was that sex was still supposed to be so bad that I think we erased it from our minds. It was the convenient mechanism of hypocrisy. You can't enjoy something or even dwell on it if it is a sin punishable by an eternity of suffering in hell.

I do remember a warm feeling of arrival when I first entered her. I felt a wonderful emotion of being part of a whole, of being in a family.

The primal cultural energy flowed through my blood for a time with her. We were in it for all the good reasons that the 1950s portrayed--children, family, country.

Most of my life with my first wife was a pleasant journey toward the homogenous oblivion that the era promised. But we were in the way of a revolution.

This revolution was not planned by anyone; it was not orchestrated. The confluence of media, the pill, psychedelic drugs, and thought-provoking rock & roll changed this world forever.

It was not all good. It was not all pretty. But it was hopeful. And, as with all of mankind's creations, we can use it to kill or we can use it to create. We have been given many two-edged swords in our history. It has always been our choice to make love or war.

I am not the kind of man who leaves anything behind without admitting its importance to my life. My first wife was what I needed and wanted at the time, and I am never sorry for any moment I spent with her. We did everything seamlessly together. We were all changing. Our break-up was my fault, yet that was also a necessary part of my life. All our roads split many times, and we often take the easy way, and then we must make do with the decisions.

My sunrise above Delphi

CHAPTER 34

# Facial Hair: The Mistaken Identity

About this time, I began experimenting with facial hair. Mother liked my lips and said I should not hide them! Today, 2012, '13, '14, the media says it is "sexy to have scratchy stubble," but I know the girls like it to be soft.

Most women don't care how macho you look, but they do care how good you feel, how well you touch them.

So I started cutting off my mustache, and left my beard or goatee. I did if for my mother and for the girls I was going down on.


CHAPTER 35

# HAIR, Infidelity And Hypocrisy

It would be "interesting" to be able to see your life before you acted it out. In some cases you would not like the outcome, so you would turn left instead of right at that juncture. But I am convinced that whichever way you turned would still produce the same results. Eventually after seeing this, a person would become so bound up in the gridlock of avoiding the inevitable that they could make no moves at all. The Oracle of Delphi does not bring good tidings; she brings the truth. It is better to live your life oblivious and to deal with the surprises than it is to live in fear at every turn.

Even though it may sound like the script of a soap opera, this chapter is another true slice of my life! It is one of those strange episodes that illustrate the sadistic serendipity of mankind and sex.

As already told, about four years into my first marriage, I became sexually restless. It had very little to do with the marriage or the desirability of my wife. It had everything to do with my being a 25-year-old male.

At the time, my wife and I were still attending the Pentecostal Church where we had met. We were members of a Sunday school class consisting of college age and young, married parishioners.

One other class member was a young, attractive, recently separated woman whom my wife and I befriended. In an effort to afford this young lady some companionship, we invited her to see a new play we had heard about. The year was 1966 or '67, and the play was *HAIR: The American Tribal Love-Rock Opera.*

Well, we did not know what we were in for. Needless to say, the performance blew our three unsuspecting minds. We went into the theater as three average young folks, just trying to live a respectable existence and make it through our lives without too much fuss. We left the performance with our immature emotions stripped of all protection, exposed to the possibilities of a life that we had not previously known existed.

I, for one, had the epidermis of my libido torn open, revealing raw nerves of sexual excitement. For the first time in my life, I questioned my status as a human and considered my animalness. Almost at that very moment I embarked upon the pursuit of my natural desires. From that encounter on, and for the next 18 years, I was a dick with feet.

One of the misconceptions held and voiced by the conservative population is that the hippie counterculture invented sex and drugs. No, they may promote them, but they certainly did not create them. God created sex and drugs, and anyone who doesn't agree with this statement needs to rethink.

The hippie counterculture uses sex and drugs, kind of like the capitalist culture uses greed and war. The counterculture uses sex and drugs to improve their emotional standard of living. Capitalist culture uses greed and war to improve their economic standard of living. But conservatives and capitalists also use sex and drugs for money and power to enhance their standard of living. If this is really a moral issue, what side do you think God would be on?

The nature of man's brain and his psyche is to absorb everything that comes within his reach. Once the door is open, once the contents of Pandora's box are revealed, mankind cannot forget it. It is in our mind.

The solution is also in that same mind. Mankind has to take the good and bad behind the door and deal rationally with it. If man lets his new awareness destroy him, he is not thinking.

The amazing spectrum of sex, the vision of something new, can bring fear, or it can excite a person to overindulge in the newfound joy. Both fear of the unknown or blindly embracing the unknown are dangerous. We must learn what our enemies are; we must use all new gifts and information if we are to grow as a species. Sex, like all gifts of God, has two sharp edges. Each will cut you in a different way.

What I did after seeing HAIR was what many other red-blooded American dicks would do if they had the guts. I took the young woman, our guest, to her home, went home with my wife, tucked her in bed, waited till she was asleep, and then went back to the other woman's apartment. I knocked on the door, and when she answered in her bathrobe, I asked her if she wanted to have sex with me.

I was convinced that she would let me in and make love with me. I was at that time and for the next 18 years so attuned to women's emotions, that I was positive she would be sexually aroused by the play and primed for sex. I was right.

But the young woman made some excuse for not letting me in. And that is when I realized that someone else was already there. I was sure someone was in her apartment with her, so I turned and left.

That next Sunday I was called into the church pastor's study. When I entered, I began to develop a suspicion. The pastor asked me to have a seat and then told me that he had received a complaint that I had propositioned one of the female parishioners. He then asked me if I was being unfaithful to my wife and if I wanted some spiritual consultation.

Well, "No," I said, "I was not being unfaithful to my wife." But I sure was trying; though I didn't tell the pastor that. And, "No, I didn't need any consultation."

It was all a blur of embarrassment and shocking realization. I knew the young woman would not have told the pastor about my visit, so at that very moment I realized that he, the pastor, was the person in her apartment at the time of my visit. And she was wearing only a robe.

Several months later it was confirmed that our pastor was having sex with that young woman. He left the church, and I was somewhat vindicated in a weird sort of way.

Shortly after that, I went on to have several very successful infidelities. My infidelities were not really the result of an unhappy marriage. The infidelities were the symptom of my being a horny young man in a very horny society; whether I admitted it or not. My marriage was sacrificed for a higher purpose, or so it seemed at the time, to get my sexuality out of my system and to get it out in the open.

Infidelity sadly, can feel very good--the vicarious fear, the intrigue, the endorphins, but it can kill some other part of your life, and something inside of you will also die.

If you want to move on, you should talk about it to your mate. Infidelity is an excuse, but it is seldom the true reason. Don't be hypocritical. Man up!

But we all know that most men are big wusses. They would rather lie and cheat than to get into a conversation that would question their integrity too deeply.

CHAPTER 36

# My First Time

It was my first time. Having just left the Pentecostal Church with which I was associated during my early life, I hadn't had much opportunity to smoke marijuana. David was an acquaintance I met when I was hired to photograph his band. He rolled it in a filter cigarette after taking out the first half of the tobacco. We drove his VW bug along the freeway with the windows all rolled down to get rid of the smell. Paranoia was rampant then. For the first few years I smoked, it was most always in the bathroom, so we could flush it if the cops broke in.

It was cold and windy, and hard to keep the marijuana "cigarette" lit while tooling down the freeway in Dave's bug. At one point, sucking on the thing, I reached the real tobacco and got a lung full. I had almost as little experience with tobacco as with marijuana. I'm still not sure if I was stoned on the weed or sick on the tobacco.

It was the Forth of July, so we went down to the beach to watch the fireworks. I was sitting in the cold sand, looking up at the stars with this unfamiliar taste in my mouth and a self-conscious feeling on my mind.

It was indistinguishable at first. Then it began to sink into my consciousness--singing. It had a strangely familiar sound. Yes, I knew that tune. Religious. They were coming toward me. A group of Christians working the beach. Walking and singing amongst the heathens. Hoping to save one lost soul. Coming toward me, me, the backslider. Getting closer. I was frozen in place! Should I get up and run? No, then they would see me and recognize a sinner. What should I do?

"Jesus loves me, this I know, for the Bible tells me so. Little ones to him..." Oh, my God, they were coming right toward me! Was it written in fluorescent lights across my forehead? "Fallen Christian." What should I do if they come up to me? I know I'll break down in tears. I'm doomed to be a Christian all my life. There they were. Young, fresh-faced, enthusiastic Christians my own age. "Yes, Jesus loves me. Yes, Jesus loves me...." Right in front of me. I'll look away, ignore them. Are they still there? What? They've gone? They walked on? They're off to terrorize someone else! I'm safe! I don't have to go back to church! I can smoke dope again!

CHAPTER 37

# Don't Worry, Baby;
# Volleyball, Beach Boys And California Coolers

In 1964, 2 years after high school, I married my first wife. As in many first marriages, we were really too young to know what we were doing. Sometimes you grow into it, and sometimes you grow out of it. We eventually grew apart, and by 1972, we separated.

I don't call my first marriage a bad experience. It was part of my life, and much of it was good. We should always look back on relationships and just say, "It was what I wanted at the time. It was good for awhile, and I don't regret it!" That which does not kill you makes you smarter, and maybe then stronger.

The most important lesson I learned during that marriage was the importance of truth and trust in any relationship. You don't really have a relationship with someone, let alone love, unless there is truth. Otherwise, you're just buttin' heads.

I was an adulterer during the last half of that marriage. I first embraced infidelity with a great deal of enthusiasm. For a time, it was an addiction, but by the time the marriage ended, I was very much opposed to the deception. That's why I ended the marriage--so I could make love with other women without having to lie, and hide, and be a hypocrite.

I wasn't really disturbed by my adultery on the grounds that it ruined my marriage. We had other problems that would have eventually dissolved it anyway. As they say, adultery is not the cause of marital problems as much as it is the symptom.

By the time we separated, I was ashamed of my unfaithful activity on the grounds...well, on the grounds that it was unfaithful. It wasn't the act of having sex with a woman other than my wife that bothered me; it was the lying about it. I have always been uncomfortable with lying, and adultery is definitely one of the biggest lies.

I won't condone my cheating by any means, but it certainly taught me a lot about myself and about life in general. My first few experiences with adultery are really good examples of life's educational system.

Between the years of 1964 and 1970, during my first marriage, my wife and I lived near the beach at different times in Los Angeles and Santa Barbara. This was Beach Boys' country, and their music soundtracked our lives.

My wife and I spent all weekend, and as much of the other days of the week as possible, on the sand. We played volleyball, rode the waves and partied.

I was involved with the birth of beach volleyball. I played with and against some of the first professional beach volleyball players. I also helped create the California cooler--cheap red wine and 7-Up--we invented it; we drank a lot of it.

My first adulterous act took place just outside the glow of a beach party bonfire. I never saw her again. The fact is, I didn't really see much of her that night either. It was dark, it was fast, and I was drunk. All I can remember is that she was a "big-boned" woman.

I was hooked from that moment. There is something about the

adrenaline rush of illicit sex that is overpowering to most men, and possibly to women as well. Endorphins, dopamine? Whatever it is?

For men in particular, it is intoxicating. I can speak only from experience or certainty regarding men, but that rush makes us selfish. It causes us to disregard wedding vows. That is, until we feel the pain and turmoil of its consequences.

In my group of friends, there was another married couple. Call them Chase and Jill. They had attended the same church as my wife and I. We all slowly rebelled against the rules of the church and eventually left together.

Chase and Jill were an interesting couple at the time because they were "mixed." He was a "WASP," and she was Jewish. They met in school and married, in spite of religion.

Jill was not very traditional as far as religion or anything else went, and she was also one of the cutest and sexiest little girls you could imagine. She was maybe five feet, two inches tall. She looked very good in a bikini, and in 1967, I began noticing.

I don't know how it started. I think we began smiling at each other and then touching each other whenever possible. She was a lot more liberated than my wife, and I was getting horny for new adventures.

In my memory the "beforeplay" leading up to our first clandestine meeting provided some of the most exciting times of my life. Feet touching feet under the table, standing close when possible, smelling each other. I remember vividly one night the two couples coming back from some function together, and Jill and I found some way to touch each other during the dark car ride home. It went on like this for several weeks, maybe a month or more.

Then I called her. She worked in a job that gave her latitude to travel around, and I worked at home. We made arrangements, and one day when our spouses were at work, Jill came to my house.

I can still remember her scent. She had showered, shaved her legs, powdered her body and dressed in nice, clean clothes just for me to remove. That realization still excites me when I think of it, even today.

I can still remember the uniqueness of her smell. Clean and fresh like a forest after rain. I still remember looking down at her beautiful little body as I pulled her underwear down over her thighs, knees, calves and feet.

When I first went down on her, she said to me, "Let's not do anything we will regret." For years, I thought she meant that cunnilingus was uncivilized, and that I shouldn't do it. You see, in 1967, oral sex was not considered proper human behavior by many people.

More recently, I have come to realize that she meant we should not get too distracted, fall in love and disrupt our marriages.

When I first slipped deep inside her, it was the most wonderful feeling I had ever experienced. I realize now that I was as high on the perilous thrill of deception as I was on the excitement of the intercourse itself.

My first few sexual encounters before marriage had been dark, cramped, quick exploits between two high school kids. The sex life created with my first wife was the amateur education of two young people who liked each other, but who never really experienced the electricity of spiritual passion.

Sex with that girl at the beach party was a quick, drunken episode. It didn't count for much technically, but it gave me pause to think. With Jill, sex all came together for me. We were experienced enough to know how to make love, we were excited by the forbidden act, and we were passionately attracted to each other.

When the head of my penis touched the opening of Jill's vagina, it met with a momentary resistance of flesh, taut by fear of the unknown and reluctance to open unto a new life. We knew we were changing our future. Deep inside, I realized it was the end of my marriage, and Jill may have known hers was ending too. The insistent thrust of my erection forced her muscles to part, and I leapt deep into her warmth and welcome. At that moment, it was where I wanted to be for the rest of my life.

We began meeting once or twice a week, at which time we would throw ourselves together into a frenzy that would last without separation for an hour or more. We thrust our bodies together with such eagerness that for days afterwards our pelvic bones were bruised and sore.

I have always been able to maintain an erection for a long period of time. It was not something I worked at. I never studied tantric yoga. It's not as if I'm an Asian guru practiced in the arts of tantric yoga. I was a horny youth, like everyone else. But for some reason I just loved being inside a woman, for as long as I could, and as often as I could.

I never meditated on my Svadhishthana chakra to control sexual energy or to postpone my orgasm. As most young men of my age during that era, I was primarily horny, and primarily concerned with the urge to achieve an orgasm.

And yet my body, on its own, had something else in mind. The physical feeling of making love was every bit as desirable as an orgasm to me. And this, I believe, is because of the type of experimental circumcision performed on me when I was born. Because of that circumcision, I experience extreme pleasure when inside a woman. I don't really want an orgasm, which would end that sensation, so I subconsciously hold back ejaculation in order to play longer.

My memories of Jill are of her sweet scent mixed with an acrid sheen of sweat, our bodies reaching out for more contact amid guttural sounds of ecstasy. We were in lust. Before her, my sex life was measured by orgasms. With her, I don't remember the orgasms; I remember the lovemaking.

Jill finally ended our affair in order to preserve our marriages. We had only one other way to go, and I think Jill knew that. She knew that, if we left our spouses to be together, we wouldn't have lasted long ourselves.

I didn't want to end it. Jill prevailed, and it was my one truly pathetic groveling moment.

But by then, I was hooked on the endorphins of adultery, and I began committing it as often as I could. It was the death knell of my marriage, but it wasn't the cause. My desire for sex with other women was not what ended my first marriage; my lack of passion for my first wife was what ended it. Our lack of chemistry was not her fault, and it probably wasn't my fault either; it was just a fact of life.

Several years after my time with Jill, I was forced to admit to my wife that I was having affairs, and within a few years, my wife had an affair of her own. I have looked upon the event of my wife's adultery many times with conflicting emotions, from anger to relief.

Never before the writing of this chapter have I stopped to think about what my wife's affair may have meant to her. I had always thought of what it meant to me.

I realize now that the moment of my wife's first illicit sexual experience may have been as exciting and as memorable to her as mine was to me. For that reason, I have now come to grips with it. Everyone deserves to feel that level of emotion at least once, whether it is with your life's partner or a onetime thing. If it ends by destroying your other relationship, so be it. If it doesn't interfere with your marriage, that also is O.K., and usually preferable.

I think everyone should have an illicit sexual experience, perhaps a few. But then I also think we should get over it, go back home, and take care of business. Most often, adultery is nothing more than just juices flowing; it's not something on which to base the rest of your life.

Being single and having an affair with someone else's wife or girlfriend is another subject. It is similar and just as exciting in its own way, but just as destructive in the end.

Is it worse for a woman to commit adultery than for a man to do so? I would definitely say that it's a more serious sign of problems in a relationship when a woman goes outside for affection, than when a man goes outside for sex. But that is taking into consideration the different basic expectations of men and women.

A man is, by nature, an unfaithful animal. Most of the time when a husband fucks another woman, it doesn't mean anything. Whereas, if a wife goes so far as to have an affair with another man, it means that she is on her way out the door.

I would go so far as to guess that proportionately wives' adultery causes more divorces than husbands' adultery. The effect that a wife's adultery has on a husband's ego almost ensures that he will not be able to forgive her and go on with their life of marital bliss, whereas women seem more willing to forgive men. The reason for this is that a man is more likely to have casual sex than a woman. Women usually aren't as casual with their affections.

The truth of the matter is that sex is more of a sacred act for women than it is for men. Besides being primal, this attitude can be explained by the physical difference between penetrating and being penetrated. To many men, it is dominance acted out; to most women, sex is the act of being receptive and nurturing.

For most women, sex is emotional; for most men, it is physical.

The possibility of becoming pregnant also makes women more selective. Men just don't have as much invested in the process, and they also don't have as much to lose.

I didn't create this situation; I am just reporting it.

*"When he left her in her bed to go back to his wife and life, she stared at the ceiling for what seemed like hours. In front of her bathroom mirror she stood and looked at her face and torso. She was still flushed from lovemaking; his bite mark still remained on her left nipple."*

*"Will he call her again? Will he come to make love with her again? Oh, I want him back again! I must wash the sheets so my husband won't know."*

*"When he caught his reflection in the rear view mirror, concerned eyes stared back at him. Is my hair in place? Did she leave any lipstick? A little smile of remembrance. Should I call her again? Will I go to her again? Is it worth the risk?"*

Dudley Griffin

What do I think about my first wife's infidelity? She had every right to be unfaithful to me, yet it gave me the excuse I needed to leave her. But also, the way she did it would have made it impossible for me to let it slide had I wanted to stay.

My wife had her first affair with the man who had been my best man at our wedding. Talk about a soap opera becoming devastatingly, ironically true!

The guy had just come back from surviving Vietnam. I felt sorry for him. I wanted to help my friend readapt to "real" life. We rented him the cottage in back of our family home.

Another bizarre facet to the whole affair is that I had also previously propositioned his ex-wife after they separated and he was in Viet Nam. I'm sure he told my wife this as part of the foreplay. By the way, his ex-wife turned me down.

Suffice to say, it was a weird time. I was a real shit, and everyone was indulging in antisocial activity. But that's still no excuse for my actions. My excuse is my male libido. I was thinking with my dick at that time of my life, and so was my friend.

Aside from my wife having an affair with my best man, the most devastating blow to my ego was that I had previously given this man a lot of help in his own social life. A major element of the male ego is status, and I considered myself superior to this guy socially.

When I first met him, he was a complete social misfit, and I contributed largely to his education. I even introduced the man to his wife, who had been a friend of mine from school. I had always been attracted to her, yet I set them up. I only propositioned her after they separated because, in my strange mind I thought it was appropriate.

When my best man and my wife started their romance, I was not only jealous, I was disappointed in the ramifications of their affair. I deserved the infidelity, but it cut deeply on several levels, and it made it impossible for me to be completely sympathetic toward my wife in our eventual separation. How she had her affair contributed to future problems in communication.

It is possible for the human mind to justify anything that it really wants to. You can have a whole panel of your friends telling you that you are out of your mind for acting the way that you are, and yet you will never see it. Perhaps it may dawn on you years later if your ego has mellowed enough, but by then the damage is done.

If I could apologize to my ex-wife in a way that she could understand my true emotions, I would try. But alas, I am afraid that there are some places men and women can never go in communication.

*"Is it any wonder that the nations of the world cannot get along, when even man and wife have difficulties maintaining harmony in the home?"*
Paraphrase of an old Irish proverb.

*"Please, please, for the sake of love in the world and your own happiness, learn these few things from my poetry and ranting, or you will die a miserable and lonely soul. You are not the center of the earth, though it revolves around you. You are on the edge of*

*everyone else's life. You can be a part of life and prosper with it, but only if you play by the rules of polite society. Love thy neighbor as your brother, respect all women as your mother, the giver of life. Don't lie, cheat and steal lest that gives others the permission to do the same to you. Acting arrogant, feeling dominant, pushing other people around, may make you feel good for a short time, but what it will give you in the end is loneliness, self-pity and a lot of black eyes! Get your act together, join the human race and have a great life." DG*

## CHAPTER 38

# Power And Wisdom

In my prime I made love continually with whomever I could find. I was not a macho man or a frightening predator.

I portrayed security. But also, most importantly, I evoked a positive aura of excitement, and a hint of the fun that was to be found in my presence.

But how and why did I exude such a persona? It was, I say,

because I possessed sincerity and self-confidence.

And how did I achieve this cocktail of seduction? Was it an act I put on? Was it something I studied to master?

No. The true nature of self-confidence and sincerity is that they are, above all, *real*. You cannot pretend to possess either of these traits. You either are or you aren't. It's like pretending to be a car when you are actually a person. You can paint yourself candy apple red lacquer and wear windshield wipers, but you are still a human being, and you will convince no one otherwise.

If you are not completely sure of who you are and that what you are doing is correct, then the object of your affection will not be convinced. If you are not doing the right thing, it will be obvious to others.

Some can fake being real for awhile, but they will eventually, and soon, fall into the cesspool of their deception. And then they will someday become morally disappointed with themselves.

In other words, if you lie, soon you will die by your own lies and the real horrible realization that others are lying back to you and laughing about it.

The whole package of self-confidence, security and fun wrapped up in one person comes from having "no fear." This is not a bumper sticker; this is the real thing.

A man who is a real "lover of women" is not afraid of who he is, ashamed or concerned about his sexuality. And he is not afraid of women, what they can do to him, or what they can do to his ego by rejecting him. A real "lover of women" will take the bad with the good and go on to love another day.

A true lover is conscious of a woman's emotions. If a woman is put off or frightened, a real "lover of women" has feelers that pick up on this, and he will retreat or change his tactics.

An unsuccessful suitor often becomes a creepy stalker if he is too insistent and doesn't know limits. Sometimes it is just a matter of timing. You have to know the variations of the word "No!" There is a coy "No," a maybe "No," and a "No" of finality, and you must read them fast and correctly.

A stalker might think that he should be with a woman, but that does not mean that his are the right circumstances for that woman.

Sometimes your brand of reality is not right for her. There are times when it is best to walk away. Don't take it personally. It can be chemistry or timing against you. It is a hair's breath between being a lover or a fool, a dirty old man or a bon vivant.

But if you are being rejected over 75% of the time, you might reassess your approach.

When you touch a woman to whom you are attracted, be subtle. Make it a soft, unaggressive touch, wait to see how she responds, moves closer or away. When you dance with "that girl" for the first time, maybe let your thigh touch her thigh, and see if she moves closer or away.

Aggression is not sexy to most, maybe all, women; it is creepy to them. Go with their lead. No one wants to be forced. Think of how you feel if someone forces you to do something. You will get better love if she wants your love.

*"A life can be short or long. It may be joy or drudgery. Yet in every life there are at least some points of brightness. Love, fellowship, beauty beheld. It may be fleeting, but it could be all you get. Hang on to those moments of vitality in life because that is all that Mother Nature promises. A few seconds that reveal how wonderful just being alive is, a few flashes of feeling that affirm the existence of your soul. "*
Dudley Griffin, 6.28.07

Self-confidence and sincerity cannot be achieved by lying, but if you can reach them through your own effort, then you are a master human.

Self-confidence and sincerity, attributes claimed by everyone, possessed by few, often parodied and never successfully faked. Self-confidence is the true aphrodisiac, the primal sexual turn-on.

Manhattan Beach model shoot late 1960's

Late 1960s, Manhattan Beach, California, waves, volleyball and girls in bikinis. It was part fantasy and all true. One of The Beach Boys lived in my uncle's apartment house! Their music, The Beatles, Judy Collins, Jethro Tull, The Doors, Carole King, Steppenwolf and The Stones were the soundtrack of our indulgences.

For about three or four years I lived one-and-a-half blocks from the LA beach. Much of that time I wore nothing but a pair of surfing "baggies," I surfed and body surfed, played volleyball and peddled my ass up and down the "strand," on my bicycle looking for girls.

We met, made love, parted and never saw each other again. That was the scenario.

**Excerpt from an earlier chapter:**

When I told the beautiful girl on the beach that I wanted to show her something, I had that look in my eyes. You know, that "I want to make love with you look." I wasn't trying to fool her into coming with me so I could get her into a position where she couldn't refuse me. It was obvious what I wanted to do. I had confidence that it would be fun for both of us, and I was sincere about that.

Many girls are fooled by fake sincerity, for a time at least.

Some people think that looking someone in the eyes as you tell them a lie is going to make it the truth. Most women get wise to that quickly enough.

Seducers use a lie to get a brief moment of love that they might be able to possess forever if they did not lie to get it.

Most girls worth winning are won only by sincerity. You have a better chance by telling the truth. Most men worth winning are also won only by sincerity; oh, and also sex appeal. This girl on the beach was in that category. She would have laughed at me if I had not sincerely thought it was right for her to come with me.

I was not ashamed of my desire to make love with her. It is a natural flow of life. Take note of the birds and bees.

If I had had hidden motives that I was ashamed of, she would have picked up on that and rejected me. But I sincerely wanted to make love with her, and it showed. And because of my confidence and sincerity, she didn't feel threatened.

I was sincere because I was not deceiving her to lead her into danger. I was confident because I was not ashamed of my actions. I was not doing something wrong.

Some people mistake arrogance for self-confidence. They are not the same. Real self-confidence is the opposite of arrogance. Self-confidence comes from within; it does not exclude others or devalue other people.

Arrogance lashes out from a place of insecurity; it ridicules others in order to build itself up. An arrogant person is a lonely person who thinks he is important because he makes a lot of noise.

Self-doubt is OK in reasonable amounts, inasmuch as it makes a better man of you. But it should never be played out in a public forum. Moments of arrogance are unavoidable to balance out the moments of doubt, but it too should never be laid before an audience.

The term body language has been overused so much that most people feel they know what it is without even thinking about it. It is not always planned. It is often inadvertent movements that tell the experienced eye what or who you really are.

Body language can be a poorly executed seduction or a well-thought-out effort at seduction. It can be an unavoidable reflex movement, and it can also be choreographed.

Some men are blind and clueless to body language. They are the ones who will miss out on romance at one opportunity and then mistakenly dive in the next time when a woman is not at all interested.

Some body code signs are too obvious and therefore not to be trusted. Others are subtle and are the real messages. Some women give out the same "available" message to every man, just to see what they can get in return. Often, if you are too eager to respond, then you are already disqualified.

Mostly, the less obvious codes are the true window into a woman. Men must remember that because women are constantly being hit on by unwanted suitors, they must mask their messages for only a certain type of man to read.

If a woman tries to keep her knees together or turns away, a true gentleman should not pursued the lovemaking. There are other body features involved in the message, pushing hands, fear in the eyes, downward mouth, or tightness of the jaw. Be a good lover and read the messages, sometimes a good lover will not try to be a lover at all.

## CHAPTER 39

# The Perfect Night: Sex, Drugs And Rock & Roll

No, it is usually drugs, rock & roll and then sex. Most people don't plan any of this. They have expectations of course, but often it is only an accident of timing and availability. It also requires some incentive, which is often the drugs, which is most often alcohol. But it is often a crapshoot! That is, unless you do plan it out. You can choose your alcohol or drug. you can drive or walk by and check the talent, and determine the time and money you want to spend. But I personally was never that contrived! I usually just ventured out and went in the direction the wind blew.

All of this activity and conclusion is also due to where you are, what you are, who you are and attitude. Good sex or bad sex is determined by what you expect. If you are real horny or real drunk or stoned, your expectations are most likely low, and often that is the same with your partner. And quality can be determined by where you are on the planet. If you were in Studio 54, NYC, Joe's Place in Monroeville, Alabama, or on the back streets of Bangkok, the experience would be different. This is not to say it would be bad or good more or less in one place or the other, yet the environment will have some influence on the experience.

Many lifetime mates first meet during these wild nights and/or "innocent" trysts in a bar at the Beverly Wilshire Hotel, so there is no shame in the process. But, I warn you that if it starts in a bar or dance hall, it can just as easily end in a dance hall or a bar.

It is an "unsupportable" fact, but fact no less, that 10% of the boys get 90% of the girls! But many times in the morning, the arrogance of the guy turns the girl off, and she splits forever. So guys, if you are looking for love, not just sex, dial down your self-importance. Is this starting to sound like an episode of *Friends* or *How I Met Your Mother*? Guys, instead of trying to improve your pick-up-line skills, you should be trying to improve your sincerity and your personality. Then you will become a "Lover" with a capital letter! Here is how you can do so.

Some people just can't handle drugs. They should be told this as soon and as often as possible. Their friends should tell them and help them to stop. It would help if the pharmaceutical companies didn't keep promoting and producing more drugs than the public can rationally consume.

Laws against drug takers are stupid and do not really address the problem! Laws and morality should address the culture of poverty and hopelessness and how that falls right into the pockets of drug capitalists.

Disclaimer: I do not advocate excesses of anything! Drugs can mean coffee, alcohol, nicotine, Nyquil, diet pills, many prescribed medications, THC, psychedelics, cocaine, and some legal herbal teas! "Use your drugs; don't let them use you!"

CHAPTER 40

# Sex: God Giveth And Society Taketh Away

*"Did God give us the ability and desire to procreate, or was it the 'Devil'?"*
Dudley Griffin, 7/7/07

*"No, It was nature, Mother Nature, if you want to know!"*
Dudley Griffin, 7/7/07, 7 minutes later

Until fairly recently (before 1960s), human sexuality was <u>not</u> outwardly spoken of, and seldom written about. The good as well as the bad aspects of sex were considered embarrassing, immoral and inappropriate to discuss. And because of that, all the ugliness in some people's behavior was ignored, and all our mistakes were relived over and over again.

Talking about sex will eventually help fix sex! If we stop ignoring it, we will make it work. If we talk about sex, I know it will make sex a normal activity, and put it in the same category with all other normal activities. But there are basic rules, and yes, even laws that we all should know, and that we should follow as rational human beings. I'm not talking about religion or social sensibilities, but about real medical responsibilities, scientific facts and common sense for our self-preservation.

In the last 50 years, sexual awareness has flipped, then flopped back again. But those of us who lived that period of time with our eyes open can never accept the reversal of those changes. The awakening of moral freedoms in the hippie era made too much sense just to be forgotten. The reevaluation of attitudes about "sins," such as drugs and sex, opened a door into the possibility of a more tolerant and enjoyable future.

Seven out of the original Ten Commandments are not viable in our society today, nor are they prosecutable. Otherwise, we would have two thirds of the world population in prison, including a large percentage of the lawyers, police and judges. Today, hypocrisy is our most prevalent moral and legal crime.

The only Commandments I worry about in this day and age are: Thou shalt not kill, steal or bear false witness, (lie).

In the 1960s and 70s, we were searching for a better world because what was happening all around us then was not good. Yes, we used sex, drugs, and rock & roll in our research, but we also employed education, religion, political activism, nature's morality, human irony and even spirits to find a new truth.

It began as just having more fun, as experiments in joy and freedom. Then it proved to be the more reasonable way in which to live.

True, there were mistakes made. It was a period of exploration into social and moral change, and, just as in scientific research, failures were a part of finding the answers. In a research laboratory, mistakes are the necessary process. Failures serve to narrow the possibilities, thus showing the path to success.

During the hippie era the counterculture experimented. We were the guinea pigs for mankind. We proved or disproved superstitions, prejudice, bad science and dogma. Some hippies died, some suffered, but in the long run the good far outweighed the bad. We came up with answers, and we documented them. We recorded and wrote them all down for mankind's benefit.

I myself wrote and published *The Hippie Dictionary: A Cultural Encyclopedia of the 1960s and 70s*. In it, I describe all the drugs of the era, what they are made of and how they affect a person, good and bad. I also describe all the religions, psychologies, fads, movements and sects. There is no excuse now for humans to fail to reach perfection with all the self-help available to them from the 1960s and 70s.

I would have to say that going through my adolescence in the 1950s, then experiencing the 1960s and 70s revolution, and then to watch the slow death of intellect in the 1980s and '90s has made me a truly evolved human being. Pissed off, but evolved.

In the mid-1960s several events took place that changed my entire perspective on women and masculinity. In the 1950s life's perfect scenario seemed simple; you found a girl, subdued her, married her, got a job and climbed the workplace ladder to the top.

I was well on my way toward fulfilling this scenario. After

high school graduation and moving to Southern California, attending some college, church, got married, and on into high-profile business, I was on the American Dream track.

At first, I thought I was following the proper masculine DNA, yet I soon realized it led me to a path untrue to myself. I was being what society wanted me to be. My life was an outline of all the traps our competitive, capitalist society creates. These traps produce people who get on the treadmill, stop thinking and start buying.

It was very much like joining the military, where you are stripped of your individuality, lied to about your patriotic duty and then sent off to fight and die.

Little did I know then that, like so may others, the life I was leading was just sublimation for my creative and sexual frustrations. Little did I know that I had died just after high school graduation. Little did I know that my salvation was just around the corner.

In each life there are defining moments that affect the rest of that life. For many, those choices lead to a trapped, unhappy existence of fulfilling other people's expectations and ignoring the desires of their own heart.

But in the 1960s we had mind-expanding drugs and poignant musical lyrics. Sometime in mid-1967 I started smoking marijuana, reading and listening to the new music. I also watched a passionate, troubled and insistent young woman sing her heart and soul out for love.

*"What do you think is the most appealing storyline in popular comedy or drama on TV and movie? Sexual tension is the most exciting back-story to any emotional, introspective or psychological comedy or drama!"*
Dudley Griffin, 8.31.13

JUNE 16·17·18 1967

CHAPTER 41

# Monterey Pop Festival, June 17, 1967

By 1967, I was a church-going Christian, an advertising industry executive, and an old man at 24 years of age. The Monterey Pop Festival changed all that. It was my spiritual rebirth, as it was for most of those of us who attended it.

I was visiting my mother in Monterey for the weekend. My cousin Diane Hildebrand, who was a songwriter for Screen Gems and *The Monkeys*, was up for the festival and gave me some tickets.

The performance I saw included Country Joe and the Fish, Canned Heat, and Big Brother and the Holding Company. Canned Heat, and Country Joe were eye-openers, of course, coming from the life I had led for the past five years. But Big Brother and the Holding Company changed my life forever.

As you may know, Big Brother's lead singer was Janis Joplin.

When Janis started to sing, I got up from my seat transfixed. I walked down the aisle and up to the stage in a trance. Standing in front of the stage looking up at Janis ten feet away, my mouth dropped open and my mind went into a spin.

Half of my emotions and sensibilities were saying, "Hey, you can't do that," and the other half of me was saying, "Right–on girl, get it on!"

Janis Joplin was the most sensual being I had seen in my life. At the same time, she exuded more power and confidence than most men I had known to that point. She was certainly the most powerful person in her band, even though all the rest of them were male.

Janis Joplin demanded to be treated as an equal. In her own way, Janis was the first feminist leader to teach me how to become a more tolerant man and person. She forced you to take her seriously as she asked for love and sex on her own terms. And yet, at the same time, her inherited insecurities exposed a vulnerability that drew your sympathy to her.

I was torn in half by Janis's sex appeal and with her power, both of which seduced me at the same time in their own way. And then from my subconscious I felt an usher's hand tap my shoulder as he asked me to return to my seat. I walked like a zombie back to sit down. I was changed!

I don't think I ever looked at women in the same old way again after that. I knew what they were capable of and what they were looking for after that moment. Before that performance I thought of women as passive creatures with little or no desires of their own.

Although it may sound stupid, arrogant and definitely politically incorrect, until then I had never before realized that women were people, just like me. Even disregarding the sexual aspects of that realization, the ramifications of that knowledge were monumental. Women were just like me; therefore, they had the same needs and desires as I had, and I should treat them the way I, myself, wanted to be treated.

I have learned since that time there are some subtle, but important, differences in women's desires and needs in a relationship. Yet, when all is totaled up, men and women are more alike than different. Men will always have better results treating a woman by the guidelines of the Golden Rule, than treating them as if they were from some other planet.

That weekend with the love, tolerance, hip art, hip clothing and the hip words of the songs of that period began to change me. I began to soften. I began to think sometimes with my head and not always with my dick. I was entering the era of men's liberation. I must also mention the influences of marijuana in this process, for it is the gateway drug to knowledge, tolerance and peace. Drug abuse comes from the person, not the drug. Alcohol is still the worst drug on all levels. If a person has an addictive personality, they will find something to kill themself with.

Everyone talks about women's liberation, yet, at the same time, another movement was born. Men's Liberation. Men began to rebel against the pressures of their macho expectations. Those of us who realized that the existing male dominance of the world was a destructive force began to rethink macho.

One thing I started to do was to question and to ask. Until then, as the masculine law states, a man did not ask for directions! I began wondering if I were doing the right things, rather than just merely doing them regardless of the consequences to others around me.

This is mental multi-tasking. It is something few people are capable of doing. Not just men. It is that ability to see a subject from the viewpoint of others. In 1967, I began to think globally, not just personally.

My wife at the time had grown up with me as the dominant alpha male. She had been impressed by my confidence as a person. When I began to change, it looked like weakness to her.

An episode at this time was a turning point in our relationship, and an indication of the reasons we later separated.

One day my wife and I were in the sand dunes overlooking the Southern California surf. A number of teenage boys were sliding down the sand hills on cardboard. I showed interest in their technique. I asked them how they did it. I may have asked if they waxed the box or something like that.

At that time in male history, a "real" man never let it be known that he didn't know something. Ignorance was considered a flaw. The strange Catch-22 of that sort of mentality is that if you don't ask about something that you don't know, then you will remain ignorant. And then you are not only ignorant, but you are also stupid.

When I asked those boys how to do something, my wife saw a

side of me that she had never seen before. She drew me aside and said, "You have changed, and I'm not sure I like the changes."

Some people are afraid of what they don't know. They are skeptical of new thoughts and feelings. The counterculture of the 1960s and '70s disturbed many people.

Why do some folks think that their God, their kind of sex and their form of drugs is better for me than the God, sex and drugs I have chosen? It is their right to believe what they want and even say what they believe, but it is not their right to force me to change my choices. My generation experimented long and hard to come up with the set of moralities we have and the attitudes on sex, drugs and God that we have. If other people don't want to join us, fine, but let us live our own lives.

One of the main reasons the establishment disapproves of mind-expanding drugs is that these drugs make people think. And when you think, you have revelations, and these revelations cause you to change. And the established society doesn't like change because it makes it harder to keep track of the things you want to buy, or read, or drive or how you want to live.

Your changes disrupt business and politics. Military and industrial leaders don't like that. After women started taking control of their lives and men started treating women as equals, the straight world took awhile to catch on, and that cost them money.

When we started smoking marijuana and dropping acid, we quit the rat race our "leaders" arranged for us to run. We realized that we never won the race anyway; the owners of the track benefited, but we just worked for them and paid them money for the privilege to work for them.

The entry fee is too expensive to continue the rat race. We work for "them" to make money to buy unnecessary, overpriced and poorly made commodities which they have advertised to us as essential. We work for "them" to be able to pay them for goods we don't really need.

Why don't we buy less crap so we don't have to work so hard to buy it? It's a vicious cycle of materialism and work that is making a few people very wealthy and the rest of us very tired.

I think having good sex, taking some safe, mind-expanding

drugs and getting closer to God is healthier for the human race than continuing the rat race. And I'm talking about the real God--not the one that lives in white churches, but the one who lives in all of us, in the earth and in the next door neighbor's ugly cat.

CHAPTER 42

# Sex, Business and Religion

*"In America, everything our society does with sex is wrong! We preach that sex is nasty, and then we promote it and advertise it to the point that it titillates all aspects of our life, leaving us no way to ignore it."*
Dudley Griffin 6.5.99

*"Why is your pocket book attached to your dick and not your brain?"* Mr. California

Common sense would seem to say that sex, business and religion should never be mixed. Sure, prostitution is a business, but really, in a perfect world, I don't think that business should have any influence on religion or sex, and I definitely feel religion should never be associated with sex or business in any way.

When I speak of religion, I mean organized, proselytizing church religion, not morality. Morality is altogether different from religion. Morality is the Golden Rule.

It doesn't sound right, yet in our society, sex, business and religion are irrevocably bound together. These three most volatile, complex and emotional activities of humankind are indeed all wrapped up together in the crazy, imaginative psyche of mankind.

The first truth that we must admit in order to straighten out this travesty of conflicting emotions is the fact that sex is by far the most important activity of humankind, not business or religion. Sex is the activity that continues the flow of life, and in Nature it is our primary function.

True, business may help to maintain life, but it is third or fourth in importance behind sex. After the basic need for food and the primal

222

reflex of self-defense, all of man's other actions are dictated by the desire for, pursuit and maintenance of sexual gratification.

There are those who would say that this is too simplistic. They might mention work, children, home and garden as the main activities of life. Yet my question to these people is, "What is the reason for work and home and what are children produced for? Are they just for our own gratification, or are we working for a better life?"

Sure, most of our active life is not devoted to sexual intercourse, yet much of our existence is involved in getting laid, supporting the product of our sexual activity and protecting the home where our children and the object of our sexual desire lives.

So how did human society get so involved in business and religion? Why do we now attribute so much importance to business and religion? No other animal does. Why do we?

The answer is self-awareness, the one thing nature gave humans that other creatures don't seem to have, or at least don't act upon.

Self-awareness makes us judge our own performance, and it forces us to compare ourselves to the performance of others. It is our strongest advocate, and it is also our most dangerous flaw.

Self-awareness sometimes makes us feel inadequate and sometimes makes us feel superior. Both of these are destructive mental states. The extreme reactions to the feeling of inadequacy are either to shrivel up and fail or to compete excessively with other people to prove oneself. The feeling of superiority that some people receive with self-awareness makes them belittle and dominate others.

A particularly volatile and often common situation is one in which a person vacillates between the two self-images of inadequacy and superiority. Alcohol or drugs often trigger this conflict. It is suggested that one not have sexual relations with this kind of person. This person needs psychiatric help.

Self-image and our sex life are irrevocably intertwined, and as with the chicken and the egg, it is difficult to tell which came first. But, most often, the self-image was reached in youth, which then affects how we interact with potential or actual sex partners. And here is where the vicious cycle starts because success in sex affects our attitude in all other areas of life.

How well we succeed in our sexual life determines whether we are self-assured or insecure, and that self-image is what dictates our treatment of other people, our competitiveness and our spiritual path. Sexual frustration often dictates how a person acts in business or religion. All the insecurity, ego and jealousy displayed by mankind can be traced to sex.

Sex, itself, is not the problem. Sex is a natural element of being a living creature on this earth. How we deal with sex is the problem. This is where the good and bad of self-awareness affect our lives. Most other animals, creatures and plants have no awareness of their importance or their worthlessness.

Only humans worry about whether they look good or are attractive to the opposite sex on a personal level. Other creatures might be instinctively concerned about appearance or performance on a biological level for the continuance of their species. They are driven by the mechanism of procreation, but they don't take it personally. Have you ever heard of a dog committing suicide because he was rejected by that foxy poodle bitch down the street?

Insecurity causes most human social problems. Insecurity is caused by self-perceived inadequacy in romantic and social associations with others. Insecurity is most often created by the treatment we receive from our own family from the beginning, and it is often increased by the ridicule we might feel in society.

The vicious cycle persists. We create activities by which to judge our accomplishments, and then we suffer from the comparisons. Ironically, the criteria by which we are judged in our family and society is established by religion and business, and then this judgment influences our sexual behavior. Yet business and religion, to a certain extent, were themselves originally created only to support and facilitate our sex and social lives.

The sad thing about insecurity-driven accomplishments is that they never solve the insecurity. Insecurity is solved only from inside a person's own head. A person needs only to say to himself, "I'm O.K."

If someone doesn't change his own mind about his own value, he will continue to drive himself to shallow rewards. He will keep on running around in circles like a silly fool, and continue to hurt others in the process. Likewise, a person who feels unlovely and unlovable because of insecurities will continue to seek the love of others for validation. Yet they will still not lose their insecurity until they take it upon themselves to quit feeling sorry for themselves and live happily with who they are.

Sex is one of the most regulated activities in our society, and that is because the people who run religions and businesses know that it is the strongest influence in human life. Therefore, controlling the morality and availability of sex is a great way to control people's time and money. Making sex a sin, which they have, strangely makes people more interested in it, almost as a mystery and/or a rebellion. And then they've got you hooked.

Men and women each have basic traits, some of which can get in the way of monogamy, morality, economy and therefore, marital bliss. King Henry VIII is an intriguing scenario and example of man/woman politics.

Many men want to produce children to prove their virility. Women want children to satisfy their mothering instincts, and often they use those instincts on their husbands if they are childless. Many women think that mentioning the need for more money is a helpful comment. Many men think that promising more money and perks will improve the sex life.

A rational woman who wants a good relationship should try to learn how to think like a man, and men should try to understand the female needs and wants as well. Dating and marriage are the most extreme examples of the necessity of trying on other people's shoes.

*"Knowing how long to hold someone's hand is a skill in the art of love. Knowing how long to hold a kiss is also a skill in love. Knowing what subjects will start an argument is a skill and a necessity to staying in love! "*
Dudley Griffin 11.19.06

## To "Ms. or Miss" Right and All Other Conservative Feminists: Birth Control and Saving the Planet

No liberal, "socialist" intellectual is asking you or any of your shiny-faced friends to use birth control or have an abortion. "We" are lobbying for all the women of the world (including in the third world and all religions) to have the freedom to use these options. This is to help save the world from over-population and to give women what we think are their human rights.

Birth control and real sex education, not abstinence, are the proper solution. By the way, anyone with a drop of brains and any knowledge of mankind's history knows abstinence is a hoax.

The real issue here is saving humankind by getting it to stop having so many children! One child per two people would slow the death of all of us, and then we would have to start working on not consuming all the food, nuts and bolts and lubricants of the world. Natural resources are necessary for life on earth. That would be water, hydrogen, sun, soil and oxygen.

The mechanism of self-preservation is not fear; it is lust for life. Man is the only insecure animal. Our mind and its recognition of itself is our "carnal knowledge," and therefore our gravest flaw.

Most anti-abortion organizations are run by men, and under the surface most men blame women for any of these procreation issues. Yet unless you are totally ignorant of the situation, you will know that it takes two bodies to perform the act of procreation. And men are usually, maybe about 97% of the time, the aggressors. So I think women should make all the rules about birth control or abortion.

Miss Wright or Right, a conservative feminist is fighting on the wrong side.

Since I have not heard from or about her for a few years, I don't know if she is still fighting that battle. If not, pardon my commentary about you yourself, but I am still adamant that women should make the decisions about what is done to or with their bodies.

CHAPTER 43

# A Miracle Of Medical Science:
# Giving God A Helping Hand

For years, it was just an interesting story that my mother told me. She was alone and pregnant in San Francisco with very little money. Her family doctor, a good friend and confidante, arranged for my birth at the University of California Medical Center at no charge. There was one stipulation. The doctors would be allowed to perform one small experiment on me.

Now, there's a frightening prospect, and also an interesting perspective on my life! I came into this world as a lab rat.

At 6:45 pm, March 5, 1943, I was born. Shortly thereafter, I was circumcised, using a new experimental procedure.

To my knowledge, I am the only man-child to receive this operation. I have neither seen nor heard of anyone else with a penis like mine, nor has anyone at the hospital ever contacted me to ask whether the procedure was a success. Perhaps they are afraid they screwed up?

Yet, if this university hospital administration were ever curious and were to ask my opinion, I would definitely shower them with praise for the little alteration they made to me. In fact, I have on occasion considered contacting UC Medical Center to suggest that they announce the discovery of a new and improved dick. I hereby name this revolutionary circumcision the "John Bassett Cut," and here is the secret of its success.

As I have said, for years it was just an interesting story to which I paid little attention until I started reading Eastern writings on tantric sex. In sexual yoga the key to true satisfaction is postponing the orgasm for as long as possible in order to achieve and experience equal and enhanced enjoyment for both partners. Hours of blissful sex enjoyed by both parties and then a simulgasm--a simultaneous orgasm. This was something I had already discovered on my own, even before studying tantric yoga, but these concepts began to give me new insights into my own body and its uniqueness.

Physically, I look no different from any <u>uncircumcised</u> man.

My foreskin was not removed, so when I am unaroused, it covers the head of my penis.

The procedure that was performed on me involved merely cutting the membrane inside the foreskin that partially attaches it to the head of the penis. This cut allows the foreskin to be pulled back all the way off the penis head. When I have an erection, I look like a circumcised man; when in repose, I look uncircumcised.

A circumcised man has an exposed penis head. This normally soft and sensitive part of the body, by being exposed and constantly rubbed by clothing, eventually becomes calloused and less sensitive. My penis head, particularly the ridge around the heart-shaped tip, is still very sexually sensitive.

Other men who have a foreskin, but who have the membrane that keeps the skin partially over the head, don't get quite as much stimulus as I do on the ridge and beneath it. And, of course, those who don't have the skin at all to protect sensitivity are even less stimulated.

Most importantly, because of this, I have always been extremely satisfied during lovemaking, and therefore I was not as anxious to rush to orgasm just to get my kicks. I often made love all night long without an orgasm and still enjoyed the hell out of it. I did though, sometimes become more selfish and animalistic in the morning just in order to have an orgasm to release the pressure.

Because I remained turned on for a longer period of time, I was usually looking for games to play to prolong my partner's interest. Foreplay, duringplay and afterplay.

As a thinking and feeling lover, I sometimes had to moderate my enthusiasm, because many women don't expect to spend the whole night in a sweaty, sensual, aerobic activity. And some women become sore from having way too much fun.

Lovers must remember that they are not making love to a machine; they are making love with a sensitive human being. That understanding can make the experience even more exciting. If a man pushes the right buttons, he can entice a woman willingly into things she has never before conceived of or considered doing. That is the sensual turn-on that gives a man the feeling of power without violence, and it is much sweeter than the masochism some men rely on for their kicks.

One conjecture about my medically-altered erection is that the foreskin that bunches up along the shaft of my penis may possibly stimulate a woman's clitoris and the lip of her labia, giving her more pleasure. I am not sure of this; it may be the subject for a little more scientific experimentation. No, just kidding, I did all the clinical research one man needs in a lifetime during the 15 years I followed my dick around the world.

I was never the obvious favorite flavor of the day. I usually had to invest some hard work for my love life, yet eventually it became clear that once I bedded a woman, there was a good chance she would come back for more. It had nothing to do with my "technique;" it had everything to do with my emotions.

I have always laughed at men who boasted that they were "good lovers." I know enough about sex to know that you can be technically excellent with one lover and then hit the bottom of the scale with the next.

Capts Costas & John and friend.

The author in the Parthenon

I used to live in Greece. I love the Greek culture, and I have a good relationship with most Greek men. The only exception is how Greek men treat women and how they relate to their own sexuality.

I often had Greek men tell me what good lovers Greek men were. After years of this, I began asking those men who said it: 'Yatee sto skefteis? Etthko sue agapo andras Elinas?' Loosely translated from my poor Greek, the question was, 'How do you know this? Have you yourself made love with a Greek man?"

It all comes down to what a woman likes. Each woman has different buttons, and a good lover is one who experiments to find them. Most guys think being a good lover is being hard, fast, and aggressive. Slow, soft, and thoughtful is usually more memorable.

Enthusiasm may put you in the running, but devotion will win the blue ribbon. It's not asking too much to give a woman's body your undivided appreciation when she is giving to you the most wonderful gift that a man can receive, her vagina, the entrance to her soul, her trust in you. Sex is a lot more spiritual to a woman than it is to a man.

Women are often turned on by a man's appearance and then turned off by his performance, but they will never forget even an average looking guy who cares for their breasts, who worships their clitoris, and who takes communion upon the fluids of their body. Well, you get the idea. It ain't the meat. It ain't the motion. It's the emotion that counts.

I don't look at screwing as a skill. I don't take credit for having special abilities. I was just turned on by the female body--the pout of her mouth, the fall of her hair, the turn of her hip. She felt good to me. I just liked to screw.

But, you know, I know the difference between screwing and making love; and making love is a skill based on emotions.

If a man's penis is more sensitive, as I believe mine is, he will enjoy the act of making love more and not rush to orgasm. When I masturbate, orgasm is the objective; when I make love with a woman, making love is the objective.

Because my enjoyment is based largely on the enjoyment of my partner, I'm primarily interested in their happiness. This is also my outlook on life in general.

If everyone around you is happy, then your life will be happier, safer and more enjoyable as well. Next time you consider cheating, hurting or stealing from someone, think about the alternative…peace, a world of no conflict, a place where we are all safe.

Consider turning 180 degrees around into good and doing everything for all lives instead of just your own selfish self. Life could be positive permanently if we all turned around, all at once and started doing the right things. This may seem hippie dippy, simplistic and irrational, but it is doable, and it is the right move for mankind. If you don't want to do this, then fuck you; you are an asshole!

*"Reducing a subject to one simple emotional response may seem simplistic. But the truth is that most problems in our world have one cause, selfishness, and one simple solution, The Golden Rule, To 'do unto others as you would have others to do unto you,' will give us all peace, love and prosperity! The most complex part of this solution is to get people to realize that it is the best for themselves, and then to give them the guts to live by it, even though others may not follow the same rule of The Golden Rule."*
Dudley Griffin, 4.4.06

*Capt. Costas and Capt. John fishing for fish and girls.*

Mankind is the only animal that has the potential of improving on God's scientific creations! Man is also the only creature with the ability to screw-up God's plan! We mostly screw it up!

What is right and what is wrong? Let's look at it from God's perspective. God or Mother Nature, take your pick, created all this. Whether she did it in 6 days or 150 million years is immaterial; he/she put a lot of time and energy into the process.

There must be some plan, don't you think? Even if the plan is no plan.

Did God know that mankind would want to stand up? Did the creator under-engineer the human body or misdesign and misconstruct the human back and knee, so that doctors now have to rebuild the knees and backs of humans?

I have considered for some time that maybe God (or Mother Nature) screwed up on the construction of man's penis. But then I realized that when man first appeared he was nude, and would continue to be nude for hundreds of thousands of years. Man needed a covering for his penis. Man survived, evolved, started wearing clothes, and didn't need a covering for his penis any more. In fact, foreskin, at times, has been a hindrance to satisfactory, satisfying sex.

Back before clothes, a man and woman didn't have time for slow, luxurious sex. They had only a few moments before the half-ton grizzly attacked. There was also nothing called marriage back then, no reason to satisfy your mate, because, after all, it was just an instinctual mating, an urge, which unbeknownst to humans was actually God-given, to ensure the species continued. Then humans started having these questions like, "Where do children come from?" or "What is life all about?" or "Should sex be enjoyment or entertainment?"

Along comes man, with his ego, which no other creature has, and his own plan, which no other creature dares to have, at least on our scale! So how do we determine which of our schemes is right, which fits into God's plan?

Well, "She" created all these trees, bugs, fish, plants, other animals and other people. There must be some reason for their existence! At least God thought so! So who are we to contradict Mother Nature's plan?

I believe that, when doing something on or to this earth and its creatures, we should treat life, all life, as sacred! Being democratic in our treatment of all creatures and other people is God's way.

Selfishness, if you are hungry, is acceptable. Selfishness for a bigger house, car, or bank account is against the laws of God and Nature.

My circumcision was definitely an example of messing with

Mother Nature. OK, what does it accomplish? Who does it affect? Does it affect them positively or negatively? Will the world care, and should it care?

Well, if my physiological assumptions are correct, I can prove the point, and if pressured to do so I could produce more "scientific" evidence, athe world would care to see. This could be one of the true breakthroughs of which mankind is capable.

What does it mean, just more sexual enjoyment for men? Well, if that were all it meant, I wouldn't give a damn!

I think it is a simple medical procedure that is capable of changing many men's attitude toward the orgasm, and that could change male and female relations in a positive way.

I think it is possible that this simple procedure could give men a better attitude toward women. And, in turn, it could give women a better attitude toward men. It could solve much of the sexual frustration in this world, thus stopping arrogance, selfishness, unnecessary competition and wars!

SNIP, just that simple.

So now you think I'm out of my mind!? They told Ben & Jerry that Cherries Garcia wouldn't fly. The first person who got up off the cave floor to sit on a log was considered crazy. New ideas are always crazy until some accountant type figures out he can make a buck on one of them.

Who can benefit from the Bassett Cut? Newborn boys, of course. Uncircumcised men of all ages. Young boys who are circumcised who have not lost sensation in their penis head can be reconstructed to give them a better sex life later in life. "The Bassett Reconstruction!"

Sorry, even with major reconstructive surgery, older men already circumcised who have lost sensation in the head of their penis may not be able to benefit.

Circumcision, other than for reasons of adherence to ancient rabbinical law, is performed primarily for cleanliness in the present day. An uncircumcised penis can harbor STD cultures unwanted in our lives. But the loss of a foreskin can also mean the loss of sensitivity, and therefore the lost of intimacy.

With just the membrane clipped, the foreskin is easily pulled back so that the smegma that collects there can easily be washed away. Yet it can still function as the protector of sensitivity.

Then, of course, with the smegma gone, some concerns about AIDS, yeast infections, and cancer in women may be resolved as well.

Win, win, win, whoopee! All humor aside, this is something that warrants close scientific consideration.

Recently, a friend approached me in confidence about a problem his son was having. This friend did not know about my unique circumcision. He just thought I might have heard of some solution to the situation.

During the 1970s and '80s a lot of people having children went for a kinder, gentler birth. No major drugs, and no circumcision. My friend's son was born within those sensibilities.

My friend's son was not circumcised and had recently, apparently during vigorous intercourse, experienced a tearing of that very membrane that was cut on me.

The doctors wanted to sew the boy's membrane back up. My friend wanted to know what I thought. I suggested that they let it heal the way it was--torn.

Let's do what we can to promote vigorous sex.

Enough about penises!


CHAPTER 44

# The Longest Chapter In The History of Writing

Women love, and men work to love.


CHAPTER 45

# Dance As If No One Is Watching

*"I would often take off my hat and show that I was bald before I walked up to seduce her."* DG

Back in the 1980s I used to tell myself, "Dance as if you're invisible!" It was part of my anti-ego mantra. I have been evolving from a macho asshole toward a good man for a long time. We sometimes forget our path, and so I would recite this to myself whenever I caught myself doing an ego trip on the dance floor.

Live as if you are pleasing yourself, not as if you are impressing others.

With that attitude you will have a good life, and I am sure you will hurt fewer people than if you did otherwise.

CHAPTER 46

# Cool

Definition: *From The Hippie Dictionary,* by John McCleary,

*Cool: Self-confident, mellow, appropriate, acceptable. The use and misuse of this word are important indications of how cool one really is or isn't. The ultimate use of cool is to describe someone who has charisma. The exact meaning of cool is defined by social values. During the hippie era, cool had one set of parameters, and today cool has other defining rules. Yet, even within any given era, there are alternative definitions of cool, depending upon the different subcultures or areas of the world. It's impossible to define what cool is to everyone, but a simple explanation is, "appropriate activity within existing social circumstances." To be quite frank, this whole definition is not cool.*

To be cool you have to "not be cool!" Real cool has a rebellious nature. If you think you are cool, you are not. You cannot make it, and you cannot fake it.

Back in the fifties, guys had a hand move that spoke of our coolness. But few could really pull it off, and most didn't even try. You snapped the fingers of your right hand then your left hand, then hit the top or your right fist with your open left hand.

Tick, tick, boom was the sound. If you were cool you could do it to fit any situation and everyone looked at you and you were truly cool!?

CHAPTER 47

# It's Not Quite Love, But It Feels Good Anyway

*Unlike women, men seldom experience the emotion of
unconditional love.
It always seems to have some price attached to it.
Guys are usually in the process of devising some way
to win some woman's affection. Girls are usually in the process of
devising some way to attract some man's attention. And because of
these, they both come with expectations and requirements.*
JOB

*"I think everything I suppose or guess in this chapter
and this book, about how or what women think, is correct, but I am
a man and I think as a man, not a woman. But, my suppositions are
based on many years and experiences with women, and that is what
I stand on as my knowledge."*
JBMc

I'm a guy. All the peace, ideals and spirituality of the hippie era aside, it was the free love that first got me interested in the counterculture.

Don't start throwing things at me! I marched, I supported the causes, I loved my neighbor--even that redneck down the block. I became a better person during that time. I am a better person today because of what I experienced then. I am more tolerant, understanding and sensitive because of the hippie era. But I'm still a guy down inside, and during that time I was a young guy, and I sure did love to make love. And I didn't always ask their age.

Today, with the sensitivities toward molestation and sexual harassment, what I'm about to tell you might just get you all worked up. But before you go any further in this book, you must promise me you will acknowledge that what happened 50 years ago should be judged by the standards and moraies of 50 years ago. That is all I ask.

During the 1960s and 70s young men in their 20s and 30s were regularly sleeping with girls as young as 15 and 16 years old. These men didn't consciously go looking for girls that young, but at that time men were not very discriminating. And the laws were much more lax then. If your sister or your grandmother showed any interest in a hippie guy, he wouldn't spoil the moment by asking her age.

Before you label us all perverts and degenerates, I must remind you of the cultural time. 1964-1967! Pandora's Box had just been opened. We were all guinea pigs in the social lab.

Most of us dudes were safe. I and the other guys I knew never forced or pressured a girl into having sex with us. The girls we met wanted to make love. They all knew what they were doing, and they often made the first moves themselves.

I personally don't think that a 14-year-old girl is old enough to be a consenting adult. I know that I never crossed that barrier.

Many of the girls had already had numerous sex partners. They were sampling the gene pool and we were contributing samples. You do realize the double meaning in this!? And I also hope you understand the sociological purity of it.

Adolescents at this point in history were all being treated by their parents in the same way, treated as children and not as soon-to-be-adults. But the movement of human society is often faster than the parents can keep up with.

We were a large national and international group of guys and girls. We guys didn't necessarily know each other, and the girls didn't know one another either. However, we had seen the same movies, heard the same music and read the same books. It worked as most peer pressure does, all of us guys were acting in the same way, and the girls were acting as girls of that time.

Men historically are randy and over-sexed for a good portion of their lives. I just happened to be at the right age at the right time in history. The hippie era was a godsend to the horny guys who lived through it.

I was a little older than many of the other hippies, being 24 in 1967, the Summer of Love. But that also meant that I was more experienced, and maybe a little more subtle. What I mean by this is that I didn't make as many mistakes in judgment.

Sexual harassment is harassment only if the attraction is not mutual. Often, the difference between being accepted as a sexual partner or being labeled as a pervert is timing and experience in reading the signs. You don't have to be drop-dead handsome, rich or well-dressed; you just have to have a little taste and intelligence. That is, unless the object of your affection has more taste and intelligence than you do.

There are times when you just have to say to yourself, "This girl has someone or something else on her mind." Not that I always followed that wisdom. I did have some maturing to do, and because of this I was rejected on more than a few occasions; graphically at times. Have you ever heard the phrase "Go stick it in the wall!"?

Yet I think I can say with impunity, and every single woman I was with will agree, it was consensual copulation. I will admit, some of my lovers were indeed not single, and that may raise a dark cloud over our bliss, yet...! And some of them may have had second thoughts the next morning for other reasons, but at the time, it was always consensual.

I will also tell you that I never used alcohol or drugs to put a woman in a physical state where she didn't know what she was doing or wasn't able to control the outcome. I also did not use my camera to get a girl to take off her clothing and into a compromising position as some guys did.

I don't fault some photographers for using their cameras as a tool of seduction, but I never did. It was a point of pride and professionalism with me.

I know some girls would let down their barriers once they were in the nude, and one of the most prevalent seductions among guys with cameras was to flatter a girl by being interested in photographing her "beautiful" body.

As a lot of guys did, I offered to give massages and introduce women to the hot tub, but most girls knew that was a seduction, and they were often looking for an excuse to let down their barriers anyway.

I won't say that I didn't take advantage of my experience in romancing a few of these women into having sex, but there was never any subterfuge, violence or restraint. As far as the youthfulness of some of my partners, that is another thing.

Hippie chicks were running around the country looking for adventure. Often, they were running from something--a repressive family, misunderstanding, mistreatment or even molestation. The guys out there who took advantage of this often provided a better family environment than what the girls left behind.

Girls knew what they were doing. I, for one, didn't look at their birth certificates; I looked into their eyes. "We cats were just spreading the love around anyway, man!"

You had to have been there to understand the purity of the intent. I actually felt that I was sharing love. You will never hear me say that I made love "to" someone; I will always say, "I made love with her."

The sky and the sidewalk were the same dirty gray, and the wind was damp and cold. I had spent the night at a friend's house in Sacramento, California. My destination was New York City, Highway 80, the cement pathway leading me there.

Hitchhiking was not forced upon us by lack of money or other resources; it was a chosen means of transportation during those times. I looked upon hitching as an opportunity to grow and to learn. I would stick out my thumb, take a deep breath, smile and think of all the adventures I was going to have and the people I was bound to meet.

Hitchhiking was a science to me. First, you had to have the right attitude. A smile on your face always helped get rides. That was no problem. I was glad to be there, and I knew someone nice would pick me up. I always thought good thoughts, and didn't have a cloud over my head that people could see or feel.

A hitchhiker also needed to understand the problems drivers would have in deciding whether to pick them up. Drivers had to have time to see you and check you out, so you stood somewhere in clear view of oncoming traffic. It was essential that it be lighted if it were at night.

Drivers had to have somewhere safe to pull off the road. You didn't want to lose your ride to a tow truck.

If a freeway was your only road, you needed to know the laws of each state on your route. In California and many states, it was illegal to hitch on a freeway, so you always stood as close to the top of an onramp as you legally could in order to be seen by cars already on the freeway. Often, they would stop.

She was all the way on the freeway, down from the onramp maybe 100 feet. Illegal, but sometimes, if you've been waiting a long time, you will take that chance.

She was wearing a white T-shirt and Levi's and carried a medium-sized grocery bag. A local, I thought, trying to get a of couple miles down the road. It was too cold for the T-shirt and threatening to rain--hell, maybe even snow.

Somehow she came over to me and we began to talk. Maybe she needed a light for her cigarette, or maybe she asked if we could hitch together. I can't remember the progression of the conversation. It was over 45 years ago.

Slowly, I learned that she was leaving home and going to live with her aunt, her sister, or someone like that. In Alabama, for God's sake!

She looked cold. I gave her my coat. We continued to stand there hitching. Brenda was her name.

She looked young, maybe 16 or 15. And somehow it was obvious that her short life had not been good to her. "Sure, we'll hitch together, maybe as far as Chicago," I said. I began feeling protective.

Her bag contained a few packs of cigarettes, some socks, underwear and feminine napkins.

What could I do? I had a daughter. I would look after her.

It started to rain. Fortunately, soon after, a car stopped. I can't remember the driver.

As we started up, we came upon another hitchhiker. He was further up ahead, and actually on the freeway as I recall. The driver was nice enough to stop for him too. I don't remember the hitcher's name. I have at least one photograph of him. He was slightly overweight, slightly awkward, but a very nice young man.

The ride ended in Sparks, Nevada. It was snowing by then. It would snow all the way to Syracuse, New York.

I think we got another ride or two, the three of us together. It began to get dark. What the hell did we think we were doing or going? That part of Nevada was nothing, going no place. It was my first trip through, and I didn't know the country. And I hadn't seen the skeletons.

This was all very common during that period of time. Casting your fate to the wind was the education, the Phi Beta Kappa of life.

A ride literally let us off in the middle of nowhere. The freeway had an overpass over a country road, and the driver took that road off into nothingness. It got darker and colder, and the snow was falling.

We stood and hitched and froze for awhile, and then started discussing the prospects of sleeping under the overpass for the night. Just before we gave up and crawled under the freeway, a Volkswagen bus, thank the Lord, stopped for us.

That young hippie couple may have saved our lives; they surely saved us from a miserable night. The couple's plan was to go on down toward Winnemucca, Nevada, and pull off into a gas station or motel parking lot for the night. We three hitchers discussed the options and decided to rent a cheap motel room.

I can't remember the financial arrangements. I know the girl had little or no money, and I had a budgeted amount. Motel rooms weren't normally within such a budget, but this was an extreme situation. We couldn't all sleep in the van.

I can't remember the sleeping arrangements exactly. I think the other hitcher slept on the floor in his bag, and Brenda and I slept in the double bed. We made love, of course. It was the natural thing to do.

I call it love, I always called it love, because I am, above all, a romantic. But, often to call sex, love is a disservice to both words. I always tried to be sincere in my lovemaking, but sometimes it is just copulating, fucking or, even less, balling.

This was one of the strangest couplings to which I have ever been a party . She made it obvious that she wanted me to make love to her, and yet during the act she showed no emotions, nor did she seem to experience any pleasure.

By that time in my experience with lovemaking, I knew enough not to be personally offended. But, at that time, I was not yet experienced enough to know all the possible buttons to push. I just may not have found her erogenous zone, but I doubt it.

Years later, I had an affair in Greece with a Greek girl. That alone was very unique since Greek girls usually marry as virgins, and most often they marry Greeks. That Greek girl had the same inattentive "style" of lovemaking, and, even though I tried every button known to man over a period of months, she never did respond.

It took me years after the Greek girl to come to the conclusion that both of these girls had probably been ignored by their families and then possibly molested by a friend or family member. They were looking for affection, they were not afraid of sex, but at the same time they were too ashamed of the sexual act to be able to respond with affection or enthusiasm. The hippie couple drove us perhaps as far as Utah and let us off. Somewhere shortly after we were picked up by a young man who lived in Salt Lake City. It must have been slow going because that was as far as we got that next night.

The young man who picked us up must have been from an old Mormon family because the place he gave us to stay that night was an old log cabin, somewhere, it seemed, on a hill right in the middle of the city. I slept with Brenda in my sleeping bag on the floor. We screwed again, of course.

Later in my life, after my first marriage, a few relationships, and a number of one-night stands, I learned that my pleasure was in direct relationship to the enjoyment of my partner. Since then I always tried to please the one I was with. I, at times, made it my crusade.

Yet, as I already stated, I was, at the time of this encounter with Brenda, still in my own sexual adolescence. I tried to open her up, for her sake and not just my own, because I knew instinctively that it was not a good thing to go through life with sexual repressions and hang-ups. By the second night, I realized how young she was and that she had some deep problems. I also think I began to realize that her relationship with me might not be the healthiest situation.

The next day we three hitchhikers traveled on toward Wyoming in the snow on Highway 80. It took us a number of rides to get out of town and down the road a way, and near the border another car stopped and picked us up. It was a nondescript, four-door Detroit model. The driver was a nondescript young man. As I recall, he was very nice in a naive sort of way. He had driven all the way from L.A., and he was tired and needed someone to drive for him. He was going all the way to upstate New York.

Hitchhiking, beyond the obvious advantage of cheap transportation and social discourse, provided a number of other opportunities. You were continually introduced to cool, new music, you could acquaint yourself with the fancy appointments and technology of various modern automotive interiors, and sample new drugs.

For me, just about the only disadvantage to hitchhiking was the fact that I preferred to drive myself rather than place my life in the hands of a perfect stranger. I was, and still am, a very opinionated driver. I love to drive. I was born to drive. I learned how to drive a WWll Jeep on cattle ranch hills at 12 years old, and forklifts, trucks and fast cars in LA at fifteen. I consider myself one of the world's best drivers. I have already admitted previously that I am opinionated, not egotistical, but opinionated!

To me, hitchhiking, stepping into someone else's environment with all their goodies, stories and vibrations, and then being asked to drive on top of all that is the ultimate. "Yeah, let's go," I said. Besides, the driver had a whole bottle of cross top speed pills, and he was willing to buy the beer.

I ended up driving, single-highhandedly, all the way to Syracuse, New York. Single-handedly in this context means that I was the only driver, and that my other hand was occupied otherwise holding a can of beer. Contrary to the dangers that might be apparent in this combination, at that time I believed that long road trips were best accompanied by beer and speed. I knew how to abuse my drugs to good purpose.

Off we went to New York, but we had a few stops in store for us along the way. Not long after he picked us up, the owner of the car needed some food and coffee, so we pulled into a restaurant just off the road near Ogden, Utah. This stop provided me with one of my first and most graphic experiences with prejudice directed at me personally. And it also taught me a good lesson in my own prejudices.

Truckers, cowboys, local businessmen and traveling salesmen looked up from the sticky Formica as we entered the restaurant door. To them, we four travelers were from outer space. To us, the other patrons were from under some rock.

I believe that one of the reasons the counterculture groomed and dressed the way we did, consciously or subconsciously, was an effort to confront straight society. Yes, we were rejecting their value system by wearing old clothes and long hair. And, yes, we were also sometimes just showing off our creative self-expression.

But, I believe, maybe subconsciously, we were also trying to create rejection in order to feel a brotherhood with other races and people who were discriminated against. To some of you this sounds hippie crazy, bleeding heart, blah, blah, but this is mankind's most damaging struggle.

For one race of people to designate themselves as the most important people on earth is stupid in the historic world experience. History will show, if you are willing to listen, that someday the oppressors become the slaves. The only way out was to play nice with the others on the playground.

We hippies also at times tried to elicit negative responses from the establishment just to prove how ignorant they were. Exposing the intolerance to be found in supposedly "God-fearing" Christian people was empowering, yet it was also disillusioning.

That moment in that roadside restaurant was memorable in a sad, yet illuminating, sort of way. As the strange quartet entered, all heads turned to observe this invasion upon their normal, blissfully ignorant existence. It may have also served as entertainment for them.

The car owner was a rumpled, yet well-dressed young Southern Californian. To some observers, he may have appeared to be homosexual. The other male hitchhiker was, like myself, a long-haired, bearded young man in Levi's, boots, strange shirt, threadbare, comfortable coat and some sort of sloppy hat.

I, myself, always wore a red bandanna around my neck, and I had that tight Levi's with-a-bulge look that prompted fathers to hide their daughters. And the girl, with her white T-shirt, no bra, and tight designer jeans, had "runaway" written all over her. She was one of those girls who caused God-fearing, married men discomfort because they wanted her, and because they also knew she was the same age as their own daughters.

As we slipped into our booth, the murmurs reached us. These travelers were not their kind, whoever they were. "Hair," "tits," "fags," and "commies" were the words that we picked out of the colloquial accented cacophony of disjointed conversations.

The atmosphere was strained, electric with fear and hate. We ordered our food and ate within a fog of mistrust.

The young waitress was leaning toward going down the road with us, while her father and everyone else in the place were wishing that lynching were still a popular sport. And then something happened to me. I began to see through the fear and hate, and glimpsed humanity in a clear light, possibly for the first time in my life.

Somehow, by the time we left that restaurant, a new realization flowed through me. As I listened to those peoples' ignorance and distrust, I saw how alike we actually were. I realized that I too was thinking the same sorts of things of them as they were thinking of me. Up until that moment, I had lived in the protected bubble of tolerant, liberal California.

These people were as fearful and mistrusting of me as I was of them. In their backwater of the world, they were cut off from the mainstream of change that was percolating around them in the rest of the world, yet they were still cut from the same cloth as I, a person who came from rebellion, revolution and change.

Something made me look at the people in that restaurant with a sympathetic eye, and what I saw was all of humanity rolled up inside a redneck from Utah. What I realized was that we all had the same tendencies, the same hopes, the same fears, the same expectations.

Part of what started my thinking down that path was sitting in the booth with the three people I came in with. In retrospect, we were also as different from one another as we could be, and yet we had been thrown together by circumstance and now had become temporary friends.

The driver and I had very little in common at that time in our lives. We were about the same age, but the driver was a businessman of some kind. I had been a businessman, but had dropped out. The one thing I did remember about him was that he seemed naive, almost as if he were just an observer. I was well past his naive period. I was now a doer. I was still learning, but I was learning through doing.

The young male hitchhiker was a student of a different kind. He was a college student. I had never liked the organized forms of education. I had only recently become a reader. This scholastic young man was a different kind of person from me. He would be considered a nerd today. I liked him, but we were on different paths.

The teenage runaway was someone with whom I would never have had any contact under any other circumstances except those exact events. She was an "Okie" child from the Central Valley of California. I was a "sophisticated" hippie from the Coast of California.

The four of us were thrown together in a coffee shop in the sticks of America, and thus found ourselves in the company of those truckers, cowboys and traveling farm equipment salesmen. We were all as different as humans of the same country could be, and yet, down inside, I saw that we were all the same. A little scared, defensive and yet curious, maybe somewhat envious.

That was one of the values of the 1960s and 70s. People got out of their inherited worlds, they traveled and met people unlike themselves, and they found that those people were really very much like themselves.

The more you travel, the more you realize that there is no such thing as a "normal" person or a "normal" family. That is found only on 1950s TV. In real life everyone is different. What is similar about people are their emotions and their natural desires.

Joyce Johnson wrote in *Minor Characters*, her book about Kerouac and the beat generation, "Normalcy in fact might be an artificial idea." Given the diversity of human thoughts and actions, I would have to say that she is stone right on.

Changing is man's strongest evolutionary weapon. It is a hedge against extinction. To be normal is to stagnate and to die. Of all the cups of coffee I have had in my life, that one in a greasy spoon on the border of Utah and Wyoming was the most memorable. We left without an incident, but with many lingering images.

Soon after we four vagabonds got back on the highway, a roadblock abruptly halted our progress. The state troopers manning it told to us that the snowstorm had closed the road, and we would have to spend the night in Evanston, Wyoming.

Off the road in Evanston, in another roadside coffee shop, we were told that several churches had opened their doors to stranded travelers for the night or until the road was cleared. We were given directions to a church.

As soon as we arrived, I recognized that everyone who had been directed to this particular church was young or looked like us--

students, hippies and radicals. Apparently, the more straight travelers were sent to other locations. All of the people at this church were freaks, kids and vagabonds. There were no families of four in station wagons.

All of the church doors were unlocked, the lights and heat were on, and the kitchen and refrigerator were stocked with essentials. We were given no instructions or restrictions, and we saw no one associated with the church or any authority figure during our stay.

We had ourselves a party. Some of the travelers had demon alcohol with them, and a sufficient supply of the devil's weed was rustled up. Guitars were unpacked, and songs were sung and played. I vividly remember a large jar of sunflower seeds and participating in a seed-eating contest and possibly a seed-spitting competition.

Soon after we arrived, I saw a young man who appeared to be attracted to "my" young runaway. I asked him where he was heading. "Into the Southern states, sir," he said politely with an appropriate accent. The die was cast. He was a well-brought-up, young gentleman, and he was heading south toward where Brenda was going.

I was concerned about the relationship between Brenda and myself. I had already broken the "Mann Act" twice and realized that I would have to do so again five or six more times before I got Brenda to her sister.

I did what any proper guardian would do when handing over a young lady to her new escort. I organized a wedding. One traveler could play the organ. Someone was a mail-order minister. I would sit in for her father and give her away.

After the most hilarious and irreverent wedding ceremony ever conducted, the happy couple was led to the only private room available to consummate their union. It may sound insensitive and definitely politically incorrect by today's standards, yet at that time in history and under the circumstances, this was the right thing to do. It was also a real hoot, a charade enjoyed by all.

I have thought about that girl many times since then. Did the couple live happily ever after? Did she ever experience an orgasm? Did her father track her down? Was there an all-points bulletin out for my arrest?

Before dawn, I awakened the other hitchhiker and the car owner, and we snuck out of the church. I didn't want to find that Brenda had changed her mind, or that the Southern gentleman had reconsidered. My friends and I drove to the roadblock. At dawn, the state police opened the road. I downed a cross-top or two with a paper cup of coffee, and we headed off toward the East Coast. The rest of the story is another story.

Girl reading in bed, NYC loft

CHAPTER 48

# Sex And Capitalism

If you're here only for the sex, I would suggest that you slide on by this chapter and go directly to Chapter 138 or 145. I can't remember; I'll tell you later. But if you are here to learn to have better sex and become a better lover, you might just read on.

> *"We got some nice girls here, they're looking at us,*
> *let's do somethin' 'bout it"*
> ZZ Top

In order for a man to have a healthy and rational sexual personality and behavior, he must have a respect for women, or for whomever is his interest. He must have had a reasonable number of successful and mutually satisfying sexual relationships. Sex is like going to the grocery store. You must know what you want, where you can find it, and you shouldn't be too hungry when shopping.

When writing a book of this type, you begin to wonder what is really important to write down and say. I can write anything, but to say something I must think about it.

One of the most damaging elements of our society today is the widespread sublimation of money for good, clean sex. Our advertising industry has fooled us into thinking that possessions are signs of sexual prowess and that the ability to buy them shows virility.

This misinformation, ironically, has led to rampant consumerism, a very destructive trend that has very little to do with sex directly, yet affects our sexuality. The greedy acquisition of shiny gadgets, flashy clothes and expensive stuff for the purpose of enhancing our sex appeal is driving mankind to excessive work hours, thus destroying health and, in the end, breaking up the family unit, which is what we are working to support in the first place.

Economic pressures are extremely damaging to a person's psyche and self-image. Insecurity created by financial pressures makes a person jealous of others whom they think have what they, themselves, don't possess. Jealousy is one of the most dangerous and destructive personality traits of mankind.

Jealousy creates extreme competition, especially among men. The need to appear virile and sexually strong causes men to be excessively greedy. Thus, jealousy breeds selfishness. Some men's insecurity drips off of them like venom, and it poisons everyone around them.

Insecurity, jealousy and selfishness are the same ugly wart on mankind. Where you find one, you usually find the others. These emotions are found in both sex and commerce, and they produce much the same result in either activity. Selfishness in love manifests itself in violence. Selfishness in business manifests itself in capitalism.

Capitalists make money on the money they invest. A capitalist does not work to make money; he works to protect his investments. The nature of capitalism is dehumanizing in that the investor is not involved in healthy, normal human work and accomplishments. He is concerned merely with the numbers on the bottom line.

This dehumanizing causes the capitalist to become insensitive to the struggles of other human individuals who bleed, sweat and suffer in the production of his profits. Just as power corrupts, capitalism eventually causes a person to place the accumulation of profits above all moral and civil laws of humankind. It also causes a dulling of other human emotions, such as love. And sex without love is just a business deal, an exchange of bodily fluids for an economic value.

Strangely enough, sexual repression is like capitalism. The sexually repressed want to control all sexuality; they want to control the market. They do not really want to abolish it because they benefit from it themselves, yet they want sex to be performed in the same limited manner in which they do it.

Just as a capitalist does not really believe in free enterprise, but prefers a monopoly instead, a sexually repressed person is jealous of the freedoms of others and wants to control their sexuality.

Their religious or social group has taught these people that sex is a sin, and although they may have been coerced into acting ashamed of sex, they are still compelled by Mother Nature to perform sexually. This dilemma often causes these individuals to construct all kinds of perversions and deviations in their own sex lives.

It would be OK if they just conducted their own kind of sex with other consenting adults in the privacy of their own space. But they often step out into society and want to change the sexuality of others.

What these people do is to try to force their prohibitions on everyone else. I believe the reason for this is that they are jealous of the freedoms of others. Fundamentalists think, "Well, if I'm not allowed to do these things (which I enjoy), then no one else should be allowed to do them."

The odd twist to what I have just said is that I am interchanging sexual perversions with sexual prohibitions. I am actually giving them both the same value and importance.

The prohibitions produce the perversions. And although perversions may seem unnatural to some people, there is really nothing wrong with a sexual perversion performed with another consenting adult.

It is when someone forces his or her sexual perversion or prohibition on another person that a sin is committed. It is when they are used as weapons that sexual right and wrong become bad for society.

I have had some problems with other people's sexual perversions. With all the sex I have had in my lifetime, you might think that I would be all right with perversions. Not so!

There is sex and then there is sick sex. Violent sex, dominating sex, sex with unconsenting minors is wrong. (I am pretty sure that no girl under the age of 15 is really consenting, but the age of a minor is different in different societies and at different times.)

Selfish sex is almost always a violation of the art and morality of sex. Hypocritical sex is a perversion.

Hypocritical sex is a sin against God, yourself, and the person you are inflicting yourself upon. A sexual hypocrite is someone who ridicules others for what they, themselves, are doing. A sexual hypocrite wants sex, but is ashamed of it. Therefore, he is too ashamed to really enjoy it. A sexual hypocrite fucks someone and then calls them a slut.

A sexual hypocrite is someone who wants it all for themselves and none for others. A sexual hypocrite is someone who has an abortion for their own personal reasons, and then later lobbies for laws so that no one else can have an abortion for their own personal reasons. You have had your abortion when you needed it, but now no one else can have hers.

I am critical of some other peoples' motivation for sex, but this does not make me hypocritical. I think there should be more sex, not less, for everyone, not just myself! But I believe in the spiritual reasons for getting it on. Love of life, love of others, love of joy.

I do not like to watch TV shows and movies that exploit human stupidity: *"Their first sex in the grass, sex with their mother's best friend, first attempt at homosexuality, their last attempt at heterosexuality, their decision to go back to homosexuality, the decision to go back to heterosexuality, the decision to be more selective!"*

Believe me, positive sexual stories will be a hell of a lot more fun and far less destructive. Let the good times roll!

Reality TV is not the right venue for expressing valid sexual emotions. Most people who are honestly living realistic sex lives would not want to be on reality TV, and most people who are on reality TV are not actually living realistic sex lives.

Some TV networks are particularly unhealthy to watch. Fox TV programming emphasizes examples of the worst human conduct, thus they are promoting dangerous, foolish and inappropriate activity. Fox never mentions the morality of conduct they advertise, nor do they warn the watcher. They like to make a joke out such things that are in bad taste. People's Court is people acting badly and getting fifteen minutes of fame for doing it. And what about Fantasy Island. Is it a reality show, a sitcom or a sex-rated and blurred porno film? What are we supposed to get or learn from these kinds of shows?

*Flashback "Hollywood bungalow 1970. My first time making love behind marijuana; Topanga Canyon overlooking Hollywood. The hippie chick, her pot, her body, her kitten playing on my ass with its sharp claws as I balled her on the vivid Indian bedspread."*
Dudley Griffin, 3.7.77

Sex is bad only if it destroys something or someone. Sex usually brings people to life...those who enjoy it and those who are conceived by it. Why would God give us such a strong and positive urge and then not want us to use it? I think it's the devil who has given sex its bad reputation.

At some point during the late 1970s, I reached a place in my sexual life where I wanted to transcend the physical part of fucking. This is not to say that I wanted to become a celibate like Gandhi or Sherlock Holmes.

I had reached a place with sex where the satisfaction of my partner was just as important to me as my own pleasure. Selfish reason if you wish, it is better sex when both feel the earth shake. I still wanted the physical lovemaking, yet I wanted to find some way to incorporate the nasty bits with a religious experience.

It was in this period of time I began to feel a spiritual uplifting in the presence of these mysterious, charming, creatures called women. I wasn't looking anymore for the virgin, slut or saint in a woman. I was looking for the average woman, the real creature. I looked no more for everywoman.

At first, this quest may have been a way to deniability. No "real" man wants a woman to think he was humping her just for her body. "It had to have some cosmic reason."

I have since realized that at the moment of sexual ecstasy, everyone subconsciously knows it is a spiritual experience, so I have written a lot about it in this book.

Who of all authors has not wanted to write the true love story, pen the most poetic jewel, or answer the questions of religion?

I foolheartedly am determined to explain sex to an animal who should already know about it...to explain sex to an animal who has too much "knowledge" to allow themselves to accept anything but the truth. And yet we are still getting it wrong.

Explaining sex is a chore less likely to succeed than trying to compile the perfect grocery list or predict how long your deodorant will last, yet I must try!

I may be wrong about other human beings. I may live in my own brain bubble thinking that everyone else knows what is right and wrong, what is good and bad. I know that sex has a sliding scale, depending on your age, your loneliness, your insecurity, but I still think it is more of a spiritual emotion than a physical need. We are humans after all. We were imbued with emotions. Sure, sex is a carnal need, but for God's sake, can't we appreciate the feelings of LOVE it gives us?

CHAPTER 49

# The Closing

I hate to do it, but I must use this one business term in relation to romance because it is contemporary, and it makes the point. **The Closing**...I use because it may be the only way to get their attention, so that some men will learn to be good and successful lovers. And, it is my intention that everyone should be successful in love, for how else will the world have harmony?

To close a "seduction" you must be obvious about your intent; you must be serious about what you want, but not violent. Don't
be tentative, but don't be demanding. Don't be giddy or too stoic.
Be warm and fuzzy cool! Above all, let the girl know that she has a
choice; it is her choice.

Girls, don't give your body to someone who doesn't deserve it,
to someone for whom it is just a game, just a second thought, or who
obviously doesn't respect you as a person with your own ability to
make your own decisions. Women, your sex and affection is one of the
most precious gifts you can give someone. Make it count for something, even if it is just for the moment. You should respect yourself by
giving it to someone who really appreciates that gift.

By the way, my definition of the act of seduction is to convince someone peacefully and emotionally you are worthy of their
most prized possession, their heart. And don't think that is a corny
thing to say, because if every sexual action were sincerely personal,
both men and women would find true love faster and keep true love
longer, perhaps forever, with much greater ease.

Using a question or asking what she wants or needs gives your
"intended" the choice, which is a good thing. Although asking is not a
"macho man's way," if you want to be a real lover, you need to know
what she wants. And to be practical you will be able to close on more
deals if she thinks it is her choice.

Now this, of course, is Business 1A. It is lesson number one
in preliminary salesmanship courses. You hear it in most sales confer-
ences you will attend: "Give them the impression it was their idea."
My codicil is that "you should actually make it their decision." Believe me, the lovemaking will be over the top of what you expect. You
may even soon find yourself happily married.

Unless you already have a history with someone, you should
be patient, less pushy, and say, "Would you like to stay the night (or
make love) with me?" Or you can say, "I would like to (make love)
stay the night with you." Never say, "I want you to stay the night" or,
"I am going to make love to you," unless you are already lovers.

If you don't know the person and you want to start the relationship with some dating time, you need to be a little more aggressive
like, "I would like to take you to dinner. Or, would you come to dinner

with me," Never say, "Would you like to have dinner with me?" The tone of voice and the timing matter too, yet you must communicate in a positive, confident voice and demeanor, not demanding or, on the other end of the emotional scale, not wishy-washy.

Humor is a winner with many women, but it should never be used in a way that gives the impression you are not really serious. A joke dissolves boundaries, but joking with a woman is often used by insecure men to give them an excuse when she refuses.

Be kind and appreciative, or "hit the road, Jack!"

To give yourself another time and chance, you must be philosophical, and if you lose, never allow yourself to appear or to actually be devastated by the failure.

Of course, the best closing is achieved only if you know exactly what she wants you to do. But that takes the sixth sense. Do you have a sixth sense? I once had it for a time.

Trying to teach the sixth sense of sex is ridiculous to suggest, since it is almost impossible to explain. But alas, I still continue to try!

CHAPTER 50

# Childhood Crises, Adolescent Crises, Seven-Year Itch Crises, Midlife Crises, And Old Age Crises

*"Be assured that all the crises and turning points in our life have something to do with sex!"*
Dudley Griffin 9/10/13

Whether we know it or not, there are going to be sexual crises throughout our lives. Not just the small daily ones you might go through, but regularly delivered hormonal crises having to do with our age and state of mind.

If we are not smart enough to recognize them, they can ruin our lives, like the seven-year-old who beats up a girl because he doesn't like her cooties, the presidential candidate who takes a lover during the campaign, or the old guy in the convalescent hospital who can't keep his hands off the nurses.

*When we are young, sex is a necessity.... In midlife, it is a delicacy.and later it is a luxury, or sometimes an obligation.*
D.G.

There is a reason that youth has no respect for the old. It is not personal. It is not just ignorance; it is God's given drive to move on. The young are hormoned into leaving their parents. They are driven by Mother Nature to leave the old behind. For this is how mankind survives, and in time evolves.

CHAPTER 51

# Alcohol As A Tool, Not A Crutch; Drugs As A Solution, Not As An Escape!

Alcohol and drugs are a valuable tool to expand our mind and body. But used as a crutch, they will destroy your mind and body.

It is basically unnatural for human beings to seek out and purposely ingest a substance that will make them stupid! We are intrinsically smarter than that, yet often we forsake all common sense.

Human cultures have used some form of alcohol or drugs to understand or deal with life since the beginning of written history. They have an educational value.

To use alcohol or drugs to escape from responsibilities is an abomination. To use them to stop and think, and look back and look forward in order to change our outcome is truly the human scientific process. We must make mistakes, and realize them as experiments in order to evolve as mankind.

Drinking is not a problem as much as it is an attempt at a solution. 4.26.14

Many drugs are not a problem as much as an attempt to heal, to forget, or to understand. 4.26.14

All stimulants and all drugs are valuable if used by rational human beings. They are tools to help us evolve.

CHAPTER 52

# Sex Will Not Be Denied

We met on the beach at Carmel, the three girls and I. Two sisters and a schoolmate. The youngest sister and I showed signs of sexual tension from the start.

The day was one of those glorious, sun confectioned affairs, with milk white seagulls, whipped cream surf and chocolate-coated girls. We flirted on the sand dunes, collected driftwood and I carved faces on seaweed bulbs for the girls to take home to remind them of me. The seaweed would eventually dry up and begin to smell bad; they would remember me.

The day ended innocently. The girls had to drive back to San Francisco. No kisses were given, but addresses and phone numbers were exchanged.

Several weeks later, I planned a hitchhiking, poster selling, trip to Northern California. I called and made tentative plans to meet at "their" apartment in the city, where I could stay overnight on my way through.

When the evening arrived, I couldn't get through on the phone and a knock on the door produced no response. I suspected that I had been blown off.

The kind of relationship I had had with the girls and the sexual tension was that unique, "catch-me-if-you-can" scenario. I was at least ten years older than the oldest, and they were just stringing me along to see if I could hang in there, push the right buttons and win the prize.

I went on up to Marin, Sonoma and Mendocino Counties in Northern California, selling my posters to book stores and head shops. On the way back south through San Francisco, I thought maybe I would take another whack at it and called the girl.

When I reached someone at the phone number I had, I was handed over to the younger sister. She had to come clean; she didn't live in the City with her sister and the other girl, who attended San Francisco State University. She really lived at home with her parents and went to high school.

We talked, and she said that she would try to stay that night with her sister at the apartment in the City. But after talking to her father, she couldn't get away from home, so if I came up to her parent's house, maybe we could see each other.

See each other! What a pregnant phrase that is. What does it mean?
I knew what it meant to me!

She lived in her daddy's big house on a hill in Millbrae overlooking the San Francisco Bay. It wasn't going to be easy getting there. Hitching on back roads usually meant a lot of walking. Was I confident enough, was I horny enough? Did I have the balls to carry it off?

She was one of those fresh faced, rosy cheeked beauties that you see only in a group of seemingly unattainable high school girls, laughing and telling stories behind your back over in the corner of the coffeehouse. She was still shedding her baby fat, but it was obvious that the large breasts she displayed were going to stay, and the hourglass figure would only get better as soon as she took up T'ai Chi, yoga, tennis, or something like that.

I trudged on up the hill. At her house we were only able to exchange a few words; her father was lurking. I pointed to a little grass covered meadow on a hillock nearby and told her I would sleep there that night and would be waiting for her with a big bottle of red wine if she could get away.

It all seemed so arbitrary, so unlikely. If the stars were in alignment, it would happen. At least the weather was ready for the occasion.

Clear skies, warm almost balmy for the coast of California. As I spread out my sleeping bag on a mattress of freshly bent grass, I began to reach a place of resolution, detachment.

There on those beautiful grass covered rolling hills, between outcroppings of granite and live oak trees, overlooking the deep blue bay, surrounded by twinkling city lights, as the orange sun exploded into the sea, I sat like Buddha.

I had my bottle of wine, I had my sleeping bag, and I didn't really care if that wonderful, soft girl found her way to my lavishly appointed nest. And yet I knew she would.

The moon and city lights cast an aura outlining dark trees, rocks, and canyons in a muted watercolor wash. When she appeared through the background haze, it was as if she were being painted into life by an unseen brush.

She wore a long nightgown that could have passed for a prom dress in that moonglow. She knelt on my bedroll. I offered the bottle, she drank deeply. My tongue tasted the wine on her lips, my fingers slipped up between her legs.

I pulled her gown off over her head and touched every inch of her body. I lay her on my sleeping bag and spread her legs to lie between. I tasted her with my wine splashed tongue.

The moonlight shone off her breasts, firm and proud in the cool light of night. I cupped them in my hands and toyed with each nipple. She rose to meet my tongue; I clung to her breasts and coaxed the blood to her clitoris.

Poised to enter her, I looked down as she lay there on the edge of the mountain in the glow of city lights. I leaned over, kissed her open mouth and fell onto her warm, damp body. Her legs rose up, wrapped around and pulled me in further.

We made love for a long time. Sometime in the middle of the night she put on her gown and tiptoed back into her father's house. I woke satiated and departed for the hitchhike back to Monterey.

At Davenport, the driver who had picked me up down the road, wanted to stop for coffee and pie. As we sat at the counter, both the waitress and the young mail delivery woman flirted unmercifully with me. It was almost as if they could smell the sex and feel the sensual energy coming from my body.

# CHAPTER 53

# **Attitude**

Attitude is your personality created by you for the public. It can be contrived or completely accidental, formed by your upbringing and education.

A self-created attitude usually comes from things and people you have seen that you respect and want to be like.

Can you handle the attitude that you have adopted? If you choose the bad boy image, make sure you can back it up. There is nothing more pathetic, potentially embarrassing, and dangerous to your soul than pretending to be what you are not. Where love is concerned it means a total loss of credibility, and that means you may be a lonely old codger all your life.

Hey, we're not just dealing with philosophy! We're also dealing here with human beings.

Hey, we're not just dealing with human beings here, we're dealing with people too!

An attitude can be your best message as long as it is sincere. If it is fake, it will be you worst mistake.

CHAPTER 54

# Fuck And Bowl

The day that my first wife and I separated for the final time, and she and our daughter drove off south to live in another town, I jumped into the fire. My next few sexual relationships were a good indication of how provocative my life was going to be for the next thirteen years. I was on a new learning curve.

She was hitchhiking in a most unnatural spot. It was actually too natural; in fact, nature was all around. It was the kind of place where a girl alone would not normally be hitchhiking. She would be walking on the rocks and beach, looking at nature's beauty. Instead, this girl was up on the road hitching.

It was Asilomar Beach, a tourist destination at the tip of the Monterey Peninsula. The road isn't really going anywhere. It's just a scenic drive, and there she was hitching.

I remember vividly, I almost didn't stop. "Where is this girl going, probably home to mom and dad?" Maybe, but I stopped anyway, because she was a strikingly attractive redhead. We spent the next few weeks in bed.

She didn't have parents in town, but a brother, who she was staying with on her way somewhere else. Somewhere else and someone else was her goal at that time in her life. She slept around a lot, just like a guy I know quite well.

Julie, I will call her, was my most open relationship. We had no commitment, no rules and no jealousy. She stayed with me when I was available, and she was available but she might be gone for a night or a week with another lover. She was so beautiful, that a man could not resist her requirements, yet I had my own requirements too.

Julie had one major drawback; she was always going off with some guy who was abusive or deranged in some way. I was the safest place she had. I had to go and rescue her several times. Once a weird mountain-man type character got her into his house, stole her clothing and wouldn't let her out for several days. Another time she hooked-up at the beach with several soldiers from a local military base who were physically abusive. How some man could become abusive toward such a beautiful, willing lover as she both puzzled and angered me. They must have been real screwed up kids.

She was young and having fun and couldn't settle on one person. I got one of my very few STDs from her. It was a minor one, but it could have been much worse. So I finally decided to cut her loose, because at the time I was looking for a more stable relationship, not exactly long term, but someone I could count on.

At one point I tried to hook her up with a young friend of mine, who I knew was safe. He was looking for a relationship, he was steady, and his family had money. They looked good together, but Julie was not into anything for the long haul at that time. One day she just left town.

I learned a big lesson through my experiences with Julie. She was not only gorgeous, but almost perfect in body and intellect, from a good family, etc., etc. Had the timing been different for me, I would have gone the distance with her. But with all her good points, she was a train wreck. You can never quite tell a flower by its petals. It just might be a flycatcher.

Several months after my first wife and I separated, I was working helping to build a tourist store in Carmel. At lunch we workers would go out on the street to watch the tourists walk buy. One day I was sitting up in my favorite tree eating my brown bag lunch and a beautiful young girl walked beneath me. I said "Hi," and we got to know each other. We agreed to meet after my work day ended.

I took her to my cottage in Monterey and we made love. Afterwords, I asked her where she was from and she said Fresno. With little knowledge of that town at that time I asked her what she did in Fresno. And she said, "Fuck and Bowl!"

Tillie's 1972

CHAPTER 55

# Tillie Gort's Coffee House: The Center of the Unknown Universe

When I moved back to the Monterey Peninsula in 1972, I immersed myself into the hippie culture. I smoked dope, did psychedelics, had lots of indiscriminate sex, and supported myself in menial, "go-no-where" jobs.

In a community the size of the Peninsula, the jobs available were limited. And appropriate jobs for a person like myself, who, at that time, didn't want anything to get in the way of my decadent life-style, were few and very specific.

There was cooking, waiting tables, carpentry and radio announcing. In all of those occupations I could get a job without a written resume. The hours were flexible, nobody looked over my shoulder and I could leave anytime I wanted without destroying my credibility, whatever that was.

During the hippie era, we worked to live, not lived to work. Sartre suggested this, yet it is as old as primeval tribal cultures.

We enjoyed life, and we enjoyed the company of others who enjoyed it too. We were young, free and self-indulgent.

We hitchhiked when we traveled, we slept where we fell, and didn't worry about next week's food and housing.

Those of you who were not a part of the 1960s and 70s counterculture might think of this kind of day-to-day existence as directionless and irresponsible. But we were doing new things. We were on a quest for knowledge. Our curiosity was boundless; our thirst for the unknown was avarice.

I, for one, was gaining experiences for my chosen occupation. I have always wanted...no, **needed**, to write. I have always been a writer at heart and soul. During this time, I was a writer in training.

I had observed that most writers did a lot of "research" early in their lives before becoming successful at their craft. This "research" most often involved travel, alcohol, drugs, indiscriminate sex and menial jobs. I wholeheartedly jumped into my studies.

One of the first places I went to work upon moving back to the Monterey Peninsula was a little coffeehouse called Tillie Gort's. "Tillie's," as we called it, served vegetarian and carnivore food as well as caffeine, but its soul was that of a coffeehouse.

The coffeehouse culture, which started as the cafe' society of the Left Bank in Paris, evolved during the beat generation of the 1950s in New York City and San Francisco. By the mid-1960s coffeehouses were the gathering places of students and intellectuals in every city that had a college or university or a liberal population.

The value of coffeehouse society to the evolution of mankind has yet to be fully recognized. The coffeehouse has become the place where divergent people with divergent ideas come together to discuss the problems of society. Often, solutions are also discussed and plans hatched to embarrass or piss off the people who created the problems.

Occasionally, coffeehouse ideas and conversations have changed the course of history.

No other casual forum exists for the development of new ideas and emotions. Some may say that the Internet is the coffeehouse of today, but my feeling is that the impersonality of chat rooms and blogs obscures credibility and impedes the natural growth and flow of valid ideas. (Written in early 2000) Too much input from people who want to remain anonymous? If you truly believe in what you say, you will put your real name and face on it!

In The Hippie Dictionary I wrote, *"Media and music were important to the development and spread of counterculture language and knowledge, but few people realize the invaluable contribution that bathroom walls of coffee houses, dance clubs and gas stations played in the proliferation of language and ideas during the 1960s and 70s. The counterculture of that period was very mobile and communicative, traveling for excitement and curiosity. Jokes, political satire and philosophy crisscrossed the United States, moving from public bathroom wall to public bathroom wall, thus helping to spread ideas and language."* (written in the 1990's)

Tillie's 40th Anniversary party photo, 2009
Coffeehouses were an important conduit for new words and concepts. The counterculture of the 1960s and 70s is due in part to these gather-

ing places, and new countercultures are brewing now in coffeehouses as I write this.

The coffeehouse, and particularly Tillie Gort's, was a debating society and a dating service. People traveling through found Tillie's, and many of them stayed for years, some for the duration.

When I first walked into Tillie's, I knew I had found a home. To answer the question before it comes up, as it did hundreds of times while I worked there, the name "Tillie Gort's" was an evolution of the high school nickname of the man who first opened the place. His name was Gil Tortalani, and in school his nickname was Gillie Tort, so "naturally" when he opened the coffee house, he named it Tillie Gort's. I would love to have been there when that name was thought up; it must have been a real stony evening.

You had to have been there in the late 1960's and early 70's to know how comforting, and also stimulating, a good coffee house could be. You could sit there and be yourself alone. Or sit there and be yourself in the company of strangers, soon to be friends. Or friends soon to be lovers. Or you could sit there and be somebody else alone.

The first woman who waited on me at Tillie's later became a girlfriend, and we eventually traveled to Mexico, Guatemala and Europe together. Once, after I became a regular customer, I was served a sandwich with a bite already taken out of it. The waitress said she was just sampling it for me. She, in particular, was just a friend and never an intimate, but that incident shows how familiar the employees and patrons could become. At one time, five of the waitresses working there were or had been my lovers.

Coffeehouses at the time were the gathering places for all the political decadents, folk singers, poetry writers, astrologers, and clitoral masseurs. There was one guy who used to come in and sit by himself with a coffee cup every day for three or four hours. He did that for ten years. He may have read books, I can't remember. He never made eye contact, he never bothered anybody, he never drooled or talked to himself about little green men. He also gave the impression that he wanted to be left alone.

One day in year eleven, out of curiosity, I said something to him. He answered me rationally, we had a conversation. He was a very intelligent person. From then on, we acknowledged each other.

He started coming out of his shell. He struck up conversations with people and even developed friendships.

At Tillie's, customers would leave artwork as tips or offer to tell your fortune for a sandwich. Travelers would sell handmade necklaces on the sidewalk out front, and when they made enough money, would come in for a tuna melt.

If you walked into Tillie's, you could expect to have five or more sets of eyes turn to see who you were. This could be disconcerting to some folks, and sometimes prospective patrons self-consciously exited backwards, thinking they had stumbled into a private club or someone's living room.

Coffeehouses were, for the most part, very much like social clubs. You went there to get out and see and be seen. You could sit at Tillie's for five hours and see all of your friends. When I would come back from a trip of three to six months, as I often did, I would go to Tillie's to get reconnected to what was happening.

Even though there was no effort at exclusivity, there definitely was an in crowd, and some people may have felt left out. But it wasn't hard to join the club. You just needed to show up a few times, and, if you could talk, smile and didn't smell bad, you were in.

Folks played chess, people painted on the paper plates, passing travelers would play guitar and sing for enough tips to buy a salad. There was always a dog or two waiting outside the door and several bicycles.

A favorite story about the beginnings of Tillie's concerns its previous incarnation. It had been a Greyhound bus stop and burger joint. When Gil took it over and converted it into a coffeehouse, he inherited the motorcycle gang that used to hang out there.

Wanting a more intellectual clientele, he approached an experienced coffeehouse owner and asked him what to do. David Walton had previously run Sancho Panza, a memorable coffeehouse in Monterey where Joan Baez and Bob Dylan had sat, drunk coffee and sung. When asked how to change the atmosphere of Tillie's, David told Gil to close the place for a week, put up barn wood on the walls and play only classical music when he reopened. Several days after doing this the bikers stopped coming.

The author as a coffee house cook

I worked as a cook at Tillie's off and on for two or three years. It was never more than subsistence living, but then it was possible to survive on a hundred and fifty dollars a month in the early 1970's.

At Tillie's, in a volatile tradition, the cook and waitress were often dating, if they weren't at each other's throats for other reasons. In one episode a cook threw a knife at a waitress; haphazardly though, for in the groovy hippie era, emotions seldom reached life threatening.

One Sunday it was very slow; Sunday afternoons were usually lazy. No customers for about half an hour, so the waitress and I went in back to make love in the bathroom.

We made it quick, maybe fifteen minutes tops. When we got back out in front, several people were waiting patiently as if nothing was wrong. It was obvious they knew what was going on, but no one would ever make comment. It was normal in those days. That was life; you just waited for the wheel of life to take its course.

A coffeehouse is one of those places where the mood or tempo can change rapidly and often. If you work at a bank or gas station, you know what to expect. When was the last time you were stimulated in an escrow office or enlightened by something while shopping at an auto parts store?

Coffeehouses create situations. Is it the caffeine? Is it the natural brown sugar? Is it the presence of chessboards, or real art on the walls, or newspapers in more than one language? Is it the people who are working there and who want to be there in spite of the fact that it pays starvation wages?

It's a bit of all of these. A coffeehouse is the milieu of spontaneity percolated by caffeine and the social aspects of sitting and drinking a warm, comforting beverage with friends. It is a Petri dish of creativity germinated from a sophisticated and cosmopolitan atmosphere. It is a fermentation of political views gleaned from intellectual expression. It is also a good place to find a boyfriend or girlfriend.

When working in a restaurant and eating most of your meals there, as I did at that time, it was not long before you would get bored with the menu selections, so as all employees did, we started experimenting. These employee experimentations sometimes ended up on the menu.

My contribution was a bagel and grilled ham sandwich that eventually made it onto the menu for several years. It was indeed a strange combination considering orthodox the Jewish religious eating restrictions. As a goy, I secretly, and only to my Jewish friends, called it *The Auschwitz Special.*

The problem of becoming overly familiar with the food available in the kitchen reached a peak one particular night. The waitress and I were hungry and bored with the available fixings.

I got an idea. The customers at Tillie's were almost as confused as the delivery boy was when he brought the kitchen staff their half mushroom, half olive and anchovy pizza.

A Brownstein party. Just for a joke I wore a tie and unbeknownst to me two of my best friends decided to do the same. We are right in the middle up front.

When I worked at Tillie's, it was owned by a lovely girl/woman named Margot. Much of the atmosphere of the place was created and maintained by her management technique and her attitude about service to the public.

As a young single mother in need of help, traveling across the United States, Margot had been befriended by a nameless waitress in a no name cafe somewhere, nowhere. Margot remembered the warmth and friendship and from that moment on, it was her desire to create that atmosphere for others who might need some hot soup or a person who would listen.

It is hard for me to fathom or to explain how someone who was almost never there could have such an effect upon the personality of a business, yet Margot made Tillie's what it was. She produced a space, set up a menu, hired good people, left them alone and created an icon.

Tillie's had a diverse and international clientele. Lawyers, criminals, artists, students, professors, doctors and Indian chiefs; as well as rebels, followers, innovators and sad lost souls.

Most of the people who worked at Tillie's had either been hitchhiking and got dropped off in Monterey, had their automobile break down there, or had been in the military at Fort Ord and couldn't think of a better place to go afterwards. Almost everyone was as far away from their hometown and family as they could get. It was a time in teenage history when the length of your hair or your choice of T-shirt art could get you grounded at home or kicked out of school.

A large percentage of the girls were Jewish from New York, New Jersey, or Fairfax, LA, refugees from religion and the indifferent, yet oppressive, control of their families. I quickly found out that I had an affinity for these rebellious young ladies, the strongest, most independent and sensual women I had ever met.

A lot of the guys at Tillie's were country boys, who left small towns to escape prejudice about their artistic or political nature. Many of them passed through San Francisco and found it too staggering for their quiet personalities.

From the core of friends I first met at Tillie's, a community of 50 to 75 people has grown. Some of these friends I have known for over 40 years. We still meet and socialize on a regular basis today.

We are still steeped in the counterculture art, music and politics. We are members in good standing of the community, and yet we have an alternative viewpoint.

I am convinced that no other period of time in the history of man created more interesting people or spawned more bizarre stories than the hippie era.

## A Poem Without Punctuation or Capitalization

i married in the depth of the mid1960s uptightness we married for the reasons people married then for sex and legitimacy she went one way I went another my curiosity for other women drove me onward sex drugs rock and roll and
i was hooked never on drugs but on freedom it was an upward spiral

toward spirituality my friends became thinkers my lovers free when my wife and i separated she went south i went north into the arms of people who needed my spirit not body or mind i went back to the roots of my grandfather the carpenter manual labor for the heart not mental contrivance for the money back to square one the dust from whence i came i picked strawberries washed dishes spun records weeded vegetables built wooden fences and constructed bridges with my mind the women were easy the knowledge was hard the drugs helped if you controlled them the music made us sweat out our poisons from our minds antiwar gave us a red star next to our names and validity to god anti-materialism put us in the temple with christ our religious tolerance put paul back up on his ass that which does not make you sell out makes you poor but stronger and wiser john mccleary 4 4 2000

## CHAPTER 56

# Remember Their Birthdays

I have very few regrets in my life. That might seem flippant to you knowing some of the ups and downs of my history, but I am very philosophical about life. I know I never meant any harm in my dealings with others, and I am also a firm believer that one fork in the road can always turn out to be as good or bad as the other.

One of my few regrets was forgetting her birthday, my first wife's birthday. Several months after we separated, it came around again.

At that time, it was still not for sure in my mind, and perhaps in hers, that our marriage was over. I was having second thoughts, as many men do. We are often the reason for the break-up, but most often we are the ones to try to re-float a ship that we ourselves have sunk. I missed my daughter very much, and I also, deep inside, longed for the companionship that her mother and I had experienced.

Siobhan, my daughter, in Paris

I made plans to drive down to celebrate my wife's birthday. It was a surprise trip. Big mistake.

But this was not a soap opera, it was real life. In a soap opera I would have gone down to my separated-spouse's house on her birthday and found her in bed with another man. No, it was worse than that.

On July 27th, 1972, I went down to Santa Barbara, California, to surprise my wife on her birthday. The problem, the tragedy, the error, was that July 23rd was her date of birth.

I can blame my undiagnosed dyslexia, my fear of numbers, my own lack of concern with my own birthday, but it was just stupid, male, thoughtlessness.

On her birthday, at the party her sister threw for her, my wife had met another man, and, most likely, because of my forgetting her birthday, she had been thrown into his arms. Had I been there, that would not have happened.

Would our marriage have survived, I don't know. I rather doubt it, but maybe. The relationship with the other man didn't last, but it broke a chain. On the night of July 27th, my wife and I made love, but everything was different. I felt it.

She told me then about her affair, and I experienced some of my lowest thoughts and highest jealousy. I had already dealt with her first affair...poorly, but I had rebounded. And now I confronted myself with my own hypocrisy.

I went through a few days of hatred toward her, self-loathing of myself, and cheap attempts at justification. I did not entertain thoughts of murder or suicide as some misguided souls do. I looked up at the beautiful sun, and contemplated the moon and realized my troubles were a speck of dust. I moved on with my life, but I vowed never to put myself or anyone else into that sad scenario again.

Remember their birthday, your anniversary, the pain they feel, and the love they need.

CHAPTER 57

# Art Or Sex

*"As Goethe wrote in 'Roman Elegy 5', But when the night comes, love occupies me otherwise. And if the result is that I'm only half as learned, I am still doubly happy."*

During the 1970s and early 80's, for about 14 years I concentrated on the pursuit of sex and forsook my art and writing. But I always felt there was nothing more educational than the ups and downs of social intercourse, and the emotional exercise of physical intercourse. I was sure that my amorous pursuits were preparing me for a very rich literary future.

For much of my hippie era, 1967 to 1985, aside from some photography and poetry, I did not produce much in the way of art or literature. I made love, smoked, dropped psychedelics, drank and traveled to new places to make love.

For the most part, sex and the pursuit of sex took up all of my creative time and energy. When a person is seriously involved in romance, searching for love is an exhaustive effort, and seduction is an extremely creative activity. And once a love affair is launched, to keep it moving forward and vital can be encompassing.

At the beginning of each relationship, the frequency of sexual activity can take up a lot of your waking hours. At the end of a relationship the turmoil can absorb much of your mental capacity and leave you physically drained.

Sometime in the early 1990s it was "discovered" that there was such a thing as sex addiction. In retrospect, I realized that I, at one time "suffered" from that affliction.

Some might say that sex is a good addiction to have if you need to be some kind of junky. I agree, but nymphomania, like most drugs, can divert your attention from other more productive efforts.

It has been said that sex and art are two of the same kind of emotions. It has also been said that it is imposable to serve both these muses at the same time. The pain and pleasure of a romance is surely stimulus for art. The definitions of sex and art are almost mutual at this place.

The selfishness which creativity often requires can make it impossible to be selfless in a romantic relationship. The time required to be an artist can also produce jealousy in a lover who wants more of your attention.

Artists recognize that the creative urge is their most demanding lover.

As with all things in life that require commitment, art and love individually, consume other activities. Creative selfishness on the one hand makes the human world go round. On the other hand, love also makes the world go round.

Humans would be better off if they, like most other animals, didn't have emotional commitments to their mates or children, and yet it is our familial ideal to be a cohesive unit. Are we an ambiguous species or a confident species?

We could be more rational if we didn't live life with our emotions, but I am sure music, art and literature would be bland and boring then. Passion is what gives our thoughts beauty. Yet it is often hard to be passionate and productive both at the same time, because one takes selfishness and the other requires selflessness.

You know how some people try to get into as many photographs as they can? I won't pass too many judgments on that fixation, but "photo bombing," is a new evolution of that kind of egotism. I have never been like that; I am always more comfortable behind the camera.

*"Someday, maybe, the excitement of tomorrow and another place won't distract me from the warmth of today and here."*
Dudley Griffin 12.7.73

CHAPTER 58

# Sex and Nudity

*"Upon your body*
*the warming sun rays playing*
*upon my body"*
John.12.29.73, haiku, Rose Lodge, Oregon

The apostles drove their 1968 Chevrolet up the dusty road. They were unrelated, yet brothers and sisters in Christ. Two young men, a middle-aged housewife and someone's grandmother.

The rutted path wound through thorny blackberry bushes, overhanging willows and second growth ash. This was new territory, un-traveled by the Lord's workers, yet judging by fresh tire tracks, someone must live here, maybe a sinner in need of redemption, and so they pushed on.

Past the massive trunk and beneath the timeworn limbs of an aged maple, the four-door mechanical behemoth broke into sunshine as the valley opened into pastures of wild grass. Two large, weathered, old, yet confident houses appeared before them. The road seemed to become smoother, and the dust dissipated as they approached the open parking area between the houses. Two Volkswagen vans, a non-descript sedan and an old pickup truck sat there comfortably.

As the Christians' car slowed to a stop just before the turnabout, off to their right their eyes beheld a large, well-tended garden, in which a number of people toiled in the sun. The righteous four gathered their Bibles and printed matter in preparation and then looked up to focus upon the potential congregation.

Granny opened her mouth and sucked in a deep breath. She turned and looked at the two young men in the back seat, and at the same time raised her hand up to block the eyes of the housewife who was the driver. "They're, they're, they are without, they have no.., they're naked!" she said, in one long, exhaled breath.

For a time in the early 1970s, I lived on a commune in Oregon. It was on a farm near the coast, south of Portland. It amounted to 8 or 10 people who shared the rent and worked together to maintain the place and an environment conducive to enjoying a free and decadent lifestyle. Two old, 2-story Victorians, a barn, some out buildings and sheds on 20 acres was our world of retreat.

It was three miles from the Coast Highway, up a logging road and then down a half-mile dirt road. We had solitude! And solitude usually meant nudity. Hippies and pagans worship the sun, wind, water and earth. The best way to worship the elements of nature is to take off your clothing and get next to them.

It was Saturday, a day of rest and work around the farm. Contrary to misconceptions of the time, hippies did work. Several of my commune mates and I were carpenters, my girlfriend and several of the other girls waited tables at upscale restaurant on the coast, one of the guys was a glass blower, and another worked as an orderly in a hospital. On Saturdays and Sundays we did what we wanted to do and what needed to be done to maintain our environment.

Five of us were working in the garden when the large Detroit-made automobile drove up the road. I was completely nude, as was my girlfriend and the other guy. The two other girls were topless, with one of them wearing a long skirt and the other in a bikini bottom.

We looked up from our work. One of us, maybe all of us, recognized at once who the intruders were, "Jehovah's Witnesses!" "Yeah, what should we do?" "I don't know." "We don't want what they've got, they don't want what we've got, let's just ignore them." "Yeah, they'll go away!"

So we ignored them. We weren't going to run and hide or clothe ourselves. We weren't going to confront them with our nakedness. We weren't embarrassed! This was our property, so we didn't think it was up to us to protect intruders from the "disgusting spectacle" of our nudity.

Hippies don't think that the nude human body is disgusting, just as we don't think a nude cat or horse is immoral. Actually, we don't even think that the nude human body is sexual. You may be attracted by it, but it is not sexual. Making love is sexual. Looking at the human form is like looking at art or a beautiful sunset. It arouses emotions, but it should not be confused with the actual act of sexual intercourse.

American Christian fundamentalist religions have created "nasty." You can go to public parks all over Europe and find families sunbathing in the nude. Most cultures in the world have less hypocritical attitudes toward sex and nudity than does the United States of America. And, also most other countries in the world have fewer sex crimes than does the United States of America. Does this show a pattern? Well, yes, make it a sin and some weirdo will pervert it into a crime.

The witnesses for Christ discussed the matter for about a minute or so and then turned the car around and drove back down the dirt road to civilization. I would like to have been a cootie on the gearshift of that car and heard what those righteous people had to say about my friends and me.

David by the author

Original instruction that came on the packaging of most religions, including Christianity, warned followers not to pass moral judgment on others. Yet, with time, the insecurities in human nature have caused many religious people to cast stones of ridicule at those who do not believe as they do. Such misguided "saints" have gone so far as to create and support laws against "immorality" and other activities they perceive as blasphemy against "their" God.

Judging by the actions of most religious leaders of today and studying the history of religion, it becomes obvious that most of the laws in religions were created by men, not by God. What God, in its right mind, would dictate prohibitions against bodily functions that they, themself, created?

The most offensive thing about all sexual moral laws is that they were originally created by religious leaders, not to help people, but to enslave people. These rules were imposed to maintain power over society, most of them, actually, to impose power over women.

Back in pre-history, because they wrote the history, some very devious and greedy men once realized that, if they could create heaven and hell in peoples' minds, then produce a vengeful "God" for people to fear, and then impose laws against <u>natural human functions</u> in that God's name, they could then make people feel ashamed and vulnerable when they performed these <u>normal biological activities</u>. Then the "sinners" would be obliged to pay these "priests" money to save their souls and forever faithfully attend church, thus listening to the sermons which contained not only spiritual, but political and moral instructions.

Suppressing sexual desire is one of the most psychologically damaging human activities. Most sexual deviations, such as rape and incest, are caused by suppressing normal sexual desires.

Sex is like the river of our lives. It flows as strongly as the desire for food or breath. Sex, Food, Breath--these are all essential elements of our God-ordained passion to preserve our species.

Until this society starts treating sex as a fact of life and stops giving it some religious "sin" value, we will continue to have an inordinate number of sex crimes and cases of violence against loved ones.

Sex, and religion--what a misunderstanding Christianity has gotten itself into here!

**Reprieve:**

*"Here it comes, here it comes, here it comes...my sex, like water down a well-worn riverbed. It flows, surging, swirling, powerful, free, unchecked, natural. But then the prohibitions of my society, like a landslide of rocks across the river gorge, block Nature's flow. And then what does my urge do when confronted by boulders of religion? It backs up; it grows stronger by weight of inhibitions building like the volume of water behind a dam. It backs up a powerful body of frustration searching for a release. And when it does release, as it will, it is a power less anticipated, less understood, that breaks the dam. Or, even worse, it deviates around the obstruction and flows into areas of dark obsession upon the object of my sex, my sex, my sex."*

Dudley Griffin, 12.7.98

Do you know who the Biblical Saul is? Better known as the Apostle Paul, he wrote one third of the New Testament, or, as we might call it, the Christian Bible. Paul wrote almost all of the Christian laws on sex in the New Testament Bible.

As an educated agnostic, I know the we have no proof that a person named Jesus ever really lived, and so all things I write about him are only speculation. But we do know that Paul did exist and we can thank the Romans' writings and fanatic attention to details and written history.

Do you know that Paul was not one of the 12 Disciples of Christ, and he never met Jesus? He became a Christian 30 years after the death of Jesus. You might remember that he was the one who fell off a donkey and saw the light. Well, I personally think he fell off that ass and suffered brain damage.

Are you aware that we know more about Paul's history than we know about Jesus Christ himself? Historically, except for the New Testament Bible and some scrolls with unestablished dates and authorship, we don't even know if Jesus was a real person or if Christ was a human creation of the ideals of perfection that we needed to reach salvation. Part of this last paragraph is highly satirical and could be called revolutionary thinking, but we can blame Constantine Emperor of Rome, from 306 to 337 AD, and his mother, for Christianity as we know it. More later!

Paul, before he hit his head, was Saul, a Jewish tax collector, gathering money from Jews for the Romans. He was a money collector for "The Man." That is how we know about him because the Romans kept good records.

Most of Christ's disciples and his other apostles were carpenters, fishermen or farmers. Paul was a banker or accountant. Jesus disliked money changers (money people) more than any other occupation of man. The only time Jesus ever got pissed off was at money changers in the temple or synagogue. So do you think he would choose a tax collector to write most of his Bible?

We also know through various writings that Paul was a misogynist. And from his sermons I see that he may have been striking out at women for his own frustrations. He may have been a latent homosexual. Jeffery Dahmer was, as most serial killers of young men are, a latent homosexual and therefore troubled and confused by his sexuality.

By the way, I have no problem with homosexuality. I do have a problem with suppressing homosexuality and what it causes some men to do. Paul is a good example of this scenario. Paul, possibly a frustrated homosexual, historically a woman-hater, wrote almost all of the Christian laws on sex in the New Testament Bible. He is responsible for creating the male dominance of our society. Oh, and with help of Emperor Constantine and his mother

I believed that Paul's writings were the beginning of a new form of destruction of a peaceful, bucolic society. With the dominance of man and his ego, came unbridled competition, wars and greed. Constantine promoted it further.

Women, historically, have been more peaceful and cooperative in dealings with others than men have.

Organized religion is a creation of mankind that possesses no obvious constructive or rational function other than to impose restrictions on our physical and emotional lives. Religion is the most complicated equation in our society.

Sex is a normal, yet uncontrollable, biological drive. Business is an intellectual creation designed to help facilitate society. Compared to them, religion is a confrontation of life.

Early, primal religion consisted mainly of emotional awe toward life, the world, sun, moon and stars, and a little fear of the power of nature. How did religion evolve into what it is today, an institution that separates us from nature and causes us to distrust people and other things that we do not understand?

Just think about it. Business has to do with economic laws, sex, with biological laws, and religion governs emotions. Emotions being the least rational element of our lives, religion should never be allowed to make any laws governing human activity.

The only exception is the Golden Rule. The admonition to "do unto others as you would have others do unto you" is the only law of conscience that is even close to being reasonable or actually doable. And the Golden Rule is the only law found in every religion of any validity.

One of the major misconceptions held by many otherwise intelligent people is that religion creates unity, tolerance and love within mankind. On the contrary, organized religion is a divisive institution. It is not uncommon to see four Christian churches in a small town, on four corners across from one another, filled with people who misunderstand, distrust and dislike the people who worship in the other three churches.

The only religion that really promotes true love and tolerance among mankind is agnosticism. Agnostics, as you may or may not know, do not know, nor do they care, whose God is the true God of this world, or in which little white church God exclusively resides. They believe that through positive actions, and through adherence to the Golden Rule, a person proves their spirituality. Worshipping a particular God does not make a person righteous, nor does it produce tolerance toward others.

## CHAPTER 59

# Cunnilingus Among Us

Most men don't know a clitoris from a cloud in the sky. Recognize it, men; get to know it; it is your best friend. If you can achieve the art of appreciation and proper treatment of this little erogenous spot, women will love you, flock to you... not just put up with you.

That tiny button of flesh just above the opening into a woman's vagina is the part of a woman's sexual organs that transmits the majority of the feelings of sexual arousal to the brain; that is, of course, if it is properly caressed during foreplay or intercourse.

Most men think that their penetration is what women want most. True, there is a certain amount of psychological arousal from penetration, and some tactile stimulation, but most of the deeper arousal comes from contact with the clitoris during intercourse.

As I have discovered in my own sexual life, both men and women experience the majority of feeling during intercourse in their groins, not in the penis or vaginal wall. The head of the penis and the clitoris are like a key on the keyboard that sends a message (a tickle) to the groin.

It is not surprising that some women find refuge in sex with other women. Other women know a woman's body better than most men, and sex among women doesn't usually include the childish penetration dominance game that men often play.

Sex comes naturally; but good sex has to be learned. If two lonely virgins were to stumble upon each other in the garden, eventually they would become ex-virgins embarking on a life of love. How that love life evolved would depend on the experimental nature of the two, or on the strength of their desire for self-gratification. But without a "good" manual or video on the subject, the likelihood is high that they would never achieve an explosive level of lovemaking. Sexual experimentation is usually limited without some form of guidance or suggestion.

Immature male lovers usually perform in a way that feels good to them and think that is good enough to fulfill the needs of their mate. Unless their mate knows what good sex should feel like, and demands it, they may never experience completely satisfying sex. The way people find out what turns them on is to have someone experiment on them or to experiment on themselves.

A key to "good" sex is a variety of lovers, or at least one partner having had a variety of lovers, and it doesn't matter which partner, male or female. But, because it is already beautiful, sex between people who really love each other does not need to have a grading system.

Actually, I think the more experience the female partner has, the better the sex will be for both partners, and that is because most men tend to get in a groove of their own pleasure and forget about their partners. However, women who have had enough experiences to know what they like are more demanding of their mates, thus raising the level of lovemaking for both.

Photo by Dave Glover, Big Sur

In the late 1960s, I published posters of my photography and poetry. These posters were sold primarily in "head shops" and college bookstores. I traveled up and down the California Coast, distributing them to stores. Sometimes, I would hitchhike with samples and just take orders along the way to be filled later. I most often traveled Highway 1 through Big Sur.

While hitchhiking north on one such trip, I met two young women, also hitching at the turnoff for Esalen. Esalen is the self-realization and Gestalt center on the coast, the home of tantric, kundalini and hatha yoga studies, and nude hot tubs.

These young women had just attended a workshop at Esalen and were headed back to their homes up north. We decided to hitchhike together. As I recall, we had a very good rapport initially.

Hitching must have been bad that day because we got only as far as The River Inn at the northern part of Big Sur. Not far from there was a spot along the river where I had camped numerous times, so we decided to stay there for the night.

At that time the camping place by the river was on a private ranch, once a Spanish land grant owned by a family named Molera. It was later to be acquired by the State of California and called Andrew Molera State Park. At that time it was patrolled by cowboys working on the ranch.

We were not bothered that night, and I had stayed there a number of times without incident. But some time later I was there with a young woman during the day. We were running around without clothing, and after we had finished making love, an old cowboy on horseback carrying a 30:30 lever action rifle came and rousted us.

I suspected that the cowboy had been watching us, and I questioned him as he escorted us back to the road. The cowboy finally admitted with a laugh that he always watched the nude hippie chicks and the sex before kicking people off the property.

But, as I said, that night the two girls and I were left alone. As our fire died down, we began sexual play, and soon I was screwing both of them, going back and forth between their sleeping bags. It became obvious after a while that I wasn't satisfying them with intercourse alone, and they began to head me into other areas of stimulation.

At that point in my sexual development I had not had much experience with cunnilingus. My primary sexual partner had been my first wife, who was a virgin when we married.

I was not too forthcoming with cunnilingus on these two girls, mostly because I didn't really know how. One of the girls got annoyed with me and stopped accepting me into her bedroll. The other decided to take it upon herself to teach me. I guess I was a bit too insecure at the time to accept such disapproval of what I though was my masculinity. I must have acted cocky and defensive.

The young woman told me she had just had sex with a man who was a practitioner of clitoral massage and tantric yoga at Esalen. I was a little amused by the idea of such a thing as seminars on creating female orgasms and suppressing male orgasms. Tantric yoga is sometimes used to control sexual energy, thus postponing orgasm to prolong the pleasure of lovemaking.

As the night progressed the women became more and more pissed off at my sexual ignorance and persistence at wanting to screw rather than make love. By the time dawn broke, we were not on speaking or screwing terms, and I couldn't wait to get out of there and on the road without them.

I hastily rolled up my sleeping bag and headed off toward the highway. As I left I could hear the two young women laughing behind my back. In response I gave a rebel yell, to feign satisfaction with just having gotten it on with two hot chicks, but as I retreated up the hill, I felt more embarrassment and less self-assurance than I had ever experienced before or since.

That which makes you uncomfortable will teach you something about yourself. At that moment I embarked on a quest to learn all I could about satisfying women.

I learned on that dark night by the campfire light that I was incomplete. Those two girls taught me that I was a selfish lover, and, therefore, a bad lover.

It is humanly impossible to be macho and be a good lover at the same time. In order to make love with feelings to which a woman can deeply respond, a man must soften his attitude. And yet, a good lover, a good man, can wield a hard cock and still express delicate emotions at the same time.

I realized through that night's experience that what I wanted to do more than anything else was to satisfy women. I saw for the first time that the feelings that make most men feel "macho" are what actually make them "unmacho." The selfishness that makes men feel dominant and strong really makes them ineffective and weak as lovers.

I had never before had a lover demand my attention and require that I perform good sex. I had never previously been with a woman who expected equality.

As time went on, I found the more I learned about a woman's body, the more pleasure I received from sex myself. It's like biting into an apple; the flavor is missed if you think only of quenching your hunger. Take time to savor the softness of her flesh as you nibble, feel her natural lubricant explode, recognize the aroma, acknowledge the texture, confront the taste and experience the droplets as they trickle down your chin.

Sex is a biological urge and will continue to be only that and nothing more for men who don't have enough imagination to make it a spiritual experience. Human beings have the creative ability to make life more than just time through which we pass. Sex is one of the elements of life that we can expand to make existence more meaningful, more spiritual.

Every once in awhile a guy needs a slap across the face to make him stop taking himself too seriously. If he's lucky, that blow will wake him up.

To those two young women, wherever you are, I am grateful. I think of you and appreciate your contribution to my awakening and to the pleasure I have experienced in my life because of your help.

Everything we know, we've learned from someone else. There's always someone out there who can teach us something, no matter how experienced we may think we are. And it doesn't matter how old you are or how young your teacher is.

Often, those most likely to teach you are those most unlike yourself or those with whom you have the least in common. In matters of sex it will profit you to listen to those of the opposite sex. Listen to everyone about everything; you can always reject what they say.

Girls…don't fake orgasms. Demand good sex; show your lover your clitoris. He will thank you in the long run because he will enjoy sex more, and he will become a man.

## CHAPTER 60

# A Strict Vagetarian

Once I learned how to "do it" properly, I began to realize how much fun giving cunnilingus could be. It gives real meaning to the philosophy that "It is better to give than to receive." There is no emotional satisfaction in life that compares with knowing you are satisfying another human being so much that they scream with joy uncontrollably.

Lovemaking, as with every other human interaction, has elements of give and take, selfishness and generosity. Human nature, self-preservation and ego often cause a person to look for the advantage in everything they do. But, in love, the giving is more productive than the taking.

There is a big difference between doing something for someone in order to get something in return, and giving to them because their joy brings you pleasure. The difference is the degree of the other person's involvement. If you expect something in return for everything you do, then your efforts are shallow.

If a man gives a woman cunnilingus just so she will give him fellatio, the exchange makes the gift meaningless. But if your only compensation for giving a woman head is her satisfaction, then you are transcending the bank account aspect of social activity.

NYC 1984: "Go ahead, touch me," she said in a matter of fact sort of way and thrust her pelvis toward me for emphasis. Without hesitation, because I am not stupid, I decided to do as she asked. Find the fantasy in this.

I chose to start at the bottom. She was wearing a pair of black leather sandals. I reached out with both hands, took them off, let them fall to the floor and began touch her feet. Caress was a better term.

I wasn't going to let this slip by in a few minutes. I took a long time to get to her knees. My eyes followed my hands, over her feet, across her slim ankles, up the shinbone, around to the firm calves. Her skin was smooth, brown and soft. That morning her razor had nicked one small spot on her shin and she missed a few hairs. Yet her legs were perfect, the hair still so soft and blonde that it seemed unnecessary to have shaved at all.

As I reached her knees, our eyes met. What we saw surprised both of us, because our eyes were glazed and sleepy, yet we both expected to find humor or embarrassment. That's when I knew!

Her vagina was cloaked in black silk, but silk reveals more than it covers. Its sheen enhances sensual shapes.

The garment was plain except for a small border of lace. Her Venus mound strained tightly against the material. The crease created by the lips of her vagina sent a chill down into my groin. Her pubic hair traced patterns beneath black cloth and circled out around and through the gossamer lace border.

I begin moving my hands down her inner thighs, and she released the strain on her legs and let them spread naturally. As she opened her legs to me, more golden brown hair sprang free from lacy confinement, and white flesh showed, contrasting brightly against the black silk.

I felt the soft down hair on the inside of her legs and caressed the straining tendons with my fingers. I was careful not to tickle her, for laughter would break the sexual tension of the moment.

I slipped two thumbs beneath the silk and into the pubic softness. My fingers rested on the delicate slip of material covering what was left of her dignity. But she cared nothing of useless dignity, and as I brushed against her clitoris with my thumbs, she gave up a sigh of complete resignation.

At this emotional release of inhibitions, she began pushing up her blouse, revealing her beautiful torso to me. Like most model-type bodies, her breasts were not large, but they were perfectly firm and enticingly perky. I would get to them later, but first her pussy was drawing me to it.

My fingers traveled over the flimsy silk panties, feeling through them the jumbled pattern of her pubic hair. I grasped the hem of the crotch and pulled it back, revealing her to my view. There is no vision more exciting than a woman's pussy exposed to you as you brush aside the crotch of her underwear. Holding the black material aside and using the fingers of both hands, I spread the lips of her vagina. My tongue dove into her as deeply as it could thrust, and she let out a scream and forced her pelvis upward.

I licked and drove my tongue in again and again, and then found her clitoris and begin to suck it with passionate intent. A thumb found its way into her vagina, and I choreographed the synchronized movement of tongue and thumb. I begin to undress myself as best as I could.

I was soon free of my clothes and considered taking off some of hers when it became apparent that she was near an orgasm. When it broke over her, the sounds that emerged from this beautiful, dignified young woman made me think of a mountain lioness in heat.

The throes of her orgasm forced her body into a spasm of pelvic motions that threatened to engulf my whole hand and face. Somehow in the struggle her silk, lace panties were torn from her body. This is not easy to do; just try it sometime.

As she panted for breath, I leaned up, pulled my finger from inside her, and replaced it with my erection. As my anxious hard–on entered her, her legs rose straight up and around me, and she began throwing off her blouse and pulling the skirt over her head. It's a good thing The Plaza Hotel's closets were carpeted, large and well lit.

CHAPTER 61

# Children Do Not Receive Wisdom Through Their Mother's Milk

*"From the light the dark is very dark...from the dark the light is very light"*
Dudley Griffin 9/16/74

Each generation must be re-educated, it seems. I look at this book as a pop-quiz for the 21st century.

By now, some of you think that you've caught on to me. Most likely, you think that I'm just using passages of lurid sex to get your attention so that I can feed you sermonettes on my views of the human psyche. Well, you are only half right.

This book also contains sermonettes thinly disguised as lurid sex. I am not in the least bit repentant about it. I want to entertain you, and I also want to preach to you. I see sex as the root cause of so much of the trauma and drama in human lives, and so I write about it to show us to ourselves.

In this effort I must use my own experiences as examples, because this is a deep subject that can be explained only from the inside out. Yet, by nature, I am a very private person. I get no ego gratification from talking about my own sex life, nor am I an exhibitionist.

As a writer, I appreciate the appeal of sex. "It" is the most provocative subject a writer can employ. But I do not get turned on writing about it, nor am I a voyeur. I do not find titillation in memories or voyeurism.

I am writing this because I have a story to tell, a very important story. I think it is a crucial enough issue to dispense with my own privacy and my credibility, if need be, in order to get the message across.

I don't consider what I write to be pornography. Pornography should be judged by the intent of the author. I'm not trying to get people worked up and frustrated. I am trying to help people reach sexual satisfaction in the way that God and Mother Nature intended. I'm trying to write the best damned description of sex that I can, so that you can almost feel as if you are involved in what is going on. I'm trying to get you to understand what good sex is.

Good sex is sharing something wonderful and valuable and pure with someone who wants to be with you, and that can be shown only by example.

I believe most deviations, perversions and sex crimes are committed because people don't know what good sex is. They were never given the chance to experience it because they were taught to be ashamed of it, or they were too insecure to find a mate or too inexperienced to know what to do when they found a lover.

Some religious folk will condemn this book as justifying and promoting sex for pleasure, but I am just trying to make sense out of a natural body function, given, if you will, to us by God. It is here to stay, and we must put it in its proper perspective, or it will eat us up. And you know, if God is truly righteous, he, she, or It will not want that to happen.

These explicit descriptions of my own sex life are meant to be a textbook on intimacy. There are much older books and ancient Eastern writings about sex, and my own sexual life was originally enhanced by reading this earlier knowledge. This book in your hand is a modern version of those books.

One of the first, most important, lessons I learned about sex was in Hermann Hesse's book "Siddhartha," when Siddhartha's lover told him to hold himself up on his elbows when making love so as not to crush her. Hurting someone isn't good sex; it isn't even a good life.

If someone enjoys inflicting pain during sex, then they are socially retarded to begin with, but they are also missing out on many of the velvet joys of love and life. Selfish love, as promoted by many male dominated religions, is conducted almost like an attack. It is domination and ego gratification. It is not romance.

Violent or suppressive sex is meant to justify having sex when you are embarrassed about it or ashamed of the desires. Primal violence seems to be a way for some men to have an excuse--"The devil made me do it!" Men sometimes use the explanation that "I am a man, and that's what I do. I am an animal when the desire overtakes me!" That is bullshit justification for not having enough intelligence and common sense to use emotional control!

Mutual sexual gratification is as spiritually high as human beings can reach within our physical life. Once a person has experienced the deep warmth of sincere love from a mate, I would think it would make it hard to ever again inflict pain or act out dominance within the act of making love. Take up paint ball, X-games or video violence, and keep it out of the bedroom.

Of course, some people who have been raised on "sex is sin" feel ashamed when they have sex. That is why they treat their mates as adversaries. The curse of the biblical story of the Garden of Eden demonizes women because "women tempt you."

1960s love-ins were the proving grounds for a whole new vision of life and love in the Garden of Eden that this world could be. Once you have felt motiveless, universal love, you will forever be trying to regain that feeling. You will spend the rest of your life promoting nirvana. It is within our grasp!

Now I'm sure you think I have gone over the edge into new-age gobbledygook, but if you knew me personally, you would know better. I do not believe anything that I have not seen or experienced personally, and I always want confirmation. Since happiness, like nirvana, is a state of mind, they are available to each and every one of us, or you can be unhappy and have bad sex the rest of your life if you want to.

For those of you who think that I have confused sex with real life, I wish to enlighten you that our problems with sex are what is keeping us from our potential perfection in all life. The greedy and competitive aspects of sex, and of business, are separating us from true satisfaction with life on this earth.

In this book I am trying to remind those of you who have experienced good mutual sex, what is good about it, and for those of you who haven't experienced it, I want you to know that it exists and maybe how you might achieve it.

These stories are meant to allow you to feel good about sex, to help you look at sex as an important and acceptable part of life. Of course, this is going to upset a certain portion of our society. There is a group of people who have made it their crusade to demonize our sexual desires. And, sadly, many people have fallen for their propaganda.

Most of those who have come to believe that sex is a sin are just good folks who have been misled by other people that they look to for guidance. It is misguided morality.

The saddest part is that this fear and hatred of sex has created more problems than it was intended to solve. The original intent of Rabbinical and Christian laws about sex was to bring men and women together in family union in order to give children a protective home environment.

The double standard and competitive sexuality, which our religious mores have created, only serve to separate the sexes and introduce deviations that complicate our sex life. Most of our problems with sex are due to the fact that this society teaches us that sex is bad.

From the beginning of our education, with one of the first lessons taught us, the one about the Garden of Eden, we are brainwashed into thinking that this basic desire is immoral. After that first negative lesson, our families ignore the subject for most of the rest of our upbringing. And then all of a sudden we reach a certain age, and we have all these hormones pumping through our bodies, and the media starts giving us new stories about how nice sex is, yet how nasty it is as well.

We get so confused by these mixed messages that we don't know whether we should love our partners for giving us their bodies or hate them for being a temptation. Sex is a fact of life; it's not going to go away. We can't pretend it doesn't exist. When we fail to prepare our children properly for its arrival, we allow them to make the same mistakes we did and all the previous generations did before us.

God, why am I ranting and raving? Because, this is all so obvious and yet so ignored by our society to the determent of all of us. I am so pissed off I can hardly contain myself!

The most prominently recognized pitfalls of sex are unwanted pregnancy and disease. These could easily be reduced or ended with education if our society had the guts to talk to our children. Some people think that talking about sex will give kids ideas. That's stupid. Sex doesn't need any advertising. It's going to happen even if we're ignorant of it. The kind of sex kids usually have is non-thinking sex. What we should be doing is helping them have educated sex.

A more realistic, positive and accepting attitude about sex would also clear up a lot of the psychological hang-ups of our lives. Pedophiles, rapists, sexual sadists and wife beaters are all created by some form of sexual frustration or misunderstanding. In my opinion, if we weren't ashamed of our sexual desires, we would wipe out these deviations and sex crimes.

Most books are about sex and love. Most movies and TV, the same. Even the books, movies and TV that are about something else have some sex and love in them. Why? Because that is what people are most interested in, and it is a primary part of our lives.

I think it is dumb, offensive and dangerous to start a sex scene in a movie or book and not take it to its conclusion to show how it's done by other people. We teach people how to read and write, to work, to cook and drive cars, yet we don't teach them one of the most potentially dangerous, yet wonderful, skills necessary in our lives. Sex!

Sex and its affect on us is one of the most important influences on our lives. Our whole self-image is seen through the mirror image we see in the eyes of a lover or loved one. If people love you, you feel good and you look good because of that, and then more people will love you. If you have no love, God help you, and God help those who come in contact with you.

But the vicious cycle of lovelessness starts somewhere, and it hinges on self–confidence. I want to help people with their confidence, not arrogance, not selfishness, but self–confidence. It's just something I want to do. You know why? Because if you're happy, the world is a better place for everyone else. I have empathy for you, and it also provides a nicer place for me to live.

*"People are strange when you're a stranger. Faces look ugly when you're alone. Women seem wicked when you're unwanted."* These lines are from The Doors' 1967 song, *"People Are Strange."* This song alludes to what I am saying. Loneliness becomes a mental illness. I believe if people were more positive about sex, they would feel better about themselves, would have better relationships with other people, and then we would have a better world.

Sex creates strange, uncomfortable and sometimes dangerous situations in every culture in the world, but no culture has more problems with it than the United States. Just look at the statistics of our sex crimes, domestic violence, unwanted teenage pregnancies and suicide related to sex compared to the rest of the world.

In this country we take sex too seriously on the one hand, yet we don't take it seriously enough in the context that we should. Because we have demonized sex, it has become an obsession. Sex and religion have been unrealistically mixed together to form a very frustrating, psychologically volatile cocktail.

Anytime you put prohibitions on a physical necessity or tell people that their natural emotions are morally wrong, you are going to create a form of schizophrenia. If a powerful authority figure asks people to restrict their natural desires, what happens is an internal battle between the mind and the soul. And in this case religion is the mind, not the soul.

Sex, like the need for food and water, transcends religion and politics. A man, and sometimes even women, will forsake all ideals or spiritual convictions to obtain the sexual sustenance that their body needs. The need for sustenance is the one true visceral urge, and it transcends all common sense in the drive to be quenched.

In order to get our priorities straight as far as sex is concerned, we must first agree on the fact that sex itself is not bad. It is a natural, God-given desire. Whether or not it was created by some deity for the sole purpose of procreating our species is immaterial. It is a drive that cannot be controlled for producing babies alone; that fact must be obvious to any thinking person.

Get used to it! Sex is an uncontrollable drive. We are stuck with that. It's not the sex that is bad; it is how we use it and what we think about it that is wrong. So what are we going to do with this fire inside us? Maybe we should start using it instead of letting it consume us?

In the year 2017 a rash of sex scandals in politics and media erupted. Sex and power is such a quagmire! How could an otherwise rational, moral person, specifically in a position of leadership or moral authority, indulge in sleazy acts of molestation, or disrespect for women? Perhaps it is because they were an animal human sometimes and a human animal sometimes.

And maybe it was the wrong time and place.

*"We bumped into each other at the wrong time. We did what we could, we tested our desires, but it was not going to happen. Not a mistake, just a glitch in timing, an example of molecules missing being in the same time and place by only moments." Rudolph Valentino or Ralph Valentine*

CHAPTER 62

# Jim And I And Jan

Jim and I are artists. He's a painter, and I'm a photographer. We often bumped into each other watching the same sunset. We ate hors d'oeuvres together at art openings and drank their cheap wine. We passed a joint to each other at parties. And we liked the same sort of women.

There was this one girl waiting tables at Tillie's, our favorite coffeehouse, Jan. I was on the prowl for some time. Jim noticed her too.

I flirted with her as she brought my cappuccino and bagel with ham. I stopped by her house from time to time to see if any chemistry was developing. I didn't drop in just before bedtime or in the middle of a drunken night. I wanted it to progress naturally.

One morning I arrived after breakfast and Jan offered me tea. She was in the kitchen talking to me as I sat on the floor of the living room in front of a warming fireplace. I was staring down at the shag rug wondering if this would ever develop into anything.

"Jim was here last night," she said with nonchalance, "We were going to split a windowpane, but he dropped it on the shag rug and we couldn't find it."

At that very moment I saw a tiny, shiny square nestled in the fibers of the rug. I was already licking the end of my finger. I reached down, snagged it, and placed it on my tongue.

I left after the tea. Went down on the rocks by the sea.

Jim got the girl. I got his acid. I hoped his trip was as good as mine.

Years later I talked to Jim about that episode. We laughed about the acid, and then he told me that he had never really connected with Jan. Their relationship had remained platonic.

I mused about that for a while! Why had Jan passed by both Jim and me? Weren't we the most attractive, eligible, experienced lovers in town?

Seriously, trying to be objective and yet humble, I will have to say that Jim and I were among the very most popular and sexually active members of the hippie community in our town.

We had numerous unique episodes competing for lovers, as I already stated, and we politely shared women friends. Jim and I still meet today, at parties, bocce and art openings, and we have had conversations about our almost comical and always congenial competitions.

Jan had somehow warded off the advances of both Jim and me. Why? Her life's history and unhappy ending held the key. You see, Jan was eventually killed by a boyfriend.

Jan left the Monterey Peninsula sometime in the mid-to-late 1980's. In doing so, she left the comfortable confines of a safe hippie community. That was her first mistake. But thinking back on the men she had dated and married, I could see a pattern.

Jan was attracted only to macho men, pushy men, "a man's man." Most of the guys she had been in relationships with were not your typical sensitive types. That left Jim and me out.

We were OK to talk with, be buddies with, but not to roll in the hay with. Jan had the typical misunderstanding many women have, that a strong man, or at least one who acts strong, must be a "better" man, therefore a better lover! Wrong!

What I am writing about here is using a pigeon hole to explain a pigeon. In my life "the sensitive hippie" is a reality!

The typical true hippie man of the 1960s and 70s was a sensitive person, artist and intellectual, but he also had the soul of a lover because he believed in love and sex as a form of positive communication between people. He was not worried about his own sexuality, he was not homophobic, and therefore, he did not try to knock girls over with his masculinity.

By the same token a sensitive man, a self-confident man, is seldom jealous. He knows that a rejection is only a minor setback. It is often lack of chemistry or just a snap decision by the woman.

A real lover of women can always find love, and he knows that rejection should not be taken as a personal attack on his ego. Besides, a true lover only wants to be with a woman who wants to be with him anyway, because he knows love and sex is best when it is mutual.

A popular misconception by many people is that the male hippie was weak and effeminate. After all, he wore flowers in his hair. Contrary to this perception, most of the carpenters I knew during the 1960s, 70s and 80s were hippies. The building trades were filled with them. And on top of that, I would venture to say the male hippie was the most accomplished and energetic of all lovers. I haven't experienced one myself, but word I got from my lovers and women friends was that the California hippie eclipsed all the Latin lovers and macho cowboys they had ever met.

What happened to Jan was an old, sad story. She reached out to the wrong kind of man, and when she decided he was not what she thought he was and left him, he killed her. This sort of thing never happened in our little circle of hippies in Pacific Grove. There were possibly 200 liberal progressives living in our little bubble of no monogamy, no jealousy and total tolerance, where we shared everything, including ourselves.

Like most women, she would have been better off with a person she liked as a friend. The appeal of macho sex wanes after a while. In any long-term relationship the deciding factor is whether the two people are compatible at the dinner table, more than in the bed.

At an early age, when I was first dating and when I first married, aggressive courtship was the norm. As I have said previously in these pages, self–confidence is attractive to women, but arrogance is a danger sign.

After Eastern religion, cannabis and psychedelics caused me to look inside myself, I became more appreciative of women's needs, and less aggressive. This didn't mean that I didn't pursue what my libido desired; it just meant that I was more sensitive in my approach.

My close relationship with my mother made it easier for me to become a better, more sensitive lover to women. I once had a girl-friend who had been through a few bad relationships. She said to me, "I will never again date a man who did not have a good, loving and respectful relationship with his mother."

Jan looked for power, not love, and she got it. When women learn the difference between aggression and sincerity, men will be forced to stop using arrogance and will have to rely on truth to obtain sex and love.

In the counterculture community of the Monterey Peninsula, many people dated and cross-dated. I called it "our incestuous fami-ly."

One little story that I often tell, apocryphal though it may be, is about a new couple who went to a party. At the party the guy greet-ed another male friend of his and introduced his new girlfriend to him. The two introducees looked sheepishly at each other and then told the new boyfriend that indeed they did know each other. In fact, they had lived together for several years and have a child together.

In my community numerous friends are ex-lovers. There have seldom been any jealousy episodes. When a relationship ends, wheth-er it is mutual or not, the principles usually take it like adults. Next week your ex may be living with your best friend.

Some people might be repulsed or embarrassed by this situa-tion, but I say, "Get real." So what are you going to do? Move? Never speak to them again? Stab them? Grow up!

This way of life is not confined to the hippies, but found flour-ishing in the middle class, upper class, poor and old. Have you ever heard the stories about retirement homes? But in most segments of hypocritical society it is lied about, denied and then used to destroy others.

Shall I go on? Today's reality shows and the old TV soap operas could be considered the most culturally destructive media ever conceived by man. Overemphasizing and glorifying bad behavior is what most media does very well. It is another form of dumbing down the public, by giving them media that stimulates only "animal" instincts and lower intellect activity.

When I first brought my second wife, my present wife, back to live on the Monterey Peninsula, she was soon confronted with my ex-lovers. At first, not being from that kind of community, she was a bit uncomfortable. Now my wife and some of my ex's are good friends. We are social animals, and we are supposed to be intelligent.

Jan didn't have to die an untimely death, but maybe she did not die in vain. Hopefully, someone reading this will be more careful about bringing home some macho cowboy. Hopefully, some macho cowboy will learn to be more sensitive to what love really is.

How soft can a man become before a woman rejects him as a man? How soft can a man become and still think himself a man? Can you ever accept me as a man if I have weakness? Will I still love you if you love me in spite of my weakness?

Sometimes it seems that man and woman will never see eye to eye until we all become blind. Our lives are continually playing out like a series of scientific experiments, mixing chemicals and suffering the explosions, until we get the right combination for the elixir of love.

Are we doing this to procreate and advance our species, for our own ego, or just because we happened to be here, and we should make the best of it?

Jim's memorial at Tillie's 2017

## CHAPTER 63

# Jim And I Again

Jim and I loved women. We occasionally shared lovers.

One night I went home with a girl only to find that Jim was visiting her roommate that night. Not only did we have connecting bedrooms, but <u>our</u> bedroom was the passageway from <u>their</u> bedroom to the rest of the house.

So all night long they had to pass through our room to go to the bathroom or the kitchen. Later the girl I was with told me that she and Jim had also been together as well. Needless to say, Jim and I have a history.

Remember, a chance meeting, a sexual encounter, can set you up for life in your dream relationship, or a broken heart, an unwanted child consequence or just a beautiful memory forever!

## CHAPTER 64

# Mom And Dad

 I have only one photograph of my mother and father together. That is strange to some people who have albums full, but I know that it is not unusual for people to have no images of their parents together, and some don't even know what their father or mother look like.

I am happy to have that one photograph. It places me somewhere, and it gives me a home for my heart.

She had an all-knowing stare with a slight, small, bit of a smirk. He had an Ironic, deep, challenging, stare with a touch of a question mark.

I did not have as much experience with my father's face and expressions because the last time I saw him, I was only 6 months old. But from the photos I have of him, I know two things about him, he was always ironic and always curious.

Ironic means to me, never take yourself too seriously, and curious means you will not stop until you are perfect. Oddly, that had been my life's direction as well. It started even before I recognized these traits in my father.

My mother's expressions were always controlled, calculated, yet somehow left open to interpretation. She smiled easily, and frowned profoundly.

The more I have gotten to know them through their photographs, the more I have come to know that it would have been hard to keep them apart. It is comforting to me to see that they were a force of nature. My parents were drawn together, as if by Mother Nature, through their unique personalities and willfulness.

## CHAPTER 65

# Sex And Ego

*"Sex without ego is impossible. All creatures mate in order to extend their essence into another generation. Ego in its most basic*

*form is the urge to be recognized. It is life's desire to continue to live."*
Dudley Griffin 5.9.12

Mating is one of mankind's most rewarding activities, but to get a mate you need to be attractive on some level. And to be attractive you must indulge your ego to some degree. To have a healthy ego you need to be self-confident and secure because insecurity is the killer of confidence. Confidence is always the best resume, but only if it is the truth, a believable confidence.

Insecure folks often look for ways to give themselves confidence and, sadly, sometimes, they pick the wrong direction. There are two paths your ego can take you--toward creativity and art, or toward arrogance.

I feel a short definition of creativity and art is required here. My personal definitions: Creativity is the parent of questioning, of experimenting, of changing, and of allowing change. Art is the parent of making decisions, of looking for new decisions, of finding new ways to decide and of allowing your decisions to change.

Ego is what makes mankind create, advance and excel. The desire to be individual, to have something of your own, to make something that will endure beyond your life, that is ego. The ego makes you want to live. And in those efforts the ego is a good thing, but the ego has another dark and sinister side. It makes some of us selfish, jealous and arrogant.

Sex and ego are interdependent. Sex strokes your ego, and ego creates the personality that either attracts or repels sexual partners.

Outgoing personalities attract most attention. Being creative, intelligent and interesting is a big turn-on to most of the opposite sex, yet an arrogant and pushy nature can turn-off sensitive possibilities.

How a person uses their ego says a lot about that person and how others react to them. Achieving recognition from potential sex partners depends on your self-confidence, which is created by your ego.

When, as often I do, I refer to how women react to certain male actions. I do so from understanding the reactions I, myself, have received from women. A woman's mind is beyond my understanding. I can only learn who they are from what they do.

One of the directions many people take to achieve social recognition is the path of arrogance. Make lots of noise, attract attention, ridicule other people and take credit for things you didn't do.

Sure, that makes a lot of sense! Draw attention to yourself with annoying, obnoxious behavior while trying to cover up your faults.

The stupid thing about this is that you fool no one. When you draw that kind of attention to yourself, people will more easily see the flaws you are trying to hide, and they will be turned off by your arrogance as well. Movies and TV shows can often show you the consequences of being an arrogant fool, and may show you what that person looks like, but many people can't see themselves, and can't recognize that they sometime act like that foolish, self-centered person on the screen.

The other direction some people take is to become a rebel against society, thinking, "Since I am flawed, and most people are ridiculing me anyway, I will cover it up by making everyone think I don't care what they think. Turn everyone off on purpose to take attention off the other flaws." Yeah, that works! Now you're a reject and an outcast.

There are two reasonable ways to deal with personality or physical faults that are causing problems with your social life. Change or evolve!

First, a person can go to the source and change themselves to adapt to the social environment they want to join. Yet, sometimes it is not possible to change yourself, and so the second way to adapt is to admit your faults, ignore them, and be a better person in other ways so that society will overlook your flaws.

The source of one's insecurity is oneself. We can work from inside ourselves to change our own opinion of ourselves--the I'm OK philosophy. Or we can work on the outside to improve the part of us with which we are dissatisfied.

But, sadly, many people employ the other techniques. They try to cover up their own faults, or they find someone else to ridicule so they won't feel like the reject themselves.

Often, insecure people seek out religions or organizations that prohibit those things that they are unable to do, are afraid to try, or of which they are jealous. Some people label immoral those activities that they can't do, don't understand, or are afraid of. It's a self-defense mechanism.

But it is really self-defeating to ridicule others for doing something you would like to do yourself, yet are afraid to try. It is easier for some people to call something a sin than it is to learn the truth about it. For some misguided folks it's less trouble to hate the unknown than to accept their own ignorance. But taking the easy way out is not the way humans advance. It is not the way we will achieve perfection.

I think human beings are capable of perfection, and I believe they can achieve it on their own, without priests and religions and gods. We created gods, religions, and priests because we didn't think that we ourselves could be perfect. We have created all these intermediaries between ourselves and moral perfection, and now these creations are keeping us from being gods ourselves.

All we have to do is follow the Golden Rule, and we will become worthy of others' love. In all things we must be welcoming if we want to be welcomed ourselves. Our ego can be our strength, but only if we use it as a window, rather than a wall.

*"There is nothing wrong with having an ego, as long as we use it as a tool and not a weapon. An ego is what gives us our individual shape. It is what creates our personality. It is up to you whether you are loved or hated; it is how you use your ego that shows others whether you are to be trusted and loved, or feared and despised."*
DG. 5.30.14

CHAPTER 66

## Sex, Business And Religion

*"Sex has a morality to it, by nature of what it is. It is creation; it is the greatest gift of God. If you have sex without a reverence for who or what you are doing, you miss the point, and you miss...well, you miss what you are! And if you treat sex only as a obligation of your groin, or only as a means to procreate, something that must be*

306

*done no matter how objectionable, then you again miss out on the pure beauty of it. The 'nasty bits' of sex are what make it fun, yet it can be a sacrament, and the spiritual part makes it eternal. Without both, we would not need to do it, nor would we want to."*
DG.10.24.11

To God: *"Are you a God of enlightenment or a God of judgment?"*
JOB

There are many people who would be offended by this chapter title. That's too bad. It needs to be here, and it needs to be discussed.

One of the most dangerous flaws with most organized religions these days, is that they do not allow rational discussions about mankind's sexuality. They just "leave it up to God," and hope the subject will go away.

Fundamentalists merely proclaim a few prohibitions and leave all rational thought out of it, so it is left to people outside religion to do the thinking.

Throughout the years, I have formulated opinions about sex and religion and the correlation between the two. This is dangerous territory; this is a taboo subject for many. There are those who will want to burn you at the stake for suggesting any similarity; yet, I am not talking about the act of having sex or the act of walking into a church. I am talking about the emotions, elations, and, yes, even the expectations.

Some will think automatically of Elmer Gantry and brush this off as my suggestion that sex is a proper sublimation for spiritual enlightenment. Some people might think that I feel the desire for sexual satisfaction should take precedence over the desire for spiritual satisfaction and inner peace. Not so! Maybe in my youth I had the priorities confused, lust for life, or lust for sex, yet, even then, I knew that this boiling inside me had more of a spiritual culmination than just a wad of sperm.

Some misguided folks think that physical sex is God's damnation. Some have faith that righteous behavior on Sunday can excuse abhorrent sexual behavior the other six days of the week.

I do not think that sex is the most important emotion mankind has, but if we deny it, we lose part of our animalness and therefore part of our humanness. To think of sex as bad negates our own life, for we were born of sex. To pretend it does not exist wipes out our forefathers and mothers, and makes of us an abomination.

Sex is one of our strongest urges for a reason...for life.

I feel that the desire for orgasm is like the desire for life. I feel that the orgasm is a momentary example of what spiritual ecstasy really is because it is the feeling of life and the desire to continue life.

*"The afterglow, the second most wonderful feeling.*
*And then as the memory fades in your rear view mirror, you start*
*wanting to relive the most wonderful feeling again. The biological*
*drive to continually refresh your memory of the ecstasy of love keeps*
*us all alive."*
Dudley Griffin, 1.6.13

Page in the bedroom kitchen

CHAPTER 67

# Hippie Chick
# Between Love And Inescapable Reality

"She was the most ethereal woman/child. Windblown blonde hair, gossamer clothing, bells on her ankle, daisy chain crown. No one who saw her was untouched by the fantasy and mystery. I was struck.

My photographs of her still give me warm feelings in heart and groin. Her smile is the eternal message of desire. Yet, she is strangely unattainable, for once you possess her, the mystery is not gone, it just moves on.

Her mystery ended two of my relationships. In my efforts to regain the fantasy, I followed her to other continents. I eventually lost her in my own desire.

When we were together she would often asked me if I wanted to make love. She asked me if I had gotten off, if I were satisfied.

Years later, I found her again. My need for her unknown quality was not gone, but faded. We loved again for a while.

And then one day she confided in me that she had never achieved orgasm with me or anyone else. We spent that weekend trying to reach her orgasm. I failed. Even fantasies are not perfect.

I wonder where she is today in her quest. I sincerely hope she has experienced inspiration with someone, man or woman. Even a fantasy deserves sexual fulfillment, no matter how it is reached."

Blue Light Aura Illuminates Rain<br>
The Image Is The Reason For The Fixation<br>
The Reality Is The Moment Moving On<br>
September 9, 1979

You wouldn't understand the sexual mores of the Hippie Era unless you were there, nor should you condemn them while living within the standards of this era. It's like looking back and ridiculing landline telephones while standing in the era of cell phones.

Our activities were the accepted norm, and we were following the standards of our peer groups. We, at the time, honestly felt that we had evolved into a better understanding of sex and love. And many of us today, hippies and others, feel that our experiment in the 1960s and 70s was a big improvement over the time before and is a better choice than the sexuality of this day and age of 2013.

The Beatles' "I Want to Hold Your Hand" hit America in January 1964, and there is a strong consensus that the subculture sexual revolution started then. That was also the year of the appearance of Andy Warhol, Bob Dylan and the topless bathing suit.

The pill had been introduced in 1960, but it took a while for girls to talk their families, or ultimately their doctors, into giving them prescriptions, so the new sexual freedom took a few years to get up to speed.

When The Doors sang "Light My Fire" in 1967, we were turned on. By the time Stephen Stills recorded "Love The One You're With" in 1971, the sexual revolution was in full swing, and we all felt it would go on like that forever.

For many, the era ran on through the '70s and ended in 1980, the year Reagan was elected and John Lennon was killed, around the same time Bo Derek was voted a "10." For some, the sexual revolution carried on into the early '80s, but it came to a screeching halt when we finally learned the source and understood the magnitude of the AIDS epidemic.

In many places in America and Europe during most of the 1960s and 1970s, sex was not obscene. The naked body was not sexual. Desires were considered natural. And the word "adult" was dropped from the phrase "consenting adults." During this period of time there was a horde of 15-to 25-year-old hippie chicks in possession of the pill running around the country. Nobody asked ages, or names for that matter.

The hippie era provided an excuse and exoneration for a great number of men to become irresponsible, and I was one of them. Dropping out meant leaving the job you hated and the wife who no longer excited you. The pressures of modern family and economics had forced men into a drudgery from which they wanted to escape.

In 1967, I was 24 years old and had been married four years.

My daughter was born that year, and I began noticing the young free spirits that were running around available for the sampling. The male ego and sex drives are wondrous and horrible things to behold.

Rationally, my life wasn't all that bad at the time. I lived in a beach community in Southern California, had just settled in to a well-paying job as an advertising executive, and my wife and I had a lovely baby girl.

My wife and I weren't getting along badly, but she wasn't as adventurous and outgoing as I would have liked, and she wasn't very exciting in bed. The sexual part wasn't her fault though; I wasn't a thrill a minute either.

When we got married my experiences were very limited and hers were nonexistent. As I have observed, lovemaking is a learned skill. Although there are basic elements that are inherent and primal, it still takes a little time to get it all together.

If you put a 14-year-old boy and girl together in a room alone for a few days, even if they had never seen a movie or a book or talked to their friends on the subject, they would find out how to have sex. But if that couple were to become monogamous life mates, their sex life would not progress very far and might never achieve any special plateaus.

Often, a woman knowing only one mate won't expect much, having no comparisons, and will consider sex a mildly enjoyable, if not distasteful, requirement of marriage. As is sometimes the case in one-mate relationships, she may never have an orgasm. Female orgasms are definitely a learned accomplishment.

In the 1950s and early 1960s, the basic nature of women and the pressures of society's mores often meant that women accepted lives without exciting sex. Female primal urges are fundamentally to raise a family and keep the home fires burning, whereas the man's primal urge is for conquest.

Though these stereotypes have changed in the last 40 years, then, as now, the man is more often likely to seek sex outside the home. I don't necessarily condone it; I am only the messenger.

Often, when one member of a couple goes outside and has sexual experiences, he or she, brings back more excitement to the marriage bed. This also is not a pronouncement of proper procedure, but it is a situation of fact viewed from experience. Sexual experimentation breeds more excitement.

What is the age of consent? Who is a consenting adult? Well, that depends, doesn't it? "Consenting adolescent" could be an oxymoron, but let's explore the possibilities.

When I hear the term "age of consent," in my mind several questions arise. I consider the literal age, then I consider someone's previous experience in the sexual world, and then I factor in that vast variable of maturity. Some humans never reach enough maturity to be capable of any rational choice. Some are mature beyond their age

Many men won't even slow down their seduction on the basis of age, let alone experience or maturity. I have never been that greedy, yet I understand the sex drive well enough to know that some men can't help themselves. This is not justification. This is just realizing the circumstances, the reality. With the upbringing of many men, it would be hard for them to be anything other than closet rapists.

First, let's drop the "adult" from "consenting adult" because you and I know there are a lot of kids and adolescents out there who have been consenting for years, with numerous people.

My moral feelings and experience tells me that no 14-year-old girl is a consenting sexual partner. And yet I have met numerous 15-year-old girls who couldn't wait to give away their virginity.

First, we must distinguish between a 15-year-old who has already had sex and one who has not. Breaking cherries was never a goal in my sex life, though to some it might be. If a girl of 15, who has already experienced sex, wants to be with an older man, then she, I believe, would seem to be consenting. If an older man pursues a 15-year-old girl who has already had sex with others, is that man guilty of taking advantage of the girl, or is he contributing to her experiences? Give and take are the operative words.

I believe a person is old enough to consent if they are aware of the nature of the activity and are conscious of the consequences of sex. But then, is it possible for any virgin of any age to be fully aware of the nature and consequences of sex?

If a 15-year-old girl gives her virginity to a 15-year-old boy, is it more acceptable than giving it to an experienced older man? In some societies it is considered desirable for an older lover, either man or woman, to assist in a person's introduction to sex.

The real issue for most people usually comes down to age difference. Fourteen-year-old girls are giving away their virginity to 18- or 20-year-old guys all the time, and no one but their fathers, and sometimes the law, really cares. What would surprise you is the number of 15- to 18-year-old girls who give their virginity gladly and freely to men who are 10 to 15 years older than they. What doesn't happen so often is two 15-year-olds giving their virginity to each other.

The next crucial point is the virginity itself. Most people don't question the morality of two 16-year-olds groping each other in their rookie attempt to dispense with that old virginity, regardless of the fact that their lack of skill and knowledge can damage the event. Also visualize two 25-year-old virgins on their wedding night. Now it begins to come into perspective.

A 16-year-old is better off with a 25-year-old on several levels. First, most 16-year-old boys are going to be so excited by the girl's pussy that they aren't going to think about birth control. Second, the 16-year-old boy is going to be so excited about the girl's vagina that he will give little thought to her lips, her neck, her breasts, her belly, her clitoris...you get the picture.

An older man is a better lover. You, as a father of a teenage girl, may not understand, but a woman does. And if you're saying, "Yeah, but an older man will 'take advantage' of a young girl. Au contraire. He is more likely to take care of her, teach her, and enjoy her. Don't you think that an amateurish, unprotected screw in the back of a car is taking advantage?

I am not trying to justify a situation from a different time and moral platform to fit into today's moral platform. I am just explaining how it was then! Give it up! You can't think the way we did then or live the way we did then. It was a different world. In 1967, many people just like you were thinking and acting as if it was 1967. Yes, get it?

Sex is the only activity, discipline or occupation in which it is considered improper to offer to teach someone who is younger and less experienced. The need for education is not obvious to everyone, but, if you have experienced the good and bad, you understand how frustrating bad sex can be. And if you understand the psychological damage of sexual frustration and the deviations it produces, you will agree with the wisdom of a realistic mentoring system.

Although some will say that offering to teach sex is a selfish offer, it must be realized that the altruistic urge to be a teacher is as strong in some people as is their sex drive.

All that conjecture aside, what is most important to determine is whether the exchange is mutual. The essential element to good sex is an equal interest by the two parties and mutual expectation and gratification.

If we didn't have all the religious crap confusing the issue, sex would be as pleasing an exchange as a stimulating conversation, a nice song on the radio or a good bite to eat.

Is it fair, morally right or biologically correct for an older man to accept the virginity of a 15-year-old when it is obvious that she wants to get rid of it? Well, that is too much of a loaded question to ask a man when the 15-year-old is giving him the eye over her ice cream or rubbing up against him on the dance floor.

During the '60s and '70s "a 30-year-old guy I know" made love with a number of already experienced 15-, 16- and 17-year-olds. In most cases it was obviously mutual consent; in a few other cases it was an acceptable outcome.

Where does the term seduction come in? What really matters are the intent and the sincerity.

Because our society has arbitrarily determined that sex is a sinful activity outside marriage, we have produced all of these problems. If we were to concentrate on the only truly bad consequences of sex, the possibility of pregnancy or disease, then we wouldn't have all of these perversions.

Men who are all wrapped up in their own sexual guilt are too frustrated to care about the needs and sensibilities of women. Our society has put restrictions on a natural, biological urge and thus created a monster.

It is obvious to a sexually liberated man when a girl is ready to have sex. A man who does not think sex is dirty is more likely to appreciate the cooperative aspects of making love. He is less likely to treat the girl like a "tramp." He is less likely to be violent, and he is less likely to force his desires on a girl or a woman.

It would almost make more sense to have an age of consent for men to be allowed to make love to a virgin. A man could be tested to see if he were mature enough and sexually well-adjusted enough to have sex with an uninitiated female.

One of the things a man must first realize is that deflowering virgins is a psychological turn-on only because of society's hang-ups. If it weren't supposed to be dangerous, it wouldn't be thrilling. Somewhere in the mythology of man, it became macho to screw virgins. Some men go so far as to think that it is supposed to be a violent activity, a rape, a taking of innocence.

What these stupid guys don't know is that it was originally a benevolent, educational, almost paternal obligation to introduce young women to sex. And there was also an educational process for young men. We would do well to consider reinstituting this realistic attitude toward one of our most important bodily functions.

I have made love with virgins, and it was a bit of a thrill at first, but it does not compare with the love that can be made with someone who knows when to bite and when not to.


One of the most interesting experiences I had with a virgin was one that got away. At least she got away from me.

You would be surprised at the statistics of the number of girls who get pregnant the very first time they make love. There is no mystery to this; it is biological.

A virgin girl ovulates, and her body produces a "hormone of desire," created by Mother Nature to help ensure procreation of the species. Girls get horny too.

Let's say a boy and girl have been dating for several months. She has been ovulating for several years, but is still a virgin. He has been trying to "talk" her into making love for weeks.

She has been reluctant and has held him off. Then one day she ovulates. She is more comfortable with him now, and, besides, her "preservation of the species hormones" kicked in.

She lets him make love to her. No birth control is available, and she becomes pregnant on this very first time she has ever made love.

It happens all the time. Even first time one-night-stands produce the same results. A girl's "horny" hormone can overcome all kinds of discretion and chastity vows.

My virgin who got away story goes like this. Sometime around 1973 or '74, I was attending a wedding in Big Sur.

Weddings are interesting parties. Usually all ages and political affiliations are present. Many memorable social confrontations occur at weddings.

This wedding was more or less a hippie affair! Unlike many marriage ceremonies of the time, this one was conducted by an officially sanctioned reverend of a widely recognized church. He was not a mail order preacher from some Church of the Broken Tablets (10 commandments or cross tops) of Levelland, Texas. He was an ordained Unitarian minister.

At this wedding there was a particularly beautiful, nubile redhead. I noticed her. Then I began noticing something specific about her, and then I began to understand what it was.

She was ripe and ready to have sex. What I didn't realize consciously, probably because of my inexperience at the time, was that she was a virgin. I think I may have known subconsciously though.

I tried to get next to this girl all through that day. I failed, mostly because her parents, whom I knew, were at the wedding as well. I probably felt it would be bad taste for me to try seducing their daughter right in front of them.

About thirty-five years later, in a conversation with that same girl, now a happily married woman, I found out that on that very night she went out to a party, gave away her virginity and got pregnant as well. I guess I was honing my instincts at that time, my anxious virgin instincts and also my instincts toward avoiding embarrassing paternity complications.

CHAPTER 68

# Me Tarzan, You Jane

Traveling through Amsterdam in the 1970s, I met a young American couple at the youth hostel. Somehow, we connected and headed off to see the city together. I was older and wiser, had been to Amsterdam before and knew my way around. I think the couple had both just finished high school; possibly they were in an exchange semester at a European school. I never did learn the exact nature of their relationship. Possibly they had met in Europe and just ended up traveling together. I did recognize that the boy had the hots for the girl, and rightfully so.

She was one of those clean, thin, beautiful girls who look as though they should be wearing tan jodhpurs and carrying a riding crop. Blonde or red hair, I can't remember which, but she had freckles; I remember them. He was a very attractive, all-American boy.

We went on the Heineken Brewery tour, to the Rijksmuseum, and then to one of my favorite pubs for some good Dutch beer and maybe a puff or two. As we left the pub, we headed off across The Dam. I glanced back, and the young man was lagging behind, looking at something. On a whim, I grabbed the girl's hand and began running. We ran till we were sure we had lost him.

I had known instinctively that she wanted to be alone with me. Instinctively, because she had not made any overt advances. She had actually seemed to show indifference to my company up to that point. But there was something.

Amsterdam is a city unlike any other city. It exudes indulgence, yet it also demands taste and creativity. As with Venice, the waterways romanticize everything, from garbage collection to prostitution. Like New York City, Amsterdam possesses an air of sophistication. Along with Paris, it oozes sensuality. As Chicago, Amsterdam has an undercurrent of the underworld, and like Disneyland, it is a playground.

Amsterdam barge

Winding through the narrow streets, over the bridges and along the canals, we finally came to the barge of a friend of mine. I knew how to get in. The friend was gone, as I knew he would be.

I took off her clothes and carried her to the bed. I went down between her beautiful, freckled legs and licked her until she cried out. From her reaction, I believe it was the first time anyone had ever put their tongue on her clitoris, or even touched it for that matter. At first, she seemed ashamed by her own outpouring of sounds and the emotions she was feeling. She was surprised by the sensations, yet pleased at the same time.

She was shivering when I finally sat up on my knees and positioned himself between her thighs, ready to enter her. The room was cold, but that was not why she was shaking. She was scared, and she was excited.

I had taken her someplace she had never been before. I had shown her a part of herself she had not known existed. I was about to fuck her, and she didn't quite know how it had happened. She was a little afraid, but even more confused because she wanted it to happen.

I leaned down over her, hands on either side of her body. Her eyes were closed. I looked at the freckles on her neck, shoulders and

318

chest. Her breasts were cute, sugar white, hand size, and not yet fully developed. The extended nipples were rose pink, not brown. She had tiny, light brown moles where the sun didn't shine, as freckled girls often do. The almost transparent white hair that covered her body gave highlights to the soft, round breasts.

I looked down at this beautiful vision as I slowly moved my pelvis toward hers. I didn't need to guide my erection; it knew where it was going.

When the head of my penis touched her vagina, she opened her eyes for a second. Seeing me, she closed them again. The look on her face did not betray anything. It was peaceful, beautiful, and curious. She licked her lips.

My hard-on found her dampness. Her legs were spread as wide as she could. Her knees were up and heels dug into the mattress. I pushed and began to slowly slip inside. Her tightness resisted in a very exciting way. As I broke through and entered completely, her mouth pursed, she released a breath of air and her eyes popped open. She raised her pelvis to meet me, and then her eyes rolled back to hide again behind embarrassed eyelids.

She was very new. Her vagina was tight, yet soft, and it held me firmly. Her tightness was stimulating, her firmness exciting.

I penetrated slowly deeper until, as she relaxed, I slipped fully into her and our pubic bones met. I then began slowly pumping in and out of her, again and again with increasing speed and aggression.

She welcomed me with pain and pleasure. Her little breasts jumped with each thrust, and her hands gripped the sheets. Her hair, unruly for the first time in her life, spilled across the crumpled bed. Her stomach muscles strained as she rose to meet each entry. I had to concentrate on enjoying the moment to keep from rushing to an orgasm.

With each penetration, her legs waved in the air, bending slightly at the knees. She gave little high-pitched grunts with the thrusts and began to smile and laugh and toss her head from side to side.

I entertained myself in this way for sometime until I realized that although she was enjoying these new sensations, she would probably not reach orgasm with just this stimulus. I wanted her to come. I wanted her to scream out in uncontrolled joy.

Without withdrawing from inside her, I brought her right leg down then slipped my left leg over it, drawing her left leg up in front of me, I rolled her over onto her right side. Our legs were scissors together, groin-to-groin. Pulling her thigh toward my stomach, I pushed deeper into her tight body. Through experience, I had found that, in this position, I was able to thrust as deeply into a woman as I could possibly go.

My first deep probe took her breath away. She was surprised by the sensation which reached far up into her belly.

I could only imagine her previous sexual encounters, which were likely painful, awkward insertions, ejaculations and quick, self-conscious withdrawals conducted within the confining discomfort of the back seat of a car.

I touched her clitoris with the thumb of my left hand, and she jumped. Our juices lubricated the little button and my thumb slipped smoothly over and around it. She began to climb a mountain from which she would soon jump into a pool of warm orgasm.

I myself become excited by her sounds of insistence. The tickle in my groin was building too.

I was deep inside her, pumping slowly, yet faster each moment. My thumb was softly rubbing her clitoris in time. She reached higher. I reached higher.

She was almost there. I was just behind her.

Quickly, I pulled out of her and lifted her up, turning her toward the bed on her hands and knees with her ass up in the air toward me. Between her legs, I rammed myself back into her vagina. Grabbing her hips, I drove myself into her, hard and fast in unison with her gasping breath. Soon, I was about to burst. Reaching around her body, I found her clitoris again with my two middle fingers and began to manipulate it with each thrust.

Within moments we both screamed and came together. In her ecstasy, all muscle control was lost, and she fell forward onto her stomach, where I pinned her to the bed, and we writhed convulsively, her pelvis thrusting against my hand beneath her.

As we walked back to the youth hostel, her disorientation was obvious. She couldn't relate to me as a lover, or as a friend. What we had just shared was too intimate for a friendship and too animalistic for a love affair.

We walked along as superficial acquaintances. She was not quite able to contemplate what had just happened to her. She was embarrassed by my presence beside her. She felt everyone we passed knew what we had just been doing.

She must not see me again, she said; she had to find her friend and apologize to him. They had plans to leave early in the morning together for Germany.

She ignored me in the dining room that night. In the morning before I awoke, she and the young man left for the train.

That day, I met a Canadian girl and took her to the boat. She was as different as could be from the small, freckled girl. The Canadian was tall and dark and knew what she wanted.

The day after that, I met a plump, blonde Dutch girl, and we made love in her tiny Dutch bed up a ladder in a cubbyhole in the wall. It was the sexual seventies; making love was like exchanging business cards, or like having a conversation, yet a conversation expressing deeper emotions, some good, some complex.

A greeting conversation, though it may contain talk of the weather, or politics or what school you went to, was very often a prelude and adjudication to sex.

This was during my "arrogant days." I was being more than normally aggressive. I just wanted to fuck. Yet I was also exploring my feelings.

During the 15 years, roughly, from 1967 to about 1982, I was functionally just an attachment to my dick, a body tagging along following it around, just for the fun of it. As the years rolled on I became more and more discriminating and less aggressive, yet more accomplished in my relationships and seduction. But in the mid 1970s, I was just plain greedy.

I never forced anyone. I wasn't going to hurt them. In fact, it was all going to be very enjoyable, so why should they object? I had learned a secret. Pushing the primal button. Women, even outwardly liberated women, respond to primal strength in men.

In the tribal cultures of our Stone Age, the man who exerted the most strength physically and socially became the chief, and he had as many women as he wanted. A powerful hunter who could feed many wives and children had many women.

The mechanism of attraction toward strength is still deep inside most women. Yet in this modern culture, today, body strength or outward power may not be the best choice in a mate. A man who makes a lot of money often has his pick of women. An arrogant person appears strong. A violent brute may seem to be a good choice because of his value as a protector.

Yet the fallacy of these choices can be that the wealthy man is often self-absorbed in his wealth, the arrogant man is insecure, and insecurity often leads to violence and spousal abuse.

But a man who knows how to use power around woman will sleep with many. And a man who really loves women will sleep with many more.

What I later learned was that using power like that was often undue force. Sometimes you can catch a woman off guard and coerce her into something she would normally not do. When ovulation is a factor or stimulants are involved, a woman can respond contrary to her normal nature. Often, she will feel shame or deep remorse afterwards, especially if she realizes that she was taken advantage of.

To the psyche of some women, it can be like suffering a rape. To many women their virtue is a very important sacrament which they hold for the proper time and the proper person. That too is primal. Mother Nature conveys to the inner women the importance of whose seed she accepts. Is this man worthy to be her children's father, will he care for them, does he have a strong will to live?

Sometimes, seduction overpowers this natural selection process, and sometimes the ecstasy of sex will divert a woman from nature's important chores. I diverted the attention of that young girl in Amsterdam. I caught her completely by surprise. She had no idea she could do those things.

The Canadian girl was altogether different; she was fearless. She had her own desires. But the American girl was not quite comfortable with her sexuality, and yet, I can tell you one thing, she would never again put up with bad sex. She would demand that her men satisfy her from that day on, or else she would find someone who would.

CHAPTER 69

# **The Rapist!**

A rapist is someone who forces their desires upon, and steals sex from another person. But that is only the beginning of the horror of the act. Even in the animal world it is not acceptable to take sex! You may deceive or coerce a partner, and that is bad enough, but to take a woman's most precious gift is to become the scum of the earth. Raping a woman takes you out of humanity. You become an aberration, you are not strong, you are not masculine, you are a weak, insecure and pathetic worm.

I understand desire! I have felt its pull, it's overpowering of one's mental capacity. Stupid is a good term for what it can make a man. But to let it take you to a place where you are not even human anymore is where the desire to steal sex takes a person.

CHAPTER 70

# Barbarians Have All The Fun

Back in the 1970's I created a bumper sticker that read: *Barbarians Have All The Fun.* I used the word barbarian as sarcasm to those who think that only perverted or immoral people party, indulge in stimulants and have sex. It is a lie and hypocritical to pretend that "normal people" don't get drunk, crazy, and screw sometimes. But often, these "normal folk" do get crazy, and then they lie about it.

The "free" in "free love" has nothing to do with economics; it has everything to do with tolerance.

Free love is not just about getting a lot of sex; it's about being free enough to give unconditional love. It is about loving freely enough to let your lover be free to love others. It is about self-confidence. People who are insecure want to control their lovers. A self-assured person is not afraid of losing love by letting a lover run free.

324

Free love is allowing others to have the same freedom in love as you take yourself. When you demand freedom for yourself, you must also give that same freedom to others. Hypocrisy has no place in free love.

Free yourself from uptight emotions. Free yourself from judging those who set their emotions free.

It was very evident during the hippie era that some people were jealous of others who were having more fun than they were. The hippies were enjoying themselves, and that gave straight society more reason to dislike them.

It's almost as if some people are afraid to feel good. It's a religious thing; they have been told by their church and pastor that certain activities are sinful. If these activities happen to be fun, this automatically creates jealousy in the abstainer when he sees other people indulging.

Jealousy is also felt by those who are awkward about a subject or by those who are unable to function properly in a situation. It is a mechanism of emotional self-preservation as old as the apes. Humans have learned to hate that which they can't do, but would like to do, because if something is demonized, that makes it easier to avoid trying to do it and failing.

People hate their own weakness, fear their desires and then transfer that fear and hatred into indignation directed at those who are doing what they can't do because of insecurity or won't do because of religious commitments. In self-defense they choose to ridicule and even hate those who are not living by the same restrictions into which they are forced.

The next step for these people is to isolate this activity, this "sin" in which they don't indulge, as something only "other people" do. In their minds they believe that they are not capable of that sin; it is performed only by others. So when they do indulge in that sin or a deviation of it, which they most often do eventually, they can lie to themselves and pretend that what they are doing is really something else which is not really sinful.

These self-righteous people will often continue to condemn others for these sins while they themselves are performing them. This, of course, is hypocrisy, and hypocrisy is actually a sin worse than the so called "original sin." Original Sin, of course, is the term most religious people use for sex, but I ask how it can be a sin if it brings life?

Hypocrisy, professing moral laws, then breaking those laws and denying it, is much more sinful and damaging than if one were just to do what felt good and accept the responsibility for what they did.

I'm not talking about actions that negatively affect others. Murder, rape and theft are understood by all societies to be morally and legally wrong. These acts break the Golden Rule, and I don't think they should ever be committed.

Moral laws created by religions that have no victim except oneself are self-indulgences by people who just want to control others and give themselves elevation. Cult leaders are people who want money and devotion (the hypocracy of religious leaders). I feel a person can choose to break, just as long as they don't lie about it later. If you lie about it, then you are ashamed of your actions, and that means you are being untrue to yourself.

When people lie to themselves, they perform the worst of mankind's sins. They are lowering humanity and denying the common sense that God gave us as his greatest gift to mankind. If you say one thing and do something else, that is deception of yourself and denial of your own common sense.

If you place moral restrictions on yourself and others, saying that they come from God, and then break those rules yourself, you are sinning against your own God, mankind and yourself. Yet, if you merely break the moral laws others have imposed on you from their God, then you are only rejecting the authority of their God.

If I reject your moral laws, I am not sinning when I break your laws. But if you break your own moral laws, then you are sinning twice--first by imposing unjust laws and then by breaking them yourself.

*"I did it, but if I pray, my sin will be wiped away!"*
*JOB*

*"Hypocrisy is possibly the worst sin of all, and this because, when you do one thing and say another you are not only lying to me, you are lying to yourself and also to your own God."*
J.5.7.14

The added twist to this scenario is that, with religion as we have created it, a "religious sinner" always has a way out anyway. He or she can just get absolution for the sin by paying somebody, or in some denominations all you have to do is get down on your knees and cry and ask forgiveness.

We humans are such weasels. We never want to take responsibility for our own faults. We always want to have a God to blame for our mistakes and then to tell us we are forgiven for those sins. We want to think that we are weak and can't help ourselves because God created these temptations. And even though we failed (because of his temptations), we still have a way to save our little butts by apologizing to our God.

We don't really apologize to the other person we hurt with our "sin" because the deed is already done. Our wife is cheated upon, the girl is raped, the guy is killed, but we feel OK because we have gone to our God, and He has forgiven us.

Do you know how many people in jail have found religion? They have absolved themselves in their own minds.

What's really strange about this is that it amounts to a process of accusing God of causing the sin and then asking for His forgiveness. How many jailhouse residents say, "God told me to do it," and then they find religion and are saved from guilt.

In so many words the church deacon who molests his own daughter is saying, "God made me do it," and now, "He has absolved me of my sins." God is a convenient scapegoat for our own greed and weakness. We have created a perfect loophole so we don't have to "Do Unto Others As We Would Have Others Do Unto Us."

Love out in the world

## CHAPTER 71

# Sperm, The River of Life

The orgasm is an interesting study. As a thorough person, I have done as much research as I possibly can.

Mother nature created this strange tickle in your groin, that uncontrollable muscle dance, the uninhibited audible sounds, the sweet, soft, caress in your brain.

So much for trying to explain the orgasm in words. This dilemma really bugs the shit out of me as a writer. My whole being wants to communicate. I want you to Understand (with a capital U) what I am thinking and feeling.

So I go and have a couple of more orgasms to see if I can get more explicit with my writing. I tried one by myself. Then I tried one with a woman.

It was Saint Patrick's Day; they were serving green beer and greener scotch. I have had very few experiences picking up women in bars that I previously didn't know. I didn't know this girl. We talked, we drank, and we went back to her place.

This girl was beautiful. She was not tall, but thin and well-formed. Her skin, smooth and darkly tanned. Her hair was full and alive, somewhere between brown and black. Her face was beautifully proportioned, nose small and unobtrusive, eyes soft, yet expressive. Her mouth was a little large, but that is appealing to me, and it made for good kisses.

Moments after we arrived at her place, her blouse, dress and underpants were off and on the floor. Her legs were open wide, knees bent and feet planted firmly on the bed. Her pelvis was thrust toward me, and her vagina, open almost inside out, the red ruffled lips of her labia spread, revealing the damp, pink opening into her.

Her breasts were large, but well shaped, and firm, her nipples reaching out wanting to be coaxed. They were both wet from my mouth. I had licked each nipple until it stood up with pride. I was standing between her legs. She was draped over the edge of the bed. I had just dropped my shorts to the floor letting my erection free. It was proud and engorged with blood.

Her eyes looked into mine as she reached down, cupped my balls in one hand and began slowly, softly pumping my hard-on with the other. She wet her fingers with her tongue to lubricate the movement. Her hands interchanged in their interest and took turns stroking and fondling in a way that made it seem as if she were worshiping my penis.

I began touching her clitoris with the thumb and forefinger of one hand and softly, slowly pushed the middle finger of my other hand into her vagina. A quick breath of air, a moan and a tiny squeal escaped her throat as her eyes shot open wide with pleasant surprise.

After some time thus employed, we both became elevated to a mutual point of excitement. Slowly, we intensified our rhythm, matching each other, and our audible breathing soon fell into unison.

It could have been minutes, it could have been hours that we played like this, but it was only the prelude to a long afternoon of lovemaking. When we finally joined together at the intercourse of our sexes, it was in a warm wash of resignation. We moved slowly, but surely, then anxiously, and then violently.

It was only after some long time that we began to consider

searching for a culmination. We moved as if suspended in space, connected only by my umbilical erection. Her hands waved in the air above her head as I ran my hands over her breasts, belly and clitoris in rhythm with our thrusting. The sounds of her squeals and my groans built with the anxiety of our approach to that wonderful and terrible experience of orgasm.

We pounded at each other in an increasing crescendo of strength. We were on the brink, afraid to fall, afraid not to fall. Wanting it not to end, and yet wishing for the champagne taste of the finish.

I leaned forward and engulfed her in my arms, and she threw hers around me as we continued thrusting. I was trying to get as much of my body as close to her as I could. It was as if our molecules squashed together and became one, yet clamped together as we were, our genitals continued massaging each other, each penetration stimulating more feeling and more want.

Her body seemed to suck me in with each of our thrusts, and then to contract, pushing my erection out with a caress. My dick seemed to engorge upon entry, and then, fully enlarged within, it massaged her vagina as I pulled out to repeat the process.

Suddenly realizing that we had reached that irreversible point of no return, we looked into each other's flushed faces and started laughing, screaming and crying as over the falls we fell together.

"Yes, yes, yes, yes, oh God, oh God, oh God" she said, and then screamed a piercing shot to my ears and soul.

I puffed and puffed and drove deeper even though deeper was a physical impossibility. Explosion!

Our thrusting slowly ran down like a wind-up doll at the end of its spring. For a moment we remained, our bodies locked together, her bare legs wrapped around my ass pulling me in, both of us as rigid as some erotic bronze sculpture. Staring into each other's eyes inches apart, our mouths were wide-open, grabbing gulps of air to refresh and cleanse our blood. The end!

And strangely enough, although I have related this in a vivid sensual reconstruction, I admit that I really don't remember any of our lovemaking that day. You know what I remember most about that event? As we lay there in her bed, satiated, sweat spent and glowing from the beautiful sex that we had just perpetrated, I looked up at a photograph on her wall and saw a friend. "How do you know Pit?" I asked in panting half interest.

Pit, a carpentry acquaintance of mine, was in jail at the time for selling a few kilograms of marijuana. "He's my husband," she said in the same sex-spent breathlessness as I had asked. Well, I got outta there as soon as it was socially possible, and you can believe I can't remember a damn thing about that orgasm. But, sure enough, just as with Chinese food, I was hungry again within an hour.

And what I remember most about her was that she could give the best rendition of the lollypop kids in *The Wizard of OZ*!


Men, today, are being criticized, rightfully, for being men. I said, rightfully, because man is the perpetrator of most of the bad things that happen on this earth. I am like a parent who wants my family to be happy and live a good life, so I must suggest, cajole, discipline and criticize my fellow sex to get their sack of shit together!


Some of you may consider this book to be too raw, explicit and perhaps profane. You may also think I am too personally involved in the story to be trusted to tell the truth, but I am telling the true story. I had to experience sex in order to know it thoroughly enough to be able to write about it. And people had to believe I knew what I was writing about to be able to listen with conviction. You shouldn't buy a knife from someone who hasn't made a knife.

CHAPTER 72

# I Was Enlightened By Rock & Roll; It Was Enlightened By Me

## The Hippie Music Chapter

Music took on a new value in the 1960s and 70s. It was not just our physical stimulus; it became our political voice and emotional expression.

"Light My Fire" was not just a sexual turn-on; it was an attitude adjustment!
"Ball And Chain" was not just a woman singing to us; it was a person asking us to listen!

Songs, albums and music that changed the world into the new world: Top 12, Déjà vu, Crosby, Stills, Nash and Young, 1970
Sgt. Pepper's Lonely Hearts Club Band, The Beatles, 1967
Surrealistic Pillow, Jefferson Airplane, 1967
Tea For The Tillerman, Cat Stevens, 1970
The Times They Are a-Changin', Bob Dylan, 1964
Blue, Joni Mitchell, 1971
Brown Sugar, The Rolling Stones, 1971
Bridge Over Troubled Water, Simon & Garfunkel, 1970
Brothers and Sisters, The Allman Brothers, 1973
Dreams, Fleetwood Mac, 1977
The Lion Sleeps Tonight, The Tokens, 1961
Light My Fire, The Doors, 1967

These pieces of music are not my top ten for their dance ability or how much money they made, but because of how they changed peoples' emotions and sensibilities. We loved more after we heard these albums, we heard more in the song of a bird or in a moonrise, we began to think man might actually be able to create beauty as well as all the wars that we were accustomed to from mankind.

Simon & Garfunkel taught us more about tolerance than about music.
Stevie Wonder had more love than we could ignore.
John Lennon was the tragic side of idolatry.
The Doors separated the men from the boys.
Bob Marley gave us all a groove.
Bob Dylan hasn't told us yet.

I wish I had the photographs I took of my only Doors concert. They were stolen by a person I shared my darkroom with. I climbed the lighting scaffolding, and I drank with the band. The negatives were hanging in my darkroom when I went to bed, and in the morning my Panama hat and the strips of black and white film were gone. His name was Random Hazard. No fooling! Don't trust him!

Some works of art and works of man's labor are sermons, and these are often more healing than words of praise or condemnation by religions of society. God, if or when he exists, would never allow the villains who run this world to continue. So we must find some way to become the power of God as a whole bunch of individuals. God would not want us to let the tyrants push us around.

It is hard, if not impossible, to predict what would have happened if something else had not happened. History is a line of circumstances related to the events before them. We can alter history, but will it create the circumstance we want? Are we strong enough or wise enough or entitled to mess with history?

But we must keep trying, and perhaps we will eventually get it right. Music is one of the most profound, yet subtle, persuasions of liberal ideology. Keep singing. It is almost as if, when you are singing a thought, you cannot lie.

I don't see the future; I only have hope for the future. I can only tell you that I know mankind is capable of healing itself and being a proper husband to this beautiful earth, our Garden of Eden.

CHAPTER 73

# Am I A Real Man If...?

Even a guy with a good measure of self-confidence will, at times, wonder if he is fulfilling his manly obligations. Procreator, provider and protector are the three basic primal duties of a man...not necessarily in that order, but heavy on our shoulders.

So far in this book I have only talked around the subject of sexual prowess and often discounted its importance. That is because I believe sexual ability is over emphasized and misunderstood. And as you may have noticed I feel that a man's sexual duty, in this modern age, is more about human consciousness than male assertiveness. Survival may depend upon mankind becoming less aggressive. Yes, I said, less God dammed competitive and less subject to stupid macho behavior!

Sexually explicit humor and even some smarmy TV shows like Friends, Jersey Shore, Sex In The City, Two Men and A Boy, Blockers and Two Broke Girls are actually good for us to experience as a back door sort of education. These examples of idiotic human behavior can, if we are bright enough to get the real joke, show us how stupid and arrogant macho posturing really is.

We are no longer living under the extreme competitive circumstances that confronted cavemen and women. It is not necessary for a man to fight physically for the right to mate with a woman, nor is it necessary for every man to grab and impregnate every woman he meets in order to ensure the survival of the species.

Competition for a mate today should be more like a dance than a battle. Sadly though, a battle often breaks out at the end of the relationship because someone has faked their abilities or overblown their value.

Man's sexual obligations are covered throughout this book. The subject of provider will be explored in future chapters, but here I want to address the protector in man's psyche. In order for a man to be a good protector, he must have a stable personality and a reasonable self-image.

The dynamics of sexual competition have changed; the elements of physical prowess are now paradoxically defined, yet greatly confused by the new and strange deviations available today. It is what causes all these endorphin freaks such frustration because of all the new sexual sublimations available. When and where does a man have the opportunity to express and exhibit his manly physical strength and guts? Perhaps jumping out of airplanes, video game violence, or cat-fishing on social networks will get you off.

If guys only knew that the excessive competitive nature they exhibit in sports is the least human of all human traits. Would macho men demur if they realized that their posturing places them back in the dark ages where animal nature, not rational human behavior, mattered? Sorry guys, I like to put a word like demur into context with a term like macho! Demur means to change your mind or object. It may not occur to some or compute to others, but men and women need to come together, or we will all blow apart.

If "rough" guys only knew they were actually throwbacks to a time and place when mankind was not evolved as we should be today, would they change? No, not likely, nor possibly, would they understand what I was talking about.

And women willingly date and marry men like this. I guess they do so realizing that it is the easiest choice! Finding a good man is, I'm sorry to say, a difficult search in this screwed-up world today. I am really not a negative soul, but it is hard to deny the problems of relationships these days. I have a lot of good male friends, yet I wouldn't marry most of them.

Even though I personally don't have an ultra-competitive nature, I have often wondered how I would react in an emergency. Not necessarily a fight or self-defense scenario, but just in a situation where quick, levelheaded abilities were required.

I have seen statistics that say in America 75% of all people will live out their whole lives without ever experiencing a mortal threat. I'm sure there are many men who are out there wondering whether they would be a wuss or a hero if the emergency arose. Minor emergencies, not life-threatening dangers, are the only way to show your protective and nurturing skills in a first or second-world nation these days.

I have been truly tested only once. That was when I was caught by the Army sergeant with his daughter's underpants in my pocket, but it never got to the critical point.

My emergency abilities test was in Afghanistan in 1978. No, I wasn't fighting the Taliban or fighting with the Taliban for that matter. I was just riding in a bus.

The bus ride was from Herat to Kabul, part of the hippie trail that ran from Greece through Turkey, Iran, Afghanistan, Pakistan and into India. It's also called the Spice, Gold or Silk Road.

I was with a girlfriend and maybe half-a-dozen hippie friends we had met over the last month in our travels. The bus was also filled with dozens of Iranians, Pakistani and Afghani travelers.

Long story short, we had a bus accident. Most of the passengers in the front third of the bus were pinned-in between seats. It took us hours to extract them all. Nobody died in the accident, but there were many broken bones and compound fractures.

That day proved to me that I was a man, not just a body taking up space. I didn't falter; I acted.

It's a valuable moment in a person's life to realize you are up to the challenges that might come. It is more than just an endorphin rush like lifting weights or beating someone up in an octagon.

Finding out that you are undeniably a useless wimp is the most painful thing a man can suffer, which is just above a lover's rejection, which is just above having your balls impaled on a rusty, medieval iron spike.

*"My name is John Bassett McCleary and I am an animal, but I am not one of those dirty rotten unfaithful, greedy, usless human beings!" JBMc, 1.25.15*

The back of the bus.

Later, after the accident, I worked with these men to save lives in the front of the bus. The big man at the back helped me tear the bench seats out of the bus floor to extract the injured.

The bus trip from Herat, to Kabul took most of a day. The road was a narrow, two-lane, with no shoulder, dropping off to a barren, rolling, hard pack vista looking north to mountains and south to the horizon. At that time, it was the main road in the country of Afghanistan.

The bus was filled with some of us hippie travelers, a few people from Turkey and Iran, and a majority of Afghans, both rich and poor. One of my photographs is of the working class gentlemen in the back of the bus. As in America, in Birmingham, Alabama, in the 1950s, the disenfranchised rode in the back of the bus. My girlfriend, Audrey, and I were in the middle. The more prestigious in front included, as I remember, one pregnant woman. The hippies rode in the middle, and the blue-collar workers, in the back.

The bus, as many in this part of the world, had two doors in front, one next to the driver and one on the other side for the passengers. At the passenger door sat the busboy with a samovar for tea and hot towels to wash the dust from your face. And there was dust. Lest you get some grand notion of this bus, it was like an old Mexican bus, without the animals. Yet, here in America, with all our amenities and pretenses, Greyhound doesn't have the niceties of tea and hot towels.

The men in back were a jovial group of mixed Afghan ethnicity; in the front seats were families, couples and traveling businessmen. Several times during the trip the bus would stop for prayers. The Muslim occupants would leave the bus, spread their prayer rugs on the hardscrabble ground facing Mecca, and do their devotions.

At that time, I didn't know what was acceptable to photograph in their culture, so I missed that shot. Given what was to happen later, it would have been a classic and ironic photograph showing people praying beside a doomed bus.

On this road you could see an oncoming vehicle for five miles or more. Just outside Kabul, our bus driver decided to play chicken with another bus coming our way. They raced each other to be the first to pass a truck that had broken down in our lane.

None of the passengers knew of this drama until we hit the truck. Possibly the most brilliant thing our driver ever did in his whole life was to hit that truck, not the bus. His other two options were to run off the road down a five- or ten-foot embankment or to hit the oncoming bus.

You do the math: a bus going 40 mph hits a bus coming at it at 40 mph, and you have a 80 mph accident. He opted to hit an immobile object at 40 mph and take his chances.

When we hit the truck, Audrey and I were bounced around a lot, and I lost my glasses. I made sure Audrey was OK and started looking for my glasses. The man in front of me handed them to me over his shoulder, and then I began to survey the wreckage.

Almost everyone in front of us was trapped. The front of the bus had been pushed into the seats, and the seats behind had, through inertia, slammed forward. The driver had abandoned the wreckage and was gone. In many middle Eastern countries, the driver in a fatal crash may be in danger of physical retribution by the deceased's family.

All of the ambulatory passengers left the bus through the back emergency window, and as soon as the dust settled, we started to remove the trapped, injured and, for all we knew, possibly the dead. We soon realized it was impossible to get to the trapped through the front of the bus, so I suggested we try from the back.

Audrey was a student nurse, on her way to work with Mother Teresa in India. Yes, this is all true. She organized the medical triage. I am not sure, but I believe we saved lives that day.

My friends and I, some hippies and Afghans, started pulling the seats out of the back of the bus. One of my co-workers was a stoic, 6' 6" Afghan, one a jovial halfwit, and the other an analytical businessman, all in turbans with earth brown skin. We learned that three strong men could rock the double bench seats back and forth and rip out the bolts that attached them to the floor.

There were compound leg fractures, some multiple, and head and chest injuries. And there was the one pregnant woman.

By the time we got up to the busboy, it was in the dark of night. He was about ten or eleven years old. I don't know his name.... I wish I knew his name. He had two broken and crushed legs. I think about him often and his prospects with two damaged legs in that land with what was coming to them in the next few years.

I do not believe that anyone died at the scene of the accident, yet some, I knew, would be in mortal danger without proper modern medical care.

After the injured had been transported to hospitals, homes or other facilities in Kabul, I scrambled up on the roof of the bus to unload everyone's luggage. One of the most memorable moments of my life happened when I was on that roof.

Spontaneously, all of the Afghan people down below began to clap and ululate. In the combination of languages that prevailed there, I realized that the locals were thanking the hippie travelers for our efforts that night.

I am convinced that that bus accident was one of the very few moments in the history of Afghanistan where the Afghan people ever saw compassion coming from the visitors to their country.

The people of Afghanistan and India will say to you if asked that, the Hippies did not come to steal from them or kill them, as most others have, 'they came to see us, learn from us and teach us!'

*"Nobody is carrying the clipboard for the world right now. My friends and I would be happy to do so. We'd be happy to tell everybody in the world what they are doing wrong, because we know!"*
Mr. California

*"You have to get rid of your ego and try out other people's shoes!" DG*

*There is a correct for every situation. Whatever is right for the most people is correct!" JOB*

In Afghanistan and the Middle East, 1978.

On the hippie trail from Greece to India, one of the countries you must travel through is Pakistan. As my hippie friends and I got off the train in Lahore, Pakistan, where we were going to have to take another train to India later in the day, a distinguished gentleman approached and asked if we would help him.

As you may know, Pakistan is an Islamic country, and Muslims are not supposed to drink alcohol. You can't buy it if you are Muslim, touch it, transport it or drink it, although it is sold in special stores for consumption by citizens of other religious faiths. A certain segment of the population has devised a way to get around this.

The gentleman said that he would pay us to buy alcohol for him. This man was immaculately dressed in a Western style suit and spoke better English than any of us. Most of the other seven or eight hippies wanted to ignore him as we would most panhandlers at bus or train stations, but I told them we should at least listen to him.

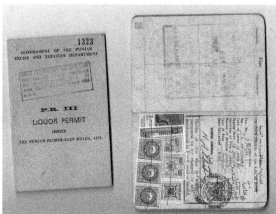

I worked for the Pakistan Mafia.

The process went like this: He would pay each of us to come with him get paperwork done, get a liquor permit, go to the liquor store, and then take the alcohol to his home. Neither he nor any other

Muslim person could touch the bottles out in public, so we had to physically deliver it into the house.

He would pay for any transportation and bring us back to the train station to catch our late afternoon train to India. I got him to pay for our train tickets in the transaction, and I, for one, wanted one bottle of beer, since I hadn't had any for several weeks. Turkey and Afghanistan are also a dry countries, and I had been able to find only one sanctioned bar in Tehran.

My fellow travelers eventually agreed, and we went off on our adventure. I have since then referred to that episode as my time working for the Pakistani mafia. As I had expected it was a good way to take up the time waiting for the train and to get an interesting tour of Lahore. It was quite a process for which, at my insistence, we used horse drawn carriages, motorcycle cabs and automobile taxi transportation. We must have been quite a parade of multiple vehicles carrying seven or so hippies and our two guides.

We needed to get a certificate filled out stating that we were Christians, then it was notarized at a card table on the street, then into a large British era government building to get the liquor permit. Then we got into three taxis to go out of town to a building in a compound surrounded by hurricane fence and barbed wire with armed guards to get the actual alcohol.

When getting the permit, we were asked what kind of alcohol and how many bottles we wanted. Our guide, the immaculate gentleman, had told what they wanted, and it was almost exclusively Johnnie Walker Red Label Scotch. He told us to get as many bottles as we could justify and that the government official would approve. As a man of a healthy stature, I was granted ten bottles, as most of the other men were. The two women got permits for fewer, and I can't remember how many.

The strangest part of the episode was when we were asked how long we were going to be in Pakistan. Our answer was three or four more hours. And the official asked if we could drink ten bottles before we left on the train. We said yes, and he stamped the permit. It was all a charade, and the officials knew what was going on. The immaculate gentleman paid the lawyer, the officials and the liquor store, in cash, from his own pocket, and off we went after physically carrying the boxes of bottles into the taxi and then into the gentleman's house. I drank my bottle of warm, green beer, and we collected our money and left by train for India.

What I figured was that the gentleman and his co-conspirators would advertise a party at their house and charge people an entry fee and/or sell shots of whisky for fifty dollars each or something like that.

## CHAPTER 74

# Break-up Sex

All relationships either cool or grow! One or the other of you may decide to go on or to end it. One or both of you can decide to make it permanent or to dissolve the experience.

Always be verbal about it. Don't just follow Paul Simon's song, "*50 Ways To Leave Your Lover!*" That may be easier, but it is spineless. You will lose part of your self-confidence if you just wimp out and leave, and you will spoil the beauty you had.

I can remember several relationships that I left, or was left, and the last sex we had was the most wonderful and added to the positive memory of that person and the time we had. Don't lose that experience, that time, those moments!

Break-up sex falls into two categories--memorial sex or desperation sex. Memorial break-up sex is if you are the one who is moving on, yet you want a good memory. Desperation break-up sex is when you really don't want the love affair to end and so you are trying to get the last taste or change the mind of your departing loved one.

There are four basic reasons for break-ups--it's mutual, or he wants it, or she wants it, or circumstances beyond your control dictate it. If you have never experienced break-up sex, then you have never broken up with someone, or they left without saying goodbye, or you have never had sex with them in the first place.

Pardon me if I get too pedantic or nit-picky-specific. Stick with me a while, because I have resolutions, maybe even solutions for your mind.

If you are the one who made the choice to break-up, then you have one set of emotions, and if you are the one left behind, another set of emotions prevail. Often at break-up neither person wants to even touch the other person again.

If you are the one who is leaving, you might be embarrassed to be the killjoy. Or if you are the one who is being left, you may rather poison the creep. Neither of these is really viable or proper, so my suggestion is that you both be rational and shake hands before, after or during the break-up sex.

When your time together is down to hours, you start to think of finality. You grasp for memories or resolutions. Well, that's not going to happen, because by now in your relationship, it is over one way or the other, no matter how wonderful your time together was or how good the sex is. I can honestly say that some of the best sex I have had, at least in the top 25%, has been goodbye sex.

*"When you are first lovers, you do not know where this thing is going. You have aspirations and hopes. And then you have realizations and fulfilments. And if the relationship ends, all aspirations, hopes and fulfillment seem to end abruptly. Yet fear not, you will have memories, and hopefully you will dwell on the good ones!"* DG

## CHAPTER 75

# A Snap Of The Fingers

There is something about the snap of fingers. It is, at once, a demand for attention and a statement of aggression. Along with that, if it is done with the right intent, it is a cool move. It is also an action that, upon this earth, can be done only by Homo Sapiens.

Back in the 1950s we had that move that consisted of snapping your fingers and hitting your fist into your palm making the sound, tic, tic, pop!

You saw it in *Dirty Dancing*, if you looked closely enough. But that tic, tic, pop can be pulled off only by someone who has the attitude.

The finger snap has always been sexually aggressive. It is a particularly male manifestation. It can only be employed properly by a man who knows what he wants. But it is a joke or a fool's mistake if done by the wrong person at the wrong time.

The sexual demand, portrayed in TV and movies with the snap of the finger, is a fantasy! I have never employed it and would never seriously use it to "ask" a woman to have sex with me regardless of the "*How I Met Your Mother*" or "*Friends*" scripting.

CHAPTER 76

# Male Mythology And Anti-Mythology

*"A man has to be truly self-confident to venture into a partner swapping episode. It is not for the faint of heart. If you are at all insecure or jealous, I suggest you rent a video instead.*
*I was only a contributor to a few of such adventures. The coolest thing I got from these experience was not new nookie, but an unqualified education.*
*After the first couple of swapping experiences, I stopped seeking them out. Not that I couldn't handle the weird aftermath myself, but because I didn't like getting involved in the jealousy dynamics of other couples. I only went into a swapping experience when I had transient girlfriend.*
*I would never consider it with a serious lover or wife. What I learned was that you had to have detachment to do it. And that was the problem; a man either didn't care deeply enough about his mate to swap her, or afterwards he would go into a jealous rage."*
Dudley Griffin, 12.31.06

*"Men actually do have ideals!*
*Taking a virgin is one of man's mythological creations that is self-perpetuating!*
*If a girl gives you willingly her maidenhead, then it is reality... I believe being given the true Camelot of sex."*
DG

CHAPTER 77

# The Rejection

Rejection is not an easy hat to wear,
but it should not always be taken personally.

Women reject men for one set of reasons; men reject women for other reasons. As a rule, men reject for more personal reasons, usually physical. Women reject for more social reasons, often economic, cultural or educational.

The process of choosing or rejecting a mate is one of the most graphic examples of primeval male/female relations. It is a capsule of our history as creatures. If you can't handle rejection, you are probably not very evolved, and most likely you don't belong in this day and age.

Rejection lines are an interesting study. "Go stick it in the wall!" was one of my favorite setbacks.

I once took a girl out on a "date," or maybe I met her at a party, I can't remember. She was a tall, dark beauty, I believe Native American. I was hot-to-trot, and from what I remember she was leading me on.

But when we got to her house she stopped me at the door with one last kiss, and laid this line on me. She said and I quote, "My body is so beautiful that once a guy sees it he becomes dysfunctional, and it never goes anywhere!"

Well, I tried to assure her that it would not happen with me, but she wouldn't hear it. I still wonder about that body. Up to that time I had touched some beautiful women, but what if she were as striking as she thought she was, and if so, would I have been able to perform? Well, I don't really question. I have no doubts that I would have risen to the challenge!

But I didn't push her anyway, because I knew it was just her ploy. It was her strange way to brush off guys.

Having said that, I must add that I think it was a very bizarre form of rejection. There seemed to be several levels of subtle humor laced with ridicule, glazed with irony.

She was dismissing me as an inexperienced lover, who would prematurely ejaculate, or worst case, not be able to get it up at all. I often wondered if that statement was a test. Apparently, I failed. I have also wondered if there were a right answer or comeback to that statement.

I guess I was more disturbed by her rejection than I realized since I have thought about it all these years. In retrospect, I have finally realized that I had the perfect rebuttal to her accusation of prematurity, and that is my circumcision.

All those years ago, this was in the early 1980s, I didn't know the significance of my medical procedure. Had I known to mention it to this girl, knowing her spunky attitude, she likely would have wanted to see it, and I would have been "in like Flynn."

Well, without that trump card, I slept alone that night. She saw something in me she didn't like, or maybe she didn't see something she needed. I didn't take it personally.

Years latter, I saw that women again, and she was acting as though she wished our night had turned out differently. But by then, I was married, and I didn't see anything in her that I needed.

It's all very subtle, the scent, the sound of a voice, the way they hold themselves, the movement of their hands.

Early in your life of love, these things don't matter, or if they do, they are subconscious feelings. Later in life we began to choose more specifically due to more profound and subtle likes and dislikes.

It is impossible to be "all lover, to all people." There are many disqualifiers, some that you don't realize exist and some that if you did, you would not be able to change anyway.

Of course, there are a few universally disliked bad traits or habits. Cleanliness is one of the most obvious, yet you would be amazed at how many men don't follow the Golden Rule in this regard.

Most men, I believe, require a certain standard of cleanliness in a mate, but many men don't pay much mind to their own filthy habits.

Guys, your percentages for scoring are better the cleaner you and your bedroom are. That realization alone should keep most red-blooded boys tidy; it is possibly the most compelling argument for soap.

Some men have weak hands; some people exude strange personal odors. Slouching, squinty eyes, shuffling walk, pigeon toes, some of these trigger subliminal detractors to other people.

But when it comes down to it, you can't really change all of these things in yourself or keep up with everybody's likes and dislikes. Then again, some people might think that slouching, squinty eyes and a shuffle in the walk are cool.

I also want to bring up the subject of inequality of rejection. I am sorry to say that in essence, it is easier for a woman to get laid than for a man. I have actually had many women dispute this, but they were factoring in selectivity. Women are usually more selective than men, so they don't "get laid" as often. But men, even though they are much less selective, have a much harder time getting laid.

Take, for example, a man and a woman with about the same level of attractiveness are sent out to proposition for sex partners.

If a woman propositions the first 10 men she meets, she will be very busy, on her back, for the next hour and a half. Fifteen minutes per. She might get one rejection (he's either gay or 82 years old), and one fellow might take half an hour to build up to his orgasm (he's 82 years old or reading Eastern religion).

The man who propositions 10 women will acquire a good number of bruises and probably end up in jail. It is easier for a woman to get laid.

Some men are more active than others. Whether it is skill, guts or desire that determines this, is not measurable. But it seems that 10% of the men get 90% of the babes.

You may have caught some confusing discrepancy in this particular discourse on the number of sex partners a man may have compared to how many a woman has. First off, it must be noted and agreed that every time a man is having a heterosexual encounter, then a woman is also having sex--with him of course! It takes two, at least. But these sex acts may be with the same person or with different people every time.

The discrepancy is that, out of any group of, say, ten women and ten men, not every one of them is having sex regularly. There are more sexually promiscuous men than sexually promiscuous women. I think everyone will agree with that statement!

But I actually believe there are a few women who are getting more sex than even the most sexually promiscuous men, and here is why. With more promiscuous men and fewer promiscuous women, the women who will are getting more action. In all of this I am factoring out married couples and prostitutes.

What is pertinent about this scenario is that there are a few women who are getting a lot of sex, some women are getting a little sex, and some women who are getting none. On the men's side, we have rock stars and sports figures who are screwing everyone. There are a few other men who are getting a lot of sex, most men are getting some sex, and a few who are getting none. For illustration I am using 10 men and 10 women in a community.

If you were able to follow that, then you now have a lot of useless esoteric information about human sexual behavior.

## CHAPTER 78

# Fear And Hate!

### Or Power Versus Force!

This is an element in male-female sexual relations. Many men believe that to be strong and forceful is the proper way to meet, win and hold a woman. But they are only thinking as a man does. Women respect and follow compassion more than violence, and understanding more than dominance.

Some misguided people think it is a sign of strength to be feared. Only a person with an insecure ego believes that.

The damnedest thing that I can think of are people who would rather be feared than loved. They just don't know what they're missing!

What most people don't realize is that fear breeds hatred. It does not create respect! If you want to be a hated person, treat other people poorly.

Having power and respect is the goal of an intelligent leader. Noblesse oblige, again, a French word meaning if you have power in a democratic country, you have a responsibility to be a good and benevolent leader.

The problem is that there are some people who are emotionally drawn to powerful and abrasive leaders: Hitler, Stalin, Trump and Putin. And the reason is because they are weak or feel weak in their lives, and they seem to think that having an abusive leader will raise them up to being a leader themselves.

The saddest and strangest misunderstanding of fear and respect has to do with love. There are some asses out there who think that they can receive love by stealing it or bullying someone into giving it to them. Love, by virtue of its name, is a sincere, freely-given emotion, the best of humankind's emotions.

Why would you ever want to be hated by the person you are having sex with? You might just as well shoot yourself and get it over with. You will never find happiness in your life!

A person is usually made into a good or bad person by outside influences; often it is their own family. It's a moment of goodness that can make a good man, or a moment of cruelty that can make a man a creature!

I believe if you care about other people and your place in society and the world, you should take stock of yourself from time to time. OK, be truthful. Above all, don't exaggerate to yourself about yourself. Are you a good person, do you like people, do people like you? Can you sing, can you dance? Can you cook, drive a car, mutually make love with someone? If not, you will be rejected more than accepted!

CHAPTER 79

# Young Stuff

The term "young stuff" has pedophilia written all over it. It is a dangerous subject to try to explain or justify.

Among most men the desire for youthful sex partners is a strong proclivity. As if the mere fact that someone very young makes them more sexually desirable.

There is nothing in life to which the phrase "It's all in your mind" applies more than to sex. The older man or woman has chosen a "younger" mate for the excitement. The fact of the matter is age has little or nothing to do with the quality of the sex. The excitement is all in the mind.

In any intelligent discussion of sexual desirability, one must begin by acknowledging that the human mind plays about 90% of the role in sex. Almost all of sex is in your mind! I'm not talking about the rational part of the mind, but the creative part.

I don't think many experienced people would disagree with me if I were to say that artists have better sex than accountants. Of course, then I might have to define "good" sex verses "bad." To that request I would have to say that many people are having bad sex, and still like it and think it's good sex, because they don't know any better. In that respect, does it really matter? They can go to their graves more or less happy with their sex life. Yet, my feeling is that an unfulfilled sex life has more ramifications than we realize.

The most disastrous effect is when a sexually unfulfilled person glimpses their missed potential and leaps off the deep end. Frustration is a very dangerous emotion. It happens all the time. The taxi driver who touches himself while watching you in his rear view mirror. The high school teacher, dedicated to their spouse and to education, and yet the right temptation might cause them to dally with a student!

Let's say a happily married, middle-aged banker is attending

352

his daughter's 12th birthday party when one of his daughter's girl-friends playfully jumps on his lap. Later that night while driving her home, he molests her.

His inexperience with titillation and where it belongs in sex has caused him to step outside his normal, circumspect personality and perpetrate a heinous crime. Had he experienced enough pure, un-selfconscious "free love" in his life, he would have been able to put his sexual emotions in their proper perspective. He would never have raped that young girl.

Education and experience produce better sex, and better sex makes for happier, less frustrated, less deviant people. Now what is wrong with that?

Oh, you protest and say that sex breeds more desire for sex, and that becomes an addiction that creates perversions!?

With all my life experiences, reading and observations, I would have to say that the statistics prove more sex does not pervert a person, but the lack of sex produces perversions. And the subject of sex addiction begs me to ask, what is the problem with that, as long as you can keep a job, have a happy home life, and it is all consensual?

In just one generation, the peace and love era, we, as humans, have learned more about ourselves, our psyche, our social life and our physical life, than ever before. We have learned that steak and pota-toes will kill us young, smoking and drinking will kill us painfully and quickly, and denial and abstinence of sex will just make us want it more.

CHAPTER 80

# Words Of Love...Words Of Sex

We often have to use alternative words to describe fucking. In pub-lic we try to be more subtle, less "offensive," by using euphemisms. Many times these words do not accurately describe what we are actu-ally doing. Making love, sleeping together, sexual relationship, what level of emotion do these word describe? How much love is involved, how much sleeping, how much of a relationship is there?

Emotions are always a part of sex, yet there are various levels of involvement. And there are various emotions from love to hate found in sex.

There are very many forms of sex. A short list of the variety is: fucking, slippin' an' a slidin', making love, procreating, doing your duty, exerting yourself, getting off, getting even. All of these words describe a different reason for or different kind of physical activity.

I like the words "making love" because that is the essence of sex to me. I appreciate the term "balling" in certain situations, because that indicates a total commitment to the physical activity of fucking. "Sleeping together" indicates a commitment to being a couple. "Having sex" is an offhand description of a non-committed relationship, dedicated only to the orgasm.

Women, when first meeting a man of interest, never voice your expectations, but always indicate the possibility of sex. Be committed to the act once you have agreed to the lovemaking. Never be passive once you start, and never pretend that you didn't want to fuck once you start. Mixed messages will get mixed results.

Men, when first meeting a woman of interest, always voice your expectations, never indicate the necessity of sex, and lie to her only if you don't want a good history with her.

**Sexual Vocabulary and Definitions:**

Affair: sex that is usually somehow unsanctioned or outside marriage
Assignation: a sexual meeting
Balling: getting down and getting sweaty
Being intimate: a sweet sexual encounter
Carnality: animalistic form of sex
Carnal knowledge: the spiritual form of sex
Cohabitation: unmarried, live-in sex
Coitus: the medical definition of sex
Conjugation: the literary definition of sex
Copulate: a very clinical form of sex
Coupling: a romantic form of sex
Fornicating: a religiously disapproved form of sex
Fraternizing: game-playing sex
Fucking: your basic sex

Going to bed: a romantic form of sex
Having: a dominating sex
Having your way: a suspicious form of sex
Humping: a joyous form of sex
Intercourse: a conservative form of sex
Intimacy: a sensual form of sex
Liaison: a meeting especially for sex
Making love: the romantic form of sex
Mating: a physical and socially responsible form of sex
Rendezvous: a cheating form of sex
Rutting: a primal from of sex
Screwing: a frivolous form of sex
Seduction: an introductory form of sex
Sexual congress: business sex
Sexual intercourse: an uptight form of sex
Sexual relations: a circumstantial form of sex
Sexual union: an arranged form of sex
Sleeping together: a euphemism for casual, occasional sex

*"Three guys were walking down the street. Coming towards*
*them was a*
*pretty girl who smiled at them as they passed.*
*One guy saw a Virgin Mary, one saw a slut, and the third saw*
*a sister.*
*Later that night, the third guy and the girl became lovers*
*and lived happily ever after."*
Dudley Griffin, 11.9.13

CHAPTER 81

# TV LOVE

People sometimes adopt a bad image rather than a good one because they think it portrays strength. They think violence is powerful, and the media supports and perpetuates this very destructive and incorrect assumption.

But if you look and listen closely, most media actually shows and teaches rational moral standards. Many people miss this even though all good literature, movies, and yes, even good TV, tells you the truth about who is good and who is bad and who will win in the end. The primary sick mistake that media makes is by overemphasizing weird and violent activity, even though they may end their stories by showing a moral balance.

The biggest social flaw in media thinking today is their treatment of sex. They are now in the process of <u>overexposing</u> sexuality because it sells. It's not that they show it or talk about it, but that they overemphasize the titillation and fixations, more so than the love and spiritual joy of sex. They do this because they are caught up in the religious hypocrisy of the act of having sex. Sex gives life, which is the plan of God and Mother Nature, so basically it is good! It is not only a God-given act, but also promoted by God! So why is abstinence considered spiritual?

Objectifying is a major activity of organized religion, and advertising and most media strengthens this horrible social mistake.

Of course, when talking about sex to other people, you are going to run into language difficulties, even with those who speak the same language, because they have emotional differences and inherited sensibilities from yours.

There is nothing wrong with sex. It is a natural act. It is the brains of some people who demonize this act, which they think is animalistic. Well, yes, it is animalistic, and we humans are really animals with bigger brains! At least some of us have bigger brains, and we should accept our animal nature and our higher intelligent nature.

Here is where I fall back on my old standby, the Golden Rule. If you want to understand the emotions, feelings and dislikes of other people, you must dissect your own, and figure that others' feelings are just like yours, but, of course, with some minor differences.

If you want to fit into society, that is, get a spouse, have a job, live an unincarcerated, comfortable, and even pleasant existence, you have to conform to a few socially acceptable requirements. Treating other people with respect is the first move toward success.

The television set, living inside your home, was the first self-perpetuating media device.

The boob tube that continually talks to us and shows us pictures is so appealing we can barely concentrate on anything else. And someone else is responsible for the content. We could just turn it off, but…?

And now the TV's little brother, the computer devices, apps and social networks, are further keeping us from meaningful relations with reality and genuine  warm human beings sitting right beside us.

Everything I have seen since the introduction of the computer screen, the cell phone and smart phone is leading me to one conclusion--that we are being dumbed down to extinction, inundated with so much useless information that we are close to a point of not caring anymore, and separating ourselves from human society.

I'm still trying to determine whether this computer thing is helping, hurting or hindering us from our divine evolution. At this point in time, my opinion is the personal computer has wasted more human hours than it has saved. If you're a research scientist, researcher or a writer of ideas, it has served us well; but people are just using it as a diversion or entertainment.

Greatly because of mainstream media and the electronic social network, our human race is dangerously close to a point of losing all reverence and curiosity toward art, love, poetry, history, ethics or spirituality. Or perhaps, hopefully, there will be a backlash, and we will put the media in its place as a tool, not a god.

All reality show sex, and most soap opera sex, give the young public the wrong impression of what sex and love are all about. Reality show and soap opera sex are usually only casual, competitive and vindictive acts of physical domination. Very little romance and forever-after are portrayed in such episodic and expedient forms of entertainment.

Reality shows seem to celebrate stupid and confrontational behavior. And that is because normalcy and tranquility do not make for good "theater." Therefore, "directors" encourage the participants to "Use the FUCK word more often," and start fights and conflicts of some sort, to liven up the action.

Most books, movies, TV dramas and TV situation romantic/comedies have a moral message about love, respect and fidelity. Not so reality TV. But still, all media is capitalizing on sex, without divulging the pitfalls of objectifying sex partners and seeking deviations for thrills.

A safe concoction of sex, drugs, and rock and roll is a difficult level to learn and maintain amongst human beings. And what we don't need is a media that is using sex as a tool to sell products, while at the same time claiming to be our primary example of proper sexual behavior. Far too often they just demonize or make fun of what they don't quite comprehend or can't master themselves.

Reality TV damages human relationships by glorifying bad behavior. It is bad for our society, creating a selfish culture. What most men don't realize is that selfishness separates them from the really good life and the really good sex.

Some day, most likely too late, we will realize this. I am ashamed of the media for pandering to the lowest form of mankind's character!

I have looked into the creation of reality TV and now realize that it came about during the TV writers' strike of 2007. Producers, who are not artists, and who apparently have less morality, created reality TV because they could save money by not hiring artists, like actors and writers, who, on the whole, have better moral compasses.

TV producers hired marginal people who would make provocative and/or smarmy TV characters. The more strange or controversial the better. But they were and are not intelligent enough or generous, or cosmic enough to be able to teach (portray) positive lessons in human nature. Of course, that is not their objective. They are just meant to attract attention, to create high ratings to sell advertising.

And then the advertising message is always speaking down to a lower IQ, in order to drag down the viewers' awareness. Speak up to someone, and they will rise; speak down to them, and they will decline in intelligence.

It is a sad process of dumbing down the American public, so that industry can sell us just exactly what they want us to buy. What the media and advertisers are doing is limiting the number of targets. If everyone is at one low level of intelligence, the advertisers don't have to spend the time and money to spread their messages over a number of intellectual demographics. They decide what they want to sell and then inflict us with mundane advertising, and we buy it.

The reduced level of education that the corporate heads and conservative politicians have created has lowered the population's curiosity, thus making them easier to sell to. This is a diabolical and damaging process caused by those we once trusted with our education.

The media and our social peer groups are where our cultural education and morality mostly comes from nowadays. The "village" and community pressures to do the right thing and follow the rules of the past are gone, and now that we don't have the village any more, we must find some other moral benchmark. And sorry, but I don't want it to be the present-day media and the World Wide Web.

*"'Do the right thing.' You have heard that comment so many times and in so many ways. Of course, it is always right to do the right thing, and no one will deny that. The problem is knowing what is the right thing.*

*The difficulty is that we, each of us, have so much more invested in our own rights than we do in everyone else's rights. In love, and in all of life, there has to be a meeting of desires.*

*Think of love as you would national politics.*

*Do you want to live in anarchy, monarchy, dictatorship, oligarchy, or do you want to live free in a democracy?"*

DG

The TV media, computer, and social networks have created a large number of new words, terms, phrases and definitions. For the sake of knowing your enemy, I would like to give you a few definitions of these terms and pitfalls:

Don't ever buy a $1,000 car; don't ever buy something online or on TV for $19.95! I don't think I should have to explain why!

My Pillow? My God! TV advertising! People laughing all the way to the bank with your money. Delivery fees, handling fees, loss leaders, you pay attention or you don't.

And now we have social media, where some people can be completely anonymous and prey on other people. A catfisher is a person who lies to people on social media platforms to get emotional energy that they don't deserve or don't know how to get in the proper way.

Catfishing is on the extreme sick list! If you are a catfisher, I suggest you look at yourself in the mirror, and no matter what you see, just call yourself a sick, insecure, selfish bastard!

Lying to people on social networks is the wimp activity of all wimp activities. So you are ashamed of yourself? That is too bad, and I feel sorry for you, but you are definitely not going to improve your value by stealing emotions from other people.

To create affection in others toward yourself, which you are not able or willing to consummate, is a waste of good love, and it only proves that you are impotent and really screwed up.

So, catfisher, how does it feel to be a minus person, a person who steals emotions and gives nothing back but disappointment?

If anybody wants to know real things about sex to be found on TV, try these shows, some of which are reruns only, yet can be found on cable. They don't seem to be obvious, but the subtle stories are more vocal than the blatant sex scenes of most movies and TV!

*M.A.S.H* always the best!

*Sex in The City* may be frivolous, but if you can handle it, it shows women's real emotions!

*Bones*, very subtle, but it shows relationships on a working level.

*Two And A Half Men* and *Two Broke Girls* are shows that are extremely realistic even though couched in humor and over-the-top sexuality! That is mainly because the writing is tasteful and informative.

CHAPTER 82

# Sex And Guns

I'm really going to get a lot of flack for this one. Men, or a certain kind of men, are wrapped up in guns and sex and violence and sexual violence.

Most of them don't know that they are perverted. They think it is all part of being a man and being a patriot.

The entitlement of men in the USA is actually a continental insanity.

Guns Do Not Protect Your Family! Stop using that as an excuse for owning firearms.

The facts prove that you are actually putting your family at risk by owning a gun. Numbers show that, for every one criminal who is subdued by a household gun, there are literally hundreds of family members who are killed in gun accidents at home, not to mention all the thousands of friends and family members who are killed with household guns in fits of passion.

This information should cause any rational person to dispose of his weapons. But then, we are not dealing with rational thought here, are we? Let's face it; we are dealing with the male macho ego.

Don't use "the right to bear arms" excuse for your reasoning. Don't dishonor the fathers of our country by saying that they meant citizens should own half a dozen assault rifles, MAC-10s and nine millimeter semi-automatics.

Don't offend the writers of the Second Amendment by thinking they intended it to be used to justify the indiscriminate sale of deadly weapons to just about anyone who could pull a trigger.

Please, let's start thinking with our heads rather than other parts of our anatomy. If you own guns, you should look deeply inside yourself to see why you really own them. Understand where this urge for weapons comes from. Could it be less to protect your family than to enhance your own image?

Men use guns, cars, clothing, sports, bodybuilding, sex, power and money to enhance their image. It's part of life, and most of those sublimations are relatively harmless, but guns are not.

We have supposedly gone beyond the days of the Wild West, but some men are trying to drag us back into those times when men were measured by the size of their guns.

Wake up! Having the bigger gun does not make you the bigger man. It makes you a weak man hiding behind a big gun. If you have such a fixation, seek help.

Although most women don't have such fixations, they often humor their men. Women, tell your men that you like them just as much, maybe even better, without that cold, steel rod. You may be saving the life of one of your family members.

But, if your man must own a gun, urge him to do so with common sense. Keep it locked up and unloaded. Teach every member of your family to treat every gun as if it were loaded, even though it isn't. Never ever, ever point a gun at another person unless you wish them dead.

Keep the gun and the ammunition in separate places. Put the ammunition someplace where anyone looking for it will have plenty of time to think about what they are doing and cool down, if need be.

So you might get robbed, but the chances are greater that you will be saving the life of a family member.

The gun lobbyists say, "If guns are outlawed, then only outlaws will have guns." The truth of the matter is that most gun homicides are perpetrated by people who were law-abiding citizens until the moment when they shot someone. Most gun violence is a crime of opportunity. The availability of so many guns is what makes the criminal and causes the deaths.

I think the NRA is misguided right now, not because they put guns into the hands of criminals, but because they put them into the hands of potential criminals. Remember, keeping one questionable freedom is foolish if it jeopardizes all of our other freedoms combined. Death ends all your freedom.

When a danger to society is recognized, a rational society will place restrictions on that danger. We have automobile speed laws, which some people feel infringe on their rights, but these laws save lives. It's about time we became civilized and started considering more stringent gun laws, too.

It is as if some people in this society don't want humankind to evolve and succeed. Often, making unpopular intellectual decisions is what human beings have to do to survive and/or to correct previous mistakes. I am ashamed of the shortsightedness of the Supreme Court judges who voted to negate local handgun laws. With each decision like this we are slipping further back into the dog-eat-dog jungle and further away from the Garden of Eden.

These are only my opinions. This is a free country, and I have the right to my opinions, as you have the right to yours. But please, use the gray matter that God gave you, and think about what I have said. Don't let your macho ego kill someone you love.

CHAPTER 83

# Sexual Revolution As A Hippie Movement

The sexual revolution was an offshoot of the hippie culture, and the hippie culture was a product of the 1950s culture. In order to talk about the sexual revolution, you must discuss the evolution of the hippie. For that I will refer you to my book, *The Hippie Dictionary: A Cultural Encyclopedia of the 1960s and 1970s.*

The pill and adolescents rebellion against their families created the sexual revolution. Don't blame sex; that is God-given. Don't accuse moral decline for children's sexual behavior; it all comes down to parents' egos, indignation, misguided discipline and shortsightedness.

The sexual revolution was one of those Pandora's box situations, so, once the possibilities were safer and promoted by the media, there was no closing the lid.

Hippies did not invent sex. God and Mother Nature did that,

and then they were helped along by the media, pharmaceutical companies, and, in a perverse twist, by religious organizations.

Most people who had sex during the hippie era will say that it was the best thing that happened during 1960s and 70s. Most people who did drugs during the hippie era, will say that it was the second best thing that happened during 1960s and 70s. No one says that going to Viet Nam was the best of anything.

> *"I had a girlfriend in Los Angeles; we made love to Van Morrison for six weeks."*
> Dudley Griffin, 1969-70

> *"I had a girlfriend in Los Angeles, one-night stand in her Wilshire Miracle Mile home, pool, jacuzzi and intercourse, but no time for intimacies.*
> *Her parents were lurking in their beds upstairs."*
> DG, 1969-70

When you think of the hippie era, unless you are a corporate, capitalist, or fanatic religious person, you think of peace, love and understanding. Now how in God's name are you going to demonize that?

In the long run, the sexual revolution has actually reduced the possibility of world overpopulation because birth control was recommended, and sexual contact was considered as a sacrament, not a duty or for growing the species.

Any revolution seems frightening to those who live in the present or past, but it is a normal process of humankind's evolution. You can live with it or rebel against it, but change happens whether you want it or not. Nobody...no, nobody is able to stop change; you can influence it rationally, or you can die trying! Influencing the future is a good thing; fighting it is a futile and destructive thing. This world will become a desert or a ball of fire if we all don't work to maintain a livable planet for all those who are going to follow us.

CHAPTER 84

# Boy Scouts And Hippies

Gilbert Shelton

Don't laugh…think about it. Most 60's and 70's hippies had a stint in the Boy Scouts during the 1950's and 60's. We learned and really believed that a Boy Scout was always: helpful, friendly, courteous, kind, obedient, cheerful, thrifty, brave, clean and reverent. We also learned to love camping on hard ground. The hippie Back-to-the-Earth Movement was not such a stretch considering the good times we had as Scouts.

The evolution of man, movements and revolutions are not born in a vacuum. We build on our past experiences and past disappointments.

In this respect you can say that the foundation of the hippie culture was constructed from the ideals of the previous generations. We accepted and used the good things and rejected the hypocrisy. THC and LSD expanded our minds and gave us insights into all the ideals and problems of our growing up years. The 50s and early 60s in America were the combination of idyllic society and hypocritical social atrocities. The hippies were just trying to show the uninformed population the dangerous path that our country was traveling, and our warnings have proven true.

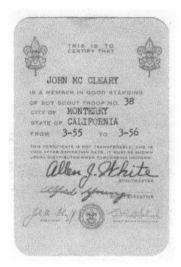

An aside and to prove my credentials as a red-blooded American boy of the 1950s, I must tell you of my personal experiences in Scouting. It is poignant in that it shows the cultural and emotional mixture of childhood influences during that time in this country.

I went through several years of Cub Scouts, as many boys did. I still have my blue uniform shirt to prove it, with all the badges and stripes and such. Living in a small town surrounded by beautiful nature, rivers, mountains and the sea, we did our share of campouts and woodcraft. I slept on the ground, ate fish and crawdads I caught, and came close to burning down the forest as so many other kids did.

I was still a manageable, respectful and patriotic young man, and then I matriculated into the Boy Scouts, just as puberty struck.

I became a member of Boy Scout Troop 38, in Monterey, California, during the years of 1954-1956. It was a brief period, because in that age and time, children were growing up fast, and I had other things to do in order to become an adult in a fast changing word. I had enjoyed Cub Scouts, experienced my share of overnight camping and nature walking, but I was over it and anxious to move on to the "real world." The real world, as it was then for a pubescent, held a lot more carousing, experimenting, high jinks, troublemaking and smoking cigarettes, not smoking beef jerky nor marijuana.

Troop 38, Monterey, California 1954-56, was not your typical bunch of helpful, courteous, kind young kids. We were an ethnically and socially diverse gang of subteen thugs. We were smart alecks, and we listened to no authority. Our troop counselors, and we went through several, suffered serious grief at our hands.

Recently, there have been many allegations and numerous class action law suits agents the Boy Scouts of America. I am sure there were cases of child abuse, and I believe that the Boy Scout management should be held to task, but from what I saw and remember in our troop all the abuse was aimed at our adult leaders. We terrorized them, and we brought weapons to our meetings

Our weapons were newspaper rubber bands and our ammo was the U-shaped pieces of wire cut from the ends of the binding that held together the bundles of Monterey Peninsula Herald newspapers.

On our way marauding through town toward the troop meetings, we would pass behind the newspaper offices and collect our arsenal. No cat or dog or smaller child was safe as we headed to our Scout House.

We met for our "meetings" on the site of the Presidio of Monterey military base in what had once been barracks for the US Horse Cavalry. Ronald Reagan once made a movie there.

Our troop "headquarters" arguably had one of the most beautiful panoramic views in California. We overlooked Monterey Bay, but still, we were just vandals attacking Rome.

And then after about a year, it all came to an end. I don't know if there is another example of this ever happening in the Boy Scouts of America's history, but our troop was disbanded in 1956, either because they couldn't find a new counselor willing to risk his sanity or in an edict coming down from the national organization judging us a bunch of incorrigibles.

One way or the other, they closed down our troop, whether it was because we were an embarrassment to them or they were frightened of us.

The members of that troop that I have kept tabs on have gone on to become hotel and restaurant owners, international drug lords and at least one hippie--me.

But to understand our present-day attitudes toward sex, you must understand the rebellious nature of young people during the 1950s and early 60s.

Keith Richards of The Stones was a Boy Scout as a young boy, and in his autobiography says that it was crucial in developing his "character."

## Sub-Chapter Religion and Hippies

Don't laugh…think about it. Most hippies had a stint in church during the 1950s and 60s. We learned and really believed that Christians were supposed to be: helpful, friendly, courteous, kind, obedient, cheerful, thrifty, brave, clean and reverent. Now we know that they are just as likely to be hypocritical and often attach strings to these otherwise pure attributes.

In my experience I have found that a Christian will be:
Helpful, *to their own kind*
Friendly, *in order to proselytize*

Courteous, *if they deem you worthy*
Kind, *when it edifies themselves and their religion*
Obedient, *unto their own laws*
Cheerful, *seldom*
Thrifty, *except to a TV evangelist*
Brave, *when standing behind their God*
Clean, *on Sunday* and
Reverent, *for several hours a week.*

My own experience with religion was typical of many Americans of that time. I have seen, I have tasted, and I have rejected it.

I was not raised in a formally religious household. My father was an atheist and my mother, an agnostic. These both are religious convictions, but there are no churches dedicated to them, and they are not willing to kill other people for their religious beliefs.

I got my Christian religious training from several of my mother's family members. For various reasons at times in my youth, I lived with my grandparents, and aunts and uncles for short periods. It is through them I got my share of Christian dogma.

Because of the time I spent with those family members, I have read and studied the New Testament several times. And, in spite of them, I have also read and studied the Old Testament and the Apocrypha. I am not a scholar, but I do know bullshit when I read it and hypocrisy when I see it.

And how do I know hypocrisy and lie? Because I have read a whole hell of a lot more about other religions, history, archeology, sociology, philosophy, biology and chemistry.

I am an agnostic. I have never had a bolt of lightning come down and tell me I must be so; I have intellectually made this decision. I respect others who think that they have, or have actually had that bolt of lightning experience. I just don't think that they should be trying to disrupt my life, forcing me to believe in what they believe.

As has been said many times by many people, I believe that religion is a very personal thing. I don't try to push my taste in food on others. I also will not proselytize my choice of cars or computers, so don't disrupt my life with your religion.

"Live and let live" is the religion of the hippie. We will accept anyone's transgressions as long as they are victimless crimes. You can fuck up your own life if you want to. We will let anyone screw around, unless it disrupts our life or any other innocent person's life.

Hippies and liberals may, from time to time, write about your mistakes and remind you that you are wrong, but as long as they are not harmful to others, we will not pass laws to prohibit your stupidity. Christians, bigots and capitalists need not fear us unless you step on mankind and our home planet.

## CHAPTER 85

# "This Is Where I Want To Be For The Rest of My Life."

### Orgasm Chapter

Sex is a tightening in the groin that keeps getting tighter 'til it pushes the juices right out of you. If it were the physical sensation alone, then we would do it once in a while and forget about it in between times. But nature added something else to sex—curiosity, craving, desire and often addiction, more than to Chinese food.

## CHAPTER 86

# The Myth Of One-Night Stands

*"If you want to be a lover, a real lover, who has sex with many women*
*and yet they still love you after you go, even if they don't*
*want you to go, then you have to watch every James Bond movie to*
*study his sincerity*
*and romantic concentration upon them,*
*and his acceptable detachment! When a belly dancer*
*gesticulates seductively around Sean Connery he does not try to kiss*
*or touch her, nor does he roll his eyes in immature adulation. James*
*Bond knows every woman wants to be with him, but he does not flirt*
*unless a consummation is*

*expected and a foregone conclusion."*
*Mr. California,*
11.20.2020

The thought of a one-night stand is exciting to many people. It is the ultimate in animalistic lust. It is the only kind of sex some people, mostly young people, have or, in some cases, want.

I have had my share. Possibly two-thirds of sexual experiences in my youth were one-night stands, one-day, or one-moment-standing-up-against-the-wall.

There is a certain appeal to anonymous sex, which can be justified and philosophized in many ways. I, for one, think that the "nasty" element, the taboo, the amoral aspect, is the most realistic justification. Thumbing one's nose at society's rules, rebellious activity and a devil-may-care attitude empower some people.

The guy may be a mild-mannered accountant by day, but those sexual exploits in the alley behind the disco give him super lover fantasies! She may live at home with her strict Catholic family, but in the back seat of his economy hatchback, she is the super slut, the Hollywood princess desired by all men!

The sad side of this scenario is that many people court one-night stands just so they don't have to be themselves. They are ashamed of who they really are, so they choose relationships that don't even require names, let alone revealing one's curriculum vita.

The next and most regrettable reason for one-night stands is the fear of commitment. This is primarily a male pathology, yet I have known women who have used anonymous sex as a condom against love as well.

I once knew a young woman to whom I was attracted, as were many other guys in town. One day I asked her why she had rejected my efforts at getting closer to her, and why I didn't know of any of my male friends who had "dated" her.

She said, without hesitation, "I don't 'spend time' with any of the men I know. I go to parties and concerts in other towns or in The City for my sex." I asked her why, and I don't remember exactly what she said, but she said something like, "Because!"

She didn't quite know why she was against having sexual relationships within the familiar confines of her little community, but I think I know why. She didn't want to get trapped with some guy who would make demands on her time and body. Her freedom was too important to her at that time.

I can understand this at some level of my own libido. At that particular time in my sex life, I didn't really want commitment either. But it is a lot easier for a woman to find sex any time she wants it than it is for a man. So men don't have the luxury to be so selective. That is why we often get ourselves into situations that make us seem shallow. Men often pick up women, for sex, that they would never want a _real_ relationship with. That is a basic difference between men and women. Women are often looking for Mr. Right. Men are more often looking for Miss Tonight.

A man usually has to put more time and socializing into getting laid, so familiar territory and familiar women make it easier to accomplish this. Even with the one-night stands I have had, most of the women were already known to me.

Random, ambiguous, one-time sex might be exciting, but people who choose to confine their emotions to that are missing out on a number of levels of sensuality!

Good sex, like a good vacation, has numerous emotions and experiences. The anticipation, planning, going, being there, sorrow at the ending, returning to reality and anticipation of a repeat performance.

If a person relies on one-night stands for their sex, it is like a vacation where you wake up one morning, sitting in a lounge chair on a beach in the sun with sticky lotion all over your body and five margaritas to drink and then wake up the next day back in your dreary bedroom with only the hangover and a sunburn on the bottom of your feet to remember it by.

Real sex, like a real vacation, should conjure up many feelings, only one of which is escapism. Sex should be, God forbid, educational! If nothing else, you should learn some things about yourself.

One of the best aspects of a new "relationship" is the anticipation of a repeat performance. You will discover that the second time is sooo much better than the first.

Think about it! The anticipation of the realization that she likes you, and your lovemaking enough to try again. And the fact that you are not quite sure how good your lovemaking together was the first time and want to check it out again.

Often, the first time you make love with someone you are so wrapped up in making sure it really happens, making sure that you perform, hoping they aren't repulsed by your body, that the bed doesn't break...the fear, the excitement, the anguish, the...well, you know.

You often don't really remember if it was satisfying, and you really don't know if they were satisfied with you. If they are willing to see you again, it should be some sort of confirmation. It gives some sort of satisfaction.

Often, first-time lovers come together in a one-night stand fueled by too much alcohol or drugs, and you don't really remember it. The second time is usually entered into with eyes more widely open and the senses more receptive. It is a whole hell of a lot more fun. And you might realize that you want to see more of her; you might even "love" her.

What you do after the second time is based on a much more enlightened viewpoint. You may just go your own ways, but I think every sexual relationship deserves a "second-night-stand."

## I Say Once Is Not Enough

One-night stands can be exciting, but they are usually based on need rather than want. Often, masturbation would be just as memorable. Of course, if you're into notching your gun, one-nighters will pad your list of conquests. Yet, they often produce meaningless scores when you realize that, to your "conquest," you were also just a conquest.

If alcohol or drugs are mixed into the equation, then the sex act is often even less fulfilling. Yes, drugs and alcohol do help to loosen inhibitions, but they often loosen other things like physical ability, concentration and memory.

In most sexual relationships the first time is often something less than satisfactory. It is the test to see if you want to do it again. If your partner pushes the right buttons, then a replay is warranted. The second time is when things really began to happen.

I don't necessarily mean the next morning. I mean the next

day or next week after you have had some time to think about the person, yes, and lust after them. If their smell on your body gives you a tremor in your groin rather then a turning of the stomach, then the next time will be even better.

That glow of fulfillment afterwards as you go through the rest of your day in anticipation of the next time, can be one of the highest points of a relationship. Expectation grows during the first part of a relationship and eventually reaches a peak, which is different in each relationship depending on the people and other influences.

I have never quite understood the men, and I have met them, who want to have sex only once with a woman. There are numerous rationalizations. Some are afraid of commitment, but more often it is that they are insecure and fear rejection. And then there are those misguided men who harbor a subconscious feeling that once they have fucked a girl she is a slut, and so they will have nothing more to do with her.

For whatever reason, some men are missing out on the best part of dating and sex, the anticipation of the next time and the learning process two new lovers experience. We can't become a better lover unless we learn to satisfy a partner, and we will never have that experimentation unless we stay with a lover for a reasonable length of time.

There is a sliding scale as to how many times a couple makes love before they reach their peak of physical performance, just as there are scales relating to their peak of satisfaction. But, to me, the factor of anticipation and longing for another person's body is one of the most exciting parts of a relationship.

Of course that aspect is also why some people are continually looking for new relationships. This thing about commitment is overplayed. Most men who go from one relationship to another are looking for that warm feeling in their groin that sexual anticipation brings.

It may be a childish quest, but it is usually driven more by Mother Nature's call than by fear of commitment. Maturity teaches the smart ones that sex chasing is an unsatisfyable urge, and that the warmth of a long-term love/friendship relationship is better in the long run.

But usually during youth, men, and in a lesser way, women,

are often chasing that wonderful cocktail of satisfaction... forbidden sex, body anticipation and orgasm. Oh yes, I remember fondly, but not with longing, that sex of two bodies who know that "once is not enough."

CHAPTER 87

# Male Silly Day

Back in "The Day" there was a men's liberation as well as a women's liberation. "The Day" is generally understood to mean the hippie era, 1960 to 1979. It was the era of great changes.

If you had fallen asleep in 1959 and awakened in 1980, you would not know what planet you were on. More cultural changes happened during those twenty years than in any other 20 years of mankind. 1895 to 1915 created scientific and economic changes, but the hippie era gave us emotional wings to fly.

For six or seven years in the late 1970s and early 80s, I had a modified commune in my home. I say modified because my housemates paid rent to me, since I owned the house, and we needed to pay the mortgage, taxes and utilities.

Communes in the hippie era were dedicated to different ideologies; politics, religion, sex, drugs and rock & roll were some of the different reasons people lived together. But economics was often the most realistic reason. Many people have a misconception that hippies didn't deal with money. They did, but mostly we reduced the acquisition, maintenance and frustrations of money and possessions down to the barest minimum.

That was the anti-materialism idealism. But even in a commune rent or a "mortgage" had to be paid.

This commune was called Lomita Street. It was on Lomita Street, and it housed an average of five to eight people at any given time. There were usually one to three female tenants, although the energy was mostly testosterone driven. There were also a number of revolving lovers, short-time crashers and traveling friends.

Due to my husbandry the house was usually a party happening or ready to happen, yet everything was always cool. Nothing ever spilled out into the neighborhood.

I have always appreciated craziness, but I abhor stupidity. This attitude created an aura around the house that, for the most part, kept out bad vibes. Given the activities within and around that structure, some people were convinced that the house was actually invisible to the authorities.

Although the house was male run, it was not "male-dominated." We were mostly evolved or becoming evolved men.

Male liberation was a process where men began to throw off the obligations and expectations of masculinity. It was a freeing oneself from the preconceptions that a man must never be wrong, must never cry, must run the family and bring home the bacon.

As I said, Lomita Street was predominantly male-oriented, as were almost all businesses and institutions of that time. During the hippie era many men were questioning that self-indulgence. This is how I got the idea for Male Silly Day.

Male Silly Day (MSD) was an effort to break the chain of seriousness and to help men come back down to being just real people. You might laugh and say that man does this all the time in fraternities and local pubs, but MSD was an effort to emphasize the irony of man's fabricated self-importance.

This is a great, retrospective, philosophical dissection of what, at the time, seemed only to be an excuse for just another party. Yet, my friends and I were genuinely trying to break down barriers of communication between the sexes.

Far too often it seems that the only true line of communications between man and woman is sexual. The intellectual man is trying to find other forms of intercourse because, believe me, most smart men are convinced that they would learn a great deal from women if they could speak the same language and get into their heads.

I started Male Silly Day to admit that men were the sillier of the two sexes. What we did on Male Silly Day was more of the same silly things we did everyday, but to excess, in order to show how vulnerable we actually are.

Taking oneself too seriously is the primary flaw most men make. And, believe me their families and the whole world suffers from man's flaws. Admitting that you do "silly man things" is a good start toward finding the balance of who you are, and not taking yourself so damn seriously. For a man to attach the word 'silly' to the word "man" is a worthy admission.

The most interesting, poignant thing about the first MSD was that we had just acquired a new female tenant. She was a black student at Monterey Peninsula College and a bit of a feminist as I recall. Not a problem, as most of my friends and I were male feminists, but!

At the time we didn't have a TV in the house and I thought we should, in the best tradition of male silliness, watch the Supper Bowl because that was one of the reasons I chose that day for Male Silly Day.

I found a TV to borrow, we bought a case of cheap beer and had a party. Well, our new house member came home as this was happing and freaked out. I wasn't able to explain the irony and humor of this party, and she moved out the next day.

CHAPTER 88

# OXOXOX X X, I Love You Mom and Dad

*"I am a tree in my mother's garden. She had desires from which I sprouted, she nurtured me and watched me grow. I was a seedling, a sapling and now a tree.*

*I am a rock in my father's garden. He had desires from which I started, he ordained me, but did not see me grow! I was sand, a pebble and now a rock.*

*I am a child of whom my mother was pleased to know.*

*I am a child of whom my father might have been proud.*
*I am a whisper and a sigh of my mother and father."*
DG, 4.17/18.06

CHAPTER 89

# Are Sex And Love Related?

*"Even their shapeless, pasty white bodies look and*
*feel good in the dark night of passion.*
*Socially recognized physical beauty might be skin*
*deep, yet it is an amateur explanation of human sexuality to use*
*beauty as the criteria for sexual attraction. How many emotions*
*are we dealing with here? Six, maybe 100! Compassion, guts,*
*independence, subservience, curiosity, fear, joy, melancholy,*
*detachment, puppy dog, well, I think you get the picture.*
*In a weak moment of egotism, I have been heard to*
*say that I could tell what kind of lover a person would be within*
*15 seconds of meeting them. Often, I know whether I would enjoy*
*making love with them within 10 seconds. These, of course, are*
*exaggerations, but they are not far from wrong.*
*If I were to choose one physical attribute as the*
*most stimulating, I would have to say the eyes. And in poems in all*
*societies, the eyes are the mirror to the soul."*
Dudley Griffin, 12.1.1999

Today, 2014, many women and some men are going before the knife to achieve the physical beauty they think they need to be a whole person. True, if it is in your mind that you are ugly, then you are ugly, because you will act insecure and therefore appear ugly.

Yes, girls, if you don't have inner beauty, no knife will make you beautiful. Achieve inner beauty first, and if you are still not satisfied with your body, then pay for the surgery. But you should know that your physical beauty will not keep a lover; it is your inner beauty that will keep them. And you should also know that insecurity and superficial beauty are ugly to most other people.

If you want to attract another insecure and self-absorbed person, then rely on your outside, but if you want someone who loves you for you, and not for their own needs, then get plastic surgery on your attitude instead of on your boobs!

> *"In weird way, reality TV could actually become a good social education for our society. In most reality shows, people are acting stupid, shallow, arrogant and/or obnoxious, and that could help viewers see how stupid, shallow, arrogant and/or obnoxious they appear to others when the viewer is acting stupid, shallow, arrogant and/or obnoxious in real life.*
> *I just hope the general public is intelligent enough to know what stupid, shallow, arrogant and/or obnoxious activity is and to recognize stupid, shallow, arrogant and/or obnoxious in themselves when they are acting stupid, shallow, arrogant and/or obnoxious!*
> DG

If we agree that sex, love, passion and romance are separate activities living in the same emotion, then we can communicate. But if you think that humans can't experience one without the others, then we must have a serious talk.

I still don't know what part sexual intercourse plays in real love. I will tell you that I have had some of the best sex with women I didn't really care for, and then, I admit, I have experienced bad sex with someone I adore.

What is love; what is sex? How do you put into words the indefinable? You turn yourself inside out and try to write down the feelings you find hidden there.

Some languages have words for different kinds of love--carnal love, romantic love, brotherly love, and love of God. Sex is a reflex, a need, like eating or breathing. Love is an ideal. Sex makes your body feel good; love makes your soul complete. I think the truth may be that sex and love are not even related.

To understand them fully, we must first separate sex and love. Although we consider sex to be a part of love, they can and do have separate places in our lives.

Love is an activity that requires some form of commitment, yet it need not be shared. Sex is an activity that requires no commitment, yet it must be shared in some way.

Love is one of the most basic joys, yet the desire for finding and keeping love is the most painful of all human struggles. Sex is one of the most basic acts of sharing, yet it is primarily a selfish act.

Love, committed to someone who doesn't want that love, can become a weapon. Sex is a selfish act which, when conducted with the proper attitude, gives joy to those with whom you share it.

Love received from others is the ruler by which we measure ourselves. Sex appeal is what we most often use to measure others.

Love is not a requirement for sex, and sex is not a requirement for love; yet, the combination of the two is the most rewarding feeling known to humankind.

> *"Love is that condition wherein the happiness of another is essential to your own happiness."*
> Robert Heinlein, in his book, *Stranger in a Stranger Land.*

> *"Sex is a selfish act that gives life."*
> DG, 7.16.12

I don't know why men have such a strange double standard where sex and love are concerned; well, yes I do, but I'm still confounded by it. It is not just a double standard; it's more like an E=MC2 standard. How can a woman be a virginal goddess when you first meet her in a bar at 10:00 p.m., a whore if she doesn't go home with you, a slut if she does, damaged goods when you kick her out of your bed at 8:00 a.m., and then, in closing, she's your most prized possession when she smiles at your roommate on the way out?

I refuse to admit being guilty of all of those thoughts toward the same girl within the same day's period, but I know guys who are. We put women up on a pedestal, and then we have to climb that damned pedestal. Once we get up there, we swear it wasn't worth it, or we swear that she came down to us instead. Of course, God forbid if we can't climb that pedestal. And you know what happens to the girl who doesn't want the pedestal, comes down on her own, or, worse yet, falls off!

I said that I know why men have a sexual double standard, so I better produce. It's the ego, with a large measure of religion added.

Sexual desire is nature's encouragement to continue our species. In the human male, recognition of self (the ego) complicates this process. Men take sex too personally. In most of nature, sex is just an impersonal fact of life. Human males want sex to be about their own selfish concept of loyalty. Down deep inside most men harbor the desire that all future humankind should come from their sperm alone. That is the power of self-preservation with a lot of ego thrown in.

The creation of sin was meant to help us protect our territory. If you are not with us, you are against us, and therefore, you are wrong. We have created religion around our desire to perpetuate ourselves and other people just like us. Religion is really a separating force and not the galvanizing influence some people think it is.

The double standard is created for the protection of the plan we have for our own selfish life. "I can do what I want to do within my plan, but if your plans don't fit into my plan, then you must be immoral." A woman can do "nasty things" as long as it is with "her man," but if she does them with anyone else, she's a slut.

In most organized religions of today, The Golden Rule has been left behind. Sins are convenient ways to separate people. By some mental gymnastics we as a society have been able to categorize many activities as sins if someone else "commits" them, but as justifiable if we do them or if they are done for our benefit.

Because of the natural drive to procreate and the human ego, most men down deep inside have the desire to be king of the world and father of all life. What this translates into is the desire to impose our will on others. That is the sexual double standard.

Men want what we want, but if we can't have it, we demonize it in order to protect our self-image from ridicule. The ego is a natural law at work; sin is a human law at work. They should never be combined to govern the same activity of life.

Women don't know how sexual they really are. Men don't know it either, but we feel it. We look for your look at us, and look back at you in anticipation. We want your sexuality, yet we also count on your physical innocence to bolster our desire for conquest.

CHAPTER 90

# To Each His Own Fetish

I never really liked my dick sucked all that much. Once a woman showed me that she was not ashamed to do it, that was the entire thrill I needed from oral sex. It was never a necessary element of lovemaking to me.

A blowjob is not a very romantic part of sex. It may be a sexual turn-on to some, but it is not intimate. Women seldom ask if they can suck your dick, but they may ask if <u>you want</u> it sucked. From my experience, I have come to the conclusion that women don't really enjoy doing it. They will, and outwardly gladly. They do it for your enjoyment or for a little prurient excitement, yet it is low on the list of sexual acts that women consider as true lovemaking.

I once had a guy tell me that, to him, blowjobs or anal sex were more intimate than vaginal sex. His rationale was that, if a woman was willing to do that to him or let him do that to her, then she was exhibiting more intimacy toward him. Get an I.Q. Her child-bearing portals are where a woman's intimacy lives. Actually, her extra actions for you are called "submission."

Anal sex and fellatio are sex acts of dominance. You might call them expressions of trust, but they are still described as animalistic dominance in the books I read and the life I have lived.

It is generally understood that sexual relationships fall into two different categories--sex or lovemaking. I actually believe that there are three--lovemaking, sex and dominance. Sadly, for many men, sex is a dominance game. To me, satisfactory lovemaking in marriage or even a one-night stand requires a mutual emotional high reached through an equality of feelings.

Upper and lower-case love comes into play here. You can love someone or you can Love them. Sure, there is a place for the "nasty bits," even in a serious love affair or marriage, but good sex requires the emotional part as well.

The "sex act" is a transitory thrill that can be experienced with any prostitute, knothole or even your own hand. Far too many people settle for shallow sex throughout their entire lives because they have never experienced real, deep, emotional sex.

Memorable sex does not necessarily have to be experienced with your one true life's mate. It can be had with a casual partner, yet it usually requires an emotional commitment.

We all like prurient sexual turn-ons from time to time, but let's not confuse them with great sex. In the long run, intimacy in lovemaking is more satisfying.

Yet, I say, "If a woman really enjoys having you in her mouth and she shows it, get into it for a while. I personally love going down on a woman, and '69' can be as exciting as it gets. I will do whatever is necessary to raise the height of lovemaking, but I have never required that a woman give me a blow job. I want sex to be our affair, not just mine."

At one time, about fifteen years ago I was doing a lot of research on sex for this book. I was married, then as now, to my second wife, and totally faithful to her as I always will be, so it was not any physical research.

I rented X-rated tapes to find out what present desires and fetishes men had at that time. And from what I can determine today, they are much the same desires most men have had forever. If you know the movie, TV and advertising industry, they always give the people what they want.

I watched hundreds of tapes, and by doing so I learned several things. First, I learned that I am not a voyeur, and second I learned that most men who watch these tapes are dominant people who like to have their cock sucked! They don't like to go down on a woman, they don't like much foreplay and they want decorative and subservient women. And this then is what women have to deal with!

CHAPTER 91

# The Erogenous Sneeze

I have an erogenous sneeze! It strikes when I am sexually aroused. Not always, but often, and quite often when least expected or wanted.

You can imagine the peculiarity, when, on a first "date" I would start going down on a new girl and break into a sneeze or two. It made for a few humorous, if not embarrassing, situations.

Eventually I got used to it and would just tell the truth. "I often sneeze when I get sexually excited," I would tell the girl, rather than feigning a cold, which could halt the lovemaking, or pretending to have an allergy to some female hygiene product.

Telling the truth also seemed to have an erogenous effect on the girls, so I stuck with that. After all, it was the truth, strange as it might seem, and it gave me a little bit of a reputation around town. I sneezed one time at a party, and had several past girlfriends look over with wide-eyed interest.

CHAPTER 92

# Signs Of The Times

It was a road sign, one of those California poppy signs that told tourists they were in a beautiful part of California, and they should look around and ooh and aah a bit and maybe get out and take a photo. It was located on Highway 1, heading south at Carpenter Street near Carmel, just north of Big Sur.

I hitchhiked there several times and noted the sign and the graffiti scratched or written on it. I now have that sign, preserved for posterity, an icon of the times, saved from replacement by an esthetic commando raid late one night.

On the front of the sign scratched into its reflective paint is written: (from top to bottom) 13; Opium (with an arrow pointing to the poppy); Mike B.; TV; 5/9/72; Lawry M; SACTO; K.R.; Pope Lost Hope. On the back written in pencil or scratched into its aluminum surface, it reads: Don't Hitch Here (skull and crossbones) no rides here; Never lose an opportunity to see something beautiful for beauty is gods handwriting; (some unintelligible scratching, possibly in Spanish); Fruitcake Cathy & Friend Paul are here in bodies only wet bodies our spirit is way ahead of us in the land of sun Grand Canyon; We love you; Vince Gipson; I longs for sex I'll never have; Peace to the beautiful people; and a very small peace sign.

As I said, I was forced to hitchhike at that sign several times over the years, mostly because the person who left me off was turning off on Carpenter, stranding me there. The spot was one that an experienced hitchhiker (which I was) would never choose, because if anyone ever pulled over to pick you up it was an accident waiting to happen. It was a long way to walk with a pack on my back to a better hitching place. so I stayed put.

Often times, standing at a hitching place like that, I would fantasize being somewhere else like Fruitcake Cathy and her friend Paul. Watching the cars whiz by, you sometimes play games in your head, make up scenarios and think up things to say as soon as you get into the next car that stops to offer you a ride.

This one time at the poppy sign, I decided I would proposition the next girl or woman who picked me up. You have to understand, I was never that deliberate in my seduction. I almost never relied on a prepared line of conversation or went about to seduce a girl sight unseen. If a chick pushed the right buttons, I made a move, but usually not unless she showed signs of interest.

During the 1970s, I was picked up hitchhiking by numerous female drivers, and seldom was there ever anything other than just a ride and a nice conversation. I would say the ratio of rides to sex approached 50 to 1. The ratio was a little different when I was driving, possibly 25 to 1.

Yet, even when I was the driver picking up a woman, I never made overt advances. I have always been revolted by the thought of putting a woman in a position where she might feel obligated to submit to what I wanted.

How can one be a real man when taking sex that was not freely given to him was his kind of foreplay. How can a man's ego feel satisfied when he steals a woman's body instead of receiving it through love? We are not animals only, we are human animals and have a conscience, one of the things that separates us from other animals.

Though I seldom initiated sexual advances, I was also seldom rejected when I did. I assume it had something to do with good instincts and my good intentions.

This time, hitching at the poppy sign, I was picked up by a young lady. I had already fantasized that, if a woman stopped, I would ask her if she was interested in a "sexual trip." I must have been both horny and pedantic that day.

Her name was not Cathy, but I will call her that, because we still live in the same community. She was cute and young, and she was taking her dog down to bathe in the river at Big Sur.

I have never used the line before or since, but I asked her if she wanted to have a sexual trip. I knew the place to do both.

We washed her dog in the lazy Big Sur River. Then we made love in the middle of the river on a rock just big enough to perch her vagina wide open for me to enter. After we grew tired of the acrobatics, we moved on to the riverbank among the soft grass and aspen trees.

The search for sex and love may take us through many adventures. Some are meaningful, some educational and some just amusing. The spot where we had sex in the river is a place where I have stopped and played many times before and since.

I later found out that the cowboys who worked the ranch near that place often went there to spy on the hippies as they frolicked nude in the river and made love in the forest. I have often wondered what Cathy and I looked liked out in the middle of that river, teetering on that slippery rock.

CHAPTER 93

# Losing a Virginity

You can give it away, you can throw it away or have it taken away, but no one has ever lost their virginity; it is usually a bit more proactive than that. And most often it's good riddance anyway.

Guys can't wait to throw theirs away, and most women give it willingly. There is a small, sad number of people, primarily young girls, who have it forcibly taken from them.

There is no accurate figure, but it is sometimes reported that

25% of all young girls are sexually molested. I don't think it's that high. Women talk to me, and I don't think it's more than 10%. But, of course, even that is tragic.

Most molestations are committed by mothers' boyfriends, then family members like uncles, cousins and brothers; then it comes down to the most heinous of all, that of the fathers.

In our society, a culture built on the particular ideals we have created for proper social behavior, if there is any unforgivable action, it is sexually molesting your own child. Yet, we must remember this is in our culture and with our set of values. Some human cultures and most animal societies have a different attitude toward incest than our Christian, Western culture.

Whether you believe for religious or biological reasons that it is wrong, or conversely, you believe it is O.K., incest is still considered improper in our society. If we lived in a closed society with no contact with the outside world, incest could be explained as a cultural reality. But in this wide-open age of advanced communications, incest and sex with children are damaging because the victim knows the about the social prohibitions. The perpetrators of pedophilia or incest in this society are sick puppies...degenerate, non-human beings.

I personally won't defend incest in any form, but as far as sex with a minor, I want to know more facts before I condemn someone. Who is a "child"? What is the age of consent?

In all of my sexual encounters, there are just two that I feel some level of guilt about. Like every young man, I was once an asshole too.

Sometime around 1972 I went through a real asshole period. I begin cheating on my wife at the time; I seduced other men's women, and applied maybe a little too much emotional pressure on potential sex partners.

At this time, I began hitchhiking around the country, traveling without my family. My soul was off to see the world, but my heart was mired in the banal mud. In other words, I was following my dick, not my conscience.

One of my trips has already been partly related in the episode of the snowstorm in Wyoming. On that same trip I went on to Boston and then to New York City.

In Boston, actually Cambridge, I stayed at a house with some university students I had met on a previous trip. The household was a revolving group of roommates who went to different colleges and universities in the Boston/Cambridge area--Harvard, MIT, Northeastern, Boston College, etc.

As was my MO at the time, I smoked and drank with the guys and tried to seduce all the girls. One particular, very attractive girl in an upstairs bedroom caught my eye. I suggested that she let me sleep with her rather than my having to sleep in my sleeping bag on the hard living room floor.

Her comment was "Go stick it in the wall!" I began noticing a lot of feminist posters and literature around the place and attributed them to her, but I didn't necessarily think she was a lesbian. I mostly suspected that she could see right through my shallowness. This prompted me to go into macho, alpha male mode.

The first thing I did was to seduce one of the girls who was also traveling through the house and sleeping on the floor as I was. This enraged the feminist even more since the girl I slept with was visiting her from their hometown.

As it turned out, I was staying in the house for several days, which included a weekend. Cambridge weekends were quite the party in those days.

The beautiful feminist and her friend went off for the weekend and I went out on the town. One bar and dance club led to another, and sometime in the night I hooked up with a young female student.

As I have said, I was a good kisser. This is not my own opinion, since I have never kissed myself. This judgment has come from my girlfriends. I was told several times that I should teach romance to men, and preferably to their own boyfriends. Once I kissed a girl, the conclusion was often forgone, especially in those days of free love.

My kisses coupled with sincerity, were almost unbeatable. That did not dispute the fact that I might have been an asshole sometimes! It didn't matter that my sincerity was for the moment, or that it was directed toward what might be considered a selfish goal. I was always able to convince a woman that what I wanted with her was going to be of benefit to both of us. I was always fun to be with. And, you know, I honestly believed that then, and still do today!

When I got the student back to my "crash pad," it didn't make any sense to roll out my sleeping bag on the floor, when there was an empty room and bed upstairs. So I moved into the feminist's room and onto her bed. Ever the alpha asshole!

Almost the moment I got the girl onto the bed, it was apparent that she was not as familiar with the proceedings as I had thought. This also put her age into question. For starters, she didn't have birth control.

In that day and age, most guys didn't carry condoms on a regular basis. Not like the 1950's when we carried them as trophy with hopes attached. In 1972, there was no AIDs to fear, and most girls who would have sex had birth control, the pill or diaphragms.

I had, for no apparent reason, just one lone prophylactic, that I had slipped into my backpack. She insisted, so I dug it out. I never liked the impersonality of a layer of rubber separating flesh from flesh.

We screwed for a while. I had an ejaculation. She thought it was over as had been the case with the other very few lovers she had had. But, she was not just being groped by some high school kid. I was going to make this an all night event.

She was beautiful, her body was perfect, and I wanted all of it. The first thing I had done, which surprised the hell out of her, was to take off all her clothes, look down on her beautiful body, and then give her cunnilingus.

She kept trying to cover her breasts or her vagina. It was a passive gesture, not at all defensive, just second nature. I began to suspect that this was all new to her. She was probably another girl who had only experienced fleeting sexual activity in the backseat of a car or in the proverbial tree house.

I got up, went in to the bathroom, cleaned out our one condom and came back to mount her again. She had put on her underpants. After that second session of intercourse, I washed the condom again, and returned to find her with her underpants on again. I then hid her underwear.

This time when I entered her it was skin to skin. In the morning she walked me to the Massachusetts Turnpike for my hitchhike down to New York City. On the way, she voiced her concern about pregnancy.

I gave her my phone number in California and told her I would help if something came of our lovemaking. I, of course, hoped she would not be pregnant and would not call. I was still married and living with my wife and daughter.

Before leaving the house, I had left a note to the feminist thanking her for the use of her bed. I knew that would enrage her more than anything. I have often wondered what she had done with the sheets. Burned them, I guess.

The irony of that episode was that I would have much rather spent the weekend in bed with the edgy feminist than both the others girls. I did appreciate them, but there was something about a woman who would reject me with rational criticism. I have always sought after the ones that got away.

That episode, the feminist's, "stick it in the wall," and the almost virgin girl, has been a constant memory and concern to me. Was I being too harsh toward a woman who saw right through me and didn't like what she saw? Did I like what I saw through her eyes?

No, I didn't like the man she saw in me, and it helped to change me. Eventually.

Was that other girl too young for me to be directing my powers toward? Did I take advantage of her?

In one sense, yes, but I think that it was not a destructive affair. And in that time and place it was a normal and natural activity.

I like to think I helped teach that girl what good sex was. But

I also think it taught her how better to protect herself. Not just from pregnancy, but also from situations that she would experience later in her life. She was safe with me; I would never maliciously harm her, aside from the threat of pregnancy.

With another unknown man from another bar, it could be different. I also hoped that our affair did not do the opposite, and drop her resistance to a future bad relationship. She had gone into that club to find someone, and deep inside, maybe she was looking for our lovemaking to happen!?

I know I was a bit of a dick that weekend, but I was learning through my on personal mistakes. I actually consider myself to be a feminist! I have female friends who call me that!
You can second-guess all of your actions. Your influence on someone, especially a young, vulnerable person, can go either way. It is a heavy load to carry. It is often too much to think about.

We can justify as right, anything we do one moment, and condemn ourselves the next. That is why laws set up by society should be the benchmark.

Many people on their own don't know when to stop. That is why the laws we have today for rape are as severe as they are.

The actions we made in the past have fathered more than children; they have begat laws that protect others from society's lack of common sense. And they have also fathered laws to protect us from ourselves.

But can we go too far with prohibitions? When do we suppress the zest for life; when do we kill individuality?

*"Volkswagen vans contributed more to the hippie counterculture than almost anything else. They stimulated travel, which enhanced cultural education. It was the meeting place for many new friends, because of the hitchhiking culture, and it was also a vehicle to lots of romance."* Mr. California

I took this photo in December, 1971, on the Acropolis, Athens, Greece, with five VW vans and hippie travelers from around the world. For 21 days my first wife, my daughter Siobhan, who was three at the time, and I lived in our van in this parking area, 200 yards from the Parthenon. During that time many other travelers passed through that spot. My daughter is the third from the right. The two young men at the back, standing and squatting, are Greek passersby.

The hill behind us, where the two people are standing is Mars Hill, where Paul spoke to the Athenians. While parked there, many days we were awakened by Christian tour groups singing "Rock of Ages."

Christmas is not Sears Roebuck's birthday

CHAPTER 94

# A New York Love Story

It started just like a 1970's "B" movie love story. We met at the pond in New York's Central Park.

I was there because I had shipped a Volkswagen van from Germany. I had to wait in New York for the boat to arrive, so I could drive it back to California.

Sitting on the monolithic rock overlooking the pond. You know the rock! You've seen it in every Fred Astaire movie.

I have mused at how the violent steel skyline and the calm, green landscape could reflect so beautifully together off the same serene waters. If you know the place, you know how private, yet exposed, that spot can be. Looking one way, you view nothing but the silent lake and uninquisitive trees. Turn your head slightly, and all of the world is looking down on you from the windows of The Plaza Hotel and 100 other buildings.

It's the kind of place where you expect to meet someone, music crescendo, bedroom scene, long, tearful kiss goodbye, and credits. Hundreds of times before and since, I have waited with anticipation in such a place for someone to give me a smile or to hear a sweet voice ask "Is this rock taken?" It seldom happens, yet this time it did.

She didn't ask to share my rock, and I am not quite sure how it did actually progress, but this is a close approximation. She was medium height and slim, dark, but light dark, short hair in the brown tones. Very pleasant to look at. I must have swallowed my basic shyness and said something inane when we got close enough for it to be uncomfortable if I didn't acknowledge her.

As usual, it must have been hard for me. For even with my inner self-confidence and a relatively good success with the opposite sex, I have always suffered from a basic social hesitation. I also never got the hang of shallow introductory spiel and canned, snappy repartee. Part of it is that I don't want to appear to be doing exactly what I am doing, which is trying to get close to a girl in hopes of making love with her. I don't like being a cliché or using clichés. No, *"Don't I know you?"* or *"What's your sign?"*

After the first few words, I've never had any problem being witty, intelligent, honest and sincere, in all honesty and sincerity. It's just that for some reason the first introduction always scared the hell out of me. I imagine it was that old adolescent fear of rejection coming back to haunt me.

When I met someone I was attracted to enough to want to get to know, I didn't want to blow it!

We talked and surveyed that most beautiful of New York City's contrasting views, the city in its grandeur, the park in its serenity. I think we went for a cup of coffee. Then we made a date to meet later because she had other obligations at that time.

This is where it becomes vague in my memory. I don't remember when I picked up my VW van at the port during our several days together. At one point during a ride to Queens through the tunnel, she commented on the casual way I drove, leaning confidently forward, resting my hands, forearms and elbows on the steering wheel.

It's odd what you remember from an encounter with someone. I don't remember her name, yet I remember a compliment she gave me. How typical of man's ego. How typical of her, the woman, to drop a simple, sensitive compliment.

I do remember one other thing; I remember that I liked her a lot. I would have taken longer to build up to the subject of sex if it weren't for the fact that I was driving back to California in the next few days.

I realize now that our meeting was an accident of nature. Even if we had both lived in the city, with our cultural differences, we would probably never have met. She was Jewish, I was an Anglo hippie, and even if we had met, it would not have been easy for us to find the place and a time to love. But I also knew that if we met under any circumstances, we would not have been able to keep our hands off each other.

From the moment we met on that rock, I started trying to get her somewhere intimate and more private. She was understanding, yet reticent. She couldn't take me home; her parents wouldn't approve. A hotel was out of the question. Too sleazy, and too expensive for my budget, or, at least, my budget would have made it sleazy.

I decided to take her to my place. My home in New York was

the loft of some friends who were letting me crash for a few days, yet it wasn't a crash pad. The friends were a young, professional couple who lived in SoHo. My other home was my VW bus.

I took her to the loft; we may have had some dinner with the host couple, and talked. And then, and then…? It was time to go to bed.

She had told her family that she was staying in Manhattan with a girlfriend. We had two options. The first was a platform bed suspended on four ropes that swung from the ceiling in the middle of the big loft room that served as my friends' kitchen, dining room, living room, studio as well their "bedroom." My young friend and I looked at the swinging bed and the creaking ropes, and thought of the vigorous and vocal love we were hoping to have that night, and opted for the second choice. Out on the street.

We made love in my Volkswagen camper van, parked down on Crosby Street in the middle of the garment district. Our lovemaking was memorable for numerous reasons.

The impression I have of that experience is that I received a great gift. In that meager place, in those humble surroundings, she gave me something of real value to cherish and remember. She was not a virgin, I knew that, but what she was giving me was even more precious to me. It was her trust.

We talked, also memorably. She told me she was Jewish from a very strict family. I hadn't even thought about her ethnic background. She wasn't my first Jewish lover, but I got the impression that I was her first non–Jewish lover, and that was a part of the gift she gave to me. Making love with me was like the loss of her ethnic maidenhead.

She was my Karla Bonoff, my Mary Magdalene.

She was not promiscuous, like many girls I have had sex with. Not using sex or promiscuity in a derogatory manner, but she was more exploratory.

Many girls, even inexperienced ones, will give you the impression that this screwing they are doing with you is not a big deal for them. You are one of the many, and one of many to come. It may be bravado, their way to prove they are mature. Or it may be their way to keep from becoming too emotionally involved, playacting as a way out, just as men often do.

But this girl made love with me only after a rational decision was made on the grounds of her affection for me, in spite of our differences and in spite of her social and religious mores. This girl, whose name I cannot even remember, opened my eyes to a new perspective. I think from that moment on, I began making love, even with one-night-stands, as if they really mattered to the flow of my life. I began to became more interested in my lovers on levels other than merely physical.

In the morning we made love for one last time, with the sounds of garment workers pushing racks of dresses, sewing machines humming and trucks maneuvering around us to deliver bolts of fabric. She then walked off into the City, never to be seen or heard from again.

I think I left for California that same day. The trip West is another story.

It is love that gives you the ecstasy and the pain. If you are afraid of these emotions, you will never live or love.


## CHAPTER 95

# What Is Truth?

There is no easy way to find the truth. You must fight for it. Many will deceive you and point this way or that. You must find your own truth, but truth really is the same for all of us.

Often only a man with everything to lose will tell you the truth. Or, only a man with everything to gain will tell you the truth.

There is often a discrepancy between your personal desires and the needs of the rest of the world and its creations. That it is the truth. It is not always comfortable. It is not always what you want, but it is the truth!

Your desires are secondary to the truth. Your wishes are registered by the cosmos, but you are just one of many.

You are important, yet the truth is more important than you. The fact that you are not the center of the universe does not matter, but, if you are trying to learn the truth, then you matter.

*Drink holy wine or decadent wine. It is how it makes you act that matters."*
Dudley Griffin, 1.19.07

## What Is Truly Right?

I define the words True and Right to mean the same thing when used in the context of human social behavior. They are the basis for personal morality. Religion doesn't really have any part in human morality. Religion is actually created by man's need for morality. Mankind is the searcher and chronicler of morality. The truth is our most sought after goal. That is, it is the goal of most people. There is a small percentage of people who are in this life only for themselves. There is often a disconnect between what you believe and what is really right. You may not like it, but you may have to rethink everything you believe!

Religious conviction is often tainted by man's thinking. True religious morals, which are always based on the Golden Rule, are truly sacred. But do not confuse religious morals with the Ten Commandments, which were, believe it or not, written by man.

There are several true moralities in the Ten Commandments, such as, "Thou shalt not kill, steal or bear false witness," because they are actually, physically harmful to a person. Commandments such as "honor thy Father and Mother" or do not "covet or commit adultery" are open to social interpretations. They may be in bad taste or intrusive upon another person's space and freedoms, but they are not sins worthy of burning in hell.

Truth is not always what you want, but it is always the truth!

Your personal desires are often secondary to the truth. Your wishes are registered by the cosmos, but you are just one of the many.

You are important, yet the truth is primary. The fact that you are not the center of the universe does not matter, (but you could be the center of "your" universe if you didn't stress about it). If you are trying to improve, then you are the truth, and you also matter.

*"I wish I could enlighten the world with just a wave of a wand. To end the pain of the world in one swoop of a hand, I would*

*give anything. Yet I guess I must toil on into this writing, to find the words that will tell the truth to everyone!"*
JBMc

Mankind cannot do what God does, and God cannot do what Mankind does! God has no hands except for our hands. God, "He or She," can keep us in check with mortality and nature's wrath, but we have free will to fuck-up if we want to. That is where morality comes in. If we are to be the shepherds of God's world, we must know what God and Mother Nature desire. This has little to do with our own needs and desires. God's world requires common sense to maintain and a moral compass to lead us away from destructive activities. The Ten Commandments are early mankind's rendition of morality, but through time and trials we have found some of them to be wrong and some to be missing.

More important to man's future and happiness would be if common sense commandments and morality commandments were divided separately with different judgments and consequences! If you kill somebody, that is a moral sin, which should be punished by imprisonment and eternal damnation. If you cuss, lust, covet, commit adultery, don't go to church, or don't honor thy parents, or use the name of the God in vain, those are social sins, and they should be treated with the disapproval of your community.

I do not agree with all Ten Commandments, nor agree with the severity of the original list! There are obvious levels of bad that are overlooked in the choices, and I don't think lusting should be a capital, *burn in hell*, crime .

Doing stupid, disrespectful or obnoxious things is not a mortal sin; it is just bad taste.

My rendition is called the "Morality" Commandments, and here they are:

Number 1: Thou shalt not Kill, other than for self-defense or food.

Number 2: Thou shalt not Steal when it threatens others' lives, liberty or happiness.

Number 3: Thou shalt not bear False Witness. This means don't lie when it threatens others' lives, liberty or happiness.

## The old "Biblical Morality" Commandments:

Number 1: Thou shalt have no other Gods besides Me.
This is very arbitrary. Which Gods are you talking about, and what about people, like myself, who believe in multiple Gods?

Number 2: Thou shalt not worship any Graven Image.
That's silly; I worship Marilyn Monroe's Blowing Dress photo, the Mona Lisa and Pieta.

Number 3: Thou shalt not take the name of the Lord thy God in vain.
Again arbitrary, for Christ's sake! And it is not in the realm of morality, goddamnit!

Number 4: Remember the Sabbath Day, to keep it holy.
All days are holy to me and to most positive thinkers!

Number 5: Honor thy Father and thy Mother.
This is a good thing to do,
but it should not be commanded,
especially if your parent is despicable!

Number 6: Thou shalt not Kill.
This should be at the top of the Commandments. It is my first Morality Commandment.

Number 7: Thou shalt not commit Adultery.
Many, many people believe that monogamy
is not a natural human ability
and that marriage is a wholly personal imprisonment!

Number 8: Thou shalt not Steal.
It is my second Morality Commandment.

Number 9: Thou shalt not bear False Witness.
This means don't lie! This is my third Morality Commandment.

Number 10: Thou shalt not Covet anything that is thy neighbor's.
You can covet it if you must, but Thou Shalt Not Steal!

**My New "Common Sense" Commandment is just one:**

Number 1: Follow the Golden Rule.
The Pieta, to me is not an image of Jesus and Mary; it is every mother and every child.

CHAPTER 96

# Use Your Drugs; Don't Let Them Use You

I started drinking beer in high school just as most everybody did. And just like everyone else it was influenced by peer pressure. I think I was introduced into male alcohol bonding by the same guy that introduced me to masturbation. "Little Richard," Richard Graham.

Lest you jump to conclusions, he didn't physically teach me to masturbate, just as he didn't drink my beer for me, he encouraged. He was the instigator of many of the marginal activities in which our little gang indulged.

Some of us became real professionals in the marginal arts, some of us dabbled. I was right in the middle. As far as alcohol and drugs are concerned I was fortunate not to have an addictive nature. Some of that was due to my mother and her influence. She was a social drinker, without the application of stigma or judgment. I drank wine with her on occasion as a child, just as European families do. To my mother, spirits were an intellectual stimulus, not a mental anesthetic.

I tried all the drugs and rejected what I could see was harmful. But some of my high school friends went deeply and some never recovered. Little Richard ended on the streets, but that was after his Viet Nam experience, which is another story.

Another of my buddies was someone we often had to drop off on his front lawn to sleep it off before he could go in to face his family. He became a lawyer, and then he was disbarred because of alcoholism.

I was fortunate; I didn't have the drinker's gene. I never aspired to be a no-holds-barred drunk, yet I have always appreciated the social and intellectual excitement that alcohol can create among people.

Most American families teach their children to be rebellious. When a parent overreacts to a normal teenage activity, then, of course, the child will begin doing it as a form of rebellion against parental control. If the parent doesn't catch on and back off, the child will continue doing it just to piss off the parent.

The prohibition of something often creates more damage than if society would just allow children to learn their own lessons!

Often, how we discipline our children has the opposite effect by giving them the idea that sex, alcohol and drugs are good to use as a rebellion. Instead of educating with compassionate, rational argument to protect children from hurting themselves, parents and society mostly just says no without rhyme or reason.

Prohibitions often push young people into addictions because they fall to peer pressure and into rebellious reactions.

Sex can be an addictive drug, just as alcohol and heroin are. Hormones, endorphins and dopamine get us excited and give us the desire to experience that sensation again. This is the basis of an addiction.

Use your drugs; don't let them use you! That should be all that needs to be said, but folks won't listen, or can't listen! Drugs are a big problem among humans, and the use of drugs, good or bad, can become a source of ridicule and condemnation by other people.

Those who don't want you to do something are often those who have been frustrated in their own efforts to do that same thing. Victimless "sins" are nobody's business but your own. No matter what God you follow, you must realize that no God worth following would want you to screw around with other people's lives.

But, of course, most of those who accuse you of something are the ones who do it themselves. They do it, so they think everyone else must be doing it. Thinking your sins are less bad than other people's sins is arrogant and will condemn you to fire and brimstone for eternity. Hypocrisy is the sin of lying to yourself, and no one can live with that curse!

Maybe the true light of God will shine down some day and we will realize that love is really the answer, not condemnation. Forgiveness and tolerance are the potential solutions to all of mankind's problems.

I think humankind has more brainpower than we are comfortable with, and we try too hard to understand our thought process. Then we have to justify our overthinking. Taking drugs to understand life is a natural course; taking them to justify your life is the start of giving up. When we are addicted to something--endorphins, morphine or gin and tonics--we make choices for the wrong reasons!

*"I believe that everybody deserves more sex! And I wish everybody could understand their drugs!"* DG

CHAPTER 97

# Un-Guilty Pleasures

*"What humans consider pleasures are mostly just facts of life to all other creatures! Sex, food, drugs and rock & roll are what any living being uses for evolution, sustenance and entertainment."* DG People with religious convictions most often believe that morality comes from God, whatever God they have chosen. And yet the deity of even one God has never really been proven. So the chances are that they may be following false morality fabricated by their priest, pastor, imam or seer.

The validity of each moral sin is recognized by a few people who have faith in the God they follow. And then, across the street or across the world, another worshiper believes in another set of moralities. Are we going to kill each other over this?

Faith is what connects many people to a belief, and yet faith does not even register in all the lists of realities in life. Gravity, death, taxes, thirst and hunger are rational things for a realistic person to have faith in, but something you can't see, feel or eat is not. Therefore, guilt by "God's" conviction is a crock of shit.

You should feel guilt and shame if you break the laws of the Golden Rule. However, if you drink too much, dance too crazy, sleep with someone you shouldn't and wake up with a hangover, you definitely should feel like an ass, but not necessarily feel guilty! You were just doing what your nature dictates.

People with guilt who condemn others for the same guilt are attempting to draw attention away from their own faults. They are trying to absolve themselves by passing judgment on others. Heal thyself before you can be a healer.

It will be so wonderful when all the people on the face of the earth can indulge in all the innocent pleasures and in the spirit of the Golden Rule. Remember to "forgive others their pleasures as they should be forgiving yours."

Insecurity is the foundation of most religious organizations. It is the creator of dictatorships and greedy corporations. Only weak people find it necessary to dominate, torture, roughen and kill others for self-satisfaction. Such people are not really human; they are barely even acceptable animals. No other animal is jealous except the insecure human.

*Stupid human mistakes:*

Insecurity is the stupidest of mankind's faults! If you are insecure, you will always fail because you are insecure! But, of course, insecurity is most often not the fault of a person. It is often created by oppressive parental expectations. That means insecurity is the stupid mistake of parents. I have said this many times, people, that a person should need a license to have children, just as we do for driving or practicing law or medicine. After all, more people are killed or damaged by parents than we are by lawyers or doctors!

*Stupid human mistakes:*

Jealousy is one of mankind's most contentious and convoluted failures! First off, most all jealousy is created by a misunderstanding or a timing error. This, of course, is exacerbated by the fact that men and women don't share the same language or sensibilities.
Also, why be jealous? If someone wants to be with someone else, why would you want to be with them anyway?

*Stupid human mistakes:*

Bigotry: Bigotry, to me, means ignorance! As human beings, other people are the most important element of our lives! Bigotry is the mistrust, fear, and/or hatred of other people. And in America, a continent of such ethnic diversity, bigotry is one of the most ignorant, self-defeating and damaging of all national mistakes.

*Stupid human mistakes:*

Greed: In order to work properly, a successful human society requires cooperation and trust. Greed and deception dismantle human society. In a greedy, anarchistic society everybody suffers; no one can trust anybody, so we all become liars, cheaters and thieves. Who wants

to live like that? If you do, stand up and give a "Heil Hitler" salute!
*"There is no room for bigotry in this country; there never has been!"* The Lone Ranger, in a 1956 TV show

*"Welcome to The United States of America, the country of bigots who should know better because they are mostly immigrants from somewhere else themselves!"* DG

*"I have very little prejudice or bias and this, because at times I, myself, have been the least desirable person in the room."* Mr. California

*Definition of screw: an insensitive form of lovemaking, or to abuse, deceive or obstruct someone."JBMc*

CHAPTER 98

# Three Degrees of Sexual Separation

*"We are so much closer than you might think; you sneeze, and I may soon get your cold. I think, and you will probably be thinking too. The truth we seek is the same; we need only to believe in the brotherhood of mankind."*
DG

I am three-degrees of sexual separation from American royalty. I once made love with a woman (actually 3 women) who eventually made love with a man, who made love with a woman who made love with John Kennedy, Jr.

We could easily make this into a communicable disease public service announcement, but I think I will just tell it as a good story. It is a very poignant and vivid story about the hippie era and the sexual mores of the time.

In the mid 1970's I had a girlfriend. I will call her Rebecca. When we first met she had recently separated from her "husband" or "ol' man," I'm not sure which, and had just given birth to their boy child. She was a lusty and well-appointed young woman, probably around 23 years old.

Rebecca was lactating, radiant and a bit crazy. So naturally, not having my own place at the time, or any common sense, I moved in shortly after our first "encounter." I soon discovered that I really loved mother's milk, and I also served a useful purpose by relieving Rebecca of the excess breast milk her son did not consume. She said I was much more efficient and enjoyable than any breast pump.

We had a passionate, confrontational, and educational relationship for over 6 months. She had unfaithful and bisexual tendencies. I had unfaithful and heterosexual tendencies. We made for quite a pair.

She introduced me to several of her bisexual girlfriends, and I looked the other way when she visited her other male lovers. It was a textbook example of a detached hippie love affair.

Rebecca was a member of the first and only *ménage a cinq* in which I was ever involved. The fivesome happened by accident one afternoon when Rebecca and two other girls and one of my guy friends all happened to accidentally converge on my little cottage at the same time.

One of the girls in the fivesome was a beautiful young local teenager (call her Jane), who was experimenting with her newfound sexuality and just happened to bump into Rebecca and me. She couldn't have met better mentors.

Another young woman who also happened on the scene at that time was from back East, Jewish and I will call her Shari. Rebecca, Jane, Shari and I became lovers and hung out a lot together for a while.

Shari was a screamer. No, I mean a real screamer! She could crack plaster.

Shari warned me about her screaming. For the first few times we made love, I must not have pushed the right buttons. When it finally happened, I was glad she had warned me. A man with a weaker constitution might have had a heart attack.

Shari and I once got a citation for sleeping overnight in a wilderness State Park in Big Sur. The ranger found us in the morning, gave us a ticket and kicked us out. The question is how did he find us in those woods. Could it have been Shari's screams, or was he looking for a wounded mountain lion?

When Shari and I went to court to pay our fine, we were also almost ticketed for PDA, public display of affection in the courthouse. The female deputy, who warned us for kissing, was partly joking, partly jealous and partly embarrassed.

The other girl in our unwholesome foursome, Jane, was "the girl next door." A real adolescent beauty, she looked only 14, but she was probably at least 17.

One day we learned that Jackson Browne was performing in Santa Cruz, so the foursome mounted a road trip. I was not photographing at that time. For a while in the 1970s, I concentrated on my human relationships. Even though I knew the magnitude of what I was involved in, I just could not take photographs; I needed to view people not as subjects. We got a baby sitter for little Christopher, Rebecca's son, and the three girls and I jumped into my 1967 VW van.

It was a wonderful concert with Jackson, David Lindley and Warren Zevon. The girls and I were having an excellent party, a party you couldn't write home about. We were at our lusty best, dancing and carousing in the audience.

At a certain point in the evening, I began to pick up some interesting vibes. When girls of that caliber get together and become sexual beings, the best thing to do is to stand back, join if you can, but don't get in their way if you must.

Guys at that level of public intoxication can become destructive and selfish. Girls on that track are also sometimes uncontrollable, but it usually means that anyone around them is going to have one hell of a good time. As the concert rolled to its end, Rebecca, Shari and Jane turned to me and said, "Let's see if we can go party with Jackson Browne!"

I could see what was going to happen. With the power and beauty of these three girls, I knew who they would be screwing that night, and I didn't want to have anything to do with it. I would only be a fifth wheel and probably end up as a flat tire.

"OK," I said, "you know where the van is parked I'll go for a few drinks and be back there by midnight. Leave me a note if you connect with Jackson." Yes, I actually said that!

At midnight I went to the van and found a note reading, "We have gone off with Jackson." I went home to relieve the baby sitter and visit another girlfriend.

**Orgasm for Six at 2**

The girls arrived back in Monterey <u>by limo</u> the next morning. Rebecca was overflowing with stories of sex and cocaine and more sex. She related to me a moment when the four of them, Jackson, Rebecca, Shari and Jane, all reached simultaneous orgasm, or simulgasm, at exactly 2 a.m. that morning.

That was memorable, I thought, because I and my other girlfriend also had a simulgasm, at that very moment. I remembered looking at the clock. Orgasm for six at 2.

In case you haven't already caught on, this little episode places me exactly three degrees of sexual separation from John Kennedy, Jr. Jackson Browne later lived for a while with Daryl Hannah, and then she eventually "dated" John-John.

Recently, I have realized it was possible that John Kennedy, Jr. might have had some of my cooties. Isn't that a strange thought?

There is a moral lesson hidden in this story. Most of you will think the lesson is that sexual decadence is--well, decadent!! Yes, that is what it is.

But my morality lessen is--so what! What is wrong with such debauchery? To my knowledge, no one was hurt by this exchange of fluids. It was a slice of life. In fact, a very funny cut of human prime rib. Admit it; it was amusing, and I think the world needs more of that kind of amusement.

We take our sex way too seriously in this country. Many other countries and almost all other creatures take sex more for granted. Sex is a fact of life; it is not to be overintellectualized. But love, love is different! That is my moral tidbit.

And if you think this story ends there, then you have greatly underestimated my strange life. And, as I have said before, this is all true! These things really did happen to me, and in most cases they happened with my own approval and cognizance.

Sometimes while recounting these occasions and writing them down, I wonder if perhaps it would be more acceptable if they were just fiction. Maybe such reality is unbelievable to some readers.

Maybe I should call this a novel and rewrite myself as a fictional character, who stumbles from one elevating, exciting, embarrassing, painful and humorous lesson into another. But, my God, that is way too close to the truth! It seems to me that's exactly what's happened to me. I guess I better stick with calling this book autobiographical, or people will accuse me of self-denial.

Shortly after the Santa Cruz concert, Jackson Browne had another gig up in San Jose. So he invited his three party girls to come up for a replay of the first night.

I suggested, rationally, that I stay at home and babysit, so the girls went off in one of their vehicles.

Five minutes after they departed I got this feeling of being left out. I looked over at little Christopher, who looked back at me and gurgled something like, "Hey, why do they get to have all the fun?"

I bundled up Christopher, grabbed some diapers and bottled breast milk and headed for San Jose. Yes, I know the way to San Jose, and I made it in record time. As a matter of fact, I caught up with the girls on the freeway and had to slow down so as not to give away the surprise.

Christopher and I were having a grand old time, he with his bottled lactose and me with my can of beer, as I recall.

In one of my earlier lifetimes, I was a rock and roll photographer. During the 1960s and early 1970s, this meant that you had to be a good gate crasher. If you didn't have recognizable credentials from Rolling Stone or some other news media, you would just sneak in to create your photographic icons.

I was kicked out of a concert only once. It was a Joni Mitchell performance in Berkeley. I have the distinction of being ejected personally from a backstage by Bill Graham, himself.

With chutzpah, I had gotten by the Black, three-hundred-pound, ex-football player bouncer, only to have Bill himself tap him on the shoulder and ask to see my media pass. Then Bill Graham walked me to the stage door and ushered me out.

At the San Jose Jackson Browne concert, I didn't have a ticket nor the money or desire to buy one. I also didn't have a camera to give me credibility, but I did have little Christopher. I knew that I could bluff my way into the auditorium by pretending to be one of the musicians or a backstage friend with a child in tow.

I was going to say that Christopher was David Lindley's son, but, I didn't even have to open my mouth. Guts and looking straight ahead to where I was going served the purpose. I even had one doorman tell me to remember to wear my pass next time I came through his entrance.

Once in the auditorium it was easy to get back stage. I went up in front of the stage and waved to the three girls who were dancing in the wings, and they got a guard to open the side door for Christopher and me.

When I arrived back stage, Rebecca was ecstatic. She took Christopher to meet Jackson and the rest of the boys. I ate good hors d'oeuvres, drank freely and met some of my heroes. When the concert was over I kissed the three girls on their cheeks, watched them walk down the stairs to the dressing room and took Christopher back home. I felt somewhat like a purveyor, but it didn't bother me. You had to have lived and loved during those times to know why.

During this time of the Jackson Brown episode in my life, I had achieved the most prestigious place that a man's ego could reach. I always had two or three girlfriends. I did not feel jealousy toward what my girlfriends did with other men or women, and I did not feel self-conscious in my own skin or in my mind.

CHAPTER 99

# Is Sex a Growth Industry?

*"First, sex is not an industry; it is the basis of all life!*
*Second, sex, is possibly the only force that cannot be functionally*

*industrialized, monopolized or controlled, no matter how powerful you are! Fortunately, neither God nor his self-proclaimed representatives have been successful in prohibiting or corporatizing sex!"*

DG, 5.22.14

Sex, if it could be controlled, would definitely have a lucrative place on the Stock Exchange. After all, many drugs are controlled by corporations and are kept illegal or manipulated by taxes in order to create a stock market value. Sex also has a market value, but fortunately for us regular folks, there is no way that the industrial complex can charge us every time we have sex.

Sex is a free commodity, but it has peripheral emotional baggage. We either treat it as a negotiated arrangement and deal with the damage that it can cause, or we respect it as a necessary emotional activity, such as eating chocolate, drinking coffee or having an afternoon nap.

Sex is so complex that it will not be an easy fix. The sexual revolution opened the debate toward accepting sex as social communication. The hippie era questioned the authority of those before them who were the twentieth generation disciples of Christianity.

The sexual freedoms of 1960s and 70s didn't solve all of the problems between the sexes, but at least that era nudged us toward starting to begin to ask the right questions.

Although at first we men thought that the sexual awakening of women was a godsend, it soon raised some uncomfortable emotional situations for many men. Some of the issues of feminism that are associated with women's sexual choices and empowerment have had an emasculating effect on some poor, misguided guys.

Many men, even some otherwise liberal men, deep inside want their women to come to them as virgins, and then when they leave them, to have them go into a convent for the rest of their lives. Most men would like to make love to as many women as they can, but that means that women have to be willing, yet the man wants the women to be willing to make love only to him.

Enough about the faults of man. How about the stupidity of man? Men who have low self-esteem or little self-confidence find it personally damaging that a woman would just as soon sleep with the next guy or the guy before. For some men, if it doesn't make them at least socially impotent or actually physically impotent, it sometimes makes them the opposite--they become sexually abusive.

The frustration of having sex with a woman who is not completely theirs forces some men into masculine games of power and pain. Some men in emasculated insecurity lash out physically and sexually to prove to themselves that they don't care about the woman, that there is no real attachment. These acts of detachment and sometimes the proverbial "lack of commitment" that many men display are their ways of insulating themselves from the ego pain of knowing that "she" was once someone else's or could at a moment's notice be with another man.

The sad part is that all this damages the really good part of sex, which is the mutual satisfaction of two people who want to be with each other for that moment in time.

If you don't think that the sex is going to be good, then, of course, it will become a so-so, or even ultimately a bad screw!

People often scare themselves in scary situations. You have heard the FDR quote, "The only thing we have to fear is fear itself."

Yes, there is some possible future for sex. It is quite likely a growth industry. But will it be a flash in the pan business that fails in the first year, sucking your life savings with it, or will it be worth the investment?

CHAPTER 100

# Homophobia Is For Pussies

*"I am 'Homocompatable.' It is a compliment for a gay guy to look at me! This means women also find me attractive."*
DG

I have never had a homosexual relationship. I have no fear of, or hatred for, men who make love with one another. It is just not right for me.

The reason I have no negative feelings toward homosexual

men is that I have no hidden or suppressed homosexual desires my-self. I am confident in my own sexuality, and I feel no shame for any-thing I do. I do not indulge in hypocrisy. I will not do one thing and preach another.

Live and let live. love and let love. But some men are threat-ened by homosexuality, and the basic reason is that they, themselves, are not sure about their own sexuality. They think that maybe if they were to be tempted, they might become what they hate.

I, personally, if a man propositions me (which has happened), I don't feel humiliated by it, I just say '"no thank you, I'm straight." I certainly wouldn't beat him up for asking. It's like, what if every time a man asks a woman to go on a date, instead of just refusing to go, she physically kicks him in the balls?

Most homophobics are deeply conflicted, weak and insecure people, and they are like that because they are worried about their masculinity.

One of the reasons people are drawn to sex, beyond the natural physical urge, is because it is a place and time that we can feel the warmth of God or Mother Nature flow over us. To want that feeling over and over again may turn some men's brains into mush. And some men who don't get enough sex will at times become anxious, worried about their virility, and too physically demanding, maybe even rape someone or use a date rape drug. But if you force or violate someone into having sex with you, then your love bank becomes overdrawn. Yeah, this is a money-to-love analogy.

Think of love as a bank account. You can't have any love (money) if you don't have it in your bank. You have to love someone else in order to get a credit back into your own account.

A basically greedy or self-centered person will not admit, to others, that they are greedy and self-centered. But, don't ever lie to yourself; that is death at your own hands! Man up and admit what you know to be true, what you know about yourself, and then you will become a better person. How in the world are you going to become perfect if you can't first admit your faults?

*"The sex you take is equal to the sex you make."*
Beatles/JBMc

415

Violent bigotry against someone who under most circumstances you will never have to deal with is often a sign of a confused psyche. Only someone who is not sure of his own sexual direction or who may be afraid of his own weakness will lash out at a homosexual, or for that matter any person they don't understand.

For all I know, I may have homosexual tendencies myself, but what I feel and what I always tell people is that I have not tried or tired of all the heterosexual possibilities yet, so why should I turn around and venture into new sexual explorations?"

Reflection on what I have just said, I think many heterosexual men should be beaten up for their treatment of women. Most macho strait men are far more obnoxious and demanding about their sexual desires than gay men are.

I believe, and it can be corroborated by the facts, that homosexuals are far less dangerous in our society than heterosexuals. Statistically, homosexual rape is a minor problem compared to heterosexual rape. The one glaring exception is in prison, where these acts are not even considered homosexual by the perpetrators.

Also, repressed homosexuality produces aberrations, such as Jeffery Dahmer. Much homosexual pedophilia is the result of suppressed homosexuality, just as most all child molestation is suppressed sexuality.

Homosexuals seldom proposition outside their culture, but even proactive homosexual propositions are usually harmless.

This is my own favorite personal homosexual proposition.

One day while hitchhiking on Highway 101 between Santa Barbara and Santa Maria, I was picked up by a guy going as far as Santa Maria.

After some small talk, I noticed that the driver was concentrating on the rearview mirror, which I then realized was turned at a weird angle. I finally caught on that it was angled that way so the driver could look at my crotch.

This only amused me. But what the driver did next really astonished me!

In one fluid motion, almost as if scripted, the driver asked if I wanted a cigarette as he reached up to the sun visor over my head knocking the cigarette pack down into my lap then reaching for it running his hand over my crotch as he picked up the fags.

I was not offended; I had seen men do much worse to women. Yet, I was greatly impressed by the creativity and choreography of the move. I broke into a fit of laughter in admiration.

When I was again able to speak, I told the gentleman that I was impressed. I may have said something to the effect that, "a performance like that deserved success," but I was sorry, I am straight! I told the driver he could let me off at the next on-ramp and go back to cruising. The driver let me off, we parted in good humor, and went on our own separate ways.

I was actually propositioned by more women than men while hitchhiking. That's not saying much since I only had four or five overt propositions while hitching. But there were quite a few other times when someone I met while hitchhiking became a lover.

I was not offended by the man and his pack of cigarettes because I was not worried about my own sexuality, and, as I have said, I know that men are far worse to women. Per capita, man-to-woman, heterosexual rape and molestation are far more prevalent than all man-to-man or woman-to-woman homosexual rape and molestation. This is to say that for every one homosexual rape there are at least thousands of women raped by men, although prison confinement ups the percentage of man-to-man rape.

Therefore, men violating women is far more a problem on this earth than men violating men!

Even though homosexual rapes occur regularly in jail, and most of the men who perpetrate them will tell you that they "ain't no fucking homo," they are just exerting power. This just goes to show how confused sexuality can get when "need is the mother of invention."

## Homophobia

One time, one day, back in the early 1980s, I put on a pair of overalls that I found somewhere and went down to the grocery store. No shirt, no shoes.

The overalls were white, cut-off and tight. I was looking good at the time. They fit and I wasn't concerned about my sexuality.

I learned a lot about homophobia that day. First, I wasn't propositioned or looked at inappropriately by any homosexual men. I did get inappropriate looks from a few young ladies and housewives.

But what actually disturbed me about that day were the looks I got and comments I heard from "normal" people. One family turned their children around so as not to have to walk by me in the aisle. In the checkout line I heard parents whispering to their children about San Francisco and fruits and nuts.

## CHAPTER 101

# Loss of Innocence

*"I can't even imagine being a girl or woman and having all these men and boys coming at me with amorous and devious intent. It definitely must be a confusion of fear and flattery, and no wonder many pregnancies and lost maidenheads occur in a state of both sorrow and joy."*
Mr. California, 5.20.21

*"From the definitions found in The Hippie Dictionary: Balling: A very derogatory term indicating the least sensitive form of lovemaking."*
JBMc

Far too often acts of flirtation and innocence lead to unwanted results because it all seems like a game. Believe me, none of it is a game unless both players know the rules.

The loss of sexual innocence is not necessarily a bad thing. Innocence is just fine as long as you reside forever in an innocent society, such as your home and supportive family. But as one ventures out into the world, which is, as we know, not innocent, one must change with the surroundings. It is a shock if innocence is lost in an unexpected and merciless manner, but its loss is not the end of the world unless it results in some irrevocable consequence, like death, pregnancy, addiction, incarceration or insanity.

Innocence is best disposed of quickly, without regret, preferably the first time it is assaulted. Certainly no one wants to make the same mistake more than once! If you are still innocent after the first time you are seduced, you could then be considered stupid.

This may sound a bit harsh, and it is meant to be confrontational. You will not learn except by your own mistakes or from lessons gleaned from your friends.

There is, of course, a place and time when the assault on innocence is not acceptable. Sexual innocence should not be taken by a family member in a way that will create social or psychological problems. It is best that it should not be forced physically or by the power of authority.

Parents should never take the innocence of their own children; that leads to psychological recriminations on both sides. Teachers or bosses should not confuse devotion with love, nor should anyone in authority over innocence take advantage of that for their own sexual gratification. No one should ever wrench a child from innocence who is too young to understand the consequences of what he or she is doing.

Loss of innocence should be enjoyed. It is a bittersweet passage. The first sexual experience can be truly memorable if a certain set of circumstances is present. First, one of the partners should be experienced. The more experience, the better.

The virgin should at least know what sex is. The innocent should not be too innocent; there must be some positive expectations. All virgins should read Harlequin novels first or watch Hallmark made–for–TV movies. In fact, in my opinion, only virgins should experience these types of entertainment. Such illusions of love and romance are good only for priming virgins. After experiencing the often-sad reality of real life, who could possibly take such dramatizations seriously?

But I am not a romantic pessimist. I believe in Love. I just believe that we should be a little more realistic about it. That is why I am writing this book, to inform and suggest that there is a good, positive, rewarding way to experience love and sex, and to assure you that it is possible to be successful with your love life. But you must also know and deal with the bad things involved in social and physical intercourse.

At least after the first fuck, a person should start realizing and preparing for reality, but there are also things to know before the first sexual encounter.

First lesson: in the first sexual encounter, there should be some element of danger. Fear of discovery is the most acceptable. The fears of pregnancy or disease are not emotions conducive to good first sex. Some first experience pre-coitus preparation is advisable.

Again I say, I don't want to destroy the mystique of sex. Even if that were possible, I would not try. Even some of the strange or difficult mental and physical aspects of sex are what make it so appealing.

Never underestimate the sensual value of illicit circumstances. Having sex for the first time in your parents' own bed, with them downstairs watching Johnny Carson reruns is a good scenario. Or in the school parking lot during class. Or with your cousin who is five years older. Or with a parent driving you home after baby-sitting their child.

The last two scenarios introduce the touchy subjects of sex with family members and the critical issue of disparity in age between first-time sex partners. First off, the taboos about cousins and siblings and sex usually concern the procreation of children. There is a natural law, and it is the medical possibility of inbreeding damage connected with cousins and siblings having children together. But there are few actual laws on the books concerning sex among family members.

In fact, the instance of loss of virginity to a family member is very high. It is the "familiarity breeds attempt" adage. I would venture to say that more people have lost their virginity to cousins than have freckles. The kid next door takes second place, and the tree houses or clubhouses would be the preferred locations for such deflowering.

A wide difference in age between a virgin and their first lover is not necessarily bad, but there are some social stigmas attached. If the experienced first lover is a "predator," someone who applies pressures for illicit sex or uses drugs or alcohol to induce compliance, the experience for the "victim" may be psychologically damaging.

Yet, on the other hand, an older and experienced lover will most likely make the experience more enjoyable for the virgin. An older lover is also likely to be more careful about contraception and disease protection.

Age and experience aside, what is most important to the loss of virginity is that it be consensual. Even if it is not well-planned or thought out, it should be experienced with a positive attitude. It may not be completely romantic or in a manner condoned by conventionality, but it should possess some element of excitement and anticipation by both parties.

What I'm saying is that loss of virginity will happen whether "we" like it or not, and often it is not under the circumstances prescribed by family or society. My suggestion is that we all help to make it as psychologically painless and even enjoyable as possible. And the way to make the process of losing virginity less painful is to be more realistic about its effect and consequences. It is a natural fact of life; it isn't a tragedy. And although how it happens and with whom are important factors, a person's psychological attitude is more important than the circumstances of who, where or when.

If sex and the loss of virginity are taught by parents and society to be a scary thing, then the event will be scary. If sex is portrayed by role models as immoral, then the event will be embarrassing and create self-persecution.

Sex has such a major effect on our human social personality. Adolescence and how we transition into sexual activity have a powerful role in creating the adult we become. We educate children for every other facet of their lives, but shy away from teaching them the hard evidence and social graces of sex. Being quiet about the facts of sex is the same as introducing our children to disaster, as is failing to tell them not to drive their car off a cliff.

Human beings thrive on information. It is what makes us different from all other creatures. A person cannot be emotionally stable within any situation unless they are sure of their footing. That is just human nature.

Sex is based on emotions, emotions that drive a physical action. That physical act of making love is the one activity in our lives that is most fraught with problems, turmoil and potential of changing lives.

Understanding sex is essential to our emotions about it, and our emotional status is most important to our sex life. Good information and a good attitude are important to good sex. Knowledge and emotions are all tied up in our sexual performance and sexual happiness, and yet it is the area of our lives for which society has failed most miserably to prepare us.

It is essential for people to reject what they learned in church about sex. That was just meant to make them feel guilty so they would give money and listen more intently to the preacher's sermon. Until we abolish sexual guilt there will be no real equilibrium and happiness surrounding love and sex.

If I have any wish for this book it is that it makes people proud, happy and realistic about sex! I want my words to somehow break the hold that "nastiness" has on sex. I want these pages to teach good sexual etiquette. I want this book to free the emotions of those who read it so that they will live happy sex lives! I want to see more smiles out there on the freeway, so that if I cut you off by accident, you won't be so dammed frustrated that you road rage me into a fiery crash!

*"The truth is not something you can play with. If you do, then*
*it becomes a lie!"*
JBMc, 6.2.14


CHAPTER 102

# What Is Indecent?

When that guy (I can't remember his name) exposed Janet Jackson's breast, was that obscene or just a public relations arrangement? If a disk jockey says "fuck" on the radio, is that obscene or just an expression of his self-proclaimed public persona?

There is an indecency code that some people adhere to because of their occupation, just as there is a code of decency that others follow because of their moral sensibilities.

We have the option to buy into other people's morality or vulgarity, or we can ignore their reality and go on with our own lives. If you took everybody else's foolishness seriously, it would drive you nuts. Have a little sense of humor about it, or you will become one of those nut cases who are always meddling in everybody else's business.

*"Even if I had the power to make a law against stupidity, I still wouldn't do it. First, I wouldn't know where to start. There is so much stupidity among humans. I prefer to lobby for education."*
Mr. California, 7.12.06

## CHAPTER 103

# Make Love, Not War

During the Vietnam War I fought many battles. I engaged in numerous skirmishes between the sheets. I breached the ramparts and drove deep into enemy territory.

I fought to stay out of the Vietnam War, partly because I didn't want to disrupt my life and partly because I didn't agree with the war and felt the USA had no business being there. I was not afraid of dying.

I stayed home and made love instead of fighting. I ridiculed those who created that war. I marched against it, created bumper stickers and slogans, and screamed those slogans.

I was not a coward. How could I be? I was too young to understand death. I was following the conscience of my era. Then one day near the end of the war, I was looking at a collection of Vietnam battle photographs, and it all came to me in a shiver of fear and realization.

No one I knew in the anti–war movement was a coward. None of them were traitors to their country. It was not easy to be a conscientious objector against the war. You were a minority, an outcast, often within your own family.

It was easier to go along with the government than to fight it. Every man I have spoken to who went to Vietnam has told me that they didn't know what they were doing. They just went along for the ride because they thought it was the right thing to do.

The fear and realization that they didn't want to be in that war came to them after they got there and saw and smelled the death. It was easy to just go to war as you were told. In many ways it was the same battle for us at home fighting against our own government as it was for our soldiers to fight for our government in Vietnam.

I had to fill out forms, write letters and feel the wrath of others to be a draft resister. Yet it was also an uplifting movement; I was part of something valuable, righteous and historic. But it sometimes concerned me that I was over here, while others were dying over there, until I saw that photograph of that war.

That photograph was a color image of a tank carrying wounded soldiers out of battle. Stretched out on the front of the tank was one boy who was being attended to by a medic. The color of that boy's face gave me a start. I knew in that moment that my decision not to go to Vietnam was the right decision. I knew right then that I would never again ridicule our soldiers for going and fighting. I knew at that moment the fear and futility.

That soldier may not have died, but to me he represented death and waste. That wounded soldier may have wanted to go and fight, he may not have considered whether that war was morally right, but he never asked for what happened to him. He never knew what was in store for him. He was a hero for going; I was a hero for staying.

Many people called anti–war protesters and draft dodgers traitors to their country. But all of them I knew were true Americans because they felt that they were doing what a true American should do. They were defending our way of life, the freedom of speech, dissent and democracy, the duty of all Americans to speak out against injustice.

Every anti-war protester I knew felt that the war in Vietnam was beneath the dignity of the United States of America. In the end it was proven that they were right.

That boy on the tank was doing what he thought was right until that bullet struck him. I was at home protesting that war. I was safe in a warm bed making love with his girlfriend when I could have been draped over that tank instead.

CHAPTER 104

# The ESP of Sex

I never used a seduction line, you know like, "What's your sign?" "Haven't we met in a past life?" or "What's a beautiful chick like you doing in a dive like this?" Not that there weren't times when I wished I had a line of foolproof chatter to lay on some unsuspecting bird, but I guess I was just too spontaneous. I never could be contrived enough to come up with a "plan of seduction."

With me, it always just happened, a different situation, a different girl, and a different approach. Most often there was ESP involved. Yet no matter how bad my approach was, the seduction was often a foregone conclusion within the first few minutes or even seconds.

Corfu, Greece, summer of 1984. She was Greek. No tourist guy ever makes love to a Greek girl unless she is a prostitute. The Greek boys make love to the tourist girls. The Greek girls are all safely at home.

The islands of Greece are saturated with love. There is a potion mixed into the air by the mischievous ancient Gods. No other place on earth makes you feel as alive, as self-confident, and as desirable.

On a hot, windless, summer day, the Mediterranean and the sky are the same color, texture and temperature. The world is like walking through molasses. Your body is slow, and yet your libido is working overtime.

Whenever, wherever a man and a woman meet, there is the hint of sex and the possibility of romance. Even on a rainy day in Duluth, Minnesota, this is true, but on a Greek island it is magnified a thousand fold.

She was thin and tall, with a nice body. Short, cropped brown hair. Small, young, childish face. Her teeth were slightly bucked. She was not a beauty, but a cute and vivacious girl.

She was a "different" Greek girl, because she was from Athens. She was the cousin of someone in the village and was on vacation. She also spoke a little English. Her name was Lula.

Over a couple of days Lula and I got to know each other. There was something there, but I knew Greek girls well enough to think that she was untouchable.

I worked on a tourist boat with my friend, Captain Costas. We took tourists from all over the world out on day trips around our island. Swimming, lunch on the mainland or at some quaint taverna by the sea, and then dancing at night somewhere at a taverna by the sea. I met a number of lovers that way.

One day I asked Lula to come out on the boat with me and some of the paying tourists. We flirted all day. At one point our boat was anchored off the coast on a shallow sand bar where we brought people to swim. I tried to coax Lula in to swim with me. She was wearing a bikini and a watch. She refused to come into the water. I went in and swam around awhile, calling out to her. She refused. I swam under the boat and came up under her feet dangling over the side of the boat.

When I pulled her in, she came willingly. When she came up for air, she said, pointing to her wrist, "See, I took off my watch." She knew I was going to pull her in; she wanted me to. I knew in that moment that we would soon be making love.

It was not natural to assume that we would be lovers, but both of our ESP kicked in. She knew I was going to pull her in, and I knew she wanted to be pulled.

That evening we went back to the taverna where my friend kept his boat. We ate, drank and danced. When bedtime came, the Greek girl let me kiss her for the first time and then went off to sleep in a large tent with the boat captain's German girlfriend and her son. I was sleeping on the boat at the time.

I waited about an hour or so and then snuck into the tent and slipped into Lula's bed. She knew I was coming. As I entered her she whispered, "Yani, I am sorry I am not a virgin for you." Later we went back to the boat and made love all night long.

We made love several times a day for three or four weeks before I left to go back to the States. You never know, and yet if you use your sensory antennae, you will always know.

CHAPTER 105

# The Macho Thing

I could easily turn into a death-dealing ninja. It is in my genes, as it is in all men. I have an arrogance inside me like most people. Yet, I have struggled to overcome it because it is not good for society. In the days of the jungle and desert, it was necessary, today it is bad for mankind.

It is always the battle of head, heart and primal nature to become the person you eventually are. Are you a good person? Are you a successful person? Are you a valuable person? Are you a person that you and the rest of the world can live with?

Survival is only one of the elements of life. Granted, it is an important part to you, but if you live to be a 110-year-old asshole, what value is your life?

It has been said that you judge a person by his friends, or if he has any friends. It is even more profound than that. You judge a person by whether people have survived him and reached fulfillment through his influence.

Again, I must say that insecurity is the most damaging human condition, and it is often caused and created by family and/or mistreatment when you are young. A curse on family members who do not treat their children with respect. And they will be cursed because it will come back to haunt them. It always does.

A curse on coaches, teachers, and fellow students who mistreat their peers and charges. And believe me, they will be cursed, if not in their lifetime, but for eternity.

There is a God. He does not play favorites, but he makes you feel good when you do good, and he condemns you to think about your crimes when you do bad. And your afterlife, if you have one, will be heaven or hell depending on whether you do good or bad! It's all in your mind, and that is your reality.

*"Have you ever dropped off a thirty-foot wave to slice across the vertical face into a froth of salt and sand?"*
Mr. California

*I have never considered myself macho or a true alpha male. I am not big in stature, I will not pump iron, and I do not buy sex. I have in moments of grandeur, called myself a lover of women, but I don't win their favors by beating up someone else physically or financially.*

*The size of your neck, bank account, or cock plays little in winning the girl. Often, the small, quiet, introspective, wimpy artist sneaks in there and gets the girl.*

*This brings up the question of stature and personality in mating. In the long run the sensitive dude does better than the arrogant guy.*

*Back in the day during one of my relationships, I was in competition with another guy. I hadn't known him before, but I got to love him as a brother because of our common girlfriend--oh, excuse me, girlfriends. You will see this cast of characters elsewhere in this book*

*I'm going to use his real name, Gordon Andrews, because he wouldn't care. He was so universally loved that I couldn't blemish his image, and lastly, he is gone now. Gordon was a tall, dark and skinny guy, somewhat awkward, always with a smile or a smirk. He was effeminate. I can't say that he was extremely effeminate. He was intriguingly bisexual in nature, and yet he was one of the most sincere and successful lovers of women that I have ever met.*

*He was the kind of guy that a Big Gun guy would invite into his house to comfort his wife while he was away on a trip. Mistake, if that wife was unhappy with her husband or in estrus, Gordon would soon be making love with her. And yet, he was a fair competitor; he picked only the ripe fruit. He was not to be despised because your woman was not yours anymore at that time when they met. She wasn't meant to cuckold you; it just happened.*

*"Don't blame the girls if you can't get laid! It is your fault for not wanting or being able to give them what they need and want."*
Mr. California

*"Most girls don't care how macho you look, but they do care how good you feel and how softy you touch them!"*
Dudley Griffin

*"How do you make somebody listen to you, then believe you and then follow your suggestion? You tell the truth!"*
Mr. California

David Avenue Commune

## The Pacific Grove Handshake

I lived and worked in Pacific Grove, California, for close to ten years in the 1970s and 80s. A sleepy little town on the coast, near Clint Eastwood and Big Sur weed.

Meeting people anywhere was an introduction to sex. In this little town at that time, making love was our most important subject. Sex was the Pacific Grove handshake.

It was casual, it was hopeful, it was exciting as hell. But, and yet, it might have led you to a heartbreak or to your golden future of marital bliss, family and fortune, or maybe an unexpected child intervention. Yet, don't let me put you off the Pacific Grove Handshake. I would do it again in a moment, if I were not bound by a moral and marital promises. The Fat Cat was a small restaurant in PG that specialized in breakfast. Any morning, and most often Saturday, half the hippies would gather there for bad coffee and great omelets. You could always find out who was sleeping with whom or what by the couples who arrived together.

We never passed judgment on others, although we may have, at times, felt some envy. Next week it might have been you with the new lover.

Most people who see immorality in others do so because they have committed the same "sins" themselves and transfer them to other people. They think that because they are sinners, others must also be. Do-gooding is OK if you are trying to help people and bad if you are doing it to excuse your own immorality, or to gain power or money by finger-pointing!

CHAPTER 106

# Sex In A Hot Tub

Sex in a hot tub is mostly just foreplay. It's exciting in your fantasies and there's some excitement connected with the threat of drowning, but it's not very efficient lovemaking.

To begin with, water is not a good sexual lubricant. In fact, water washes away vaginal lubricants. And most hot tub owners don't want a lot of massage oils, or any other fluids for that matter, floating around in their tub.

Hot tubs are a very good place to start a romance. It is where all those Playboy Mansion grotto fantasies come to life. But after the first touching and near drowning experiences, it is on to a more compatible surface, such as the hard, pebbly pool coping or a squeaking chaise lounge.

If you're a real pro, you will have a chaise lounge mattress lying about somewhere, or better yet, a pool house and bed.

Many folks have fantasies about making love in a weightless environment, but unless you are astronauts don't try it. I am sure someone, possibly the Russians, did an experiment, either officially or on the side. Trying to have weightless sex in a pool or hot tub is courting disaster. Fellatio and cunnilingus are definitely drowning propositions.

I admit to only one or two sexual hot tub encounters. One was a long relationship that started in a hot tub. I was working as a carpenter at a very lovely lady's house. One of the jobs was to put a fence around her hot tub. Well, after I built the fence, we hopped into the tub and had sex for our first time.

It was the same as all such attempts are. Floating in the comforting hot water, getting chummy, kissing, messing around, a little awkward intercourse and then into the bedroom. From then on, our whole relationship revolved around the hot tub, but we only attempted to make love that one time. We met in the tub each evening, or often in the middle of the day, drank wine, relaxed, touched, and then retired to the bed.

My other hot tub affair was at Esalen in Big Sur.

*"I have always respected the tranquility and sanctity of the Esalen baths. I do not speak loudly of my most recent real estate killing. I do not offer massages to all the women. I do not pretend to be more spiritual than I really am.*
*I did make love in the baths once back in the 1970's, but we came together, that is to say we arrived as a couple, and then we drove back to Monterey in the nude, in the full moonlight with the headlights off."*
Dudley Griffin 8.15.05

Making love in a hot tub is like making love in a car. It has the fantasy factor, that nasty side, the surreptitious scenario. In our youth a car was often all that was available, and now, if we as adults "do it" in a car, it is mostly for a nostalgia turn-on. But as far as sex in a car and or hot tub, it is mostly in your mind.

That brings up one of the most subtle aspects of sex. The fact is that sex is mostly in your mind.

That is why men can make love with their wives of 35 years and do it with vigor while they fantasize on the latest swimsuit model. That is why some men will be impotent, when there is no medical or physical reason why they should be.

Fantasy or fear in sex. One is very important to sex, the other is very damaging to sex. Fantasy can make a plain girl feel like a movie star. Fear can make you impotent in bed, even with a movie star.

I say that if you do want to make love in a hot tub, the best position is to have the man sit on the bench with the woman sitting on his lap facing away from him. He enters her from the rear "doggy style." I always preferred, vaginal sex, but it could be anal.

In this position, a couple can have either intimate or energetic sex without the threat of drowning. After all, sex in the hot tub is usually the beginning of a relationship; it would be nice if everyone were still around to experience the rest of their sex life.


CHAPTER 107

# Busted For Sex

For a number of years I worked as a radio programmer. Some people know that position by its more banal name of disc jockey. Most of my radio experience was as a volunteer in public radio, but some was in commercial radio where I actually got paid for having all that fun.

During my public radio period I met another programmer, who eventually became a live-in lover. I will call her Sheryl.

Sheryl was the most talented voiceover personality I have ever known. She could record any commercial using any obscure accent, employing the proper conviction and perfect timing.

Sheryl was also a great writer and storyteller. She is the only person I have ever considered plagiarizing. She gave me several premises for stories, which I still, to this day, want to write.

Sheryl, as far as I know, is now a programmer in some large city and is probably still writing articles for music publications. She was the purest creative person I ever met. And we had a hell of a lot of fun because we were both ready and willing for any new or quirky life experience.

We did programming together at two stations. At one she was Sheryl the Shark, and I was John Jellyfish to fit the ocean theme of the station. One show we did together on the public station was a jazz show. She knew a lot about jazz. I learned most of what I know about jazz from her.

Working together, we often did off-the-wall things to combat boredom. One show we did in the nude and invited the audience to take off their clothes as well. We were well ahead of Howard Stern.

Sheryl and I also once made it into the police report in their local newspaper. The report read something like this. "Monday, noon: Officers responded to what neighbors thought was a domestic altercation. Upon arriving at the location on 17th Street, they discovered that it was only a couple making love."

Yes, it made it into the paper just about like that. It was a small town rag, and the editor had a sense of humor. That's a hard thing to believe nowadays. But again this is a moral lesson; consensual, non-exploitive sex can be humorous. And in those days we thought sex and humor were good for people.

Sheryl's neighbors called the police about the ruckus. When the policeman came to the bedroom window just above the bed, he knocked and asked, "Is everybody OK in there?" My answer as I pulled the curtain open just above Sheryl's head was: "Yes, everybody's just fine. Everybody's making love!" We were indeed doing OK. It was a beautiful day in the neighborhood.

My relationship with Sheryl eventually ended badly. Of course, when most relationships end, there is something bad about the ending.

By nature, all endings of a good thing are bad. Most of my romantic relationships dissolved or resolved into an end of some sort, or else, of course, I would still be in my first relationship.

My thing with Sheryl ended badly because it didn't end due to normal circumstance, such as growing apart or moving on, but for a stupid guy reason.

As I said, Sheryl and I met in radio. I was a programmer on KAZU public radio in Pacific Grove, California around 1982 or 83 when Sheryl arrived at the station.

Sheryl was an extremely attractive girl. Dark, yet bright brown, electric curly hair, great smile, shapely body and eyes that spoke to you. I met her at a programmers' meeting at which a new list of the programmers and their phone numbers was given out to all the volunteers.

And here is where a unique twists of fate altered our lives. Another bizarre scenario of social intercourse.

At a radio station, with program schedules as they are, it is possible to work at the same station with someone for a long time without ever seeing them. After the programmers' meeting I remembered this girl and within the next week or so I took out the phone list I had been given at the meeting with the intent of calling Sheryl to ask her out for a coffee or something.

When I unfolded the paper upon which the phone numbers were written, I discovered that Sheryl's number was in the crease. The exact place where her phone number was printed was on the fold, and I couldn't read the digits. Obviously, I didn't call her.

Within the next weeks or months I failed to bump into her, and she faded from my radar. As I remember, at that time I was doing one of those extremely uncomfortable and dangerous girlfriend balancing acts. I had two, maybe three, lady friends who I was "trying out" to see what would develop.

Then several months later at the Monterey Jazz Festival, I bumped into Sheryl and we began "seeing" each other. Later I told her about the phone list episode and the fact that I had wanted to call her, but couldn't.

Sheryl's commentary to that was that within days of the volunteer meeting and the distribution of that phone list, every eligible male at the radio station except me had called her asking for a date. She turned them all down and said she would have done the same to me, had I called. It was way too obvious that these guys were just using the radio station as their dating service.

Well, playing hard to get does work, even when it's unintentional. You often stumble into a life's lesson at the most unexpected times.

Sheryl and I had a strange and exciting relationship. Within a month of our meeting and starting to spend exclusive time with each other, I had a trip planned to Europe. She was not disposed to go, so I went alone.

When I returned three or four months later, Sheryl kicked out her interim boyfriend. As I arrived back at Sheryl's apartment, I met the young man at the door and watched the poor guy leave, with his bags and his head hung low.

Sheryl loved music, and, as I said, she knew as much about jazz as any living person I ever met, but she didn't dance. I love to dance and it was a requisite that any girlfriend of mine must dance or let me go out to dance on my own when I needed to.

Sheryl learned to dance for me, and she eventually moved into my house.

And that set up the menage a trois with Sheryl and her female cousin. At some point Sheryl's cousin came to visit her. Well, one glass of wine led to another, and we eventually found ourselves making love together.

Sheryl was what is known as a dark, exotic and full-bodied person. Her cousin conversely was blonde with a thin and supple body. That night I had a realization about my own preferences that later resurfaced to end the relationship between Sheryl and me.

I have always preferred slight and bright to dark and voluptuous. It is a shallow, male thing, and I know it, but it is with me and I can't shake it.

One of the reasons, I will tell you, is sexual performance. Most voluptuous women are less callisthenic in their lovemaking. I really enjoyed sensual gymnastics.

On a few occasions where a large woman was extremely enthusiastic, I felt like a train wreck victim the next morning. I am not a small person,. I would be called average size at, 5' 9", 170 lb. at that time. I have never excluded a potential lover on size alone, but I preferred making love with a very active person with whom I could easily lift, move and manipulate.

That night with Sheryl and her cousin, two situations arose which were on the one hand conflicting, and yet poignant in our relationship. When making love with Sheryl's cousin I began to notice that she did not bend her back into my penetration or cunnilingus. She did not perform gymnastically as most of the supple types I preferred. She was the body type that I liked, but she did not react as most of my other, like-sized, lovers had.

I wanted to instruct her and guide her, but the situation was not appropriate for that. I could not concentrate on just her. I was very careful to treat both of the girls equally, as I always did in such circumstances. I was always careful in sexual triangles not to make anyone jealous, and especially my primary lover.

The next morning, Sheryl had to open the radio station, so she left before her cousin and I were awake. When I woke up, Sheryl's cousin was asleep on the floor where she had slept after our night's romp. I was on the bed.

I tried to coax her into the bed so we could make love, but she refused to join me. I wanted to find out if I could get her to open up and bend to my lovemaking, but she refused my advances. After much cajoling I finally realized that she had probably been uncomfortable with the situation the night before, and that was why she hadn't completely submitted to my sexual leading.

But, as I will tell you, the experience pointed out a problem in my relationship with Sheryl. No lover had been more intellectually or creatively compatible with me than Sheryl. Yet her body type was a mental obstacle to committing completely to her. What a lame excuse! And yet, it was the big, green elephant in the middle of our bed that couldn't be ignored.

As I said, she was very attractive. In fact, she was the type of woman who would turn all the heads when she walked into a room. To be frank, she had big glorious breasts, which stood up and natural all by themselves. Real breasts. This was before silicone!

After all, as I said, every one of the unattached males at the radio station (except me, by default) had called to try to get next to her.

Sheryl was also very well-proportioned. She had an hourglass figure. She was short, but she stood straight and proud.

The most interesting and peculiar thing was that she did not dress to accentuate her body or breasts. She never showed cleavage in public, and her slacks and blouses were always loose fitting. She seldom wore dresses. She wore clothing almost as camouflage for her body and her beauty. In fact, I remember a stylish young woman once asking Sheryl, "Are those pants really yours, or are you borrowing them from someone else?"

Our relationship ended badly. It was a bad ending because my reason for ending it was silly. I told her that I didn't really like her body type. I loved everything else about her, but her breasts got in the way. Stupid male human fault!

Our relationship may not have survived anyway. In fact, I think not.

I do know for sure that I did eventually find the only woman I will never find any fault with. I don't even know why I find her flawless, because I know rationally she has faults. True love is not definable. It doesn't make any sense.

My wife, the woman I live with now, may have flaws, but

there is something that I see in her, and love, that transcends all definitions or emotions.

Sheryl was one of my most interesting interludes, but in the end, I was too slippery to stick around. It wasn't her; it was my search for that indefinable!

KAZU radio staff 1979, by Don Gruber
I am kneeling on your right.

KAZU radio staff 1980, by Don Gruber.

CHAPTER 108

# Hair And Clothes; *"Dahling, you look mahvelous!"*

Statements like "Clothes make the man" or "You are what you wear" can be nominally true, but are often not literally true. A person, by applying a thin veneer of clothing, can appear to be anybody they want to be. But they may also be lying to you with their "costume!"

The most graphic examples of this are the young "gigolos" in Southern European countries who chased "rich" tourist women in the 1970s and 80s.. Most of these boys spent all of their money on expensive European fashions and went home to sleep in hovels that were without indoor plumbing. In these cases the ruse was not important when sex was the only expected outcome, but to begin a real relationship, this kind of subterfuge is death to love.

Clothing is often the first impression people have of you.

Clothing can also be your first opportunity to disappoint them. Being dishonest about who you are is the most monumental betrayal in a love relationship. Looking marvelous is often the deceptive approach, especially if you are only beautiful, yet not nice or intelligent.

Looking marvelous is often not really the goal you should be seeking. It can actually be a detriment. Being overdressed is by far the worst fashion mistake. It is also a social faux pas. Setting yourself apart from other people gives the impression that you are looking down on them. It doesn't make them love you. It often makes them despise you.

To look "marvelous," different or exaggerated have almost the same effect on many people. They tend to push people away. The point is not to look marvelous, but to look confident, to look comfortable with who you are, and, if your ego can handle it, maybe to look "interesting."

Overdressed, over-made-up, or over-colorized, is an obvious turnoff to someone who wants a lover that they can relate to, someone who is approachable. "Trying to be fashionable" can leave you "marvelous," but alone.

Leisure suits are the brunt of jokes today! I wish gold lame, push-up bras and leopard skin would go away as well. The only time to wear such things is to a costume party.

But there are other dressing habits which, if taken seriously, will prove to be your romantic downfall. Of course, "taken seriously" are the key words.

## Men: I'll pick on the men first!

Gold chains! One is bad enough, but multiple examples of egotistical bad taste are abhorrent to me. I'm sorry, but I cannot see any "serious" occasion when they are warranted. Then you add medallions, and you are through the roof screaming, "Look at me! Look at me! Please, somebody, look at me! I'm so insecure I need some envy!"

Even celebrity rappers don't pull it off. I don't know who they are trying to impress. Someone else who can afford to put that much money around their neck is not going to be impressed! And someone who can't afford it will just bad mouth it.

If you're buying a guy's CDs because he wears "sick" chains, you've got a value deficiency. If he's wearing the chains to make his fans jealous, he doesn't understand how fan loyalty works or the value of those loyalties. Somehow, it always turns out being about, "Look at me!" 2020 Ice this, and can't touch this are working as TV ad actors to pay for their gold chains.

Two or three top buttons open. It better be awfully hot. Otherwise, you might as well be wearing gold chains.

Hair plugs, hairpieces! I've already said my piece about the stupidity of looking for love if you don't even love yourself. If you don't like the way you look naturally, how can anybody else like you?

Nice, sharp creases in Levis! If you're gay, that's one thing, but if you are straight, I can't help thinking that any prospective girl-friend will turn away thinking she might have to be ironing those some day.

Tie-dye shirts! I have one or two tie-dye T-shirts. One has Jim Morrison on it and the shirt is cut off at the navel and shoulders. It is worn only as a statement and never a very serious one. At a party or rock and roll concert, you can wear anything with Jim Morrison, Bob Marley or Jerry Garcia on it. Anyplace else, you are dangerously close to the line.

Tie-dye in general is a fashion statement open to numerous forms of ridicule and prejudice. Contrary to what most people think, the majority of hippies didn't wear tie-dye. Weekend hippies and hard core Deadheads did.

Men wearing hairspray! What can I say? It has already been said over and over. Men wearing hair mousse! What can I say? The jokes abound. Men wearing perfume!

These are all past styles, which reappear from time to time. I suppose it could be said that I am being derogatory because I no longer have enough hair on which to use these things, but, believe me, I am not jealous one bit about not being able to wear them.

Hair manipulation is a fashion that, for men, can be viewed as a necessity or an annoyance. I think that distinction is what makes combing or styling your hair either acceptable or excessive. If you, as a man, feel that styling your hair is essential, then you are probably over the edge. If you are resigned to combing your hair out of courtesy for others, then you are a real man. If you refuse to touch it, you are a rebel.

Shoes on the beach! This is a dead give-away, girls. If he insists on wearing his shoes, or worse yet, socks on the beach, then run "barefoot" in the other direction. Someday he will have you color-coding and folding his socks and underwear. Remember *Sleeping With The Enemy*?

Some people say that "shoes make the man," or at least you can judge a man's wealth by his shoes! Well, maybe so, but girls, do you really want to be in a relationship with a man who cares more about shoes than you do?

The female shoe fetish is one of woman's most amusing transgressions. Shoes that are expensive, ugly <u>and</u> uncomfortable. Transport that fetish to man, and you then have a person wearing expensive shoes that have no intrinsic reason to be ugly and uncomfortable.

Checks, spots, paisleys and stripes! Most everybody has been warned about mixing contrasting designs, but for some reason many men either forgot or are suffering from pattern blindness.

If garish clothing and mismatched designs are a natural innocent misunderstanding of fashion sense, that is almost forgivable. But if a man wears gaudy or clashing styles consciously to attract attention, it is a sad confession of deeper problems. Overdoing anything is a red flag indicating insecurity. It is a call for attention by a person who is unaware of the proper channels for attracting love or friendship.

Only a very few men can pull off extravagant clothing. It usually requires a sense of self-effacing humor. Most men who can succeed in doing it are gay. If you are going to call attention to yourself, you better be well-grounded, self-assured and able to take the barbs.

But, understatement is also a psychological façade!

I often see people, men in particular, who seem to be trying to repulse others by their appearance. Sorry but, short hair, cut in the "sidewall" style is a very awkward look. A person with this hairstyle appears to be lost, unaware of what to do next, out of their element, and perhaps incarcerated. This is the institutional, military and prison hairstyle.

Guys with shaved sidewall cuts would be better cutting off all their hair, but even the "bald cut" look is hard to pull off unless you have a perfect head.

Men wearing a polo shirt with a white t-shirt underneath! This is not a style! This is not a fashion! This is not even clothing! It did not come from the '50s, '60s, or '70s! It is not cool!

Men pretending to be more than who or what they really are usually are out of their element! That often shows in the discomfort they display wearing unfamiliar styles. "God, what do I do with my hands if I can't shove them into my pockets!?"

## Women: I'll pick on them now.

Women who wear dresses with hemlines just below the calf and above the ankle are also, lost, uncomfortable and possibly institutionalized. You don't need to be a Hollywood fashion guru to see this.

That old commentary that "women dress for other women" is as true as anything ever said. In this society if women dressed for men, they would be wearing edible bikinis.

Contrary to fundamentalist Christian belief, nudity actually dampens sexual arousal. If this were a nude society, sex crimes would decrease, and man's respect for women and their bodies would be greatly improved.

But if men want women to be sexually appealing, which most men do in this sexually charged society, they want them to wear provocative clothing. In a rating chart of sexy clothing, a small amount of material that calls attention to, yet covers up, the "nasty bits" is the most libido- provoking.

Yet sex is only one aspect of clothing and adornment in the eyes of a complete man. A man looking for a life's mate is not looking for sexy as much as stability, fidelity and frugality.

Yes, girls, believe it or not, down inside the primal pea brain of every man is a rational being trying to get out and to do the right thing! There is a real man with reasonable expectations of women buried by this society's pressures down inside of every man. But often times, women and the clothing that they choose to wear serves only to awaken the most prurient and dangerous aspect of man's nature.

If we were still living in the jungle and dealing with the struggles of life and death every day, the macho, competitive nature of sexual conquest would make sense. But today in this Western, industrial society, sexy for sex sake is self-defeating, definitely for women, and in the long run for men as well.

Most men I converse with don't take seriously a woman who dresses sexually to indiscriminately provoke men. We may lust after her body, but we aspire to, and we love, a woman who has our own idea of taste and style. Sure, there are places and times for sexually explicit messages, but on the subway or in the grocery store, it is a blatant form of misdirected advertising.

If what I'm saying makes you think I am a prude, then you don't know my sexual history. I have had my share of sex toys, but they have been outgrown and rejected in favor of serious love.

To say that women dress for other women is true, but simplistic. They follow predominant styles accepted by other women that are thought to be appealing to men. Most women's clothing styles are created by designers who are women themselves or gay men. This is not PC, I know, but these are the facts.

If women's clothing designers ever decided to confer with guys in the bleachers at sporting events or around the office coolers, we would see fashions more "desirable" to men. But I'm not saying that would be a good thing.

Most men like cleavage and short skirts at the right time and place on women whom they visualize in a certain category. Thank goodness men don't design most women's clothing. It is left to the artists of the fashion industry to create styles that are tastefully seductive and romantic in order to temper the raw sexuality some people put on clothing. Gay men are most suited to designing women's clothing.

Gold lame, leopard skin and push-up bras: Women who wear them are often biting off more than they can chew! As I have said before, a push-up bra is a lie that will most often come back to haunt you.

High-fashion shoes: Why would anyone pay too much money for something that is both ugly and uncomfortable?

Cleavage: In the right context I am all for it. It is not proper or in good taste in school. It is not proper or in good taste in the work place, unless you're selling cars. It is not proper or good taste for going down to the bad side of town to buy a refrigerator or an ounce, unless you want the wrong kind of attention.

But for some women, showing cleavage is a way to compensate for other failings that they perceive to have. Excessive breast display is an insecurity alert, just as a sausage down the pants of some guy is showing that he is insecure.

Now I know that all of this discourse on clothing might give you the impression that I am overly concerned by appearance, but anyone who knows me will dispute that. What I care about clothing most for myself and for others is that it should make others feel comfortable, maybe entertain, maybe amuse, and definitely give people the indication of personality.

Creativity is the core of human nature. There is no reason why it shouldn't be expressed in clothing ourselves. Individuality is human nature, but as with all creations, if you are ahead of your time or too far out, your efforts have a tendency to repulse. Knowing what society will accept and embrace is the science of a true artist.

Peer pressure creates styles. Some styles are enduring, and some are fringe.

The Goth style is an enigma to me. I guess that's what it's meant to be, and possibly should remain.

This multi-pierced, multi-tattooed generation does not feel right to me either. Although we hippies started the piercing and tattooing in this culture, I find most of the young people who have adopted it to be uncomfortable with themselves because of a lack of conviction. Rebellion without a purposeful message is just psychodrama.

The hippies were comfortable with their rebellion. Our clothing was a celebration of life and individuality, not something to hide behind. Our tats and ear piercings were a rebellion, a statement, our freak flag!

I tattooed myself and others! I got people drunk to give a tattoo, and I got drunk to get a tattoo. But my first tattoo was by my own hand in L.A. in 1960. I was 16 or 17, I was sober, but immature, the tattoo was a sword on my left forearm. Before it, as an experiment to see if I could do it, I embossed a small circle on my left hand, just to see if I could do it. When the light is just right I can still see that circle in blue on my hand.

The goths, the punks, and the extravagant body adornments

appear to be a cover-up for insecurity. Most of these young people don't seem comfortable in their skin, or clothing or tats. It is a statement without conviction.

As a young person in the 60s and 7os, I dressed to make a statement that I was different, and not because I was ashamed of who I was or wasn't.

As hippies, we rebelled in order to create change, positive change. But we made one fatal error. Our clothing style, which was a major element in getting the attention we wanted to make people listen to us, was the one thing that made them not listen.

As hippies, we were outraged by prejudice, war, materialism and religious intolerance. We tried to separate ourselves from those who indulged in such things by changing our appearance. We dressed to offend uptight people, and we grew our hair to make a statement against conservatives.

In retrospect, I now believe that those avenues of rebellion were counter-productive. We made statements, which our opponents would not listen to because we repulsed them by our appearance.

Our truths, our well-thought-out, well-intentioned information was unheard by those who could have made changes, because they would not listen to someone who was physically abhorrent to them. It was our youthful arrogance that made them reject us. They may have thought we would insist that they dress like us in order to accept our ideals. No, further than our thoughts, we wanted them to think, and change, not change and think.

The establishment also thought we were dirty and smelly, which lost us respect. We didn't use antiperspirant, and we did smell "natural," but honestly, we bathed when the opportunity arose and washed our clothing as often as we could afford to. We just wore old clothes that looked dirty.

In retrospect, I now realize that you must not only speak the same language as those you wish to enlighten, but you must also appear to be the same species as they are in order to achieve their respectful attention. We must accept the preconceptions or misconceptions and overlook the limitations of those we are trying to convince.

In this respect the present counterculture is missing the point even more than hippies did. The hippie clothing rebellion had a smile on it. We didn't take our clothes too seriously. They were a light-hearted addition to our personality, and I guess that is what adornment should be.

During research for and development of this chapter, I stumbled onto an aspect of clothing that had eluded me before. I have mentioned in this chapter and elsewhere how some people compensate for their unfortunate appearance (or their self-perceived unfortunate appearance) by wearing outrageous or even shocking clothing. I now have new awareness of and observations on this activity.

Where once I thought that people were making a mistake by drawing attention to their flaws through use of "costumes" or adornment, I now have tempered my judgment. If a person, no matter how socially attractive or unattractive, wants to reach out and communicate with others for purposes of love and fellowship, it is commendable that they use whatever vehicle they have at their disposal.

Peer pressure is one of mankind's primary motivations. To be acceptable and accepted is a prominent social need for most rational people.

Humans are a more peaceful and compatible creature when they have companionship. To seek love, fellowship and friendship is a normal and natural human desire. It is a need that we display more than most other animals do.

I withhold my approval at obnoxious behavior to attract attention, but my opinion is not necessarily the last or best judgment. Because of my age and background, I may not fully understand the social order of younger people today.

I know that the activities and clothing styles of myself and my friends during the 1950s, 1960s, and 1970s greatly disturbed the older generation. In retrospect, I can understand their discomfort, but I know that our path was necessary for us, just as the present younger generation's activities are for them.

Peer recognition and acceptance is a natural necessity to adolescents. If one has to adorn oneself in a particular way to achieve notice and therefore love, it is understandable.

Some might consider alternative dress codes as eye pollution, but as long as the young do not eat their parents, smell bad in public, or cross against the light in front of me, I will accept their eccentricities and appreciate their need to attract the attention of their peers.

CHAPTER 109

# Sexual Tension

After dropping out of the advertising industry in the early 1970s, I dabbled in photography and carpentry. I couldn't be both a hippie and an advertising executive. It would have, sort of, blown the anti-materialism commitment.

I eventually settled on carpentry to keep from starving to death on the anti-materialism diet. It was creative, productive and Christ was a carpenter, so it couldn't be all that bad, unlike money changing.

During those years I could work for six months and travel for six months or a year. I made good money. Sometimes as much as $30 an hour, (the equivalent today is $204+ per hour). And it didn't look bad on my resume, because carpenters seldom worked in any one place for long. You could get hired by just showing the quality of your hammer and that you knew how to braid a power cord.

For much of that time I advertised and did odd carpentry jobs for homeowners. I have always preferred working for myself.

Sometimes, I would be hired by a single or divorced woman. Sometimes we would end up having an affair. It was part of the program. It all had to do with sexual tension. Don't call me *The Carpenter* because I nailed a lot of women! That's a bad joke, and I personally don't like the term "nailed," which I think has disrespectful connotations.

I made love with many of the women I worked with or was in contact with for any length of time. It was more comfortable that way, it relieved the sexual tension. It allowed both of us to function properly within the job or business in which we were mutually involved.

This may sound strange, or strangely familiar, but for much of my life it was difficult for me to be friends with a woman I was sexually attracted to. It was also often uncomfortable working with someone with whom I had not been intimate. A lot of men were that way.

There are various ways to deal with this. You can be miserable in her company. You can stop being around her. Or you can get it on with her and get it over with so that you can carry on a normal conversation and conduct a reasonable relationship without all the sexual innuendo and tensions. That's the way I liked to solve this socio-sexual conundrum.

Yet, you must realize that many guys are exactly the opposite. They freeze up once they <u>have</u> had sex with a woman. These guys have an all-too-common hang-up called religious dogma. They can't carry on a normal friendship with someone once they have had a clandestine or "out of wedlock" sexual relationship with them. The first three reasons are:
1. They feel embarrassed, based on religious prohibition.
2. They are ashamed of the girl, based on religious prejudice.
3. And/or they are afraid it means commitment and want to split.

If this guy also cannot have a friendship with someone they <u>haven't</u> slept with, then they are really in for a shitload of loneliness.

But <u>I</u> was quite capable of having a short sexual relationship with someone and then slipping into a platonic relationship with them. I didn't expect special treatment. I wouldn't react strangely if they started up with someone else, and I would never embarrass them by mentioning our experience if that were not appropriate. If they wanted it that way, it was as if it never happened. But it did happen, I knew what they felt like, I had seen their body and the tensions were dissipated.

Yet, I would do what I could to continue a sexual relationship until its proper end! And that meant I was not afraid of commitment. Back in the 70s and early 80s, I knew that ending a relationship was easy, and it needn't be done before both of us had become satiated ourselves, and it needn't be embarrassing or contentious!

One aspect of this scenario which I have now recognized, and am finally able to admit, is that having made love to a woman, I am then less susceptible to jealousy if by chance they should take up with someone else. It is better to have loved and lost, or given away, than never to have loved at all.

The subject of jealousy has always been sensitive to me. I have seen men do such stupid things because of it that I don't ever want to be involved myself.

Sexual tension is often used to drive movies and TV story lines. Sexual tension can be portrayed as humorous. It can be the vehicle for drama, and it is often the introduction to a love story.

But in real life, sexual tension is also often an introduction to sexual frustration and jealousy, and it ain't pretty what frustration and jealousy can do to a man.

CHAPTER 110

# Venereal Disease Dance Tonight!

In the mid 1980s when I was a radio programmer, my co-host/girlfriend and I did a lot of strange and wonderful on-air pranks. These pranks also dabbled in social consciousness. I was way ahead of the alternative curve.

One of the ideas that Sheryl and I suggested as a benefit for their Public Radio station, was to hold dances specifically for people afflicted with sexually transmitted diseases (STDs), a VD dance so to speak.

Now, you are going to have to suspend all uptight feelings of propriety, dignity and morality in order to understand the genius of this idea. A combination of humor and common sense are necessary to appreciate such a premise.

These parties would be specifically for people with, say, herpes or HIV to find a sex partner with whom they could be intimate without fear of giving someone else their diseases or contracting another affliction themselves. This may be a bit alarming to people with cretin sensibility, yet if you think about it, it was a rational way to keep people from spreading such diseases.

At each dance party people would wear name badges that would list the diseases they possessed and the last date of their testing. A perspective dancer or sex partner could peruse the badge and assess whether they wanted to take a chance. Under the circumstances this was a much better rating system than checking to see if they had a nice ass or not.

Sexual desire has no conscience. By bringing these diseases out in the open, we could more responsibly and rationally deal with the problems of infecting others and give people alternatives to one-night-stand murder.

This realistic approach would also serve to get people to admit they were sick and get on with their lives or deaths, whichever applied, and do it with a partner who understood their problems. For those who had only a minor STD, it would be a way to be promiscuous while still maintaining a moral conscience.

Denial and ignorance are two of mankind's worst faults. Admitting we have a problem is the first step, as they say, to finding a solution.

To be sick with a disease that frightens other people, cuts a person off from meaningful contact with humanity. To compound illness with loneliness is a real death sentence.

Pretending these kinds of problems don't exist is the province of fundamentalist Christianity, not the brains of two wacky radio disk jockeys. This is what some people might think was a silly and maybe even perverse idea, but it was concocted with humor and pathos. In retrospect, it was an idea before its time when Sheryl and I thought it up in 1983.

Sadly, the idea never reached fruition, but the advertising promotional concepts were a real hoot. VD or STD dances are something that should be considered today. A rational society would do so.

CHAPTER 111

# Lovers Don't Come With Resumes

It would be so much easier if, before any of the sticky stuff started to happen, all prospective partners and lovers were required to hand over a bio, a real one, not like those written for dating services or personal ads.

A curriculum vitae for a prospective sex partner or mate should include several basic "truths," and I emphasize "truths!" Your sex, your sexual proclivities and a "real," "current" photograph and family history.

Yes, family history! Not just, you had a father and mother, but did you love your father, and did you love your mother, and did they love you back?

In the development of a lovable person, the relationship with their parents is the primary influence. Good childhood, good person, bad childhood, bad person, is not just a generalization.

Relating back to the previous chapter, a good resume for a prospective sex partner would list their diseases, their sexual position preferences, and their police rap sheet, specifically showing any charges of sexual battery or spousal abuse.

Of course, this was some sort of fantasy dream. Most women who were trying to find a mate would not want to scare off a prospective husband by giving them paperwork at the beginning of a relationship. And most men, when they are trying to get laid, will tell a girl anything, even if it is not the truth, or maybe the truth, but only if it promotes his agenda.

*"To write this book with the expectation (intent) that it will reach, translate to, or change the minds of those I am writing about is a fantasy, a hope, a prayer. Mankind has iconic moments when it does the right things. Mostly we fuck-up, but if we stopped and thought awhile, we could change and become responsible and rational human beings."*
Mr. California, 6.7.14

Any man who says he understands the sexuality of women does not really know anything about women or sex. You can't go in with the same attitude or scenario every time. You have to adjust to the woman you are with, and the time and place, because they are constantly changing.

I have been with women who were aggressively sexual the first time, and the next day didn't want to have anything to do with me. And then some who were exactly the opposite. Turn you down at night and wake you up with wet acceptance!

I've known women who would agree to lovemaking and then act as if they didn't enjoy it. And then the next day agree again, and then again show little appreciation of the act itself.

I have the knowledge to turn most any woman on, but then I have little or no idea how they're going to react sexually. I have at times said that I could tell how a woman will make love by looking at her, but I was just profiling by their look or smile.

Most women do not know what sex they want until they have the buttons pushed. Each woman will make love differently with each man. Don't take it too seriously. If you are a good lover, you can make something happen. If you are not good, it is a toss up.

I give recommendations and advice based on my own experiences only. I generalize and sometimes offer hearsay, but I do not promise results, nor will I wager on what I say. My experience quotient is my only guarantee of reliability. And my only real suggestion is that you be conscious of the woman and don't be greedy or violent.

> *"With all my experience with women, I still cannot say that I understand the whole thing! It's like, the closer you get to the subject, the further away it appears. Just don't ever bet on it. You're better off just giving in to the inevitable confusion and conflict, and enjoying what you can of the rest of it."*
> Dudley Griffin,
> 4.13.06

> *"Losing a lover, spouse, or paramour is one of the most devastating events in your life. It is the same if they die, you leave them, they leave you, or you kill them."*
> Rudolph Valentino

CHAPTER 112

# Cycles of Sex

I'm not talking about two-wheel transportation here.

Women go through their menstrual cycle, and that's the one cycle men are most familiar with. But women also go through an ovulation cycle, and that's the puppy men should be most aware of.

At the beginning of a woman's "monthly" cycle, a new egg develops and passes down the fallopian tubes to the uterus, where it waits to be fertilized. Waits? Well, no it doesn't just wait there. The girl who is wrapped around that uterus and egg is out there at the bars, going to parties or in the back seat of her boyfriend's car. And this is the cycle that I'm talking about. This is a girl's horny cycle!

Twelve to 14 days after a woman has her "period," you may call it "monthly," or "curse," a new egg is in place, and fertilization is possible again. This is the part of a woman's cycle that men should be thinking about; this is the important part.

Whether you want to make love and get pregnant or just want to have fun and avoid pregnancy, this is the crucial period. It is a time when women are most receptive to sex and also most susceptible to pregnancy.

Do you have any idea how many young women get pregnant the first time that they ever make love? Lots!

Urges. We can't outsmart Mother Nature. Urges are what propel life. Hunger, thirst, procreation.

This little 16–year–old girl had been dating the captain of the chess team for six months. He had just beaten the best that their rival high school had to offer. She was impressed. He was feeling virile and assertive. For months, she had been putting him off, holding him off. Her church and her parent's dictate that she should push him away, but she was ovulating, and her body said yes. Nine months later little Josh was born.

I don't consider myself to be particularly psychic or intuitive. At least I don't rely on it. I think of myself as observant. I see things, I feel things…, and too freaking often they are right.

Particularly, I know of numerous occasions when I recognized a virgin on the day of her deflowering. Disclaimer here: I was involved in only a few myself, and they were justifiable.

The wonder of watching a girl approach womanhood, of seeing her flirt with the future, so fresh and excited, so hopeful. It is exhilarating and also somehow nostalgically mournful.

To be able to smell and sense something about to happen is a blessing, as long as you do not cross over the lines of propriety.

*"The curse, the monthlies, on the rag, historically a time when woman were banished, and made fun of. We make note of, and bring attention to this time in a woman's cycle, yet we don't even acknowledge the opposite end of the cycle. In this culture we don't celebrate ovulation, the time when a woman is fertile, and most attractive. Perhaps we should."*
Mr. California, 6.7.14

Men, it seems, have a sexual cycle as well. Or at least that is what I am now going to tell you. Much the same as women's ovulation and menstrual cycles, I think men have a horny cycle. I discovered this observing my own masturbation habits.

I noticed I had periods of time when I masturbated a lot and times when I didn't at all, and it had no correlation to the amount of other sexual contact I was having.

I first recognized this when living for long periods of time in a small Greek village, where I had no contact with appropriate available sexual partners. These times without a sex partner gave me reflection on the phenomenon. People adapt sexually to the sexuality available.

Without a woman present to allow, offer or initiate appropriate sexual contact, I found that I had a natural sexual desires that ran in cycles. This was indicated by my masturbation habits.

I went so far as to try to map it out on a calendar to determine if it was a 27-or 30-day or whatever duration. I never could quite figure that out. What I did know was that I could go for two weeks or so without the desire to perform, and then I would have a week when I had the urge at least once a day.

As I grow in stature, wisdom and age, I have less of an urge less of the time. And thank goodness for the future of mankind!

Unlike women who produce an egg on a particular schedule, men produce sperm on demand. If a man uses up his supply, the body produces more. Some men say they masturbate to release sperm that has built up causing "blue balls," or pain in the testicles. But I'm skeptical. I think they are just having fun.

## The Monthly Turmoil

This is as good a time as any to bring up this very contentious subject. The issue is the monthly emotional struggles that some women display during hormonal activity. There is really no easy way to address this subject, yet it must be dealt with or it can destroy an otherwise good relationship, as it has many times.

First, it is a medical problem more than an emotional problem, and it can be dealt with medically through hormone adjustments. See a medical doctor, not a psychologist.

Second, it is not personally directed at a particular mate. If she were living with Mahatma Gandhi, she would still go through the same scenario.

## CHAPTER 113

# The Confessional

"I confess, I've never done this before," she said, as I pulled her shorts down below her knees.

"Will we burn in hell?" the other girl said, as she lifted her blouse for me to caress her breasts.

"Hell no!" I said. "This is a confessional. It's where you come to be forgiven for sins. We're just cutting out all the extra steps by bringing the transgression to the absolution."

Until recently, I didn't believe in suppressed memory. I had never experienced it, or so I thought, and I had never known anyone else, in my estimation, who had experienced it.

But not long ago I had an intimate conversation with a former lover; let's call her Adrian for purposes of the story. Adrian reminded me of an episode we had shared years before. It was something I had completely forgotten, maybe even suppressed.

As soon as she related the circumstances, it all came back to me. I had completely suppressed the memory. And why, I asked myself, had I buried that particular affair, even though it had been exciting, humorous and even poignant?

The former lover and I had a relationship that spanned perhaps three or four years. Our affair also spanned other lovers.

We were never a couple. We each had several live-in lovers and numerous other sexual encounters during our relationship. You had to be there, where we were during that time, the 1970s, in California, to understand.

Adrian lived and played with a group of people who included another girl with whom I was intimate. I was making love with both of them. Separately, yet irrevocably, entwined.

For clarity the other girl must have a name. I will call her Tracy. Our leapfrog love affair incorporated some of the most humorous, exciting and yes bizarre human episodes I experienced, dreamt, or heard of. Some of these activities are related elsewhere in this book. They have been separated and dispersed herein, because no one would believe they could possibly reside in the same relationship.

*"Love is looking for someone who feels like you do!"*
DG

My suppressed experience is this: Tracy, Adrian and I went down to Big Sur one day for some adventure. We may have dropped some LSD, checked out some friends or communed with nature.

On the way back to Monterey, we stopped at Carmel Mission. It was an ecumenical field trip for the girls. They were both Jewish.

The sanctuary was empty. No priests. No worshipers.

I have no clue how the idea came to us, but one thing led to another. I remembered the confessional from a previous photographic expedition to the mission. I had shot up all my film so, on that occasion, I popped into the confessional and quickly reloaded film holders, uninterrupted in the pitch black little cubicle.

So on this hippie adventure, Tracy, Adrian, and I slipped into the confessional to experience some carnal knowledge. I can't remember how we accomplished this exactly, within the confines of the space, or the duration of our dalliance, since I apparently suppressed it, but knowing the girls as I did, it must have been a hoot.

Was this a sacrilege, I ask? Will we indeed burn in hell? I don't think so! First, do you really think that you can hurt the feelings of, embarrass, or offend an omnipotent, omnipresent, omniscient God? He already knew what you were going to do before you did it. If God had any emotion about what you were doing, it would be either indifference or boredom. Yet, he could have been laughing.

A backslidden Protestant screwing two Jewish girls in a Catholic confessional. You have to admit, anyone, no matter how pious, would at least consider a chuckle in spite of themselves.

Also again I say, you had to be there, where we were, during that time. Hippies, young people, the counterculture of the 1960s and 70s were continually asking God to stand up and show himself. And He did, yet not in the traditionally expected ways.

Adrian, Tracy, and I, were doing what we were doing in celebration of God and his creations. God was there. We were not having sex in the confessional to make God angry or to see if He would strike us dead, although we may have been doing it to see if he would take notice. And God did, but he didn't show himself as the omnipotent, vengeful deity that so many people fear he is. He was there and he gave us joy, and then he smiled at our exuberance.

All three of us had been blessed in our own way, and to our own needs.

God showed himself in the 1960s and 70s as a ray of sunlight, a drop of rain, a laugh, a tear, an orgasm, or even a pain in the heart. God can still be felt in the same ways today by anyone who cares to experience him. God is nature to many evolved humans.

I once dabbled in Fundamentalist Christianity, and at that time I thought that God lived exclusively in my little white church building. But I moved on and become an agnostic, an evolved Christian.

As an agnostic now, I don't think anyone owns God. I think God is in all of us and in all things, and I don't think God is critical of anything humans do, unless they screw with God's other creatures and creations.

*"At first I thought, 'Maybe I had forgotten this event because there were so many such incidents.' No! I have always remembered my lovers and all our episodes. This one circumstance was suppressed into the depths of my memory, I presume for some religious necessity. I still don't know why."*
Dudley Griffin,
7.12.06

CHAPTER 114

# Sex, Drugs and Rock & Roll Society

Rock and Roll Haiku

the music strikes us
we stagger under the beat
that lifts us upward

the movement to dance
predates other desires
to sit back and rot

A reasonable society would realize that sex, drugs and rock & roll are normal human activities. A culture with a conscience knows that you don't criticize and ostracize people for doing what comes naturally as a human being. A thinking government is aware that prohibiting God-given physical drives is stupid.

OK, do without sex, drugs and rock & roll for the next 6 weeks!

So why are we still doing these imbecilic things to ourselves and our fellow humans? Why are we criminalizing human weakness instead of softening their damage by educating and loving the victims? Religious fanatics and conservative control freaks are the reason. People who have to butt into other people's business are exacerbating the problems of our society. Sex, drugs and rock & roll are not the problem. How we deal with them is the problem.

You don't cut off a child's hand because he wants to stick it into the fire! You tell him what the fire will do to his fingers, maybe let him singe himself a little, and then give him comfort and medicine to sooth his pain.

If you have been a trustworthy parent, your child will believe you when you warn them. They still may try the forbidden. That is human nature. But if you are understanding toward their human frailties, then they will most likely learn from their mistakes.

But if parents or society try to force young people to stop doing what is natural for them, they will rebel. And that short-sighted dogma and the rebellion it creates will cut off communication until there is no family relationship. That blind discipline based on ego is what creates most of the conflicts in our society.

Is it worth losing your children to be able to exert your ego's power over them? Your separation will prove to be more destructive than your acceptance.

Sex is not dirty. It may be messy, but it's not dirty. If a person is given the proper preparation for sex, it will become just what it is, a natural and essential part of a satisfactory and fulfilling life.

Drugs are not immoral. They may not be sanctioned by present-day popular churches, but they are not immoral. Drugs have been used for millennia in most cultures to enhance spiritual enlightenment.

Rock and roll will not rot your brain. It may distract your mind, but it will not rot it. Dancing and playing music are important elements in the enjoyment of life.

Life is difficult enough without creating more problems by making sex, drugs and rock & roll into sins. Hate, greed, competition and corporate crimes are sins. Sex, drugs and rock & roll are the things we do to make life enjoyable.

Any of the real problems surrounding sex, drugs and rock & roll can be solved by education. Humans will turn any activity into an addiction or obsession, but with understanding and education, a sincerely helpful society can soften the obsession.

We cannot erase the urge for sex, drugs and rock & roll, but we can reduce their psychological danger by accepting the fact that they are just normal human activities. And then we can reverse any physical damage created by them with education and medicine.

The way that churches go about battling human fragility is wrong. It actually makes the problem worse. By making a sin out of a normal human desire, the person ends up with two problems rather than just one. They have an addiction and they are also a sinner.

I want to start a new country, one where sex, drugs and rock & roll are normal accepted activities, but where war, hatred, intolerance and greed are sins and treated as the crimes they are.

*"I don't know, I might like it.*
*Then again, I may just enjoy it because it's the thing to do".*
DG, 1.23.02

CHAPTER 115

# All The Wrong Things

There is a point in a dying relationship when a guy cannot help but do or say all the wrong things. It is the black hole of communication. It is an anomaly unbelievable to behold and sadly unavoidable.

Those things that he said or did with positive results last month are met with disdain this month because he is on the way out. Now she accuses him of stalking when he sends her flowers. Last month that got him laid.

When he compliments her on how thin she is, she will bristle because she thinks, "Compared to what, how fat I was last month?" He buys her perfume, and she thinks he is telling her she smells bad. He takes her to a chick flick about love, and she sees a mixed message in that too.

When he doesn't compliment her, she is hurt. When he doesn't bring a gift, she is inconsolable, and when he takes her to a man's movie, she reads a message into that. At that point, there is nothing a guy can do. Every time he opens his mouth to patch things up, it tears the fabric of their relationship even more. The only thing a man can do to retain his dignity is to turn and leave, preferably without trying to explain why he is leaving. Leaving, of course, will not mend the breakup. At this point jealousy or absence does not make the heart grow fonder.

If you do leave her, she may try to get you back just so she can leave you, thus mending her bruised ego. But as far as getting a lost lover to come back by becoming scarce, it doesn't happen.

And you know what, it goes both ways. Men play the very same rejection games. Those cute little silly things she used to say or do that made him horny now produce a roll-of-the-eyes or an outright rebuke.

My sage advice, "Just walk away, Renee." Cut the breakup time, save the money of unappreciated gifts and wasted candle wax. But I know most people won't follow this advice. They will hang in there until the bitter end. They will eat meals in silence and reach out to a limp hand. Then one day, after a sufficient amount of time and pain, they will pick a fight with their mate, pack and leave with great fanfare, proclaiming that they have been faking it for months and months.

There! Their ego is safe. But sadly, they now need to go out and buy some new candles.

*"Self-pity and self-pride, may I be spared the folly of both."*
*Dudley Griffin*
*10/3/82*

Alvin, champagne and me

This photo was taken in the late 1970s to early 80s. I was at the top of my form as you can see. Italian Riviera straw hat, Hawaiian shirt over a turtleneck sweater, champagne and my faithful dog Alvin. It is also my favorite photograph of me. Partly, of course, like everyone, I choose a photo that makes me look better than I really do.

As a photographer by trade, occupation and nature, I have no illusions. I know photography can make a person look better or worse. Sometimes it has nothing to do with the photographer or the subject. We must remember that people get what they see. If we would be more philosophical and positive about our own appearance, then we would be happier with who we are, and therefore a better package for others to see.

## CHAPTER 116

# Don't Tie An Anchor Around Your Social Life

I had two different dogs over fifteen years during the 1970s and 80s. First, Thumper Underfoot, the quintessential hippie dog, red bandana and all. It is reported that he ate a gram of hash as a puppy. Then Alvin. Both of these characters were "Benjie" dogs. They looked alike and acted alike. I called them Walt Disney dogs.

Aloof, but friendly if you were worth their time. Everybody's favorite dogs. But you had to be cool. You had to have soul, or they rejected you.

I didn't get either of my dogs just because they were a cute and fluffy thing to attract women. It didn't really work that way anyhow because they both smelled like dogs, but they also didn't repel girls, nor did they interrupt romantic moments or bite sleepovers.

Some people, both guys and girls, saddle themselves with big, slobbery, destructive, crotch-sniffing animals, and then wonder why they can't find a lover or a prospective mate.

Driving a car that your girlfriend has to push to start, having a dirty bed, a smelly bathroom or an obnoxious dog is a buzz kill for any relationships. My dogs didn't posture, but they also didn't repulse.

466

CHAPTER 117

# I Yam Who I Ya
# I Yam What I Yam

*"Unanimously, people agree that truth is necessary to achieve acceptable love or exceptional sex. Yet why does our society suppress the truth about love and sex, and why do most people lie about it?"*
DG, 1.16.02

Lying is one of mankind's most overrated accomplishments. In the early evolution of the mind of human animals, lying was developed to help gain some advantage in a dangerous world by impressing some other creature or human. It was most often employed to save your life.

Yet in this day and age, lying is used to impress someone with something you didn't do and/or to get something you don't deserve. The fact of the matter is lying is now an activity that actually works against the person who uses it.

Most often, liars end up disgusting other people, and what they get from their lies are shallow rewards because of how they were obtained. So you alienate people and acquire ill-gotten goods, and what does that make you?

Lying means that you are not happy with who you are, and it gets you something you don't deserve. Boy, that sure makes you a big Zero! This applies to all areas of life, home, school and work, and it's even truer in love.

Liars are usually insecure people. They don't think that who they are or what they do is good enough. They think that if they can impress someone, they will get that person's love. What they don't know is that those lies are the one thing that will ultimately deny them the love they crave.

The simple explanation is that, if you set someone's expectations too high, they will be doubly disappointed and disillusioned when they find out what you really are like. And the fact that you lied to them puts another nail into your coffin. You are better off portraying yourself as less than what you are, and then your true value will impress the hell out of them. That is, unless you want a whole life of one-night stands.

One of the reasons so many relationships fail is because of disillusions. Here is a visual analogy to describe this phenomenon. Let's just say that a person is like a hand with five fingers, or in this case, five personality traits. Humans have far more facets than just five, but for the purpose of this analogy, let's use the five fingers.

The five fingers or traits could be cleanliness, attitude toward money, political leanings, sexual preferences and feelings about parenthood. These five are on the top of the list of problems in relationships. Religious preferences are also important to be on the same page with a live-in partner.

Capitalist personalities are crucial to watch for. If you love money, the battle for money, and have a competitive nature, you might fit with a partner who is the same, but, and it's a big but, there are a lot of problems living with a greedy or competitive person. Often, even two people who are the same in this category are incompatible.

So there is a man and a woman at a party or bar somewhere, and they are like clenched fists hiding their real personality traits from each other. She wants to be Britney Spears or someone like that, so she shows that fist which creates the appearance of that kind of person. He wants to be Justin Timberlake, so he fashions himself into a fist that looks like that.

So they meet each other and like what they see, and end up going home together. Now they have started a relationship based on the phony personalities that they have fabricated.

Well, two hours later or two weeks, two years or two decades, these two hands made up of five personality traits finally have opened up to each other, and what do they find? That their fingers or traits don't match up. So they break up and go their separate ways.

If we walked around like open hands so that everyone could see our fingers and who we really are and see if their hands matched up, then relationships would be a lot easier to maintain.

The only time that lying about who you are is acceptable is when you love someone enough that you intend to change yourself into the person they are enamored with and you are pretending to be. But that's a dangerous game. Changing yourself to win and maintain the love of another person is very romantic and can possibly be attainable, except for few subtle problems.

If you change yourself for another person, it is possible to lose yourself and what makes you unique. This is not necessarily wrong by any laws of man or nature, but it could have some emotional consequences within yourself.

Compromising your personality in order to fit into the life of another is OK if you are going to feel good about it for the long run. But if you wake up one day and discover that you haven't done what you wanted to do with your life because of your mate, then you may begin to resent them, and this can lead to the dissolution of the relationship.

Not maintaining your true personality in a relationship can lead to one of two possible causes for the ending of that relationship: 1. If you change so much that a part of you is lost that first attracted your mate: 2. If you become so disillusioned with your own watered-down self that you fall apart or run away.

There are a whole slew of physical and emotional traits that we as humans can have which may be considered undesirable or strange, but that is what being human is. I, as yet, have never met a perfect person. We love each other as we are, or we become very lonely people.

A danger is that, if you are ashamed of something about yourself, others are more likely to be ashamed of you too. If you ignore it, oddly enough, others will ignore it as well. This, of course, means that you must ignore their flaws also.

Having physical or emotional flaws is human. We all have them! But it is easier for others to accept your flaws if you don't bring attention to them by being embarrassed by them.

This is a major mistake some people make. They bring attention to their flaws by being ashamed of them, when someone who loves them, or would potentially like to love them, would gladly ignore the flaws.

Just think back on any relationship you have had with someone. It could be a romance or just a family member. You never cared that your mother had a wart on her chin. You never cared that your father had nose hairs. You never cared that your first lover had a little cellulite on her hips or too much hair on his back. If you did notice these things, soon, if nothing was said about them, you forgot all about them in your love for that person.

I am bald. I have been balding since I was 23 years old, but it never obstructed my love life or sex life. The reason is that is that I don't care that I am bald. I never talk about it, or care about it.

I have never had a woman tell me that she wouldn't be with me because I was bald. I assume there are women who are turned off by baldness, but as far as I can see, it has never been an issue in my relationships.

When I asked girls to dance, most of them said yes. The ones who didn't, may have refused me because of my baldness, but they never said so. And I never cared if they rejected me for that, because I didn't want to be with someone who is that shallow anyway. I would have been sorry for them because who knows what might have been?

Why would you want to dance with someone who didn't like the way you looked? They just might not want to dance with themselves if they could really see how <u>they</u> looked to other people.

I have my own set of preferences in women, but I have never rejected a woman, up front, because of these traits. I don't particularly like large breasts. I don't like big thighs or big hair. Oh, and I'm not attracted to bald women. But I have dated women with all of these features, including the baldness.

If a woman is not ashamed of herself, I will accept her as she is. Personality is much more important in the long run. Just don't lie to me. That will come out eventually, and as far as I'm concerned, lies blow away everything else about someone's personality.

*"We can function without lies."*
Dudley Griffin, 12.19.78

# CHAPTER 118

# **Competition**

Competition is found in all walks of our lives--survival, greed, ego and entertainment. It can be found in the fight for life in the jungle, the fight for sex in the city, the fight for money and dominance in the business world, or in sporting events.

I must say here that competition in itself is not a bad thing. It is the intent that is either good or evil. To compete to save your life or the lives of others is good. To compete for the love of someone is necessary sometimes. To compete for economic stability and free will is also necessary at times, and in sports it is most often the reason for sports. But the ego can screw these all up, make you a monster, and make what you do an abomination.

In a life-and-death battle, your winning is essential, but in the safe confines of the Western World, death by violence or by predator seldom occurs. Losing in business can be uncomfortable economically and a little painful to your ego. Losing in a sporting competition is usually bad only for your ego, unless you are betting money on yourself, or if it means the loss of a paying job. Losing in love is mostly just damaging to your ego.

You compete when you are happy, you compete when you are sad, but the objective is different depending on your mood. You compete to make yourself feel good by winning, and if you lose you feel worse. You compete to impress someone, and when you lose you choke up and lose her, yet she really didn't care if you won or lost.

Mixing competition with your ego is always a bad investment. Overworking your ego is a big mistake. It will disappoint you more often than it will elevate you. We could save ourselves a lot of pain and make the world a better place for everyone if we humans could get off our high horse and stop screwing others because we feel entitled to do so.

*"If we can't teach fathers to stop laying gilt trips, promoting extreme competition and having unreasonable expectations of their sons, then we are doomed as a race!"*
DG

CHAPTER 119

# To Do Or Not To Do

Surprisingly, in my life I have toyed with celibacy. For this reason, I believe that it is a natural, though sporadic, often "religiously" motivated desire of humans. I can't speak for all women, but I have seen this tendency in some women.

In the mid 1970s I had a girlfriend, or should I say a part-time lover. We never went on a date, but literally every time we met, we made love. We would hug, and my arms wrapping around her body would bring my hands in touch with the sides of her breasts from behind. You will remember this if you have ever felt it. Your right hand inadvertently reaching around her perfect form and feeling the swelling of her right breast, and your left hand feeling the presence of her left breast, and it was all upwards to lovemaking from there. Even today, years later, when I greet her with a hug, I have to check myself.

She was a mime. She was another of my Jewish lovers. She carries the brand today on her wonderful ass from the searing hot wall heater in my cottage.

During one period in our sporadic involvement throwing our bodies together, we decided to become celibate for awhile. The subject came up because we both were feeling a little self-conscious about our decadent lifestyle.

We both abstained for perhaps a week or so and then accidentally met in the Santa Cruz Mountains at a music event. She was there as a mime, and I was there as an acid-eating dancer, and we decided that sex was too wonderful an exercise to give up.

Mime on bike

CHAPTER 120

# Red-Haired Frustration
# Power Politics in Bed (1980s)

*"There are some experiences that are best to have later in life and some best to have early. Ego-crushing events are tolerable once you have had other masculine-building incidents. For some people, having their ego crushed early in life can be a life-threatening scenario."*
Mr. California

Every once in awhile I think of one particular girl, and I really get pissed off. It was one of my relationship failures that still affects me to this day. I am embarrassed to say that I can't remember her name, but maybe that is a form of detached self-preservation. Yet I can remember with pain and frustration how I felt at not being able to touch her the way I wanted to.

She lived in a small back yard cottage rental on the hill above Monterey. I can't remember how we met, but somehow we did and I started visiting her and taking her out to dance or for walks. I would kiss her from time to time, but it never seemed to lead anywhere.

Usually, if I could kiss a girl, she soon warmed to the idea of sex. I was complimented and compensated often for my oral succulence. But this girl didn't bite. Soon we started talking about why not. She just said she didn't "feel it." "Chemistry?"

For possibly two or three months, we got together once or twice a week. I kept hanging around, although I knew that the longer the period of time, the less likely that sex would happen. We had good talks, we liked each other, I began to think that maybe she was one of those girls who would rather have a nice guy friend, than exchange him for a lover and lose the companionship.

Although it might appear shallow of me that I seemed to equate sex with every girl I knew, you had to have lived at that time to understand. Sex was an intimate handshake. The brothers did the cool five's. The brothers and sisters made love.

I did have close girlfriends that I never made love with, nor attempted to. It was just that some women were on your radar screen.

This girl didn't seem to have any love life that I could see, or too many friends. She was from elsewhere. She worked as a waitress in several very nice restaurants in town.

Before I go much further I must try to describe this beautiful girl. Rust red hair that billowed out from a smooth, round, freckled face in thick curls and ringlets. Her eyes were green, as I recall, with eyelashes that fanned the air across the room.

Above-average height with long, beautiful legs, well-designed pelvis and ass. To some eyes she may have been deficient in breasts, but that had never been an essential attraction to me. Rolling foothills can be explored just as well as mountains, and with far less macho intensity.

She was very clean; she must have come from a good family. She spoke well and would have showcased in any country club in the world. She had real class, but it was subtle, yet I got the feeling she didn't think I was quite good enough for her. She would never be unkind and was never flagrant with her rejection. She liked me enough to put up with my visits, but not enough to sleep with me.

When I first met her, I got the impression that she wasn't affected by her own beauty, meaning she didn't treat the rest of the world as inferior, and she didn't seem to expect more out of life simply because she was good looking.

Gorgeous women fall into three main categories. The least prevalent are the ones who almost seem as if they are embarrassed by their good looks and sometimes try to hide them. Then there are the opposites, the arrogant ones. The other, the most prevalent and most desirable, are women who seem to ignore their appearance, are comfortable with their looks, and do nothing obvious to enhance or detract from them. This is the group I felt she occupied.

When I say she was clean, what I mean is she was tidy in dress and appearance. She wore almost classically conservative clothing. At the time I was going through a thrift shop phase, and, in retrospect, that may have been why I was "not her type."

I have never been a clothing snob, nor have I any clothing prejudices, especially with women. If she were a nice person, intelligent, and at least physically washed, I didn't care if she wore Dior or back door.

As for myself, I often went out of my way to be anti-style conscious just so girls would take me for myself, not for my clothing labels. I know good clothes and would often buy good, or stylish, used clothing, but it had often been cleaned or laundered more times than was socially acceptable for some folks. But mostly I didn't even think about my clothing or appearance. My body and its clothing were just a vessel for my personality.

*"It's not about how my body looks, but how my body acts!"*DG

I wanted to make love with this girl so badly that I continued visiting, against all odds, just on the off chance she would eventually accept me as a lover. I thought I could put up with any affront to my manhood. I was wrong.

There are situations into which a person sometimes stumbles that have no silver lining. It's a bust to begin with. I could see it coming. With each visit, I became less desirable, like a shabby dog living on the street that visits for a bone, but never gets any of the meat from the table.

After a period of time, I began to realize that, even had she finally let me into her bed, that shabby dog would never have turned into a purebred in her eyes.

Most every woman I have slept with has wanted more of me. It has nothing to do with prowess; it has everything to do with sincerity. I don't believe in the "good lover/bad lover" value system. I do know the good moves, but in the end it is how much you want to please the other person that makes you a good lover or a bad one.

It's strange how you can succeed with nine relationships in a row, and then, for no apparent reason, the tenth girl will reject you, no matter what you do. Why would one girl that you really care about just refuse to accept your offer, when a whole line of previous women, some you didn't care that much for, all loved you?

This could all be sour grapes. If she had fallen for me, I may, in the end, have just lumped her in with all the other memories. But I don't think so, at least not this time.

Sometimes a woman will get to know you too well to be able to take you seriously as a lover, and after that point, your desire for her starts to annoy her. You're not a mystery anymore; your intense interest is not flattering any more. Soon, if you keep coming around, you start to look like a stalker. When once you might have been a knight in shining prophylactic, you eventually become the court jester.

Had we made love the first or second night after our meeting, it would have been a wonderful relationship. "It's all in the timing." You can quote me on that. We may have dated for six months, we may have lived together for a few years, may have even married, though I think that is a stretch. Even though I could have easily stepped up to her standards, I still think that she saw me as below her from the very beginning.

And that is why what happened next was so devastating.

I have my own value system. I think nice, clean, country club girls should occasionally go slumming. I think they deserve to experience forbidden pleasure and previously unknown indulgences. But I don't feel that the actions and attitudes of some unsavory men warrant the reward of the soft companionship of a girl like this one.

There is a difference between letting yourself get seduced by a "bad boy" and falling for a sleaze. You can see where we are going with this, can't you? I am building up my anger.

One night, after several months of frustration, I dropped by this girl's place again. The frequency of my visits had become fewer and fewer, but I was still interested enough to occasionally re-jeopardize my ego for the chance to make love with her. I brought a bottle of wine, as I often did. Knocking on the door of the studio apartment, I was answered from behind closed curtains by an obviously nude occupant.

I don't remember how it all transpired, but she invited me in, even though she was with another man. And I, like a stupid fool, accepted. I must have been curious, and possibly I wanted to exhibit my self-esteem, of which I had a fair amount. But, as I learned, I had not near enough to withstand such an attack on my ego.

If I had handed her the bottle of wine, said, "Enjoy," and gone home without entering, I may have fantasized that a better man had won the day. But instead, I entered, expressing my open-mindedness, only to experience some of the most humiliating moments of my life. I spent the next half hour or so sitting at the foot of her bed as she cuddled under the covers with an arrogant, sleaze ball, Latin lover type.

He was her boss from the restaurant. I believe he was several years older than myself, and that would make him at least 15 years older than the girl. I had nothing against that. What did bother me was that I knew from the man's attitude that one of the reasons he was a restaurant manager was so that he had the economic power to seduce any of the girls who came to work for him.

I believe he was also married. And he was boning one of the most beautiful, "sweet," "unspoiled" and sophisticated girls available on the streets of Monterey. Or so I had thought.

Well, you can imagine that it took me awhile to get over that night. I'm not sure, but I believe I never saw her or sought her out again. I still can't believe the inequities of this world sometimes. Of all my relationships, good and bad, of all the triumphs and disappointments, that single episode affected me most.

I have no idea how their relationship progressed, nor to what end it evolved, but I will tell you one thing and I will bet everything I have on it. Her relationship with that slime was far less satisfying and far more damaging to her than the same amount of time with me would have been.

You can tell I was disappointed, can't you? I was and still am. It had something to do with the total scenario. Here I was thinking that she was a sensitive, intelligent woman, someone with self-respect and instincts toward fairness. And then I learned that she was actually flawed, capable of relinquishing her precious body for financial considerations, and susceptible to seduction by someone who used the power of his position to gain sex.

I was crushed, and as I started relating this, I began to realize what a profound effect that experience really had on me. The more thought I put into that episode, the more memories were excavated.

I now realize that this was a turning point in my relationships with women. I remember shortly thereafter beginning to treat some women with less respect for the first time in my adult life. As a teenager, I had moments of insensitivity, but for most of my sex life, I have had the greatest respect for the opposite sex.

To a great extent, from that moment on, I became disillusioned with the dating game. Up to that time, I had always been optimistic about new women and enthusiastic about the mating dance; yet, starting around that period of time, I become painfully blunt concerning my intentions and none-too-subtle about my needs in relations with women. If a girl wouldn't sleep with me on the first date, I was gone. In a strange sort of way, it prepared me for my eventual marriage a few years later.

Because I was so dissatisfied with the courting game after that experience, I became more black and white about relationships. I began looking at women as someone to sleep with on the one hand or as someone to live with on the other.

Because of my disillusionment, I was not into relationships as much for the fun any more as I was for the necessity. I became much more discriminating, and I believe I subtly started seeking a long-term mate.

I can't really thank that girl. That kind of disillusionment is too painful, even if it brings a positive change. Yet I will say that I would love to have seen what our relationship might have produced. I think it would have been good.

But, of all my lovers and/or women friends, that girl is the one I would not be truly comfortable meeting again. I have very few regrets in my relationships. I feel no embarrassment about how any of them ended, and I truly believe that I could look any of them square in the eyes, say I loved them and wish them well, but I might have a problem with that girl.

Her image and my ideals of women were so severely crushed by that episode that I could feel only sadness in her company. In the end, though, I do hope she found satisfaction and real love in her life. But most of all, I hope she found someone who truly appreciated her as a woman, as I did, someone who would love her as a sensual being, of course, but mostly as a woman and a companion.

I used to think that there was a virgin within all women; now I feel that there is a woman within all virgins. The lesson I learned from that beautiful redheaded girl is the basis of my respect and tolerance toward women today. I no longer think that women are totally pure as I once did, but that they are human, and their impurity, although disturbing, is one of the most compelling aspects of man's desire for them.

And, if I were to extrapolate that idea further, I would have to admit that the biological influence of the law of survival of the fittest is a major reason women pick certain men. I may not like it, but a man who exudes money and power is a more desirable mate to most women, even in this civilized society.

Having said that, I must add that women are just going to have to accept what they get if they continue to use lots of money as the criteria for a mate. Sensitivity, which is one of the traits women most often state as important in a mate, is not prominent in type-A men. That is a fact supported by almost every sociologist, and well-documented by the employees of most rich men.

Women suffer inconvenience loving a poor and powerless man; but they suffer more from a man who loves money and power more than he loves them.

*Narrow grows our path*
*now through dark woods we must walk*
*closer together*
JBMc 1.14.73, Rose Lodge, Oregon

CHAPTER 121

# Love Without Jealousy

Most people don't understand jealous-free love or jealous-free sex. The reason? Because they have not experienced it. Before the 1960s when hippies rediscovered it, pure love had been obliterated by Christian doctrine.

Christianity and its accompanying insecurities have complicated what was once a simple act of life. Sex is now a sin! And therefore, it is to be ashamed of. And it is to be repented for, over and over and always. A woman made you do it, and therefore she is to be abused.

One of the largest categories of murder in America is jealous rage, not to mention all the battery and spousal abuse. It's not a pretty sight what religion has done to love. It isn't very civilized the way a possessive ego can obliterate romance.

Religious doctrine, such as "Saint Paul's" 1 Corinthians 7:9 *"But if they cannot contain, let them marry: for it is better to marry than to burn" and* other, out of context, quotes cherry-picked from the Old Testament have changed our attitude about sex and coupling. Until Christianity interjected sin, monogamy and sexual possessiveness were based on necessity and not psychological needs.

Paul's pronouncements in 1 Corinthians 11:8-9 *"For the man is not of the woman; but the woman of the man" "Neither was the man created for the woman; but the woman for the man"* has given generations of men pretentious powers and a psychological push toward jealousy.

Being possessive toward a mate for procreative reasons is at least a natural activity and found in all species. But jealousy is exclusively a human trait. And jealousy is a very destructive form of "love."

To abuse or kill someone because you love them is a demented rationalization. It will take a reversal in attitude about what love really is to change this ugly trend in human domesticity. The kind of love that makes a person happy and keeps them sane is unconditional love. Selfish love is not really love; it is not an emotion that fulfills your life.

To really love someone you have to be willing to "set them free" if that is what they want. I keep harking back to Robert Heinlein's almost perfect definition of love, which is found in his book, "Stranger in a Stranger Land," *"Love is that condition wherein the happiness of another is essential to your own."*

Sex is just the animal in us; love is the human in us. You can force someone to have sex with you, but you can't force them to love you. If all you crave is the shallow experience of sex alone, then insecurity and jealousy are probably part of your personality. And with these traits you will find it hard to attract a life's mate.

After all, believe it or not, in every relationship the sex becomes secondary to friendship. It may take 3 months, it may take 30 years. Eventually, sex is gone completely, but the unconditional tolerance of a companion is what makes a couple cherish each other forever.

> *"How can a man call himself a man, be a man, unless he has earned the love of a woman?"*
> Dudley Griffin, 1.24.02

## CHAPTER 122

# A Train Full of Amazons

It was during one of my trips to Greece. I think it was in the early 1980s. Leaving Paris for Italy by train, I found an empty 2nd class compartment and settled in for the departure.

It would be an overnight ride to the South of France and the border of Italy. I wanted to be sure to have a place to stretch out and sleep, so I was pleased to find a compartment to myself.

But then, just as the train began to leave the station, a horde of Amazons descended upon my sanctuary, and a new adventure unfolded.

A dozen, beautiful, trim, athletic, six-foot women had just entered my train car, my compartment and my fantasies. Was it my pheromones, or was it just my very good fortune? Whatever it was, I was up to the challenge.

Bottles of wine began to appear from backpacks, and food, and then basketballs! Basketballs? I had the great good fortune to be introduced to a girl's basketball team from Marseille returning home from a national tournament in Paris. And they had won!

Well, the evening evolved into a party. Basketballs were dribbled up and down the train car, wine was consumed, music played and dances danced.

My French has always been elementary, but such celebrations do not require deep communication. Other people on the train may have joined the revelry, but I can only remember myself and the twelve or more French female basketball players.

At least one of the girls was black, one from Morocco, several were classic blond swimsuit models, and others were farm girls with big hands and big breasts. I remember a lot of flirting, touching, and some kissing, but it was mostly a celebration of being young and successful at life.

When our exuberance and energy burned out, I fell asleep intertwined in the arms and legs of half the team in one of the compartments. When I awoke to the Mediterranean sun shining onto my face through the train windows, I was alone.

The obvious answer is that the girls got off at their station, and I slept through it. But I will tell you that I had never before slept through a girl leaving my bed without making love one last time. I sometimes think the whole episode might have been a dream, yet in my mind I still taste the cheap wine, Brie and French lip-gloss.

*"Life has its limitations; we can go only as far as we travel,*
*and travel only as far as we dream."*
Mr. California,
1.24.02

CHAPTER 12

# The Insanity Of Alone

Human beings are social creatures. They crave and seek out the warmth of others. If you want to drive a person insane, isolate him.

There are a lot of people living in this world who are mentally disturbed in various degrees, because they have cut themselves off from love and companionship. Most did not do this consciously, but due to some childhood trauma or flaw in their personality development. They acquired an attitude of distrust or fear, which eventually caused others to distrust or fear them.

These people are the walking wounded. They push away the thing that they need most--the love of others. These unloved and unhappy people are the cause of much of the hatred in this world. It is sad for them, and it's sad for all of us.

Insecurity is our worst enemy. Fear of rejection is the gun we hold to our own head. The moment we become happy with ourselves, the moment we stop taking rejection personally, people will come to us with their affection.

Being happy with yourself is its own reward. Kill that insecure person inside you who is killing you.

*"From my vantage point perched on the handle of a cup of*
*cappuccino,*
*I am a God of men and above suspicion."*
JBMc, 11.8.77, Corfu

CHAPTER 124

# The Toilet Seat Chapter

Sitting on a closed toilet lid in the dark is, for a man, as traumatic as sitting on a toilet seat up bowl for a woman.

Was the toilet created with the seat up or down? This is not a question designed to start a fight or determine probability factors. I really want to know. See, I don't mind lifting, then pissing, and then lowering the seat afterwards. I just don't want to do it if it doesn't make any sense.

*First, we must agree on several simple truths:*

Women (almost) always sit on the toilet seat.

Men sit sometimes and stand most of the time, unless it's too dark, or they are too drunk, stoned or tired to stand, or they just left bed with an erection.

A real woman would, without regret, joyfully piss on the latest issue of Popular Mechanics that sits in that little niche next to the toilet. A real man would never purposely piss on a toilet seat because he knows there is going to be a time when he will need to use it himself. A man may never consciously piss on the seat, but we know from experience that accidents do happen, so it makes good sense to lift the seat.

No one knows the gender of the first person to use the first toilet seat.

*Some questions I have:*

Was the toilet installed with the toilet seat up or down?

What if the next person to use the toilet is the same gender as you?

Is this a gender issue or a democracy issue?

Is this an area where women should demand and exercise equality?

Is chivalry the reason for conflict?

*Here are some solutions I propose:*

Men and women both put the seat back the opposite of the way they found it.

Leave it the same way you found it.

Leave it the way you have used it.

Leave it the opposite of the way you have used it.

Men should always leave the seat down.

Women should always leave the seat up.

Get out your calculator and determine which of these is the most democratic. Are we getting silly now?

*Another option:*

Try to calculate which gender is going to come in to use the bathroom after you.

Although this toilet seat issue is seldom the cause of a couple's destruction, it is still an indicator of larger problems and a foreboding of future friction in a relationship.

Although I tend to be confrontational about the concept of putting down the toilet seat, I would never think of failing to do so. As a matter of fact, thinking has a big part to do with the misunderstanding. A man, particularly a young man who has had his mother cleaning up after him or who has lived in guy houses or dorms for a long time, just doesn't think about such things as the position of the toilet seat.

To fail to follow seat etiquette in a two-gender household is often just thoughtlessness, so if a man continues to do so even when he is in a relationship, the problem is usually selfishness, and that is an issue which will really destroy love.

Though, as I said, I will most always, out of courtesy to women, put the seat down, I do not recognize the logistical fairness of it. Also, there are some women's lib and equality issues here.

OK, I will concede that when the toilet was installed in the house, its first configuration was with the seat down. When the first person walked into the bathroom, the seat was properly closed with the "seat" and the "lid" down. But, who first walked in, a man or a woman? Who was the first person to use the can? I'm disregarding construction workers and the likes, and we know how they use toilets!

So was it a man who had to raise the lid and the seat, or a woman who had to lift only the lid? Here's where the women's equality and liberation issues enter in. Do women want to start raising the seat every time they finish on the off chance that the next person who uses the toilet will be a man, or do they want to just leave it as is when they finish? It's a 50-50 chance that it will be another woman. And then there is the issue of whether the man wants to sit or stand when he comes in.

I have installed more toilet seats than I can remember, and I can say that after all installations I put the seat and lid down. I would have to admit that when the world was created the toilet seat and lid were probably down, so I think it is proper to return it to its original state.

Since writing this chapter I have decided to "always" leave the seat and lid down when leaving a bathroom. The exceptions are when no lid exists, when I am the only user of the toilet or when the toilet is in an "animal house."

Let us all, men and woman, put the seat and lid down when we are finished. That way we will all get our exercise and no one can complain.

*"Then later in life it hit me that the one toilet seat concession has given me credence whenever I suggest something of much more importance, such as, equal pay, equal respect or abortion rights by the possessor of the fetus and its obligations and requirements of motherhood."*
*DG, 3.31.15*

CHAPTER 125

# OJ Could Have Been A Hero

If OJ Simpson had the right publicist, killing his wife and her friend could have had a silver lining. With all due respect to the Brown and Goldman families, I am grieved by their deaths, and I would never condone their murder or anyone else's. However, there could have been an up side to this tragedy. As it is, OJ compounded a personal tragedy into a national disaster.

If I had been Orenthal James Simpson's publicist, accountant, lawyer, tax man, friend or pimp, I would have told him to confess to the murders and start apologizing immediately. If he had any brains, he or an advisor with brains should have started condemning domestic violence and campaigning against spousal abuse. OJ could have come out of this more popular and more famous than being a football player or media star ever gave him. One catch. He would have had to be genuinely sincere about it because he is not a very good actor, and everyone would have known he was lying.

He would have kept most of his money, all of his self-respect and the respect of others, and he may have gotten off with 12 years in jail instead of eternity in the hell where he is now. He may not have been able to seduce as many women in his lifetime, but they would have been nice women instead of the bimbos he now has to sleep with. No woman with any brains or self-respect would let him touch her now.

I am not a prude or a religious person by nature, although I am a moralist. But there are times that even nonjudgmental person like myself must use the term, "Burn In Hell!"

It is now too late for OJ's publicist to help him. He will go down in history as one of the most detestable of all once famous people.

There is nothing wrong with infamy or notoriety as long as you handle it well. Bob Dylan became infamous when he went electric at the Newport Folk Festival. He prevailed. It depends on what your offense is, of course. Murder is a bit of a stretch, but if OJ could have been contrite enough, he might have survived with flying colors. If he had truly repented and done something to change the world by his admission, he could have survived with respect, dignity and some of his money. Of course, there are some completely ignorant and warped people out there who still look to Hitler as a role model, just as some people feel OJ was framed.

OJ set back race relations at least a hundred years! And he has also probably been responsible for the murders of hundreds of other spouses and lovers by husbands and boyfriends who thought they could get away with it too.

Most tragically, if he had admitted his frailty, asked forgiveness and campaigned against spousal abuse, he could have helped to avert the deaths of many women and the imprisonment of many misguided men. But his macho personality could never have allowed him to stand up and be a real man.

There are some men who feel so entitled that they don't believe the people or the courts would ever blame, convict or prosecute them for their crimes. This is the worst transgression a man can commit. To think that you are above the laws of God and man, you have to be a real scum bag.

*"If I must preach to you, I insist on saying something that is really instructive, not religious. Not for your soul, but for the safety of the people you intend to terrorize!"*
Mr. California

## CHAPTER 126

# A Slave to Endorphins

*"For years, I have been hearing about Twinkie highs, caffeine buzzes, and all the legal stimulants and their influences on human nature and eccentricities. Well, I have a complaint about the new drug of choice among the yuppie, the dot.comers, the nouveau riche and nouveau bored.*
*I'm concerned by this endorphin thing that makes all*

*these young people run around, steal your parking place, remodel the architecturally historic house next door, or try to sell you stocks. It's this exercise fanaticism some folks are into right now. We're not talking about running jackrabbits out of the bean field, chopping wood, or making love all afternoon, we're talking about endlessly lifting chunks of pot metal up and down, up and down without getting paid for it, or riding a bicycle 40 miles in your living room while watching Seinfeld reruns.*
*What is the point in creating obstacles over which you yourself must jump?"*
Dudley Griffin, 7.12.05

CHAPTER 127

# Do the Right Thing

Be helpful, friendly, courteous, kind, obedient, cheerful, thrifty, brave, clean and reverent. In life, but more than ever in your sex life. If you act in this way, you will have a healthy, productive and long love affair or love affairs or marriage.

CHAPTER 128

# Back Tats and Tramp Stamps

*"You take a sweet young thing with a perfect body and luscious innocence and stick some ink under her skin, branding her as a slut, or someone who wants to appear to be a slut. What a waste of exciting romantic mystery."*
Mr. California, 8.3.06

*"You may think that what I say here is due to an age and cultural difference, but don't forget that I was a hippie, and I had tattoos and piercings long before any of this current bunch of goths, punks and rebels were born."* DG

Tattoos are not, I repeat, not, sexy. They may be a statement, a rebellion, or meant to be an adornment like clothing, but they are not intrinsically sexy, though they can definitely be trashy! I'm not talking about a flower on the foot or a butterfly on the shoulder or pierced nose, but facial tats, ass tats, clit rings, and legs that look like a jungle with snake crawling up. These give a different message than intimacy!

Tattoos on a girl or a woman may make a man think that he is getting a person of some sexual or social experience, but where is the romance in this?

Like most of us who lived through the free love 1960s and 70s, I am afraid for young girls who put tattoos on their perfect bodies to make themselves look like skanks. It's their body, and they can do what they want with it, but do they really know what they are doing?

These girls will tell me that it's a modern fashion, everyone is doing it, and I'm too old and don't understand. But I understand all too well where it is coming from and where it leads.

In the 60s and 70s a girl smiled in a certain way when she was interested in your affections. It was pretty straightforward. No one had to guess or make embarrassing mistakes.

Now all these girls with back tats and very few smiles are getting unwanted attention from all kinds of confused guys. The courtship game has become like a TV commercial. And advertising what you don't know or don't have is a bummer for the future of a relationship. If you attract someone with your feathers, you better be the bird that they want underneath.

CHAPTER 129

# To "Ms." Wright and All Other Conservative Feminists, JBMc, 8.12.06

No liberal "socialist" intellectual is asking you or any of your shiny faced friends to use birth control or have an abortion. "We" are lobbying for all the women of the world to have the freedom to use these options. This is to help save the world from over population and to give women what we think are their human rights.

Only conservatives force laws on people. Liberals are fighting for all women's rights and freedoms found in the US Constitution. We are not asking to change the Constitution, as you are.

No, silly girl, there is no mention of abortion in our Constitution, but it is explicit in our Constitution that women have the right to have one if she wants it. And, by the way, there is no mention of fetuses in The Bible.

The liberal community and Planned Parenthood have <u>never</u> considered abortion a proper solution to population control or family planning. Birth control and real sex education, not abstinence, are the proper solutions. By the way, anyone with a drop of brains and any knowledge of mankind's history knows abstinence is a hoax.

If you conservatives would allow realistic sex education and birth control in the world, we could humanely reduce the population and unwanted pregnancies, thereby saving the world!

Your naive rhetoric about sex education creating promiscuity is yet another self-deceiving pronouncement. Sex does not need advertising! Young people will find it no matter what "grown-ups" do. It is God's gift of creation. Only rational understanding of the pitfalls will slow it down.

Conservatives think only in one dimension. They are concerned solely with their own survival. And be damned with the problems of others who are poor, trapped in oppressive societies, or ignorant (usually because of conservative meddling).

Liberals think about the problems of other people and other generations. Note the term you have given us: Bleeding Hearts! But what is the opposite of Bleeding Hearts? Heartless! And that is what conservatives are.

I doubt that you will read this, but if you do, your mind will not be able to handle it. So I will tell you with the wisdom of spiritual knowledge far older than Christianity, you and those like you are so out of touch with the realities of life that you have become the Antichrist that you fear so much.

Our liberal position on a woman's right to birth control and abortion does not infringe on your right not use birth control or abortion, or to oppose birth control and abortion. Though I can't figure out why you, as a woman, would oppose your own freedom.

> *"Peace, the Golden Rule, and may you change before*
> *your soul is lost."*
> DG, 8.12.06

All creatures are born with a one-dimensional mind; self-preservation is its concern, and its job is to consume and procreate--eat and have sex! From crickets to snakes, to deer, to cougars and man, selfishness is our first rule. At birth, we are all concerned solely with our own survival.

As human beings, the second dimension is the recognition of other human beings. But, depending on our family politics and social dimensions, we are taught to look at others as either leaders, equals or slaves.

The third dimension of human social development is caring about other people, having compassion!

The fourth dimension for humans is doing something for others.

The fifth, and this is achievable only by saints and gods, is giving your life to help others. I realize that this is all very close to the Eastern philosophy of self-realization. By the way, self-realization does not mean that you look at yourself in a mirror and decide that you are more beautiful than others. Self-realization is when you see yourself in a mirror and think that you are god, <u>just as</u> all other people are gods, and that is all right with you!

## "Dear Wendy" On Returning to Modesty

It would be wonderful if we could return to a time when we thought that sexual relationships were more romantic, quaint and safe. Yet the reality was never really as sweet as we would make it in our selective memory or in the limited accounts put down on paper.

The first error in your thoughts was the word "return," for once the cat is out of the bag, it is only forward that we can go. Even if the Victorian view of love and sex had really been as idyllic as you fantasize, going back would be impossible.

I won't belabor the fact, but you realize that the "Harlequin novel" image of gallantry and modesty before the 1960's was not as widespread or bucolic as you think it was. Suffice is to say that maybe only 10% of the population in our "civilized" western world had the luxury of education and money to live a genteel, modest and "proper" life, not to mention the rest of the world's population, which had, and, in some cases still has, sexual mores as varied as accepted incest and rape as a means for acquiring a wife.

But, even if sex had truly been perfect before the pill, and now after the pill it is imperfect, going back is out of the question.

Sex is by far the most complex, confusing and misunderstood human influence. Religion is by far the most complex, confusing and misunderstood human subject. They are both mired in incredible irrationality. It is natural and also tragic that they should become entangled in our lives.

It would be a boon to mankind if we could somehow separate these two aspects of our existence. That is my challenge and effort.

Religion was devised originally as a way to separate human beings from the rest of the animal kingdom, to make us more important (God-like?), a mechanism to raise us above other creatures in our own minds.

Sex was one of the reasons religion was concocted. Prohibition of sex was one of the first sins concocted. It was created by a priest who wanted all the girls to himself.

CHAPTER 130

# Sun's Gossamer Gift

The morning broke clear, but cold. My sleeping bag held me for a little while longer until I felt the sun on my face. My breath vaporized, making me look just like a smoking caterpillar.

I sat up to face the rising ball of heat and light and was greeted by a beautiful apparition. Sometime in the night she had rolled out her own bag thirty feet away between me and the rocks, sea and rising sun.

She was combing out her straight, blonde hair. When she stood up the pink sun shone through her hippie dress, revealing a beautiful body. Yes, that is really what it looked like, the cover of a bodice-ripping, Harlequin novel. But this is how I would write it. "Combing her straight, blonde hair glistening long silk strands, the X-ray sun shown through her gossamer dress, revealing Venus."

The opposite of having the breath sucked out of you--I was filled with a gust of life. The opposite of having my heart broken. I was pumped with fresh, hot blood. How could she perform such a mundane act, unaware of my watching and still fill my heart in such a way.?

I introduced myself, we talked, and I offered her my shower, which was three blocks away. You see, I was preparing to go on a long hitchhiking, third-class traveling trip, and was trying out my new sleeping bag. She (and I can't remember her name) was in the midst of her third-class accommodation trip through California.

We spent the next three days together...my cottage, Big Sur, off she went back to Galveston.

The next year I took the long way to Europe by way of Texas just to see her. When I got to Galveston I found out she had a boyfriend. She let me stay at her house, but she had a boyfriend and so I couldn't touch her again. Such is life. So I sewed her a new pair of drawstring pants to show my appreciation for knowing her. Several days later I continued hitchhiking to New York and then flew on to Europe.

CHAPTER 131

# Satire and Shame

I just liked the sound of these two words together. We needed a change in direction here, and I thought by writing a chapter title that sounded good to me, I could get some ideas.

The interesting thing about sex is it is so prevalent in our lives that any situation or emotion can be applied to it. And, just the same, by using any word as a subject, a whole episode can be written about sex.

Now, of course, the words satire and shame, though they may sound good together, have almost the opposite meanings when connected to sex. Satire, in short, is the act of poking fun at wickedness for the purpose of drawing attention to its folly. Shame is self-inflicted accusation of your own folly or wickedness.

Satire is accusing others of sin; shame is accusing oneself of sin. The other difference between satire and shame is that one is almost always humorous, and the other almost always tragic.

The next thing I need to do to lead into this chapter is to give you my definition of sin. Sex is not sin; sex is a natural element of being alive. Intolerance is sin, hypocrisy is sin, hatred is sin, and violence for any reason other than self-preservation is sin. Shame, itself, is sin if it is not accompanied by apology and rehabilitation.

Remorse is worthless self-mindfucking over something in the past that can't be changed. Repentance to God is misused time. But if it involves apology to someone else for your mistakes, then it is good. Shame is like kicking yourself for something you have already done and can't do anything about anymore.

If you did something bad and you knew it and do it again or find out it was bad and do it again, then you deserve punishment. But shame is stupid punishment for ignorance. If you were ignorant, you shouldn't blame yourself. And shame is useless punishment for wickedness because what we really need to do is to get over our self-incriminations, straighten up our act, and change our lives for the better.

As you can see, shame is not one of those human emotions that I care for. It is influenced by religion or the traditions of family and social status, both of which I consider to be detrimental to human enlightenment.

Shame came to us in its present state partially from our Victorian ancestors, and mostly from the Christian traditions of self-denial and flagellation. The old school that says, "If it feels good, it must be wicked, and therefore I must punish myself for indulging in it."

The human being is often such a silly animal, and shame is really one of its most destructive follies. Human self-awareness carries two sharp edges. Unlike other animals that are just living their lives without anticipation or regrets, mankind has expectations for himself and feels disappointment for his failures.

On the one hand this is what make us so creative in our life-style, yet it is also what creates our selfishness and hypocrisy. Satire and shame! We are capable of making fun of our humanness, and yet we also indulge in self-recrimination.

When I first separated from my first wife, I felt a great deal of embarrassment about my treatment of her. I made several efforts at reconciliation, but each time, I was soon reminded of why I had instigated the split in the first place.

My shame was slowly resolved by the realization that the process of destroying my marriage was somehow preordained. It wasn't pretty, and it wasn't something that either of us wanted, but the circumstances of that period of time and my biological pressures made it inevitable. The only way to move on was to become philosophical about it.

This satirical attitude about love and sex started to grow into a new pathology of life. Like Voltaire's Candide, I slowly learned that there was good and bad in the world in almost equal measures. And I began to realize that the good and bad were not always planned by the perpetrators. It was often just human nature or uncontrollable reactions to the situation at hand.

Then, not as a cop-out, but as a process of moving on with my life, I began to laugh off those things over which I had no control and forgive myself for my past ignorance. I also began forgiving others for their humanness.

Candide in French means a naïve or innocent person. I was no Candide. I was not guiltless. But each of my mindless transgressions taught me a lesson. The pain I inflicted often came back to haunt me, so I stopped doing that. It was a natural reaction to being hurt by my own actions. It was the process of growing up and the development of wisdom. Call it the "oops" factor. "That didn't work out, I won't do that again."

But you have to have a satirical sense to see irony that allows you to laugh at your mistakes and change your actions. People without humor never change.

Conservative seriousness precludes accepting one's own faults. People wrapped up in false morality or self-doubt somehow never forgive themselves and move on because they usually just blame the other person. It is somehow too painful to admit error themselves. These people are often insecure by nature.

Admitting a flaw in oneself is too damaging to an already fragile ego. They cannot admit they are wrong, and therefore they never change that part of them that made the mistake.

Laughing at your mistakes doesn't make them go away. They are still there, but you have risen above them. They won't haunt you, and you most likely won't repeat them.

Taking yourself too seriously is not good for a true, deep, romantic relationship. If you find two people who are perfect, I want to meet them! If you find two people who think they must be perfect, I don't want to meet them. If you find two people who know they are imperfect, but are trying, I will know them by their love.

We must have a sense of satire to understand love. We must abolish shame to keep love.

CHAPTER 132

# How To Give Up On A Relationship
# How To End A Relationship

Breaking up! There are two lessons to be learned here. There are two different reasons why all relationships end. Either your partner wants it to end, or you want it to. If you are the one who is leaving, there is one way to act; if you are the one being left, there is another set of proper moves. We must take into consideration that because each and every person is different, there is never only one answer; there is only the best answer for the circumstance.

I can give a man advice on male/female relationships because I have experiences as a man.

I cannot give a woman advice on male/female relationships because I am a man, and I have not experienced them as a woman. I can give my opinions as gleaned through observation, but I will not bet on the outcome of my opinions!

Sometimes relationships just don't work out. Even if you are still committed to the love affair, maybe she wants to bail on it. When this happens you have two basic choices. You can:

1. Get pissy, stalk her, have a restraining order filed against you, make a fool of yourself, and never be able to get over it, thus never get your head straight and never find true love.

Or:

2. You can suck it up, act like real a man, move on and love another day!

## Giving Up On a Relationship With Dignity When He Or She Leaves You

When she leaves you, you are offended, your heart and your ego are crushed! You question if you will ever love like that again.

But you must realize and sympathize; she also has feelings. Her heart is sad, her heart is glad! She is looking forward to the next adventure, and yet she is afraid that leaving you was a mistake.

If you are the one being left, you must be the most rational person, or else you will become the asshole!

## Ending A Relationship With Dignity When You Leave Her

She is devastated, her heart and soul are crushed! She is also wondering; what she did wrong or what did she not do? And she will also question if she will ever love like that again!

But, if you admit your own emotions, your heart is sad, and your heart is also glad. You are looking forward to the next conquest, and yet, you are afraid that leaving her is a mistake.

If you the one leaving, you must be the most apologetic person, or else you will become the asshole!

Any woman who wishes to may transpose this previous chapter to be able to view it through female eyes.

*"One of the most serious things I learned in the hippie culture was not to take sex so seriously. Love is a serious aspect of life, but sex can and should be treated with a lot less uptightness.*

*And love... when a mate tells you that they don't want
to be with you any more by words or actions, then love ceases to be
as serious as self-preservation.
Let them go and get on with your life.
When a lover leaves, it is most likely not who you are
as much as what you did or didn't do. Learn from it, grow and move
on to a better relationship."*
Dudley Griffin, 6.8.06

## CHAPTER 133

# Male, Female, Drugs, Seduction

Women can and will be seduced with drugs. It is immoral in my estimation. I preferred seducing them with my sparkling, humorous, amorous love.

Women don't need drugs in the same way men do. Believe me, we all need some form of relief, diversion and introspection, but if you have to try to forget what you have done, you are an asshole and you have to change or you will die alone and broken.

## CHAPTER 134

# Love is Love, Sex is Sex

*"You do not make true love with your body, you do not even
do it with your heart, it is the soul that truly loves."*
Mr. California, 6.12.11

When we were young we believed that sex was the foundation of love. When we were in our middle age, we believed that sex was what kept love alive. In our old age many of us believe that love is the foundation for sex, and that love keeps sex alive. Yet the truth is that sex and love are often in conflict with each other. Both take a lot of work, and we must figure out which one is most important to our own and our familial happiness.

## love... Love... or LOVE

*The Beatles sang, "The love you take is equal to the love you make." How hard is that to understand?*
Dudley Griffin, 10.30.12

A woman giving her body to a man is a sacrament, whether she knows it or whether he knows it. The man should be infinitely grateful

I admit, I have fallen in love a lot. I am susceptible to love. Now, I have one LOVE. But I can still fall in love on a momentary basis.

How far I take my love is commensurate with the situation. I smile at a girl who interests me. I talk to someone who is exciting. I watch many women as they walk away.

In the past I loved many, Loved a lot and LOVED a select few. I could have been called a slut, and I admit to that designation. But I have never been a "whore."

I fell in love a lot! It was my most vivid way to communicate. It wasn't as if I were giving my emotions away cheaply. That is too painful in the long run. It seems that I really cared about those I offered my Love to.

I have known myself as who I really am for only a short time. It is interesting to begin to know someone this intimately now, after thinking I knew him for so many years. I am a person who has, through the circumstances of my birth, good fortune and timing, known mostly the blessings of love. In this, I am in the minority, maybe too few to mention.

Few people are blessed with a socially and sexually normal upbringing. Many of us are assailed by the egos and expectations of our parents. I dodged certain childhood projectiles through a series of events beyond my understanding or control. I was just a child, after all.

As a sperm, I did not know that I would be chosen. As a fetus, I did not know where or when I would arrive. As a child, I did not have a choice of my teachers. I was lucky that those who taught me loved God's creations because God made them. I was lucky because the people who showed me the way, made way for me.

I have had three lesbian lovers that I know of. That means we had sex. One of them I still know, and bump into from time to time. She is what has been called a "bull dike," no offense intended. The other two I have not seen or heard of for many years, but at the time in the 1970s they all professed the lesbian lifestyle.

One of these girls was definitely bisexual because of her history, I knew of her with other men. The other two were "hard core!"

But I have a theory, controversial as it may be to feminist and egotistical men. I believe that most women who are lesbians have been driven to that lifestyle by the macho, aggressive and self-centered activities of the men in their lives.

I have said many times that I am glad I am not a woman, purely for the reason that I would not want to have to deal with the social flaws of men. George Carlin said, "There are only two things about men and women. Women are crazy, and men are stupid!"

Love is love no matter where it comes from, and sex is a need which we will seek out and find where it is available. If we can't find heterosexual sex, as in prisons, humans turn to same sex. If sex with the opposite gender comes with too much trauma, we will turn to our same sex to feed the urge.

Love is the same. It has always been the most constant thing in the world. We have called it many things, but you know it when it knocks. I say knocks because it never barges in. It always asks to come in. It is up to you. Are you ready?

Love is not a guessing game! Love is not a competition! Love is not pretending!

*"Love for real not fade away,"*
Buddy Holly

*"I don't scrimp where love is involved. I will give the most expensive ice cream, the most opulent sunset, the best ear rub."*
DG

Graffiti as seen on a wall somewhere, "You are my love…my love you are… are you my love? Love you are my…!? (punctuation)

**Victimless Love**

I know what victimless love is. I know love without pain because I have felt it with my daughter, a couple of dogs, and then a cat. But, of course, the cat did scratch me from time to time!

The use of the negative word victim is counterintuitive, but if I said to you "I know what wonderful love is," you would walk away with an indifferent disgust, thinking of me as a new age, warm and fuzzy, cultist, kook. I am really trying to get your ear by using key emotional terms.

Sad to say, victims are often the product of our present human love scenarios. The word "pain" is associated too often with "love" in humankind's histoire l'amour de la vie (love life story), but love and pain should never be associated.

Procreation is naturally painful, in all of its stages, but why does that wonderful feeling that drives to sex carry pain? The light of our life becomes a cloud blocking the sun. Objects of affection can morph into objects of revulsion.

> *"Love is not a game, but we insist on playing it!"*
> Dudley Griffin, 7.3.12
> *"Love is not a gift, it is a requirement!"*
> JBMc

> *"It's Not All Just One Big Pastoral, Bucolic Bed Of Whipping Cream. Not everything I have to say about love is positive. Not everything I have done is framed in roses. This is life, after all."*
> Mr. California, 12.31.06

> *"We have an enemy keeping us from Love, and it is sex. We cannot prohibit sex, but we can learn to put it in its place, and keep it out of the way of Love.*
> *Sex and love are subjects that men and women will never agree upon, and we should never try to discuss them amongst each other, we should only do them amongst each other."*
> DG., 2.24.13

> *"Anybody who says they do not have an alter ego is either lying to you, or they don't know what a fantasy friend or surrogate is."*
> JBMc, 12.27.20

CHAPTER 135

# Coitus Non-Performus

*"I was never any good at flirting. Flirting is like stepping into a fast, beautiful car, starting it up, revving the engine a few times, and then turning it off. I like to drive. I don't like to flirt."*
Dudley Griffin, 1.13.07

Of course, some people believe flirting is a fun little game and an essential element of courting. It can help you gauge another person's interest in you. It can allow both parties to show their level of intellect or humor. It also often spoils the moment and turns a potential love affair into a sitcom.

Don't toy with her affections! If you are attracted to her, let her know your intentions, sensitively, of course.

If she is not interested in you, your best defense is always having mounted a 'good' and respectful offense. Your reaction will then be, "Oh, OK, I understand. I'll see you later."

Don't ever say, "Maybe next time?" and especially not "You will come around."

Everyone you meet will have a different opinion of you, many of them probably wrong, but a first opinion is often etched in stone. You will never, ever talk someone into loving you. You can easily talk someone out of loving you.

CHAPTER 136

# Less Than A Rock Star Or A Sports Hero!

After all, I was only a California hippie.

I can almost remember all of my lovers. I couldn't pick them all out of a crowd, but I remember the general place and circumstances of all of my sexual experiences. And I have emotional memories of them as well.

In education and science the number of experiments usually equates to the achievement of knowledge or perfection. But it is also assumed that over-indulgence can create a jaded or bored outlook, i.e., even too much of a good thing can twist your perspective, just as too little of a good thing creates obsession.

> *"As a hippie I learned that it was not the sex itself we craved, but it was the satisfaction we sought."*
> JBMc, 4.1.10

Numbers are not important, satisfaction is. I had just the right number of sexual partners to learn needs and limits. In California during the 1960s and 1970s I could sit in one place for one day, and it was as if every girl in the world was coming by to get to know me.

*"I don't know which came first, but I was 'with a little girl in a Hollywood bungalow.' Her kittens jumped on the bed and scratched my ass."*
Mr. California

CHAPTER 137

# Facial Hair, The Mistaken Identity

The confusion about beards should have ended with Abraham Lincoln. Mustaches and stubble are another conundrum.

Here and now in 2011-2021 should society automatically arrest and imprison every man wearing a beard, or woman for that matter? Should we automatically consider a man with stubble to be a bum or a macho fox? And are mustaches the indication of homosexuality or of a sleazy car salesman?

If you watch movies, TV and advertising, you might fall into these traps of prejudice. Granted, styles change with time, but the pigeonholing applied to choices of facial hair is rampant and most often wrong.

In the 1960s and 70s, many of us younger men stopped shaving as a rebellion against the conservative thinking of our parents. In essence, we did it to piss off the establishment. But many of us also grew beards to experience the prejudice that we knew would come our way by doing so.

As pampered, white, middle-class kids, we wanted to be able to empathize with the other "downtrodden" races, and to be made to feel the disenfranchised attitude that the poorer "classes" felt.

In the 1970s with long hair and a beard, I hitchhiked with my 5- or 6-year-old daughter from Oregon to Southern California. We were having a blast, meeting new people, listening to their music, and riding in the luxury of their automobiles. Somewhere in Northern California as we were standing there with our big thumb and little thumb out, a man in a suit in a big Detroit gas guzzler drove by and yelled out the window at me, words to the effect that I was a bad father, submitting my daughter to such degradation.

He didn't see me as the educator that I was. I was showing my daughter new experiences, just as I had shown her Europe the year before. In Europe we were in a cozy VW van. Here we were in my home state, in my own country, traveling in a way that I had already traveled over 10,000 miles.

CHAPTER 138

# Is This a Fantasy or Am I Remembering?

Most of this book is non-fiction. Four-hundred and fifty pages of truth, history and reality. To write a 450-page fantasy novel about sex would take me maybe two months. This book that you are reading now, with the interruptions of life, other work, and family, has taken me 20 years to write. But I want to show you the difference between fantasy and fiction, so I have included two fictional stories that also are sex education. One of these is based on a girl I met in China. I call her Ming and it is all true except the sex. And the other fantasy is based on Mary Lou and Betty Sue, two girls whom I have met many times with different names and places. You will meet them other places in this book.

**Mary Lou and Betty Sue**

I used to have a recurring fantasy. As much as I can tell, it is also basically the #1 fantasy of every other heterosexual young man in the whole world.

It was a combination of a few real episodes in my life, as all fantasies are. The place was sometimes Winslow, Arizona, or sometimes outside Levelland, Texas, and the year was either 1978 or 1983.

I was hitchhiking through Texas on the way to Galveston to visit a girlfriend and then on to Europe. I don't know the name of the town, but it was somewhere in the panhandle.

They drove past me several times before stopping to pick me up. They were pretty little things. They were corn-fed girls with perfect complexions and classically cute appearance. Let's call them Mary Lou and Betty Sue. After all, they were from Texas. I later found out they were fifteen and sixteen years old.

It was Sunday afternoon, and they had just left church. Mary

Lou was carrying her bible, and she kept it with her for the total twenty hours I knew her. We had about as much in common as a Volkswagen van and a flatbed Ford, which is what they were driving.

I threw my kit in the back and got up into the cab next to Mary Lou. We were real close on that bench seat in the truck.

They were cousins. I asked if they knew of a place I could stay for the night. They hemmed and hawed with embarrassment, and then came to a conclusion. Their grandma had just died a few months before, I could stay at her place out on the old farm. They took me there.

In the musty old house, they showed me around and when we got to the bedroom, I asked if they wanted to "fool around" a little. They said that they were Christian girls and didn't have much experience with boys.

I told them I was a heathen and I would teach them how to French kiss. They agreed. We lay on the bed, and I took turns making out with each of them for a while. They were indeed very inexperienced, but they were curious.

I had intended to end it at kissing, and I would have if it had felt as if I were taking advantage of them, but they were very intelligent and self-assured. I began to feel up their breasts and started talking to them about their bodies and the sensual feelings created by kissing and caressing a woman's breast. I determined to make this an educational experience for these two girls. I was beginning to like them a lot and thinking about their life locked away in that dusty little town.

I felt them up through their clothing. There are few things more exciting than the feel of a firm, young breast held tightly in its bra, longing to be free. I got the impression that they had already allowed their boyfriends to go that far, but it was still very new to them.

They were both wearing white short-sleeve blouses, tucked into medium length pleated skirts. The outfits were alarming similarly to girls' school uniforms.

Back and forth I went between the two, keeping them both in a state of excitement. After a while I started slipping my leg over between their legs and pressing my thigh up against their crotch.

Betty Sue was more anxious to indulge, so I said to her, "Let me do something that feels just like real sex. Believe me, you'll enjoy it." She nodded sheepishly. So, like the wolf I was, I got between her legs, on top of her and started rubbing my, by then, fully-grown hard-on against her crotch.

As I did this I looked down at her, smiled, threw my head back and arched my body into her, pushing my erection up between her legs, forcing her head into her grandmother's pillow. She caught her breath, and I slipped my tongue back into her mouth, and we drove our bodies against each other in rhythm.

As we did this, her skirt began to riding up, and eventually I was rubbing against her underpants. My dick and her vagina were separated by just a few thin layers of cloth. It started getting hot and heavy.

Mary Lou wanted to try it also, and when I rose up off Betty Sue, I looked down at her pubic mound. The thin material of her underwear was pressed into the crease of her cunt, and I thought I could see a little dampness. I had definitely gotten in contact with her clitoris. Her eyes were glazed.

I was wearing my usual light material khaki shorts, and I never wore underwear, so I was having a hard time keeping my pecker inside my pants. To Mary Lou I showed the woman-on-top position.

I rolled over, swung her leg over me, put my hands around her waist, and began rocking her up and down on top of my hard-on. The moment I touched her clitoris, she melted into a trance. We were soon thrusting methodically against each other, forcing our sexual receptors together as tightly as they would fit. Of course, her dress slipped up, and eventually I was holding her soft round ass clothed only in thin, nylon underwear.

I began to worry that the zipper on my shorts would tear through her panties and into her flesh. It was time to take it to the next level.

It was a shame to break this spell they were already in, but I wanted to show them all the experiences. I began to slow Mary Lou down and asked them what they thought of those feelings. They were both almost speechless at that point.

I then told them that they were so beautiful and sexy that I was now one horny son of a bitch. I asked if they had ever given a guy a hand job and they pleaded ignorance, but offered to learn.

I lay back on grandma's lace pillows and told them I would teach them how. I started by taking each one separately by the hand, rubbing over the bulge in my shorts, and then letting them rub by themselves for a while. I then had them unbutton a button or two until they could stick a hand inside and feel it skin-to-skin.

They chuckled and smiled at each other as they took turns reaching in to rub my hard-on. Eventually, they were both doing it together. They did this for a while and told me how they liked the smooth feel of the hard "thing." I asked them to call it my cock, which they did from then on.

I then took off my shirt and asked them to pull off my shorts. This they did slowly in unison. As I lay there naked before them, they looked in wonder at me. It really was wonderment in their eyes.

I then taught them the art of male masturbation. I first demonstrated on myself, then guided their hands and then left it up to them. They practiced and experimented for some time. I told them what felt good, eventually teaching them to run their hands also over my scrotum and testicles. I had a few mock orgasms for them.

I then suggested that they try something else. It would be fun for them, and it would also turn me on so I could have a real orgasm. I asked them to take off their blouses and bras, and I would show them something really interesting.

As I watched them remove their clothing, I mused at what a wonderful world this was. These two beautiful young girls were about the same height. One was blonde with long, down-the-back hair, and the other was a red tint brunette with slightly shorter hair up in a ponytail.

The blonde, Mary Lou, had put her Bible on the bedstand. She had smaller, one-hand-size breasts that stuck out in perfect points with a little upturn to the sharp pink nipples. The brunette had larger breasts, the kind that drive men wild, completely round and firm, that pouched out on the sides under her arms. They were the firmest and roundest in my memory.

I asked the blonde to come closer so I could feel her tits. She complied without hesitation. I reached both hands up and cupped each breast in a hand. She snuggled up close. We kissed, I fondled her nipples between my fingers, and she began to whimper. As we progressed I could feel Betty Sue had returned to playing with my cock. I observed later that she had a fixation with my dick.

I soon broke off the petting with Mary Lou and asked Betty Sue to come so that I might feel her boobs. I always called hers "boobs," and Mary Lou's "tits."

Betty Sue's boobs were indeed glorious, and I soon was sucking on them while she masturbated me. I could have come right then, but I had other plans.

Tearing myself away from her beautiful flesh, I then showed each girl in turn how to rub her nipples on the heart of my cock. They got a real kick out of this, laughing and joking with each other. Arousal!

I then introduced them to fellatio. How a woman sucks your cock is a great indication of how adventurous she is. Mary Lou, the blonde, was shocked when I suggested it, but Betty Sue jumped at the opportunity to do so.

I gave her some instructions. I sucked her middle finger to show her how. "No teeth," I said, "until you learn how!"

She grabbed hold with both hands and licked and sucked, took it deep into her throat and had a grand time. After Betty Sue gave it her full attention for a while, Mary Lou caved in to peer pressure and tried it. She was not going to be ridiculed for being a bad sport, but I could tell she was not all that enthusiastic. I was later to find that Mary Lou had her own fixation.

I was never insistent about any one position or sex game. Whatever turned on the girls, was what I wanted to do. I liked to hear them squeal.

So I told Mary Lou to come on up to my mouth and let me suck her pointed breasts, and did they ever get pointy as I caressed her nipples with my tongue.

While I was doing that Betty Sue went back to gobbling up my dick and caressing my testicles. It was fun for a while, one girl attending to my lower half and the other one giving my hands and mouth a thing or two to do. This lasted for some time. It was time to move on.

At this point I pushed Mary Lou up into a kneeling position above me. I looked her up and down as she sat there sheepishly in her pleated skirt with her tits pointing into the next county.

"Would you take your skirt off for me?" I asked. She looked into my eyes, looked away, rose up on her knees and slowly, awkwardly unzipped it. She then tentatively slipped it off over her head.

I was drinking in her beautiful, white body with my eyes. Embarrassed, she pulled her arms together over her breasts and placed her hands in her lap. Betty Sue was still enjoying the feel of my hard-on inside her mouth.

I reached up and brought Mary Lou's arms and hands over to her sides. She continued to look away as I ran my hands down her body over her brief nylon underwear. I placed a hand between her thighs and pushed them apart slightly. She cooperated. She looked wet, very wet.

In the slight crease of her panties, there was a jumble of pubic hair that could be seen through the thin damp material. She was obviously a natural blonde.

"Pull down your panties. I want to finger fuck you," I said with affection and authority. I think Mary Lou hesitated only a moment and then slowly reached up to the hem of her underpants. She turned and looked directly into my eyes in defiance and started to lower her panties.

I watched as her pubic hair slipped from its confinement and sprang to life in a golden nest of thin, wispy feathers. It was indeed thin and sparse but extremely long. I could see her pearl white skin and goosebumps under the hair in that place the hot sun never ventures.

As she lowered the hem below the crotch, I watched the gash of her vagina come into view. But what made me catch my breath were the pink and protruding lips of her labia engorged with blood.

Instinctively, without hesitation my right hand reached out and middle finger slipped between the folds of skin. The moment my finger touched her clitoris, she gasped and squatted down on my hand, forcing the finger up into her vagina. I had found Mary Lou's fixation. She had the most responsive clitoris I had ever known.

Her eyes and mouth opened wide. She began to rock back and forth on my hand and finger forcing them in contact with her soft button of erogenous flesh. She fell forward on her hands and knees, placing her nipple within reach of my mouth.

She began to moan and squeal, and Betty Sue, still at my dick watching and hearing all this, began to moan with her.

"Oh, God, no, sinful, don't make me, I'm soo sinful, ah, yes, I love it!... God" Mary Lou began a conversation with herself and her God and she moaned and whimpered. Betty Sue got into the rhythm with Mary Lou humping my hand, and she began to suck my cock in unison. We were all accelerating.

I was making an effort to rub Mary Lou's clitoris with my hand and tickle her nipple with my tongue as she rocked back and forth. I also had a hand on Betty Sue's head, guiding her mouth.

Our movements continued building in intensity until I realized two of us were going to have an orgasm. Mary Lou was oblivious to everything but her impending damnation and the warm tickle building deep inside her. I looked down at Betty Sue and said politely, "I am going to ejaculate now. If you would, please swallow the cum."

A few moments later, Mary Lou screamed out, "Ahh yee yes, oh, daddy, daddy, I'm sorry, sorry, sorry," intake of breath, "eeeeeeee," and then she began to cry.

I ejaculated during this discourse and I heard Betty Sue gag slightly, then swallow and begin to lick and suck and swallow hungrily. And then she made that familiar "yumm" sound we all make inadvertently when we first see the golden brown Thanksgiving turkey come out of the oven.

I didn't let the moment slip away. I rolled Mary Lou over onto the bed next to me and sat up onto my knees. I brought Betty Sue up to me and kissed her deeply.

It is not a fixation with me, but the taste of my own sperm in a woman's mouth or in her vagina is a bit of a turn-on. (It's the only way I could ever imagine tasting the stuff.)

Not that I needed anything to keep me excited at this point. I still had several places to go. As I kissed Betty Sue and fondled her breasts with one hand I ran my other hand down her smooth, flat stomach into the waistband of her panties. I was amused to find that she had already removed her pleated skirt.

She too was damp, but not quite enough. I coaxed my finger into the folds of her vagina and soon found some lubricant hidden there. When I stuck my finger deeply into her to find warmth and acceptance, she let out a deep breath of air, "Ahh," and then a timid, "yesss."

I fingered her for awhile, and found that her G-spot deep inside her brought her most pleasure. I then lay her down on the bed and knelt above her.

Looking down at this incredible body, I began to muse at how different two girls could be and still create the same lust within a man. Betty Sue's hair had long since broken free from its ponytail. It fell across her forehead and face in waves of red and brown watercolor paints.

Her face, shadowed and half hidden, was voluptuous, eyelashes stark, long, intriguing. Eyes, brown, deep, inviting. Mouth, full, wet, encompassing.

Mary Lou was a waif, eyelashes, thin, light, fluttering. Eyes, blue, damp, emotive. Mouth, pert, pink, appealing.

As I looked down upon Betty Sue's body, her breasts were fertile, nipples rich, warm comfortable. Vagina pink, wet, encompassing.

Mary Lou's breasts were fun, nipples exciting. Vagina, like a flower, soulful, inviting.

Betty Sue's hands had not left my erection for the last half hour. She was still caressing it as I lay her down on the bed. I slowly played with her nipples as I looked at her.

Betty Sue was vulnerable, yet not defenseless. My right hand wandered down her torso over her belly to the hem of her underpants. Black. They were bunched up around her brown hips, showing a tan line revealing lighter, yet still tinted, skin.

Mary Lou wore pure white panties against pure white skin, but they were now crumpled around her knees. She was defenseless, curled up in a ball.

I slowly pulled Betty Sue's underwear down her legs, over her feet and tossed them to the foot of the bed. I spread her legs and moved between them. I caressed her thighs as she caressed my dick.

Lifting her knees, I moved forward. Directing her hand wrapped around my erection, I placed the tip on her clitoris. She froze. I moved her hand, she ignited.

A whimper, and she began moving the head of my penis around her clitoris. Without realizing it, she slowly directed me into her vagina. First a little nudge, then an inch, then she arched her back and I drove deep inside her. She screamed a short breath, and we rammed our bodies together.

We forgot Mary Lou was there. We became fixated on our movements, excitable, almost violent, fucking. It was as if she were born to do this. She was a vessel for my juices, and she wanted it all.

I don't know how long we carried on. Oblivious to our surroundings, we trashed the bed, pillows and blankets flew everywhere. When she finally came I was fucking her dog style with my cock and finger in her vagina and on her clitoris.

She screamed into the mattress and clutched the sheet, her tail in the air with my pelvis pounding her beautiful, round ass. I was about to orgasm again, and I wanted to be deep inside, so I quickly turned her over and drove back in as far as I could fathom and began vigorously thrusting until I erupted. In a fantasy, no one worries about pregnancy or disease.

Betty Sue and I convulsed in each other's arms. Our excitement wound down like an old forgotten watch in a drawer. We lay there panting, and I turned to take a breath and found Mary Lou's eyes as big as half dollars looking straight at me. She had been in the fetal position facing the door when I started screwing Betty Sue, now she was curled up facing our tangled bodies. She was watching intently, and her facial expression said nothing. She was also now clutching her Bible again.

It was almost as if she had her thumb in her mouth, but her Bible provided that comfort. Her innocence and vulnerability were both pathetic and sexually charged at the same time.

The innocent lamb before the slaughter, teetering on the edge of her freedom from the prison of ignorance. Say what you will about the deflowering of a virgin. Better me than some crude cowboy on the tailgate of his truck.

It is never without sin unless free of hypocrisy. If the parties of a good fuck are without deception, guilt or malice, it is ordained!

I smiled at Mary Lou. Her face softened, and I saw something in her eyes that I recognized. I withdrew from Betty Sue and turned to Mary Lou.

My erection sprang out damp and full. I reached over and took the waistband of Mary Lou's panties and pulled them down over her feet and threw them to the foot of the bed. She did not resist; as a matter of fact she helped. I slid between her legs.

She voluntarily spread her legs as wide as they would go. Her eyes were still riveted on mine; she clutched her Bible between her pointed breasts. I moved between her thighs.

I grabbed a pillow, lifted her body up and placed the pillow beneath her firm, soft ass. Her white, blonde, pink crotch opened to me. I balanced over her upturned vagina.

Placing fingers on either lip of her labia, I parted the skin and looked into the dark red inside of her. Wishing my penis as large as I could, it engorged in anticipation. Hands on either side of her hips, I rose up on my toes and slipped into her cunt.

She became a warm kitten. We made soft, but powerful love for a long and liquid time. Only when I touched her clitoris did she explode with lust. Otherwise, she was soft and malleable like a flannel robe encompassing me. When she reached orgasm it was a quiet whimper and tears.

The sun had fallen into the dust of the Panhandle. It became a long Texas evening! Several times they told me that they had to go home. I diverted their attention with new sexual positions and games before they finally insisted.

I watched them dress slowly. They were not ready to leave. They drove off down the dirt road after promising to come back for me in the morning to take me to the highway heading south.

In the middle of the night, Betty Sue drove back and snuck into grandma's bed. I pinned her to the mattress for the next few hours. She told me not to tell Mary Lou.

In the morning they both came back to pick me up before going to school. I invited them in. Against their half-hearted objections I began to remove their clothing.

We were soon fucking again. At one point I placed Mary Lou, who was the smallest, on top of Betty Sue, both facing up toward me. I got between their outstretched legs and began screwing them both at the same time. I would enter one, then the other, then the other, and then the other. Faster and faster, in and out, in and out until I was fucking them both together.

And at that moment, with all the hot, moist breathing, the wallpaper on the ceiling lost its holding glue and started peeling off down around us. They both screamed, and we all laughing together. Our damp breath had dissolved the ancient glue holding the paper. After our mirth and brushing aside the wallpaper, we continued a variety of other exercises. But my personal favorite was screwing one and eating the other. Oh what beautiful sounds this produced.

After almost two hours of demonstrating all twelve sexual positions on the Zodiac poster, they were finally able to impress upon me the urgency of leaving. They were already late for school and getting later. Soon the town would be sending out a posse to look for them.

I finally gave in. This time they dressed quickly. I could have kept their underpants if I were a pervert.

Grandma's farm was just off the old road that bypassed town. We drove south toward the main highway leading to Houston and Galveston. I sat between them with my hands roaming up and down the inside of their smooth, soft legs. We joked and laughed a lot. Several times I had to bend down to hide from passing cars driven by their lifelong friends. Our fun enticed them to drive ten more miles down the highway and further from the lynch mob that was sure to be on my trail.

When they finally let me out to turn around and return to their little town and little lives, I said "Don't pick up any strangers now!" As they drove off, I left them laughing and crying.

Back to reality.

The girl I was going to see in Galveston had been a hitchhiker in California that I picked up. We made love for three days, and I showed her around Monterey and Big Sur, as ever the tour guide and Chamber of Commerce member.

CHAPTER 139

# The Hitchhiking Chronicles

For a time hitchhiking was a way of life in the 1960s and 70s. It was not just a mode of transportation. It was a form of amusement and therapy, and it verged on becoming a new religion. The dream of being treated nicely by perfect strangers was a hippie hope. Treating perfect strangers with love and respect was a hippie devotion.

I traveled by thumb across the USA twice, up and down California and Oregon many times, in England, Scandinavia, France, Italy and Australia. Some of these adventures are related in this book.

It is hard to describe an emotion in words. It is harder still to describe a spiritual revelation. Hitchhiking was a revelation and a revolution. Breaking down barriers, giving in to curiosity, allowing others to see some of your most intimate moments. That was what it was like to be the driver or the rider in a hitchhiking experience.

We weren't all capable or able to do this, and that is why some people stayed at home and others passed me by as I stood there with my thumb out.

There are those who stay at home not knowing why they do, and there are those who travel not knowing why. But in the hippie era, we stayed or went because we wanted to.

We humans don't have all that much self-confidence. We have been the hunted for much of our history, and now that we are the top predator, we must stop being so defensive!

As the cartoon character Pogo said, "We have met the enemy and he is us."

We can start the conversation at any point, but the truth is the truth. We humans have fucked it up so far. Mankind has had some high points. Democracy was one. Humility was another.

What more can arrogance and violence get us when compared to peace, tranquility, camaraderie and understanding? Hitchhiking was a way to break down our differences and get to know people we would otherwise never meet.

I had people stop and pick me up who would come right out and say, "I don't know why I picked you up. I don't pick up hippies, but you seemed OK." And we became friends in transit. If not friends, at least we learned tolerance from each other.

Getting out and meeting people is the most exciting and stimulating thing a "human" person can do! We are a social animal, perhaps the most social animal. We need to commune to succeed and to evolve. Why would we learn to speak if we were not trying to communicate?

For a short period of time in the 20th century, 1965 to 1975, people gave a ride and took a ride for free from someone that they did not know. It was all very innocent and bucolic until a small number of bigoted, sick, sexual deviates destroyed hitchhiking by preying on female hitchhikers. May they rot in hell

CHAPTER 140

# My Body

As a child I was never strong, tall or burly, but I was adventurous. I climbed the tallest tree, the highest hill or most interesting conversation. As a teenager, I was more of a dancer than football player. I was quick at short distances, and had exceptional hand/eye coordination. I won all the hand-slapping contests, and I can still drop a full glass from shoulder height and catch it before it hits the floor.

None of this is an ego trip. I just want you to know that I know what I'm talking about, so you will listen closely with intent to learn.

I would have made a great shortstop, but I was never committed to competitive sports. As a young man I was a very good volleyball player for my size, and an excellent body surfer in Manhattan Beach from 1960 to 1972. I invented upside down body surfing, by accident, by the way. I body surfed Waimea Bay several days as the only haole in the waves. I have shredded in Australia, France, Mexico, and up and down the coast of California. I was and still am an avid bicycle rider and I have ridden on five continents for distances and for days. I have legs and calves that draw comments wherever I expose them. I believe they were created in my youth on the hills of San Francisco.

One of my hand constructed, hand painted, parts bicycles. A descendent of the around-the-world bike that I took to Hawaii, Japan, Australia, and Greece, where I left it as a gift to a girlfriend. Painted in multi-colored abstract designs and with one (the front) brake, so no one would steal it. These bikes were stolen only once, and I found it a short way off, wrecked but easily fixed at the bottom of a steep hill with blood on the pavement.

I have worked with my hands and arms all my life, and for most of my adulthood have been a strong man in the room. Yet, I abhor sculpted muscles or lifting weights, and I am definitely an anti-macho man.

To begin with in my peer group at the time, an overly muscled body was considered "gay." And during that era most body builders were gay. It was narcissism, and it was not cool. Even if the guy weren't gay, he was definitely weird. Looking at Schwarzenegger and his aberrant sexual behavior now, we realize that we were right.

Surfers were never musclebound. They were strong and fit just like volleyball players. Most standout athletes were muscular, but not to the point of ego. Later *Baywatch* set a standard that wasn't achievable or realistic, and that is why I couldn't watch it when it came out.

This fixation with visual value is out of sync with reality. Beauty is only skin deep. And if you get involved with somebody who is self-absorbed, then you might try to hook up with someone because of their soul, not for their body, next time. If you like them below the skin, your relationship will have a better chance at life!

Clothing, hair, makeup--they are all advertising for something that may or may not be underneath that veneer. Lying about oneself often indicates insecurity.

Proclaiming to be what you are not, and self-promoting what you are, both fall into the same, sad, insecure package.

Hippies were seldom bodybuilders or musclebound. We were to a large extent active and fit. Some hippies were proud of their hair or beard, but that was just a statement of freedom and rebellion. No hippie said, "Hey, let me take my shirt off so you will want to make love with me." We used our minds to seduce most often.

I have been very fortunate in the body I was dealt. I was never judged gorgeous, but my looks have never disqualified me with anyone. Even after I lost the hair on the top of my head, I never experienced any obvious rejection, and my own attitude was always to act as if I were the most desirable man in the room

Even if I were to be rejected for my baldness, my whiteness or my credit rating, I would not care, because I do not care to be with someone who doesn't want to be with me.

The most important issue with my body is its general health, and with that I have been very fortunate. I know you can live a good and pure life and still die young of some random illness. Who knows who or what chooses who is to die?

Emotional diseases kill more people than consumption. Debauchery can often be the physical reason for a person's death, but it is most often not the real cause. Depression kills almost as many people as heart disease! Self-hate opens the door for mental illness, giving up and suicide. Conversely, self satisfaction and strength of character give back the will to live.

No one has both a perfect mind and a perfect body! We have these in various degrees of good or bad. We are successful in life if we can use the right one at the right time. And then there are the few people who prosper against all odds.

In the 1960s and '70s most women didn't care about your six-pack. They were more interested in your mind, not your body! We guys during that era didn't care that much about what she looked like in clothing, but what she felt like in the dark.

As a man grows older and begins to gain weight in the midsection, as most men will do, women, do not despair. Do not create a physiological disaster by hounding him about it. Love him, or leave him, or help him trim down.

Women, considering an older man, look at the legs, the shoulders and the hands. Those are the most valuable parts of a man's body! Most men will say, and many women will agree, that for lovemaking, a man's penis is the most important! But don't forget the hands, his tongue, shoulders and legs in the physical part of lovemaking. Sure, if the belly is too big, lovemaking skills can be hampered, but a normal amount of male midsection expansion, just as male pattern baldness, has no negative effect on carnal abilities.

*"Self-confidence, without the wisdom to temper it, is Russian roulette!"*
DG

*"And as far as life is concerned, much of it is luck. So if you are arrogant with pride, just know that today was your lucky day. Tomorrow may be the shits"*
Mr. California

CHAPTER 141

# Computer Sex And Other Deviations

I include a chapter about computers in this book about sex and human relations because I think that the Internet, the computer and social networks are an extreme danger to real sex, sincere love and rational human relationships. 3/27/14

**Computer**: A device that takes human information and puts it into an organized human observation. Only two things hamper the computer's deity: The sporadic tendency of "electric" power and the mistakes, ignorance and stupidity of those who use it. Stupid in, stupid out!

**Facebitching**: Facebook confrontations between one or more people or one person against the system.

**Facebook**: A binary system of social networking that tends to make three-dimensional humans into two-dimensional, inanimate objects with egotistical tendencies.

**Geek**: A person who is considered socially inept or inappropriate, computer aware, yet socially inept.

**Sensory Overload**: Sensory overload is what the computer does to us that stops our thinking process. It gives us so much information that our brain cannot process it without reaching gridlock. It has not yet been recognized as the negative force that it is or analyzed for the damage it is doing to our youth and likewise to our society.

**Social Network**: A path or device for communication of social feelings and facts. The computer Social Network as it is today is neither fact nor feelings. Recently a much-heralded movie was produced called "The Social Network." What a load of bollocks. The term "Social Network" could be the first great oxymoron of the 21th Century. There is nothing since before the invention of the printing press that has separated people more than the computer.

I'd love to continue with this dictionary of computer terms, but it is a prosaic punchline. Computers are the dehumanization of humankind. Sure, we will be well-entertained while we punch the keys and watch the screen to our extinction.

In my estimation E-communication could be the end of society as we know it. It is like the nuclear war threat hanging over us again, only this time it is a weapon that will not necessarily kill you outright, but will kill your creativity, spirit and time.

The vision of where it is taking us is not a pretty sight. Have you read any science fiction? Whole books, trilogies, and series of books have been written about the future disconnect between people created by technology.

The only area I can see that could be expedited by social networking is matchmaking. To me, anything that brings people together is good for humankind. But web dating has already proven to be a very sharp, double-edged sword.

First, never trust what a person writes or says about themselves unless you are looking into their eyes. Second, you must know a person's mind and body for it to be a successful conventional love affair. If you have something else in mind, then I guess cyber sex and literary affection are what you need.

From what I can see to this point in time (6/22/14), on-line dating has created far more travesty and tragedy than it has produced true romance. Of course, it is flawed by that human factor, and any mechanism that enhances a person's ability to anonymously stalk, deceive and seduce is just multiplying that person's character flaws and making them more dangerous.

Liberal intellectuals don't want to be the bearer of bad news nor the wet blanket on your parade. We would rather use positive enticement and encouragement, but if mankind is going to ignore all common sense, some chastisement and rational warnings are necessary. We don't want to stifle technology, but we want our technology to be used for positive, life-giving, and society-enriching purposes, not to hide our own flaws, steal money or seduce adolescents.

We humans need to look behind ourselves from time to time in order to check on our progress and see if we are heading in the right direction.

You have heard the quote, "Those who do not pay attention to history are destined to repeat it." Documenting our mistakes and our success is history's job. If we ignore this education, then we are fools.

A small number of people study humanity's mistakes in order to take advantage of them, but the majority of us have a more rational use for history, and that is to learn to create a better world for all of us in the future.

The computer takes our minds off those things that are so much more important. Hiding behind a computer monitor will not solve your own flaws or the flaws of our society; it will exacerbate them.

Anonymity cannot create love, friendship, morality and honor. If you are hiding, then you have something to hide that would eventually turn other people off. Network socializing hides your flaws, but it also hides what makes you an individual someone could love as a special person.

In the world of electronic anonymity, it is so easy to become immoral and dishonest. A person with a weak ego and low morality will generally take advantage of others if he or she thinks they are insulated and won't being caught. Rules, oversight and transparency strengthen man's moral and social correctness and sensitivity

I predict that the personal computer will someday be recognized as possessing the same dangers to mankind as do gun powder, nuclear fusion and fossil fuels. Someday the computer will be known to be as deadly to mankind as radioactivity, guns and global warming.

Don't count on technology to answer all your needs. A blackout or computer virus can make you impotent, and unimportant as well.

Talking used to be the way to communicate personally, then letters were personal, then the phone was personal, and even email could be personal! But Facebook, texts, tweets and blogs are definitely not personal, and so they make it easier for people to become more deceitful and secretive.

And now what? Should we go back to talking?

The computer industry was so lucrative that venture capitalists took it over. The web became a business, and that is a shame because it could have been such a boon to mankind's clarity of purpose and search for the truth. It is harder to lie when you are face to face and your words are formed by the color and texture of your voice

The Computer 5/20/2020: The computer is still wasting more

time than it is saving. Even with the entertainment factor, that is not a good trade-off.

It looks as though man has found another tool and "labor-saving device" that is going to take us quite a few decades to figure out. The entertainment qualities of computers are established by this time, as indicated by the number of folks gaming and watching cats chasing lights and dogs chasing tails. But entertainment isn't always good for humankind. Sometimes it diverts our attention from the truly important things, like survival and companionship. As of right now, if we don't figure out the positive uses of the computer, then it will serve only to bring us to our destruction faster than if we had not discovered it!

Contrary to all the hype about the social network, the computer is pushing people away from one another, not closer. Computer daters are lying to you. Catfishers are trying to get their jollies off by posting pictures of themselves that are the inaccurate age, gender or race, and stringing you on.

Back in the 1990s I saw marriages break up because the husbands wouldn't leave their offices, their computers and the new programs to learn. Women lost their families to on-line romances that they never consummated, with people they never met.

## CHAPTER 142

# Profanity Is For Pussies

Profanity is an interesting study! People usually use profanity because they are insecure and want to gain attention.

There are two more or less rational ways to use profanity:

1. To disgust, embarrass or make other people uncomfortable.

2. To get attention in order to emphasize what you think is an important issue.

Men, and sometimes women, use profanity because they don't really have anything intelligent to say. Profanity is for people who are really not very strong but want other people to think they are. If you can't start or finish a sentence without a cuss word, you are probably weak emotionally and educationally. You are a pussy!

CHAPTER 143

# Stalking and Sexual Harassment

This could be two chapters taking up 20 pages each, but I will condense. Even so, I am not sure if the perpetrators of these crimes could understand how smarmy they are, because these activities are forms of insanity! My hope is that our society will make these activities so anti-human that they will stop happening. A stalker is someone who thinks they are more important to someone else than they actually are! If this is too much for you, then maybe you should become celibate.

Sexual harassment is the activity of a person who is so lame that they don't know they are being un-cool and are a reject-bug on the windshield of life.

"Maybe" does not mean "yes." A smile does not mean yes! You must earn sexual favors from a woman, and that means you have to learn what each woman's sensibilities are. Some women like being whistled at, bumped into in the hallway, called stupid names, or touched every chance you get, but most women don't like these harassing activities. You must at least be smart or aware enough to know when a woman likes something or not.

Following or "stalking" can be very creepy to a woman, and it automatically disqualifies you. Read the signs early, or you may never regain the opportunity. And if a woman actually says, "stop bothering me," give up, because it is already too late.

At that point, change your tactics by using "no new tactics." Just stop! Smile, be nice, don't send them notes or put things on their desk. More or less ignore them unless it is part of your job or they come to you. If there is a chance for you, doing nothing is your only chance. Maybe if you act naturally they will see something in you, and then they may, I say may, initiate something themselves. But don't expect it. Move on; don't put all your eggs in one basket. The weight of the eggs will break those eggs underneath. Besides, there are many hens in the barnyard. Maybe one of them may find your oppression mildly interesting!

And don't get your ego bruised. Self-pity and negative personality traits are the biggest turnoff to a woman. Smile and move on, or go directly into the creepy guy jail!

A catfisher is a person who lies to people on social networks. They are a social media stalker. Catfishing is on the extreme sick list! If you are a catfisher, look at yourself in the mirror, and no matter what you see, just call yourself a sick, insecure, stupid bastard!

Lying to people on social media is the wimp activity of all wimp activities. So you are ashamed of yourself. That is too bad, and I feel sorry for you, but you are definitely not going to improve your value by stealing emotions from other people.

To create affection in others toward yourself, which you are not able or willing to consummate, is a waste of good love, and also it only proves that you are impotent and really screwed up.

So, catfisher, how does it feel to be a minus person? So seek help or kill yourself.

## CHAPTER 144

# Sexual Etiquette

*"A line of B.S. must be humorous if it is to succeed.*
*If you give the impression that you don't take your own bull*
*shit too seriously,*
*she may cut you some slack."*
Mr. California

Guys, there are things you should not do or never say to your wife or lover early in your relationship, if you wish that relationship to be long, pleasant and sexually successful. You should instinctively know these things, but the macho advertising industry has made most men sensitivity deprived.

Don't compare her sexual performance to anybody else. That is a can of worms, whether you think it is a compliment or not!

Don't ever mention any negativity about any part of her body.

Don't blow farting noises on her bellybutton.

Don't insist on her performing any act if she shows distaste, by saying, "Yuck" or "Go stick it in the wall" or "Is that the kind of girl you've been with?"

Be prepared to say, "Sorry, that was a slip of the tongue, 'or whatever'."

Don't buy her anything crotchless. Don't buy too small a bra or panties too large. As a matter of fact, only give her gift certificates from *Vitoria's Secrets* or any lingerie store.

Early in your sex life, sometimes, try to wait for her to orgasm first.

She is who she is, and you should love her for that. Yet, if you wish to improve your love for her by making your relationship better and you wish to suggest an improvement in her "performance," be loving and diplomatic! My suggestion is that you speak to her as you would have her speak unto you!

A female, girl, woman has the same emotional levels as you do, though she may exhibit them differently than you, so don't say something to them that would embarrass you, yourself, frighten you, make you mad or make you leave.

These are deep romantic secrets, but if you use them just for momentary satisfaction, then you are a scab!

*"We still don't know about Happily Ever After. We may have seen people who have, it seems, attained it, at least at the date of this publication, but we are still not sure that it exists. There are no percentage figures on its possibility or probability, but it is reported to be out there, and we will continue to pursue it!"*
DG

*"The love you take is equal to the love you make!"*
The Beatles

*"This means if you want love, you must love!"*DG

## CHAPTER 145

# Fantasies and Fantasy

*"Fantasy, if it becomes an obsession, can destroy you. If you get too good at it, it will make you dissatisfied with the real thing."*
Dudley Griffin, 10.30.12

Most fantasies should be kept as fantasy. They should never make it into reality. In many cases the reality of a fantasy is destructive, the actual acts are immoral, sometimes deadly, and they can ruin your life and the lives of others. Stick with sex that is not perverse, but never ignore nor deny Love that you desire.

Desire and fantasy are two different things. Desire is something that is realistically and safely achievable. Fantasy is usually unrealistic and often too dangerous for you to make into a reality.

Yet fantasy, kept as fantasy, is a harmless and almost necessary part of our lives. We cannot stop our minds from thinking these things, and we would be hypocritical if we said we didn't think them. We needn't be ashamed of these thoughts because everyone has them, but they are only "what if," and they should stay there in our minds.

Like most of us I have balanced on the edge between fantasy and reality for all of my life. Yet I have teetered, but never fallen, either way as many others have! Does that sound convincing?

What are you searching for, a fantasy or a reality? Fantasies are easy to construct, but hard to live. Face up, man up, this is your life, this is what has been dealt you. Do something with what you have, or don't do anything. Just don't be a hypocrite. Maybe you care if you don't excel in this world, but the world does not care. All it requires of you is that you do not do more damage than you do good!

*"Dude, some fantasies are best left unfulfilled. Often if they do come true they can put you in jail or at the wrong end of a divorce."*
Dudley Griffin, 12.24.13

There is so much more to love than we can ever fantasize. If we have weakness or fear, love can heal even those. Fantasizing can make you happy for awhile, but then you go back to that loneliness or feeling of worthlessness, but a real live companion will fill in most of the holes in your life.

Never mind the The Mother Fixation: Oedipus, we men have so many more fantasies and fixations about women than that. The Whore/Virgin fantasy. The Someone Else's Wife complexity. The Two-woman fantasy. The Mile-High Club. The Young Girl fantasy, which is extremely harmful if you make it reality. The bathroom or closet, on-the-table or under-the-table fantasy, these can become reality without being too dangerous, but watch out for grandma's valuable tea cups or falling into the toilet bowl.

There is no need for embarrassment in your fantasies; they are only in your own mind. There is no need for beauty in your fantasies, for they are only in your mind, and it creates what it wants. There is no need for status in your fantasies. They are only in your mind, and you can create whatever persona or social status you need for yourself.

The Ones Who Got Away, Ran Away, Or, Flat Out, Didn't Want Anything To Do With You. The ones who got away I now use as fantasies. I feel no regrets or bad feelings for the girls who rejected me or slipped through my fingers. I think of them fondly and with visions of how pleasant it would have been.

*"Dude, believe me, the expectation and fantasies of sex are often more long lasting and valuable than the actual act. Memories of the event do not last and are clouded by desire for the next encounter. That is Mother Nature's way to make sure that you do it again."* DG 12/24/13

My primary fantasies (four) are all iconic male desires and are also based on some of my own previous encounters.

1. A young lover. Virgins are most men's fantasy. You are their first. No   man has been there before. They are reliant on your strength and knowledge.

2.   Multiple-partner sex.  To have two women intent on your pleasure.

3.  The reluctant wife or committed woman. To win the affection of a woman away from another man.

4. The lesbian lover. To "turn" a lesbian away from women to wanting you.

The fallacies of fantasies becoming reality.

Virgin lovers do not make you a man. The real test of a man is being chosen by a woman because of her previous experiences with other men.

Having previous relationships should never make a mate jealous. The last man to live with a woman is the winner; the last woman to live with a man is the winner of the contest for mating.

Multiple-partner sex is very difficult to perform without jealousies arising. To have two women intent on your pleasure, you must treat them both equally or as one lover.

Making love to a reluctant wife or an otherwise committed woman who is willing to give sex to you is not the person you will have a good history with. You are opening yourself up to a myriad of problems.

A fantasy is allowing yourself to do with impunity in your mind what you should or could never actually do. A fantasy is doing today in your mind what you didn't do yesterday, and because it is only in your mind, you don't have to pay the consequences. Fantasy is not necessarily an undone desire nor an accomplished desire. Fantasy can be a destination.

*"So, I am making love with Jacqueline Bisset, our arms and legs and genitals entwined. And then I open my eyes to find that it is only Marilyn, my girlfriend. Well, the climax and my lust for Marylyn was diminished by the experience, and she and I broke up the next week, and I went off looking for Jacqueline."*
Mr. California

It is obvious to most of you, I hope, that it is unhealthy and destructive to fantasize about another person while making love with your steady mate! Humans are so fickle that we are always looking for something better, or something over the next thrill. Well that does not work within a true loving relationship.

No one can ever match up to your fantasy lover. You don't want to call your partner by another name while making love. Don't lose a lover overnight because you are thinking of someone else, who may not even reach your expectation if you found them.

"The grass is always greener elsewhere" is a farce. Many, many, many people have ruined their lives chasing fantasies.

Another fantasy mistake is fantasizing about someone who is too close at hand. The first possible negative aspect of that is you might try to make the fantasy reality and therefore get into an embarrassing situation. Also, don't fantasize on someone you are already with or are expecting to have a relationship with. Unfulfilled expectations can kill a relationship! The sex is not necessarily better on the other side of the hill.

A man should never have preferences as to body type, hair color, or religion. It should always be the inner person that you love. Yet a casual relationship might sometimes have different prerequisites. I did have a preference in women for lovemaking, and that was Jewish girls.

Politically incorrect as this might be, I liked Jewish princesses! That term may mean different things to me than to you, so I will define my feelings. A Jewish girl is usually the underdog in their family, being that male sons are doted over. A Jewish daughter must be aggressive to make her way. Jewish girls, then, were usually a little more sexually aggressive than their sisters of other ethnicity or religions around the world. Some people think aggression and self-indulgence are the same. I don't necessarily agree.

Aggression was not the turn-on. It was the fact that they seemed to know what sex was all about, and they were not afraid of it. Most Jewish girls were not really aggressive as much as realistic. They didn't worry about what their families would think, nor what the neighbor would think. They seemed to know that sex is a rational and acceptable part of life. I believe they may have received this through their DNA, coming originally from one of the parts of the world with the highest child mortality rates. Also, in the Hasidic cultures rape or sexual violence was not a major occurrence because of moral standings.

In many ancient cultures stealing a girl and forcing sex was the way to get a wife. Often, it was a violent and unwanted outcome. I don't believe the tribes of Israel generally acted in this way. Well, am I getting too pedantic?

If I were to construct my fantasy woman, I would end up with four basic outlines. 1. New York or Southern California Jewish princess. 2. Southern California blonde beach girl. 3. Hispanic/NativeMesoAmerican/European. 4. Asian/African.

But the truth is, for me, none of the physical or ethnic types was ever any more appealing than any other. I was always open to the moment, and to whoever came along. Most people at the right time and for a span of time, can be appealing, attractive, or even desirable.

One of my favorite Hispanic/European women is Joan Baez. I met "Joanie" three times, and have been at least three of her concerts. She was a fantasy for many young men in 1960s and 70s.

My first meeting with Joanie was in Big Sur in the 1950s. She was sitting on a tree stump singing to a bunch of us kids. She was 14 or 16 and I was 11 or 13.

I do remember another concert. It was held in the Monterey Peninsula College football stadium. She was recording her performance, and she sang an a cappella *Amazing Grace* that made us all cry. It may be the recoding we have all heard on one of her albums.

The next time I saw her was at Tillie Gort's Coffee House in Pacific Grove, California in the mid 1970s. Joan would come in from time to time when she was in town. She was sitting with a young man, and I respectfully approached and commended her on her rendition of a Jackson Browne song that she had recently recorded. Her comment was, "Thank you. Isn't he a great new musician. We are all very impressed with him."

My next communication with Joan Baez was in 2002-3 when Bush and Cheney were going to invade Iraq looking for non-existing WMDs. It was one of the largest public demonstrations for or against anything in the history of mankind.

My wife Joan and I went by bus with the Monterey Peace Coalition up to march in San Francisco. It was a glorious day of peace, camaraderie and wonderful, insightful signs and banners promoting anti-imperialism and exposing the crimes of our government and corporations. There were demonstrations all over the US and the world against Bush's planned war.

As we were waiting for the bus to pick us up afterwards, I looked across the street and saw Joan Baez and a few of her friends coming to their parked car. I recognized her and told my friends, I then whistled to her and we all waved and we said, "Thank you Joanie. We love you," and she waved back. She had been one of the speakers in front of the city hall that day.

After a few minutes I realized that Joan was having a problem starting her car. The battery was dead. She got out of her car opened the trunk and took out her jumper cables. I went across to help.

Talking to her, I realized I would have to flag down a passer-by to jump start her car. I stopped a young couple in a truck, and they did the job. I still to this day wonder if they knew who they were rescuing.

I then asked politely if I could take a photograph of her. I have that prized photo of Joan Baez at the trunk of her Mercedes with her jumper cables, wearing a tee shirt that reads, "Fuck George W. Bush And The Supreme Court He Rode In On." I love that girl.

Joan and her jumper cables

My Jewish fantasy and reality is well documented in this book already. Half of my fantasies are based 25% on visual and 75% personality and the other half is based on 75% visual and 25% personality. If you can figure that out, you are one up on me.

My Asian/ African fantasy is not well defined, but it is mostly based on a visual look I had in my head. I didn't really have a strong Asian woman fantasy, but I acquired one on a trip I took through China.

This Asian fantasy was my one foray. Yes, Asian girl fantasies are prevalent in White Male society. Some "gui jing, gwailou" will only date or marry Asian girls. That is because of a perceived subservience that is attributed to Asian women. I am definitely not attracted to any women for that reason, nor do I believe the characterization is true. I'm non-committal and ambiguous, but I will tell you that I do not prefer subservient women or men, or people for that matter!

**Ming, my fantasy**

The circumstances of my meeting Ming were exactly as I write here. Only much later did the fantasy sex occur to me.

1984, I was in Guilin, China, and found the only hotel that would accommodate un-escorted American tourists. I settled into my hotel room for a night of watching television. After months of traveling around the world with little or no media, I was looking forward to it. Unlike many places I had stayed in China, this upscale hotel had a TV. The number of channels was limited, but it was all new stuff, and at least one channel was in English.

I watched a farm production report, lots of propaganda parades, and a program on electrical generation. I think it was all in Chinese. I also saw a Chinese circus, with young girls contorting their bodies while balancing glasses of wine on their heads, feet and hands.

Early in the evening a Chinese maid knocked on my door and came in to see if she could help me in any way. Our common language was mostly hand signals.

I told her "no" I didn't need anything, I was doing fine with my Tsing Tao beer and television and released her from any obligations. She was beautiful, as precious as a porcelain Ming vase. This was more service than I had seen in quite a while and better accommodations than my traveling budget usually allowed.

Of course, at that time China was trying to attract tourism. Foreigners were allowed to visit only 25 or 30 cities, and there were very few "authorized" hotels where tourists could stay. During most of my trip through China, I slept on trains or in train stations. In this hotel I had TV, a nice double bed, not too lumpy, a ceiling fan, and the bathroom was only a quarter mile down the hall.

It was 1984, and U.S. President Ronald Reagan was also visiting China at the same time I was there. I assume that the president's accommodations were at least as opulent as mine.

I was intrigued by the cultural differences between America and China. Ronald "Rayguns" was trying to get the Chinese people to stop eating dogs and spitting on the streets.

The second time the China doll came into my room, she brought more towels. In the humid heat I was sitting on the bed wearing nothing but my walking shorts.

Watching TV in another language is a strange experience in frustration and discovery. If you really concentrate, it is possible to understand most of what is going on, and it's interesting to note how much of the visual media is purely visual and therefore translates into all languages.

To many English speakers, the Chinese language is ugly or awkward. To me it is like singing and laughing at the same time.

The third time the maid came into my room, she offered to turn down my bed sheets. I still didn't get the picture, and I don't think I did for a few months or years after that. I am really a very trusting person. I try not to read anything into what someone does unless the chemistry tells me otherwise.


**Here the fantasy starts**

I had some extra money, and the experience would have been a blast. Conducting a business transaction and having sex in sign language. Also, did I tell you she was very beautiful?

But then I began to wonder if it was entrapment. I have always been careful not to run afoul of the laws of any country where I traveled, and this was Communist China. I wondered if this form of capitalism was mentioned or excluded from the list of transgressions in Mao's Little Red Book. I have tried to read it several times.

First, I must inform you that I have never in my life hired a prostitute. I have never had a lap dance, unless it was free of charge, nor have I seen more than a couple of "girlie" shows. That's me, can't help it, all of my sex has been free, consensual and non-voyeuristic. That's the way I liked it. I wanted my lover to want to be with me and to really want to make love with me.

When the Chinese porcelain doll slipped back into my room for the third time and gestured to me that she would be willing to turn down my sheets, it finally sunk into my naive, thick skull. She was offering some form of sexual favor. All the scenarios and repercussions sped through my brain in one or two moments as I looked back pleasantly at this young girl's quizzical face.

What made me so dense in the first place was that I never consider prostitution when looking at a woman. And I never took it for granted that a woman who was nice to me automatically wanted to get into my pants, especially if it was her job to be nice to me.

I considered the possibility that this all might be a communist plot to entrap the arrogant capitalist, arrest me and throw me in jail for the rest of my miserable life. Then I realized I shouldn't worry, the President of my country, The United States of America, was in China also at the same time and would, of course, intercede on my behalf, thus effecting my release. Not!

Perhaps, by chance, this girl just wanted to have sex? Or was she trying to find a husband who would take her to America, away from the poverty of China? Would I embarrass her or enrage her by offering money?

What I did know was that if I proceeded slowly and carefully, following my instincts, I could most likely determine whether the girl was a plant, wanted money, a husband, or just liked my blue eyes and broad shoulders.

She was still waiting. I smiled at her and crooked my finger, motioning her to come closer to me. I was wearing only my walking shorts remember, sitting on the end of the bed watching TV when she came in. She smiled with a questioning frown and took one tentative step. This told me several things. She was not a provocateur. She most likely was not just horny or looking for a husband, but she still might be seeking money for favors.

I then reached into my pocket, pulled out my money clip and placed it on the bed. Ming looked at the money. She did not smile. She hesitated for several seconds and then took two steps forward placing herself almost within arms reach. This told me something else. She was willing to do something for the money, but she was new to this. Or she was a government agent waiting for me to incriminate myself.

Still sitting on the edge of the bed, I motioned her closer. Ming made the last step and then knelt down on the floor between my legs. But she did not reach for the money and this told me the last two things I wanted to know. Ming was not a communist spy, and the night was going to be wonderful.

She placed her hands on my knees. My heart rate jumped twenty points.

Ming was truly beautiful! Her hair, as black and shining as a show horse, was tied in a tail behind. Her features were framed by a face, both Chinese and Caucasian.

Her eyes were slanted, yet open, and crystal clear, dark green with golden brown flecks. Her long, thick lashes flipped up like a frisky house cat's. They fluttered as she spoke with her eyes. Her brows were peaked high and thick, tapering to thin, perfect proportion.

Her nose was broad, yet with familiar dimension, and turned up slightly showing her nostrils. She possessed a rich, full mouth with a smile turned downward, yet in anticipation of happiness. Peeking through unsure lips were perfect teeth. The overbite was there, yet only served to entice. She had dimples that deepened with each expression.

Her body was thin, but landscaped with curves, and a waist so small she looked pubescent until you saw her breasts. Have you ever noticed how a woman with a really breathtaking form usually has breasts that spread across her whole torso? Together, they are actually wider than her body and bulge provocatively out on either side. She is usually so perfectly thin that when you hug her, your arms reach all the way around, and your hands inadvertently encounter those breasts as they spread wide from your hug.

As I had watched her leave twice before, I observed the roundness of her bottom pressed lightly against the fabric of her pants. The circle is a perfect shape when illustrated in the human body. She was perfect in her roundness!

She appeared to be between 18 and 22 years old, but acted much younger from her lack of experience, possibly due to a childhood on a farm in the country. She seemed to be playing everything by ear.

Her skin was like white Ming Dynasty porcelain, her clothing was Ming blue. She was slightly tall for Chinese, her neck long and sleek, matching the perfect proportions of the rest of her body that I could see.

Her pantsuit was made, not of silk, but from some soft synthetic. It was the typical Mao style uniform worn by everyone in China at the time, who was at all official or in a service capacity.

The suit style and material also proved to me that she was not a phony prostitute whose job it was to entrap me. If she had been, she would have worn silk in a more Western style.

Ming began softly rubbing my legs. She looked into my eyes for confirmation. I smiled, and she sheepishly smiled back then looked down at her hands as they slowly moved up my thighs. Her hands were calloused, yet tender, the last indication of her amateur status and innocent sincerity.

When she reached my shorts, she began rubbing the mound that was already growing there. After only a few moments of this, she moved to my belt, unfastened it, and began unbuttoning my fly. Ming was a little surprised to find my penis right beneath the buttons, unclothed by underpants.

After all, I was a hippie! I didn't wear underwear. When Ming first encountered my erection, she measured it with her eyes and then tentatively stroked it a few times. I could not tell if it was strange to her, longer or larger than her experiences or expectations. She ran her hands over its length and then pulled my foreskin back and leaned delicately forward.

Holding the erection strait up with her two hands, she rose on her knees, solemnly bent at the waist, and touched the tip of it with a beautiful, pink tongue.

She was extremely feminine in her touch and movements. Like an empress testing the sweetness and bitterness of a persimmon, she ran her tongue and lips over my head-on. It soon became florid and sleek from the nectar of her mouth, and she slowly began sucking and moving in unison with my vocal appreciation.

I ran my hands over Ming's soft, black hair. I released her ponytail and began combing my fingers through its silky texture. She rocked back and forth, engulfing the full length of my erection within her mouth.

Ming knew the games to play with her tongue and teeth. She had at least done this before. She was quite good and very kind.

I began to get the impression that this was the sex she thought I was paying her for. But I could not just stop with fellatio, and it has never been my goal merely to ejaculate in someone's mouth.

After a few minutes Ming began to increase speed and intensity in order to bring me to orgasm. I let her proceed for a while, and I did enjoy it. And then I began slowing her down by guiding her head. She showed some confusion at this and eventually looked up at me with her big, round lash-framed eyes. I smiled down at her, pulled her head up and then brought us both up to standing.

She was really perplexed by this. And when I kissed her she was even more undone. She did not resist, and in a moment she closed her eyes and gave in to it. Within a few more moments, she began melting into my lips and soon was toying with my tongue.

My arms slipped around her tiny waist and my hands caressed her back. She placed her arms over my shoulders and was soon rubbing my neck, head and hair with appropriate affection.

We progressed like this for awhile, kissing more deeply by the moment, and exploring new places for our hands. I had kicked my shorts away, and I was standing naked in her arms.

I then began to reach up under Ming's shirt, touching the soft skin of her back. The feeling of my hand on her bare skin sent a shock through both of us, and she became more animated, pressing her body against mine.

Our tongues and hands explored more deeply. We began the slow advance toward more sensitive spots of our bodies. When I reached around her back and felt the side of her bulging breast, I caught my breath.

She was pressing herself against me, and I could feel fullness and firmness and excitement. She wore no brassiere. When I reached back around to the front of her and cupped an appropriately small but firm Asian breast in my hand, she whimpered and bit my lip. No blood flowed, but desire.

In a moment of fast moving fingers, I removed her blouse, and my mouth was suckling one breast as my hand massaged the other.

She reached down and began caressing my erection again. In a second my hand slipped into the waistband of her pants, down between her smooth belly and the hem of her underwear. Through her pubic hair between the lips of her vagina, my middle finger slipped deep inside her.

Ming voiced a sharp, breathless, quiet scream. She didn't resist, yet pulled her head back slightly, and opened her eyes wide and stared at me in disbelief. She then dove back at my mouth as her hand increased her vigorous coaxing of my erection toward its expectation.

I slipped my other hand inside and down the back of her pants to hold her wonderful, soft ass. With pressure from that hand I forced Ming's pelvis forward against my other hand and finger that slipped in and out of her vagina and over her clitoris. Within a moment Ming's knees buckled.

She was whimpering, sucking my tongue and manipulating my erection. We both began to slip toward the floor. And then, in a moment of physical strength and mental clarity, I lifted Ming off the floor and placed her in the middle of the bed.

I looked down at her for a moment. She was bare to the waist. Her full, well-shaped breasts were white as snowcapped mountains, each with a round, pink Buddha meditating on top. She lay there looking back at me, her arms askew on the bedspread beside her. Her pants were still on, her legs spread, one knee cocked up in an awkward nonchalance.

Her blouse and slippers were already abandoned on the floor. I reached out and began pulling her flimsy pants down by the legs. They slipped off easily with a little help from Ming as she arched her pelvis and raised her legs. The look on her face was surprise and bliss, as if she didn't know this would be so good.

I slipped up onto my knees next to her on the bed and hooked an index finger over the hem of her panties. They were cotton, white and virtuous. They must have been the height of feminine fashion in the 1950s. As I began to pull them down, Ming's eyes got bigger as she looked at my erection standing up, proud and awaiting.

Her panties came down easily, delicately, like a petal slipping from a flower.

She was gorgeous. No flaws, all smooth and pure. Her dark black pubic hair was the only interruption in an otherwise white expanse of porcelain.

I pulled the panties over delicate feet, and they joined her other clothing on the floor. I placed my two hands between her thighs and gently spread her legs. Slipping over her leg I sat back on my haunches between her outstretched feet.

Standing erect before her. I coaxed her legs wider and raised her knees slightly. Reaching out, I spread her labia even more and looked down at her. My fingers softly wandered over the fleshy start button, and Ming lifted her pelvis, rolled her eyes and began to whimper.

I ran one hand down between the petals and inserted my finger deep into her body. She gulped a breath, began to rock back and forth as I worked it slowly in and out of her. She was soon up on her feet and shoulders, arching her back into the devotion of my hands.

After a few moments I leaned forward and replaced my hand with my mouth on her clitoris. With one motion I sucked the sensitive fleshy button in and began circling it with a conscientious tongue. Ming exploded. I was grateful for the thick concrete walls.

The skin on the inside of a woman's labia around her clitoris is the smoothest surface on the face of the Earth. When it was lubricated by my saliva and her natural juices, it was a tongue's playground.

With my hands and tongue I made love with Ming's body for half an hour as she lifted toward her first orgasm, raising higher and higher toward overflow.

Ming crested the wave and began falling through the kaleidoscope of feelings, still reaching for every last bit of sex. I ran my tongue up her stomach, breast, neck and to her lips. Our bodies slipped together, lubricated by our sweat, and I entered her in the dance of eternity.

I dove deep, slowly and methodically, and it was almost too much for me to fathom. She was still hanging on to her orgasm, and she bounced on the end of my hard-on as I drove the feelings deeper into her body.

I was building faster and faster, and she accelerated with me as we rammed our bodies together. Within a few minutes of this crescendo, I had my first orgasm, and she was still there, and it was as if she had a second coming.

Ming and I did not disengage for the next three hours, and made love in every speed and position that we could devise. Most all were unique to her, and many were new for me.

Ming sang and laughed for me. She must have thought I had a better grasp of Chinese than I did. People who have never traveled often speak loudly thinking that will help you understand them. I understood her clearly and, but for the cement walls, our neighbors would have also.

In the middle of the night, Ming finally convinced me that she really had to leave, so I withdrew from her sore, satisfied body. It was a sweat-spent night.

Before she left the room, Ming tried to wash me out of her in the enamel water bowl as she squatted over it on the floor. She would not take any money. I was divided over this. I knew she needed whatever money she could get, but I wanted ours to be a love affair, not a business deal. So did she. We were both happy. (End of fantasy)

I never saw Ming again. But I made love with her sometimes in masturbation fantasies, which I developed throughout the years. This then was my fantasy.

When I left the hotel I thought I saw two men in bad suits watching me suspiciously, but then, I knew I had done nothing wrong.

## NYC 1972, not a fantasy

You know, as I do, that some lovers will step into, or bump into your life, and you slide together for a day or two, and you can't forget her for the rest of your life. I spent an active night with two graduating senior girls from The Chapin School, in a dark walk-in closet in The Plaza Hotel. I can't tell you that I remember the names or the moments of time together, but because of them I can trace every inch of the body of every woman in the world with my mind and my hands.

For many men, sex is a conquest, a violent adoration of their banal desire to reproduce. They usually do this reproduction ritual without consideration for their mates.

Most men "fall in love" on an average of twice a day. They lust about three times an hour. At this point in my life, I just have moments of good feelings and memories once in a while.

CHAPTER 146

# Men Behaving Badly

"Boys Will Be Boys!" That's the excuse for all man's bad behavior.

The drive, the power, the selfishness of man is natural. It is Mother Nature's drive to survive and procreate. But, it is man's obligation to temper this violence and use the brain, also given us by Mother Nature, to adapt to our environment in order to survive. But she forgot to give us the common sense to use our power appropriately to the world we live in. Most of us don't live in the barren desert and dangerous jungle anymore; we must learn to live in civilization and act civilized.

Selfishness is mankind's worst sin, and it will eventually, probably destroy us. Insecurity is what causes most people's selfishness, and then their ignorance causes the rest. If only we all knew that we must all be together to survive. Co-operation is our only chance for eternal life. We are all living eternally as long as mankind survives.

Male aggression is not always a male pathology. Sometimes we are just trying it out to see if it works. God help us and those around us if we decide it works for us. I've had my bad sides and times. They were usually from frustration. Then I learned that I am not a force of nature; I am nature.

*"Girls, I want to tell you that if you're making love with a guy and he's not paying attention to your needs, you should just slap him across the face and tell him to shape up."DG*

**Sex and Jokes**

If you are still joking about women and sex after the age of 30, you are retarded or you are hanging with a crowd who is dragging you back into a junior high school mentality.

What is funny, what is cruel or crude, what is immature, what is insincere and what is insecure?

There is no other aspect of human life that is more misunderstood by human beings than sex. There is no creative endeavor of human beings more misused than humor. There is no subject in humor more explored than human sexuality. There is no part of human life more misrepresented in humor than sex. Why is it that so many people decide they are going to make fun of things they know the least about?

Joking about sex is something you do only if you have not had enough of it. Because, believe me brothers, sex deserves more respect.

Only a good satirist can tell a respectable sexual joke. Good sex jokes are self-effacing, whimsical, and they never place blame or judgment on another. No shame!

Bad sex jokes bring shame to someone. Good sex jokes don't pass judgment, but they may leave it for each person's own God. Hypocrisy is one of a satirist's best messages in a sex joke!

Sex is not the subject of humor. It can be fun, hilarious, stimulating, and outrageous, but it is also very serious. Sex is important.

You can have fun with sex without ridiculing or making fun of or it. So stop it, grow up and live with it. Sex is here to stay. It is very serious and essential!

And making fun of women regarding sex is a stupid man's joke. You will respect them, or you will never know true love. It is not that they will turn from you, but that you will have never face them!

## No-Harm, No-Foul Rule

Women don't understand it, men live by it, the "no-harm, no-foul rule." This is not an attempt to justify it; this is an attempt to explain it.

Entitlement was not something men planned. We were born into it because we were at the top of the food chain. Our arrogance is a tradition. We have often thought we were in when we were out, and when we became out, we were often in.

"No harm, no foul" means: If I didn't kill someone or damage them, but only stole or cheated, then my moral standing is still OK. There is no foul, and therefore no sentence, and I can go on and do it again.

I know that "no harm, no foul" is another example of men using sports mentality and terminology to describe real-life situations and somehow make them acceptable.

But quotes like this fit into the sensibility of men. We need a way to justify, wiggle out. We are less moral than women; we don't think that deception is a sin. We also think that any aggression conducted within a game, by our definition, is acceptable. We believe that morality should not get in the way of our own personal game.

But the real dilemma that man has is the moral issue: Are we to be moral to God's laws or to Man's laws? Are we splitting philosophies and ideologies here?

## Pick-Up Lines

Don't be a prehistoric man. Never grab a girl and drag her with your hands or force her with your voice anywhere she doesn't want to go.

Always say, "would you like," not "I want you to!" Refrain from using words like, "Sit on my face," and never, never ask a girl what her bra size is!

Well, you get the idea. Many men use shit pick-up lines. I can't believe it. Most men actually think lines that would work on them as a man should also work on women.

There is no perfect pick-up line except maybe, "Do you want to go to bed with me?" That line is masculine, expedient, and a great time and money saver, but it is often met with rejection and sometimes with violence. P.S. I personally have never used that line.

All pick-up lines are subject to low success rates, just like all first meeting between boys and girls. My suggestion is sincerity; that is the best approach. Sincerity, humor and a bit of detachment.

Let's take the restaurant/waitress scenario: First, don't stare unless you are willing to back it up! And by back it up, I mean that you are willing to give her a good tip, talk politely, and ask her if she wants to make love with you? Always be bold, but with respect! Don't ask them where they came from unless you are really interested, or are prepared to find out that they actually own the restaurant.

As you may suspect, I believe all male bad behavior is based on his misdirected ego. I say misdirected in that it has not caught up with the world realities that we cannot fight each other as we did in the jungle 1,000 years ago or even in Europe in the 1940s, or now in the Middle East, and survive as a race!

I don't think the male ego is undernourished or undereducated, for that would make it more competitive for its self-knowledge.

An ego is too difficult a thing to sustain and to still remain human! As I have written before many times, the male ego is the most dangerous weapon on earth.

Most men judge themselves by their own perceived sexuality or portrayed, or presumed virility. Most women and other men judge a man by the virility he portrays.

Male ego, masculinity and the money game, are indulgences by those who fear they might only be regular people. It's all right to be a regular person, live your life, have children, and not kill anyone else, with a weapon or a fountain pen.

We need our ego to push us to accomplish our best, but it need not be used to pummel others into submission.

Compete only with yourself. Don't create enemies just to feel bigger and better. That only reveals your insecurity. And think of this: Enemies just reduce your own self-worth by creating negativity around you. Duh! Did I really have to write this down? Do you mean that people didn't already know this?

I know, I know, there are many people and many cultures who are still catching on to the benevolent intellectual male mentality or the 19th, 20th, and 21st Centuries. It will take some time, but please, not too long, or we will not survive as a race or maybe even as a planet!

The male ego is sometimes driven by needs, but most often driven by expectations of our family and society. The drive to be productive influences all men's nature. In many cases, if we did not have to prove ourselves to our father, wife, or society, we could truly be more productive. I'm not talking about the GDP. Being productive is necessary for survival of the species, but what kind of product is the morally correct one?

Never take advantage of a person who is weaker than yourself. I think God first said that. But what happened to this truth/law? This could actually be one of the commandments that were lost from the tablet.

Women as a rule, when sober, send messages. They don't grab your hair and drag you off. That's the man's presumed job!

Most women, unless they are very needy or drunk, don't talk

loudly at parties and restaurants so that everybody in the room can hear them, including the real needy guy with his face in a glass in the corner.

## I May Have A Shot

Many of us men have made the mistake of thinking she was a "slam dunk." But sometimes the message that a girl is giving is not the same message that we are reading or wanting to read. You can be a bulldozer, completely misunderstanding, or you can go slowly and listen to her heart.

> *A woman's heart. You may not think of such a thing.*
> *It may be mumbo jumbo to you,*
> *but if you get into a woman's heart,*
> *you have reached the center of the earth!*
> Mr. California

Some women are naive to the ways of the world. And that naiveté is a beautiful thing to be protected forever.

Many girls will look at you with affection that does not mean anything except friendship. You must recognize this form of female communication for what it is!

Many men see this warm and fuzzy as a sexual come-on. It is most often just being a nice person.

You, yes you, as a man, who has the power, must suppress your desires and wait for the real green light. It's not easy, and many fail.

The worst behavior that men display is stalking! It is not sexy to have someone following you in the dark or calling you in the middle of the night with suggestive comments. If you go to a restaurant just to watch someone, you are a stalker. If you follow, spy on or drink too much in the bar where they work, you are a stalker. If you don't walk up to them and say, "Hi, my name is Dudley, and I want to spend time with you." within the first three contrived meetings, then you are a stalker!

If she says "no" twice, and you keep asking, you are a stalker! And that makes you a dumb son of a bitch!

*"Sex isn't a desire as much as it is a hope. Marriage isn't a goal as much as a beginning. Alcohol isn't a crutch as much as a prosthetic! Money isn't a tool as much as it is a toy. Happiness isn't as much an achievement as an acceptance. Man's journey is all too often confused by his ego."*

DG

*"Never let your exuberance overcome your dignity."*

JBMc, 2010

*"The real measure of intelligence is knowing when to talk and when not to. The real measure of wisdom is knowing when to act and when not to."*

Mr. California

*"Everybody has their own level of ego and greed, and that is O.K. But when it begins to bleed over into other people's life and has negative effects, then it is a moral problem for society, the world and democratic governing."*

DG, 4.20.20

CHAPTER 147

# Interviewing For A Wife

*"You and I are Jesus and Mary. Mary is woman, man is Jesus. And that philosophy will get you into a lot of confusion and trouble"*

JOB, 1.18.07

I chased romance from 1955 until about 1984. At first, I didn't know that romance was my real goal. I was just a guy. Emotionally, I was in it for the nasty bits, but I was seeking more than just sex or vindication or even satisfaction.

I don't think I rationally knew what I was looking for most of that time. I am now more equipped to see myself as I was then. It is easer to look backward than forward with all the wind and dust blowing in your eyes.

550

In the mid-1980s I began discriminating, but I was still a hound dog, I didn't like being without a girl or woman close at hand. I didn't want to be alone. "Alone," that was the operative word.

I remember vividly an episode around 1983 when I called a girl to ask her to spend some time with me, and she declined. I was polite to her and chatted respectfully, but I beat the phone to death after she hung up. It was a classic, collectable phone that I really liked, and I trashed itI

I didn't care as much for the girl as I did for the phone. And at that moment I began to realize I wasn't into the sex as much as I was into the companionship, the relationship, and the reality.

Sometime in the mid-1980s I began to worry about whether I would ever find a woman with whom I could be satisfied to live forever. I hadn't thought much about the subject of forever before. I was just following my desires up to that time. In 1984, whether I knew it or not, I began interviewing for a wife.

At that point in my life, I owned my own home, I had three vehicles, a bicycle, an everyday car, and a work truck. I had also traveled extensively around the world, and yet I wasn't actually a big spender. I had money because I worked hard and spent carefully.

I also had most all of the sex I could ever want. A guy is never really satisfied in that category, but by most standards I was successful in love.

I had already been married for seven years and divorced. I wasn't anxious to repeat the bad parts of that scenario.

So why would I even want a wife? Maybe it was because something resounded within me. It was not my clock ticking. It was like a bell ringing in my head. DING! DING! DING! Like a school bell telling me it was time to move on to the next classroom.

Of course, finding a wife is a completely different activity than finding someone for sex on a Friday night. The investment is considerably more complex, both financially and psychologically.

The first thing I had to do was assess the package, me, my own qualifications. To be a lover, one does not need to have deep values, just an attractive demeanor. To be a life's mate, one must possess substance, both emotionally and materially.

I stepped back and looked into a mirror, figuratively at least.

Mirrors were never a part of my self-gratification. The mirror I now looked into was more like a magnifying glass.

I knew, by what I saw in that image, that I would have to present a more successful, profitable front, so I went about to improve myself in an attempt to attract likely prospects for marriage. I improved my record collection, changed the sheets every two weeks and bought a classic Porsche.

Ironically, within a few years, tapes replaced records, and CDs replaced tapes. The woman I married wanted the sheets changed every week, and she didn't care an ounce about my Porsche. But those are all academic now.

Me and my Porsche

I will categorically say right here, right now that a car does not make a man! It doesn't even get him laid! A personality gets you laid!

Neither a car, a new coat, a haircut, a candlelight dinner, nor even a diamond ring will get you laid without you having the personality that speaks to her at the time.

When I bought that 1966, 911 Porsche, I had already made love to many women. My stats after that car came to around less than five. Don't blame or credit your car for your success or failure in the realm of romance. It is all up to your personality.

Within a few years after I bought my Porsche, I made some other changes that had a far greater effect on my love life than any possession could make. I started looking at women in the context of their emotions, not how they looked or what they said, but what they believed in. I started looking at women as prospective wives, just as they might look at a man as a prospective husband.

Every once in awhile I would take another look at myself in that figurative mirror. It was as if I looked at myself as if I were a woman looking at me.

Impartial choices are almost impossible. We have prejudices implanted early within our childhood. Watching others without positive or negative assessment is difficult. How can you fall in love with someone rationally without knowing their faults and then overlooking them?

One of my romantic interests at the time was a small business owner in my town. She was possibly ten years younger than I. She was blonde or of a blonde spirit. Well-read, well-dressed, well-designed. We dated on a sporadic basis. I never kissed her. Yes, folks, I never kissed her. I never even tried.

For the previous 18 years, every woman who came within body heat of me was subject to probable make out, heavy petting and often intercourse. Yet for this particular year I suspended the libido and approached girls and women as socio/sexual equals.

I really learned a lot.

It was not exactly disillusioning. I did not lose respect for women. Actually, I acquired more respect for them, grudgingly though it might have been. What I learned was that women, given the freedom and the space to do so, would choose their own mates. It is not easy for a man who is an experienced lover to acquiesce and allow women to make their own choices without giving them hints.

I found out, again, that women were much like men, only different. Only this time I learned they were different because they were supposed to be so, not because they wanted to be contrary. Mother Nature had a plan. It was no less a plan just because she didn't inform me and the rest of the male population of its particulars.

1984 was a banner year for me. I dated a woman who would not ride in my Porsche because it didn't have seat belts. I had a stalker. I don't want to talk about it. And I had my first fling with a girl who lived in a trailer.

Screwing in a trailer had its own unique emotional and psychological aspects for me, since half of my family, the fundamentalist, uptight side, came from what might be considered a poor, white, trailer park trash background.

I had another purely platonic relationship that year. She was yet another thin, wispy blonde, my favorite type. This was the year I went out looking for my type, since I figured, if I were to marry someone, she should be the complete fantasy package. But best laid plans often look contrived in retrospect.

This girl was also the appropriate ten years younger than I. We had very good conversations, but no sex. I did kiss her, and she toyed with me, by saying, "I guess this means we should go into the bedroom and fuck all night long, but I just don't think it's right!" I thought she had lesbian tendencies or perhaps emotional issues, but those are probably just my justifications for the reasons she wouldn't sleep with me.

I seemed to be tying up loose ends in preparation for a life change. I went on one last around-the-world trip in 1984-85.

China was an interesting episode. Most of the time I was the only gui jing (white person) around. On a train trip I was given several offers of marriage, but that was too much cultural exchange. Having sex would have been all right, but marriage?

In my hotel in Guilin, the young, beautiful maid came in three times to see if she could help me in any way. I finally realized after the third time, she was offering more than just to turn down the sheets. But I didn't.

It was refreshing to me that I was so unjaded that I didn't automatically think that she was willing to sell her body. I had never been into prostitution anyway, and never paid more than a dinner and some wine for sex with a woman.

In Chungking, now Chongqing, I did connect with a tourist girl. We didn't have any birth control, so we made love in every other possible way. 69 can be an extremely intimate form of lovemaking, in that you are both trying to pleasure each other, and that your pleasure is increased exponentially by how much you stimulate your lover.

中国重庆人民路175号

175 PEOPLE'S ROAD CHONGQING CHINA

Our room was the whole top floor wing of the Renmin Hotel. The hotel was modeled after the Temple of Heaven in Peking, now Beijing, and our room was the round palatial tower. I am convinced that, because of the exotic surroundings, we were spurred on to invent a galaxy of new sexual activities not involving intercourse. And we had numerous beds to employ.

When I returned to my home from that trip, I was as lost as I had ever been. It wasn't as if I wanted something I couldn't have, but I needed something that wasn't there. You know "You don't always need what you get, but you get what you bump into!"

Well, I knew what I needed! It may not have been what I wanted, but maturity was starting to tell me that I was getting too old for the games I was playing. But changing wasn't as easy as staying put.

I knew that a wife and family life would be the best for me. Yet at times I considered the possibility that I would never find a true mate, and began looking at a life and old age as a "confirmed" bachelor. It didn't look pretty!

One of the girls I "interviewed" for a wife was a lot younger then I was, but she was very bright and creative. Call her Ann. We bumped into each other often, some of which I contrived. This was not my style, but since I was in a search of a certain type of mate, I considered it appropriate. We talked and liked each other, so I asked her out. It didn't fit into her schedule. I asked a few more times and the same thing happened, so I quit "bumping" into Ann.

Needy is an overused term in today's social intercourse. But needy sometimes means that you need to give affection to someone whom you love. It doesn't always mean taking away something without giving back.

Around this time, I started assessing my needs. I needed affection, just like everyone does, but I started realizing that my needs for a mate had a lot to do with my own need to nurture. Nurturing, a trait generally known as female, it is also primal in men, yet pushed aside in our aggressive culture.

The post-war testosterone culture brought back by horny soldiers after World War 2, was eventually countered by the intellectual world of Europe, India, Africa and Asia as seen by many other soldiers during the war. The beat generation was born, and then the hippie culture from it.

The 1960s and 70s introduced a big change in many men who had traveled elsewhere in the world. During that time, we became softer creatures, we realized love was a both-way agreement. We realized that we had the need to nurture and sacrifice for our loved ones, just as women did.

It was the psychedelic and cannabis education that brought us to male liberation! Expanding our minds made us see the stupidity and destructive nature of our male dominated, aggressive culture.

I began looking for a woman whom I could nurture and who would nurture me as well on the same plane.

Social taste, by definition, means choosing something based on a set of ideals or peer pressures influencing artistic, spiritual and/or intellectual life! It can be a bad thing because it might make you exclusionary, which indicates prejudice and the possession of a God-complex. Well, I am definitely not that way, by choice or nature, but one day I realized that I did have some preferences

I actually started using some discretion in choosing a woman. I realized that I did have some taste after all! I developed some level of judgment. I still love and loved all women, but I decided that some were good for me and some were not.

I started realizing that there were some deal breakers to my ideal relationship. One, I didn't like high-maintenance women, someone who was late most of the time, or put on too much make-up. I found that I liked no scent rather than too much perfume, and that I actually preferred the natural smell of the female body. I won't go so far as to say that I liked to smell them sweat, but I didn't want someone who smoked tobacco or drank more than I did! I needed intelligence and humor in a mate!

During that year of interviewing, I was confronted by almost total rejection for the first time in my romantic career. Later, much later, I determined that it was because my motives had changed and subtly, women picked up on that. Apparently, there was an anxiety, a desperation about my approach.

I had a few more attempts at finding a wife, and then one day I just gave up. I actually said to myself, "Self, it's going to be just you and me, babe!"

And then the 1985 Monterey Jazz Festival happened. It is interesting to note that two of the major changes in my life happened 18 years apart at the same music venue. The Monterey Pop Festival in 1967 and the 1985 Monterey Jazz Festival were both performed on the same stage at the Monterey Fair Grounds.

In 1967 I discovered a new dimension to women in general when I saw Janis Joplin at Monterey Pop. In 1985, I found my wife at the Monterey Jazz Festival.

Within minutes of that meeting we both knew that we would be married some day. Three weeks later I bumped into Ann, that young girl who had been rejecting my offers to go out on a date.

But this time she came on to me. She made it obvious that she was very interested in seeing me. But I found some polite way to excuse myself.

As I walked away from my past life as the predator, I shook my head in disbelief at the ways of romance. When you are in need you will die of thirst. When you have plenty, you may drown.

CHAPTER 148

# Marriage and Bitching, and Wishing and Hoping... Also "The Mothering Syndrome and Henpecking"

*"No marriage is the salvation of mankind."*
Manhattan MacGandhi

*"Women are Man's only hope for becoming a real Man."*
Dudley Griffin, 5.31.11

What came first, the drinking or the bitching?

Life within marriage is a balancing act. You may have to give up some of the things you think make you a man in order to become a successful, functioning husband. How much are you willing to give up in order to fit into society's parameter of manhood? How much are you willing to give up to be acceptable as a husband?

In many cases in this conversation, you can transpose the female with the male references, but in some of these, if you do that, you may find yourself in  deep, politically-incorrect shit and deep intellectual scat!

We are seventy years old. We don't necessarily need anymore sex, we have had lots of sex. What we need now is love, and someone who will be willing to change our diapers.

*"Air guitar as therapy. Sometimes it is appropriate to wuss out!"*
Mr. California, 2014

*"I don't drink to party, I drink to think! And Marijuana strips away your ego!"*
Dudley Griffin

## The Bitching

Who's bitching here? The wife, or the husband because <u>she</u> is bitching?!

What came first, men drink because women bitch, or women bitch because men drink?

The most common name for it is henpecked! For centuries it has been immortalized in poetry, drama and song.

Man's disdain for bitching is not so much a complaint as it is a pleading for its end.

I once had a lover who told me to stop whining about her whining! My thought was, "Would she rather have the alternative, the back of a hand from a man who didn't really love her?"

I don't know which came first. In early stages of a relationship there are things and situations that occur and alter the dynamics of the relationship. At first you don't know, care or understand what they are or what their consequences would be.

But my theory is that some men feel the need to drink to deal with the stress of being the "head of the household," the provider, the one expected to produce. And then it is also stressful to have to support and protect our own egos, of course.

In marriage and long-term relationships, arguing can become a habit.

It is quite possible that if it weren't for alcohol, women would be the dominant sex in human society. I'm not saying that would be bad. I actually think that it would be better. But we can't put the spirits back in the bottle.

When I say, "if it weren't for alcohol, women would be the dominant sex in human society," I don't mean that women are limited or hindered due to their drinking. I mean that men are often elevated by their dominant character and verbosity by their drinking.

We have to deal with the situation as it was dealt to us. Maybe someday with a little more education and soul-searching, men and women won't be so hard on each other.

Women...men's drinking habits? You can help or you can be the reason. Husbands are constantly, continually, consistently forced to fulfill the expectations of their wives, while maintaining their own self-esteem. It is not an easy conflict for the male ego. Many men drink to fortify themselves, which makes women bitch, which then defeats the fortitude of the alcohol, making their man want, and sometimes need, to drink more.

The basic natures of man and woman are not very compatible. The sex, the intriguing diverse companionship and supposed economic advantages bring man and woman together. But sex does not make a relationship. Time makes a relationship! Being able to stomach being in the same room together is a good criteria to start with!

How are our wives able to do this to us, to drive us to the brink of leaving and then within a moment's reversal of criticism, they are able to convince us that they are genuinely sorry? And why do we fall for it every time, and allow the problem to build without true conciliation, until that last time when we finally explode, to everybody's detriment?

But this bitching thing is not restricted to men's drinking habits alone. There are eating habits to be changed, and clothing habits, and TV watching habits (all of which have nothing to do with how much your man loves you)!

And gentlemen, these pleas for more responsible, healthy living are so you won't die on her, because of your debauchery, but the bitching is in many ways as stressful and deadly as the debauchery!

"The children are launched and doing fine. Must I still be held up to such scrutiny as a provider?"

Why don't you believe me when I say, truthfully, that the sky is blue? I would never lie to you unless it were for your own well-being.

We can never quite reach her expectations. We will always come up short. It is not her fault, it is not our fault, it is the nature of humankind, and it is Mother Nature's way to get the best for the children and the future family of mankind.

As far as I can say with my experiences, my amount of love for someone is in direct relationship to the time I want to spend with them. If I am faithful and come home and sleep at night; if I cook for you and vacuum the floors and talk to you about just anything, then I think you are my mate, and I am yours. If you will have me!?

Prepare for the eventuality that at some time through nature or circumstances, you may have to live without sex. It doesn't have to be a bad thing. It might be more respectable than chasing skirts at seventy-one years old, or paying dearly for it.

I am not stupid enough to think, nor ignorant enough to believe, that men don't bitch too. Men bitch. I ought to know, I've been in locker rooms! Yes, we bitch! We just bitch about a different part of the pie!

It is far worse to underestimate your mate than to overestimate them! The poor husband who is continually being told he could do better in the work place, begins to feel unappreciated. Even his triumphs are ignored. He will overwork to compensate and can die young and frustrated, or drink himself to death from his wife's dissatisfaction! Duh! So how many movies and TV sitcoms have you seen about this and still don't get it!? It's not just a catchy script plot!

## And Wishing, And Hoping...

*"Women are searching for chemistry rather than just fluids."*
DG, 2014

How can a woman understand raging, testosterone-driven ego any more than a man can understand raging estrogen-driven depression?

These things I am saying might sound disparaging, but they are what we need to hear right now in order to save our culture, sanity, and our egos.

Women influence us toward peaceful co-existence, yet we speak separate languages, and there are few interpreters or translators! Most thinking men know that women are usually correct and willing to indulge us, but we also know that they are weak to our lies and susceptible to our power trips. So of course, we men, being animals, will take advantage of them even if we don't need to be deceptive to get their love.

Motherly love is recognized as the only pure form of emotion of which humans are capable. Some might say that agape, God's love, is the ultimate, but you don't see that very often. Women often "mother" their mates, co-workers, ex-mates and sometimes even ex-mate's partners. But it doesn't usually work positively on anyone other than their own children, and then only to a certain age.

Because men do not naturally have the mothering instinct, their love is a question of give and take. But with women, because of an uncontrollable urge to mother, love is a forgone conclusion.

Women have the capacity to love a man without reason or expectations, yet they can also ask us for more than we can possibly get for them. And then one day, one or the other, man or woman, will stop putting up with the bullshit or can't take it any longer, and will leave, or tell you to leave.

Both men and women have their unreasonable requirements for a love partner. Neither of them can forget their own needs long enough to listen to their partner's needs. But these are all curable shortcomings.

I think if we both agreed that we didn't really know what was the best way to live, your way or mine, then we could get on with the business of just living!

I am convinced that many wives can never be truly satisfied with their husband's accomplishments. It is primal, imbedded in the DNA of women, to continually seek a better mate for the family, her nest and her $40,000 kitchen.

I am convinced that many men can never be truly satisfied with their women. It is primal, imbedded in the DNA of men, to seek out more sex in order to fulfill their inbred mission to procreate and even populate the world. As Freud said, "Sublimation is one of the most destructive sex toys! (no close quote)

**Advice:**

To men, accept who you are and demand they love you for who you are.

**Advice:**

To women, accept who they are and love them for who they are. No more, no less!

**Advice:**

To women, accept who you are and demand they love you for who you are.

**Advice:**

To men, accept who they are and love them for who they are No more, no less!

Both men and women have basic gender personality traits that make it almost impossible for them to live peacefully together. Men may be immature, never make enough money, drink too much and don't shave or bathe as often as they should. And women bitch about it!

This is not a chicken or egg first issue! These gender specific activities are more or less motivated independently of each other, yet related to each other, except maybe the drinking. Bitching or work stress make men drink. But it also seems as if women would still bitch if their men made too much money or bathed too often.

At this point I want to make a deniability statement. I will say that this does not necessarily or specifically apply to my own marriage.

> *"Male and female homo sapiens wear two different sets of blinders. Or, if you wish, they are motivated by two different lost causes. Men are trying to make it through life without being discovered to be the fraud that they actually are. And women are trying to legitimize their men."*
> Dudley Griffin, 5.22.06

There is a pitfall in trying to understand and accommodate both sides of the pie. You can lose your male perspective in trying to learn the female perspective, and vice versa! You could actually learn to sympathize with the other sex!

I always hope that I am doing the right thing, or not doing the right thing at the wrong time. It's a crap shoot whether she approves. Or, I hope I'm doing the wrong thing at the right time.

Women are mothers by nature, barefoot and pregnant. Men are rapists by nature, shallow and unfeeling!

On the surface these gender generalizations would seem to be irrational commentaries, but if you listen closely to them, you will realize that they are personal miscalculations or misunderstandings on both sides.

First, men don't need to, nor can they, defend being men. They are just men! Second, women can't really change or legitimize men because, as it has been said many times over, men will be men, and boys will be boys!

Bitching at a man for being a man is definitely one of the most frivolous (what I really mean is foolish) endeavors womankind has taken on. This is not a criticism of their efforts or of the validity of their endeavor. It is a question of whether the effort could ever be productive. This is not an observation on the foolishness of women as much as a statement about man's inflexibility, his insistence on being a man.

Early in a relationship if a woman lets it be known that she is unhappy with certain behavior, the man just might change. Many men do make changes in their habits to accommodate women, but there is a limit. After three or four years of cohabitation, a woman should realize that the man has changed about as much as he is capable of doing.

If her well-intended suggestions of personal improvement go on for too long, they mysteriously transform into bitching. The man has already heard it. He has processed the complaint and has decided to try to ignore it or work on it in his own time. If a woman actually loves her man and wants to keep him, she will do well to curtail the ragging. Your man is not going to start acting like a woman just because his being a man bothers you!

Besides, being a man, just like being a woman, is not intrinsically bad. It is just different. But this is just downright scrambled thinking if you are at the other end of the gender helix.

Unshaved, unwashed, with beer on his breath, man still has his uses. Remember ladies, there was a time in your naive, yet primal, life when you didn't care about all his annoying flaws, which now drive you crazy.

After years of cohabitation and familiar contempt, relationships often come down to needs. If your mate does not satisfy your needs, then you become bitchy and stubborn. Both men and women do.

If male stubbornness and female bitching continue, divorce or separation may be the result. So try again! And if you still won't change, adapt or be quiet, it may happen again. If a man or woman has had three or more divorces, they might consider that they are incapable of flexibility and therefore realize that marriage is not right for them.

There are many people in both genders who are wrong for marriage. Call it selfishness, call it individuality, but some folks are better off as good friends, good sex partners, but not mates.

Some of the male traits that women start to complain about after several years are the reasons that they were attracted to the guy (poor sod) in the first place. "Immature" is also called "fun-loving" or "devil-may-care!"

To appear exciting and economically "devil-may-care" is what made us suitors buy all those flowers and weekend get-a-ways for you. The romantic side of men is what often eventually makes them marginal providers or quirky individuals. Women want to marry the fictitious and endlessly rich movie character who seldom exists in reality. Contrary to sitcoms and TV reality shows, men actually have to work, supply a financial foundation and follow some semblance of political correctness to be of any value. If a man stays around and does those things, he is a keeper!

After 15 or 20 years of marriage, there should really be no disapproval left in a marriage. If you don't truly like the person, you should be gone by then. If you can't live with their quirks, get out. But stop bitching at them. They are not going to change any more than they already have, and all you are doing is diminishing the quality of your relationship.

Bitching and male/female conflict make for good TV sitcom dialogue, but not good marriage. Love is living with the imperfections of your mate. We all have them, even you, even I!

A type-A husband might buy that Jaguar or expensive perfume, but he is often unavailable to enjoy them with you because he is too involved in loving himself. The perfect mate is somewhere in between the cowboy and the stockbroker. Your perfect husband is the strong, individual type, yet with an attentive affection for you.

There is a syndrome that eventually occurs in perhaps 50 to 70% of all marriages. Call it a jaded relationship. Familiarity breeds contempt or just plain boredom. One or both partners reach a point when their old mate is old hat. You have seen and heard what they can do, and you are bored and want to find some other excitement.

The truth about this syndrome is that it happens on both sides of the marriage.

When a man loses faith in a relationship, he may wander and test other options. If and when he fails to find something better, he will try to return to his mate. At this point he may be forever disillusioned. Women, don't let this happen, Keep him interested, not just sexually, but intellectually and emotionally.

Women it seems are more resolute and less forgiving. When a woman loses respect for her mate, it is really a death knell: A man can seldom change a woman's assessment, whether her judgment is true or false. When you as a man screw it up, you might just as well get used to the disrespect or leave.

Men, don't let this happen. Keep her interested, not just sexually, but intellectually and emotionally. For both men and women: if you have invested 10 or 20 years in a marriage, the chances are that finding a solution to your problems will usually be easier than trying to finding another person to beat up or put up with.

*"The true proof of a man's love for you is not what he gives to you, or even his sexual attraction to you from time to time. His true expression of love is how much time he wants to spend with you!"*
DG, 2014

I heard a man friend say, "You can't quite describe or define why a man can love a woman so much that he will put up with all of her emotionally insulting bullshit."

I also heard a woman friend say, "You can't quite define or describe how a woman can love a man so much that she will abide all his typical macho scat."

There is a popular new Americana/folk song that states, "It is hard to kiss the lips at night that chew your ass out all day long!"

Ladies, please get the picture. If you want your man to be loving and feel physically amorous toward you, you <u>must not</u> emasculate him. Men have emotions too, and their emotions are connected to their erections.

It takes desire for a man to perform as a lover. Women on the other hand can be the receptacle without having any desire. Any man, no matter how self-assured, can fail to perform, or will not muster the desire to perform sexually because he has been emasculated by the woman who is supposed to be his sex/love partner! Even guys want to know they are wanted too!

Growing old has never been easy! The whole thing about not being physically able to do what you once could do is thought-provoking, and to some, devastating. The aches and pains of the body and soul reveal themselves. Hemingway could not accept it!

If you hang your masculinity on being able to do 43 push-ups at 43 years old, then you will be, by your own admission, less of a man when you can only do 42 push-ups later in life.

With age and wisdom you are better at many things of more importance than push-ups. Like aged Scotch you will not get people more drunk, yet you will taste better than in your youthful form. With age, hopefully, you will gain rationality to know that push-ups are not the measure of a man.

It is the same for her as it is for you. She has her wisdoms, and she has her faults. Neither of us is without our faults, and after decades of living together, we should all cut our mate some slack.

I am not convinced that it is ever possible to keep a wife happy. It is imbedded in their primeval DNA to always want more. The mother's drive is always to "Get the best you can for your family's gene pool."

*"I lost you someplace along the line. I don't know if it was my fault or just a happenstance. I have always tried to be acceptable, conscientious and helpful. Somehow I must have failed."*
JBMc, 2010

*"It's primal; many women may seek out only the best situation for their family. Therefore, you may not quite match up to their expectations, because there is, quite possibly, someone out there who might treat them better and produce a better family."*
DG, 8.3.10

## CHAPTER 149

# My Last Affairs

One of the last sexual relationships I had before I married Joan was with a girl who should have just been a fantasy. She was the sister of a friend; she was very young and inexperienced. My guess of her age was seventeen or eighteen, and by her own admission she had only "fooled around" before, and then only once. From that I gathered she was a virgin or part virgin.

She was awkward in her skin as a woman. She wore baggy, androgynous, monochromatic clothing and a Bob Dylan hat. She called herself Astar, or I will call her that, though her given name was probably something average and flowery. She appeared fragile, yet she acted curious and open to experiences.

I don't remember how we came to be alone at my home on Lomita Street, but there we were. It was in the afternoon. We talked and it became obvious to me that she was curious and interested in social experience, yet did not know how to proceed.

So I asked her if she wanted to take a bath with me. I don't believe, that at the time, I was thinking of it as a prelude to sex, as I remember I was merely trying to help her open up to her sexuality.

In my home at that time I had two tubs, both standard, old-fashioned iron and porcelain clawfoots. One was outside on the deck; it was a small, one or two friendly person tub, and another large one in the bathroom.

I chose the inside tub for her privacy. I never knew when someone would come truckin' into the back yard to visit. Also, I didn't want to crowd her dignity and make it sexual. It was a big tub, yet I would rather have had a hot tub for her coming out party.

When we got in the tub, it was awkward at first. She hugged her knees and looked down at the water. We began to talk, she looked at me, I looked at all of her. She was about 5'7", slim, rounded, white, soft, beautiful without her camouflage of drab clothing.

Within a few sentences it was obvious that we wanted more than even the bliss of our conversation and caress of our hot bath. I said, "Come with me!" We dried ourselves, and she followed me into my bed.

I had already fumbled and barged and fallen into sex with many women with various enthusiasm on both our parts. I think I was determined to make this one be perfect, for her, not necessarily just me!

At this time in my life, I always preferred silk or satin sheets on my bed. It was for me as well as for her. I had a black set that I particularly liked, and I remember they were on the bed that day.

She was beautiful, un-assured, yet gorgeous in her lack of understanding or profile of arrogance. I was at my sexually tutored best in 1985 at age 42. I knew my foreplay was good, because I played to please, and I honestly enjoyed it as much as my lovers did.

I have an image of her white against the black of my sheets. Skin stuck to skin when we both were damp! The tongue has more receptors of touch and taste than any other part of our body.

Knowing her inexperience, I rationalized, and probably asked if she had contraception. At the time, the pill, diaphragm or implant were the most popular. She had none.

I remembered a few prophylactics, rubbers to you throwbacks, that I had in a dresser drawer. They fell apart upon opening them; they were at least six years out of date. I don't like rubber getting in the way of my feelings of love anyway, and I definitely didn't want to destroy the intimacy of that relationship.

I told her I would be careful, and we would bath again afterwards. I was a purist; I didn't think putting on a condom in front of a virgin just before her first romantic experience was complementary to the beautiful moment.

I could not remember a better entry. I have a few others that mean as much to me, but I think I learned more and felt more deeply from that affair than any of those before it.

So I had been given the ultimate sexual reward, but I knew I would not live the rest of my life with this woman. I would cherish what she gave to me.

We had sex several more times over the next few weeks before she was scheduled to go back East to her family and on to school.

We did a few other things together. We walked on the beach, talked, hitchhiked around town.

One day while hitchhiking, a car stopped, and we walked up to it. The woman driving was someone I had previously flirted with and somewhat dated. We were not sexually introduced yet, but I was still trying.

The driver was arguably one of the most beautiful and desirable young women on the Monterey Peninsula at the time. On the few occasions I had met with her before I had cleaned myself up, but on this day I was "slumming" you might say. Astar and I were dressed for walk along the railroad tracks between Monterey and Pacific Grove.

The driver apologized that she couldn't pick us up, because she was in a two seater' with one of her other "gorgeous" friends. And then she said something to me like, "What have you done. You look like a hippie." and "Who is this, is it a girl or a guy?"

Well, my first feeling was of shame and defeat. I knew I would never see that "gorgeous" girl again. And then my feelings turned and became a revelation. I didn't need, nor really want that "gorgeous" girl. I wanted a girl who loved me for who I was, not who I appeared to be or tried to be."

I knew I would not live with that gorgeous girl for the rest of my life. I might relish her temptation; yet, provocative as she was, I was heading somewhere else away from her glow of perceived perfection.

Also, I knew I would not live the rest of my life with that innocent young woman. I would cherish what she gave to me; yet, sweet as she was, I could see she was heading somewhere else with that Bob Dylan hat.

Dredging up my emotions and spilling them out to you.

This was an all-around interesting time in my life, 1980-1985. After 35 years of age, I was growing up! And in order to grow up, you must have lessons! Some educations are sought after, institutionalized and paid for, and other, often more important lessons, sneak up on you and pay you something in the end.

I went to a party right around this time. I went with one current girlfriend, S. who I was in the process of breaking up with. At the party there was another current girlfriend of mine, with another man, and Astar was there with her brother, and she was leaving the next morning. I could have run around and tried to screw each of them that night, but I was wiser and a more perfect man by then!

I learned more about life, and myself within life, within that night, than any other night of my life.

The intoxication of California, The Coast, Big Sur, Pacific Grove, it was the lack of hype! What you saw was what you got. Hopefully, it will come again. Love in all its shapes was real. No one lied; no one lied without the consequence of expulsion from Paradise. Let us all hope it will come again.

That evening was a wonderful point of education for me. I synthesized the sum total of my requirements in a mate. The question was, "Who did I want to be with most, and how much of a commitment was I willing to make?" That became the determining factor in my eventual successful coupling.

That night was the beginning of the process of re-evaluation my priorities. How many more women did I need in order to finally feel like a complete man? Maybe it was time to accept myself as who I was inside, not who I perceived myself from the outside.

During this time of my growth in the mid-1980s, the highs were very high, but there began to be lows. That was the shock. I started having questioning feelings. My emotions went beyond the party emotions toward questions of whether the partying was worth it! Was I doing the "right thing"?

These lows were not in my plans for the future. No mainstream love story I had seen on screen had mentioned these emotional setbacks except *The Days of Wine and Roses*.

Have fun for awhile, then find somebody you love, get hooked up and live happily ever after. That's what I wanted, and that was even the accepted scenario in the hippie era.

Free Love. I have always wondered why some people try to steal what they can get free if they show the right emotions.

If you think you have to deceive someone just to get her love, then you are the one deceived. In order for it to be love, you have to feel that certain something. And even if it really doesn't make sense, it can be love! You can contrive to appear to be good in order to gain a woman's love, or you can really want to be good to earn a woman's love

I know what love Is. After all I have been through, I finally know what love is. It may be something different for other people, but for, me at this age, I have an understanding.

I have read a lot of words by people trying to wax poetic about this most elusive of human emotions. I have seen a lot of people acting out what they think love is, including myself. I now think I know what it is.

Love is giving someone else what they want, within your limitations and also giving them what they need, without your need of recognition!

Many people say that giving someone else what they want is love but if you ignore what they need, it is a fumble.

Lying by omission is a real gymnastics act. It could actually be an oxymoron, and at the most extreme, considered impossible to do. But men still do it often with some success, yet most often, only as a good try.

For men, it is often an attempt to postpone or delay a discussion or argument, about one of the same conflicts that come up in all marriages--money, sex, drinking, health and cleanliness.

Now it is not that men don't want to talk about, better yet solve, the conflicts of money, sex, drinking, health and cleanliness. It's just that we don't want to revisit the conflict on a regular basis.

Lying by omission, or even verbally, has several acceptable

times. As I've said, lying to get into someone's pants is a definitely a moral hiccup. But lying to keep from hurting someone's feelings is something even your pastor, the Pope, or God would overlook.

"I am told" that, as a husband or lover, lying to put off an argument is sometimes acceptable, but I know that the most acceptable lie is this one. If you as a mate have an emotional or physical problem with something that your mate does, and just can't seem to stop doing, and yet you lie by omission by not harping on that problem, then you really love that person and will avoid anything that creates a rift in your relationship.

I will not say that women are innocent of using lies by omission or of resorting to a "no harm, no foul" mentality, but they are learning by dealing with men, and so have adopted some of our follies.

Lying by omission is compassionate, and it is diplomatic. It is often necessary to protect someone or to protect your relationship with someone whom you cherish. But it's a bitch! I would rather have full disclosure, and then go on with our love.

There are things about your mate that you will never be able to change. If they are not deal-breaker issues, then live with them. If you can't do that, then move on because you are too anal, or they are too rigid. Remember though, you may live the rest of your life alone if you are too rigid or too anal.

The man who can cry is a feeling person. I cry for the dead and dying, as most people do. I cry when I see love and redemption, but I also cry for my own frailty. I cry to mother nature, my maker, that I will be humble enough to make my place on this earth a peaceful place. 10/5/14, I've never met a man who was more of a man than I am! This is not false ego speaking. This is my own true confidence even with my lack of a competitive nature. 10/7/14, I've met only a few competitors, but that was their definition, not mine. But if I were living in prehistoric times, I would be the best hunter and the best leader, if it were necessary.

2015, Just like the questions I asked myself at age 45 about the relevance of my party life, now at 72 I am asking myself about the relevance of my quiet, monogamous life. Should I eke out a little more fun in my life? Should I stop worrying about the eating, drinking or smoking improperly?

Maybe we should not try for perfection, or maybe we should demand perfection in ourselves as we wish for it in others? What is the satisfaction of perfection? That is the outcome of being perfect. Will it help ourselves? Will it help others? Yes, if each and every one of us were perfect, it would be a perfect world, and any imperfections would stand out and be changed by peer pressure. Then none of us would have to suffer imperfection.

Some married people continually make social mistakes that end up in unwanted baggage, conflict, troubles and divorce. I don't like these sorts of things!

Love is a wave of energy, just as hate is a wave of energy, and both can be powerful forces like an ocean wave. Like a wave in the ocean, they have a counter or conflicting action that comes back at you to knock you off your feet or your high horse.

Which would you want to be struck by? Which would you want to come back at you, love or hate? Would you like to live in an ocean of hate or an ocean of love? Like the parable of perfume or water.

Emotions are not something you learn. They are created within you from the lessons you learn.

Everyone thinks they know what love is. Sadly, most don't. Regardless, many people have a definition of love by which they try to live.

If your personal wants, your needs and your desires are primary in your definition of love, then you have missed the point! Love is not something you expect; it is something you give freely without expectations. And what you get back is frosting on the cake.

The best love is balanced, going both ways.

Strangely, only the person getting the love can truly judge its value. The person giving love may not be able to determine what the other person wants in the form of love!

I have two definitions of love; one is old and well-publicized. It is from Robert Heinlein's book, *Stranger In A Strange Land*, and it reads basically, "Love is the condition in which the happiness of another person is essential to your own." My other definition of love is from my own experiences and feelings. I believe that you can only truly measure a person's love by how much time they want to spend with another person.

In fifteen years between the time I separated from my first wife, Kathleen, and the time I met and married, Joan, my second wife, I had sex with many girls, babes and women. I am glad I experienced that when I did. I got over sex as a sport, as a challenge, or as an ego trip. You can't give up eating or breathing, but sex can be put into a dietary place, saved for when the time is right.

## CHAPTER 150

# What's It All About, Dudley?

A man does not have the power to give birth as a woman does. He has the power to impregnate, yet physically or cosmically that carries no requirements or obligations. Familial satisfaction can be a wonderful reward, and this reward may also give us men some power and soul. However, all things being equal, man does not have the power to do much of anything except to work for his family's support and protection. And work, as we know, has no guarantee of success.

> *"Life is the primal urge, not just for oneself, but for the continuation of our species. Anything else is frivolous. But then, what is life without a little fun?"*
> Mr. California 3.2 10 9:02pm

> *"If you don't have compassion and a social conscience, you may be a robust animal, but you are not really a human being!"*
> DG

What More Can I Say?

I have opened my mind and mouth, coming with all of what I have within me and my experiences. I know that we humans find advice and criticism difficult to take, but sometimes we need a foil challenging our thought process. Listen to the objectivity of those who may not know your exact life, but who have lived parallel experiences.

Two things I'm not going to do. I'm not going to make excuses for myself, and I'm not going to blame others for who I am! If we are not our own creations, then what are we--a puppet, a slave, a fake?

> *"I really liked to turn women on. It used to be my joy, but as a married man, I will only remember it. I will not allow someone to get interested in me.*
> *Flirtation may be a game, but it is a dangerous game for a man who wants to keep his happy married life."*
> Mr. California

I still like to be a subtle flirt. It is almost a deniability issue. I don't want them to know that I am flirting. I am only giving them a invisible compliment. I even use it on men, and it is all sincere. I do it with smoke and mirrors. Humor, smiles, questions, no direct compliments, low key, sincere and chivalrous. Something like a British, French, Italian combined movie plot. Very much like I was when I was seducing for real.

I never was aggressive as a pursuer. Most often I let the woman think it was her idea and make the first move. It was always a better love affair if the woman invested in the seduction.

Now, as a married man, I do it so subtlety that women don't know why they like me. It is a hidden agenda. I like women, and I want them to like me, but I don't need to shake up lives over it.

Several months after writing this chapter, I read Keith Richards' biography, "Life," in which he wrote something like this, "I didn't pursue… I made it known that I was available! It was their first move to make!"

Now, with me, it is my game to make them like me, yet at the same time know that I am not available.

## I Was a Bird Dog!

At one time, and for 14 or 15 years, all I cared about was touching the next girl, and I was good at it! I make no excuses because it was pure, it was primal, yet it was moral. As long as there is not deception, hypocrisy or force, then it is moral. You will not burn in your hell or their hell!

Selfish arrogance is a form of mental delusion, insanity maybe! If life were really just about you, then you would have all the fame, fortune and love you wanted. But most of us don't have them all, or at least at the same time, and never forever without the fear of losing them.

I am not the center of the earth, you are not the center, nor is she or he. We may think so from time to time, but unless we are certifiably insane, we really know that I am, you are, she is, he is and they are all of the same value.

What made me a prolific lover was my self-confidence. What made me a good lover was my sensitivity.

My pains are no less painful than yours, my love is no brighter, my needs no more critical, my value no higher. The fact that I am alive is no more important than the fact that you are alive. I am forever virtuous, except for my faults!

Much of our lives are defense and/or reaction to what is happening to us and around us. Even by this time in the development of human kind, we have not been able to create a perfect world for ourselves to live in. Maybe it's our ego that separates us from perfection.

But it is possible to create a perfect world. "Do unto others as you would have them do unto you." Speak out whenever you see wrong, and soon there will be no wrong!

The macho thing and sports! I think sports could be, and maybe should be, an education in human nature instead of human violence. I am not a sports fanatic. I am a San Francisco Giants baseball fan. Three reasons: 1. San Francisco is the place of my conception and birth, my City of Love. 2. City of social and cultural diversity, gay guys gesticulating for the Giants. 3. Baseball is the purest, most cerebral and least cutthroat competitive team sport.

*"It's not hard to be an obnoxious, selfish, scab of a person.*
*All you have to do is forget that you are only one of 7 billion people*
*on this earth. You are only one of everybody!"*
Mr. California

This past page or two may have seemed like a monolog of a sort of rationalization of my life. Well, it ain't that simple! As I have said before, a writer about the past or history should write his own experiences with the past as much as possible, and to make it real, he must not lie! And in order to do that, a writer must learn to dissect himself, and in the spirit of truth, he must admit being wrong at some times in his life. You can't see the dark side of the moon without going there!

I know that it is not possible to teach sensitivity or love or even morality. It is inherited more than learned. But there are things that we must learn on our own: To move away from upbringing, to find a new way to look at sensitivity, love and morality. It is a painful rebellion, but it will allow evolution.

There are things we can learn only on our own time. They must come from within, based on the outside influences of family and village.

1985, Just when you think you got it all figured out, that's when all of your well thought out conclusions and profound perceptions end up in life's dumpster of misconceptions.

In 1980 I bought a 1966 911 Porsche, one of the first 911s that was imported to the USA. I kept that beautiful car for about 35 years! It outlasted a number of girlfriends, and gave me many wonderful and exciting moments: Driving the California coast on Highway One from Monterey to LA at 3 a.m., racing Corvettes over Pacheco Pass, trying to keep my moving violations to a minimum while driving a sports car.

One of my misconceptions was one that is held by most young men concerning the attraction that females have for men with "special" cars. It is a myth that women have rating systems for vehicles.

Most women are OK with any motor vehicle as long as it is clean and has a radio that works. I cannot remember one time that my Porsche actually got me laid or helped me keep a lover for that matter. My work truck and my old clunker transportation vehicle saw more sex than the Porsche ever did. Space limitations factored in!

The topper was that when I met my wife, to whom I am still happily married, she was not impressed. I was riding my bicycle when I first bumped into her, and she never did like riding in my sports car. But that was OK. I really had that car for myself, anyway. I had it for the driving experience.

I have seen so many men make fools of themselves over women. I have seen important and powerful men destroy their lives by having some stupid, sexually-related episode. Presidents, senators, and church pastors acting like adolescent kids.

My suggestion when you are tempted by such things, is that you say to yourself, "I will forget the orgasm by the morning, but any repercussions or damage will be with me for a lifetime!"

My first marriage was my proving ground. I learned the damage of deception. In my second marriage I would never do something like that; I have never done anything like that, though I have had the opportunities. I am 72 now in 2015 and have been married over thirty faithful, wonderful years

I have been faithful to my wife all these years because I had as much sex as I could ever want when I was younger. Not that a man ever gets tired of sex, but a person with a healthy sex life when young, and common sense, will usually know that having just one more fling isn't worth losing what you have and cherish.

In this era, the 2000s, the appearance of youth seems to have more importance than the virility of youth, the freshness of youth or the accomplishments of youth. Anybody can get a new chin or knockers if they can pay for them, but you can't get a new morality or a new positive attitude just by paying for it. The uptight attitude of our society is causing false desires and expectations, and creating deviations.

"It's All In You Mind You Know!?" When you think about it, now think about it, the things that you see are all translated and created in your mind from what your eyes are looking at. What your ears pick up as sound is filtered through your brain. And what you touch, smell and taste are all somewhat altered by that gray matter sitting above your shoulders.

So it is no real stretch of the imagination to consider that everything around you in your life is altered by your mind and may not actually be what is really happening. Yes or No?

The truth is that you really have more control of what your life is or turns out to be than most people think. If you have a positive frame of mind, your life will be positive. If you have a negative attitude, then your life will be more negative.

This is commonly understood by most intelligent people, and yet many folks still live negative lives and continue to spiral downward. This is something that humans as a race should be able to agree upon and solve. But the problem is that it, like domestic violence or alcoholism, is passed on from generation to generation. Is it in the genes or in the lifestyle?

There was a period of time when I could not be completely comfortable with a woman until we made love. Of course, there were the "friend girls" and the girls I was revolted by or was afraid of! But in that era, though we didn't know the term "sexual tension," we were experiencing it. And because of that tension, I found it easier to be real with a woman once we had gotten past that tension. It might have been a one-time thing, but it allowed us to talk about the other important things and work together without that hanging over our heads. That period of time spanned about ten years, in increasing and diminishing amounts of insight and growth.

Although men are often accused of being ready for sex at any time, and with anyone, you must remember that for a man to perform sexually, with an erection, there must be a mental arousal in order to create a physical arousal!

*"You are not stupid if you don't know that others are older and wiser than you, but you are a fool! If you are over 16 years old, you should be able to realize that you know today what you didn't know yesterday. That is the natural process of getting older and wiser! If you are still too self-absorbed not to know that tomorrow you will be more intelligent than today, then you are not there yet. You are still a baby, a lump of unthinking flesh. Respect those who have had more hours on this earth."*
Mr. California

WRITTEN & PHOTOGRAPHED BY
JOHN McCLEARY
400 LOMITA ST
MONTEREY, CALIFORNIA

## My Travels

I love Sweden. I have been there only once. The old churches, the cold light, the tepid sun. I made love "to" a teenage girl there; she said she was a witch. In a photo I took of a group of us together, her image did not appear, only a bright flash of light!

I love Greece. I have been there many times. Once, I made love with a tourist girl I met in Athens. I got her away from her friends, and we spent the night in a tourist hostel. She placed me inside her. When we rejoined her friends the next day, my lover began to ignore me. She didn't speak to me again, I walked off into the streets of the Plaka. Some situations are hard to understand. I don't think I did anything wrong, but, who knows, there might have been a gorilla in the room I couldn't see.

I love New York City. I have been there many times. I smiled on the subway when others frowned and looked away. I was on a northbound subway, smiling, when I saw her smiling back at me. I got off at my stop, she followed me. We faced each other, she spoke in her Hispanic whisper, I love your nose. May I kiss it?" She kissed my gringo nose and got back on the next train to Spanish Harlem.

Sacramento, California. She was young, of legal age, I think! We were hitchhiking together, and I did travel with her over state lines. Some guys will call me a pervert, but that is what they would have done themselves. Some in glass houses do throw stones!

## Sex in the Workplace

Sex is everywhere! Ignore it, and it will bite you in the ass! Take it too seriously, and it will destroy your life!

Of course, in every association involving a man and a woman, there is some sex involved. It is natural, it is primal, it cannot and should not be ignored, but it should be placed into perspective.

There will always be sex involved when men and women come together. Get used to it, accept it, admit it. I am not responsible; I am only the messenger, the one stable, concerned, voice of reality.

Why is it that when a person tells us the truth about male/female relations, he becomes a sexist, while all those who are standing around silently are left alone to their own distorted imagination of reality?

To deny the presence of sexual energy whenever a heterosexual man and woman are together is to ignore one of the great truths of nature. To deny the sexuality within yourself or suppress it when social laws are not in the way, is to deny your humanness, let alone your animalness.

All this is paraphrased by the previously mentioned social laws and restrictions. Rape or coerced sex is not acceptable, and certain other moral and legal taboos, such as pedophilia and close family incest, are wrong.

If you are married in a workplace, and want to stay married, you have to be careful. As a married man, you must always appear untouchable. Make an agreement with yourself and follow it religiously. Do not show any interest. Be nice but do not flirt! And above all, don't try to be funny with a sexual joke or innuendo! That only works in sitcoms.

You can't separate sex and life, because everything that happens in our life, somehow affects our sex life and everything that happens in our sex life affects our social, economic and emotional life. That's why I say that we must be invested in finding the solutions to every problem of society, politics, religion and economics in order to protect the purity of our sex life. And I also say that we must be invested in finding the solutions to our sexual problems in order to protect the purity of our of society, politics, religion and economic life.

CHAPTER 151

# The Theory of Human Relativity, Life, Sex and Baseball

*"The more we slow down, the more we see the world relatively. The more we speed up, the more we can see the world as it relates to our relativity. The more we move, the more we can see the real world relative to who we are.*
*Did that confuse you? Well, welcome to the world of relativity!" DG*

Albert Einstein is not celebrated as a sociologist. He received his PhD in Physics, yet he may have been looking deeper into humanity than even he knew. We create from our personal experiences.

Albert was a human being possessing all the foibles, flaws and joys of all other people. Einstein was from a typically awkward family. He suffered ridicule in his youth, fathered a child out of wedlock, was unfaithful, divorced, etc., etc. Einstein was a man affected by the relativity of life just as all of us are. And he may have been subliminally philosophizing life rather than light, time and matter in his theories.

I have followed his quantum theories of light, speed and time into human life and the life of all of us. Suspend your knowledge, misunderstanding or ignorance of E=MC2 for this chapter! You see someone, you feel attraction, you move toward them, they move toward you, or maybe away from you. You meet, have children, live happily ever after, or none of the above. The relativity of life is that a body falling does not feel its own weight; the speed is relative to your perspective, whether you are on the train or looking at the clock!

View it this way, you are a set of eyes looking one way, moving at one speed, and the rest of the world is moving at a different speed in a different space. Can we actually assign reality to anything under those circumstances?

One other thing we can't trust is the speed of light. Although we have been taught that it travels 186,000 miles per second, we are also informed that if we were likewise traveling at 186,000 miles per second, we could never catch up with that light; the ball will never stop falling!

Gravity has been called physical attraction. Isn't love the same?

The one thing that we usually agree upon is time. We most often concur that when we observe something in real life, it is actually happening at that time--real time. But that all changes when you start bending light.

Regardless of whether you have a scientific or a carnal mind, the most important thing in our lives is our relationship to other people, not to how fast or on what curve time is traveling.

A small child who, tragically, may live for only a short time, could still be the most fortunate of humans, based on how deeply their family loved them packed into that abbreviated life.

Beauty is said to be skin deep, but it could be timing, and, of course, good lighting that attracts the attention! People often wake up with a dog, when they went to bed with a movie star.

As many authors and song writers have written, "When you experience orgasm, the earth moves!" I would add that light, time and space explode together. Reality is suspended, and relativity sends you mixed messages, all of which you want to believe.

God and Albert Einstein gave you relativity. People in love speak of being on the same wavelength. Is it a wave or moving particles of emotion?

Sex is definitely a relative thing, definitely relative and relatively definite! You can be making the best or the worst move of your life by making love with someone. I am not able to give you the formula for choosing a lover. I have made a few mistakes myself. I am not even telling you to be careful! I am just asking you to keep your ego out of it, your insecurity out of it, and your family lessons and history out of it!

You can give your lover many things--the clap, a baby, a black eye, a tie, a Cadillac, but the other things you give--ideas, laughs, respect, your soul--those will last for eternity.

Make love with anyone who(m) you feel is right, but have an exit strategy. Yet always give a love affair the opportunity to be the right choice.

The uncertainty principal is something we live with daily. It is life. God does not play dice with the world, but that authority does allow us to create our own game of reality and relativity!

In baseball, unlike most other team sports, you literally cannot play the game without all the other team members. You rely on each specialist to do their job, or you lose.

When that little white ball is hit, all eyes are upon it. It is light, it is space, it is relativity. We know that it will come down, that is a given. Where, when, and at what speed? Some of us see it as a tiny speck; some see a big paycheck and some of us as the balance of their career upon being able to catch it.

The player might be thinking of how he looks to his new girlfriend in the grandstands. Then he boots the catch, and they lose the game, and he loses the girl! In baseball everything is seen and reviled. You cannot lie or cheat, and you can steal only a base or two.

We may think that we hold our own destiny in our hands, but we are only players on a baseball field. We miss the pitch, or the catch or the tag, and our world is disrupted, but it is all relative!

If I could tell people how to be perfect and how to live a perfect life, I would. But it is relative to each of us, where we live, who our family and friends are, and what pressures have been placed upon us.

God bless all of you! And I don't really know what that means, because I don't know if there is a God. We may be here all by our-selves, and the answer might be that we must come together in order to make it work, so that we can each survive all of us. Cooperation and socialization are two of the things we are best at as humans, as a race. But if we don't care enough to save ourselves by becoming sisters and brothers on this world, then I hope that whatever God is in control will save the rest of life on this planet as we humans commit our own suicide.

What we call God is just an arbitrary authority figure! I say this because few religions agree on God's importance, appearance or powers, yet all religions say their God is the real God! Can any of them prove this?

I think God is a creation of our own mind and soul, and *IT* is the arbiter of a morality that we already know. This means that the commandments are already known by our souls.

Think, observe, remember, wonder and create! If you are not doing these things, you are not a whole person! These few activities are what separate human beings from all other living creatures! With them, we can build or we can destroy! The difference between a good person and a bad one is how they use these gifts from God. It is not a hard choice. Any God, yours or mine, who supposedly created man-kind would never give a gift to mankind to be used to destroy that which it created!

Everything we observe in this world and in this life is relative to who we are or where we are. If this world and mankind are to suc-ceed and prosper, all mankind has to agree on a few things, and then live by them.

My suggestion of a list of these universal truths and laws starts with:

1. Love is the supreme solution.
2. Greed is the supreme disaster.
3. The Golden Rule is the supreme path.

All things good will come if we follow these simple truths. The hippies were right! Too bad we didn't follow them originally. So many have suffered and died because of that. Perhaps we can follow them now and clean up the mess made by the "Greatest" Generation!


CHAPTER 152

# Sex and Religion, Sex and Dominance, Sex With Morality

The reason sex is one of the most prominently demonized human activities in Christian and most religious societies is that the people who run religions know it is the strongest influence in human life. They know this because they suffer from this sexual ambiguity and frustration themselves. And yet they know that they can't control people if they can't control people's sex life, and that bugs them because they want to be God themselves and take your adulation and money.

Since Paul the Apostle's writings in The Bible and the male-dominance that Constantine created in the Christian church, that institution has demonized sex. Not because these men didn't like sex, but they wanted to be, and stay the dominant sex.

The way the Christians deal with sex has a tendency to make sex even more desirable by making it a sin.

After all these 500 plus pages, it comes down to this. Sex is a natural human activity, which is uncontrollable by mind or religion. Humans will destroy themselves if they even try to control it. We must accept it and learn how to deal with it rationally.

This is the realization of a simple problem that is almost insurmountable, yet one that could be solved if man and woman would put their hearts and minds together to resolve it.

Men and women each have one basic trait, which will always

get in the way of marital bliss. Man's problem is the urge to conquer women and eventually to "corral" the perfect woman. Women's flaw is their continual search for the perfect man to create and protect the perfect home and family.

Man's desire to spread his seed to extend his lineage and women's search for the proper bloodline for her children could possibly destroy us. These are both primal urges that cannot be stopped with the wave of a hand, no matter how anguished the plea or violent the argument.

Women are emasculating their men by trying to improve them or threatening to exchange them for a better model. Men are betraying their women by continually looking for the newer model.

The solution to our shared plight is that we must banish all blame! We are both flawed, and neither of us is aware of our faults or see them as faults. Only our shared pain and shared forgiveness will bring us together forever.

In a long-term relationship the time you spend apart is almost as important as the time you spend together. It need not, and should not, be long-term separations, but being alone and/or introspective is rejuvenating to human emotions.

Couples who have been together for awhile begin to repeat their stories until there are no real conversations anymore. Couples should go out and have new experiences apart so that they have something new to bring back to form conversations.

Companionship is eventually the most important part of a relationship. If you don't have the ability for casual conversation with your lover, you will soon became bored with them. The nuts and bolts of life with a mate are what round out your lives together. If you cannot work out the dirty dishes problem, or the snoring problem, or the money issues, then life together may never last. There are four or five facets of relationship that must be dealt with and solved, or a true marriage will never exist. These issues may not have anything to do with sex or even love. They have to do with respect!

You must stand back to see a picture. If looking back on your life moves you to change your life, then so be it. It is right. All this intellectual truth is completely based on common sense thinking, intelligent thinking. But, as we know, people's motives and even people's common sense are based on their environment!

Paul Simon's "50 Ways to Leave Your Lover" illustrated a few of the possibilities of deception of which human beings are capable. Thank you, Paul. Before that song, sleaze had not yet been defined. Human beings are the thinking animals, and so we can find the words to make commitments and then also find the words to break them.

A person's concept of themself is more important than the reality of who they are and what others think of them. It has its limitations though. If you have only the genetic brainpower to do X, or the physical genetics to do Y, then all your confidence and striving will never allow you to exceed a certain level of accomplishment. But if you always do your best, then on any given day you can reach the level of competence of almost anyone, if they are not doing their best.

The key is doing your best. I, for one, have had a very interesting early history of not doing my best with confidence. In a summer camp swim meet, I was winning and stopped to see how I was doing. I was way ahead of everybody else, but I was disqualified for stopping and standing up. That experience made an impression on my competitive nature. I never rely on other people's opinion of my ability, and I don't need to be given a medal to show or to know my abilities!

## Adultery And The Reasons To Be Faithful

In my opinion and with some actual life and scientific observations involved, I believe that it is possible for a marriage to survive if the man is unfaithful, but not if the woman is promiscuous. Women make love with their hearts, and men, with their dicks. It is primal.

You should be faithful if you love someone and you want to be with them. But, if you don't really care about eternity, go ahead, be unfaithful and it may last a few years more.

The heart is a person's spiritual leader, the mind is the rational leader of a human being, and the dick is the primal leader of men. A relationship requiring love cannot survive on thinking and primal urges alone! Love, real love, requires a spiritual commitment.

In this society, it seems that men and women can be equal only during sexual love. How sad. There is so much this world could do if men and women really became partners in the culture of this ecosystem.

Even if it could be bottled, branded and correctly advertised, real LOVE would still be a failure in the inventory of any market place. Most people are unwilling to pay the price, even though it is technically free.

Love is the enigma of all ages, and it can be a real problem for many people to love and stick with one person forever. You have to admit, in this day and age it is a strange concept!

I am trying to make it past this page onto the next few pages. This page has kept me for maybe four months. Have I made it yet?

As a child, the moment we received knowledge of self, we began to seek love, but often our knowledge of self makes us selfish, and we become cheapskates and don't want to give as much love as we receive. Capitalism and love do not live well together. Love means you share. You must be a socialist to love truly. We can debate on this later.

It is the big question of mankind. Will we stop being selfish and survive, or will we continue being greedy and destroy ourselves?

This translates into human sexual attitudes and stability as well as our economic stability. Sexual ego insecurity is the IED, which explodes into arrogance and overcompensation!

People who are insecure make poor lovers. First, sinse they don't like who they are they, they try to become someone else, thus confusing the whole process of love and they over compensate, which often ends their relationships. And then they become even more insecure at work or at school. Which came first the sexual insecurity or the insecurity we received at home, work or school?

Love is a commodity more valuable than the weight or image of gold, and yet it does not look good on the shelf. Love is the opposite of selfishness or greed. As Robert Heinlein said in *Stranger In A Strange Land*, "Love is the condition in which the happiness of another person is essential to your own happiness." (slightly paraphrased)

If you love someone enough to place yourself second, put your wishes aside and acquiesce when something matters deeply to them, then you know love, and you have evolved. You will have the perfect ego when you love someone so much that you will forego your own ego!

Both Masters & Johnson, who wrote the book *Human Sexual Response*, and Barash & Lipton, the couple who wrote *The Myth Of*

*Monogamy,* said, in different words, that it is never politically incorrect to call a cheater a cheater, an abuser an abuser, a rapist a rapist, or a bad singer a bad singer.

It is always politically correct to bring attention to socially incorrect activities.

Follow a man's heart to know what he really loves, follow his mind to know his philosophy, follow his money to find his fixations.

But a man's heart is not easy to find. He hides it passionately. In our male dominated society, it is not profitable for a man to show his heart, because that might mean he would have to give up his delusions of power and dominance. Women of wisdom will always follow strength that exhibits reason before they submit to power that uses violence.

In the social game of adultery and betrayal, the unfaithful man is never correct and seldom secure. Insecurity is a primary flaw in many men. It makes them do things to allow themselves to feel good while at the same time, disappointing others. Whereas a self-assured man will seldom be cruel, a weak and insecure person tends to be domineering.

Boys who want to become real men, please ignore all the media images of manhood--*Jersey Shore, Duck Dynasty, Ax Men, Gator Hunters, Bounty Hunters, Fast & Furious,* etc. They represent false efforts to become self-confident. And when you add sci-fi into that mix, you come up with *Game of Thrones, Hunger Games, Avengers, The Purge, Walking Dead,* etc., which portray a level of violence and masculinity in which no one in their right mind would want to be personally involved in or would ever be able to achieve. And in the video game world, kids are taught that death and destruction are not serious, and yet to lose the game is a humiliation. These games are not good for the psyche of the players. This does not bode well for the future of humankind.

I will never advocate completely killing your ego. It is an essential weapon in survival in this business world today, as it was in the jungle of our history. However, ego can be the most dangerous double-edged sword because it cuts you just as it cuts your competitor.

Trying to dominate others is a basic male aggression created by expectations and insecurity, forced upon us by pressures in childhood. Mending the damage to one's ego by childhood misdirection and abuse is mostly beyond our control. Violent self-preservation was a path on which human beings were sent early in our history competing with bigger and stronger predators. Today, being overly competitive is a dangerous and self-destructive direction for humankind. It is a downward spiral that creates all forms of conflict. It produces a worldwide social and economic climate which is damaging to all of society and creates wars that no one can win and destruction that no one can repair.

These self-preservation competitions often create over-expressed national, ethnic and religious pride which promote ugly conflicts and violence. It is important to protect our own cultural and spiritual values. But be careful, for if you try to force your own values onto others, outside your small town, race, religion or country, you will find that their values are also not wrong within their own town, race, religion or country. Learn to allow them their differences, and possibly they will allow your "strangeness" too. If not, we will soon all kill one another.

If you want to be a real man, you must find some way to ignore your fears of failure, for men will fail. But failure is not as bad as cheating to win or killing to succeed, because then you become a hypocrite, for you, yourself, would not want anyone else to beat you with violence or deceit.

Often, the humiliation a man feels makes him unable to think straight, and therefore, he will start thinking crookedly.

The rebellious outlaw life or its image might seem romantic, but usually it is a pathetic effort to rationalize greed and self-indulgence. The real outlaw does not break laws as much as he asks society to rethink its laws.

## Marriage, Mating and Dating As a Competitive Game

Women seem to judge the unfaithfulness of a husband as childish stupidity, when it is often a desperate attempt to regain perceived lost masculinity. Men seem to view a wife's infidelity as a calculated rejection, when it is often research to see if they made the right decision in choosing you! The sexes seem to have different planets, yet deep inside us we are still amoebas with mostly the same needs.

Women seem to judge their own unfaithfulness as an attempt to find real love. Men seem to view their own infidelity as a primal prerogative! Sure, sexual aggression seems to be necessary for the survival of humanity, but no one man should try to take on the obligation of impregnating every woman on earth.

I think it is possible to have a workable "marriage" relationship where love and devotion are not present, but then that is just a business relationship! Companionship is the key element to human society and therefore all our triumphs. Friendship within couples is a foremost value.

I have seen first hand marriages that were of convenience. After the passion fades, you have to find another good reason to be together and stay together.

Often, people are not introspective enough to realize that trying to find the perfect mate, another mate, a better mate, than the one with whom you now reside, is far too often a futile, out-of-the-frying-pan, into-the-fire move.

Domestic bliss is not quite as it was advertised in the 1950s, and it never was even then! It has always seemed a bit hokey to most men, a little too mushy. It's definitely not for the majority of younger men, but it has its appeal. If you ever achieve it, it is something to be nurtured and protected.

The economics of relationships cannot be ignored! Money problems can be overcome, but only if both members of a couple are committed to making it work, and if they can get a bone to chew on, and a blanket to cover their bed.

"All We Need Is Love" is found only in the fantasies and dreams of The Beatles!

It's not easy folks, no matter what the movies or romantic novels say. You must step up, make a commitment based on devotion, and follow it to your gold star for being true to love.

I am a subversive within the male gender, a spy for the army of cohabitation. Many men, I'm sorry to say, are suffering from Male Ego Syndrome, Male Fear-of-Failure Syndrome, Male Laziness Syndrome or Human Emotions Deficiency Syndrome! Society will not progress if the male ego keeps us in conflict with each and every other person, religion and society on earth.

Women, I have observed, suffer from a different set of syndromes or deficiencies. Female Insecurity Syndrome? Overzealousness Syndrome? Female Fear Syndrome? Society will not progress if the female angst keeps us in conflict with each and every other angst on Earth.

Here, at this point in the narrative, when I say marriage, I mean your final attempt, the one that lasts. Sometimes, for men, our first marriage is the effort to achieve a more or less reliable source of sex.

And for women, the first marriage is often a way to become a mother or find the family you did not have as a child.

Marriage can be a way to become a mother or father, but it is not always the way to find a family. The family is often elusive. It means putting yourself aside at times, thinking about the future, and not just the next party, drink or fuck.

Marriage, or even just coupling, is a process of searching for home. Home is the safe cave, the warm fire and food of our prehistoric drives. We are not gods, but we are of the same cloth of life as all the gods and saints, lovers and politicians that have made this world good and bad.

Marriage is finding a companion to share your daily experiences and realizations with. Someone to ask, "Hey, did you see that?"

> *"I decided when I got married for the second time to be the best husband I could be. I had heard about compromise."*
> JBMc

> *"I don't have a problem with my erection! It comes when needed. Desire to have intercourse (the insertion of the male genitalia into the female genitalia) for a man means desire. He has to be erect to insert. A woman can be entered without her consent."*
> Dudley Griffin

## Second Marriages

It is commonly believed that second marriages are, in many, most, or all cases, better than the first marriage. We must agree, with common sense, that this is a marital legend.

Of course, you should learn from your mistakes, but what if you never find the same situation again and you are given a different circumstance to fuck up? The old lessens are not going to help you with your next problem. What if the next scenario is completely different than your last relationship? It is obvious that we can make different mistakes with different people, yet we keep thinking it can be better next time. That's good to be positive, but you may have to change your viewpoint and requirements a bit.

Statistics show that in The United States, first marriages fail 41% of the time, second marriages, 67% and third, 74%. This in no way proves anything unless you factor in so many things that it becomes a jumbled mess. But I am convinced that maturity, wisdom, and learning your true likes and dislikes better can help with your next marital attempt. At least it will help you with your own knowledge of self, and from there, good luck with all the other stuff.

Several circumstances of second marriages are most particularly interesting to me because I am personally involved in one that I want to maintain. I have observed, in my own second marriage and in those of others, a few things on which I hang a theory.

I think that many divorced women who were originally married to overly dominant or egotistical men, were not taken seriously, or ever had their opinions considered by him. She may, in her second marriage, try to assert herself more, even if it is not necessary, because her new husband is likely more diplomatic and approachable, because she chose those traits in him.

This is not necessarily a complaint, but an observation. I sympathize with the frustration women must have felt, and I would try to ignore their criticism unless it creates ripples of discontent that can cause irreparable damage to the family and marriage.

Alone for a long time anyone can become an opinionated, messy, hoarding curmudgeon. And if you don't change, you may live the rest of your life alone, just because you have a personality trait that repulses mates. Suggestion, don't get an obnoxious pet, big, slobbery dog, or a cat that you talk to more than you talk to a human partner.

Married 35 years, I have learned a lot toward perfection as a husband, but I still think making the bed is a bloody waste of time.

In my youth I use to be bad for six days a week and make up for it in one day, and I don't mean Sunday in church. Now I am good six days a week so I can be bad one day.

## Falling Out Of Love

It is possible to fall out of love, but it takes a very bad set of circumstances. That is, if you were ever in love in the first place.

Men are more likely to "fall out of love" or not have been in love than women. Women are tolerant, but each of them has their limitation. And once you have overstepped that limitation, you better just shut up go away or be prepared to be hurt by your own selfishness. When she finally rejects your deception, it will hurt like a hot iron of your hypocrisy burning through your own heart, and maybe lower down in your anatomy.

Sexual problems within a couple are "mostly" a two-person problem. They are usually caused by a lack of communication and a momentary lapse in remembering to make sure to satisfy both of you. It is a common death of a relationship when one or both forget that "the love you take is equal to the love you make." L&M

> "I wish we could kill the ego without killing what makes a
> person an individual."
> God

Insecurity breeds jealousy, arrogance, and selfishness, and these are the worst sins of mankind. Insecurity is the foundation of most religious organizations; it is the creator of dictatorships and greedy corporations. Only weak people find it necessary to dominate, torture, ruin and kill others for economic gain and self-satisfaction. Such people are not really good humans; they are barely even acceptable animals. No other animal expresses greed or jealousy quite like the insecure human. Some people say dogs, cats, chimps and a few other primates do, but that is just primal urge of fight or flight.

We have to learn about our human personality and about our creations. We must do that if we want to survive as a species.

If you don't know what you're doing, turn and walk away. Ego, pride, and insecurity are the most damaging flaws to a good relationship with a lover.

The age-old question, what do women want? Maybe they don't want anything that you could supply or even understand! Maybe they just want a life free of trauma and drama. If you want to be a real man, then you should create that for them. Can you do that, or are you the cause of the drama, and just can't live without it?

Women and children don't have the same expectations of us that we have of ourselves, nor do they care. Most men think that they are deficient in some way, and that is probably so, but their wives would not agree with them on the deficiency.

I cannot speak for women, for I am a man, and sometimes I cannot even speak intelligently for my own gender. I have intuitions about women, but those are ideas gleaned from my male perspective. I use my own male sensibilities when negotiating with the female gender, as most men do.

There is a difference between lying and not telling the truth. "Not telling" something is a more passive than telling a lie. If you lie, you are actually proclaiming something you know not to be true. If you don't tell something to someone, you are not lying, you are "protecting" them and yourself from the truth. That may sound like a cop-out, but it is not a deception, it is diversion.

There is an "if" in life! If only, if only, if only.

I haven't always been truthful to myself and therefore to my mate. I am a romantic, but I am also a realist. I know rationally that I am not the center of the earth, but when the lights go out I am the only thing I have. People will do anything to survive emotionally or physically. Husbands and wives are not always what they seem. Believe me, this is not a negative thought. The common sense answer would be for all of us to lighten up, step back a pace, dissect the circumstances and assess our chances outside the relationship. If you truly would be doing better elsewhere, then go! But if you miscalculate on your chances, you can be screwed.

Hunting and gathering were the real first profession. What people call prostitution was first called mating! Men hunted, and women gave birth to children so that the family or tribe could prosper. Of course, then as now, women had to hunt, gather, cook, clean, and birth and raise the children. Men had to hunt and supply sperm.

> *"Opposites attract, yet they also often repel each other.*
> *Night Follows Day, or Does Day Follow Night?"*
> Dudley Griffin

The husband-wife relationship is different from all other man and woman relationships. Duh, that sounds like a sophomoric and obvious statement, but it is deeply poignant. That cohabiting relationship needs to be explored and understood for what it is and why it is different.

When a man and woman meet, for the first moments, minutes or hours, they don't know what their relationship really is. They may just be classmates, fellow workers or people who bump into each other at the coffee shop or bar. When they first date they are reaching for enjoyment, getting the most out of the experience.

When couples finally settle in to a commitment of time and space, they begin to spar for positions, and to contemplate the possibilities. This is the real decision time. If a mutual arrangement is reached, they marry.

You realize I am exploring only heterosexual coupling in this discourse. I know very little about the emotions and inner workings of same-sex relationships.

Marriage changes everything. Maybe it shouldn't, but historically it is a fact that the paper affects the parties involved.

Here is where I step on thin ice. When I use primeval influences as a theory, I often lose some people. Women have a deep DNA drive to protect children, home, and hearth.

This profound genetic obsession in women often excludes her mate, just as the primal male urge to procreate does not always consider his mate.

Women push men to advance, while men treat women as objects. Men suffer from the expectations of women, and women accept mistreatment as some form of love.

If we could become more alike, we could get along better. However, we might become boring to each other. Opposites attract, and they attract on a tense level. I might say here that we are glad for the sexual tension, but it would be an oversimplification of the male-female dynamic.

In our society we are programmed to believe that sex is the barometer of love. I beg to differ. Mutual respect is the foundation of love, companionship is a primary reason for it, and chemistry is the amorphous glue that creates it. Sex for procreation is the biological prerogative, and sex for pleasure is one of the celebrations of love.

We should all read Masters and Johnson again!

In my observations of other marriages and the experiences in my own marriages, I find that men and women sometimes, and for short times, can see what the other is feeling.

I don't think a women can truly understand the effects of emasculation on a man, any more than a man can understand the effects of infidelity on a woman. Yet, I believe these are similar in how they affect each of us.

## A Primal Truth

It is a sad thing to admit that most men, myself included, are failures. We fail as husbands and providers because we are unable to keep our wives happy. But sadder still is the fact that most wives are strangely incapable of being satisfied (happy) with their husband's efforts, no matter how vigorous.

We all have expectations, but it is best if they are directed at ourselves! Men expect more from their wives, and wives expect more from their husbands.

> *"More alcoholics have been created by wives*
> *than by alcohol."*
> God

> *" I don't know that if I had been Betty Friedan's husband or*
> *significant other or Gloria Steinem's lover, I could have understood*

Mother's Heart, Father's Mind

*all they were saying then.*
*But now I see it, because I have lived it."*
Mr. California

It is in the primal DNA of every woman to look for the best procreator, provider and protector for their young. It is in the primal DNA of every man to lie, cheat and steal to appear to be the best procreator, provider and protector for that woman's offspring!
        *"Of course, there are some men who are not trapped in the male ego. They really do want to satisfy and appease the female. But all too often they are painted by the history of their gender and their sex! And then accused of being another worthless fucking asshole man!"*
Dudley Griffin 1.24.07

*"My God, My God, why have you forsaken me?*
*"My God, My God, why have you lifted me up"?*
J.O.B


CHAPTER 153

# The Secret To Finding True Love Is...

Just kidding!

Good writers and bad have been trying to create true love in their stories (and, I'm sure, in their own lives, I might add) since the very first story was told around the first campfire. The misconception has always been that eternal love is something you find, or bump into, that it is a matter of being in the right place at the right time and meeting the right person.

Well, the truth of the matter is that true love is something you create yourself, not something you find. Conversely, it is something you can blow yourself. Meeting mister or miss right is important as the first step, but, most often, love requires work to create the final bliss.

The problem is that most stories about love concentrate on the idyllic elements of romance and never discuss the negative parts concerning bad taste and selfishness. Most writers are too subtle for the most part, too kind, and the truths have been wrapped up in morality plays which are often overlooked by the reader in their search for the juicy parts.

I'm not going to be so subtle. I'm here to tell you that, if you act like an asshole, you will live and die a lonely, shriveled-up person. In countless books, movies and TV sitcoms, writers have been trying to tell you how you should act in relationships. They do this by having a good guy and a bad guy. The good guy gets the girl, and the bad guy walks. No one is talking about how the guy got bad or what makes him obnoxious.

True love starts first with a positive self-image created by a good childhood. This self-respect will allow you to have the proper emotional tools to love and respect another person. It will make it unnecessary for you to be selfish in order to enhance your own self-image.

In other words, if you can't love yourself, no one else can love you. In most good book or movie plots, the selfish, abusive lover never ends up with the girl, so why in the hell do guys continue acting that way? Possibly because that kind of activity appeals to their insecurity, they think that rough exterior will hide from the world that they really have nothing inside. Only in rap videos do the assholes get the girls, but do they get to keep them in the end?

The question remains that, if self-image is lost in childhood, is it possible to regain it? Sure it is, but it takes guts!

## God Made Me Do It!

Criminals have been saying this for centuries, blaming their frailties on God. God is only the creator; "it" is not the corruptor of man. Do not use God as your excuse for being deceitful, immoral or insane. Stand up like a man, and do the right thing! And don't tell me you don't know what that is!

Until Christianity finally accepts that sex is a God-given, God-ordained human activity, I will continue to remain an agnostic. I certainly don't want to become a Christian and therefore turn into a hypocrite like so many other Christians.

What is life all about?

    Are you being successful at life?

    Is there such a thing as success or failure in life?

    How do we measure success?

    Does success matter?

    What's it all about?

These are some of the questions that go through a person's mind when they've had a couple of glasses of wine. That doesn't mean they aren't relevant questions. It just means they are intellectual pursuits that are not always considered. And probably they should never be considered. Life is complicated enough without attaching a pass/fail grade to it.

First, there are two viewpoints on your success. Yours and everybody else's. When it comes down to it, your own assessment of your life is the only one that matters to you, and theirs is the only one that matters to them.

How a person feels about the success or failure of their own life has to do with their own value system. And yet, that value system is obtained through the influences of others.

The predominant male criteria for success are usually defined as: Making lots of money, creating children and maintaining a mate. From what is written here most people might believe that my viewpoint leans toward: Making lots of fun... period. But that would be a shallow and deceptive assessment.

## Talk or Die

What you say to a person can make them remember you or forget you, love you or fear you. It may depend on how intelligent they are, or how gullible, and it also may depend on whether you mean what you say.

In the realm of romantic conversation, there are two kinds of language, the serious and the sarcastic. Timing decides which one of these to use. Learning timing is the most elusive of romantic skills.

There are some phrases that you should never say to someone you really want to impress. They are "trust me," "in your dreams," "be careful, you might get what you wish for" or "read my lips."

Another phrase not to use is "it's now or never" even though I did once use it to positive results, but then that was in 1961.

Earlier in my life I had moments of frustration with my circumstances. There were situations where I felt as if I were being picked on by God or situations. I eventually realized that there was no vengeful God, nor were circumstances ever personal. All creatures have the same possibilities of success or failure.

If we can't be critical of ourselves, we will never evolve. Who among us will listen to someone else anyway?

Until now, the ticking of the clock was always a positive thing. The moving of time was anticipatory. I was looking forward to the next moment and what it would bring.

Now, the sound of the clock reminds me of the shortness of remaining time.

It is a little uncomfortable to admit and definitely politically inappropriate to say so, but I chased nookie for a large portion of my early life. That's honestly what I did for the majority of my waking hours between the age of 13 and 42 years old, I was in the pursuit of sex. But remember, there is a difference between thinking about it, pursuing it, or getting It!

## College career and the night I kicked a girl out of my car.

The night I kicked a girl out of my car because she wouldn't "put out" was the night I expressed my manhood and rejected my manhood at the same time.

In the last semester as a high school senior I signed a piece of paper in my civics class, and that got me into my first semester at the local junior college. I matriculated with such glowing reports from my teachers and administration from high school that I was given the honor of taking bonehead English and Introduction to Marriage and Family (basically, Psych 1A). But I beat them at their game and decided not to be at all cooperative. I spent most of my college experience playing whist with "the boys" in the student union. Oh, I did try out all of the classes. Some lasted up to my first yawn, and some ended when they moved the class location, and I failed to make an effort to seek out the new room number.

But *Marriage and Family* was something I did hang in for.

I suppose the reason was that the word marriage held some sexual prospects. You see, it was 1962, and we weren't gettin' much...very little...hell, weren't getting' any!

There were also a lot of cute, want-to-be-mothers and chicks in that class, and that's where I met Margaret Mead.

Three of my high school girlfriends became the local junior college cheerleaders. I went to see them at a football game when I was still in high school. I have always been blessed to be near women of great beauty and great spirit.

So what do I think now at my age, after all I have survived and after what I have seen others go through? It is still just my male observation, and my experiences. I don't think monogamy is a common or necessary social requirement for human beings. It is a wonderful thing when it works.

The spiritual connection between a woman and her mate is beautiful. And when a man recognizes that spiritual high for what it is and accepts it, their life together can be better than it would be if they were apart.

Some men at certain ages will have sex at any time and with almost anyone. I have learned, or I surmise, that women have to have a bit more incentive. Girls who are new at sex are often driven by curiosity and peer pressure. They also have the desire for love deep inside.

My love for women resides in a combination of respect, lust and wonder. In my early youth I was comfortable with girls as friends due to my closeness with my mother. And because I did not have a domineering father who departmentalized women as wife, employee or toy, I respected women as people.

In adolescence I had no problem "seducing or talking up" girls because of my comfort with them, but then lust became an issue. There was a 23-year period of time when I could not be a real good friend to a woman until we had made love.

On one hand, seduction was a challenger, on the other, it was an equalizing factor. It was almost like getting it over with. Sex between genders is such a detriment to rational life. You see it in every book, movie and sitcom.

I know instinctively that "the act of procreation" is one of the most important things we do as human beings. But I also know the act of "procreation" is one of the most spiritual experiences we have in life.

I could not explore my wonder of women until I got over my lust for them. And now my wonder of women is one of the most fulfilling experiences I have.

*"What is life about? What is a successful life? I can speak only for my own needs and my own values. Life is breathing, eating and producing something to be left behind. If you don't leave something behind, then it is hard to prove or to believe that you ever existed. Leaving children could be called proof of existence, but leaving a good poem is just as good. Success? Above all, don't leave the world with anyone in it wishing that you had never lived."*
DG,10.16.06

## Good Man, Smart Man, Stupid Man, Dumb Lover Syndrome

There are some words that I reserve for the most extreme situations, and some that I won't even utter. Some terms I use only in jest and some that are saved for capitalists, politicians and rapists.

Nixon's favorite word was cocksucker. I sometimes wonder what his history with that activity was. I never use that word except on Nixon, Reagan or Trump.

Slut, I use on men more than women. Sack of shit is my strongest condemnation. Any man who seriously calls a woman a slut is a sack of shit.

Talking about a woman behind her back makes you a sack of shit. A man being disrespectful to a woman is a sack of shit, except if she is being disrespectful to him. I stopped making sexual jokes and nasty comments about girls when I was thirteen years old. Grow up, guys!

There are some men who did not get enough James Bond! They did not learn the suave thing. But they still could be your bright, productive and attentive mate.

Women have to do something related to this. I touch on this subject lightly, but women have to lose their James Bond or Mick Jagger fantasy if they are ever going to find a good mate.

All of life is not a movie script. We are all not going to get our fantasy as a mate. Say this another way, your fantasy is non-existent, and if you chase that your whole life, you will be alone or unfulfilled all your life.

In the Western World there are plenty of women and plenty of love to go around for all men! So why are some men alone? And also, I might ask why are some women lonely? Find a nice un-socially connected person and hook up!

Are we too dumb to make the move, or do we want to be alone? Sex is not just something you check off your list! Affection is not something you learn from a void. Companionship is not something you learn from a family member.

You know the phrase, "and they all lived happily ever after." Disney promoted it, Palmolive, GMC and Richfield Oil all promoted it. Happily ever after and the American dream are attainable, but that is mostly in your mind!

Nothing is perfect, but you don't have to be a quitter to feel happy in a less than perfect world. Your positive attitude is adding to the happiness in this world!

The most important step in being happy is to not be stupid, in love and in all parts of life. Stupidity is a selfish act, because when you do something stupid, everyone loses, your family, the people next door or those on the other side of the city and country or world. Step into other peoples' shoes, think as they might think. Don't just think of your own needs because then you make enemies out of people who could be your friends or family.

## Dropping names

I have lived a very nice life, just enough excitement, enough quiet time, met some very nice people, most of whom were just people, bumped into some celebrities and accumulated a whole bunch of funny and interesting stories. I drop names sometimes to draw attention to personalities and give perspective.

I have two more stories to tell.

I once bumped into Elvis Presley in LA. I was leaving my advertising agency job on Sunset Boulevard going home to Manhattan Beach, sitting at the stop light at Santa Monica Boulevard on La Cienega. I noticed the black Cadillac town car next to me, within arm's length. It's a narrow street at that place, with narrow lanes. In the passenger seat one foot away from me with the window down and his elbow inches away was Elvis. We looked at each other smiled and he said, "Nice car." I was driving a new model that year, the 1967 Mercury Cougar.

New York City date unknown. You see, I used to travel through once or twice a year for ten years. I met a girl going to the Chapin School in Manhattan and spent some time with her, including one night in her dorm room upstairs in the school building. At breakfast downstairs in the morning she was showing the walls of classical oil portraits of notable students of the past. Trisha Nixon, and Grace Slick of Jefferson Airplane went to school there. I don't know what dates they attended, but I did know at the time that Grace Slick had attended previously. The girl I was with asked me if I would come to dinner that night, so I spent some time trying to find a good poster or photograph of Grace to surreptitiously put up on the wall when I came back. I didn't find Grace, but I had a sumptuous meal or two with the girl.

## CHAPTER 154

# Joan's Chapter

Love keeps me alive. A lot has been said about how much longer a married man lives. It goes even deeper than merely a medical salvation. Having a mate's companionship gives one reason to live.

Companionship feels like the warmth of a family. Having a history is a window into each of us.

Wife...what a nice word! I like the sound of that word, and the name Joan. We have been together in our love for so long that it is as natural as breathing in and out. If that sounds like a statement of boredom or jaded repetition, not so, friend! I have never been bored for a moment in my life, and living with a woman will not allow your life to get boring.

In the long run, I have had only one monogamous relationship, this last one!

I have made love with just one woman in the last 35 years. Albeit numerous times, of course, but this is still a major frustration of a man. It goes against our basic primal nature, but in the context of today if you are able to make love with only your wife, you are a more sensitive, secure, rational, strong and realistic man! Plus, you do not have to pay numerous alimony checks, get followed by PIs, dodge bullets from husbands and catch unmentionable STDs.

Do you really want to be a tabloid story that is old and irrelevant in a week's time? And do you want to be, shunned, laughed at, and spoken about in whispers in your own town?

*"It makes me happy to make her laugh!"*

*"I didn't marry Joan because she was a trophy,*
*I have been with them.*
*I wanted to be with her for the rest of my life because of*

*something that defies words or explanation!"*
JBMc


*"Most women have no idea what effort, pain, anguish and love it takes for a man to accomplish the normality that a wife requires and often demands."*
DG


A man must be emotionally committed to be able to have sexual intercourse with a woman. A woman does not even have to know nor like a man to have sexual intercourse with him! Most women don't understand this concept, and mostly because they cannot understand the intimate connection a man has with his penis. A man must have blood flowing to his phallus, or it can not perform.

Not to be disrespectful, but sometimes men and women both think they could have done better. Some men have affairs an/or have fantasies, and sometimes leave their families. Some women have affairs, but few of them leave their home for their lover, and that is because women's prevailing influence is the protection of house and family. Many women are insecure about and critical of their mate's economic productivity, and that plays into his insecurity, which is need for ego gratification. This is the point at which many marriages end.

The eternal story of a new romance or marriage: She was uncomfortable with his language. She didn't say so, but he knew she was. His eating habits were too...too bachelor. She didn't say, but he knew. He started taking food out of the can and putting it onto a plate when she was around. And he began exploring real cooked food.

She chafed when he didn't shave. He invested in more blades. Her clothing was cleaner and fresher looking. He acquired a wardrobe. She liked driving a clean car. He found a bucket and sponge.

She preferred broccoli. He ate broccoli. Vacuuming strained her back. He hated vacuuming, but it became his penance. Washing dishes was the next cross to bear.

He knew she forsook some of her own habits. He knew she changed some 'wishes to maybes,' some 'oh nos, to OKs.'

It is the way of love. As long as the love remains, these compromises will not become an issue. We must always remember that upon this give-and-take our love swings.

We're not given the option to choose who we fall in love with. It happens! Sometimes it is heaven, sometimes hell, but hopefully it will be a manageable balance of both.

If you are lucid enough and when you realize that that person is your soul mate, just hope that you have the strength and knowledge to hold on to them. One day when the two of you are old and dying, one of you may be wiping the others butt and combing their hair, and that is better than being alone when you die!

"Everybody loves my wife, but they are not quite so sure about me."

I am in a love affair that will take up the rest of my life.

Joan is one of my few successes. Not just finding and marrying her, but being faithful to her. The true proof of a man's love is not what he gives to you, or even his sexual attraction to you. His true expression of love is how much time he wants to spends with you!

"True Love Ways" by Buddy Holly is one of the most romantic songs ever written. I had my friend, Dave Love, sing it to my wife, Joan, on our wedding day, December 21,1985. Over the years, I have sung it to her from time to time on the occasion of our anniversary or her birthday.

No love affair is without its trauma and drama. Buddy Holly wrote that song to sing to his wife on their wedding day. Their story was one of the most star-crossed, beautiful and yet tragic love affairs. Buddy didn't marry "Peggy Sue." He moved away from Lubbock, Texas, to New York City to pursue his music career in 1958. He met a young woman there and married her. Maria Elena, his wife, was pregnant with their son when Buddy was killed in that plane crash with Ritchie Valens and The Big Bopper in Clear Lake, Iowa on February 3, 1959.

That song reveals, "Sometimes we'll sigh, sometimes we'll

cry, and we'll know why, just you and I know true love ways."

*"I would lie, cheat and steal to keep you from running, but the one thing I will not do is to change the nature of the man I was the day you fell in love with me!"* JBMc 4.14.16

*"I can understand your feelings only if I have experienced the same feelings myself. I can return your feelings only if I have the same feelings for you!"*
Dudley Griffin, 4.16.16

A man alone has no expectations placed on him, but from himself. A man married and in an economic relationship with a woman has expectations from all sides. After ten or fifteen years of marriage, depending on how old the couple is respectively, sex is not an issue, but the money issue is still there! From a man's perspective, at this point, it is devotion that keeps you here, fighting the fight!

When your wife or girlfriend has more of an ego than you do, it is normally not the same kind of ego that men display. It is usually defensive rather than offensive. Men kill far more often than women, and it is usually senseless, about greed or ego, whereas women usually kill only to protect their children, themselves, and yes, to protect their husband or lover.

You will not put me on the spot to pronounce unequivocally male and female relationships are pre-ordained by God, nor doomed. I am not always a romantic, but I am always a realist. And yet fight it as I have, I have become smitten of love, and now believe that it is the most valuable thing in life. I am married, and now they tell me that I may even live longer because of it.

She kept me alive, she led me toward vitality, and she confirmed my validity.

I look at my life as it relates to my wife. Joan, it is impossible to imagine life without you.

It was my good fortune to have met and married one of the nicest people in this imperfect world. I feel sorry for those less fortunate that I.

*"I know I could not do better, and she probably would have a hard time replacing me, but perfection is not for mankind to possess."*
Dudley Griffin, 6.11.11

*"Joan, 80% of the time I want to be by your side, 20% I want to be with myself."*
JBMc, .5.31.11

*"I did not marry you for your body, your sexuality or your cooking! I married you because I love you... just you!"*
DG, 10.3.14

*"There are few things more valuable than a friend! There are few things more valuable than a lover! There is nothing more valuable than a friend who is lover!"*
JBMc, 9.29.14

*"What is bad manners for the gander is bad manors for the goose."*
Dudley Griffin, 8.27.15

That thing called love is hard to define! Many people have given it a shot, but few have succeeded in my estimation. Here is my profound effort.

"Love is indefinable, it is chemistry and sweat, it is blue skies and black and blue egos, it is diamond rings and rings around the tub, it is eyes that do not falter and words that will not waver. If it is true love, it is like trusting the rest of your life to thin, soft, white silk as you jump out of an airplane!"

In a good relationship there must be periods of discovery, long sessions of familial discussion, comfortable peace and quiet, and then moments of conflict that resolve a misunderstanding. In a long love affair you must give yourself completely many times, but for the love to be real between equals, neither must lose themselves, or then it is a life indentured!

I can dissect this now, after all these years, why I chose Joan as my mate for life. I wasn't carrying a list, and I didn't check it off when we met. But I wanted someone I could laugh with, someone naïve enough, to the point just before you deceive her. Someone everybody loves, yet who does not make every man feel as if he should take a chance. Someone who could help me raise my aspirations as my mother did. I found her in Joan.

I was blessed by the best mother and blessed by friends and lovers, and now I am blessed by the best wife. It is a progression of what I consider to be my wonderful life.

You must realize that in order to write the truth, you must give up your lies. I cannot tell you the truth unless I have lived it. In order to appreciate the truth, you must realize that the truth is the best life and the best story.

I am sorry about my indulgences of food or drink and sometimes being economically challenged! I am not sorry about drinking, we all indulge in some form of escape. I don't stick anything into my blood stream, nor snort it up my nose. I am sorry you "worry," about my male indulgences. I'm not sorry that I am not a "type A" person.

This is not a criticism, just a sad observation, but I think that women are genetically predisposed to demand from their man more than he can produce, no matter how well he is providing. It is primal for women to want a strong provider, and it worked in the jungle. But I'm afraid it often succeeds in breaking up families in this day and economic age.

Many men cannot battle and win in this competitive world today, when the bar is being raised as fast as you reach it. And few men can predict what next requirement their wives will impose. It is not an unsolvable dilemma. All it requires is love, companionship and the desire for happiness to survive as a family in this world today.

How can I explain happiness to those who have not known it in their families and their lives? Happiness is a lack of pressure and an absence of conflict. Those who know nothing but conflict will accept the discomfort of negativity, and that is a dysfunctional love affair or marriage.

Each moment in our lives is a slice of hope. Some do better

than others. Some aren't even given a chance. Some are given more than they can handle, and some more than they deserve.

A real marriage is not just a business contract! A real marriage is shared goals and companionship; people with the same purpose, having a warm glow of knowing someone who wants to be with you, of knowing that they will gladly change your diapers and you will gladly change theirs.

How can you ignore the purity of love when living in this world where money, diamonds, fast people and fine china are speaking seductively to you? There is love if you want to find it, but to find real love there is a cost. You must give in, acquiesce at times, you must demand compassionately sometimes, and you must refuse when the emotional cost is too high.

Old couples, truly in love and who have been together for a long while, are each conflicted. They don't want to be the first to die to leave their mate, whom they wish to help in their old age. And yet, at the same time, no one wants to see the decline of their loved one.

*When I think of my wife, I see the two sides of her that sparkle.*
*Naiveté born of trust, and compassion born of motherhood.*

I can say one thing as a husband to my wife of 37 years, in all truthfulness, "I have been faithful to you all these years," but, and this may be a condemnation of my sex, I know most men cannot say that!,

There is one conundrum (weird question) having to do with men and women that will pretzelize your mind. It is hard to understand why women demand too much of their men and why men do not appreciate their women for being motherly. In many cultures the mother, most often the grandmother is worshipped, yet the girlfriend or wife is treated poorly, and yet the girlfriend and wife are mothers as well, now or in the future.

Primeval mentality or the chromosomes dictate that women will reject a man who seems to them to be weak, even a man whom they love and adore, who is just trying to make them feel comfortable by being warm and fuzzy. It is in woman's nature to think there is a stronger, better man out their somewhere.

And primeval mentality or the Y chromosome dictates that

men will shun a woman who seems to them to be too strong, even a woman whom they love and adore who is just trying to please them by being a good sport. It is in man's nature to believe that the perfect woman is out there still waiting for them.

The sooner you get over these delusions and realize that this could be the greenest grass and accept the things that are good in your relationship, the better your days will be. If your relationship is over 50% good, then my experience tells me that you should stick with it. There are a lot of 25% out there.

But you must note that this may only be a valid benchmark, and then only if you went into the relationship with your eyes open in the first place. Choose wisely early in a relationship if you want it to last forever, and then stick with it.

But in my observation, most men take a long time to become adults and that is why many first marriages don't last. I think many men are at least in their late thirties early forties before they are marriageable. Yet the problem is by that time, many men as well as women are too set in their ways to be good partners.

My wife and I have been married now for 35 years. We are as happy with each other as any two people can be. Our relationship looks so good that, I am sure, some people can't believe it is true, and some others are jealous. Don't be jealous of the success of other people. They have had to work at it, compromise and step up.

I have to admit that at times I, myself, am jealous of the image we portray. Standing on the outside, everything looks neat and tidy, like a nice, white egg, but inside is all that gooey, sticky stuff.

Of course, from the inside it's always a different story. No relationship is perfect. The perfect relationship would be me, just me, with everything I want, whenever I want it, even orgasms, and the last word and the perfect sleeping conditions.

But there still is something maddeningly intriguing about relationships of opposites, and so I'll stick with it. Maybe I will get to comfort my wife in her last moments, or she will comfort me in mine.

## Second Wives, Second Husbands

You have heard the term "baggage"? Sometimes a wife on her second husband or a husband on his second wife will not be able to forget the mistakes of their previous spouse and will expect their new mate to repeat those mistakes. Second marriage couples often punish the new spouse for the mistakes of the last. Some wives on their second husband will not be able to appreciate the good things about their new husband, because they were imprinted with bad experiences. They may not realize that a man can be a good man. They may not be able to recognize that a man can be kind and still be strong, can be a man without being a bully. And this can go both ways.

If you add multiple marriages or committed relationships, then you can see the stepping stones of mating in the world of human beings.

"I know that I can never be everything to you, and you can never be everything to me. And if you know that I can never be everything to you, and you can never be everything to me, then now we may begin a new and lasting love."

Most men at some point fantasize that they need a combination of three women. We want to possess the slut, be loved by the mother, and elevated by the muse.

Many men want it all ways. Polygamy, bigamy, infidelity and cult power over women are appealing to many men. But all I have ever really wanted, and at one time unbeknownst to me, was a friend.

Every married person wishes they were single from time to time. If the fantasy takes up more than half of the time, then it's time for a change. If you are not happy for most of your marriage, if the sum total of happiness does not match up to the unhappiness of your relationship, then that relationship has proven to be a deficit and negative in your life.

If 51% of your time together is good, then you are still a winner. I know for a fact that when I was single, I spent 98% of my time trying to hook up with somebody. When you are married, you have a hookup available 80% of the time.

Being comfortable with a person, having companionship with a partner 51% of the time, is a winning situation as far as human relationships go!

Men living with men, and women living with women would be a better arrangement than bad marriages! After a certain age and numerous relationship experiences, many people give up on heterosexual marriage happily ever after. And some of these disillusioned, decide to cohabitate with same sex partners, for economic, social, sometimes sexual benefit.

This arrangement is not a revolution against marriage; it is a statement against hypocrisy. The only thing I am morally against in sexual or marriage relationships is slavery!

Knowing Joan from our middle school days, I knew that she was a flirt, naïve, of course, but still a force to be dealt with.

The male mind and female mind are different in numerous ways. Most men take flirtation as an offer of something more physical. Back in 1957 it was almost never more than a kiss, but if you continue your 1957 flirtations into the 1970s and beyond, you will come in conflict with the deeper male ego.

Joan and Bugs, the cutest of the flirts.

Flirting is fun, but you have to know the consequences and understand the motivations of the person you are flirting with.

Since my wife and I re-met in 1985, I have never flirted with anyone because before that time when I flirted, it was for an end result. So I don't lead people on, and I don't make it look like I could become unfaithful because I never will be, this time.

I, for one, cannot be intimate with someone who does not respect me, and as in many relationships, for a time, Joan seemed to show more respect for others and appeared to shutting me out. So I began to retreat from intimacy, but my love for her and my desire to be with her has never lessoned.

Yet, for a time in the late 90s, I was looking at other options; not acting on them, but testing the waters of my desirability and looking at my own desires. I soon rejected the possibilities of any deviations. I have never wanted anyone else's companionship, other than Joan's, ever since September 1985.

Joan, at this place in our lives, all I am trying to do is to keep everything happy. We need to be with and for each other to survive the rest of our lives in comfort and dignity. For us to begin harping on each other right now would only mean that one or both of us have gone mad.

Soon one of us may have to be wiping the other's ass and toweling their drool. Now is the time for us to be getting even closer together. I just know that no matter what lies ahead, all I want to do is take care of Joan for the rest of my life; and beyond.

*Sweetheart,* you are the only woman I have ever been faithful to. *John*

> "My God, my God, why have you forsaken Me?"
> JOB

> "My God, my God, why have you lifted Me up?"
> JOB

CHAPTER 155

# The Snoring Chapter

In this book I have usually refrained from placing blame on one sex or the other, and definitely not on the opposite sex. I will accuse my own sex, though, when it is obvious that we are wrong or acting badly, stupidly or ignorantly. Yet this is one case where I am going to cast some aspersions against the "fairer sex,"

My experience is that wives (partners) often treat a snorer as if they were snoring just to annoy them, or that somehow they are doing it for some nefarious reason. For the most part, if not totally, a person has no control over their snoring! For a bed partner to blame a snorer is cruel and insensitive!

There are times when a person's body weight will create snoring. In some cases what you eat or drink contributes to snoring, but mostly it has to do with a physical cause that is not a person's own fault.

In my experience, and it can possibly be proven, women's snoring is somewhat less common and often with less volume, but it is a fallacy that women don't snore. I recorded my wife once or twice, and she was most embarrassed and in denial. She finally realized it when one night she woke herself, accused me, and then found that I was not even in bed at the time!

I personally have suffered as much or more from my own snoring than others have from my snoring. For years, I have had to move from my own familiar and comfortable bed to avoid interrupting the sleep of others.

In the effort to protect my partner's sleep, I have bedded down on thinly padded floors, cold cement floors, in closets with smelly shoes, on short bunk beds, some with urine stained sheets, in back seats of cars, and several times, outdoors.

What was even worse, if you can believe this, I often didn't sleep at all, or I slept fitfully or in a shallow sleep! Sleep deprivation is a technique used by torturers.

I have suffered through the use of nose strips, plastic and rubber mouth devices, cold, irritating nose sprays, horrible tasting throat sprays, and yes, even, self-hypnosis!

I found it interesting not too long ago while vacationing in Mexico. I went looking for nose strips, only to find none! In Mexico, as I suppose in many third-world countries, everybody snores, men and women, and it is ignored and nobody cares.

They just sleep through their partner's habits and "flaws." Part of the reason is that third-world houses are much smaller, and in many cases the whole family sleeps in one room. No one can hide from snoring, night sweats or sleepless thrashing unless a separate house or island is provided as in Sicily near Palermo where "it is said" that women during menstruation were banished to the small island just off the coast called Isola delle Femmine!

This brings me to my real point. I, for one, am awakened only by a threat to my home, family or self. My partner's snoring does not awaken me, nor does the garbage truck, my neighbors arriving home from a late party, or the water heater turning on, etc. My sleeping psyche makes decisions. I wake for unnatural sounds, but continue to sleep through normal sounds.

My conclusion is that my sleeping partners have been guilty of having shallow sleeping habits, which is not my fault. They are not living in the jungle, so therefore they needn't awaken from "noise" only, and definitely not by the snoring of their loving bedmate. This, of course, is tongue and cheek, but true.

There is a long history of married couples sleeping in separate rooms when it was economically or physically possible. In my situation, I do not consider this to be the perfect arrangement since I want to sleep next to my wife. But when sleep depravation starts to set in, occasionally we do sleep separately for two or three nights in order to balance or recoup our sanity from sleeplessness.

Some activities, temperatures, this or that situation do cause snoring. And solutions should be explored, rather than just arguments and divorce!

The answer to this problem is not going to be solved by one chapter in this book, but maybe a discourse will be initiated by this introduction!

*"It is godlike to give less than you take. It is godlike not to expect more than you give. This means that if you believe in eternity and/or heaven, it would be better for your retirement plan to take a loss in this world today."*
Dudley Griffin

CHAPTER 156

# Media's Contribution Toward Bad Sex, Sex Crimes, and Immorality

Today on your idiot box, there are numerous TV dramas and reality shows that are dumbing down the public and, worse yet, glorifying the stupid, and ignorant.

Much of the new science fiction, horror and terror fiction like: The Walking Dead, Purge, Twilight, Resident Evil: Extinction, A Haunting and Hunger Games is taking you nowhere good and teaching only evil. These shows also confuse the young and malleable mind of what is true and what is false science and morality.

The relationship shows, such as: 90 Day Fiancé, Married at First Sight, The Bachelors and The Bachelorette, will do nothing for you except confuse you about what is real love and commitment.

The economy shows like The Profit and Shark Tank teach nothing but greed is good for the greedy.

Our ethnic life, economic life, religious life and sex life are all tied together. If any one part is shaky, the other parts suffer.

No one is easily able to think beyond their education or experiences nor think below their present place. It is hard or impossible to go back to a point where you could have changed your mind and gone up or down or left or right; the moment is lost forever. Aside from a properly regulated psychedelic rejuvenation of memories, we are sometimes going to have to take the word of others, call them teachers or loved ones.

The media has gotten lazy, thinking that they can put out any crap and the brain dead will watch it and buy whatever is advertised. I was in the media when we tried to stimulate minds, not kill them. I was in the advertising industry when we tried to attract the rational and common sense part of the consumer.

There are three different personality categories that the media has defined and exploited. They are: the capitalist personality, religious personality, and moralist personality. The status of these is expressed by the media as good, bad or problematic, and these judgments change with the times and the political administration in power. My basic definitions of these people are: capitalistic personality emphasizes that greed is good. A religious personality judges others, although blind to themself. The moral person defines morality by what it does or does not do unto others. To be capitalist you must be ruthless. To be religious you must not think too much. To be moral you have to live in everyone else's shoes.

*"Nothing is more important to a human being than a teacher. I believe that a real good teacher is the one who is somehow, miraculously able to break you out of you here and now with a thought that is true and real and which you cannot deny."*
JOB

*"Believe me, there are some people who don't want to learn anything new. They think it is too hard and a waste of time. But the one thing that is most important in order to be a human being is to have more information. That is the job of humankind, because that is how we will eventually get it right, learn the truth, become perfect and save the world and ourselves. "*
Mr. California, 6.27.21

*"Morality is the standards of conduct that are accepted as right or proper by humans as dictated by common sense, or by God, if we need a middle-man.
There is a place in our society for business, but not predatory greed. They can say that it is not illegal, but it is definitely immoral.
There is a place in our society for religion but not religious bigotry. They can say that it is their spiritual faith, but it is immoral in a true God's eyes.
Immorality is a sin against yourself, or your GOD, whatever god you worship."*
Dudley Griffin, 6.27.21

CHAPTER 157

# Researching Sex, A Dangerous Misadventure

During the first years of developing this book, I tried numerous ways to learn the things I needed to know to write a book as diverse and poignant as I wanted it to be.

I started doing some experimenting, some very productive, and others ill conceived. One of my efforts was a sex questionnaire, trying to get a current wide view of peoples' sex history and likes and dislikes. I displayed them at coffee shops with a box for the participant to deposit their completed form.

My intent was to get a couple of hundred returned valid questionnaires, tally the answers up, and print the "scores" and my conclusions in the book. It turned out to be too time consuming and difficult to organize and justify, so I left it out, although it did help me organize my own thoughts and contributed to many of the things I wrote in this book.

Another effort to learn people's likes and dislikes was to watch as many X-rated videos as I could handle. I am definitely not a voyeur, and that was a chore for my sensitive tastes. I kept a list of the number of each sexual activities displayed. Straight intercourse, fellacio, cunnilingus, foreplay, anal sex, etc. In the media, which those tapes represent, the producers offer what the public wants, and so it gave me a good outline on public interests.

Around that time my wife and I were having a little rocky period. Something I will call mid-relationship doldrums or second thoughts! If you have never had a rocky patch in your marriage, then you are fortunate. It seems that losing sight of your love and what brought you together can be a periodic event. Think about the definition of the word marriage, which means the bringing together of two objects or people! A couple must continually re-affirm their relationship by growing closer together in order for there to be a marriage.

From time to time as many wives do, my wife was not completely satisfied with the productivity of the man she was married to.

I didn't bring in enough money, I snored, or maybe I didn't bring her coffee in bed, or get her a glass of wine the moment we got to a party! She may have started thinking she could do better.

At the time, we had a tenant in our studio who was tall, dark, handsome and charming. I liked him very much too, but often it appeared that she was paying more attention to him, than me. I know in my mind that no physical contact ever happened. But I felt left out, I felt less respect toward me and my feelings in my own home sometimes.

The result of that was, I felt under appreciated! I have said many times that I usually suppress my ego. But if you know the self-preservation nature of all animals, including man, you know that men will sometimes react drastically in some way when their home is threatened. Fight or flight.

I understand the knee-jerk reaction, but I have never been one who would punch a guy out for looking at my girl. But only if she seemed to be reciprocating would I even consider taking other measures, and the first action I usually took was to try to be even more desirable than my competitor.

That didn't seem to work this time. So as in my past history, when that tactic failed, I started pulling back in my own affections for her, not to be cruel or vindictive or to create jealousy in her, but because her lack of respect naturally triggered my own cooling of feelings for her. I don't want to be with a wife, friend or lover who doesn't want to be with me.

This is not the only place in this book that you will read this line from a country western song, "It is hard to kiss the lips at night that chew your ass out all day long!"

Even at that time I knew that Joan was my "soul mate." I had no desire to move on, but how she was treating me hurt my soul, not my ego, but my soul.

She seemed to be showing indifference toward me, and that came close to pushing my detachment button, which in some of my past relationships had started me looking for another source of love or satisfaction!

In my relationships with people, women in particular, I've always wanted to know for that moment, at least, they cared about me, and I was, for that time, their "center of the earth." With a wife or live-in mate, I want, most people want, to be the center of their life.

That is the way I felt toward women. While I was with them, they were the center of the world. It is why I was a successful lover.

If a woman didn't want me, I would stop desiring her. It is a simple hormonal reaction.

A man tries to satisfy his wife because a happy wife means a happy man, and a happy man is more likely to look for ways to make his wife happy. We all win!

This first and only rocky period with Joan was between 1999 to 2004, our ages were for Joan 55-60 and for me 56-61. Late mid-life crisis time.

When I turned 59 years old I had a thirty-five-year-old daughter, a gray beard and a bald head. I looked younger than I was, but that still put me in the 45 to 55-year-old range.

I have had numerous, and beautiful girlfriends, but my extravagant life ended when I married my wife, Joan, fifteen or sixteen years earlier. I hadn't missed the fast lane much, and apparently it didn't miss me at all.

At 59 years of age, I could walk into a room full of women between 14 and 30 years old, and none of them would look up with interest. I used to be considered a sexy man, or so I have been told at least. And with my sexual history, I would think a woman with good instincts should be able to look at me and see me as the exciting lover I once was. But they don't seem to notice.

It doesn't bother me; I have no major ego problems with being invisible to young women. Yet I began wondering, what would it take, in the new millennium, and after the sexual revolution, for a man of my age to get laid by a young woman? I had to find this out; how would I do it? Ask a women in person or with a questionnaire, or read more about women? All too difficult and time consuming, plus there was the problem of getting self-serving answers or answers they might think I want to hear.

A seduction game appeared to be the only answer. I would just show my interest to someone, maybe flirt a bit, and then ask them point blank if they would sleep with me. Strangely I didn't consider all the sticky problems attached to such a plan.

First I had to get my research done without jeopardizing my marriage, which I cherish, and that meant there could be no actual "sexual" contact which meant to me, no sensual kissing or beyond. No first base, second base, third or homerun.

At that time I seemed to believe that most women had a kind of ESP that quantified a man's values and calculated what the future might be with him. I simply thought women chose a man consciously while stimulated by hormones and aided by a divining subconscious.

I was eventually to find out that I was partially right about two-thirds of the time, and the rest of the time the reasons a woman does what she does couldn't be calculated by the flipping of a coin, not even a ten-sided coin. So I hope now you understand how confusing human coupling can be.

Since the day my wife and I re-met I had not flirted with or led-on anyone. But I was curious why I got so little interest, and whether or not it was because I was not flirting. Was it all up to us men to make the first move or say the first words? And did my age or married status matter? I had to find these answers, but I found instead that I was searching for too many answers. I knew that if I told my wife or even if she heard of this crazy effort to do research for a book, I might jeopardize our then tenuous relationship. I would try to do my research, keep Joan from learning about it and sustain my moral foundation all at the same time. And our marriage is really a moral foundation.

I have mentioned my mother's final rejection of my father's marriage proposal, because of his legendary infidelities. Well, I didn't want to follow my father into that abyss.

For one thing I have often wondered what my life would have been like had my father been the faithful kind and my mother had agreed to marry him after my birth. All this moot -point conversation about what might have happened is stupid. It might have been much worse. But I am curious! Yet, I am not going to be socially like my father, I love everything else about him except his early sex life. I have found out recently that he was fairly faithful and sober in his later years.

But, after my first divorce, I decide that if I got married again I was going to be faithful, to a fault.

Part of my research dealt with what flirtation meant. In order to study this, I had to get close to a flirtation episode. I could not do that watching over other people's shoulders. I looked around at the girls who had outwardly been "nice" to me, or at least in my perception had been maybe flirtatious. Of course, perception was one of the things I wanted to learn. Was she just being nice, was I being too literal?

I perceived that a few girls had flirted, and I chose three or four to pursue. My plan was to take them to the point of sexual contact and then tell them that this was a test for them and me, and stop.

They were all girls who knew I was married and who knew my wife. I realized that if I had to stop it, when they were willing, they might be hurt or embarrassed, and so I prepared for that.

Have I mentioned that this plan of mine was brilliant yet ill-advised?

I cannot remember the order or time lapse of the episodes with these girls, yet I will relate them! One was in Santa Barbara, and three were in Monterey. Always aware of my wife's sensibility and not wanting to hurt her, I had roughed out an explanation I would give to these girls, stating that my intentions were research.

During this time, I was also dealing with my feeling of disenfranchisement at home, and it was only a few years later when I realized that my actions were part of a mid-life crises that I as all men had to traverse. Only my strength of character would save me, and I can even laugh at that!

My script of seduction was, with certain alterations, I would arrange to meet with each of them, in a mutual place, or someplace unthreatening, and ask them point blank if they would like to make love with me.

One said she had just started a new relationship and didn't want to divert her attention. One looked at me as if I was some kind of a stalker and walked away. One said no, even though we went out and ate and danced all night, and we both learned a lot about relationships. The fourth I decided not to pursue. By then I could see the stupidity of the project, and I had already learned all I needed to know for this book and had seen enough about myself.

The problem and shame of it is that I was only able to tell one of the three girls about it being a test, and a research project for my next book. Later, it was also obvious to myself that it was also a test of my resilience, morality and love of my wife.

I tried to contact each of the other two "guinea pigs," but they would not talk to me or take my letters. I applaud them for treating me like the stalker they must have thought I was.

It all ended up well. The things I thought my wife was feeling didn't come to anything. And, with time, I have also realized that her activities were not flirtation. Being the mother of two boys, she has always been comfortable with, and interested in young men in general.

After this time we became stronger, and our marriage is working as it should be. We are actually marrying closer every day. For what I thought was happening, I apologize to my wife, Joan, and for any discomfort the others felt, I ask forgiveness. It was an unusual time and not my best behavior.

I was busy building our house, more or less by my own hands and working on my careers as photographer, ad agency owner and building contractor, all of which were stressing my common sense a bit.

Around this same time, I was also doing another experiment, and that was actually homework to learn what I needed to know to write my three complex books. The project of educating myself to write so I could be understood was facilitated by getting a lot of "good" books and reading them and reading more and more again.

Vulnerability is something we all possess at times, and to recognize it is a lesson we should all learn. If we learn our faults and failings and find out how to avoid or suppress them, life will be sweeter and contain fewer booby traps.

## Sexual Questionnaire

Please be totally truthful. This survey is completely anonymous, so you would only be lying to yourself. Exaggerations or omissions will serve merely to damage a valuable study. Questions may overlap. Please answer all that apply to you. The responses will be tabulated for a book.

Age _25_ Male _✓_ Female ____ Single _✓_ Married ____ Divorced _No_ # of Marriages _0_

Heterosexual _✓_ Homosexual ____ Bisexual ____ Do you cross-dress? _No_

Have your ever been raped? _No_ or molested? _No_

Total length of sexual life Months _1_ Years _6_ Approximate Number of Sex Partners _4_

Length of sexual life with present mate before marriage _N/A_ Years of marriage _0_

Do you have a steady lover other than a spouse? _No_ Do you have multiple sex partners? _No_

Frequency of intercourse per week _0_ per month _0_ per year _0_

Would you prefer more or less frequency? _More_ How many extramarital affairs have you had? _0_

If single, number of sex partners per week _0_ per month _0_ per year _0_

Do you insist on condoms? no ____ sometimes _✓_ always ____

Do you object to using condoms? _No_ Are you circumcised? _Yes_

Do you enjoy performing oral sex? no ____ it's OK ____ very much _X_ more than vaginal ____

Do you enjoy receiving oral sex? no ____ it's OK ____ very much _X_ more than vaginal ____

Have you ever had a homosexual experience? _No_ Would you consider it again? _N/A_

Do you enjoy anal sex? no ____ it's OK _X_ very much ____ more than vaginal ____

Do you have a tongue stud? _No_ Did you get the stud for sexual purposes? _N/A_

Do you enjoy a partner's tongue stud? _Yes_

Do you have any other piercings for sexual stimulation? _No_ What and where? _N/A_

Do you enjoy bondage or rough sex? no ____ it's OK _X_ very much ____

Do you masturbate? _Yes_ How often? per day _0_ per week _2_ per month _10_

Do you use a dildo? _No_ Do you enjoy pornography? _Yes_

Do you have any sexual fantasy or activity of which you are ashamed? _No_ If so, and you wish to explain, please do so. _N/A_

Please place this questionnaire in **THE BOX**, or send to: Box 114, 484-B Washington Street, Monterey, CA 93940

**What is your sex?**   **Sexual Questionnaire**

Please be totally truthful. This survey is completely anonymous, so you would only be lying to yourself. Exaggerations or omissions will serve merely to damage a valuable study. Questions may overlap. Please answer all that apply to you. The responses will be tabulated for a book.

Age _47_ Male _✓_ Female ____ Single ____ Married ____ Divorced ____ # of Marriages _0_

Heterosexual _✓_ Homosexual ____ Bisexual ____ Do you cross-dress? _no_

Have your ever been raped? _50%_ or molested? _no_

Total length of sexual life  Months ____ Years _30_ Approximate Number of Sex Partners _300_

Length of sexual life with present mate before marriage _3y_ Years of marriage ____

Do you have a steady lover other than a spouse? _no_ Do you have multiple sex partners? _yes_

Frequency of intercourse  per week _5_ per month ____ per year ____

Would you prefer more or less frequency? ____ How many extramarital affairs have you had? _0_

If single, number of sex partners per week _1_ per month _2_ per year _4_

Do you insist on condoms?  no _✓_ sometimes ____ always ____

Do you object to using condoms? ____   Are you circumcised? _yes_

Do you enjoy performing oral sex?  no ____ it's OK ____ very much _✓_ more than vaginal ____

Do you enjoy receiving oral sex?  no ____ it's OK ____ very much _✓_ more than vaginal ____

Have you ever had a homosexual experience? _no_ Would you consider it again? _yes_

Do you enjoy anal sex?  no ____ it's OK ____ very much _✓_ more than vaginal ____

Do you have a tongue stud? _no_ Did you get the stud for sexual purposes? _me_

Do you enjoy a partner's tongue stud? _no_

Do you have any other piercings for sexual stimulation? _no_ What and where? ____

Do you enjoy bondage or rough sex?  no ____ it's OK _✓_ very much ____

Do you masturbate? _✓_ How often?  per day ____ per week _4_ per month ____

Do you use a dildo? ____ Do you enjoy pornography? _yes_

Do you have any sexual fantasy or activity of which you are ashamed? _no_ If so, and you wish to explain, please do so. ____

Please place this questionnaire in **THE BOX**, or send to: Box 114, 484-B Washington Street, Monterey, CA 93940

Detach and keep this strip of paper for a 20% discount on the book
*Loveseat Fantasies: The Sexual Documentary of a Young Man,*
when purchased directly from the author.

To be published in 2004.

630

*Definitions of Sexual Preferences:*

**Bisexual***: A person who is sexually attracted to both sexes*
**Bad Boy, Rough Trade:** *A guy who is perceived to be economically poor and socially rebellious*
**Gay***: A homosexual; a male or female who is sexually attracted to the same sex*
**Gay Pride:** *The promotion of dignity, equality and equal rights for all, regardless of gender*
**LGBTQA:** *For those or you who don't know what the acronym means, it initially stood for: Lesbian, Gay, Bisexual, Transgender and Queer, and Ally. Now as of 1/20/21 there is* **LGBTQ Plus / QIAAP** *Questioning, Intersex, Asexual, Allies, Pansexual*
**Heterosexual***: Someone who is sexually attracted only to the opposite sex*
**Homosexual***: Someone who is sexually attracted only to the same sex*
**Lesbian***: A female homosexual*
**Transgender***: Someone who considers themself to be the opposite gender of the one they were designated at birth or indicated by their sexual organs. This is not a transvestite, or cross-dresser, who may not be a homosexual, yet just likes dressing in the other sexes' clothing. As a heads up, when referring to a transgender person, it is probably best to use a simple pronoun, like they, he or she, rather than he/she or she/he. Follow the lead of the clothing. If a person is dressed in male clothing, use he, and if dressed in female clothing, use she*

**Definition of Sexual Activities, Body Parts, Nouns, Pronouns and Slang:**

*"There are more names for and ways to describe sex than for any other activity of human beings. More than for food and eating, breathing, going to the bathroom or dying! And that is because sex is what we do, think about and like or hate, and everybody does these things in one way or another."*

Mr. California

**Affair**: *Sex that is usually somehow unsanctioned and outside of one's committed relationship*

**Anal Sex**: *penis inserted in the rear of a woman*

**Assignation**: *A sexual meeting*

**Balling**: *A very derogatory term indicating the least sensitive form of lovemaking*

**Being Intimate**: *a sweet sexual encounter*

**Carnality**: *animalistic form of sex*

**Carnal Knowledge**: *sexual intercourse, sometime considered a spiritual form of sex*

**Catfisher:** *a person who lies to people on social networks for some perverted sexual reason*

**Cohabitation**: *unmarried, livein sex*

**Coitus**: *the medical definition of sex*

**Conjugation**: *a literary definition of sex*

**Copulate**: *a very clinical form of sex*

**Coupling**: *a romantic form of sex*

**Cunnilingus**: *oral sex on a woman*

**Feeling up**: *touching a woman's breast*

**Fellacio**: *oral sex on a man*

**Fingering**: *inserting a finger into a woman*

**Fornicating**: *a disrespectful form of sex*

**Fraternizing**: *game playing sex*

**Fucking**: *your basic sex*

**Going to Bed**, *a romantic form of sex*

**Getting it On**: *yeah, you get it*

**Having**: *a dominating sex*

**Having Your Way**: *a suspicious form of sex*

*Humping*: *a joyous form of sex*
*Intercourse*: *a conservative form of sex*
*Intimacy*: *a sensual form of sex*
*Liaison*: *a meeting especially for sex*
*Love:* *Greek or Aramaic forms of love:*
    Eros: *The sexual passion*
    Philia: *The deep friendship*
    Ludus: *The playful love*
    Agape: *The love for everyone. Also known as the love of God*
    *toward his creatures, humankind included*
    Pragma: *The longstanding love*
    Philautia: *The love of self*
*Making Love*: *the romantic form of sex*
*Mating*: *a physical and socially responsible form of sex*
*Nookie*: *a woman's vagina, it is also an extra-colloquial word for sex*
*Rendezvous*: *a cheating form of sex*
*Rutting*: *a primal from of sex*
*Screwing*: *a frivolous form of sex*
*Seduction*: *an introductory form of sex*
*Sexual Congress*: *business sex*
*Sexual Intercourse*: *an uptight form of sex*
*Sexual Relations*: *a circumstantial form of sex*
*Sexual Union:* *an arranged form of sex*
*Sixty Nine, 69*: *oral sex performed simultaneously*
*Sleeping Together:* *a euphemism for casual, occasional sex*
*Slut:* *A man or woman who is sexually promiscuous*
*Shall I go on?*

**Movies To Watch**

**Movies To Watch If You Want To Improve Your Sexual IQ and Social Intellect:**
*Alfie 1966*
*Barbarella 1968*
*Blow-up 1966*
*Bob and Carol and Ted and Alice 1969*
*Everything You Always Wanted to Know About Sex, But Were Afraid to Ask 1972*
*Easy A 2010*
*Harold and Maude 1971*
*Fast Times At Ridgemont High 1982*
*There's Something About Mary 1998*


**Books To Read In Order To Improve Your Sexual IQ and Social Intellect:**

*Art of Loving, The* Eric Fromm1956
*Decameron* 1700
*Everything You Always Wanted to Know About Sex, But Were Afraid to Ask* David Reuben 1969
*Human Sexual Response* Masters and Johnson 1966
*Looking for Mr. Goodbar* Judith Rossner 1975
*Magus, The* John Fowles 1966
*Myth of Monogamy* Barash and Lipton, 2001
*Siddhartha* Hermann Hesse 1922

John Bassett McCleary

*I have taken numerous photographs of myself
with the purpose of showing myself within history
and travel, but this is technically
my one and only selfie, because it was taken in the spirit
of Selfies.*

Photo by Zach Weston

## About the Author

Mr. John Bassett McCleary has worked as a writer, art director and photographer in the newspaper, music, publishing and advertising industries for the last fifty-three years. He is a third-generation journalist. His father and grandfather were muckrakers, newspaper owners and political speechwriters. John's grandfather, J.M. Bassett, owned *The Golden Era, Oakland Tribune* and *Los Angeles Herald*, and was the secretary/advisor to California Governor Leland Stanford. John's father, W.K. Bassett, owned, wrote and edited the Carmel newspaper *The Cymbal* between 1926 and 1942, and owned and worked on other papers in Boston, California and Hawaii. W.K. was also the secretary/advisor to Honolulu Mayor John Wilson.

636

During the 1960s and 70s, John McCleary was a music industry photographer in Los Angeles and was on stage and in the dressing
rooms with The Doors, Jimi Hendrix, The Stones, Tina Turner and others. In the early 1970s, he produced a series of twelve posters and *The
People's Book*, a photographic essay of the counterculture of the era.
John participated in and photographed many civil rights and anti-war
demonstrations across the United States during the 1960s and 70s. His
photographic essay of the 1960s counterculture was published in 1972
by Celestial Arts in San Francisco, and in 1998, he self-published *Monterey Peninsula People,* a book of photographs and bios of Peninsula
residents. John is also the author of *The Hippie Dictionary: A Cultural Encyclopedia of the 1960s and 1970s*, published by Ten Speed
Press in 2002, revised in 2004, and now published by Crown Publishing Group, division of Random House. Mr. McCleary is considered
"The Authority on the generation that questioned authority." John has
published three books on the hippie counterculture: T*he Hippie Dictionary* (2001), *Common Sense and Reason Again* (2019*),* and this book,
*Mother's Heart, Father's Mind* (2021). These three books complete
*The Hippie Trilogy.*

In his own words John will tell you, "In this book, *Mother's
Heart, Fathers' Mind,* I do not describe to you my accomplishments
or revelations for my own gratification or recognition: I do so as a

messenger or teacher. I write what I write so hopefully someone will find some truth in it and then find a happier life and pass it on to the next few people. The word sin is a religious word and concept that, for a price, promotes only heaven and hell. I, for one, believe in morality, which is a word and concept that promotes personal value. Morality is the common sense way to live and treat other people, and it is approved by the majority of mankind. The Golden Rule is its foundation."

"What I hope you have learned from this book is that sex is not a sin or even immoral. The worst thing about sex is that many people cannot control their desire or put it in the right perspective. That is what causes most of the world's frustrations, insecurity, greed and violence. If we do not get our emotions and common sense thinking straight, we are in for more insecurity, selfishness, religion based bigotry and wars to come."

Oh, P.S. Right now in America we are on the brink of a race war that was created by capitalism from the very beginning during the slave industry, which started over 300 years ago, and came to a head during the Civil War. Feudal capitalists created bigotry for economic reasons, and then to justify slavery they taught it to the working class, so they would fight in the Civil War. The rich are now continuing to promote bigotry to control the poor whites, so they will vote for Republicans. This is stupid voting, because dollar for dollar and word for word, the right-wingers are stealing more from and lying more to the poor than the Democratic, left-wing, socialist bleeding hearts. But what is the opposite of bleeding hearts... heartless! And that is what conservatives are.

I have been a guinea pig most of my life. When I was born in the first half of the 20th century, doctors experimented on me. When I went to school, they tried new math on me, and phonetic spelling. In the 1960s I was expected to experiment with birth control and new forms of drugs and rock & roll. Also, in the hippie era we experimented with tattoos and body piercings.

Then at the end of the last century and now in the new millennium I am being bombarded by the multiple and continually changing forms of computer, cell phone and Internet learning curves. Not to mention, I am being tested by the new forms of capitalists' cheating and stealing techniques.

For thousands of years mankind didn't even know that sex produced children. And for thousands of years after that, humans could not seem to control their horny desires enough to keep sex from being more trouble than it was worth. Finally in the last few thousand years, but mostly only in Asia, did people started to control their urges for the sake of common sense. Then in the 1960s and 70s after the invention of easy and trustworthy forms of birth control, a culture arose that started taking sex seriously as positive activity and a pastime that could be controlled to bring about only good results. So now we can celebrate sex as being a possible success story for the human race.

"Nobody is carrying the clipboard for the world right now. My friends and I would be happy to do so. We'd be happy to tell everybody in the world what they are doing wrong, because we know!" Mr. California

"You have to get rid of your ego and try out other people's shoes!" DG

There is a correct for every situation. Whatever is right for the most people is correct!" JOB

I am not afraid of needles, yet I have fainted during blood testing and intravenous procedures. I am vaccinated. Are some of you afraid of needles and the embarrassment fainting might cause you?

We need to rethink the human being and how we act as human beings. Are we going to continue conflict with each other, or to destroy our world, or are we going to start thinking beyond our own life and agree that the next generation has the right to have the same chances we did?

We all know that fear can kill us. "Nothing to fear but fear itself." But aggression can kill us just as dead. We kill more family and friends with guns we own than strangers who come to rob or kill us!

Angela

Do it

*"If you want to have a perfect world for yourself, you can't just let some things go. You can't ignore the human ego, the crimes of religion, the abominations of capitalism or the good and bad of sex, drugs or rock & roll. Humankind has prevailed by being pragmatic. When something is a problem, we have fixed it; or if we didn't fix it, we have had to suffer from it later. None of us are safe, as long as any of us are threatened. "*
Dudley Griffin

Our sexuality often clouds our rational thinking.
It would be helpful at many places and times in our lives if we could
become temporarily  neutered.
JBMc

JBMc

CPSIA information can be obtained
at www.ICGtesting.com
Printed in the USA
JSHW061805300622
27492JS00001B/1